THE ROUTLEDGE COMPANION TO COPYRIGHT AND CREATIVITY IN THE 21ST CENTURY

T0384731

These collected chapters and interviews explore the current issues and debates about how copyright will or should adapt to meet the practices of 21st-century creators and internet users.

The book begins with an overview of copyright law basics. It is organized by parts that correspond to creative genres: Literary Works, Visual Arts, Fine Art, Music, Video Games and Virtual Worlds, Fashion, and Technology. The chapters and interviews address issues such as copyright ownership in work created by Artificial Intelligence (AI), the musical remix market, whether appropriation is ever a fair use of a copyrighted work or if it is always theft, and whether internet-based platforms should do more to deter piracy of creators' works. Each part ends with an essay explaining the significance of one or two landmark or trendsetting cases to help the reader understand the practical implications of the law.

Written to be accessible to both lay and legal audiences, this unique collection addresses contemporary legal issues that all creators need to understand and will be essential reading for artists, designers, and musicians as well as the lawyers who represent them.

Michelle Bogre, Esq., is a Professor Emerita from Parsons School of Design in New York City, where she taught photography and copyright law for artists and designers. She is the author of three other books: *Photography As Activism: Images for Social Change*; *Photography 4.0: A Teaching Guide for the 21st Century*; and, her newest, *Documentary Photography Reconsidered: Theory, History and Practice*.

Nancy Wolff is a partner at the bi-coastal firm Cowan, DeBaets, Abrahams & Sheppard, LLP. She is co-chair of the firm's litigation department, Past President of the Copyright Society of the USA (CSUSA), and member of the American Bar Association (ABA) IP Task Force on Copyright Reform. She is the author of *Best Practices in Image Licensing,* published in the Licensing Journal, and *The Professional Photographers Legal Handbook*.

THE ROUTLEDGE COMPANION TO COPYRIGHT AND CREATIVITY IN THE 21ST CENTURY

Edited by
Michelle Bogre and Nancy Wolff

Routledge
Taylor & Francis Group

NEW YORK AND LONDON

First published 2021
by Routledge
52 Vanderbilt Avenue, New York, NY 10017

and by Routledge
2 Park Square, Milton Park, Abingdon, Oxon, OX14 4RN

Routledge is an imprint of the Taylor & Francis Group, an informa business

Library of Congress Cataloging-in-Publication Data
Names: Bogre, Michelle, editor. | Wolff, Nancy (Editor of Routledge
companion to copyright and creativity), editor.
Title: The Routledge companion to copyright and creativity in the
twenty-first century / edited by Michelle Bogre and Nancy Wolff.
Description: New York, NY; Milton Park, Abingdon,
Oxon: Routledge, 2021. | Includes bibliographical
references and index.
Identifiers: LCCN 2020025645 (print) | LCCN 2020025646 (ebook) |
ISBN 9781138999251 (hardback) | ISBN 9781315658445 (ebook)
Subjects: LCSH: Copyright. | Copyright—Art. |
Creative ability. | Creation (Literary, artistic, etc.)
Classification: LCC K1420.5 .R685 2021 (print) |
LCC K1420.5 (ebook) | DDC 346.04/82—dc23
LC record available at https://lccn.loc.gov/2020025645
LC ebook record available at https://lccn.loc.gov/2020025646

ISBN: 978-1-138-99925-1 (hbk)
ISBN: 978-1-315-65844-5 (ebk)

Typeset in Bembo
by codeMantra

Nancy Wolff

To all the creative people I have met and who have inspired me: my love of copyright comes from what you do. To all my copyright law colleagues: your insights inspire me to keep learning more every day.

Michelle Bogre

This book is dedicated to creators everywhere and the IP lawyers who work tirelessly to keep the system functioning.

CONTENTS

Contents

Contents

Contents

PREFACE

The idea for this book originated a few years ago, when I was teaching an elective class in copyright law to art and design students at Parsons School of Design in New York City. Although my students were keenly interested and engaged in the material, I knew that my law class was an anomaly among art and design schools, even though, in this digital age, all artists and designers should have some understanding of copyright law and what it protects as it forms the underpinnings of their livelihoods.

Understanding copyright is more important now than ever before. Copyright issues in the twentieth century were primarily reserved for two entities: those that created work and those that produced or published the work, such as publishers, music companies, motion pictures, and software companies. Creators and producers were seldom the same person, but now, we are all creators and publishers. We wake up to an alarm that plays our favorite song, we check our various social media accounts and share with our friends what we see and read, we create videos and download music for the background, we stream television and video games, and we create memes with text and images we have downloaded. We participate in a culture that blithely creates, borrows, remixes, and shares copyrighted work many times every day without a thought about who created it or if we are doing something wrong.

Digital copying and distribution through the internet has transformed the marketplace for copyright in music, games, and videos. With a simple right click of the mouse, most content on your screen can be on your computer, without any technological restrictions on what you can then do with it. These changes in how society uses copyrighted work have been propelling calls for change. Copyright law needs to emerge from the past and morph into something that works today. There is a disconnect between the rights that the law confers and the rights that are asserted in practice. If we assume that the goal of the Copyright Act was to promote creativity and innovation while allowing some access for the public, maybe things are out of balance and skewed too much to the producers and publishers, not the creators—those students I was teaching who were about to embark on a creative life.

But rather than write another book about copyright, I thought, why not write a book about the current issues that these artists and designers are facing in the twenty-first century? And why not write it for those artists and designers and young law students engaging with this world, rather than a legal audience?

So, that idea became this book, molded and crafted to what it is now, and Nancy Wolff agreed to be the co-editor. Her deep knowledge of the law, and her ability to make complicated ideas accessible, guided the focus of the book. This is not a typical book about copyright law. It is a riff on issues that intrigued the artists who agreed to be interviewed and the lawyers who agreed to participate. We encouraged them to write in any style they wanted as long as they wrote about an issue more pertinent to the twenty-first century than the twentieth century. Knowing that many of our readers would not be lawyers, we included a short overview of copyright law basics. We would suggest that non-lawyers read this first.

And, in the end, we hope that maybe this book will help readers make more sense of copyright law than Mark Twain thought possible.

Michelle Bogre and Nancy Wolff

ACKNOWLEDGMENTS

Nancy Wolff

I thank my firm for giving me the support to edit this book (even after I spent two years as President of the Copyright Society!). It is a pleasure to be surrounded by other IP and entertainment law geeks. Thank you to my team who brought this over the finish line, Rachael Jenison, Sara Gates, Elizabeth (Lizzy) Altman, and Lindsay Edelstein, and my former intern Anton Nemirovski for his research and writing. Thanks to all my colleagues who agreed to write essays, despite all being too busy. My apologies to anyone who was not asked to participate; there is always next time. My thanks to Michelle for being the driving force and inspiration throughout this project, believing we would get it done. And a special thanks to my patient husband Jack for when I ignored him to work on this book (and who inspires me every day) and to my extended family, who always help me out.

Michelle Bogre

First, I am deeply indebted to Nancy for saying "yes" when I asked her if she wanted to work with me on this book. Her keen intellect and nuanced understanding of the law guided us. I couldn't have found a better person to be my co-editor. I profoundly thank all the people who agreed to be interviewed or to write essays and share their knowledge and ideas about copyright law. And since no book is ever the endeavor of one person, to my Australian-based assistant, Ella Colley, and to Nancy's team—Rachael, Sara, Lizzy, and Lindsay—this book literally would not have been completed without you. Maybe the most important thank you goes to Natalie Foster, Jennifer Vennall, and the editorial team at Routledge for believing in this project and for being so patient with us when we missed deadlines. Finally, to my friends who have supported me throughout this process and to my husband, Peter, for his understanding when I also ignored him repeatedly to work on this book.

CONTRIBUTORS

Elizabeth Altman is an associate at Intellectual Property, Media, and Entertainment firm Cowan, DeBaets, Abrahams & Sheppard, LLP, where she counsels clients on copyright and trademark matters. Elizabeth has experience across a wide range of entertainment fields, including digital and traditional media, where she litigates on behalf of clients leading the way in interactive digital art and advertising as well as illustration, film, publishing, and photography.

Joseph T. Baio is a litigation attorney practicing in New York City with the firm Willkie Farr & Gallagher LLP. He served as lead trial counsel for the plaintiff in *Morel v. Agence France Presse* and was lead trial counsel for the defendants during the damages phase of *Arista Records v. Limewire*, cases which are discussed in this chapter. The views expressed are his own.

Michael A. Bernet is an attorney at the law firm Brutzkus Gubner in Los Angeles, California. Michael practices in intellectual property and general civil matters, including copyright, trademark, and complex business litigation.

Michelle Bogre, the former Chair of the Photography Department at Parsons School of Design in New York, is currently Professor Emerita after a 25-year career teaching almost every type of photography class and copyright law for artists and designers. She is also a documentary photographer and author of three other books: *Photography As Activism: Images for Social Change*; *Photography 4.0: A Teaching Guide for the 21st Century*; and, her newest, *Documentary Photography Reconsidered: History, Theory and Practice.*

Alex Branczik is a Senior Director and Head of Contemporary Art, Europe, at Sotheby's London. He was closely involved in the sales of major collections, including the Collection of Jean-Yves Mock and the groundbreaking Bear Witness single-owner sale. He drove the transformation of Sotheby's October Contemporary Art sales from mid-season events into high-profile auctions, which included several record-breaking sales.

Daniel J. Brooks is a partner at Scarola Zubatov Schaffzin PLLC. He was counsel for the plaintiff in the well-known appropriation art case *Cariou v. Prince*, 714 F.3d 694 (2d Cir. 2013). He has written and lectured extensively on appropriation art and the related fair use defense to copyright infringement, including a recent *amicus* brief for a leading fair use case, *Oracle America, Inc. v. Google LLC.*

Dale M. Cendali is a partner in Kirkland & Ellis's New York office and is firmwide head of Kirkland's Copyright, Trademark Internet and Advertising Practice Group. Dale has received numerous accolades, including being named by *IP 360* as one of the 25 "Icons of IP" and by *The National Law Journal* as one of the "100 Most Influential Lawyers in America." Dale also teaches Copyright and Trademark Litigation at her *alma mater*, Harvard Law School.

Bob Clarida advises clients in a wide range of industries, including software, publishing, film, music, and photography. He has also litigated a number of high-profile copyright matters and argued significant federal appeals in several circuits. Bob speaks and writes frequently on copyright issues. He co-authors the regular copyright law column in the *New York Law Journal*, teaches a seminar on emerging intellectual property issues at Columbia Law School, is a past chair of numerous bar committees, and has served as an expert reviewer for the Multistate Bar Exam.

Jonathan Coulton is known for his eclectic catalog of masterful songwriting on subjects from zombies and mad scientists to sad parents and dissatisfied software engineers. He's written songs for *The Good Fight* and *Braindead* TV series as well as the *Portal* video games. He is the house musician for the NPR show *Ask Me Another* and the host and namesake of the annual JoCo Cruise.

Cheryl L. Davis is General Counsel of the Author's Guild, where she oversees the organization's legal affairs, including its in-house corporate affairs, its government relations and policy initiatives, and its legal services program. In addition, she is responsible for developing a wide variety of the organization's written positions, policies, statements, submissions to government agencies, and legal briefs as well as participating in public speaking engagements and conferences.

Michael Donaldson founded Donaldson & Callif with Lisa Callif in 2008. The firm focuses on independent films, specializing in fair use opinions and other clearance issues in scripted and documentary films. In 2007, Donaldson negotiated with insurance companies to provide errors and omissions policies to cover material used pursuant to fair use. Donaldson also successfully argued to the Copyright Office at the Triennial Digital Millennium Copyright Act (DMCA) Exemption Hearing that documentary filmmakers should be exempted from criminal portions of DMCA, relating to ripping DVDs, Blu-rays, and streaming services to obtain material to be used pursuant to fair use.

Phil Galdston is a songwriter, producer, and music publisher. More than 130 million copies of his songs and productions have appeared on more than 70 million records worldwide. *Save the Best For Last*, recorded by Vanessa Williams and co-written with Jon Lind and Wendy Waldman, is undoubtedly his best-known song. He is a Music Professor, Director of Songwriting, and Faculty Songwriter-in-Residence at New York University's (NYU) Steinhardt School. He is also one of the founders of musicanswers.org.

Joseph C. Gratz is partner with Durie Tangri LLP in San Francisco. A Trustee of the Copyright Society of the USA and an Advisor to the forthcoming ALI Restatement of Copyright, Mr. Gratz litigates cutting-edge cases at the intersection of copyright and new technology. Currently, he represents Amazon, Facebook, Microsoft, and a variety of other companies in intermediary liability matters.

Brandon J. Huffman is an attorney and founder of Odin Law and Media, a law firm focused on counseling video game and interactive media clients on issues related to intellectual property and corporate growth, content, licensing, and publishing. Brandon also serves as general counsel to the International Game Developers Association, the largest nonprofit membership organization focused on serving the needs of individual game developers. He is a frequent speaker on legal issues related to game development, emerging technology, and creativity.

Justin Hughes is the Hon. William Matthew Byrne Distinguished Professor of Law at Loyola Law School, Los Angeles, where he teaches international trade and intellectual property courses. From 2009 until 2013, Professor Hughes also served as Senior Advisor to the Undersecretary of Commerce for Intellectual Property. In that capacity, he was the US chief negotiator for two multilateral copyright treaties: the Beijing Treaty on Audiovisual Performances (2012) and the Marrakesh Treaty for the Blind (2013).

Umair Kazi is a lawyer, writer, translator, and Director of Policy & Advocacy, Authors Guild.

Terence P. Keegan is a partner at Miller Korzenik Sommers Rayman LLP in New York. He represents news organizations, publishers, artists, and others in copyright, trademark, defamation, and commercial cases. He helped obtain the Second Circuit's affirmance of a fair use summary judgment in the fashion parody case *Louis Vuitton Malletier, S.A. v. My Other Bag, Inc.*

Jeffrey A. Kobulnick is a Partner and Chair of the Intellectual Property Practice Group at the law firm Brutzkus Gubner in Los Angeles. He is an experienced copyright and trademark attorney and regularly litigates claims for copyright and trademark infringement and related causes of action.

John Koegel is an attorney and founder of the law firm The Koegel Group LLP. Since 1982, Mr. Koegel has specialized in Art Law, exclusively representing artists, galleries, and others involved with visual art in most areas of the law. Mr. Koegel also served as General Counsel and Secretary at the Museum of Modern Art. He helped draft the Visual Arts Rights Act of 1990 and represented Jeff Koons in the landmark fair use cases *Rogers v. Koons and Blanch v. Koons.*

Barbara Kolsun, professor of practice and director of the FAME Center at Cardozo Law School, is a leading fashion industry attorney and co-editor of the seminal texts on the subject, *Fashion Law – A Guide for Designers, Fashion Executives and Attorneys* (Bloomsbury, 2nd ed., 2014) and *The Business and Law of Fashion*, to be published by Carolina Press in 2020. Kolsun started the legal departments and was the first general counsel of Kate Spade, Stuart Weitzman, and Seven for All Mankind.

William T. McGrath is a member in the Chicago law firm of Davis McGrath LLC. His primary areas of practice are copyright and trademark law and litigation, including publishing, visual arts, and Internet law issues. His practice involves issues relating to the ownership, licensing, protection, and infringement of intellectual property rights. He teaches courses in Copyright Law and Copyright Litigation at The UIC John Marshall Law School.

Olivera Medenica is an attorney at Dunnington Bartholow & Miller LLP whose practice covers the fashion industry. Dunnington Bartholow & Miller is a New York City law firm with domestic and international practices spanning several sectors, including in the areas of intellectual property, advertising, art, and fashion law. Dunnington's Fashion Law Group represents domestic and foreign businesses, individuals, and estates in fashion, retail, media and entertainment, transactional, data privacy and technology, litigation, and arbitration matters.

Peter S. Menell is a Professor of Law, Berkeley Center for Law & Technology, University of California at Berkeley, School of Law. His research and teaching span intellectual property across the digital technology and entertainment fields as well as environmental law and policy, property law, and law and economics. He has authored more than 100 articles and 15 books, including leading casebooks, intellectual property treatises, and research handbooks.

Cameron Mizell, Brooklyn-based guitarist and composer, has been part of the New York City music scene for the past decade-plus, performing a variety of genres from experimental improvisation to bluegrass musicals. He also works on the industry side, managing operations for Destiny Records. As an artist, Mizell has released seven albums ranging from jazz-funk to Americana to avant-garde. "Quietly and efficiently, Mizell has put together a remarkably tuneful, eclectic, understatedly cinematic body of work" (New York Music Daily).

Mickey H. Osterreicher serves as general counsel to the National Press Photographers Association (NPPA) and is *of counsel* to Finnerty Osterreicher & Abdulla. He is an award-winning photojournalist with over forty years' experience in print and broadcast. The Society of Professional Journalists (SPJ) honored him in 2015 as a "Fellow of the Society," its highest professional honor for extraordinary contribution to the profession.

Marcia Paul was a national leader in media and entertainment law, and a partner in Davis Wright Tremaine's media and entertainment group. Widely honored for excellence, she handled many high-profile copyright, trademark, and First Amendment matters over her forty-year career. Ms. Paul passed away in February of 2020.

Judith B. Prowda is a New York attorney, mediator, and arbitrator focused on art law, copyright, entertainment, and commercial law. She has been a member of the Sotheby's Institute of Art Masters of Art Business Faculty since 2007. Her book, *Visual Arts and the Law: A Handbook for Professionals* (Lund Humphries 2013), is in its second printing and has been translated into Korean. She is a founding member of Stropheus Art Law, a collective of art law and business specialists who offer unbundled services to the art community.

Mary E. Rasenberger is the Executive Director of the Authors Guild and the Authors Guild Foundation. Prior to joining the Guild in 2014, she practiced law for over 25 years in intellectual property, media, and technology, with an expertise in copyright law, counseling authors, artists, and their estates as well as publishing, media, and internet companies. She is a recognized copyright expert, a frequent speaker and writer on authors' rights and copyright, and an adjunct professor at Columbia Law School.

Christopher S. Reed is a lawyer in the entertainment industry focusing on intellectual property, content protection, antitrust, and litigation. He previously served as the senior policy advisor to the U.S. Register of Copyrights and a trial attorney for the Antitrust Division of the U.S. Department of Justice. He is the author of *The Unrealized Promise of the Next Great Copyright Act: U.S. Copyright Policy for the 21st Century*, published by Edward Elgar in 2019.

Shanti Sadtler Conway is a partner in Kirkland & Ellis's New York office. She focuses her practice on intellectual property litigation and counseling, including copyright, trademark, false advertising, and right of publicity. She has been recognized in *The Legal 500*, sits on the Unfair Competition Committee of the International Trademark Association, and is the Secretary of the Copyright and Literary Property Committee of the New York City Bar Association.

Chrissie Scelsi is U.S. General Counsel for Wargaming, an award-winning online game developer and publisher that is a leader in the free-to-play MMO market across PC, console, and mobile platforms. She is responsible for legal and business matters for the company's operations in the United States, including IP, advertising, privacy, esports, licensing, events, and basically any question involving what can be done with a tank.

Scott J. Sholder is Co-Chair of Cowan, DeBaets, Abrahams & Sheppard, LLP's Litigation group and focuses his practice on litigation, counseling, and dispute resolution in connection with entertainment, media, and intellectual property matters. Scott represents and advises clients across various industries in copyright, trademark, right-of-publicity, unfair competition, domain name, and commercial and business disputes. He has appeared in federal and state courts around the country as well as administrative and arbitral tribunals, and has handled cases from pre-suit negotiations through trial.

William Stafford is the co-founder and the Executive Director of the music publishing company Missing Link Music. Previously, he was Vice President, Copyright, at SonyBMG in New York, overseeing the mechanical and synchronization licensing activities of Arista, RCA, Jive, Bad Boy Entertainment, and J Records. Prior to that, he held the position of Director, Copyright Licensing, at PolyGram Records, with earlier experience as a Licensing Agent at The Harry Fox Agency. Throughout his career in the music industry, he has focused on music theory, analysis, and performing as a pianist.

Kenneth N. Swezey is partner at Intellectual Property, Media and Entertainment firm Cowan, DeBaets, Abrahams & Sheppard, LLP. He has substantial experience representing companies and individual clients in the emerging fields of digital media, social media, and transmedia. He represents clients ranging from broadband television companies, well-known authors, publishers, entertainers, literary estates, and visual arts agencies to not-for-profit organizations in the areas of intellectual property and entertainment.

Francine Ward is an intellectual property law and estate planning attorney. Her IP focus is on copyrights, trademarks, social media, and publishing law issues. She also counsels clients regarding the protection of their estates, with an emphasis on trust-based estate plans and special needs trusts. Admitted to practice in California, New York, and DC, Francine represents business, entertainment, and publishing clients.

David Wolfert is a GRAMMY- and EMMY®-nominated songwriter, composer, orchestrator, and producer who has worked in all areas of music, including film, records, advertising, and television. As a music activist, he regularly advocates on behalf of musicians and songwriters, including through musicanswers.org, of which he is a co-founder. He is also an adjunct professor at New York University, where he teaches both undergraduates and graduates.

Nancy Wolff is a partner at Cowan, DeBaets, Abrahams & Sheppard, LLP in New York. Frequently ranked as one of the top women in IP, she represents a wide range of creative individuals and companies in all areas of digital media, art law, licensing, and publishing. She serves as counsel to the Digital Media Licensing Association. She is the Immediate Past President of the Copyright Society of the USA (CSUSA) and member of the ABA IP Task Force on Copyright Reform.

Caroline Womack Carroll is an associate at Morrison Rothman, a Los Angeles-based firm that specializes in video game, esport, entertainment, and intellectual property law. She received her

Juris Doctor degree from Quinnipiac University School of Law in 2019 and served as the Executive Managing Editor of the Quinnipiac Law Review, where she was recognized as an Emerging Scholar for her extensive studies on the boundaries of fair use and the application of the DMCA in the context of let's plays and live-streaming. She is interested in and passionate about the intricacies of the video game industry.

PART I

Copyright Basics

1.1

COPYRIGHT BASICS

What You Think You Know May Not Be True

This chapter is intended to be an overview of copyright law for those readers who do not have a legal background. It will provide a reference for terms used and ideas discussed in this book's essays.

Legal Systems

Law is country-specific, so the legal principles discussed in this book apply to the United States (US). There is no worldwide intellectual property (IP) law that applies to all countries; however, many US legal principles harmonize with laws in other countries. Also, the US is a signatory on international copyright treaties that establish obligations that treaty members must adhere to and include in their national laws. The two main copyright treaties to which the US is a signatory are the Berne Convention for the Protection of Literary and Artistic Works[1] (Berne Convention) and the Universal Copyright Convention.[2] The US is also a member-state of the World Intellectual Property Organization (WIPO), an agency of the United Nations that serves as the global forum for IP services.

Generally speaking, there are two types of legal systems in developed countries: civil law, used in most countries around the world today (such as Europe, Russia, China, and most of Central and Latin America), and common law, used in Britain and most former British colonies, including the US (where common law applies to all states except Louisiana, which bases its state law on a civil law code, due to its French origins). In a common-law system, laws usually originate in the legislative branch, but are developed, honed, and parsed by the courts. Great weight is placed on judges' decisions, which have the same force of law as a statute and, in fact, courts have the authority to make law where no legislative statute exists. In copyright law, for example, the fair use doctrine, which we will look at in greater detail, originated in the courts before being added to the Copyright Revision Act of 1976.

Copyright Is Federal Law

As a Federalist system, the US has both state and federal courts, with hierarchical structures for each. Because copyright law is federal law, all copyright cases are heard in federal courts. The federal court system has three main hierarchical levels: district (or trial) courts; circuit courts that hear appeals; and, finally, the Supreme Court, the highest court in the land. Federal courts are organized geographically or regionally. There are ninety-four district court jurisdictions and twelve regional circuits (including the District of Columbia), each of which has one court of appeals.

In a common-law system, interactions between court decisions, constitutional law, statutory law, and regulatory law can be complicated; however, *stare decisis*, the principle that similar cases should be decided according to consistent principled rules, and that similar facts should not be treated differently, lies at the heart of all common-law systems. In cases where the parties disagree on what the law is, a common-law court looks to past decisions of relevant courts. Supreme Court decisions are binding on all courts. In most jurisdictions, decisions by appellate courts are binding only on lower courts in the same jurisdiction and on future decisions of the same appellate court, but decisions of lower courts are not binding on appellate courts. A decision by a court in a different jurisdiction is only non-binding persuasive authority. So under the doctrine of *stare decisis*, if a similar dispute has been resolved in the past, the court is bound to follow the reasoning used in the prior decision in the same jurisdiction. If, however, the court finds that the current dispute is fundamentally distinct from all previous cases (called a "matter of first impression"), judges have the authority and duty to make law by creating precedent. Thereafter, the new decision becomes precedent, and will bind future courts in that jurisdiction.

Copyright Protects Creative Expression

Copyright law is a form of protection provided for most types of creative work. It falls under the umbrella of IP law, which protects "creations" (property) of the mind. IP is rooted in the concept of real property rights. The philosophical basis for protecting private property ownership is well entrenched in Western society: Laws protect private (real) property from interference by others. For example, you can sell your property, you can loan it to someone, or you can exclude someone from using it. You can touch real property and because it is real, that is, composed of atoms, etc., it can only occupy one place at any given time. This means that possession of a physical thing is exclusive; if I have it, you do not. Private property ownership has been viewed as a foundation for an ordered economic system, and historically, as a vehicle for the accumulation of wealth. IP also has an extraordinary value. In 2017, core copyright industries added $1.3 trillion to the US economy and employed almost six million people.[3]

IP, by definition, is intangible. You cannot touch it. However, even though it is intangible, it is something you own, just as you own a car or a camera. It belongs to you, the creator, and you alone decide how it can be used. Because it is intangible, protecting IP is a more complex philosophical question than protecting tangible property. Should IP rights be the same as real property rights? How long should they last? Why do we protect it at all? The essays in this book explore these questions.

Copyright law is enshrined in the US Constitution, article 1, section 8, clause 8, which grants Congress the power to ". . . promote the progress of science and the useful arts, by securing for limited times to authors and inventors the exclusive right to their respective writings and discoveries." A simple reading of this language would suggest that the framers were interested in striking a balance between protecting creative work, by giving creators an economic incentive to create, and protecting the public's right to benefit from those creations in a reasonable time frame. The first Copyright Act, passed in 1790, protected work for only fourteen years with one fourteen-year renewal, but only if the work was published and had a proper copyright notice affixed. Unpublished works were protected only by state common law. Work that was not protected, or lost its protection, entered the public domain where it became free for use by the public. Published meant offering copies to the public, even if those copies were offered for free. The copyright law was first updated in the Copyright Act of 1909 and that Act still applies to works created before 1978. The most current law, the Copyright Revision Act of 1976 (which became effective in 1978), applies to works created after 1978. While the subsequent versions of the Copyright Act increased the length of protection for works (for example, the 1909 Act had an initial term of twenty-eight years with a renewal term of another twenty-eight years), the distinction between published and unpublished works continued until the current Act. This Act extended the term of copyright to life of the author, plus a term of years, initially fifty and now seventy, and for works owned by entities, the term was initially seventy-five years from publication, but was later increased to ninety-five years. For works made for hire (discussed below) or pseudonymous works (that is, works created under a false name), the duration runs ninety-five years from first publication or 120 years from creation (whichever is shorter). The 1976 Act still required that published work bears a copyright notice. Significantly, when the US joined the Berne Convention in March 1989, the requirement that work have a copyright notice affixed was eliminated, a formality that caused many works of authors to inadvertently fall into the public domain. To avoid the harsh impact on foreign authors, works of foreign authors regained copyright protection that was lost for failing to follow the US formalities.

To understand the impact of a long copyright duration (the US term is consistent with most treaty countries), if a creator is twenty years old when she creates something, but lives to be 100, that particular work would have copyright protection for 150 years. Because it is difficult to keep track of duration, and with works still in copyright under the 1909 Act and the current Act, a good chart to rely on is Cornell University's public domain chart.[4]

The law initially protected only "authors" and "writings," which then included maps and charts. The term "author" is not defined, but it has been interpreted to include only human authorship. Copyright currently covers:

- Literary works (including computer programs)
- Musical works and accompanying words
- Dramatic works and accompanying music
- Pantomimes and choreography
- Pictorial, graphic, and sculptural works
- Motion pictures and audiovisual works and sound recordings
- Architectural works

It does not cover:

- Names
- Titles
- Slogans and short phrases
- Ideas, concepts, or facts
- Themes
- Works created by the federal government
- Fashion

While trademark law may offer protection for some titles, slogans, and short phrases under specific circumstances, copyright, as a form of monopoly, does not protect things that should be available to the public. For example, copyright law does not protect ideas; it protects the "expression" of the idea the moment the idea is fixed in a tangible medium. While this is not defined in the statute, it has come to mean fixed (preserved) in any form that can be perceived (read or heard) directly or by use of a machine or device for a period of more than transitory duration. For example, a copy can be fixed even if it only occurs in a computer's RAM for a few seconds. However, televising a live event would not be fixed unless it is simultaneously being recorded.

However, because copyright is an intangible right, it does not "attach" to the object itself. For example, if a photographer sells a print, made from a photographic negative, the purchaser only owns the print. The purchaser can display or sell the print, but does not acquire any of the exclusive rights of the photographer under copyright, so the purchaser cannot, for example, make any reproductions of the print, or use the print as the subject for a painting, without the consent of the photographer. This separation of copyright from the object is often misunderstood by both creators and the public.

The elements for copyright protection are minimal: In addition to being fixed, the work has to be original, which means that the author created it rather than found or identically copied it from another work, and it has to be creative, not utilitarian, but the bar for creativity is very low. Because the current law does not require publication or notice, all work that fits these minimal standards currently has copyright protection for the full term of copyright. This means that most creative work found on the internet has copyright protection. It is not necessary to register the work with the Copyright Office for the copyright to be valid, although there are good reasons to register works (discussed below).

Joint Copyright

If there are two or more creators, the law allows for a joint copyright, defined as a work prepared by two or more people "with the intent of merging their contributions into inseparable or inter-dependent parts of a unitary whole." Intent is the key. All creators must intend at the beginning of the project that they are collaborating as equal creators.

The problem with a joint copyright is that all parties are considered equal owners, so either party may exercise any of the copyright holder's exclusive rights without needing the other's permission, unless one party wants to grant an exclusive license. A joint copyright holder may only grant exclusive rights in the work to third parties if all coauthors agree. For all other rights, the joint copyright holder's permission is not needed, and the only requirement is to share any money that might be made. This sounds good in theory, but often creators have conflicting interests. Except for true joint projects where the works cannot be separated from each other, it is often better to have a collaboration agreement where the dominant party holds the copyright and shares revenue and credit with other participants, and to seek the advice of an attorney to draft the agreement.

Work Made for Hire

The only exception to the rule that copyright belongs to the creator is when an employer-employee relationship or a work made for hire—commonly known as work for hire—agreement exists. Generally, the employer-employee relationship is defined by law as a relationship governed by whether the party who commissioned the work has the right to control how the work is created. Simply being hired to do a job does not necessarily make someone an employee. The law considers whether the employer takes taxes out of a paycheck, where the work is performed, and how much of the work is controlled by the employer. The more control the "employer" has over the work duties, workplace, and work hours, the more likely the arrangement will be considered to be employee-employer, in which case the employer owns the copyright, absent an agreement to the contrary. A single job would not likely create an employee-employer relationship, but someone who has an ongoing relationship in a regular workplace where all the work is done under the employer direction *might* be considered to be an employee, even if the employer never made a formal job offer. Work for hire is a legal fiction that allows a person, company, or organization to claim authorship of a creative work they did not create, and as the "author" they own the copyright. Work for hire occurs more frequently in today's work environment because many contracts, even for a single job, contain a work for hire phrase or clause. Understand that if you sign a work for hire agreement, you are irrevocably transferring all of your copyrights to the commissioning party. To be valid, a work for hire agreement (outside of an employer-employment agreement) must be in writing, and must fall under nine categories of specifically commissioned works as defined in section 101 of the Act: a collective work, part of a motion picture or other audiovisual work, a translation, a supplementary work, a compilation, an instructional text, a test, answer material for a test, or an atlas. If you have not signed a work for hire agreement, and you are not in an employee-employer relationship, you own the rights to the work you create. If a company desires to be the copyright owner, the rights must be assigned in writing.

Copyright Holders' Rights

The copyright holder has the absolute and exclusive right to control the reproduction, distribution, adaptations (derivative works), and all public performance and public displays of her work for the duration of the copyright. What does this mean?

- **Reproduction rights** allow you to control when, how, and where your work is reproduced, either in print, or electronically via the internet, because downloading work reproduces it.
- **Distribution rights** allow you to control how, where, and when your work is distributed, including in print and via the internet.
- **Derivative work rights** allow you to control any use of your work in a new work. Common types of derivative works include paintings based on photographs, a screenplay from a novel, or collages using more than one original work. The new material added to make the derivative work may be entitled to a separate copyright if the additional material contributed to the original work is also original and sufficient enough for copyright protection. The new copyright extends only to the material contributed by the second creator. Derivative work rights are important rights for creators today, as are the creation of unauthorized derivatives, more common today in our digital environment with software programs such as Photoshop that make it so easy for anyone to copy, modify, and reuse a visual image.
- **Performance rights** apply to public performances of dance, music, and theater.
- **Public display rights** address how, when, and where a work is shown publicly.

These rights are independent of each other, which means that a copyright holder can sell or license one right, but not the others.

Registration

Although a work does not have to be registered to be entitled to copyright protection, copyright registration is recommended and encouraged because: (1) filing an application for registration is required for any legal action (for a "United States Work" as defined in the Copyright Act), (2) copyright registration provides evidence that the copyright is valid, and (3) if the work is filed in a timely manner (to be defined below), the copyright holder can elect to seek statutory damages (instead of actual damages) and reimbursement of attorney's fees, awarded at the court's discretion. Statutory damages generally range from $750 to $30,000, or up to $150,000, in the court's discretion, for willful infringement. Timely registration is defined as a work being registered before it is infringed or, if the work is published, within three months of publication.

What constitutes publication? We would all agree that something printed in a magazine or a book is "published" and that kind of publication is clear in copyright law. What about works posted on a website or on a social media platform? What constitutes online publication is often confusing, and is the subject of a Copyright Office study. The current definition from the Copyright Office offers some guidance:

> "Publication" is the distribution of copies or phonorecords of a work to the public by sale or other transfer of ownership, or by rental, lease, or lending. The offering to distribute copies or phonorecords to a group of persons for purposes of further distribution, public performance, or public display, constitutes publication. A public performance or display of a work does not of itself constitute publication.

As a *general* rule (but not always), a work posted online, or included in an online portfolio on a creator's website, would be considered "published" only if the copyright owner authorizes users to download and retain copies of that work either for a fee or free of charge. So a notice that a creator puts on her website that viewers are allowed to download work and reuse it in any way could be construed as "offering to distribute" copies to the public. In this instance, posting on a website would probably mean that the work was published for copyright registration purposes. However, if an author puts a copyright notice and an "all rights reserved" notice on her website and states that people are not authorized to download the work, she is not offering the work to the public for further distribution simply by posting it on the website. In this instance, posting work would not be construed as "published." Intent matters here, so if notices on a site clearly state that the work is copyright-protected and should not be downloaded without permission, the fact that someone downloads it anyway does not render the work published. It is unclear if sharing work on a social media site such as Instagram is a publication as the work can be "shared."[5] Distinguishing between published and unpublished images is important because when an author registers an image, he must confirm whether it is published or unpublished. Filling this out wrong can void the registration, which, if the author ends up in a lawsuit, could be costly because if the registration is voided, it is not "timely" anymore.

If a work is not registered in a timely fashion, the author cannot seek to have his attorney fees reimbursed and can only seek actual damages and/or "any profits of the infringer that are attributable to the infringement and are not taken into account in computing the actual damages." Measuring actual damages is not defined in the statute, but case law has established benchmarks: Courts compute damages based on real numbers, such as documented sales, so if the copyright holder does not have robust licensing or sales of their work, damages may be hard to establish. Copyright holders can also show lost revenue, but that is often impossible to prove. Proving how much of a defendant's profits are attributable to using a work can also be difficult, particularly if the work is not used in a product, but merely displayed on a website.

The registration process is not complicated. It can be done electronically, and there are tutorials on the Copyright Office website located at www.copyright.gov. The Copyright Office also publishes various circulars that answer common questions and has published its registration practices in an online Compendium. Some categories of works—such as newspapers, serials, periodicals, and photographs—qualify for group registrations to make it more affordable for creators. Just remember that published works and unpublished works must be registered separately.

Infringement

Infringement occurs when someone violates any of a copyright holder's exclusive rights without the copyright holder's permission (subject to limited exceptions such as the fair use doctrine, discussed below). It does not matter that someone used the work without making money from it, or that the user credited the copyright holder. If it is done without permission, it is infringement, absent any exceptions.

Enforcing copyright can be very expensive as all cases must be litigated in the appropriate federal district court. While Congress is currently working on legislation to create a voluntary and centralized tribunal for copyright claims of $30,000 or less, as of this writing, no legislation has passed. Infringement cases, particularly if a case proceeds to trial, can range in the hundreds of thousands of dollars. While infringements online are rampant—because so many people think it is okay to download work from the internet or to repost something sent to them—it may not be practical or possible to enforce all infringing activities. If the work is not registered before the infringing activity begins, damages may be limited, and the cost of enforcement may be too high.

If a copyright holder chooses to proceed with an infringement claim in the US, they must first register the copyright in a work before filing any claim.[6] Then, in order to prove infringement, they must first establish access to their work and second establish that their work was copied. If the allegedly infringing work is not an exact replica, the copyright holder must establish that the secondary work is substantially similar to their work. Proof of access is required because courts recognize that similar works could have been independently created. Proving access does not literally mean putting the work in the infringer's hands, but copyright holders do have to prove that there is a reasonable chance that the infringer had access to their work. One famous case involved George Harrison's song "My Sweet Lord," eerily similar to songwriter Ronnie Mack's song "He's So Fine,"[7] sung by the Chiffons. Even though Harrison testified that he was not consciously thinking of Mack's song and was rather thinking of an old Christian hymn "Oh Happy Day," and that he wrote "My Sweet Lord" in praise of the Hindu god Krishna, the court ruled that Harrison was guilty of copyright infringement of a particular musical combination because "his subconscious knew it already had worked in a song his conscious mind did not remember"[8] but he must have heard because the Chiffons' version of Mack's song had been No. 1 on the billboard charts in the US and No. 12 in Britain when it debuted in 1963. Today, with YouTube and such a vast amount of music available online, the internet has become a large digital jukebox, and courts may infer access if a song has more than an insignificant amount of viewers.

Copying and substantial similarity are more complicated concepts because copyright does not protect all elements of a work. It only protects what is unique and original. This is most evident in works of visual art, such as fine art and photographs, which usually contain expressive and non-expressive elements, that is, elements that are copyright-protected and elements that are not. For example, in a photograph, expressive elements, which are protected, would include lighting, point of view, angle, focus, and the arrangement of objects in the photograph. Non-expressive or commonplace elements, such as a couple kissing, a sunset, or someone jumping, are not protected. With fiction, courts consider whether more than the general plot sequence or theme is copied, and look at specific copyrightable (expressive) details about the characters, places, or a unique turn of phrase. The courts distinguish between the ideas and how the ideas are expressed. For example, two young lovers meet, one from the wrong side of town, the family disapproves, and the young lovers die rather than be apart. This plot could describe Romeo and Juliet, West Side Story, or countless other stories. The law will not give a monopoly to one author for an idea, but it will for unique detail about characters or places. For example, the idea of a magic school with witches and wizards is not protected, but the unique description of the characters of Hogwarts that makes the Harry Potter stories so unique is protected.

When comparing expressive elements, the law requires that the two works be "substantially similar," which is a more complicated concept, because it is subjective. Specifically, substantial similarity does not mean that the work is identical. It refers to whether there is a strong resemblance of more than minor similarities between the works. The courts use two very different legal tests that yield different results. One older and more commonly used test asks if an ordinary observer would be predisposed to overlook similarities between the works unless she deliberately tried to detect them. A second test used in other circuits essentially asks: If the non-copyrightable elements are extracted, are the elements that remain substantially similar?

Even if the work itself is copied, or someone adapts a work, there are defenses to copying, such as fair use that may permit the use or adaptation of the work.

Fair Use

Fair use, a doctrine created by the courts to permit some use of a work without permission in circumstances when the use furthers the purpose of copyright, is a "defense" against infringement, or an exception to the rule that all unauthorized uses are infringement. The doctrine, now codified in the statute (17 U.S.C. § 107), strikes a balance between the First Amendment (the right of free speech) and copyright protection because commentary and criticism are essential to a functioning democracy. For example, if you are a literary critic reviewing a new novel, you will need to quote from it to substantiate your criticism, but the author may not want to grant permission to quote from the book or may condition permission on a favorable review. You want to quote from the work without compromise and do it anyway. Or you are an appropriation artist and you are challenging the idea of authorship, so you knowingly make a derivative work of other artists' materials without permission. In both cases, you have infringed the existing work. The fair use doctrine provides some legal protection in such circumstances because the law specifies that the fair use of a copyrighted work for purposes such as criticism, commentary (including parody), comment, news reporting, teaching, scholarship, or research is not an infringement of copyright.

Since fair use is a defense against infringement, it can only be invoked after the finding of infringement. It is always fact-specific, with courts deciding the outcome on a case-by-case basis, which means the outcome is never predictable. It also is not a free pass. It allows for reasonable uses in the public interest. For example, just because "teaching" is mentioned in the statute does not mean that a faculty member of a college or university can copy entire books and pass out the copies to all of her students.

Rather than being a definitive quantitative standard, the fair use doctrine identifies four "factors" that courts should consider in analyzing whether an infringement is a fair use:

- Factor One: The purpose and character of the use (for new work), including whether it is for commercial or nonprofit purposes.
- Factor Two: The nature of the copyrighted work (the original work).
- Factor Three: The amount and substantiality of the portion used in relation to the copyrighted work as a whole.
- Factor Four: The effect of the use upon the potential for or value of the copyrighted work.

Because the law provides no further guidance on how courts should "consider" these factors, fair use is a highly litigated issue reliant on the facts of each case. It is almost impossible to provide any bright-line facts upon which creators can rely. Not all factors are treated with the same weight, and different courts have interpreted these factors differently over time.

What do these factors mean? Generally speaking, the first factor looks at the reason the secondary work was made. Is it commercial or non-commercial? Does the use fulfill the objective of copyright law, which is to stimulate creativity and add to public information? Courts might consider how "transformative" the work is, which means that the new use must be productive and must employ the original work in a different manner with new information, new aesthetics, or new insights, or for a different purpose. This factor has been given the most weight in many recent cases, and if this factor favors fair use, the remaining factors weigh toward fair use.

The second factor is concerned with protecting the incentives of authorship. The more creative the original work is, the more protection it receives, and the more factual the work, the less protection. This factor is rarely the one that tips the scale and is often considered neutral.

The third factor does not set absolute amounts. It looks at both the amount of what was taken (quantitative) and the significance of what was taken (qualitative). Generally, the more the user takes or if the user takes parts of great importance —the "heart of the work"—the less likely that taking will qualify as a fair use. The courts do acknowledge that a parody, which gets strong protection because it is "commentary," might require a taking of all, or a significant portion. With visual images, courts often permit the taking of an entire work, as it is difficult to comment on only a portion of a visual work. You might have heard that you can only take "10 percent" of a work, up to 150 words, or eight bars of music, but those are not legal standards and there are no "safe harbor" formulas based on amounts or percentages.

The fourth factor looks at market harm to the original work by the secondary use. It looks at both actual market harm and potential harm if the infringing use became widespread. Before the Supreme Court case of Campbell v. Acuff-Rose Music, Inc., 510 U.S. 569 (1994), in which the court found that 2 Live Crew's rap parody "Oh Hairy Woman" of Roy Orbison's "Oh Pretty Woman" could be a fair use, most commercial uses were not considered fair use because of harm to a licensing market and a creator's income. However, for uses such as parody, or some collage art, where even if a licensing market exists, fair use is favored because it promotes the purposes of copyright, and a creator is unlikely to grant a license to a secondary user who wants to parody a work. Generally, if there is no ill effect on the market for the original work or for licensing derivative works, the courts will find the use to be fair and non-infringing.

One of the challenges of relying on the fair use doctrine, or thinking you might know how the court is going to rule is that fair use is the most unpredictable of all legal doctrines. Courts do not agree on which factors are the most important, how to weigh the factors, or even what transformative means. The Copyright Office maintains an index of fair use cases, and breaks them down by types of works, which is helpful as courts have tended to be less liberal in finding fair use with taking of music samples in copyright cases and more permissive with appropriation artists using works of other artists.

Digital Millennium Copyright Act

The Digital Millennium Copyright Act (DMCA), which became part of the Copyright Act in 1998, was passed in response to the growth of technology and the internet. It created a cause of action not just for infringing the exclusive rights of a copyright owner, but for activity that could encourage or increase infringing activity, such as the removal or alteration of copyright notices, credits, and metadata (copyright management information under section 1202). Section 1201 created a separate cause of action for circumvention methods intended to bypass measures implemented to control access to copyrighted work, known as digital rights management (DRM). Damages for removal of metadata or circumventing technology measures include statutory damages of between $2,500 and $25,000 per work and potential attorneys' fees at the court's discretion. While copyright is primarily a civil action, there can be criminal liability in limited circumstances, primarily to prevent piracy where there is no financial gain, which can result in egregious cases of up to five years in jail.

The DMCA also limits the liability of qualified online services for copyright infringement by their users, or due to content being cached. That is why YouTube, Instagram, and Facebook, for example, are not directly liable for infringements that occur on their sites, provided they have policies in place to remove repeat infringers and promptly take down infringing content after receiving proper notice. The DMCA allows a copyright holder to send a takedown notice to the service provider's registered agent for user-generated content that infringes a copyright. Before sending a DMCA takedown notice, the copyright holder must establish a few things:

1   The copyright owner owns the copyright or has the right to assert infringement of a copyright licensed.
2   The alleged infringement is not covered by an exception such as fair use or free speech laws. This requires a statement of a "good faith" belief that the alleged infringing use is not covered by any law which would permit its use.
3   The content is capable of being infringed online. That means the work must be something in digital form.

The takedown notice must be in writing and be signed; identify the work(s) that have been infringed; identify the material (place) that is infringing the work; include the copyright holder's contact information; include a statement that the complaint is in good faith; include a statement that the information in the notification is accurate; and include a statement that under penalty of perjury the person submitting the takedown notice is authorized to act on behalf of the owner of an exclusive right that is allegedly infringed. There are many services online that provide free or low-cost takedown notice generators.

Upon receipt of a proper takedown notification letter, the website or service provider is on notice of the claim and is required to "expeditiously" take down the allegedly infringing material and to send a notice to the customer saying that it received a DMCA takedown notice and is taking down the user-generated content.

Unlike other aspects of copyright laws, the DMCA takedown process does not require that the work be registered. However, if the user files a proper counter-notification claiming non-infringement and the web host notifies the copyright owner that a counter-notification has been received, the work will be put back up on the site unless the copyright owner files a copyright infringement suit within ten business days against the alleged infringer. The problem is that the work has to be registered to file an infringement suit. Since the recent Supreme Court decision in Fourth Estate, it is clear that authors cannot file a claim with only an application and must have the final copyright registration from the Copyright Office. Depending on the backlog, it can take months after filing with the Copyright Office to receive the copyright registration. While there is a provision for expediting the application process, it takes a week to a couple of weeks to attain an expedited registration, and the special handling fee is significant.

Termination Rights

What happens if you transfer all your rights early in your career and later you realize you made a mistake? The Copyright Act allows you to reclaim those rights under § 203, entitled "[t]ermination of transfers and licenses granted by the author." Any transfer or license of copyright granted by the author on or after January 1, 1978 can be terminated, or revoked, under certain circumstances. The rights can then be renegotiated or the copyright holder can enter into new agreements. This does not apply to rights transferred in a work for hire agreement.

The rules governing termination rights are complex, and since the rights to terminate only became effective in 2013, courts are still carving out the contours of the law. Thus, what follows is a brief overview of the basics to help you know if you might qualify for termination rights, in which case, it would be best for you to contact a lawyer.

Generally, termination rights apply at any time during a period of five years at the end of thirty-five years from the date of the execution of the grant or from the date of publication.

Only the original grantee or her heirs can challenge the termination rights by serving an advance notice in writing not less than two or more than ten years before the date of termination, stating the effective date of the termination. If the proper notice has been served (subject to limitations) on the effective date of termination, all rights will revert to the author(s) with the following limitations: A derivative work prepared with permission prior to the effective date may continue, but no rights extend to new derivative works.

Termination rights apply even in instances when a copyright owner has signed a contract with conflicting terms—often the case with musicians and recording companies—because federal law supersedes state law.

Moral Rights

Moral rights (from the French term, *droit moral*) are additional rights granted to creators of copyrighted works to control the eventual fate of their works. They protect the personal and reputational rather than purely monetary value of a work. Moral rights often include the right to share in the increased value of work when it is sold, known as resale rights (*droit de suite*) which provide that visual artists or their estates receive a royalty generally ranging from 3 to 5 percent on the resale of artworks.

Moral rights are usually recognized in civil law jurisdictions, and, to a lesser extent, in some common-law jurisdictions. Moral rights recognize that a creator deserves respect for creativity, with a right to:

* Be recognized as the author of a work or to decide that the work should be published anonymously.
* Be properly attributed as the author.
* Prevent others from modifying, distorting, or otherwise interfering with the integrity of that work.
* Determine if and when material is made public.

Moral rights are distinct from any economic rights tied to copyrights and were first recognized in France and Germany before they were included in the Berne Convention. Even though the US was a signatory to the Berne Convention in 1989, it still does not completely recognize moral rights as part of copyright law, but rather as part of other bodies of law, including the Visual Artists Rights Act of 1990 (VARA), and laws of defamation or unfair competition. In Europe, moral rights are inalienable, which means an artist cannot voluntarily give them up, or contract them away. Even if an artist has assigned his or her copyright rights to a work to a third party, he or she still maintains the moral rights to the work. Canada, the UK, and the US are among a handful of countries that allow moral rights to be waived.

Visual Artists Rights Act

In the US, moral rights receive protection through judicial interpretation of several copyright, trademark, privacy, and defamation statues, and through 17 U.S.C. § 106A, known as VARA. Under VARA, moral rights automatically vest in the author of a "work of visual art," but only if that work is of "recognized stature." VARA defines visual art as paintings, drawings, prints, sculptures, and photographs, existing in a single copy or a limited edition of 200 or fewer signed and numbered copies. However, a photograph is protected only if it was taken for exhibition purposes. VARA specifically excludes posters, maps, globes, motion pictures, electronic publications, and applied art. VARA applies to works of art created on or after June 1, 1990. Protection expires when the artist dies, or for a joint work, when the last surviving artist dies. The moral rights for works created before June 1, 1990 are only protected if the artist still has title to the work and are coextensive with and expire at the same time as the copyright. Under VARA, moral rights are not inalienable; authors may waive their moral rights and often do so in exchange for a sale or for gallery representation. VARA also does not include resale rights.

VARA grants the right of attribution and the right of integrity. The right of attribution allows an author to prevent misattribution of a work—that is, to prevent her name from being attached to art that she did not create, to require that the authorship of the work not be disclosed (i.e., remain anonymous), and to prevent her work from being attributed to her if it has been modified in such a way that damages her "honor" or reputation. VARA also prevents the intentional or grossly negligent destruction of any work of recognized stature. Therefore, if someone paints a Jeff Koons sculpture a different color, he will have violated the artist's moral rights under VARA.

For VARA violations, artists may seek actual damages and the profits of the violator which result from the infringement, or statutory damages of between $750 and $30,000 per work (similar to copyright statutory damages) and up to $150,000 if the VARA violation was done willfully or in bad faith. If the violator can prove she did not know that she was committing a VARA violation, then the damages can be reduced to as little as $200. Artists can also seek attorney and court costs, awarded at the court's discretion.

Works Integrated into Buildings

Works, such as murals, which are a part of a building have their own specialized set of VARA rules. If a work cannot be removed from a building without being modified or damaged, and the artist consented to the installation of the work before June 1, 1990, or signed a contract along with the owner of the building after June 1, 1990, acknowledging that the removal of the work may damage it, then the artist has no VARA protection. If the work can be removed without being modified or damaged, then the artist has VARA protection unless the building owner makes a diligent good faith attempt to notify the artist within ninety days of the removal. If the artist removes the work at her own expense, she has title to the work as well as moral rights.

Notes

1 "Berne Convention for the Protection of Literary and Artistic Works," September 9, 1886, as revised at Stockholm on July 14, 1967, Art. 1, 5(1), 828 U.N.T.S. 221, World Intellectual Property Organization (Paris Text 1971), accessed May 20, 2020, https://www.wipo.int/treaties/en/ip/berne.

2 "Universal Copyright Convention, with Appendix Declaration relating to Articles XVII and Resolution Concerning Article XI 1952," Legal Instruments, United Nations Educational, Scientific and Cultural Organization (UNESCO Constitution), accessed May 20, 2020, http://portal.unesco.org/en/ev.php-URL_ID=15381&URL_DO=DO_TOPIC&URL_SECTION=201.html.

3 David Robb, "Core Copyright Industries Added $1.3 Trillion to U.S. Economy in 2017, Employ 5.7M Americans," *Deadline*, December 7, 2018, https://deadline.com/2018/12/core-copyright-industries-added-1-3-trillion-to-u-s-economy-in-2017-employ-5-7m-americans-1202516240.

4 "Copyright Term and the Public Domain in the United States," Cornell University Library, accessed May 20, 2020, https://copyright.cornell.edu/publicdomain.

5 Sinclair v. Ziff Davis, LLC, No. 18-CV-790-KMW, 2020 WL 1847841, at *3–4 (S.D.N.Y. Apr. 13, 2020) (holding that the photographer could not sue a website for embedding images posted on Instagram).

6 Fourth Estate Pub. Benefit Corp. v. Wall-Street.com, LLC, 139 S. Ct. 881 (2019).

7 Bright Tunes Music Corp. v. Harrisongs Music, Ltd., 420 F. Supp. 177 (S.D.N.Y. 1976), *aff'd sub nom.* ABKCO Music, Inc. v. Harrisongs Music, Ltd., 722 F.2d 988 (2d Cir. 1983), https://law.justia.com/cases/federal/district-courts/FSupp/420/177/1738901.

8 *Id.* at 180.

PART II

Literary Works

Introduction

Books and other writings are the touchstone of our nation's copyright laws. The US Constitution, the source of federal copyright law, referred specifically to writings in granting Congress the power "to promote the Progress of Science and useful Arts, by securing for limited Times to Authors and Inventors the exclusive Rights to the respective Writings and Discoveries." The current Copyright Act, enacted in 1978, identifies categories of works of authorship eligible under copyright, and the first category listed is "literary." The definition of a literary work under the Act is intentionally broad to cover software and includes all works other than audiovisual works that are expressed in words, numbers, or other verbal or numerical symbols. However, the chapters in Part II primarily focus on issues arising from traditional literary works and do not address issues unique to software. Even though the term "author" is used throughout the Copyright Act, there is no definition of author in the Act itself. The Copyright Office, in its Compendium of US Copyright Office Practices, does clarify that the Office will only register works of human authorship.

Literary works have always served the purpose of copyright in promoting the progress of science and useful arts as books, articles, poems, plays, and other writings have throughout the history been used to educate, inform, entertain, provoke, persuade, and incite the curiosity and imagination of the public. Literature in all its forms has added to our society's cultural riches and helped create an educated democratic society. The twenty-first century and the digital age offer authors the promise of many new possibilities for publishing works, as the internet creates a platform that allows anyone to be a publisher, whether it is a blog, poem, or other form of communication. Traditional publishers still play an important role in publishing, serving as a gatekeeper and filter for literary works with the resources to review, edit, and promote selected works of authorship. But the opportunity for self-publication provides new avenues for many authors that might not otherwise be published.

The chapters here in Part II look at opportunities as well as the challenges that authors of literary works face in the twenty-first century under copyright law, but many of the issues such as fair use address broader categories of works. As the internet opens many publishing avenues, it will also provide fertile ground for the mass distribution of pirated works and unauthorized copies. Copyright doctrines such as fair use play an important role in reviewing and critiquing others works but those lines need to be deftly navigated as the distinction between making a fair use and an infringing use can be confusing to lawyers as well as non-lawyers. As with other types of authorship, the line between what is protected by copyright and what is an idea that can be freely written about by others continues to be an ongoing question for authors.

In Chapter 2.1, "Piracy of Books in the Digital Age," co-authors Cheryl Davis, the General Counsel of the Author's Guild, and Umair Kazi, the Guild's Director of Policy and Advocacy look at the impact piracy and the sale of unauthorized books have on the livelihood of authors and what tools are available to authors to try and protect their rights under copyright. They address the challenges with both print and e-books, that can both be reproduced with ease, and end up competing with authors for the sale of authorized books, depriving them of royalties, harming both publishers and authors. They examine the cause of these challenges, including the ability for anyone in any part of the world to be able to sell counterfeit books and the difficulty in keeping these books off of legitimate sales platforms such as Amazon. They also look at the Digital Millennium Copyright Act (DMCA), now more than twenty years old, and how it has been interpreted by the courts, tilting the burden to uncovering these counterfeit copies on the publisher and author, and allowing internet service providers to escape liability for the sale of these copies, provided they merely remove the copies after receiving a proper notice for each time an infringing copy is uploaded, with no obligation to filter for these counterfeit books or to monitor the platform. They suggest changes in enforcement that may help, support the proposed Copyright Alternative in Small-Claims Enforcement Act that has passed the House and, at this writing, is waiting to be brought to the Senate floor, and provide steps authors can take to protect themselves.

In Chapter 2.2, "Is a Picture Really Worth More Than A Thousand Words?," Marcia Paul looks at the question of whether a fictional character featured within a copyright protected work can be afforded protection outside of the work. She provides an overview of the law and seminal cases that have looked at protection for fictional characters to determine how developed the character must be to be afforded stand-alone protection and where the cases differ in how central the character is to the plot line or whether the character is merely a "stock" character, akin to an idea than anyone can write about. This chapter asks the question whether characters should have protection as a category of work, outside of literary works, or whether the Copyright Act, as interpreted by case law, provides sufficient protection under a traditional analysis of substantial similarity and provides enough protection to sufficiently delineated characters.

In Chapter 2.3, "Fair Use: The Judicial Mix-Up over 'A Mixed Question of Law and Fact,'" Terence P. Keegan looks at the role of the judge and jury in deciding fair use cases. While this chapter is not limited to literary works, it raises an important issue for everyone, as jury trials are very expensive and, if a judge can decide whether a use is a fair use or not, the costs of litigation, while not inexpensive, are certainly reduced. Most cases settle if a decision cannot be decided by the court based on questions of law. If there are questions of fact in dispute, the issue is generally left to a jury. Keegan presents a history of fair use cases and concludes that courts misuse the legal phrase "mixed question of law and fact" to relegate too many fair use decisions to a jury and instead, he believes that fair use, as it touches the outer boundaries of copyright law, is better decided by the court.

In Chapter 2.4, "Fair Use: The Linchpin to the Future of the Copyright Act," Michael Donaldson holds out that reasonable use of the fair use doctrine will meet the needs of creators and users and keep the Copyright Act relevant in the twenty-first century. Donaldson sees the fair use doctrine as providing the flexibility needed in the Copyright Act to permit uses without permission if it serves the purpose of the copyright law to promote new works, but is not reverse engineered to create a business model that competes with the underlying works. The ability of judges to decide whether fair use applies based on the facts of each case permits the court to allow the use of copyrighted works, and, in particular, works of nonfiction, where the use is justified as it was used to illustrate a point. Donaldson created his own "safe harbor" outside of the four-factor test that looks at the point being made, the reasonableness of the amount used, and whether the connection between the work used and the point being made is clear to the viewer. While this method is often applied by Donaldson in films, it may be transferred to other creative mediums. This chapter also looks at cases that address parody and the importance of fair use to allow the creation of a parody work as permission from the work being parodied is unlikely to be granted. In sum, Davis demonstrates how fair use gives the Copyright Act the freedom to maintain its relevance in the twenty-first century.

In the last chapter in Part II, "Self-Publishing Revolution: Copyright Pitfalls for Writers Who Go It Alone," Francine Ward offers practical advice to authors who choose the self-publishing route and helps the reader navigate the many roles an author must perform in successfully self-publishing a work. Ward reviews the importance of hiring competent counsel, registering copyright in the work, and using contracts with collaborators. She also explains commonly misunderstood questions such as what is in the public domain and what can be used under the doctrine of fair use.

2.1

PIRACY OF BOOKS IN THE DIGITAL AGE

Cheryl L. Davis and Umair Kazi

- piracy
- noun

1   the practice of attacking and robbing ships at sea.
2   a practice similar to piracy but in other contexts, especially hijacking.
3   the unauthorized use or reproduction of another's work.[1]

The meaning of piracy has changed over the centuries, as commerce has moved from on sea (and on land) to online. Its impact has not changed; property owners are wrongfully deprived of their property, be it tangible or intellectual. Governments once pursued maritime pirates and attempted to bring them to justice. Now they pursue them in the equally murky waters of the internet. The law has to adjust to recognize new ways in which copyrights can be exploited and appropriated, and now courts and legislatures are scrambling with how to combat internet piracy without unduly limiting the freedom of the internet.

The theft of property has existed since objects have been owned, and the theft of intellectual property has existed for hundreds of years. So, why then make such a fuss about internet piracy? Theft is far more common on the internet than in the physical world, because digital technology and the internet have made rampant the theft of intellectual property. It is commensurately easier for pirates to roam the internet looking for works to steal than it was for them to roam the high seas. In an Author's Guild Piracy webinar, Sarina Bowen stated: "When you empower publishers to publish, you also empower pirates to pirate."[2] This chapter examines twenty-first-century piracy by looking at the issues that book authors face and how the law has tried to balance internet efficiency and creator's rights. (This piece draws from Authors Guild Advocacy materials.)

Piracy in the Digital Age

In anticipation of issues that would arise with digital technology and a growing and expanding internet, Congress passed the Digital Millennium Copyright Act (DMCA) in 1998. Recognizing the possibility (actually, near certainty) that once copyrighted works were circulated on the internet, they would be infringed there as well, Congress attempted to strike a balance between protecting copyrighted works without stifling technological innovation or the efficiency of the internet by providing a safe harbor for internet service providers (ISPs). The legislative history explains Congress' attempt to keep pace with technology while still protecting content:

> Copyright laws have struggled through the years to keep pace with emerging technology from the struggle over music played on a player piano roll in the 1900s to the introduction of the VCR in the 1980s. With this constant evolution in technology, the law must adapt in order to make digital networks safe places to disseminate and exploit copyrighted materials . . . [T]his bill[] provides this protection and creates the legal platform for launching the global digital online marketplace for copyrighted works. It will also make available via the Internet the movies, music, software, and literary works that are the fruit of American creative genius.[3]

The DMCA established a system to limit the liability of qualified ISPs so that they would not face liability for copyright infringement under certain circumstances, namely if an ISP:

A   i   does not have actual knowledge that the material or an activity using the material on the system or network is infringing;

     ii   in the absence of such actual knowledge, is not aware of facts or circumstances from which infringing activity is apparent; or

     iii   upon obtaining such knowledge or awareness, acts expeditiously to remove, or disable access to, the material;

B   does not receive a financial benefit directly attributable to the infringing activity, in a case in which the service provider has the right and ability to control such activity; and

C   upon notification of claimed infringement as described in paragraph (3), responds expeditiously to remove, or disable access to, the material that is claimed to be infringing or to be the subject of infringing activity.[4]

As laudable as was Congress' intent to protect both creators and ISPs, the DMCA generally has protected ISPs more than it has protected creators. Authors in particular have disproportionately felt the impact of internet pirates and have experienced the substantial loss of income that results from the activties of these modern-day Blackbeards. The DMCA is now more than twenty years old and the internet has substantially changed. Some would argue that it no longer needs protection from liability because it encompasses virtually all global commerce and content. The incomes of authors and other independent creators have been substantially reduced by others appropriating and selling their works with impunity or using their work without paying a license. At what point is it no longer necessary to protect ISPs to the detriment of creators? Let's look at some realities faced by authors today and understand how books are pirated online.

The most pervasive type of piracy for physical copies of books is the unauthorized reproduction of books in their entirety—cover art and copy included—that are sold on online marketplaces by third-party sellers. Since pirates are attempting to pass these books off as authentic copies, they copy and use (and thus misappropriate) the publisher's trademark, the author's name, copyrighted to cover art, as well as other proprietary and trademarkable attributes from the book covers. A number of US-based self-publishing services will provide printed copies of any book that is uploaded without, checking to see whether the copyright to the uploaded book is owned by the customer uploading it or if they infringe a copyright. The counterfeiter can scan a book, upload it to an online print publishing service (such as Amazon's Kindle Direct Publishing), and print out and sell the books on demand directly to consumers by setting up third-party seller accounts on Amazon, eBay, and Google Play.

While counterfeiting is not new to the internet, the internet has enabled and emboldened this type of piracy. The prevalence of reputable online platforms (such as Amazon) through which third-party sellers (including some pirates) may sell their wares means that counterfeit copies can be sold thousands of miles away from the pirate's location; in fact, many piracy sites are located abroad, in places such as Ukraine.

Amazon's book marketplace also allows third-party sellers to sell new and used books (the seller designates whether the books are "new" or "used") alongside publisher copies; and unlike other products sold on Amazon, third-party book sellers need not prove that their books were legitimately obtained. While copyright law permits the owner of a physical copy of a book to resell that book under the first sale doctrine, previously such used books were sold in different physical locations (such as separate bookstores, or in separate areas in a bookstore that also sells new books). Today, Amazon and eBay have completely changed the book market and permit books from many different sources to be sold through their online marketplaces, often intermingled on the same web page as a new (and royalty-bearing) copy of the same book. This means that used books and pirated copies are competing with new, legitimately sourced books.

Unlike someone buying suspiciously cheap products being sold on the sidewalk who knows the products are knockoffs, consumers of counterfeit books bought on a reputable platform assume that they are buying a legitimate book and, unless the quality of the reproduction is particularly poor, will not know any better when they receive the counterfeit copy. Even if the quality is poor, consumers may blame the publisher and author, rather than realize that they have fallen victim to a pirate.

Piracy can be philosophically difficult to battle in this age of the "copyleft" movements that promote the idea that authors should surrender some of their copyrights so that the public may freely benefit from their work. There are pirates who self-righteously argue that "information wants to be free"[5] and believe that they are serving some greater good by liberating works under copyright. Pirates are not "Robin Hoods"; they are thieves who take from authors who make a living only from writing.[6] What these pirates do not consider is that there are real people who are harmed by their cavalier acts of theft.[7] Whether authors are published by a traditional publisher or are self-published, they are dependent on sales of their books to earn money. Thus, whenever a consumer buys a pirated rather than a legal copy, the author loses income. This loss of income is not insignificant. Authors are already struggling financially. Their book-related income has dropped 42 percent in the last decade,[8] but the recent surge in book piracy and counterfeiting is stealing even more money out of their pockets. Many books that add to our collective culture require a large amount of research and are the product of at least two or three years of work, if not more. The piracy of a single book can amount to theft of years of full-time work. Few other crimes can compare to this in terms of how they affect the victim's livelihood.

Pirating of e-books is particularly rampant as they are already digital. It is even easier (and cheaper) to copy and electronically distribute e-books through pirate websites dedicated to just that purpose.

E-book pirates come in all shapes and sizes. There are large pirate repositories such as Libgen, Sci-Hub, Pirate Bay, and Torrent sites, which have been a cause for concern for some time for authors and publishers, as well as governments. There are also individuals and relatively smaller groups that use legitimate services such as Amazon, CreateSpace, Google Books, and Barnes & Noble to sell pirated e-books and even counterfeit physical books to consumers. Other websites allow users to upload and share copyrighted works, and despite their efforts to paint themselves as legitimate, these sites are just as illegal as the big pirate repositories.

Changes in the publishing marketplace in the twenty-first century have facilitated online piracy because online marketplaces are now a central part of the American book industry. Amazon alone controls 64 percent of online sales of print books,[9] about 89 percent of all e-book sales,[10] and approximately 76 percent of sales of self-published e-books.[11] As a result, American authors and publishers cannot simply choose to not sell their books through online marketplaces like Amazon. They are compelled by the marketplace to make themselves prey to digital pirates.

Some of the factors contributing to the rise of book counterfeiting and piracy are the low cost of entry into the e-book marketplace, the online platforms' volume-driven business model, the extraterritoriality of the actors involved in the production of counterfeit and pirated copies, as well as weak piracy enforcement and significant gaps in the legal and regulatory framework governing online marketplaces.

The low cost of producing a counterfeit copy allows counterfeiters to dramatically undercut the price of authorized (and royalty-bearing) copies, allowing them to steal customers from legitimate vendors. Counterfeiters anywhere in the world can use cheap print-on-demand (POD) services to remotely print and ship unauthorized print copies to customers. Those pirated books can be sold more cheaply because counterfeiters are spared the cost of design, editing, copy editing, and marketing, as well as author royalties and advances. POD publishers are not incentivized to alert authors or publishers that someone is counterfeiting their books, since Sales of counterfeit books still increase POD revenues. Transactions conducted on many internet platforms earn listing fees and commissions, whether or not the product sold is authentic or counterfeit, legal or illicit.[12] The combination of the focus on volume and the lack of platform accountability[13] provides fertile waters for piracy and other copyright infringement scams such as selling an existing book with a new author, title, and cover,[14] as well as scams, including "doppelganging" and "title-cloning"—using an existing author's name or a confusingly similar title to sell lower-quality books. While all of these practices violate Amazon's policies, and Amazon does try to keep up with the scams and counterfeiters, the volume of these illicit practices is difficult to reign in.[15]

Third-party marketplaces also can conduct business worldwide, and, while this makes the marketplace more appealing for consumers and therefore sellers, it also makes it easier for pirates in other jurisdictions to profit from their illegal sales in the US. If a pirate is located in a foreign country or its profits from piracy are placed in a foreign bank, these profits are out of reach to US authors making it too difficult to sue the pirate or recover any damages.

The Impact of Online Piracy on the US Marketplace

In 2005, Marybeth Peters, the then-Register of Copyrights, testified before Congress and said: "International piracy poses a tremendous threat to the prosperity of one of America's most vibrant economic sectors: its creative industries."[16] Approximately fifteen years later, this threat has only grown. The value of trade in counterfeit and pirated goods is estimated to be approximately half a trillion dollars per annum, with roughly 20 percent of this trade infringing upon intellectual property belonging to the US persons. In April 2019, the President, in his Memorandum on Combating Trafficking in Counterfeit and Pirated Goods,[17] requested that certain federal appointees and agencies draft a report on piracy, including the role of third-party marketplaces and intermediaries (both in facilitating and combating piracy), and identifying administrative, regulatory, and policy changes that might lead to more effective detection of and combating piracy. Clearly, the concern about the harm piracy does to the US economy[18] has reached the highest federal levels.

According to a 2017 Digimarc/Nielsen survey, the US publishers lost approximately $315 million in sales because of online piracy. The piracy alerts the Authors Guild received from its members increased by 300 percent between 2009 and 2013, and by another 76 percent between 2013 and 2017. As with physical piracy, government and industry studies suggest that there is substantial economic harm from online piracy. While piracy of physical books was originally concentrated in the higher-priced textbook and higher education markets, it has now spread to commercial fiction and nonfiction, with best-selling books particularly at risk. As POD technologies and services have improved in quality, the cost of printing books has decreased, and counterfeiting has become significantly easier.

How Does the Law Combat Online Piracy?

Unfortunately, the law has not solved the issues of online piracy as much as it could (or should). While physical marketplaces are held accountable for the sale of counterfeit and pirated goods conducted in them,[19] internet marketplaces are not. To encourage internet entrepreneurs and to ensure that the internet would flourish, our legislatures and courts have placed far less responsibility on online marketplaces than on physical ones. Therefore, internet platforms have little to no legal or financial accountability for the piracy and counterfeiting that occurs through their marketplaces; we believe that this is a primary contributing cause of the surge in piracy and counterfeiting through online marketplaces. The DMCA has given favorable treatment to ISPs and, over the past twenty years, courts have interpreted the DMCA in a way that expands the protection granted to platforms by the legislature, at the expense of copyright holders.

Internet platform terms of service, including those of third-party marketplaces, often place the burden of discovering and reporting infringements upon rights holders. As a result, authors spend time and effort better spent creating new works on combating pirates and counterfeiters. This reactive approach to policing for infringement, piracy, and counterfeiting puts the burden on writers and publishers to invest time and energy in scouring the internet.[20] Some marketplaces encourage buyers and sellers to use third-party payment services like PayPal, which can add another layer of anonymity further protecting pirates.

One of the main issues with respect to online piracy is just how liable an ISP should be for copyright infringements that occur through their websites. The rationale is that websites should not be automatically liable when wrongdoers act through them —but does that mean they should never be liable? Courts have wrestled with this in several high-profile cases.

In Viacom International Inc. v. YouTube, Inc.,[21] YouTube argued that it should not be held liable for the approximately 79,000 infringing clips at issue in the lawsuit, which were posted on the site by YouTube users between 2005 and 2008. The Second Circuit held that the DMCA required YouTube to have an "actual knowledge or awareness of facts or circumstances that indicate specific and identifiable instances of infringement" to be disqualified from sheltering in the safe harbor.[22] The YouTube plaintiffs argued that there was still a possibility that YouTube had "red flag"[23] awareness of specific instances of infringement under the law and if so, should be liable because Congress had expressly stated that although "a service provider would have no obligation to seek out copyright infringement, [] it would not qualify for the safe harbor if it had turned a blind eye to 'red flags' of obvious infringement."[24] The plaintiffs cited evidence that YouTube employees estimated that 75–80 percent of all YouTube streams contained copyrighted material and Google's own financial advisor estimated that "more than 60 percent of YouTube's content was 'premium' copyrighted content—and that only 10 percent of the premium content was authorized. These approximations suggest that the defendants were conscious that significant quantities of material on the YouTube website were infringing."[25]

The Second Circuit sent the YouTube case back to the District Court for the Southern District of New York, which then looked to the rationale behind the relevant provisions of the DMCA:

> Title II of the DMCA (the Online Copyright Infringement Liability Limitation Act) was enacted because service providers perform a useful function, but the great volume of works placed by outsiders on their platforms, of whose contents the service providers were generally unaware, might well contain copyright-infringing material which the service provider would mechanically "publish," thus ignorantly incurring liability under the copyright law. The problem is clearly illustrated on the record in this case, which establishes that "site traffic on YouTube had soared to more than 1 billion daily video views, with more than 24 hours of new video uploaded to the site every minute," and the natural consequence that no service provider could possibly be aware of the contents of each such video.[26]

The court rejected the plaintiffs' argument that YouTube had been willfully blind to the red flags, stating:

> Here, examples proffered by plaintiffs (to which they claim YouTube was willfully blind) give at most information that infringements were occurring with particular works, and occasional indications of promising areas to locate and remove them. The specific locations of infringements are not supplied: at most, an area of search is identified, YouTube is left to find the infringing clip.[27]

The interpretations of the DMCA set forth in YouTube, and UMG Recordings Inc. v. Shelter Capital Partners,[28] and subsequent cases effectively eliminated the "red flag" language in the DMCA and scrolled back protections in the Second and Ninth Circuits (respectively) for copyright holders in order to protect service providers. The "safe harbor" standards set forth in the DMCA were essentially reduced to "the infringed gives the service provider notice of the infringement on a specific URL and the provider then takes down the specific URL," ad infinitum.

The result of these decisions has created a version of the game "whack-a-mole," now a term often used to describe online piracy and the never-ending effort the DMCA notice and takedown procedure imposes on copyright holders. Many pirate sites do not have any contacts to receive DMCA takedown notices to begin with. Some do, but the forms do not work, and others comply, but the infringed books just pop right back.

While the expanding safe harbor for service providers may not, strictly speaking, enable pirates, it does make the "waters" in which they operate much friendlier, since there is no disincentive for ISPs to engage in any efforts to deter pirates. The incentive, as is the burden, is all on the copyright holders. Ensuring that the DMCA protects rights holders as well as internet providers is essential for authors in their fight against online piracy.

After a decades-long pattern of courts stripping away all protections for copyright holders in DMCA safe harbors, the US Court of Appeals for the Fourth Circuit, in BMG Rights Management (US) LLC v. Cox Communications, Inc.,[29] took an important (and long overdue) step to hopefully reverse that trend. In that case, the Fourth Circuit required ISPs to have and enforce reasonable repeat-infringer policies. The plaintiffs there tried to compel defendant Cox Communications to terminate subscribers engaged in high-volume infringement. At the time, Cox had a "thirteen-strike policy" in place, which meant that only after a thirteenth suspension would Cox even consider terminating an infringing user's account. This created a particularly egregious whack-a-mole situation. The Fourth Circuit's opinion in BMG astutely observes that "[a]n ISP cannot claim the protections of the DMCA safe harbor provisions merely by terminating customers as a symbolic gesture before indiscriminately reactivating them within a short timeframe."[30] That court also acknowledged the profit motive behind Cox's inadequate policy, quoting a comment by a Cox manager instructing an employee not to terminate a repeat infringer's account: "[t]his customer pays us $400/month . . . [e]very terminated [c]ustomer becomes lost revenue."[31] While the binding effects of this decision are limited to the Fourth Circuit, the Authors Guild hopes that sister jurisdictions will consider and apply its reasoning on similar cases within their purview.

Suggested Changes to Better Combat Online Piracy

Increased Accountability for Online Platforms

Third-party marketplaces should be held responsible for the sale of counterfeit and pirated goods though their platforms, since they are best situated to detect and control the sale of counterfeit and pirated books. They, not the rights holders, profit from the sale of illegal books through their platforms since they collect commissions and fees from the sales. Further, since they have contractual privity with both third-party sellers and their customers, they are in the best position to address piracy and counterfeiting. Since these platforms now possess an astronomical portion of the country's wealth, it is fair to say that they no longer need the belts-and-suspenders protection from liability that the laws and court decisions have given them. It is time to revisit our laws, along with the way courts have interpreted them, and place more responsibility for combatting counterfeiting and piracy on the internet marketplaces, just as we have for physical marketplaces.

One way to truly combat internet piracy would be to enforce the DMCA as written, or to modify the law to create a "notice and stay-down" process, rather than the much-abused notice and takedown procedure. Other modifications to the statute that would benefit creators include adding a standard of "general awareness of infringement" where the service provider does not have actual knowledge or "red flag" knowledge of a specific infringement, which general awareness will be presumed when the service provider has received over 1,000 takedown notices, and providing for differing technical requirements for service providers with revenues greater than $10,000,000 per year.[32]

The European Union Copyright Directive adopted in April 2019 includes stronger online copyright protections than the US law currently provides. Since each EU member state has a two-year period in which to enact its own version of the Directive—and it remains to be seen exactly what each version will look like—it will be some years before we learn how effective these new measures are in terms of protecting the interests of copyright holders.

Increased Criminal Enforcement

Counterfeiting and piracy at the commercial level are crimes and law enforcement should treat them as such. If someone's purse is stolen or their house is broken into and robbed, the police will come to their aid. But if an author's book is counterfeited, they have little hope of getting law enforcement engaged even though the damage they suffer can be far greater and more devastating. US authors who are harmed by criminal levels of piracy or counterfeiting should be able to obtain the assistance of criminal law enforcement just as easily as they can call the police and seek assistance when robbed.

To this end, the federal government should provide more resources to government agencies responsible for enforcement for intellectual property crimes. As a nation, we need to start treating intellectual property theft as a real crime. This is particularly true when dealing with foreign-based counterfeiting operations where the author or publisher often will not have the means to effectively sue or obtain an award of damages from abroad. Increased collaboration among the US law enforcement and financial institutions with their foreign counterparts could make it easier to fine or bring civil cases against counterfeiters in any country and allow victims of counterfeiting access to counterfeiters' illegally obtained assets.

Regulation of Online Marketplaces

The history of litigation surrounding copyright on the internet over the last two decades indicates that our courts are not well-equipped to shape rational, effective rules and policy regarding piracy and counterfeiting. At the same time, the marketplaces and counterfeiting and piracy practices change too rapidly for federal legislation to keep up.

Ideally, an existing federal agency would be charged with regulating internet platforms, including third-party marketplaces. This agency should be empowered to create regulations, provide guidance, and issue administrative rulings in matters concerning not only deceptive commercial practices, but also those involving intellectual property and consumer privacy. Regulations could *require* online marketplaces to use anti-counterfeiting and anti-piracy measures—which would include artificial intelligence, as well as human intervention—to police their platforms, and promptly remove violating accounts. If and when malicious activity is discovered, affected rights holders should be notified accordingly. Online marketplaces could also be required to institute certain requirements for all third-party sellers using their platforms, including requiring sellers to provide purchase orders of books proving they were obtained from approved, verifiable wholesalers. Publishers would be given the opportunity to provide lists of authorized wholesalers and retailers, and purchase orders from those not listed would not be approved and/or subject to further investigation. This agency would also notify the counterparts of the Departments of State and Commerce and the Office of the US Trade Representative in the foreign countries where the counterfeiting activity is concentrated to aid in extraterritorial enforcement and exert diplomatic pressure.

Recommended Changes to the Industry

Many books sold as "new" on the Amazon marketplace are not actually "new," nor have they been sourced directly from the publisher; Amazon's definition of "new" books does not require them to be so. Yet, despite the fact there are no authorized channels of trade through which a third-party seller should be able to acquire a truly "new" copy of a book at a price low enough to compete with the publisher copies furnished by Amazon, Amazon's listing for any given book often lists a dozen or more "new" copies available from resellers at prices lower than those offered by the publisher.

The provenance of these books is somewhat of a mystery. Publishers and others have suggested that these books must be unlabeled review copies or copies contractually obligated to be sold in a foreign market, or books bought cheaply from big box stores, or overstock sold off cheaply by publishers.[33] If publishers would clearly mark such books as review or overstock, or remaindered copies, they could not enter the Amazon marketplace as "new." Sometimes (especially for recently published books), there are so many "new" copies available in the marketplace from third-party sellers that there is a reason to believe that many of these purportedly "new" books are actually counterfeit copies. Since Amazon will remove counterfeits if notified, publishers and professional organizations can help by policing the marketplace.

A Small Copyright Claims Court

The proposed Copyright Alternative in Small Claims Enforcement (CASE) Act[34] would enable an author or other individual content creator or small business copyright holder to obtain some redress for copyright infringement by creating an administrative tribunal within the Copyright Office to handle small copyright infringement claims at a minimal cost to rights holders. Even without the CASE Act, authors can and do bring lawsuits against individual alleged (and occasionally admitted) pirates in court. For example, author John Van Stry brought an infringement lawsuit against Travis McCrea, the operator of the site Ebook.bike.[35] However, few rights holders can afford such expensive lawsuits, which are the only means of intellectual property rights enforcement and restitution. The goal of the CASE Act is to change that and shift the internet landscape toward greater accountability for intellectual property theft.

What Authors Can Do to Protect Themselves

While the very notion that someone may attempt to take (or may successfully take) their work is understandably extremely upsetting to authors, the more authors know about the potential risks, the better they may be able to prepare themselves and protect their work from pirates. Here are some actions authors can take to protect their work:

- Educate themselves about the DMCA takedown process and issue takedown notices as needed; sometimes, they do prove effective. (The Authors Guild provides DMCA takedown forms to its members and helps members file them.)
- Set up a Google alert of both the author's name and the titles of the works (since a pirate may not have the grace to properly credit the author while trying to sell a stolen book).
- Make sure a personal website has the most recent and best information, because this will enable the Google algorithm to move it to the top of the search; Google representatives have stated that pirate sites can rise to the top of searches because there is no website with better, more recent information.
- Include pirate SEO language on the author's website (such as "download [title] here," "PDF," "free epub," or "read [title] book for free (at your local library)"; this may divert potential consumers searching for the book from pirate sites to the legitimate one.
- Report copyright infringements to Amazon, which generally removes counterfeit books.
- Watermark e-books; this will make it easier to prove infringement.
- Employ paid piracy monitoring services (Muso, Blasty, etc.) that will send notices to search engines asking them to remove infringing URLs (i.e. website addresses).

Conclusion

Hopefully, with changes in the law and certain industry practices, authors, publishers, and ISPs will be able to work together to combat pirates. As Marybeth Peters, the former Register of Copyrights, testified:

> [I]n the nearly forty years that I have worked in the Copyright Office, piracy, and especially global piracy, is probably the most enduring problem I have encountered. As with some other illegal activities, there will always be at least a small segment of any population who cannot be deterred from this theft of others' creativity . . . What we can and should strive for is the reduction of piracy to the lowest levels possible; levels that will not rob authors and copyright owners of the incentive to create and distribute the works that have made America's creative industries the envy of the world.[36]

Notes

1 "Definition of Piracy in English," *Lexico*, https://www.lexico.com/en/definition/piracy.
2 Seminar Recordings, "Changing Tides: Novel Approaches to Combating Digital Piracy," Authors Guild (webinar), presentation commentary by Sarina Bowen, uploaded April 10, 2018, https://www.authorsguild.org/whats-new/seminars-member-events/webinar-recording-archive.
3 S. Rep. No. 105–190, at 2 (1998).
4 17 U.S.C. § 512(c)(1)(A)–(C) (2018).
5 Joshua Gans, "'Information Wants to Be Free': The History of That Quote," *Digitopoly*, October 25, 2015, https://digitopoly.org/2015/10/25/information-wants-to-be-free-the-history-of-that-quote.
6 The number of piracy complaints the Authors Guild has received has multiplied over the past few years. It should be noted that these complaints are not from best-selling authors—although they have certainly suffered from piracy as well.

7 Katy Guest, "'I Can Get Any Novel I Want in 30 Seconds': Can Book Piracy Be Stopped?" *Guardian,* March 6, 2019, https://www.theguardian.com/books/2019/mar/06/i-can-get-any-novel-i-want-in-30-seconds-can-book-piracy-be-stopped.

8 According to the Authors Guild's last two surveys, authors' incomes are decreasing at alarming rates, to the point where many are forced to take on other work or forgo writing for a living altogether—indicating that the copyright incentives are not working as they should. Writing-related earnings, for example, plummeted to a median of $6,080 in 2017, down 42 percent since 2009. Full-time US authors, meanwhile, earned a median of only $20,300 from their writing. That is well below the federal poverty line for a family of three or more. Over half of the authors surveyed earn less than the poverty level for an individual from their writing. See "Authors Guild Survey Shows Drastic 42 Percent Decline in Authors earnings in Last Decade," Industry & Advocacy News, Authors Guild, January 5, 2019, https://www.authorsguild.org/industry-advocacy/authors-guild-survey-shows-drastic-42-percent-decline-in-authors-earnings-in-last-decade

9 Polly Mosendz, "Amazon Has Basically No Competition among Online Booksellers," *Atlantic,* May 30, 2014, https://www.theatlantic.com/business/archive/2014/05/amazon-has-basically-no-competition-among-online-booksellers/371917.

10 Matt Day and Jackie Gu, "The Enormous Numbers Behind Amazon's Market Reach," *Bloomberg,* March 27, 2019, https://www.bloomberg.com/graphics/2019-amazon-reach-across-markets.

11 "Six Takeaways from the Authors Guild 2018 Author Income Survey," Industry & Advocacy, Authors Guild, January 5, 2019, https://www.authorsguild.org/industry-advocacy/six-takeaways-from-the-authors-guild-2018-authors-income-survey.

12 Professional sellers on Amazon, for example, pay a $39.99 monthly subscription fee and a per transaction commission. See "Let's Talk Numbers," Pricing, Amazon, accessed May 19, 2020, https://services.amazon.com/selling/pricing.htm/ref=asus_soa_faq_p. eBay charges variable fees depending on volume and categories. See "Selling Fees," Customer service, eBay, accessed May 18, 2020, https://www.ebay.com/help/selling/fees-credits-invoices/selling-fees?id=4364.

13 Unlike direct retailers, the law does not view third-party retailers to be "sellers" and, as such, they do not owe affirmative guarantees of authenticity and merchantability with respect to products sold by third-party sellers.

14 For example, romance author Becky McGraw accused author Laura Harner of plagiarizing her same-sex romance books by changing names, places, and the sex of one of the characters. Jonathan Bailey, "When Romance Meets Plagiarism," *iThenticate,* January 18, 2016, http://www.ithenticate.com/plagiarism-detection-blog/when-romance-meets-plagiarism#.XT8LjXt7l9M. In addition, Nora Roberts accused fellow author Janet Dailey of having plagiarized Roberts's book *Sweet Revenge.* Laura Reeth, "Plagiarism, Then and Now," *Fall into the Story,* February 22, 2019, http://fallintothestory.com/plagiarism-then-and-now.

15 These pirates profit off of authors' hard work and reputations by engaging in scams such as manipulating Amazon's Kindle Unlimited pay-per-page scheme, where an author is paid for each page read (as measured by the Kindle or other reading device). They buy Amazon ad space, use click farms, and write fake reviews in order to promote their books on the best seller lists and draw readers (and income) away from hard-working authors.

16 *Piracy of Intellectual Property: Before the Subcommittee on Intellectual Property, U.S. Senate Judiciary Committee,* 109th Cong. 5, testimony of Marybeth Peters, Register of Copyrights (May 25, 2005), https://www.judiciary.senate.gov/imo/media/doc/Peters%20Testimony%20052505.pdf (hereafter Peters *Testimony*).

17 Donald J. Trump, "Memorandum on Combating Trafficking in Counterfeit and Pirated Goods," (official presidential memorandum, Washington, DC, April 3, 2019), https://www.whitehouse.gov/presidential-actions/memorandum-combating-trafficking-counterfeit-pirated-goods.

18 Copyright industries (those industries whose primary purpose is to create, produce, distribute, or exhibit copyrighted materials) play a large and growing role in the US economy. According to the International Intellectual Property Alliance's (IIPA) "Copyright Industries in the U.S. Economy: The 2018 Reports," core copyright industries have contributed more than $1.3 trillion to the US gross domestic product (GDP) in 2017, and accounted for 6.85 percent of the US economy. They employed nearly 5.7 million workers in 2017, accounting for 3.85 percent of the entire US workforce, or 4.54 percent of total private employment in the US, while the total copyright industries' share of private employment remained near 9.3 percent for the entire period. See Stephen E. Siwek, "Copyright Industries in the U.S. Economy," *IIPA* (2018), 3, https://iipa.org/files/uploads/2018/12/2018CpyrtRptFull.pdf.

19 See, e.g., Fonovisa, Inc. v. Cherry Auction, Inc., 76 F.3d 259 (9th Cir. 1996).

20 Sean Gallagher, "Amazon Caught Selling Counterfeits of Publisher's Computer Books—Again," *ARS Technica*, February 14, 2019, https://arstechnica.com/information-technology/2019/02/amazon-caught-selling-counterfeits-of-publishers-computer-books-again.

21 Viacom Int'l Inc. v. YouTube, Inc., 676 F.3d 19 (2d Cir. 2012).

22 *Id.* at 32.

23 Section 512(c) requires that a service provider not "be aware of facts or circumstances from which infringing activity is apparent," which is commonly referred to as "red flag" knowledge.

24 S. Rep. No. 105–190, 48.

25 Viacom, 676 F.3d at 32–33.

26 Viacom Int'l Inc. v. YouTube, Inc., 940 F. Supp. 2d 110, 114 (S.D.N.Y. 2013) (internal citation omitted).

27 *Id.* at 116.

28 In *UMG*, the court was dealing with a website that allowed people to upload and share video content. UMG Recordings, Inc. v. Shelter Capital Partners LLC, 718 F.3d 1006 (9th Cir. 2013).

29 BMG Rights Mgmt. (US) LLC v. Cox Commc'ns, Inc. 881 F.3d 293 (4th Cir. 2017).

30 *Id.* at 304.

31 *Id.* at 305.

32 Interestingly enough, one of the objections raised to Article 17 of the 2019 European Union Copyright Directive is that smaller ISPs would not be able (either financially or as a practical matter) to perform such takedowns on a global scale. The Copyright Directive contains a limitation that this requirement would not apply to ISPs with annual revenues of less than 10,000 euros, and which have been available to the EU public for less than three years; this calls back to the original concern of the DMCA to encourage the growth of new websites.

33 "Amazon's Taking another Bite of the Publishing Pie," Industry & Advocacy News, Authors Guild, May 8, 2017, https://www.authorsguild.org/industry-advocacy/amazons-taking-another-bite-publishing-pie; "Amazon's Buy Box Shake-Up: An Update," Industry & Advocacy News, Authors Guild, August 7, 2018, https://www.authorsguild.org/industry-advocacy/amazons-buy-box-shake-update.

34 Copyright Alternative in Small-Claims Enforcement Act of 2019, S. 1273, H.R. 2426, 116th Cong. (2019–2020), introduced in House May 1, 2019.

35 Van Stry v. McCrea, No. 19-CV-0104-WCB, 2020 WL 1911391 (E.D. Tex. April 20, 2020).

36 Peters, *Testimony*, 1.

2.2

IS A PICTURE REALLY WORTH MORE THAN A THOUSAND WORDS?

(The Scope of Copyright Protection for Fictional Characters)

Marcia Paul

Courts across the country have acknowledged that, at least on a theoretical basis, copyright protection can be accorded to a particular fictional character who appears in a copyright-protected work, provided that character is sufficiently delineated, whether verbally or pictorially. However, in practice, courts have granted that protection sparingly and, even then, much more readily to those pictorially depicted than those only verbally described. Is there a rational basis for the distinction, and is the entire treatment of this subject consistent with the underlying purposes of copyright? Those are the questions that this chapter will try to address.

Consider the following scenarios:

- I draw a mouse with floppy ears, big round eyes, and lascivious red lips fixed in a wicked grin, clad in a floral T-shirt, with tiny arms each with four fingers sporting violet nail polish, and squat legs capped by platform sneakers. I register my drawing of that mouse for copyright protection as a pictorial work.
- I write a novel about a family who decides to leave the city and move to a ramshackle barn in the country. The family consists of a mother, a father, and two kids, a boy and a girl. The plot is about the adjustments they have to make to rural life and their travails. The narrator of the novel is a mouse who lives beneath the barn. I describe her in my novel in exactly the same words I used earlier to describe the picture that I drew. The story of the family's adjustment is told through her eyes and voice from start to finish, but we learn nothing more about the mouse herself, except to the extent that we can hazard a guess about her views from her narration of their story. I register my novel for copyright protection as a literary work.
- I write a novel about that exact same family, with the exact same plot, except that the story is narrated by the daughter, a young girl. In one chapter, she encounters the same mouse and frightened, races to tell her family that they have company in the barn. In telling them, she describes the mouse in precise detail, down to her platform sneakers and violet nail polish, once again exactly as depicted in the drawing. Her dad is pretty sure she did not actually see the creature she describes, but he tells her that she has nothing to fear. Time and numerous other scares pass. Soon the girl forgets both her fright and the mouse, and the mouse never reappears in the story. I register that novel.

- After my first novel is published, I write a second novel about the flip-side travails of a different family, who decide to move from a small farm outside a town of 800 people to an apartment in a major metropolitan city. This family also consists of a mother, father, son, and daughter and, once again, the daughter encounters that exact same mouse in the bathroom of the apartment. Although she grew up in a rural setting, seeing a mouse in a city apartment frightens her. Again, she runs and describes the mouse to her father in exactly the same way, and once again, dad is somewhat dubious but reassures her. In time, she forgets the mouse and the mouse never again appears in the story. I register that novel.
- I license the rights in that second novel to an animation studio which gives visual life to my mouse in a movie. The movie is true to my verbal character description and the story line does not provide any more information about the mouse than in my novel. The studio registers the movie as a derivative work.

In each of these five scenarios, the mouse is my original creation. In all five, she has exactly the same attributes. The only difference is that in the first scenario she is described pictorially in a drawing, in the next three she is described in words, and in the last, my original verbal description is amplified by her visual depiction in the movie. As we will see, copyright protection is available for the first. My mouse may be entitled to copyright protection when she is a narrator because of her central role in the story even though it is not about her. The law is least likely, if at all, to grant protection in the third scenario because she plays a bit role in the story of the family and is not the driver of the narrative or the main character in it. Although she neither narrates nor is the focus of the fourth and fifth examples, she has a better chance of being protected because she appears in more than one work (my second novel) or because the studio added a pictorial description (the movie). In each of these scenarios, I created the exact same distinct mouse, with particular features and characteristics. Why is it that the law treats those depictions differently, and should it? Is the mouse who appears as a character in each of these works copyright-protected, standing alone from the work in which she appears? To answer these questions, we first look at how the law on point has evolved.

Overview of Existing Law

Any discussion about copyright protection for fictional characters must start with *Nichols v. Universal Pictures Corp.* (a case cited most often for Judge Learned Hand's famous "abstractions" test to determine whether a work is expression rather than idea), because it is oft-cited for his parameters for copyright protection of characters.[1] He noted that when an infringement claim concerns a character rather than a story, the idea/expression dichotomy is especially illusive. To illustrate, he said:

> If Twelfth Night were copyrighted, it is quite possible that a second comer might so closely imitate Sir Toby Belch or Malvolio as to infringe, but it would not be enough that for one of his characters he casted a riotous knight who kept wassail to the discomfort of the household, or a vein foppish steward who became amorous of his mistress. These would be no more than Shakespeare's 'ideas' in the play, as little capable of monopoly as Einstein's doctrine of relativity, or Darwin's series of the Origin of Species. If follows that the less developed the characters, the less they can be copyrighted; that is the penalty an author must bear from marking them too indistinctively.[2]

While Judge Hand's *Nichols* quote has been repeated by courts around the country, much of the law on point has been created by the Ninth Circuit. Initially, that court came down firmly against a broad view of copyright protection for characters, drawing a distinction between when a character "is only the chessman in the game of telling the story," in which case no protection attaches, and when a character constitutes "the story being told" when the character may be protected.[3] Hammett sold the motion picture rights to his novel *The Maltese Falcon* to Warner Bros., which produced a very popular movie featuring Humphrey Bogart as the main character, Sam Spade. Thereafter, Hammett granted CBS the right to make a radio series entitled *The Adventures of Sam Spade.* Nothing appeared in the radio series from the novel except for the Sam Spade character. Warner Bros. argued that its exclusive right to the novel precluded CBS's use. The court found that there was no protection for fictional characters like Sam Spade, reasoning that literary characters are difficult to delineate and therefore may be nothing more than an unprotected idea: "The characters of an author's imagination and the art of his descriptive talent, like a painter's is like a person with his penmanship, are always limited and always falls into limited patterns. The restriction argued for [protection for the character] is unreasonable, and would affect the very opposite of the statute's purpose which is to encourage the production of the arts."[4]

The Ninth Circuit revisited this question in *Walt Disney Prods. v. Air Pirates*, where the defendant published an underground comic book with well-known Disney characters engaged in activities "antithetical to the accepted Mickey Mouse world of scrub faces, bright smiles, and happy endings."[5] Noting that comic book characters have "physical as well as conceptual qualities, [and are] more likely to contain some unique elements of expression," the court struggled to limit the *Sam Spade* case to its particular facts, in effect cabining that decision to literary characters, not illustrated ones.[6] Subsequently, this distinction was extended to characters visually depicted in a television series or a movie[7] and to characters that "have displayed consistent, widely identifiable traits."[8]

District courts in the Ninth Circuit have evinced considerable difficulty trying to apply those various authorities. For instance, in *Anderson v. Stallone*, the court characterized the Ninth Circuit law as "fraught with uncertainty."[9] It noted that although subsequent Ninth Circuit decisions (*Air Pirates* and *Olson*) implicitly limited *Sam Spade*, those cases concerned visually depicted rather than purely literary-depicted characters. With that backdrop, the court found the *Rocky* character at issue, depicted visually in film, entitled to protection as a highly delineated character with specific character traits and sufficiently central in three movies to constitute "the story being told."[10] Reviewing the aforementioned Ninth Circuit cases, the court summarized:

> In determining whether a character deserves copyright protection, courts look at many elements of the character—visual depictions, name, dialog, relationships with other characters, their actions and conduct, personality traits, and written descriptions—to determine whether it is sufficiently delineated such that it is a unique expression.[11]

That court also rejected the defendant's argument that, in order to perform this analysis, it had to dissect the various elements of that character to strip out the unprotectable stock elements before deciding whether the two characters are substantially similar, because "it is the unique combination of elements that makes up a protected character."[12]

Most recently, the Ninth Circuit in *D.C. Comics v. Towle* considered the protectability of the Batmobile from the Batman television shows and films, a fictional, high-tech automobile with external bat-like features, equipped with futuristic weaponry and technology.[13] The court traced the history of character protection for cartoon characters from *Air Pirates* through *Halicki* and concluded that a three-part test exists for determining whether characters in comic books, television programs, or motion pictures will be protected: (i) it must have "physical as well as conceptual quality"; (ii) it must be "sufficiently delineated"; and (iii) it must be "especially distinctive" and "contain some unique elements of expression."

Meanwhile, in the Second Circuit, primary focus remains on the level of character development. In *Goodis v. United Artists Television, Inc.*, the court concluded that the defendant-publisher, who had serialization rights to a novel and used the characters from that novel in new plot situations in the television series *The Fugitive*, was contractually entitled to do so.[14] The concurrence focused on the importance of granting authors stand-alone character protection so that characters could be used in sequels, because divesting the original author of that right "would be clearly untenable from the standpoint of public policy, for it would effectively permit the unrestrained pilfering of characters."[15] In *Burroughs v. Metro-Goldwyn-Mayer, Inc.*, the successor to the author of the book *Tarzan of the Apes* licensed MGM the rights to use the Tarzan character in a screenplay and a remake.[16] The court determined that the Tarzan character, apart from the book in which he appeared, was sufficiently delineated to be protected (and therefore that license could be terminated), based upon this very general description of the attributes of the character: "Tarzan is the Ape-man. He is an individual closely in tune with his jungle environment, able to communicate with animals yet able to experience human emotions . . . He is athletic, innocent, youthful, and gentle and strong. He is Tarzan."[17]

In *Warner Bros. Inc. v. American Broadcasting Companies, Inc.*, the court noted that since *Nichols*, copyright protection had occasionally been granted to a literary character but more often to cartoon characters.[18] According to Judge Newman, most courts consider not only visual resemblance, but the totality of the character's respective attributes and traits and the extent to which the allegedly infringing character captures the "total concept and feel" of the copyrighted character: "A character is an aggregation of the particular talents and traits his creator selected for him. That each one may be an idea does not diminish the expressive aspect of the combination."[19] To reconcile the paradox that, in copyright law, generally, the defendant cannot escape infringement by pointing to elements he did not copy, but when considering character infringement courts pay attention to *both* similarities and differences, Judge Newman relied on the distinction between literary and graphic works:

> A story has a linear dimension: it begins, continues, and ends. If a defendant copies substantial portions of a plaintiff's sequence of events, he does not escape infringement by adding original episodes somewhere along the line. A graphic or three-dimensional work is created to be perceived as an entirety. Significant similarities between two works of this sort inevitably lessen similarity that would otherwise exist between the total perceptions of the two works. The graphic rendering of a character has aspects of both the linear literary mode and the multi-dimensional total perception. What the character thinks, feels, says and does and the descriptions conveyed by the author through the comments of other characters in the work episodically fill out a viewer's understanding of the character. *At the same time, the visual perception of the character tends to create a dominant impression against which the similarity of a defendant's character may be readily compared, and significant differences readily noted.*[20]

Silverman v. CBS, Inc. was a copyright and trademark challenge to the defendant's efforts to create a Broadway play using characters from the famous radio and television series *Amos 'n' Andy*.[21] Some but not all of those programs were in the public domain. Having concluded that CBS had abandoned any trademark rights in the characters,[22] Judge Newman held that since the still-protected works were derivatives, all that the plaintiff could protect under copyright law was the incremental original additions in those derivatives, and concluded that: "we have no doubt that [the characters] were sufficiently delineated in the pre-1948 radio scripts to have been placed in the public domain when the scripts entered the public domain."[23]

Most recently, in *Salinger v. Colting*, a Swedish comic book writer decided to write a sequel to J.D. Salinger's renowned novel *The Catcher in the Rye*, the story of the iconic Holden Caulfield character.[24] The defendant aged the teenaged Holden Caulfield and put him in a new plot, using many elements of the back story from the novel. The district court (affirmed on point by the

Second Circuit) held that plaintiff was likely to succeed on both his claims for the creation of a derivative work and infringement of the character, on the grounds that the book was substantially similar to the original novel and that the character was entitled to stand-alone copyright protection and infringed, and that the sequel was not a fair use. To reach that conclusion, the court relied on both the depiction of the character and the use of other plot elements from the novel, illustrating the difficulty courts sometimes have in trying to define a fictional character, separating the character from the context in which he appears.

Appellate law on point is not limited to the Second and Ninth Circuits. In *Gaiman v. McFarlane*, Judge Richard Posner held that two comic book characters were entitled to protection, but acknowledged the difference in the level of abstraction between literary and graphic expressions:

> The description of a character in prose leaves much to the imagination, even when the description is detailed—as in Dashiell Hammett's description of Sam Spade's physical appearance in the first paragraph of the *Maltese Falcon*. 'Samuel Spade's jaw was long and boney, his chin a jutting v under the more flexible v of his mouth. His nostrils curved back to make another, smaller, v. His yellow-grey eyes were horizontal. The v *motif* was picked up again by thickish brows rising outward from twin creases above a hooked nose, and his pale brown hair grew down— from high flat temples—in a point on his forehead. He looked rather pleasantly like a blond satan.'[25]

According to that court, even given that rather vivid verbal description, one hardly knows what Sam Spade looks like, in contrast to Humphrey Bogart playing the role: "[a] reader of illustrated fiction completes the work in his mind; the reader of a comic book, or the viewer of a movie is passive."[26]

Judge Posner revisited the issue in *Klinger v. Conan Doyle Estate, Ltd.*, concerning *Sherlock Holmes*.[27] As in the *Amos 'n' Andy* case, some but not all of the *Sherlock Holmes* works were in the public domain; the defendant sued for a declaratory judgment that he was entitled to create a sequel using the character. The estate argued that there is a distinction between "flat" and "round" fictional characters, arguing that because the former were complete in their original formulation, when the first work in which they appear entered the public domain, they too entered the public domain, but "round" characters—developed over time and over a series of works—should remain protected until the last work lost protection. Judge Posner rejected this distinction on policy grounds and found *Sherlock Holmes* to be in the public domain.[28]

What can be distilled from this body of case law? Several principles emerge:

- Copyright protection can attach to a particular character standing apart from the copyright-protected work in which it appears.
- Courts take different positions on how to define a character and whether and at what point to divorce the character from the story in which it appears.
- Courts generally do not dissect the elements of a character, but rather view it as a unified whole, unless some aspects of the character are no longer copyright-protected.
- The more delineated the character, the more likely it will be granted copyright protection.
- If the entire story revolves around the character, it is more likely to be protected than if the character, no matter how fully delineated, is less central.
- The more integrated the character is in the story line (maxxing when the character is "the story being told"), the more likely a court is to find infringement of the work without reaching the issue of infringement of the character.
- Characters that are depicted both verbally and pictorially are most likely to be accorded protection.

- Characters who are depicted pictorially only are more likely to be accorded protection than those depicted verbally only.
- Using the same character in multiple works makes it more likely that it will be accorded protection, even if those works are in different media or by different authors.

What, If Any, Protection Should Be Available for Fictional Characters?

Should there be any copyright protection at all for a fictional character who appears in a work, independent of the protection accorded that work? If so, what should be the proper scope of that protection, and should it only be accorded in certain circumstances? Does it depend upon the mode of depiction of the character, or on the nature of the character's appearance in the work? How should the "character" be defined or separated from the context of the work in which it appears? In this author's view, while there are rational bases to support distinctions in response to these questions, the only distinction that *should* make a difference is how delineated the character is (isolated from the plot), i.e. where it falls on the idea/expression dichotomy.

Should Stand-alone Protection Be Accorded?

There is no principled reason why protection for a fictional character who appears in a work but is not the work itself should not attach, at least in some circumstances, as a fictional character can be an original work of authorship. If no such protection was available, the creator would be wholly deprived of the ability to create or license the creation of derivative works based on that character, as exemplified by the Holden Caulfield character in *Colting* and the "fugitive" in *Goodis*. If the character is but a stock character, or otherwise has a public domain status, or is insufficiently delineated, then it does not qualify for protection. But assuming that it crosses the line from idea to original expression, whether verbally or pictorially or both, protection should be available. A contrary view would argue that if a literary character can be protected, then other stand-alone elements of a literary work, like a setting (e.g. Jurassic Park) could likewise be protectable, divorced from plot. Perhaps so, but settings are more likely scènes à faire and even if not, why should Universal Pictures not have the exclusive right to create a theme park based on the setting of one of its movies? The originality, expression, and delineation requirements will narrow the number of qualifying aspects of a literary work that are independently protectable and the substantial similarity tests and fair use will leave ample room for use of ideas or themes, rather than concrete expression.

Should There Be a Separate Registration Requirement?

Since registration is required in order to sue for infringement,[29] is a separate registration requirement for fictional characters necessary? While works of pictorial, graphic, or sculptural nature can be registered, as can literary and audiovisual works,[30] fictional characters are not enumerated as protected works of authorship.

Over half a century ago, the US Copyright Office rejected the idea of creating a separate category for fictional characters, explaining:

> There are undoubtedly some characters that are developed in detail and with such breadth and depth that they emerge as separately identifiable parts of the copyrighted work in which they appear. Others, perhaps the large majority, cannot be said to represent independent creations apart from the particular literary or pictorial works depicting them. As is equally true in the case of detailed presentations of plot, setting, or dramatic action, we believe it

would be unnecessary and misleading to specify fictional characters as a separate class of copyrightable works.[31]

In the past half-century plus, the monetary value of characters, particularly with respect to their use in sequels, prequels, and remakes, has increased exponentially. If a stand-alone category for characters were created, the deposit copy accompanying the registration would have the salutary effect of putting third parties on notice of the precise scope of the claimed protection, but it would also raise a host of issues. What would an author actually register? A verbal description of the character exactly as it appears in the underlying literary work? How would the author/registrant divorce the character from the setting, plot, and interactions with other characters in the underlying literary work? Is the character a published work if it has never been used by the author independent of a published work in which it appears? Does it matter whether the character was created prior to its appearance in a published literary work or contemporaneously therewith, or whether the attributes of the character are defined not only by the original work, but also in a sequel or a movie version? While questions like these have been explored in many copyright infringement cases, creating a separate category of protection seems unnecessary and unduly complicated. The registration of a magazine protects each article in it, so too the registration of a novel should suffice to protect the characters in it.

How to Define the Attributes of the Character

That the level of delineation of a character is key directly derives from the idea/expression dichotomy. The amount left to the reader's imagination matters because without defined parameters, it is unclear what is protected and therefore whether or not a similar creation might infringe. What should a court consider in order to answer the question of whether a character has been sufficiently delineated? In the *Great American Hero* case, Judge Newman endorsed looking not only at the visual resemblance of the characters, but also at the "totality of the character's attributes and traits." In the *Jonathan Livingston Segal* case, the court listed "visual depictions, name, dialog, relationships with other characters, their actions and conduct, personality traits, and written descriptions." If these wide parameters were the proper focus, analysis of character infringement would merge with the overall substantial similarity analysis for the works at issue. Holden Caulfield's experiences with his prep school teacher are not part of the character, but are rather how that character functions within the context of the underlying work.[32] Of course, a fictional character in literature does not exist in a vacuum; it appears in the context of a story and, consequently, drawing the line between character and story may be difficult in some cases and probably most difficult to draw when the character is "the story being told." But the more you look at the interactions between the character and the story, the closer you come to comparing the substantial similarity of plot rather than substantial similarity of the character.

When a character—even a relatively minor character in a book—can be lifted and be put in another plot and yet still exhibit the same attributes it is capable of living, it should be allowed to live an independent copyright life. When it has actually been used for that purpose, such as in a sequel, that is proof positive of that character's independent copyright existence. This is important because lifting a character from a novel and putting him in a totally different plot (e.g. detective series in which same detective solves totally unrelated crimes) may not be an "adaptation" sufficient to qualify as a derivative *of the original novel*, but if the character is stripped of plot and settings, the second use may well be a derivative *of the character*.

Another issue in defining the scope of the character is authorship. Consider this example: I write a novel that delineates a character who is neither the main character in, nor the focus of, the novel and then I license the right to produce a movie based on that novel to a studio that selects a particular actress to play that character. More than one work featuring that character has now been created by or under authority of the author, and viewers of the movie have a visual depiction of the character. But as the court said in the *Amos and Andy* case, it is the owner of the derivative work—the studio in our example—who adds the incremental delineation of the character. Absent a contract to the contrary, the original author still only owns the copyright in the verbal depiction, so to define the character, focus must also be on the question of who is the author of that character, rather than the author of the work in which the character appears.

The Proper Character Infringement Analysis

Once a character is deemed worthy of protection, there is nothing unique about the analysis of whether it has been infringed. Substantial similarity can be determined by "comprehensive nonliteral" copying, for example, tracking the plot of a novel, but putting it in somewhat different words. Alternatively, it can be "fragmented literal" similarity, meaning although the overall structure or form of the original work was not copied, there was a taking of an important part(s) of the original work on either a quantitative or qualitative basis. In some circuits and with respect to some works, courts look at the "total concept and feel" of a work. Applying comprehensive nonliteral similarity or total concept and feel to a character would likely cast too wide a net, as a somewhat different expression of the same general character attributes might encompass similarities in idea rather than expression. Applying fragmented literal similarity makes the most sense, as taking a fragment (in this case, a character) can be sufficient to ground a finding of substantial similarity, but only if the fragment is the same or virtually identical, and qualitatively and/or quantitatively important to the work from which it has been taken.

Does It Matter in What Mode the Character Is Expressed?

A distinction based on whether the character is drawn pictorially or verbally has a certain logic. Judge Newman's comparison of the linear dimension of a story and the unitary perception of a graphic work in the *Great American Hero* case rings true, as the creator's claim for protection of the pictorial depiction is clearly defined, as opposed to a more open-ended verbal depiction. Think about the relatively high level of detail in the verbal depiction of Sam Spade in Hammett's novel quoted earlier, and then think, as Judge Posner noted in *Gaiman*, how much more room even that narrative leaves for a reader's imagination than watching Humphrey Bogart play that role in the movie.

Here's another way to think about the issue: Describe a character in detail and then ask five people to draw that character. It is highly likely that you are going to get five very different drawings of that same character. Then show the drawing of a character to those same five people and ask them to verbally describe what they see. While there will probably be some difference in choice of words, their descriptions are likely to be substantially similar. When you read a book, do you form a picture in your mind of characters in it? Most people, most of the time, do not. However, in some ways, a reader may form a more detailed—albeit subjective—definition of a character from a novel than from a picture of that character: The reader will likely learn a lot more about all of the attributes of that character because he or she can extrapolate more about that character from the plot, the character's interactions with other characters, the settings the character appears in, etc. But how a reader fills in the interstices while reading a novel or what a licensee adds by furnishing a visual depiction in a derivative work is not part of the original author's "work of authorship." All of these questions and distinctions may come into play in any particular case, but the mode of expression should not matter; how developed the character is by the author should control.

In conclusion, let us revisit the five scenarios at the beginning of this chapter. In all five, the mouse has the same degree of delineation, but the mode of expression and the role of the mouse in the stories differ, and, in the case of the second novel and the movie, the mouse appears in more than one work. There is no reason that any of these five scenarios should be treated differently because the mouse has been delineated by the author to the same extent in each and is *capable* of leading an independent copyright life, whether or not that independent life has yet been exploited. The necessary limits on the scope of protection in order to ensure that other creators have sufficient space are already built into existing law. If the mouse is not sufficiently delineated based on her characteristics or attributes (not based on how she functions in the story), then she is not entitled to any protection at all. The less detailed the delineation, the narrower the scope of protection. And the less prominent the mouse is in the work, the less likely it is that a second comer will be found to be infringing because the mouse is neither qualitatively nor quantitatively important to the original. And, of course, a second comer can make fair use of our mouse. These basic concepts of copyright law are more than ample to prevent undue extension of the copyright monopoly and yet reward and incentivize the creator of a fictional character, the twin goals of our copyright laws.

Notes

1 Nichols v. Universal Pictures Corp., 45 F.2d 119 (2d Cir. 1930), *cert. denied*, 282 U.S. 902 (1931)
2 *Nichols*, 45 F.2d at 121. (This has been labeled by courts and commentators alike as the "distinct delineation" test.)
3 Warner Bros. Pictures, Inc. v. Columbia Broad. Sys., 216 F.2d 945, 950 (9th Cir. 1954).
4 *Id.*
5 Walt Disney Prods. v. Air Pirates, 581 F.2d 751, 753 (9th Cir. 1978).
6 *Id.* at 755.
7 Olson v. Nat'l Broad. Co., 855 F.2d 1446, 1452 (9th Cir. 1988) (no protection for unit of three Vietnam veterans described in three to four lines, citing the *Sam Spade* case, but noting that a character could be protected if "especially" distinctive).
8 Rice v. Fox Broad. Co., 330 F.3d 1170, 1175 (9th Cir. 2003) (holding that the magician at issue, although visually depicted, was not sufficiently delineated and had not displayed consistent widely identifiable traits); see also Halicki Films, LLC v. Sanderson Sales & Mktg., 547 F.3d 1213, 1225 (9th Cir. 2008) (finding a car featured in a film to be more akin to a comic book character than a literary character because it had widely identifiable traits and was actually depicted in the film, but remanding the matter to determine whether the car's physical and conceptual qualities were sufficiently unique).
9 Anderson v. Stallone, No. 87-0592, 1989 WL 206431, *6 (C.D. Cal. April 25, 1989).
10 *Id.* at *6–8; see also, Toho Co. v. William Murrow & Co., 33 F. Supp. 2d 1206, 1215–16 (C.D. Cal. 1998) (*Godzilla* character sufficiently delineated even though changed over the years, because he had a constant set of distinguishing traits); Metro-Goldwyn-Mayer, Inc. v. AM Honda Motor Corp., 900 F. Supp. 1287, 1296–97 (C.D. Cal 1995) (*James Bond*) (same). And in Bach v. Forever Living Prods. U.S., Inc., 473 F. Supp. 2d 1127 (W.D. Wash., 2007), defendant used plaintiff's character *Jonathan Livingston Segal* as a corporate logo and in advertising.
11 *Bach*, 473 F. Supp. 2d at 1134.
12 *Id.*
13 DC Comics v. Towle, 802 F.3d 1012 (9th Cir. 2015).
14 Goodis v. United Artists Television, Inc., 425 F.2d 397 (2d Cir. 1970).
15 *Id.* at 406 n.1 (Waterman, J., concurring).
16 Burroughs v. Metro-Goldwyn-Mayer, Inc., 519 F. Supp. 388 (S.D.N.Y. 1981) *aff'd* 683 F.2d 610 (2d Cir. 1982).
17 *Id.* at 391.
18 Warner Bros. Inc. v. Am. Broad. Cos., Inc., 720 F.2d 231 (2d Cir. 1983).
19 *Id.* at 243.
20 *Id.* at 241–42 (emphasis added).
21 Silverman v. CBS, Inc., 870 F.2d 40 (2d Cir. 1989).

22 There is some overlap in protection under copyright and trademark laws for fictional characters. See Professor Jane C. Ginsburg, "Intellectual Property as Seen by Barbie and Mickey: The Reciprocal Relationship of Copyright and Trademark Law," *Journal of the Copyright Society of the USA*, November 13, 2017; see also Frederick Warne & Co. v. Book Sales Inc., 481 F. Supp. 1191, 1196 (S.D.N.Y. 1979) (mere fact that the works were in public domain under the copyright laws did not mean that they could not acquire trademark significance).

23 *Silverman*, 870 F.2d at 50 (citing Nichols v. Universal Pictures Corp., 45 F.2d 119 (2d Cir. 1930)).

24 Salinger v. Colting, 641 F. Supp. 2d 250 (S.D.N.Y. 2009), *vacated on other grounds*, 607 F.3d 68 (2d Cir. 2010). The author of this essay represented the plaintiff in that litigation.

25 Gaiman v. McFarlane, 360 F.3d 644, 661 (7th Cir. 2004).

26 *Id.* at 660–61.

27 Klinger v. Conan Doyle Estate, Ltd., 755 F.3d 496 (7th Cir. 2014).

28 *Klinger*, 755 F.3d 501–03; see also Columbia Broad. Sys. Inc. v. DeCosta, 377 F.2d 315, 320 (1st Cir. 1967) (rejecting argument that fictional characters are inherently uncopyrightable).

29 See 17 U.S.C. § 411 (2018); Fourth Estate Pub. Benefit Corp. v. Wallstreet.com, LLC, 139 S. Ct. 881 (2019).

30 17 U.S.C. § 102.

31 US Congress, House of Representatives, House Committee on the Judiciary, *Supplementary Report of the Register of Copyrights on the General Division of U.S. Copyright Law*, 89th Congress, 1st sess., 1965, 6.

32 Some commentators have argued that isolating the character from the plot for purposes of delineation actually increases the risk another character will be found infringing, because the character is more narrowly defined. See, e.g., Samuel J. Coe, "The Story of A Character: Establishing the Limits of Independent Copyright Protection for Literary Characters" *Chicago-Kent Law Review* 86, no. 3 (2011): 1316–17.

2.3

FAIR USE

The Judicial Mix-Up over "A Mixed Question of Law and Fact"

Terence P. Keegan

Referring to fair use as "a mixed question of law and fact" fuels confusion over the court's role in safeguarding new expression. It is high time that judges retire the phrase. This essay explores courts' early references to "mixed questions" outside copyright in the nineteenth century and the phrase's creep into judges' fair use opinions over the last thirty-five years, which is inconsistent with how the Supreme Court has used it. This essay argues that a refocus of fair use analysis on the Supreme Court's guidance in *Campbell v. Acuff-Rose Music, Inc.* would avoid the "mixed question" fog and better position judges to decide fair use issues as matters of law.

The US judges have only relatively recently begun to label fair use in copyright as a "mixed question of law and fact." The phrase's appearance in courts' opinions is roughly contemporaneous with Congress' recognition of fair use in the 1976 revision of the country's copyright law.[1]

Judges had devised the concept of fair use more than a century before, as a means of determining the unwritten boundaries of copyright ownership. They had long regarded claims of one having appropriated another's copyright in a new work as especially "difficult" to resolve. The very decision from which the 1976 Copyright Act drew its four fair use "factors" perceived copyright (along with patent) as engaging "the metaphysics of the law" more than any other type of case.[2]

But neither that touchstone 1841 decision, nor the text of the current copyright law, speaks of fair use as a "mixed question of law and fact." Reliance on that phrase over the last half-century—namely, in repeating without examination a piece of Supreme Court dictum from 1985[3]—has only made pretrial consideration of fair use cases more "difficult."

When judges employ the phrase—especially when considering pretrial dismissal of an infringement suit on fair use grounds—they do so in passing, without explaining what exactly a "mixed question of law and fact" means in the fair use context.[4] More than fifteen district and circuit courts did so in 2019 alone.[5]

The phrase seems to invite questions into the roles of a judge and a jury (or trier of fact) in a fair use case. For example, is each of the four factors that Congress listed as among those "to be considered" in fair use cases—the first being, "the purpose and character" of the defendant's work—a question of "law" for a judge, or a question of "fact" for a jury?[6] Is each factor "a mixed question"? Who decides it? What about "weigh[ing]" the factors together as the Supreme Court has instructed, "in light of the purposes of the copyright,"[7] to determine whether a use is "fair"?

Judges in fair use rulings generally do not acknowledge these questions. As a result, commentators have noted, "the dividing line between questions of law and fact in the fair use area can be manipulated across a very broad range of relevant issues."[8] This is an invitation to confusion and obscured decision-making.

Copyright plaintiffs may voice concern over a court improperly taking "fact" questions away from juries, and papering over infringements by pronouncing a defendant's work "transformative" in purpose and "fair" as a matter of law.[9] But the judicial presumption of fair use as "a mixed question of law and fact" is more concerning from the defendant's perspective—for the phrase casts a fog in which artworks, articles, songs, films, plays, and other endeavors deserving of vindication can easily get lost. That, in turn, threatens the very "progress" that the US Constitution calls upon copyright law to "promote."[10]

At its worst, presuming fair use to be a "mixed question" misleads judges into abdicating their decision-making power. It can make fair use cases appear more inherently fact-bound than they are. And it can confound courts into misperceiving cases as "close calls" that cannot be dismissed on the pleadings or on a motion for summary judgment when they perhaps should be. But fair use cases should not be seen as exempt from pretrial dismissal—especially where *legal characterizations* of the facts, rather than the facts themselves, are often what's really at issue. There's nothing so "mixed" about the questions fair use cases pose. Many of the facts are often manifest on the face of the works at issue.[11] And the ultimate fair use determination—weighing the "results" of factor exploration "in light of the ends of the copyright law"—has long been recognized as primarily a judicial task.[12]

Disputes over the limits of a copyright, and vindication of the use of one work by another, are no less entitled to a "just, speedy, and inexpensive determination" than any other civil case.[13] In fact, there is greater, constitutional justification for ruling upon fair use early: not only to advance "progress" under the copyright clause, but also to respect the First Amendment freedom of expression that is superior to copyright law's monopoly restrictions.[14] The phrase "mixed question of law and fact" should play no part in such rulings.

Nineteenth-Century Roots of Misunderstanding "Mixed Questions"

"Like other controversies of a similar character," wrote one US court in 1869, fair use "presents *two* questions, one of fact and the other of law":[15] "Stated in brief terms, the question of fact is, what use did the respondent . . . make of the complainant's [work]? And the question of law presented, inasmuch as it is conceded that he used the same to some extent, is, was that use allowable, or was it of a character and to such an extent that it infringed the complainant's rights."[16]

By that point, "fair use" had already begun to serve an umbrella term for several judicial doctrines, including "fair abridgments" and "new and different use."[17] Judges had already been developing those doctrines for decades.[18] At the same time, notions of "mixed questions of law and fact" had already been voiced in American jurisprudence by the mid-nineteenth century, albeit outside the fair use realm. In 1829, for example, the Supreme Court affirmed a judge who had refused to instruct the jury that it could make certain inferences in a commercial case if it found certain facts: "Presumptions, from evidence given in a cause of the existence of particular facts, are in many, if not in all cases, mixed questions of law and fact. If the evidence be irrelevant to the fact insisted upon, or be such as cannot fairly warrant a jury in presuming it, the court is so far from being bound to instruct them, that they are at liberty to presume it, that they would err in giving such instruction. For why give it, when it is manifest, that if the jury should find their verdict upon the fact so deduced, it would be the duty of the court to set it aside, and to direct a re-trial of the cause?"[19]

The question there was "mixed" in that the court had anticipated the *legal* insignificance of an impermissible *factual* inference. The trial judge had, therefore, not instructed the jury on something that was entirely within the court's province to determine on its own.

But by the end of the nineteenth century, the legal theorist and professor James Bradley Thayer observed that judges were expecting the phrase "mixed question of law and fact" to do more than it should. The phrase had by then become "almost universal," according to Thayer.[20] However, he pointed out: "All questions of fact, for a jury or for a court, are mixed questions of law and fact; for they must be decided with reference to all relevant rules of law; and whether there be any such rule, and what it is, must be determined by the court. Now since this mixture of law and fact is thus common to a variety of different situations, it is an uninstructive circumstance to lean upon when one seeks for guidance in discriminating these situations."[21]

The specific "situations" Thayer was commenting on were assessing the respective duties of judge and jury in malicious prosecution cases.[22] It had been easy to be "inexact" about them, Thayer allowed.[23] Yet, at least as far as malicious prosecution cases went, the "mixed question of law and fact" phrase had "only added to the confusion," Thayer wrote.[24] He approvingly cited to an 1853 New York court decision in which the judge warned of another "deceptive" effect of the phrase in malicious prosecution cases (where "want of probable cause" was an element of the tort):[25] "[M]isled by this statement, it not unfrequently happens that judges content themselves with defining a probable cause, leaving the jury to decide whether the facts of the case correspond with the definition, which is, in effect, leaving the whole matter to their determination."[26]

It would be as if a modern court instructed a jury on fair use simply by handing it the four factors from the Copyright Act. That would be "a fatal error," the 1853 New York court concluded.[27] Unfortunately, that is often just what judges do when they hand fair use to a jury. The pattern of jury instruction for fair use in the Ninth Circuit, for example, lists the Copyright Act's four factors as those the jury merely "should consider" in "determining whether the use made of the work was fair." In its comment, the Ninth Circuit admits to the instruction being "basic." But the Ninth Circuit only offers that it "*could* be supplemented" by a judge "to suggest how the presence or absence of any particular factor may tend to support or detract from a finding of fair use."[28]

Notably absent from the Ninth Circuit's instruction is the Supreme Court's requirement that the results of exploring the four factors be "weighed together, in light of the purposes of copyright."[29] Of course, to explicitly include such a legal evaluation would betray the inherent error in passing the entire bundle of questions to a jury.

When a judge "leaves it to the jury to determine not only whether the facts alleged by the plaintiff are true, but whether, i[f] true, they prove a want of probable cause," the 1853 New York court found, "he abjures his own functions."[30] In malicious prosecution cases, the phrase "mixed question of law and fact" was "either wholly unmeaning"—or it was "intelligible and true only in a sense which renders it just as applicable to every question of law that a judge in the progress of a trial can be required to determine."[31]

What was true in the nineteenth century for malicious prosecution cases applies equally in the twenty-first century for fair use. The "mixed question" designation is either meaningless or trivially true.

Fixing the "Mixed": Contemporary Supreme Court Approaches

The Supreme Court has sometimes placed more stock in the "mixed question" phrase. In a 1995 criminal case, it even cited Thayer's treatise for the seemingly broad proposition that "the application-of-legal-standard-to-fact sort of question . . . , commonly called a 'mixed question of law and fact,' has typically been resolved by juries."[32]

That was only partly true. Thayer discussed how the phrase had sown "confusion" in areas of the law such as malicious prosecution. "[I]t is true," he also had conceded, that "whenever the facts and all just inferences of fact are once ascertained," the function of applying a legal standard to facts "belongs, in strictness, to the court."[33] If "at the outset, both sides admit all these things, *there is nothing for a jury to do*. In such a case," he wrote, "the questions raised in the application of the law to the facts are questions of law."[34]

More recent opinions by the Supreme Court recognize this. A 2015 case examined whether a trademark owner could "tack" its use of an older mark onto a new one to assert priority of rights. The legal test for permissible trademark "tacking" operates from the perspective of "an ordinary purchaser or consumer."[35] Therefore, the court ruled, it was the province of the jury to apply the legal test to the facts and answer this "mixed question."[36] It agreed with the Ninth Circuit, which had reversed the district court's grant of summary judgment on the issue and remanded the case for jury trial. But the Supreme Court quickly qualified: "This is certainly not to say that a judge may never determine whether two marks may be tacked. If the facts warrant it, a judge may decide a tacking question on a motion for summary judgment or for judgment as a matter of law."[37]

A March 2020 Supreme Court immigration decision drilled even deeper into how the court has understood "mixed questions of law and fact."[38] It identified two types of "mixed questions" that the court has historically contemplated.

The first type concerns "[w]hether the historical facts found satisfy the legal test chosen."[39] This was the type at issue in the case: The Fifth Circuit had determined that it could not consider whether two men had diligently sought to reopen their respective deportation proceedings, because diligence was a "factual question" outside its congressionally sanctioned purview.[40] But a majority of the Supreme Court's justices held that because the facts in the men's cases were "undisputed or established," the application of a legal standard to such "settled" facts was a "question of law" that Congress had expressly permitted courts to consider.[41]

In contrast, the second type of "mixed question" centers on "the proper standard for appellate review of a district, bankruptcy, or agency decision that applies a legal standard to underlying facts."[42] The Supreme Court has "often used the phrase 'mixed questions'" in such instances:[43] "The answer to the "proper standard" question may turn on practical considerations, such as whether the question primarily "require[s] courts to expound on the law, particularly by amplifying or elaborating on a broad legal standard" (often calling for review *de novo*), or rather "immerse[s] courts in case-specific factual issues" (often calling for deferential review)."[44]

For this type of "mixed question," the province of the jury—so often on the minds of judges weighing pretrial dismissal of a copyright infringement case on fair use grounds—is not the focus.

Over the last 120 years, the Supreme Court has heard a handful of fair use cases. Among those, it appears to have employed the "mixed question of law and fact" phrase only once: in a case brought by Harper & Row Publishers, Inc., the publisher of President Gerald Ford's memoirs, against *The Nation* magazine, which contended that it had fairly excerpted passages about Ford's pardon of Richard Nixon in an article before the book's release.[45]

"Fair use is a mixed question of law and fact," the *Harper & Row* court's majority opinion pronounced.[46] For that proposition, it cited a footnote from an Eleventh Circuit opinion in an earlier case—which, in turn, had attributed the phrase to no one.[47]

Nonetheless, in the words of fair use commentator William Patry, the *Harper & Row* majority "carefully limited the characterization of fair use as a mixed question of law and fact to bench trials"—i.e. the specific procedural posture that the Supreme Court, like the Eleventh Circuit case, was considering.[48] "Where the *district court* has found facts sufficient to evaluate each of the statutory factors," the *Harper & Row* majority wrote, "an appellate court 'need not remand for further factfinding . . . [but] may conclude as a matter of law that [the challenged use] do[es] not qualify as a fair use of the copyrighted work.'"[49] Hence, the Supreme Court used the "mixed question" label to justify a *purely judicial* determination of fair use—not, as many now use it, to justify leaving the matter to a jury.

To use the Supreme Court's own terminology, *Harper & Row* simply concerned itself with a "'proper standard' question"—not an "application-of-legal-standard-to-fact" sort of question.[50] The *Harper & Row* majority's use of the "mixed question of law and fact" phrase signified nothing to lower courts about the availability in fair use of pretrial dismissal as a matter of law under the Federal Rules of Civil Procedure.[51] If anything, it suggested that these are legal questions largely manageable by district and appellate judges.

That was driven home in the last fair use decision the Supreme Court issued: a 1994 decision in which "mixed question of law and fact" played no role.[52]

In *Campbell v. Acuff-Rose Music, Inc.*, a unanimous court reversed the Sixth Circuit, which had ruled that 2 Live Crew's rap parody of Roy Orbison's song "Oh Pretty Woman" was presumptively unfair because of its inclusion on a commercial album. "No such evidentiary presumption is available," the court held, "to address either the first factor, the character and purpose of the use, or the fourth, market harm, in determining whether a transformative use, such as parody, is a fair one."[53]

Of the first fair use factor, the court endorsed the concept of a "transformative" purpose proposed by Judge Pierre Leval in his 1990 law review article on fair use adjudicative standards.[54] It located that "transformative" purpose inquiry in the touchstone 1841 fair use analysis was conducted by Justice Joseph Story, after which Congress had fashioned the Copyright Act's factors.[55]

"Although such transformative use is not absolutely necessary for a finding of fair use," the *Campbell* court wrote, "the goal of copyright, to promote science and the arts, is generally furthered by the creation of transformative works. Such works thus lie at the heart of the fair use doctrine's guarantee of breathing space within the confines of copyright."[56] Assessment of the transformative character of a defendant's use engages a court in examining the "ends of the copyright law"[57]—a purely judicial task that no jury should be enlisted to judge. It is not analogous to, say, weighing the degree of risk as might be called for in a negligence case, or the determination of a person's state of mind in a fraud case.

Of the fourth fair use factor—here, harm to the prospects of an authorized rap version of "Oh, Pretty Woman"—the *Campbell* court commented that the district court, in granting summary judgment to 2 Live Crew, had "essentially passed" on this factor, silent as the evidentiary record was on the issue. The Sixth Circuit, meanwhile, "went the other way by erroneous presumption" of market harm.[58] "The evidentiary hole," the court concluded, "will doubtless be plugged on remand."[59]

But unlike in the later *Hana Financial* trademark case—whose question, the court held, "must be decided by a jury" when "a jury trial has been requested and when the facts do not warrant entry of summary judgment or judgment as a matter of law"[60]—the *Campbell* court expressed no concerns that courts were invading the jury's province on factual issues. The court made a point to dispel the ostensible "presumption" against commerciality, and relegated to a footnote the supposed prerequisite of "good faith" on the part of the user—both of which *Harper & Row* had repeated. But in its restatement of legal considerations for lower courts—now considering a work's "transformative" purpose, among other factors, "in light of the purposes of copyright"—the unanimous *Campbell* court voiced no expectation that judges should foist these considerations onto a jury. No "mixed question" confusion here: *Campbell* stands as a manual for consistent adjudication of fair use as a matter of law.[61]

Do Not "Shy Away"

The earliest opinion to pronounce fair use a "mixed question" acknowledged that, "even where there is a right to a trial by jury, the applicability of the fair use doctrine may not be a jury question."[62] The "mere fact that a determination of the fair use question requires an examination of the specific facts of each case," it added, "does not necessarily mean that in each case involving fair use there are factual issues to be tried."[63]

The year after the Supreme Court handed down its *Harper & Row* ruling, Harper & Row Publishers, Inc. found itself on the defendant's end of the fair use question. Yet even though a

Second Circuit appellate panel in that case repeated the notion that fair use involves "numerous issues of fact and law," it emphasized the utility of summary judgment in such cases:

> When the law requires a judgment for defendant, . . . the difficulty of the fair use question is not a valid reason to shy away from summary judgment. In the case before us, the parties frequently offer different *characterizations* of the facts, but generally do not seriously dispute the relevant sequence of events preceding the controversy. The distinction between the portrayal of the facts and the facts themselves is subtle— some might say elusive—but without it the summary judgment tool would be rendered a nullity.[64]

Campbell followed, re-centering the legal frame for the fair use inquiry (on a motion for summary judgment, no less). Yet, a curious thing has happened over the last twenty-five years. For all of fair use courts' seeming grasp of *Campbell's* "transformative" construction, they often reach back past *Campbell* to the older pronouncements of fair use as a "mixed question of law and fact."

Even the Second Circuit, which in 2013 had little trouble finding twenty-five Richard Prince paintings and collages transformative of a photographer's prints, still saw fit to label fair use a "mixed question of law and fact" in passing.[65] That appellate panel even withheld summary judgment vindication for five of the Prince works, stating, "We cannot say *for sure* . . . whether Prince has transformed [the plaintiff's] work enough" to render them transformative.[66] Why was *Campbell's* "reasonably [] perceived" measure—cited by the Second Circuit in this very opinion— insufficient to vindicate the remaining five?[67]

The Second Circuit's most recent upholding of a "transformative use"—a Drake song's sample of a spoken-word passage from a jazz recording—saw no need to even discuss the "reasonably perceived" standard.[68] Once again, the ease with which the appellate court affirmed the sample's "transformative" purpose and fair use overall should continue to encourage lower-court judges to not "shy away" from pretrial vindication of fair use as a matter of law. However, the appellate court still followed the fashion of couching summary judgment for fair use in subservient terms— as if it was only an occasional means of resolving "a mixed question of law and fact."[69]

As a result, even lower courts that grant fair use summary judgments continue to defer to the "mixed question" notion.[70] For others—even those that acknowledge *Campbell's* analytical focus on the ultimate purposes of copyright law—the "mixed question" language is so strong that it conjures looming issues for a jury.[71] One such court, after weighing the statutory factors together—which, again, *Campbell* had described as principally a legal task[72]—went so far as to hold that fair use was "not so obvious" a result "that the Court can conclude that no reasonable jury could find to the contrary."[73]

Conclusion

Judges should not "shy away" from pretrial consideration of fair use as a matter of law.[74] Nor should they "shy away" from dropping the "mixed question of law and fact" language from their analysis. It is an empty phrase that confuses courts' fair use evaluation. It stokes judicial misperceptions over the supposed complexity of copyright questions. It makes fair use more expensive to resolve and threatens to put pretrial resolution all but out of reach. Those days, as one appellate court resolved decades ago, are behind us.[75] In furtherance of the "progress" at the heart of copyright law's constitutional charter, judges should end the era of the "mixed question."

Acknowledgment

I am grateful to David S. Korzenik, partner at Miller Korzenik Sommers Rayman LLP, for sharing his insights into fair use case law and for his valuable thoughts and comments on drafts of this essay. I also thank Zachary M. Press, associate at Miller Korzenik Sommers Rayman LLP, for his helpful comments and research assistance.

Notes

1 See Meeropol v. Nizer, 417 F. Supp. 1201, 1213 (S.D.N.Y. 1976) ("The fair use defense generally raises a mixed question of law and fact."), *aff'd in part, rev'd in part on other grounds*, 560 F.2d 1061 (2d Cir. 1977).

2 See, e.g., Folsom v. Marsh, 9 F. Cas. 342, 344, 348 (C.C.D. Mass. 1841); compare *id.* at 348, with 17 U.S.C. § 107(1)–(4) (2018).

3 See Harper & Row Publishers, Inc. v. Nation Enters., 471 U.S. 539, 560 (1985); see, e.g., Cariou v. Prince, 714 F.3d 694, 704 (2d Cir. 2013); Worldwide Church of God v. Philadelphia Church of God, Inc., 227 F.3d 1110, 1115 (9th Cir. 2000).

4 See generally Howard B. Abrams and Tyler T. Ochoa, *The Nature of the Fair Use Defense—A Mixed Question of Law and Fact*. Vol. 2, § 15.29, *The Law of Copyright*. Thomson Reuters, 2019; see, e.g., Estate of Smith v. Graham, 799 F. App'x 36, 37–38 (2d Cir. 2020); Cariou, 714 F.3d at 704; Blanch v. Koons, 467 F.3d 244, 250 (2d Cir. 2006).

5 See, e.g., VHT, Inc. v. Zillow Grp., Inc., 918 F.3d 723, 739 (9th Cir. 2019), *cert. denied*, 140 S. Ct. 122 (2019); Brammer v. Violent Hues Prods., LLC, 922 F.3d 255, 261 (4th Cir. 2019).

6 See § 107. Congress did not expressly state whether any of the factors is "to be considered" by a judge or a jury. § 107. Of course, under the Seventh Amendment of the Constitution, "the right of trial by jury shall be preserved, and no fact tried by a jury, shall be otherwise re-examined in any Court of the United States, than according to the rules of the common law." U.S. Const. amend. VII. Jury trials are often demanded in copyright cases. But neither the Seventh Amendment nor the fair use provision of the Copyright Act sheds light on whether fair use considerations are factual or legal in nature.

7 Campbell v. Acuff-Rose Music, Inc., 510 U.S. 569, 578 (1994).

8 Abrams and Ochoa, *The Nature of the Fair Use Defense*, § 15.29.

9 See generally Cariou, 714 F.3d at 705–06 ("'[T]ransformative works . . . lie at the heart of the fair use doctrine's guarantee of breathing space.'" (quoting Campbell, 510 U.S. at 579)).

10 *See* U.S. Const. art. I, § 8, cl. 8.

11 This is so across at least the first three fair use factors. And even the fourth, which examines harm to the market for the original work, categorically excludes the plaintiff's potential market for derivatives that are of the same "transformative" character as the defendant's work—for example, self-parodies. See, e.g., Campbell, 510 U.S. at 592. ("Th[e] distinction between potentially remediable displacement and unremediable disparagement is reflected in the rule that there is no protectible derivative market for criticism. The market for potential derivative uses includes only those that creators of original works would in general develop or license others to develop.")

12 See Campbell, 510 U.S. at 578, 581.

13 Fed. R. Civ. P. 1.

14 See generally Harper & Row Publishers, Inc. v. Nation Enters., 471 U.S. 539, 582 (1985) (Brennan, J., dissenting). (Limitation on copyright scope "ensures consonance with our most important First Amendment values.")

15 Lawrence v. Dana, 15 F. Cas. 26, 56 (C.C.D. Mass. 1869) (emphasis added).

16 *Id.*

17 *Id.* at 58, 59.

18 See generally Folsom v. Marsh, 9 F. Cas. 342, 348 (C.C.D. Mass. 1841) (discussing cases).

19 Bank of U.S. v. Corcoran, 27 U.S. 121, 133 (1829).

20 James Bradley Thayer, *A Preliminary Treatise on Evidence at the Common Law*, pt. 1 (Boston: Little, Brown and Company, 1898), 224–25.

21 Thayer, 225.

22 See Thayer, 222.

23 Thayer, 222.

24 Thayer, 224; see also William F. Patry, "§ 7.6. Appellate Review: Applying the Proper Standard," *Patry on Fair Use* (Westlaw, updated May 2020), n.32 and accompanying text (citing Thayer) (hereafter "Patry").

25 See Thayer, 225 n.1.

26 Bulkeley v. Smith, 2 Duer Super. Ct. Rep. 261, 271 (N.Y. Super. Ct. 1853), https://cite.case.law/duer-super-ct-rep/2/261.

27 *Id.* at 272.
28 See United States Courts for the Ninth Circuit, "§ 17.18 Copyright—Affirmative Defense—Fair Use (17 U.S.C. § 107)," Comment, *Ninth Circuit Manual of Model Jury Instructions Civil*, September 2006, 388, https://www.rid.uscourts.gov/sites/rid/files/documents/juryinstructions/otherPJI/9th%20Circuit%20Model%20Civil%20Jury%20Instructions.pdf.
29 Ninth Circuit, *Model Jury Instructions*, "§ 17.18 Copyright"; cf. Campbell, 510 U.S. at 578.
30 Bulkeley v. Smith, 2 Duer Super. Ct. Rep. 261, 272 (N.Y. Super. Ct. 1853), https://cite.case.law/duer-super-ct-rep/2/261.
31 *Id.*
32 United States v. Gaudin, 515 U.S. 506, 512 (1995) (citing Thayer, 249–50).
33 Thayer, 252.
34 Thayer, 252 (emphasis added).
35 Hana Fin., Inc. v. Hana Bank, 574 U.S. 418, 420 (2015).
36 *Id.* at 420, 423–24.
37 *Id.* at 423 (citing Fed. R. Civ. P. 50, 56(a)).
38 Guerrero-Lasprilla v. Barr, 140 S. Ct. 1062, 1069 (2020).
39 See *id.* at 1074 (Thomas, J., dissenting) (citing U.S. Bank Nat. Ass'n. ex rel. CWCapital Asset Mgmt, LLC v. Vill. at Lakeridge, LLC, 138 S. Ct. 930, 966 (2018)).
40 See *id.* at 1068.
41 See *id.* at 1068–69.
42 *Id.* at 1069.
43 *Id.*
44 *Id.* (quoting *Vill. at Lakeride*, 138 S. Ct. at 967).
45 Harper & Row Publishers, Inc. v. Nation Enters, 471 U.S. 539 (1985).
46 *Id.* at 560.
47 *Id.*; see Pacific & S. Co. v. Duncan, 744 F.2d 1490, 1495 n.8 (11th Cir. 1984); see also Patry, "§ 7.6. Appellate Review," n.4 and accompanying text.
48 Patry, n.5 and accompanying text.
49 Harper & Row Publishers, Inc., 471 U.S. at 560 (citing Pacific & S. Co., 744 F.2d at 1495).
50 Guerrero-Lasprilla v. Barr, 140 S. Ct. 1062, 1069 (2020).
51 See Patry, "§ 7.6. Appellate Review." ("Neither court intended to be announcing broad rules . . . neither *Pacific & Southern* no[r] *Harper & Row* involved a jury.")
52 Campbell v. Acuff-Rose Music, Inc., 510 U.S. 569 (1994). The Supreme Court has been poised to reexamine a jury's finding of fair use in the long-running dispute between Google and Oracle over software interoperability. But in April 2020, the court postponed oral argument in the case to its fall term, as part of its case management response in the wake of the coronavirus pandemic. See Docket, Google LLC v. Oracle America, Inc., No. 18-956 (March 16, 2020).
53 Campbell, 510 U.S. at 594.
54 *Id.* at 579 (citing Pierre N. Leval, "Toward a Fair Use Standard," *Harvard Law Review* 103 (1990): 1111).
55 *Id.* (citing 9 F. Cas. 342, 344 (C.C.D. Mass. 1841)).
56 *Id.*
57 *Id.* at 581.
58 *Id.* at 594.
59 *Id.*
60 Hana Fin., Inc. v. Hana Bank, 574 U.S. 418, 423 (2015).
61 *See generally* Pamela Samuelson, "Unbundling Fair Uses," *Fordham Law Review* 77, no. 5 (2009): 2537 (analyzing how fair use case law "is more coherent and more predictable than many commentators seem to believe"), https://ir.lawnet.fordham.edu/cgi/viewcontent.cgi?article=4447&context=flr.
62 Meeropol v. Nizer, 417 F. Supp. at 1213.
63 *Id.* at 1208.
64 Maxtone-Graham v. Burtchaell, 803 F.2d 1253, 1259 (2d Cir. 1986) (emphasis in original).
65 Meeropol v. Nizer, 417 F. Supp. 1201, 1213 (S.D.N.Y. 1976).
66 Cariou v. Prince, 714 F.3d 694, 711 (2d Cir. 2013).
67 See *id.* at 707 (quoting Campbell v. Acuff-Rose Music, Inc., 510 U.S. 569, 582 (1994)). The appellate court remanded to the district court "to determine, in the first instance, whether such relatively minimal alterations render [the five Prince artworks] fair uses (including whether the artworks are transformative)." *Id.* at 711. It was unclear what exactly the appellate court expected the district judge to do at that point. The case had turned so upside down by then that the plaintiff was seeking a judgment of no fair

use as a matter of law, and the defendant was seeking a jury trial on fair use. See Cariou v. Prince, No. 08-CV-11327-DAB, Docket Nos. 85, 89 (S.D.N.Y. Aug. 1, 2013 & October 15, 2013). But the parties settled the case before the judge made any further determination. *See* Cariou v. Prince, No. 08-CV-11327-DAB, Docket No. 129 (S.D.N.Y. March 19, 2014).

68 See Estate of Smith v. Graham, 799 F. App'x 36 (2d Cir. 2020).

69 See *id.* at 37–38 ("Although fair use is a mixed question of law and fact, this court has on a number of occasions resolved fair use determinations at the summary judgment stage where there are no genuine issues of material fact.") (internal citations omitted).

70 See, e.g., Solid Oak Sketches, LLC v. 2K Games, Inc., --- F. Supp. 3d ----, 2020 WL 1467394, at *8 (E.D.N.Y. March 26, 2020).

71 Philpot v. WOS, Inc., No. 18-CV-339-RP, 2019 WL 1767208, at *4, 7 (W.D. Tex. April 22, 2019).

72 Campbell, 510 U.S. at 578 (citing Leval, "Toward a Fair Use Standard," 1111).

73 Philpot, 2019 WL 1767208, at *7

74 Maxtone-Graham v. Burtchaell, 803 F.2d 1253, 1259 (2d Cir. 1986).

75 *Id.* at 1258 n.5.

2.4

FAIR USE

The Linchpin to the Future of the Copyright Act

Michael Donaldson

Time and again, litigators have used the fair use doctrine to defend the innovative actions of their clients. This is especially important for cases dealing with innovations not clearly addressed in, or anticipated by, the Copyright Act of 1976.

Fair use is the single mechanism that can mold copyright law to meet the demands of this new technological landscape and still achieve the constitutional objective to promote the creation of new works. Those who ignore this important role of fair use do so at their own peril. Fair use protects certain otherwise infringing uses of protected works against claims of copyright infringement. It emerges as the centerpiece to keep US copyright law relevant to the digital era because it is the only aspect of copyright law that, by explicit statutory language, is to be determined on a case-by-case basis by the courts. The statutory balancing test through which fair use has been adjudicated has empowered the courts to apply it in a way that serves the constitutional purpose of the Copyright Act and the realities of the brave new world of digital technologies.

The limitation of the Copyright Act was considered by the Supreme Court in 1975 in a case involving the performance of music on a restaurant radio before the new Copyright Act was passed and way before the game-changing technologies became front and center in American life. "Creative work is to be encouraged and rewarded, but private motivation must ultimately serve the cause of promoting broad public availability of literature, music, and the other arts . . . . When technological change has rendered its literal terms ambiguous, the Copyright Act must be construed in light of this basic purpose."[1]

Forty-five years later, this tension was best illustrated in *Author's Guild v. Google*.[2] That case highlighted the divide between those who hang on to certain literal phrases of the Copyright Act and those who look to fair use to provide breathing room for an amazing achievement that benefits authors and society as a whole.

Google Books digitized 100 percent of more than 20 million books and allowed the public to access very brief passages that contained words or phrases selected by searches. Without leaving the comfort of your living room, Google Books allows you to type in a phrase and find books that use that phrase. You can also ask Google Books how many times a certain word or phrase is used within a title you provide. Many works, including two of my own, have been discovered by curious folk using Google Books. The Author's Guild, well-versed in the Copyright Act, brought suit because copying 100 percent of a book surely required a license and payment. They were, of course, absolutely correct had anyone tried to copy a book in 1978, 1979, or 1980. When the Act was passed and for quite a few years thereafter, copying millions of books was not possible. The court wisely evaluated this new possibility, the degree to which it could benefit the public, the careful restraints placed by Google to prevent access to the entire book or a substantial portion, and the benefit to society under the fair use doctrine. No other doctrine in the Copyright Act could have done this.

Critics of this case give the knee-jerk, unthoughtful, unhelpful response: "Well, Google copied the whole book, so it cannot be fair use," without consideration of the benefits to society and, frankly, to authors: I myself have received phone calls from people who have discovered one of my books through Google Search. In that way, I have benefitted from this ruling, as have others who are members of the Authors Guild. Those who believe themselves to be pro-author by lamenting the court's ruling are letting their backward grip on copyright law lead them to a harmful and destructive conclusion. Judge Pierre Leval has said that if Google Books was organized differently—to allow public access—it would have been decided differently.[3]

For some reason, public reaction was greater to Google Books than previous cases which countenanced the copying of an entire work. In 2009, *A.V. ex rel. Vandergye v. iParadigms, LLC,*[4] the court held that schools may preserve copies of independently created student papers in order to detect and prevent plagiarism by students whose competitive spirit took them across an ethical line. Even earlier, *Bill Graham Archives v. Dorling Kindersley Ltd.*[5] approved the use of 100 percent of various concert posters to illustrate a picture book on the band, the Grateful Dead. It created the greatest stir because the lawsuit was so hotly litigated. Other examples in which courts had similarly found the creation of complete digital copies of copyrighted works to be transformative fair uses when the copies "served a different function from the original" include *Perfect 10* (a digital, thumbnail copy to provide an internet pathway to the original) and *HathiTrust* (justifying the noncommercial digital copying of 100 percent of the books for the purpose of preservation and permitting searchers to determine whether its text employs particular words).

However, fair use is not the panacea some would like you to believe. Particularly, there are two areas in which this occurs. The first group is composed of folks who simply throw out the words fair use as though they were a shield against any miscreant behavior. Particularly common is the user who grabs something off the internet, which they can do for free, and want to call it fair use. People become more and more accustomed to making use of virtually all the knowledge in the world without ever leaving their sofa. No fees. No waiting. Just turn on a smartphone and ask a question. They can listen, learn, make notes, use what they learn in writing a paper for school, and tell their friends about what they learned—all without giving one moment's thought to the creator of the material that has been viewed, absorbed, and used in some way or another. Without much effort, various things found on the internet can be combined or used to create new things for their personal enjoyment. So far, so good. All that is legal.

If their creation is cool, they want to share it. Sharing their work with friends and family is legal. Friends and family are excited, supportive, and encouraging. "Everyone will love this," they say. Naturally, the creator wants to share it with more people. They go public. They put it on the internet. That is not allowed. Often, the copyright owners of the underlying material are simply not knowledgeable enough to respond intelligently.

The urge is as understandable as it is abhorrent to a copyright holder. If someone who paints a picture in a traditional manner can show it off, why not show off an equally creative work cobbled together from things found on the internet? What could be wrong with that? Just the Copyright Act, that's all. To a lay person who grows up with the internet and its rapid access to just about everything in the world, and who enjoys tinkering around and creating things, the urge to share more widely is easy to understand. Later, I will provide an easy way to challenge the urge.

The second group should know better. They reverse engineer aspects of the fair use doctrine in order to build some newfangled money-making venture. Courts have been pretty good at sniffing out the motives and false logic behind such efforts. ReDigi, Inc. wanted to come up with a system whereby owners of a digital download could sell their download. They bought it, they ought to be able to sell it under the first sale doctrine, right? Wrong. Under the first sale doctrine, the logic might very well have been approved, but Congress did not adopt the judicially created doctrine. It adopted something narrower, more constrained, and very specific, and it did not cover digital anything—it only covered physical copies, clearly and unequivocally. So ReDigi looked to fair use to bail them out. They looked to Google Books and focused on one element: the fact that 100 percent of millions of books were copied. And what is the benefit to society in ReDigi's plan akin to the enormous benefits of the Google Books plan? Their reasoning? It is a work-around for the omission of digital material from the statutory first sale doctrine that was enshrined in the Copyright Act. Judge Leval who wrote the *Google Books* decision also wrote the decision in *Capitol Records, LLC v. ReDigi Inc.*, in which he had carefully pointed out in a well-reasoned opinion[6] that the court was not the place to amend a statute. It was Congress who ReDigi had to persuade, not the Second Circuit. If the statutory first sale doctrine were not so specific, the case might very well have gone the other way.

Not very different in terms of its desire to develop a new business was TVEyes, which copied all television content. Subscribers to their service could locate content identified only by a keyword or phrase. So far, the process looks an awful lot like Google Books. The paying customers of TVEyes were mostly commercial enterprises who were very interested in where and how their product was being mentioned somewhere on television. They would not subscribe to the service if they could not access the entire program. So that feature was added. Clearly not fair use, but they tried anyway. Fox and all the other studios sued. The court had no trouble shutting down that operation.[7] TVEyes had not transformed the programs one iota. They had just figured out a way to market and sell any program that contained a name such as Tylenol, wiping out a market that belonged to the creators of the programs.

The entrepreneurial graveyard is filled with a lot of corpses. Napster[8] and Grokster[9] are probably the best-known companies who pushed the copyright envelope too far. Napster facilitated peer-to-peer (P2P) file sharing knowing some (or most) of the material was infringing. Napster was found to be secondarily liable. Grokster went a step further and actually promoted their software as capable of infringing. Grokster was found liable for the resulting acts of infringement. Other start-up companies will continue to try to create a new and different business or business model justified on the basis of fair use. Some will work; most are just too clever for their own good. If the motive is purely money and not the good received by the general public, they will and should fail to pass muster. The starting point of all things copyright is acknowledging the constitutional purposes of copyright, which admittedly creates a very real tension: to encourage authors to create new works and to benefit the public. The use of someone else's work for a profit motive is not in service of the intention for copyright laws that the founding fathers or Queen Ann had before them.

Another Way to Advise Clients and Predict Results

The wide acceptance of fair use has changed the landscape for every creative medium from film to computer codes, and from photographs to hip-hop music. Many folks who turn their attention to fair use begin to read all fair use cases and become very confused. They do not realize that cases involving films, for example, are so different from computer codes cases, and that reading cases outside of the subset of creative works in which they are interested is confusing and often misleading. It is far better to look closely at the exact material that is being challenged in a given case. For example, our office works on more than 300 films a year. Most contact us initially about some sort of clearance or rights issue with their film, so we try very hard to read and study every fair use case involving film and—equally important—to collect the actual footage or issue that was being decided because seeing the footage helps make the decision of the court much more realistic and understandable. Being able to show actual clips to clients certainly helped us communicate more clearly what was found to be fair use or not fair use.

By reading hundreds of cases, it should be possible to discern patterns that can simplify the process of deciding when something can be considered safe fair use with such confidence that it can be called a safe harbor. Statutory and judicial safe harbors that reduce or eliminate a party's liability have been enacted in other areas of the US law, including securities law, patent law, Medicare/Medicaid regulations, accounting, online infringement, and even certain torts. Our office has developed a de facto safe harbor for fair use in nonfiction works, which is based on more than 175 years of published court decisions. It has been reinforced by an examination of many of the actual works that are the subjects of these decisions.

In order for the use of copyrighted material in a nonfiction work to fall within the fair use safe harbor protection from copyright infringement liability, three safe harbor questions must be answered in the affirmative. (This approach was eventually set out in a law review article.[10] Judge Pierre Laval generously vetted the approach, urging a replacement of the timid word "necessary" in the second question with the more accurate words "reasonably appropriate" to describe how much of the work can be used within the fair use doctrine.)

The three questions are:

1   Does the asset illustrate or support a point that the creator is trying to make in the new work?

The use of the word "illustrate" is important. If you are using original material to make a point through voiceover, interviews, or on-screen cards, and you are using the material to illustrate the point you are making, the answer to the first question will be "yes." However, if you are relying on assets owned by others to tell your story, the answer to the first question would be "no," and therefore, the answers to the next two questions would be "no." This would cause the use to fall outside the safe harbor even though it still might constitute fair use for a variety of other reasons. Remember, fair use falls along a spectrum.

2   Does the creator of the new work use only as much of the asset as is reasonably appropriate to illustrate or support the point being made?

Put another way, is the material used primarily in service of the point you are trying to make or does it continue on after that goal has been accomplished? The phrase "only as much as is reasonably appropriate" is elastic, but the published court opinions often explicitly defer to the artist to determine how much is appropriate when the discussion focuses on just the third factor in the statute.

There are a lot of mythologies to the effect that there is some magic amount you can use to always be safe. That is never true. Fair use is often a function of how much is being used, but, much more often, it is a function of *why* you are using something. What is your purpose? Have a reason before using someone else's work. The better you explain your use of an asset, the more likely it is that you will be in the safe harbor for fair use.

3   Is the connection between the point being made and the asset being used to illustrate or support the point clear to the average viewer?

The "average viewer" refers, of course, to the average viewer in the intended audience for the new work. The third question helps you move your work toward the safe harbor.

After the appearance of the law review article, our office began receiving requests to clear scripted films that were biographical in nature or otherwise based on true stories. We handled those just like the documentaries based on the safe harbor approach even though no court decisions were exactly on point. But the decisions came quickly on films we were not involved with. The megahit musical *Jersey Boys* used a clip from *The Ed Sullivan Show* to illustrate the point that The Four Seasons came to national attention when they appeared on *The Ed Sullivan Show*.[11] This was considered a fair use as it was used as a historical anchor.

The Weinstein Company recreated two scenes from the famous porn film *Deep Throat* in its biopic on the film's star, Linda Lovelace. The court said that it was fair use.[12] Woody Allen claimed fair use of a famous quote from Faulkner in a fictional work. The court approved.[13] In totally original works, the opportunities for fair use do not arise as often, but often there are possibilities which should not be shied away from. Keep in mind that even though my examples are film-centric, the law's application is not. Dance, paintings, computer codes, and any other work created by a human can turn to fair use for use of prior components in the new work.

The safe harbor approach developed in our office and gently mentored by Judge Leval was borne of creative works and applies solidly to such works. Practitioners and users alike can use the approach to move marginal uses to safety and adjust uses that do not fall within fair use in order to fit them into the territory of acceptability. This safe harbor is not applicable to the utilitarian uses of creative works such as discussed earlier in *Google Books*, *ReDigi*, and similar cases. Practitioners often claim that judges decide their fair use cases impulsively, instinctually, or instantaneously and then go through an analysis of the four factors in a way that supports their conclusion, while other practitioners jump to the defense of judges and insist that they work carefully through their analyses. Malcolm Gladwell has written an entire book (Blink) in support of the notion that all of us—lawyers, doctors, CPAs, and firefighters—make decisions in the blink of an eye and then rationalize the decision after the fact.

Parody

Of course, one cannot talk about fair use and its future in the development of copyright law without some attention paid to the widely misunderstood subset of fair use which is parody. Parody is a very specific legal concept with very specific requirements. Technology has not impacted parodic uses to the same extent it has impacted other fair uses. Our firm's legal definition of a parody, drawn from an examination of the materials being litigated and all court decisions we could find in this area is the following:

1 A new, copyrightable work,
2 based on a previously copyrighted work,
3 that uses enough of the previous work so it is clearly recognizable,
4 but not taking more from the previous work than is reasonably appropriate for the purpose of reference and comment,
5 that criticizes or comments on the subject matter or style of the previous work, at least in part, and
6 is not likely to invade the market for the previous work.

Statistically speaking, most examples of parody turn out to be humorous. But parodies rarely put a smile on the face of the owner of the underlying work. Judges often go out of their way to say that they do not think that the parody before them is funny.

The Supreme Court did not issue a detailed decision on parody until the 2 Live Crew case in 1994.[14] The reason for the lawsuit was that 2 Live Crew wrote, recorded, and released a song that they thought was a parody of Roy Orbison's 1964 hit song "Oh, Pretty Woman." Not surprisingly, Orbison's publisher Acuff-Rose Music was upset. Here are selected lyrics from Orbison's "Oh, Pretty Woman" compared to 2 Live Crew's "Pretty Woman."

"Oh, Pretty Woman" by Orbison and Dees vs. "Pretty Woman" by 2 Live Crew

Pretty Woman, walking down the street,	Pretty woman, walkin' down the street,
Pretty Woman, the kind I like to meet,	Pretty woman, girl you look so sweet,
Pretty Woman, I don't believe you,	Pretty woman, you bring me down to that knee,
You're not the truth,	Pretty woman, you make me wanna beg please.
No one could look as good as you.	Oh, pretty woman.
Mercy.	Big hairy woman, you need to shave that stuff
Pretty Woman, won't you pardon me,	Big hairy woman, you know I bet it's tough
Pretty Woman, I couldn't help but see,	Big hairy woman, all that hair it ain't legit
Pretty Woman, that you look lovely as can be	'Cause you look like Cousin It.
Are you lonely just like me?	Big hairy woman.
Pretty Woman.	

As in virtually all parody cases, the first three factors in my definition were clearly established by 2 Live Crew. These lyrics are (1) a new creation (2) that is based on Roy Orbison's "Oh, Pretty Woman" (3) to such an extent that the original "Oh, Pretty Woman" is clearly recognizable—even on the written page without the music.

The fourth factor brings in some subjective judgment as to whether 2 Live Crew did or did not take more from Orbison's "Oh, Pretty Woman" than was reasonably appropriate. Courts tend to defer greatly to the artist on the question of amount in all fair use cases. In this case, the court remanded on the question of whether the amount of Roy Orbison's guitar riff was too much. Courts try not to second-guess creative judgment. The case settled and there was no decision on this question.

Supreme Court Justice Souter wrote:

> It is true, of course, that 2 Live Crew copied the characteristic opening bass riff (or musical phrase) of the original, and the first line of the Orbison lyrics. The "heart" of the original, [but] the heart is also what most readily conjures up the song for parody, and it is the heart at which parody takes aim. Copying does not become excessive in relation to parodic purpose merely because the portion taken was the original's heart.

The fifth factor concerning commentary on the underlying work is the focus of most of the opinions. Almost any commentary on the work can qualify. Commentary on society in general, however, will not qualify. That would be a satire and would not enjoy the extra leeway afforded a true parody to meet the third factor in my definition of being able to recognize the previous work.

As the first five factors are solidified, it almost always follows that the new work seeks a different audience from the audience sought by the previous work. While courts spend a lot of time on this factor and most scholarly writers believe that this finding is essential, we view it as much less bothersome than the rest of the elements since it is hard to imagine a circumstance in which the parody would be seeking the same market as the previous work.

Another example of parody seeking a different audience from the audience attracted to the original work is an episode of the animated television show *Family Guy* entitled "I Need a Jew." The show's goofy central figure and patriarch, Peter Griffin, finds himself in a financial pickle. Taking advice from his friends, Peter decides that he needs to find a Jew to solve his financial troubles. Peter breaks into the Disney song from the film *Pinocchio*, to the tune of "When You Wish Upon A Star": "Nothing else has worked so far so I'll wish upon a star, wondrous dancing speck of light, I need a Jew."

Disney sued. They lost.

Finding that the tones and messages of the songs were "strikingly different," the court held that "I Need a Jew" parodied the sweetness of the idyllic message of Geppetto's song because

Peter ignorantly sang about stereotypes of Jewish people, while at the same time earnestly and innocently wishing for a Jew. The court concluded that the two songs served different market functions and appealed to different audiences.[15]

Two cases from the book publishing world shed some light on parody and how direct commentary on the underlying work is the key factor in deciding whether a work qualifies as a parody.

Not too long after O.J. Simpson's criminal murder trial and before a civil jury found him responsible for killing his ex-wife, several books came out about the case. Simon & Schuster had what they thought was a parody printed about the case and shipped to stores when a court halted the delivery. Very few copies ever saw the light of day. We own one. The book was called *The Cat Not in the Hat*. Defense lawyers argued that it was a parody based on Dr. Seuss's famous *The Cat in the Hat*.

Keep in mind that the fifth factor (criticizing or commenting on the subject matter or style of the previous work) is the key. Although Simon & Schuster tried to argue that *The Cat Not in the Hat* was a commentary on the innocence of the Seuss book, it was crystal clear that the book was really just taking a humorous look at the murder trial. And the thing that made it humorous was the relentless, start-to-finish taking of the style and rhyming of Seuss and even the look of the illustrations in Seuss's book. Once that factor went against the authors of *The Cat Not in the Hat*, nothing else mattered much. One could view the taking of *The Cat Not in the Hat* as excessive. After all, even the Seuss drawings were mimicked in the new work. And there is a strong argument that the existence of this work would have been very confusing to the young audience of *The Cat in the Hat*. Certainly, it would have been easy for someone to grab the wrong book because of the similarity in how the covers looked. It would have been natural for someone to believe that there was some sort of endorsement or approval from the Seuss estate for the new work. But the important reason that the copies of the new book had to be destroyed was that the commentary was not on the underlying work, it was on a completely different subject—no matter how hard the lawyers tried to twist things after the fact.

The Cat Not in the Hat was clearly a satire. The lawyers did not go there because the authors took way too much from the famous Dr. Seuss book to pass muster under a straight fair use test. That is why they tried (unsuccessfully) to convince the court that *The Cat Not in the Hat* was a parody. If the authors wanted to write humorously on the O.J. trial, they should have created their own work, not merely rewrite the Seuss text, using many of the phrases of the original in order to create a wry look at what the authors believed was a miscarriage of justice.[16]

For works with no shred of humor, return again to the publishing world. The most famous such case involved *The Wind Done Gone*, Alice Randall's small and powerful 2001 novel about the slaves who populated Tara, the cotton plantation, in Margaret Mitchell's popular 1936 novel *Gone with the Wind*. In Mitchell's book, the only characters who came alive on Tara were white. The furniture was described in more detail than the many black people who made the place run. The Mitchell estate sued Randall and her publisher—and won an injunction at the trial court level—on the theory that *The Wind Done Gone* was an unauthorized sequel.

The estate lost on appeal. *The Wind Done Gone* was allowed to be published based on the fair use doctrine.

When you compare the two books using the six factors at the beginning of this section, it is easy to see why *The Wind Done Gone* is available for purchase today. It clearly makes commentary on the subject matter of *Gone with the Wind*. It takes thinly disguised characters, particularly black characters, right out of Mitchell's book and tells their rich stories, including the pain they felt by being treated as less than human by Mitchell's white characters who loom so large in American literary life. The key factor of commentary is very much in favor of *The Wind Done Gone*. Having read both books, my opinion is that *The Wind Done Gone* could have used even more material from *Gone with the Wind* than it did.

This case also illustrates the powerful forces that seek to broaden the fair use area. The following news organizations all filed amicus briefs, joining the fight on behalf of *The Wind Done Gone*: Cox Enterprises, Cable News Network, and the owners of *The New York Times* and *The Boston Globe*, *The Wall Street Journal*, the *Chicago Tribune*, *The Los Angeles Times*, and *The Tampa Tribune*.

While parody cases and the support they are receiving from the publishing community are rapidly widening the understanding of, and therefore the acceptance of, parody, the concept is not likely to have a significant impact on copyright law in general, and certainly not to the extent that other cases involving non-parodic fair use have had and will continue to have in aiding copyright law to live in the technological world so very far from its time of birth.

Conclusion

The Copyright Act is loaded with all sorts of finely tuned, precisely worded, detail-loaded sections for everything from registration of works to termination of license grants. From the birth to its death of copyright, there seems to be no shortage of highly specific guidance. That is, until you get to § 107, fair use.

The fair use statute is only specific in its declaration that the fair use of material is not an infringement. Otherwise, fair use determination is left to the courts with the only command being that they consider four not-very-specific factors, and anything else that comes to mind. This has caused many commentators and practitioners to shudder, claiming that fair use is unpredictable, and nothing is a fair use until a judge says so. There is widespread reluctance to advise clients without so many weasel words that clients are left confused and uncertain as to how to proceed. However, this flexibility and lack of any bright-line rules are the strengths of fair use. It allows courts—nay, pushes courts—to mold the Copyright Act to adapt to the new technological world that did not exist in 1978 when the modern Copyright Act became law. Nowhere else in the Copyright Act has such freedom been accorded to the courts or anybody else to keep the Copyright Act current. This transfer of responsibility to the courts on a case-by-case basis gives some validity to the phrase "Congress, in its wisdom. . . ."

This essay on a fair use safe harbor gives practitioners a tool to guide clients to safer uses of material pursuant to fair use and permit productive use of prior materials in both nonfiction and fictional storytelling. This can make it easier for creators to obtain errors and omissions (E&O) insurance, even for films that use over 50 percent of a song, are made up of one-third of clips from a single major motion picture, or deconstruct Beatles albums with heavy reliance on the music being discussed. Applying these principles should lead to reduced apprehensions over responsible fair use.

Notes

1 Twentieth Century Music Corp. v. Aiken, 422 U.S. 151, 156 (1975).
2 Author's Guild v. Google, 804 F.3d 202 (2d Cir. 2015).
3 Pierre N. Leval, "Fair Use in the Digital Age: Reflections on the Fair Use Doctrine in Copyright Law," Fourth Annual Peter A. Jaszi Distinguished Lecture on Intellectual Property at American University Washington College of Law, Speech (November 12, 2015), http://www.pijip.org/judgeleval.
4 A.V. ex rel. Vanderhye v. iParadigms, LLC, 562 F.3d 630 (4th Cir. 2009).
5 Bill Graham Archives v. Dorling Kindersley Ltd., 448 F.3d 605 (2d Cir. 2006).
6 Capitol Records, LLC v. ReDigi Inc., 910 F.3d 649 (2d Cir. 2018), *cert. denied*, 139 S. Ct. 2760 (2019).
7 Fox News Network, LLC v. TVEyes, Inc., 883 F.3d 169, 177 (2d Cir. 2018), *cert. denied*, 139 S. Ct. 595 (2018).
8 A&M Records v. Napster, Inc., 239 F.3d 1004 (9th Cir. 2001), *as amended* (April 3, 2001), *aff'd sub nom.* A&M Records, Inc. v. Napster, Inc., 284 F.3d 1091 (9th Cir. 2002), *and aff'd sub nom.* A&M Records, Inc. v. Napster, Inc., 284 F.3d 1091 (9th Cir. 2002).

9 Metro-Goldwyn-Mayer Studios Inc., v. Grokster, Ltd., 545 U.S. 913 (2005).

10 Michael C. Donaldson, "Refuge from the Storm: A Fair Use Safe Harbor for Non-Fiction Works," *Journal of the Copyright Society of the U.S.A.* 59, no. 3 (2012), https://www.researchgate.net/ publication/256052051_Refuge_from_the_Storm_A_Fair_Use_Safe_Harbor_for_Non-Fiction_ Works.

11 SOFA Entm't, Inc. v. Dodger Prods., Inc. 709 F.3d 1273 (9th Cir. 2013).

12 Arrow Prods., LTD. v. Weinstein Co. LLC, 44 F. Supp. 3d 359, 372 (S.D.N.Y. 2014).

13 Faulkner Literary Rights, LLC v. Sony Pictures Classics Inc., 953 F. Supp. 2d 701 (N.D. Miss. 2013).

14 Campbell v. Acuff-Rose Music, Inc., 510 U.S. 569 (1994).

15 *Family Guy*, season 3, episode 22, "I Need a Jew" (song) from "When You Wish Upon a Weinstein," directed by Dan Povenmire, written by Ricky Blitt, aired on September 9, 2003, on FOX, http://www. clearanceandcopyright.com/ch3/2 [LINK DOESN'T WORK FOR ME, https://www.youtube.com/ watch?v=ebajv8mjPTo is clip on YouTube but not official from FOX so maybe we shouldn't use].

16 Dr. Juice, *The Cat Not in the Hat* (Newstar Pr, 1996), http://www.clearanceandcopyright.com/ch3/3.

2.5

SELF-PUBLISHING REVOLUTION
Copyright Pitfalls for Writers Who Go It Alone

Francine Ward

While not new, self-publishing has, more than ever, become a viable alternative for many authors. Webster defines self-publishing as publishing a book using the author's own resources. Self-published writers essentially assume the sole or primary responsibility for financing, creating, publishing, distributing, marketing, and selling their books. This includes securing editors (if they are smart), graphic designers, photographers, and anyone who will assist in the creation and ultimate distribution of the work. The writer is also responsible for securing lawyers to draft agreements, offer counsel, and vet the manuscript, if the writer is wise enough to realize that this should be done.

Why do authors choose self-publishing? The primary reasons include having total control, wanting to retain all the money, sometimes because the author was unable to secure a traditional book deal, and for some, retaining creative control is of the utmost importance. These authors want to be able to decide not only the content of the book, but what, when, where, and how the book will be delivered, published, and distributed. Others are more concerned with the money. They want to get and keep all of the proceeds from the sale of their creative content, minus expenses. Publishing is a business. Because publishers are in the business of making money, they extract hefty sums from any money that a book earns. While the financially successful author is in a position to negotiate favorable terms to his book contracts, the average traditionally published author will have to be satisfied earning pennies on the dollar. Finally, for other authors, self-publishing is less a chosen alternative, and instead, a choice made for them. They are unable to secure a traditional book deal and unwilling (or unable) to pay the tens of thousands of dollars demanded by the many subsidy and vanity publishing services that have popped up over the years.

The good news and the bad news is that self-published authors are responsible for everything. It is their job to secure people who can help them get their book published, from cover and graphic designers, to editors, to distributors, to marketers, and more. These Authors often neglect hiring lawyers and this can be a costly mistake.

There are many challenges faced by self-published authors, but for the purpose of this chapter, we focus on copyright-related issues. They fall into four categories: protection of content, avoidance of lawsuits, collaborations, and contractual issues.

Protecting Creative Content

Investing in Legal Counsel

Many self-published authors like to go it alone. But going it alone can often be hazardous to one's health and pocketbook. The self-published author who chooses to operate without legal guidance is like the person going into the rain—unprotected—without rain gear, or, like the armchair investor who makes investments, without doing his research. It is just not smart. Also, while the internet is filled with advice, it should never be the first place to look for accurate legal information.

Investing in competent legal advice will save you money in the long run. If money is an issue, consider contacting one of the many organizations that offers pro bono or low-cost legal services.[1] Among them are Electronic Frontier Foundation, Volunteer Lawyers for the Arts, and a host of other groups,[2] as well as law school clinics and entrepreneurship programs, such as Stanford Law School's Center for Internet & Society, Columbia Law School's Entrepreneurship and Community Development Clinic, University of Washington School of Law's Entrepreneurial Law Clinic, among others. Many law firms and solo attorneys may also be willing to help, by offering pro bono or discounted assistance. The smart self-published author would be well served by getting accurate and current legal advice from a lawyer specializing in publishing law issues.

Making Sure that the Content Can Actually Be Protected

Not everything can be protected by copyright. As a self-published author, when you are writing your novel, memoir, or self-help book, make sure your work is original. The law says that copyright protects only *original* works of art or authorships that have been reduced to a tangible format.[3] If you have copied any portion of someone else's protected content, you will not be able to claim ownership of that.

Ideas are not protected.[4] Authors often mistakenly believe that their ideas are protectable and that no one can copy them. Wrong! Copyright law specifically states that the expression of an idea, and not the idea itself, is protected. What does this mean? Let's say you want to write a book about a boy meeting a girl, but their families do not want them to be together. That is a great idea, and one shared by millions of authors—including Shakespeare. In order for your work to be protectable, the expression of your idea must be original. That can happen through the development of your plot (if it is fiction), through your characters, through the tone, and by use of other creative devices.

There are a number of other unprotectable elements that self-published authors should be aware of, such as concepts, processes, systems, methods, book titles, stock characters, character names, undeveloped characters described in words, and *scènes à faire*, which are general themes commonly found in a variety of works. In *Cavalier v. Random House, Inc.*, 297 F.3d 815 (9th Cir. 2002, authors of copyrighted children's works about the "Nicky Moonbeam" character sued the defendants for publishing books containing artwork, text, and characters virtually identical to materials previously submitted to Random House and CTW by the Cavaliers. The court held, among other things, that the night sky setting constituted unprotected *scènes à faire*.

In *Williams v. Crichton*, 84 F.3d 581 (2d Cir. 2009), the author of the *Dinosaur World* children's books sued the author and the creators of the novel and movie, *Jurassic Park*. Among his other claims, the plaintiff alleged that the defendants used a dinosaur zoo as the location of *Jurassic Park*, and that it infringed on the author's dinosaur books. Both the lower and appellate courts held that the concept of a dinosaur zoo was an unprotectable *scènes à faire*, material filled with trivial and scattered details.

I cannot tell you how often, as a lawyer, I have had authors, of all types, insist that they can copyright their book title. Let me be clear, a book title can never be protected by copyright.[5] If at all, it will be protected as a trademark. For a book title to be protected as a trademark, it will either need to be a series, such as *The Chicken Soup for the Soul Series*, or have acquired a secondary meaning—i.e. seen as something other than the title of the book. In *Tanksley v. Daniels*, 902 F.3d 165 (3d Cir. 2018), the copyright holder of a three-episode television pilot sued Lee Daniels and others alleging that the series, *Empire*, infringed on the plaintiff's copyright. In affirming the lower court decision, the appeals court held in favor of defendants and, among other things, held that book titles are quintessentially unprotectable by copyright.

Affixing Proper Copyright Notice to the Work

In 1989, the US joined the Berne Convention,[6] and the use of the copyright notice no longer became a requirement. Nonetheless, affixing some type of copyright notice[7] on your self-published work is a smart business decision. Why? It lets the world know you claim ownership in your copyrightable work of authorship so it puts potential infringers on notice.

If you choose to affix the copyright notice symbol to your work, make sure you do it correctly. Proper formatting includes the word (copyright), abbreviation (copr.), or symbol (©) for copyright. Next, the year of first publication or the year of creation if the work is unpublished, and then the name of the copyright owner. You can feel free to add the phrase "All Rights Reserved," but you do not have to.

The following are examples of proper formatting:

- Copyright 2020 Jeanne Doe. All Rights Reserved
- Copr. 2020 Jeanne Doe. All Rights Reserved
- © 2020 Jeanne Doe. All Rights Reserved

Why Registration Is Important

As with the use of the copyright notice symbol, registration of the copyrightable work with the US Copyright Office is not mandatory. Under the Copyright Act,[8] an author gains "exclusive rights" in her work immediately upon the work's creation. That being said, it is a smart idea to register your work because registration confers a number of benefits:

- It establishes a public record.
- The copyright owner receives a *Certificate of Registration*.
- The owner has the right to claim ownership nationwide.
- It is easier to get an international registration.
- By far the most important benefit, *in this author's opinion*, is the right to sue for copyright infringement. (Without a registration (and not just an application on file), you cannot sustain a copyright infringement lawsuit.)[9] Furthermore, if the work is registered in a timely fashion (within 3 months after publication), the owner can possibly recover lost profits, treble statutory damages (3×), court costs, and attorneys' fees if the work is infringed.

Registration is not a complicated process, but it is one that requires knowledge. If done incorrectly, it can be costly because the registration may be voided. As with anything related to the law, what you do not know can hurt you, when going it alone. For the self-published author who chooses to go it alone, the Copyright Office has a number of useful circulars designed to assist in the process.[10] But again, they will not provide legal advice.

Another great resource issued by the Copyright Office is the *Compendium of U.S. Copyright Office Practices*.[11] The Compendium comprises 1,182 pages of information on everything from what can be protected, to how to protect your work. On the Copyright Office website (www.copyright.gov), the complete Compendium is searchable, and it is also available as a PDF download. Each chapter can also be individually downloaded.

The Poor Man's Copyright Is a Ruse

The "poor man's copyright" is the false notion that an author, in lieu of registering his/her original, protectable, creative content, can simply mail a copy of the work to him/her and retain the sealed envelope. The argument is that this proves that the author owns the work and substitutes for a valid copyright registration. It does not, nor does it provide an author with the protection of a properly registered copyright. There is no provision in the copyright law for this.[12] In a recent case decided by the US Supreme Court,[13] the court held that, in order to file a copyright infringement lawsuit, the work had to first be registered. For years, federal circuit courts were split on this issue; now, the Supreme Court's ruling is the law of the land. The self-published would be well served by ignoring any commentary stating that the poor man's copyright is a good idea.

Protecting Derivative Works

More and more entrepreneurial authors are thinking beyond just books, and thinking of derivative works—turning the core of their self-published work of authorship into new products. These spin-off derivative products might include videos, CDs, DVDs, blogs, articles, screenplays, scripts, music, and merchandise. These ancillary works also need to be protected. The Copyright Office provides several useful resources for the author who chooses to go it alone.[14] But licensing rights for derivative works are complicated, so it would be best to consider consulting a lawyer who specializes in this field.

Avoiding Lawsuits: Do Not Infringe Someone Else's Copyright

Another common mistake made by self-published authors is believing what they read on social media websites. Armchair lawyers have taken over the internet. The amount of inaccurate information they disseminate on a daily basis has increased, but because they act like they know what they are talking about, innocent authors get caught in the web of their deception. This is most evident when the discussion focuses on what and how much of someone else's copyright-protected content an author can use without permission. There are so many erroneous notions, such as "It is okay to use thirty seconds of someone's video," or "Thirty words from someone's written content is legal," or better still, "If it is on the Internet—it is free." None of this is legally accurate. The most effective way for an author to avoid being sued is not to take what does not belong to her.

For the self-published author who wants to avoid being the defendant in a lawsuit, assume the following: If you did not create the content, presume someone else did. And, if someone else did create it, assume you need permission to use it. While there are a number of exceptions to the need to ask for permission, such as public domain and fair use, asking for permission is still the safest way to avoid landing in court. And do not forget to secure the permission in writing. The person who gives you oral consent today may not be the person in charge a year later. Plus, any transfer of rights should be done in writing. Get it in writing!

Depending on how the self-published author wants to use the material, the copyright owner will likely be amenable to granting permission. However, going beyond the scope of the permission granted can lead to trouble. For example, if a copyright owner grants the author permission to use three images, in her book, in the print publication only, that is the scope of the license. If the self-published author makes her book available as an online digital product and she incorporates seven of the copyright owner's images, the author has likely infringed the copyright owner's work by going beyond the scope of the license. In Penguin Random House LLC v. *Colting, 270 F. Supp. 3d 736 (S.D.N.Y. 2017)*, the court held that while the author permitted an online version of the reference guide, she did not permit the publication of the Lexicon, so that version infringed her copyright.

What Rights Does a Copyright Owner Have?

The law confers upon the copyright holder a number of exclusive rights. Knowing these will help the self-published author to better understand the ways these rights can be infringed. The Copyright Act[15] provides that the owner of a copyrighted work has the following exclusive rights:

1   To reproduce her original work of art or authorship. For example, if the author writes a book, she can duplicate it as often as she chooses. She has the right to make one copy or 50,000.
2   To display the work publicly. The author has the right to post chapters of her book online. If she takes photographs to go along with her self-published work, she can also post those photos on Facebook, Instagram, or some other social media site.
3   To distribute copies of the work publicly by sale, rental, lease, or another form of transfer, ownership, or by rental, lease, or lending. The author has the right to sell her book or license some or all of the rights in the book to others.
4   To perform the work publicly. The author can read from her book publicly or create a performance based on the book.
5   To prepare derivative works based on the original work. The author has the right to create a number of products derived from the original work of art or authorship.
6   To grant others the right to use the work. For example, take self-published authors who get a traditional book deal—as has happened with a few authors, such as Andy Weir of *The Martian*, Meredith Wild of the *Hacker* series, E.L. James of *Fifty Shades of Grey*, and Nicholas Sparks of *The Notebook*. In order for the traditional publisher to be able to do anything with the self-published author's work, the author must grant certain rights to the publisher. By granting these rights, the self-published author allows the traditional publisher to stand in her shoes. The traditional publisher can now reproduce, display, distribute, and, in some cases, create derivative works, or license others to do so.

What Is Infringement?

Section 501 of the Copyright Act of 1976 provides, in part, that, "Anyone who violates any of the exclusive rights of the copyright owner . . . is an infringer of the copyright or right of the author." The general rule is that any unauthorized use of someone else's work is infringement, unless an exemption applies. A simpler way to look at infringement is any use of someone's copyright-protected content without permission unless it's in the public domain or that use falls within the scope of the fair use doctrine.

Direct, Vicarious, or Contributory Infringement

An infringement of someone's copyright-protected content can generally occur in one of three ways:

1   As a direct infringement, where the owner of the copyright had a valid copyright and the infringer copied the work.[16]

2   As an indirect or third-party infringement, where someone had a controlling relationship with the infringer and benefited financially from the infringement (vicarious liability).

3   As an indirect or third-party infringement, where someone, with knowledge of the infringing activity, induced, caused, or materially contributed to the infringing activity (contributory liability).[17]

A self-published author can easily find himself in an infringement quagmire, because he violated one of the exclusive rights of a copyright owner, by incorporating photographs and other images into his self-published work, or by taking other protected content and incorporating it into his self-published work, without permission. The self-published author can also find himself liable for copyright infringement if someone he hires uses content without permission. Whether the self-published author *knew or should have known* is the benchmark standard for third-party liability. So whether the author knew or not, if he should have known, he will be liable for the actions of his hire. His job is to adequately supervise that employee or contractor. An example might be if the self-published author hires a ghostwriter to write his book. If that ghostwriter incorporates content taken from another source, without garnering consent, the self-published author who hired that person can be held liable for third-party infringement. Again, that occurs when the author knew or should have known about the ghostwriter's behavior.

So, what should an author do to protect herself? An author should always secure permission before using anyone else's protected content. If you are unsure who owns it, take the time to find out. Diligence will pay off in the long run. A final word, carefully supervise anyone who creates content on behalf of the author, regardless of the nature of the material.

Not Every Use Is an Infringement

Aside from getting written permission, self-published authors can avoid being sued for copyright infringement by confirming that the work they want to use is in the public domain or that their use is a fair use (see section below).

Public Domain

Public domain works are those copyrighted works that have either lost their protection or never had it. Any work in the public domain can be used without permission. That being said, if you incorporate a work found in the public domain, you will only be able to claim protection for that part of the work that is your original content.[18]

Another word of caution: Just because you think something is in the public domain does not mean it is. The self-published author has a responsibility to do his due diligence and make sure what they want to use is free and clear of encumbrances.

Works find themselves in the public domain in one of several ways:

1   Works generally published before January 1, 1925, (as of January 1, 2020)
2   Works not fixed in a tangible format,
3   Works with no original content,
4   Works that lost protection because they had no copyright notice, as required before March 1, 1989,
5   Works that were not renewed, as required,
6   Historical facts,
7   Works created by employees of the federal government within the scope of their employment.

Fair Use Doctrine

Section 107 of the Copyright Act provides, in part, that:

The fair use of a copyrighted work, including such use by reproduction in copies or phonorecords or by any other means specified by that section, for purposes such as criticism, comment, news reporting, teaching (including multiple copies for classroom use), scholarship, or research, is not an infringement of copyright. In determining whether the use made of a work in any particular case is a fair use, the factors to be considered shall include—

- the purpose and character of the use, including whether such use is of a commercial nature or is for nonprofit educational purposes;
- the nature of the copyrighted work;
- the amount and substantiality of the portion used in relation to the copyrighted work as a whole; and
- the effect of the use upon the potential market for or value of the copyrighted work.

Fair use is perhaps one of the most misunderstood concepts in copyright law. Lawyers do not always agree on the legal theory of fair use, and judges certainly do not either, as evidenced by the different opinions interpreting the concept. The Supreme Court has spoken on the issue; yet, different jurisdictions have come up with a variety of interpretations. For that reason, the self-published author should use caution when relying on the doctrine. Make sure you have substantive legal information to back up any decision you make.

So what is a self-published author to do? What I can say for sure is that there is no one-size-fits-all. If you are ever going to hire a lawyer, this is the time. A good lawyer can assess the use in light of fair use case law in the jurisdiction. It is not as simple as assuming that if something is not used for a commercial purpose, it is okay to use without permission. And what is "transformative"— which speaks directly to the "purpose and character of the use"—to one person is not transformative to another. If a lawyer, after reviewing the facts of your situation and researching the relevant law, gives you a written opinion that it is okay to move forward, you can rely on that opinion. Then, if something goes wrong, your defense could be that you relied on the written legal opinion of your attorney.

Collaborating without Clearly Defined Expectations

Many authors love the idea of collaborating with others. They can share the responsibility of creating an entire work. In some cases, it allows the self-published author to brainstorm and acquire a new or expanded expertise that they otherwise would not have. The thesaurus uses "collaborative" and "joint" interchangeably, but in legal parlance they are not the same. The Copyright Act's definition of "joint work" is that the contribution of each joint author must be copyrightable, so it is not enough that the combined result of their joint efforts be copyrightable. In addition, each contributor must intend, at the time their contributions were created, to be treated as joint authors.

Why is clarity around joint ownership so important? Getting it wrong may create unintended consequences. Suppose the self-published author hires an editor to work on her manuscript. Because of the editor's contribution, she incorrectly assumes that she has an equity stake in the work; thus, she sees herself as a joint owner.[19] Or assume a consultant is hired without clear expectations of who owns what. She, too, incorrectly assumes that she is a joint owner.[20]

In both instances, the editor and the consultant assumed that they were joint owners. But the self-published author has made no such assumption. To her, she is the sole owner of the work and simply hired an editor or a consultant as a contractor. Without an agreement clearly defining the terms of the relationship, a conflict would surely develop, especially if the editor or the consultant files a copyright registration in their name as coauthor.

A consequence of a work being deemed a joint work for copyright purposes is that both parties share in the spoils of the work and both parties have the same rights as the other. Either party can exercise any of the rights without the other's permission, unless an exclusive right is being assigned, in which case both parties must agree. The joint owner can sell, license, distribute, and even create derivative works based on the self-published author's work, and the self-published author would not be able to intervene.

When hiring contractors or even when working with someone else, always have a well-drafted, enforceable agreement that clearly defines the terms and scope of the relationship, and one that expressly and explicitly states that there is no <u>intent</u> to create a joint relationship.

Make sure the contractor understands the terms; do not just have the contractor sign a piece of paper. A well-written agreement clearly defining terms of the relationship keeps you in control, not the courts.

Contracts, Agreements, Letter Agreements—Whatever You Call Them, They Are Necessary!

This last section of pitfalls deals with contracts, the result of not having them, or having the wrong kind. Perhaps the most important thing this attorney will say about contracts is that the self-published author should have agreements with everyone they do business with—without exception. They may push back on this and say, "But it's my friend," or "I like doing business with a handshake," or "I want people to know I trust them." That may very well be the perspective, but I remind those who come to me that every party to a breach of contract lawsuit started out either as friends or colleagues who liked one another. Now they do not.

Almost every contract a self-published author enters has intellectual property law implications, particularly who owns what. Such an important issue should not be left to chance or a judge.

A short list of some of the agreements a self-published author might need to enter into includes:

a   Graphic designers
b   Ghostwriters
c   Cover designers
d   Editors
e   Distributors
f   Videographers
g   Photographers
h   Virtual assistants
i   Social media influencers
j   Marketing professionals

Here are a few things to think about, regarding agreements:

1   One size does not fit all. Contract law is state law and every state has its own rules. Know what they are or invest in someone who does know.
2   While downloading a template from the internet is cheap and easy, it is rarely wise, unless the contract has been vetted.
3   Make sure agreements are enforceable and well-drafted. A poorly drafted agreement is as useless as no agreement at all.
4   Make sure every agreement addresses the protection of intellectual property.

5   Read and understand all agreements before signing. This may seem like a no-brainer, but the average person appears not to read documents before signing them. Whether they are doctor's consent forms, car rental agreements, terms of use, or business agreements, most people simply sign the contract. This is a bad habit to get into and one land mine many self-published authors step onto.

6   If the self-published author licenses her work, make sure the work is first registered; then, make sure the licensing agreement is one favorable to the author (i.e. you). A carefully drafted agreement is always the way to go.

Self-publishing, for many, is a viable option and one that can render great benefits. But, as with anything, what the self-published author does not know can hurt them. Take heed of the warnings in this essay, and enjoy the ride.

Notes

1   The author of this article does not have the ability to vouch for, or endorse, every one of these resources. This list is a starting place, but it is up to you to do your due diligence.
2   "Arts and IP Volunteer Lawyer Organizations," New Media Rights, accessed May 7, 2020, https://www.newmediarights.org/lawyers_arts.
3   U.S. Copyright Office, Library of Congress, *Circular 1: Copyright Basics*, revised December 2019, https://www.copyright.gov/circs/circ01.pdf.
4   U.S. Copyright Office, *Circular 33: Works Not Protected by Copyright*, revised September 2017, https://www.copyright.gov/circs/circ33.pdf.
5   U.S. Copyright Office, *Circular 33: Works Not Protected by Copyright*.
6   The Berne Convention is an international copyright treaty that was first adopted on December 5, 1886 in Berne, Switzerland. Its official name is *The Berne Convention for the Protection of Literary and Artistic Works*. It was later adopted by the US through the Berne Convention Implementation Act of 1988 and made effective as of March 1, 1989. The Act deals with the protection of creative works of art and authorship, providing creators of content a way to manage how, by whom, and on what terms their content is used.
7   U.S. Copyright Office, *Circular 3: Copyright Notice,* revised September 2017, https://www.copyright.gov/circs/circ03.pdf.
8   17 U.S.C. § 106 (2018).
9   Fourth Estate Pub. Benefit Corp. v. Wall-Street.com, LLC, 139 S. Ct. 881 (2019).
10   U.S. Copyright Office, *Circular 2: Copyright Registration*, revised October 2019, https://www.copyright.gov/circs/circ02.pdf.
11   U.S. Copyright Office, *Compendium of U.S. Copyright Office Practices,* § 101 (3rd ed., 2017), https://www.copyright.gov/comp3.
12   U.S. Copyright Office, *Copyright in General*, https://www.copyright.gov/help/faq/faq-general.html#poorman.
13   *Fourth Estate,* 139 S. Ct. at 892.
14   U.S. Copyright Office, *Circular Update Guide*, https://www.copyright.gov/circs/circular-update-guide.pdf.
15   17 U.S.C. § 106.
16   17 U.S.C. § 107.
17   See generally, e.g., VHT, Inc. v. Zillow Grp., Inc., 918 F.3d 723, 745 (9th Cir. 2019), *cert. denied*, 140 S. Ct. 122 (2019); A&M Records, Inc. v. Napster, Inc., 239 F.3d 1004, 1020–23 (9th Cir. 2001), *as amended* (April 3, 2001).
18   Skidmore for Randy Craig Wolfe Tr. v. Led Zeppelin, 905 F.3d 1116, 1126 (9th Cir. 2018).
19   See generally Childress v. Taylor, 945 F.2d 500 (2d Cir. 1991).
20   See generally Aalmuhammed v. Lee, 202 F.3d 1227 (9th Cir. 2000).

2.6

LANDMARK CASE

Authors Guild v. Google, Inc., 804 F.3d 202 (2d Cir. 2015)

This case centered on Google's reproduction and display of snippets from tens of millions of books through its Library Project and Google Books project. Google acquired these books through major libraries (which had submitted them to Google for the purpose of making digital copies) but never received permission from the individual authors and rights holders. These rights holders brought a class copyright infringement action against Google, to which Google responded by arguing that its copying and public display constituted fair use.

The process by which these snippets become publicly available and the scope of the snippets themselves is part and parcel to the resolution of the case and is worth a closer look. Under Google's agreements with many of the world's major libraries, Google is provided with millions of books for inclusion in its Library Project and Google Books project. Google digitally scans each book, and creates an index of the machine-readable text of each book. As of 2004, Google had scanned and indexed over twenty million books. Most of these books are nonfiction and out of print. Some are copyrighted, while some are in the public domain. Google's scans are stored on computers that are isolated from public internet access, and shielded by the same security systems that Google uses to protect its most confidential information.

The snippets themselves are horizontal segments constituting about an eighth of a page in length. Each page includes eight snippets. The Google Books project search engine allows users to search for a word, and then see snippets from the book that include that word. Each search for a word will reveal the same three snippets, and only the first usage of the word on a page will be displayed. Searchers may view more than the same three snippets from a book by searching for different words. However, Google "blacklists" at least one snippet on each page, and one complete page out of every ten pages. This process of blacklisting means that these portions of the book are permanently blocked from public access. Google also disables the display of snippets from the types of books where access to a single snippet may stifle the searcher's need for the book—these types of books include dictionaries, cookbooks, and collections of short poetry. Moreover, Google is also willing to withdraw any book from snippet view altogether if the author or rights holder submits an online form. Finally, Google's search function does not display any advertising, and Google does not profit off of searchers using Google's links to purchase books.

The class of rights holders suing Google argued five points, two of which occupied the bulk of the Second Circuit's analysis. The plaintiffs first contended that Google's digital copying of entire books and subsequent display of portions of those books were not "transformative," and provided a substitute for the authors' underlying works. Next, the plaintiffs argued that Google's commercial profit motivation and dominance of the global internet search market cut against fair use. As such, they argued that Google's fair use defense must fall, and that the reproduction of the books and display of the snippets constituted copyright infringement. The plaintiffs also raised concern about Google's impact on the authors' derivative works, as well as whether Google could adequately protect the digital copies from hackers. However, the first two fair use points constitute the heart of the opinion, and carry the most significant implications for copyright law.

Writing for the court, Judge Leval ruled for Google on all counts. The court found that Google's snippet search function was transformative because it expanded public knowledge by making certain useful information about these books available online while also ensuring that these snippets did not provide the public with a substitute for the books themselves. Emphasizing the significance of the first fair use factor (i.e. purpose and character of the use), the court quoted an earlier Second Circuit decision that concluded that "the creation of a full-text searchable database is a quintessentially transformative use . . . [as] the result of a word search is different in purpose, character, expression, meaning, and message from the page (and the book) from which it is drawn." *Authors Guild v. Google, Inc.*, 804 F.3d 202, 217 (2d Cir. 2015) (quoting *Authors Guild, Inc. v. HathiTrust*, 755 F.3d 87, 97 (2d Cir. 2014)). The court noted that the snippet view contributes to the highly transformative nature of the search engine by assisting searchers in determining whether they are interested in a particular book. Pointing to Google's commercial profit motive also did not do the plaintiffs much good, as the court concluded that a mere profit motive is not sufficient to overcome Google's transformative purpose.

The court also found in favor of Google on the (less important) second and third factors, ruling that the overwhelmingly factual nature of these books and the inherently limited scope of the snippets cut in favor of a finding of fair use. Turning to the issue of commercial harm in the fourth fair use factor, the court conceded that the snippet function may lead to some loss of sales. However, access to a snippet is unlikely to satisfy the searcher's interest in the protected elements of an author's work (in other words, a snippet may reveal an unprotected fact but is likely insufficient to cover copyrighted expression), and the snippet certainly does not provide a substitute for the book. As a result, the possibility of loss of sales is insufficient to hold in the plaintiff's favor on the fourth factor. In the end, Google prevailed on all four fair use factors.

Authors Guild v. Google, Inc. reflects a growing concern among authors and other rights holders about how readily available their work is on the internet and about the seeming ease with which an internet giant may use such work to strengthen its grip on the market. The Second Circuit's decision suggests that courts are hesitant to trade technological advancement for more robust protections of copyrighted works in the digital age. Moreover, the Second Circuit's focus on the fact-heavy nature of the overwhelming majority of the books raises questions about the scope of this decision and how it would mesh with a future case addressing the potential use of fictional works (i.e. works that are traditionally perceived as more expressive than nonfiction titles) in a similar search engine.

PART III

Visual Arts Introduction

Introduction

Part III highlights some of the challenges illustrators, animators, photographers, and videographers face living in this twenty-first-century digital environment. The Copyright Act was overhauled in 1976, and the last significant update, other than the recent Music Modernization Act, was in 1998, when the Digital Millennium Copyright Act was passed. It was drafted primarily to deal with immunity for online service providers and the protection of technology measures. While it was intended to be content-neutral, the Act, in many respects, has not kept up many of the current issues that have altered the lives of professional visual artists. Ironically, visual imagery has never been more important or prevalent because online publishing demands an insatiable amount of visual content to feed and refresh the 24/7 news and popular culture information cycle. Professional visual artists, and in particular photographers, once distinguished by expensive equipment and lenses not used by everyone on the street now compete with citizen journalists, designers, and amateurs armed only with a smartphone and creative software programs that allow them to create visual works that are good enough for online publications. Even worse, once a work is posted online, it can be easily republished and redistributed by a simple right click, without the owner's consent. With the ease of republication and the accepted practice of users sharing every moment of their lives via still images or video, the public's understanding of what copyright protects, what is public, and what ownership of a work means has shifted. These chapters look at copyright cases and issues that creators are grappling with today: what does copyright protect, who owns a work, how much of a prior work can be borrowed, when do you need permission, how much human authorship is required if you use drones or other technology as tools to create a work, and what do you give up if you choose to post your work on social media? The courts may not always have the answers, and decisions often lag years behind social practices and technology measures, but at present, these cases serve as helpful guidelines that will shape future decisions.

In Chapter 3.1, "How Close Can You Get: Substantial Similarity in the Context of Works of Visual Art," Dale Cendali and Shanti Sadtler Conway examine one of the most difficult copyright questions in the visual arts—what is the line between inspiration and copying? Throughout history, artists have built on the work of prior artists, and explaining that copyright does not protect ideas, only the expression of the idea to an artist ends up sounding like abstract legalese without any clear guidelines to follow, as all expression incorporates some ideas. This chapter looks at a few recent cases where courts have had to compare two images side by side for substantial similarity to decide if protectable "expression," which is infringing, has been taken, or if just the underlying idea was taken, which is permissible. The essence of this legal doctrine is that the courts don't want to give one photographer or artist a monopoly on an idea. Cendali and Conway look at seminal cases involving photography, illustration, applied arts, textile, and sculpture, and highlight the factors that were important to the courts in each instance. Looking at the facts of cases and seeing which factors tip the scale from infringing to not infringing provide some boundaries that may be applied in other situations.

"Gorgeous Photograph, Limited Copyright" by Justin Hughes, the Hon. William Matthew Byrne Distinguished Professor of Law at Loyola University, explores what makes photographs "original" and subject to copyright protection. It begins with the Supreme Court case examining the portrait of Oscar Wilde that decided for the first time that the photographer's choices in creating a photograph, including the selection and arrangement of elements, make a photograph an original work of art. He looks at the factors the court considered to find originality and questions whether some modern photographs, such as Google Street View, or selfies taken with a smartphone that records factual information would, if strictly examined, meet the criteria of originality. The chapter examines the limited protection offered photojournalism, or what is described by the courts as a thin copyright, to avoid giving a photographer a monopoly over the subject matter depicted in the photograph. It also addresses some of the thorny issues arising from technology and imagery, such as deep fakes, in which an image a public figure is inserted in place of another, often a porn star to give the false impression that the public figure is engaged in some activity, and posits whether copyright is strong enough to prevent this malicious use of software. Other issues addressed include the copyrightability of selfies and how courts often misapply the fair use doctrine when dealing with photography cases, stumbling over what it means to use a photograph for a different purpose under the first fair use factor. Hughes highlights how various copyright issues are highly nuanced when applied to photographic works that serve as both an art form and a record of authentic events.

Chapter 3.3, "Copyright Concerns for Visual Journalists," by Mickey Osterreicher, looks at the challenges faced by photojournalists in the twenty-first century. It begins by exploring whether the Copyright Office's rules that copyright applies to human authorship (and not to monkeys) will limit protection to photojournalists who use drones as part of their toolbox in capturing photographs. It looks back to the nineteenth century, when the first aerial photographs were taken from hot air balloons, and traces the history of aerial photography to the present day. The chapter highlights the toll that piracy plays in the livelihood of photojournalists, because the ease with which photographs can be infringed cuts into the photographer's licensing revenue. Osterreicher also looks at how the fair use defense is misunderstood by internet publishers as well as the courts, and the misperception that if a photograph illustrates a newsworthy article, the fair use defense is applicable because the use is deemed newsworthy, or is considered transformative, even though the photograph has not been substantially altered. He further explores the difficulty of registering photographs with the Copyright Office as photographers create large volumes of works which are required to be segregated by published or unpublished for registration purposes, a definition that worked in the print world, but does not so easily transfer to the digital world. That difficulty, coupled with the common belief that photographs that are online are public and free for the taking, creates a perfect storm of rampant infringement that leaves the photojournalist with little ability to enforce his or her rights under copyright.

In the final chapter of Part III, "Social Media: Use It and Lose It?" Joseph T. Baio looks at the opportunities and risks associated with using social media platforms by photographers desiring to share and promote their works with a larger population than was ever before possible. He explores a key twenty-first-century case, *Agence France-Presse v. Morel*, that involved a photographer who posted images on his Twitter account, documenting the recent earthquake in Haiti. Another Twitter user downloaded the images, reposting them under his own name. Those photos, identified under the wrong Twitter name, were then syndicated by Agence France-Press directly and through its distributor, Getty Images, and published by media companies around the world. While the photographer eventually won a significant statutory damages award for copyright infringement and violation of the DMCA, the court did not award him any attorney's fees because the issue before the court was a novel question that needed to be litigated. The chapter takes the lessons learned from this case and looks at the challenges faced by photographers sharing images using social media, where identities are hard to verify, images can be reposted without consent, and broad terms of use employed by many platforms permit sharing among the users of the platforms and could even include the use of third parties. Baio examines the terms of service of many popular social media sites, and provides tips for obtaining compensation for works used without permission without resorting to litigation, sending takedown notices, and examining some recent cases where photographers have elected to litigate the infringement of images, focusing on the costs of litigation, the amount of damages received in these cases, and the likelihood of recovering any attorney's fees.

3.1

HOW CLOSE CAN YOU GET

Substantial Similarity in the Context of Works of Visual Art

Dale M. Cendali and Shanti Sadtler Conway[*]

A common question that comes up for creators is: How do you draw the line between inspiration and being found liable for copyright infringement? The key to answering this question often rests on the well-established copyright principle referred to as the "idea/expression dichotomy," which provides that copyright does not protect *ideas*, but rather only protects specific creative *expression*.[1] As a result, in comparing works for substantial similarity (a required element of infringement), courts ask: "Are the works substantially similar beyond the fact that they depict the same idea?"[2] This principle allows creators to use the ideas of others and build on them without going too far and infringing the creative expression that is another artist's property and vision.[3]

Courts apply the idea/expression dichotomy to all types of copyrighted works, including visual arts. This Chapter will illustrate this dichotomy by comparing example cases in the field of visual arts, some of which found infringement and some of which found no infringement. As shown by these cases, the application of the idea/expression dichotomy and its impact on the ultimate finding of infringement depends on the particular facts of the case.[4] Depending on how the facts are presented, a court may find that the defendant's work only took general ideas, and thus does not infringe, or that it copied specific expression, and thus does infringe.

Photography

Various photographers over time have brought copyright infringement claims alleging that other photographers or creators of other types of visual works have copied the creative expression in their photographs and thus infringed. In deciding these cases, courts have compared the works for substantial similarity and applied the idea/expression dichotomy.

For instance, the US Court of Appeals for the Ninth Circuit recently considered claims relating to Nike's photograph of Michael Jordan taken in or around 1985, which formed the basis of its iconic "Jumpman" logo, which continues to be used on shoes and apparel today.[5] The plaintiff, photographer Jacobus Rentmeester, claimed that Nike had copied his 1984 photograph of Jordan, which Rentmeester took when Jordan was a student at the University of North Carolina preparing for the Olympics and published in *Time* magazine. The Ninth Circuit affirmed the lower court's ruling that Nike's photograph and logo did not infringe Rentmeester's photograph as a matter of law because Nike did not copy protectable expression. This decision was reached simply by the court's own comparison of the works at issue on a motion to dismiss, before the parties engaged in discovery.

In its decision, the Ninth Circuit noted that while "[b]oth [works] capture Michael Jordan in a leaping pose inspired by ballet's *grand jeté* . . . Rentmeester's copyright does not confer a monopoly on that general 'idea' or 'concept'; he cannot prohibit other photographers from taking their own photos of Jordan in a leaping, *grand jeté*-inspired pose."[6] The Ninth Circuit found that: "Just as Rentmeester made a series of creative choices in the selection and arrangement of the elements in his photograph, so too Nike's photographer made his own distinct choices in that regard. Those choices produced an image that differs from Rentmeester's photo in more than just minor details."[7] For instance, the court noted that "[t]he position of each of [Jordan's] limbs in the two photos is different," with Rentmeester's photo "convey[ing] mainly a sense of horizontal (forward) propulsion," while Nike's photo "convey[s] mainly a sense of vertical propulsion."[8] Similarly, while both photographs were taken outdoors, the scenes had "stark differences," with Rentmeester's photo "on a grassy knoll with a whimsically out-of-place basketball hoop," whereas Nike's photo, shot against the Chicago skyline, had "no foreground element at all" and the "hoop . . . appears to be easily within Jordan's reach."[9] The court noted various other dissimilarities, such as the "cloudless blue sky" featuring a large sun in Rentmeester's photo, as opposed to "the Chicago skyline silhouetted against the orange and purple hues of late dusk or early dawn," without a sun, in Nike's photo.[10] Ultimately, the various choices that Nike's photographer made "produced an image unmistakably different from Rentmeester's photo," and thus there was no infringement.[11]

The same copyright infringement principles were applied by the US Court of Appeals for the Second Circuit in *Rogers v. Koons*, but led to a different conclusion in the context of the facts of that case.[12] The court found that Jeff Koons's sculpture infringed the plaintiff's photograph of a couple sitting on a bench holding eight puppies because Koons borrowed not just the idea of the photograph, but rather copied the photographer's specific expression. The Second Circuit recognized that "ideas, concepts, principles and the like found in the common domain are the inheritance of everyone. What is protected is the original or unique way that an author expresses those ideas, concepts, principles or processes."[13]

With respect to the works at issue, the court found: "It is not therefore the idea of a couple with eight small puppies seated on a bench that is protected, but rather Roger's *expression* of this idea—as caught in the placement, in the particular light, and in the expressions of the subjects—that gives the photograph its charming and unique character, that is to say, makes it original and copyrightable."[14] While Nike's photograph in *Rentmeester* simply used the same general idea of Michael Jordan dunking in a pose inspired by ballet's *grand jeté*, the court in *Rogers* found that Koons had "used the identical expression of the idea that Rogers created."[15] For instance, unlike Nike's photo—which used a different pose, clothing, positioning of the subject, background, and other elements as compared to Rentmeester's photo—Koons instructed his artisans to meticulously copy the precise poses, expressions, clothing, placement, and composition from Rogers's photo. While Koons argued that his sculpture was different because he added flowers to the hair of the couple and made the noses of the puppies more bulbous, those differences were "insufficient," given the various details that Koons had copied.[16] The Second Circuit noted that "[i]t is only where the points of dissimilarity exceed those that are similar and those similarities are—when compared to the original work—of small import quantitatively or qualitatively that a finding of no infringement is appropriate."[17] Thus, "[b]ecause of Koons' extensive use of the same expression of the idea that Rogers created," the Second Circuit affirmed the finding of infringement on summary judgment, meaning the decision was reached after discovery, but without requiring a trial.[18]

Paintings and Drawings

Courts have applied these same copyright infringement principles in deciding claims relating to paintings and drawings. Accordingly, courts have found that such visual works of art do not infringe when only an idea or concept was borrowed, but that infringement may occur when specific creative expression is taken. In making such decisions, courts carefully consider and compare the works.

For instance, in *Franklin Mint Corp. v. National Wildlife Art Exchange, Inc.*, the US Court of Appeals for the Third Circuit considered an infringement claim concerning two paintings that both featured two birds (specifically, cardinals) perched on apple tree branches.[19] The cardinals and branches were positioned similarly, but the body shapes and coloring of the birds were somewhat different, the leaves and flowers on the branches were somewhat different, and the plaintiff's painting featured a butterfly, whereas the defendant's painting did not. The appellate court affirmed the district court's finding after trial that the defendant's painting did not infringe because "while the ideas are similar, the expressions are not" as each artist depicted the concept of cardinals on apple tree branches differently.[20] The court recognized the need for copyright protection in order to encourage artists, but also the need to leave room for other artists to explore similar subject matter. The court wrote that "[t]he similarities here are of a nature not calculated to discourage an artist in the development of a specialty yet sufficiently distinguishable to protect his creativity in that sphere."[21] In other words, a finding of infringement would have effectively given the plaintiff a monopoly over paintings of two cardinals on apple tree branches, and thus would disable other artists from contributing their own versions of that idea. As a result, the court found that the trial court, which had made its decision after a bench trial, had not erred in finding that the defendant's painting did not infringe.

The US District Court for the Southern District of New York applied the same copyright principles, but found that defendant's work infringed, in *Steinberg v. Columbia Pictures Industries, Inc.*[22] The case considered the defendant's poster for the film *Moscow on the Hudson*, and compared it to the plaintiff Saul Steinberg's iconic cover illustration for *The New Yorker*. The plaintiff's drawing depicted "a parochial New Yorker's view of the world," showing a street view of New York City facing west and a "telescoped version of the rest of the United States and the Pacific Ocean," with China, Japan, and Russia far away.[23] The defendant's movie poster showed a street view of New York City facing east, with "[t]he parts of the poster beyond New York . . . minimized, to symbolize a New Yorker's myopic view of the centrality of his city to the world."[24] The court found that the poster infringed as a matter of law because it was substantially similar to the plaintiff's drawing, and thus granted the plaintiff's motion for summary judgment.

Like the court in *Franklin Mint*, the court in *Steinberg* recognized the need to have a balance between protecting creative works and leaving enough room for others to create as well. The court noted the "delicate balance between the protection to which authors are entitled under an act of Congress and the freedom that exists for all others to create their works outside the area protected by infringement."[25] The court also discussed how the idea/expression dichotomy reflects that balance as it attempts to "'reconcile the two competing societal interests that provide the rationale for the granting of and restrictions on copyright protection,' namely, both rewarding individual ingenuity, and nevertheless allowing progress and improvements based on the same subject matter by others than the original author."[26]

With respect to the works at issue, the court in *Steinberg* found that the defendant infringed because, unlike the defendant in *Franklin* and more like the defendant in *Rogers*, it meticulously copied specific, creative expression. The court acknowledged that "defendants cannot be held liable for using the *idea* of a map of the world from an egocentrically myopic perspective."[27] In other words, the defendant could have used that same idea, but depicted it differently. But the court held that the defendant's poster went beyond that idea and used the plaintiff's "expression," noting "the striking stylistic relationship between the posters" and that the defendant's poster "was executed in the sketchy, whimsical style that has become one of Steinberg's hallmarks."[28] The court discussed the numerous specific similarities, such as that both feature a bird's-eye view across the edge of Manhattan and a river bordering New York City to the world beyond; four city blocks in detail and then become increasingly minimalist; a narrow band of blue wash across the top to represent the sky; and a brand of primary red to show the horizon.[29] Importantly, the court found that there were significant similarities in the details of the New York City blocks, such as the water towers, cars, and the ornaments and facades of the buildings. The defendant even copied the shadows, which did not face in the ways that would have been dictated by nature. As a result, the court found the works substantially similar and granted summary judgment for the plaintiff.

Textiles

One subject matter that has seen much copyright litigation over the years is textile designs. Textile cases also provide an opportunity to illustrate the idea/expression dichotomy as one can argue that a particular visual theme for a design is an "idea," which one creator should not be able to monopolize. For instance, in *Boisson v. Banian, Ltd.*, the Second Circuit considered quilt designs and found that one of the defendant's quilts did not infringe, but that another of the defendant's quilts did infringe.[30] The case was on appeal after a bench trial before the lower court. Each of the parties' respective quilts featured the letters of the alphabet in capital letters, arranged in 5 × 6 horizontal rows and vertical columns, with some squares filled with pictures or icons instead of letters. The court recognized that "copyright protection extends only to a particular expression of an idea, not to the idea itself."[31] With that in mind, the court proceeded to compare each of the quilts at issue. The defendant's "ABC Navy" quilt did not infringe the plaintiff's "School Days" quilt because, while the defendant also used the concept of a quilt showing the letters of the alphabet in a grid with pictorial graphics, that idea was expressed differently. For instance, while the plaintiff's quilt showed each letter in the alphabet sequentially, with the images of a dog, house, American flag, and basket in the last four squares, the defendant's quilt interspersed its images of teddy bear, cow, star, and ship throughout the alphabet. The court also noted, for instance, that "for the most part," the colors chosen by the defendant for the "ABC Navy" quilt differed from the ones in "Schools Days." While the letters themselves appeared in a similar font, the court found that that alone "cannot support a finding of infringement" as fonts are not copyrightable, and the details of the letter shapes differed.[32]

However, the court found that the defendant's "ABC Green" quilt did infringe as it did not only use a similar idea, but rather copied specific creative expression. The court viewed the "ABC Green" quilt as more similar to the plaintiff's "School Days" quilt than was the "ABC Navy" quilt, which the court, in turn, found did not infringe. For instance, the court noted that the alphabet blocks were grouped in the same exact manner in "ABC Green" and "School Days," as each letter appeared sequentially, with images at the end. And while the images in "ABC Green" and "ABC Navy" were similar, and both were different from the images in "School Days," the court noted that "ABC Green" placed the image of the teddy bear with an American flag in the same block as the American flag in "School Days." In addition, the court found that "ABC Green" used the same color backgrounds on each letter and the same unique shapes for several of the letters, whereas the colors and specific letter shapes for "ABC Navy" were different. As a result, the Second Circuit reversed the trial court's prior finding of non-infringement with respect to "ABC Green," but affirmed its finding of non-infringement with respect to "ABC Navy."

Sculptural Works

Courts also have applied the same standards for copyright infringement to sculptural works, including fine art sculptures, toys, and dolls. As with cases involving other creative media, courts carefully distinguish between unprotected ideas, on the one hand, and protected expression, on the other.

For example, the Ninth Circuit considered competing stuffed dinosaur dolls in *Aliotti v. R. Dakin & Co.*[33] The Ninth Circuit affirmed the lower court's decision that the works were not substantially similar as a matter of law and thus that the defendant was entitled to summary judgment. The court stated that "[n]o copyright protection may be afforded to the idea of producing stuffed dinosaur toys or to elements of expression that necessarily follow from the idea of such dolls."[34] Thus, the plaintiff could not rely "upon any similarity in expression resulting from either the physiognomy of dinosaurs or from the nature of stuffed animals."[35] With respect to the particular dinosaur stuffed dinosaurs at issue, the court noted that neither the similarities in "postures and body designs," nor "the fact that both lines of dinosaurs are gentle and cuddly" could not be relied upon because they were un-protected.[36] The court suggested that "the eye style and stitching" of the stuffed animals could be protected, but found that the defendant did not incorporate those aspects of the plaintiff's products. Accordingly, the works were not substantially similar and there could be no infringement.

The US Court of Appeals for the Seventh Circuit applied the same copyright standards, but found that the defendant infringed in *JCW Investments, Inc. v. Novelty, Inc.*[37] The court found that the defendant's doll was substantially similar to the plaintiff's doll as a matter of law, and granted summary judgment for the plaintiff. Both parties' dolls depicted middle-aged, overweight men with black hair and a receding hairline, sitting in an armchair and wearing a white tank top and blue pants that make a farting sound when their fingers are pulled. Consistent with the court in *Aliotti*, the Seventh Circuit noted that "the idea of a farting, crude man" is not protected, but that the plaintiff's "particular embodiment of that concept" is protected.[38] But while the dinosaur dolls in *Aliotti* did not share similarities that went beyond the concept of a dinosaur stuffed animal, the defendant in *JCW Investments* copied numerous expressive details of the plaintiff's doll. The court found that the similarities between the works "go far beyond the fact that both are plush dolls of middle-aged men sitting in armchairs that fart and tell jokes."[39] Rather, both works "have crooked smiles that show their teeth, balding heads with a fringe of black hair, a rather large protruding nose, blue pants that are identical colors, and white tank tops."[40] The court clarified: "The prob-lem is not that both [the dolls] have black hair or white tank tops or any other *single* detail; the problem is that the execution and *combination* of features on both dolls would lead an objective observer to think they were the same."[41] The court noted that the defendant could have used a different combination of elements, such as dolls with "a blond mullet [that] wear flannel," which would have used the same idea, but a different expression.[42] As the defendant copied the plaintiff's specific expression, however, the Seventh Circuit affirmed that the defendant infringed.

Conclusion

As can be seen in the above cases, in analyzing works for substantial similarity, courts carefully compare the works at issue and consider whether the defendant's work merely reflects the same idea or whether it copies specific, creative expression. Where the defendant uses the same particu-lar visual details, flourishes, and the like, infringement will be more likely, whereas it will be less likely where the defendant used the same general idea or concept but expressed it in a different way by using different creative details. As a result, it is safer for a creator to merely borrow an idea or concept but then make his or her own creative choices and thus depict the idea in his or her own creative, expressive way.

Acknowledgment

★ The authors thank Summer Associate Aaron Schroeder for his helpful research assistance for this essay.

Notes

1 See, e.g., 17 U.S.C. § 102(b); Golan v. Holder, 565 U.S. 302, 328 (2012); Feist Publ'ns v. Rural Tel. Serv. Co., 499 U.S. 340, 350 (1991); Peter Pan Fabrics, Inc. v. Martin Weiner Corp., 274 F.2d 487, 489 (2d Cir. 1960).

2 Mattel, Inc. v. MGA Entm't, Inc., 616 F.3d 904, 917 (9th Cir. 2010).

3 See, e.g., Rentmeester v. Nike, Inc., 883 F.3d 1111, 1117 (9th Cir. 2018) certiorari denied, 139 S. Ct. 1375 (2019). ("[A] defendant incurs no liability if he copies only the 'ideas' or 'concepts' used in the plaintiff's work. To infringe, the defendant must also copy enough of the plaintiff's expression of those ideas or concepts to render the two works 'substantially similar'"; Apple Computer, Inc. v. Microsoft Corp., 35 F.3d 1435, 1443 (9th Cir. 1994). ("[S]imilarities derived from the use of common ideas cannot be protected; otherwise, the first to come up with an idea will corner the market.")

4 See *Peter Pan Fabrics*, 274 F.2d at 489 ("[N]o principle can be stated as to when an imitator has gone beyond copying the 'idea,' and has borrowed its 'expression.' Decisions must therefore inevitably be ad hoc.")

5 *Rentmeester*, 883 F.3d at 1111.

6 *Id.* at 1121.

7 *Id.*

8 *Id.* at 1121–22.

9 *Id.* at 1122.

10 *Id.*

11 *Id.*

12 Rogers v. Koons, 960 F.2d 301 (2d Cir. 1992).

13 *Id.* at 308.

14 *Id.* (emphasis added).

15 *Id.*

16 *Id.*

17 *Id.*

18 *Id.*

19 Franklin Mint Corp. v. Nat'l Wildlife Art Exch., Inc., 575 F.2d 62 (3d Cir. 1978).

20 *Id.* at 67.

21 *Id.*

22 Steinberg v. Columbia Pictures Indus., Inc., 663 F. Supp. 706 (S.D.N.Y. 1987).

23 *Id.* at 709–10.

24 *Id.* at 710.

25 *Id.* at 711 (quoting Warner Bros. Inc. v. Am. Broad. Cos., 720 F.2d 231, 245 (2d Cir. 1983)).

26 *Id.* at 712 (quoting Durham Indus., Inc. v. Tomy Corp., 630 F.2d 905, 912 (2d Cir. 1980)).

27 *Id.*

28 *Id.* at 712.

29 *Id.*

30 Boisson v. Banian, Ltd., 273 F.3d 262 (2d Cir. 2001).

31 *Id.* at 268.

32 *Id.* at 275.

33 Aliotti v. R. Dakin & Co., 831 F.2d 898 (9th Cir. 1987).

34 *Id.* at 901.

35 *Id.*

36 *Id.*

37 JCW Investments, Inc. v. Novelty, Inc., 482 F.3d 910 (7th Cir. 2007).

38 *Id.* at 917.

39 *Id.* at 916.

40 *Id.*

41 *Id.* (emphasis added).

42 *Id.*

3.2

GORGEOUS PHOTOGRAPH, LIMITED COPYRIGHT

Justin Hughes

Evocative, expressive, joyful, full of pathos, beautiful—often more beautiful than the things they portray: Photographs can be all these things. Photographs are also records of reality, whether the short-lived reality of fashion shoots and birthday parties or the enduring reality of the Grand Canyon and the Taj Mahal. This duality—creative expression and record of the real—shapes the nature of copyright protection for photographs. This essay explains when photographs are protected by copyright and what that protection practically means for different genres of photography.

1884: Photographs Are Copyrightable (Sometimes)

Congress extended copyright protection in the US to photographs in 1870, but the question of whether photography *could* be protected by copyright was not settled until 1884 when the Supreme Court decided *Burrow-Giles Lithographic Co. v. Sarony*.[1] In *Sarony*, a trial court had found that the Burrow-Giles Lithographic Company made and put up for sale 85,000 unauthorized copies of *Oscar Wilde No. 18*, a studio photograph of Oscar Wilde taken by noted portrait photographer Napoleon Sarony.

There was no question that Burrow-Giles had violated copyright law if there was a valid copyright in the *Oscar Wilde No. 18* photograph, so Burrow-Giles argued to the Supreme Court that photographs could not be protected by copyright at all.[2] Copyright law is grounded in the provision of the US Constitution that gives Congress the power to "secur[e] for limited Times to Authors . . . the exclusive Right to their respective Writings." Burrow-Giles's constitutional argument boiled down to "only this question: 'Are Photographs the writings of Authors?'"

One might think it is obvious that photographs are not "writings" but by 1884 a series of congressional acts had extended copyright to engravings, musical compositions, paintings, drawings, sculptures, and models for works in the fine arts. Since all these art forms had already been accepted as "writings," the bulk of Burrow-Giles's attack on the constitutionality of copyright protection for photographs was the argument that photographs were not the products of "Authors" because photographs lack originality. Citing Webster's definition of an "author," Burrow-Giles argued that "[a]ll these synonyms and definitions presuppose the idea of originality"; that for copyrighted engravings and prints, the copyright protected "only such as are original, and are founded in the creative powers of the mind"; and that under the American copyright law, both before and after the Constitution, "the matter to be protected must be ORIGINAL. This test has been kept steadily in view by the Courts of the United States, and is still the principal test."[3]

With this originality-imbued understanding of "Author," Burrow-Giles argued that "a photograph [was] not a . . . production of an author" because a photograph was "a reproduction, on paper, of the exact features of some natural object, or of some person."[4] Burrow-Giles described the process of photography as "the reproduction of existing objects, by means which are merely applications of scientific principles."[5] In other words, Burrow-Giles claimed that a photograph was only a recordation of facts ("the exact features of some natural object or of some person") and that there was no creativity or originality involved in a machine recording whatever facts are put in front of it.

But Justice Samuel Miller, who wrote the Supreme Court's opinion, was unwilling to view the fact-recording nature of a photograph as a bar to copyright. He pointed out that the first Congress, which included many of the Framers, passed the first copyright statute that "not only makes maps and charts subjects of copyright, but mentions them before books in the order of designation." Why did Justice Miller think that order was important? Because maps and charts are prototypically fact-recording expressions. Justice Miller reasoned that "[u]nless, therefore, photographs can be distinguished in the classification on this point from the maps, charts, designs, engravings, etchings, cuts, and other prints, it is difficult to see why congress cannot make them the subject of copyright as well as the others."

Once Justice Miller had rebuffed the argument that photographs could not be copyrighted because they are factual records, *Sarony* was actually quite easy to decide. By the time this case reached the courts, Napoleon Sarony was a celebrated portrait photographer and it was known that Sarony "posed and directed his sitters, using flattery, threat, [and] mimicry, to bring out their histrionic powers."[6] The Supreme Court recited the trial court's findings of fact that drew fairly express parallels between portraiture *painting* and portraiture *photography* in the conclusion that *Oscar Wilde No. 18* was: "a useful, new, harmonious, characteristic, and graceful picture, and that plaintiff made the same . . . entirely from his own mental conception, to which he gave visible form by posing the said Oscar Wilde in front of the camera, selecting and arranging the costume, draperies, and other various accessories in said photograph, arranging the subject so as to present graceful outlines, arranging and disposing the light and shade, suggesting and evoking the desired expression, and from such disposition, arrangement, or representation, made entirely by plaintiff, he produced the picture in suit."[7]

Armed with that description, Justice Miller was confident that Sarony's photograph was "an original work of art."[8] Of course, Justice Miller was also implicitly saying that Burrow-Giles misunderstood the process of photography. For Burrow-Giles, the photographer's process was only the taking of the picture: Sarony setting up the tableau—the drapes, props, and pose—had no relevance. In contrast, Justice Miller clearly thought that everything Sarony did in his studio to produce *Oscar Wilde No. 18* was part of an integral creative process.

Yet, it would be a serious mistake to say that the *Sarony* decision stands for the proposition that "photographs <u>are</u> copyrightable." The court only says that a photograph *can* be copyrightable, not that every photograph is or probably will be copyrightable. Indeed, after hearing Burrow-Giles's argument that photography is "simply the manual operation, by the use of . . . instruments and preparations, of transferring to [a] plate the visible representation of some existing object," the court acknowledged that that description might "be true in regard to the ordinary production of a photograph," and "that in such case a copyright is no protection."[9]

Limited, but Meaningful Copyright Protection

So where do we find this elusive "originality" that can justify copyright in a photograph? When judges in the US and other common-law countries tell us about the originality in a photograph, they almost always recite a *Sarony*-like laundry list: Original expression can be found in "the photographer's selection of background, lights, shading, positioning of subject, and timing"[10]; "posing the subjects, lighting, angle, selection of film and camera, evoking the desired expression, and almost any other variant involved"[11]; the "angle of shot, light and shade, exposure, effects achieved by means of filters, developing techniques"[12]; or "the choice of light sources, filters, lenses, camera, film, perspective, aperture setting, shutter speed, and processing techniques."[13] Originality comes from the photographer's "decisions regarding lighting, appropriate camera equipment and lens, camera settings and use of the white background."[14]

If one reads these decisions carefully, it becomes clear that courts are finding original expression in photographs by considering *the process of creating the photograph* as much or more than the photograph itself. There are good reasons this happens. First, as soon as a judge starts assessing originality in the visual image *per se*, it is easy to slip into a murky zone of artistic judgments. In the 1903 *Bleistein v. Donaldson Lithographing* decision—a case about copyright in a circus poster—Justice Oliver Wendall Holmes admonished judges that "[i]t would be a dangerous undertaking for persons trained only in the law to constitute themselves final judges of the worth of pictorial illustrations, outside of the narrowest and most obvious limits."[15] Those thundering words are often cited: A judge who takes them to heart can quickly become uncomfortable trying to describe the nuanced elements of a photograph; it is safer to use the artistic process as evidence of originality. Second, it is easier for a judge to receive objective evidence on the choice of camera, film, and the like than to receive subjective evidence—often entailing expert testimony—on the originality in the image.

This eliding of a photograph's original expression with the photographer's creative choices should generally be a harmless error.[16] As an influential court of appeals said in a 2000 decision, "[c]ourts today continue to hold that such decisions by the photographer—or, more precisely, the elements of photographs that result from these decisions—are worthy of copyright protection."[17] If it does produce errors, those errors are probably to the benefit of photographers: In close cases, judicial focus on the *process* of creating the photograph helps courts side with photographers in protecting what is undoubtedly the photographer's investment of time and energy, even if the originality of the photograph is hard to pinpoint.

Despite the tendency of courts to recite sources of original expression in photographs in laundry-list fashion, we can organize those sources with a little more rigor into three categories: [a] creative choices in constructing the scene; [b] creative choices in initial image capture; and [c] creative choices in manipulating the image. These categories will help our understanding of copyright's search for originality in photographs *and* how different photographs will have varying amounts of protection based on varying amounts of original expression.

Creative Choices in Constructing the Scene

Composing the scene or subject captured in the photograph is the first category of potential originality in a photograph, occurring before, and independent of, any photographic processes. In terms of copyright doctrine, this is the "selection" and "arrangement" of what will be photographed, including the posing of objects.

This selection and arrangement can have the elaborate production values of a Cindy Sherman self-portrait, an in-studio or on-location fashion shoot, or the highly staged Vanity Fair celebrity group photographs (that have become a style in their own right). It could also be the selection and arrangement of fruit and foods in a still life or of the books and papers on an intellectual's desk. Less elaborately, it can also be the arrangement of sports team members or conference attendees for a group photograph. These less elaborate arrangements will, by their nature, have fewer creative choices available to the photographer and, therefore, less original expression by the lights of copyright law.

This pre-image capture selection and arrangement is also a matter of framing, particularly when it comes to fixed objects. The photographer taking an image of the skylines of New York, Hong Kong, or Chicago decides which structures she will include and how they will occupy the frame. The same for a photographer capturing street scenes or eerie images of a cemetery. Although the skyscrapers, brownstone staircases, and tombstones cannot be moved about by the photographer, there are ample creative choices available for what to include in the frame and the angles from which things are shot for the resulting photograph to have at least *some* originality in the pre-image selection and arrangement.

Creative Choices in Initial Image Capture

The creative choices mentioned by courts that properly fall into this category are pretty straight-forward: effects from choice of camera, choice of lens, use of filters, control of exposure, etc. We can also include in this category—*or* in the first—the lighting choices a photographer will make for a photographed scene or image.

Creative Choices in Manipulating the Image

The last broad category for original expression in a photograph includes all the things that can be done after capturing the image. This includes a range of processes that can take the image beyond what a purist may consider *photography*. "Composite" photos reminiscent of classic paintings appeared by the mid-1800s along with "doctored" photographs of Abraham Lincoln and Ulysses S. Grant. Throughout the twentieth century, Communist propagandists and Hollywood publicists made opponents and wrinkles, respectively, disappear from photographs. Post-image alteration software is now so ubiquitous that it has become a common verb: An image is or is not "photoshopped."

Short of alterations that take the image beyond a "legitimate" photograph (whatever that is), the important point is that a variety of choices that prior generations of photographers could only make (or only make easily) while shooting can now be remade later. Digital filters essentially act as lenses by passing the data set of the photograph through an algorithm that alters the image globally. Colors can be shifted or intensified; focus can be sharpened (to imitate what would be produced by specialized types of lenses); lighting can be changed, and apparent time of day altered—something that used to be a process during filming.

Is there Anything Else?

A rigorous application of copyright doctrine would say no, but there is also no question that an originality standard—even our low one—does not completely fulfill the general policy objective of giving people incentives to create non-original photographs and films. Indeed, we want people taking exhaustive photographic records of political campaign events, natural disasters, public demonstrations, and thousands of other kinds of events. We want them to turn on the camera when things get interesting, remarkable, or newsworthy.

That causes two things. First, some countries have expressly extended legal protection to non-original photographs. Although French courts recognized copyright in photographs as early as 1862, photographs were not expressly included in the copyright statute until 1957. The 1957 amendment to the law provided for the protection of "photographic works of an artistic or documentary character." Reflecting prior French cases, photographs of the first group ("artistic") could be likened to paintings, while photographs of the second group were those where the photographer's intention was to capture an image of public interest—for reasons other than the image's aesthetic appeal. In July 1985, the French copyright law was revised to eliminate the artistic/documentary distinction, but other European jurisdictions—among them Germany, Italy, and Norway—now provide separate, statutory protection to non-original photographs, always with a substantially shorter term of protection than copyright.[18]

Second, in countries that do not have two tiers of protection—the US, the UK, and most common-law jurisdictions—courts will struggle to find original expression where they can, ensuring that photographs get at least "thin" copyright protection against mechanical reproduction. Sir Hugh Laddie, one of Britain's most distinguished judges in intellectual property matters, believed that there could be at least *some* originality in a "worthwhile photograph by being at the right place at the right time" or an image of "a scene worth preserving because [the photographer] made a special effort to go and find it."[19] The celebrated American jurist Learned Hand also seemed disposed in that direction, finding in 1921 that industrial photographs of trademarks could be copyrighted "because no photograph, however simple, can be unaffected by the personal influence of the author, and no two will be absolutely alike."[20] There is some judicial sleight of hand in such reasoning, but the legerdemain is to the benefit of photographers, both professional and amateur, so we should not complain.

What Does this Mean in Terms of Modern Practices?

Both lay people and lawyers frequently lose sight of the originality requirement and assume that there is copyright in all photographs. But the truth is much more complex. There are many photographs that will have robust copyright protection. Other works, including some iconic twentieth-century photography, may have "thinner" copyright protection that essentially protects them against unauthorized reprographic reproduction and little else. Finally, nowadays, it is possible that *most* of the world's photographs and video—made only to record information—should not qualify for copyright protection *at all*. Let us consider these two situations and then work through a couple of puzzles of how copyright law *should* be applied to some modern disputes.

Museum Postcards, Google Street View, and ATMs

It is important to recognize that when the content of the photograph has an independent reality (meaning it would exist without the photographer's project), and the photographer seeks only to achieve (and does in fact achieve) an accurate representation of that independent reality, there is a good chance that the photograph has no copyright protection at all. That includes identification photographs, security camera videos, many industrial product photographs, numerous satellite imagery, museum postcards of public domain paintings, crime scene photographs, and Google Maps's Street View.

Judge Lewis Kaplan reached this correct result in the 1999 case *Bridgeman Art Library, Ltd. v. Corel Corp.*,[21] in which the library tried to assert copyright over photographic transparencies of paintings that were in the public domain. Because "plaintiff by its own admission ha[d] labored to create 'slavish copies' of public domain works of art," Kaplan concluded that "there was no spark of originality—indeed, the point of the exercise was to reproduce the underlying works with absolute fidelity. Copyright is not available in these circumstances."[22] Similarly, the Nimmer treatise advises that a "photograph should be denied copyright for lack of originality" if it "amounts to nothing more than a slavish copying" and gives the example of "[a] photograph of a painting or drawing" captured in this manner.[23] Many museums (or their postcard suppliers) continue the vestigial practice of claiming copyright in postcards of public domain paintings, but that is not what the US copyright law teaches.

We need to have the same rigor as the *Bridgeman Art* court when we consider copyright claims for what is produced by surveillance cameras, driver's license cameras, New York taxicab cameras, and Google Maps's Street View. The surveillance camera captures as much of the hallway as possible or as much of the facial features of the person operating an ATM as possible. If it is a poor or distorted image of reality, it is because the camera was not well-maintained or because the lighting was suboptimal, not because of some aesthetic choice. The selection of the image is garden-variety—adjusted for purely utilitarian, information-gathering purposes. The parameters for Google's ambitious Street View project are about the technology, its improving accuracy, and the completeness of coverage, not about any expressive decisions.[24]

With all these photographs, including photographs of museum paintings, images captured at ATMs and by immigration officials stamping passports, Google Maps's Street View, and aerial reconnaissance photographs, these images may have copyright in the few countries that still base copyright protection on "sweat of the brow,"[25] but not in the US or the European Union. Susan Sontag captured the point nicely: "[I]n the vast majority of photographs which get taken—for scientific and industrial purposes, by the press, by the military and the police, by families—any trace of the personal vision of whoever is behind the camera interferes with the primary demand on the photograph: that it record, diagnose, inform."[26]

This function—to record, diagnose, and inform—produces what is really a pixelated database and there is insufficient "trace of the personal vision of whoever is behind the camera" for us to grant copyright.

One exception to this observation *may* be photographs that *appear* to be simple recordations of fact, but are actually skillful composite efforts. One of the suppliers for Google Maps says that a person looking at those images is "often looking at multiple layers of data such as satellite imagery, aerial photography, synthetic ocean imagery, roadways, location names, addresses and more, which come from many different data and imagery providers." Apparently, even "[t]he 'Satellite' layer consists of a mix of mid-resolution and high-resolution satellite and aerial imagery from multiple providers for a given area."[27] Such integration of visual information from multiple sources is not uncommon in satellite and space photography, as in NASA's iconic 2000 "Blue Marble" image of planet earth.[28] But that may or may not mean there is enough original expression to support copyright protection. If the layers of data are compiled in a way that serves the ends of making a more factually accurate satellite image, i.e. what a perfect satellite would see on a perfect day with absolute fidelity, then these choices would seem to involve only the same skill and effort at issue in *Bridgeman Art Library*. However, if there were aesthetic choices on what blues to use for different parts of the ocean or choices that create a "perfect" picture that could never actually be captured by a satellite's mechanical operation, there may be sufficient original expression.

Limited Protection for Photojournalists

Photojournalists typically do not get to make as many creative choices as studio photographers. Indeed, that is almost definitional to photojournalism: In contrast to the studio session, the photojournalist is supposed to be photographing independent *reality*, a reality that would exist with or without the photographer's presence. The result may be what is called a "thin" copyright. The nature of this thin copyright may mean that the photograph is effectively protected from slavish, reprographic copying, but has little protection against unauthorized copying of many of the photograph's elements.

A 2011 district court decision from Massachusetts correctly understood how to analyze this problem. In *Harney v. Sony Pictures Television*,[29] the plaintiff claimed that an audiovisual image from a made-for-television film infringed a still photograph that he had taken of a father and daughter leaving their Beacon Hill church on Palm Sunday. The father turned out to be Clark Rockefeller—a.k.a. Christian Gerhartsreiter—who later "absconded with his daughter following an acrimonious divorce." After the kidnapping, the FBI and Boston Police used the photograph in "WANTED" posters.

When Sony created a made-for-television film based on the Rockefeller kidnapping, it used a similar image of the actors playing father and daughter, both as a moving picture sequence in the film and as still photographs on the "WANTED" posters used in the film. Although Judge Zobel found the Harney photograph to be copyrighted, she also found that Sony had not copied any of the protectable original expression:

> Harney captured a moment in time of a father and daughter passing through Beacon Hill. The Rockefellers were not models. Harney did not select their clothes, give them a church program and palm leaf as props, or ask them to pose. Those aspects of the Rockefellers' appearance are factual realities that exist independently of any photo. They are not Harney's original expression, and they are not copyrightable elements of his photograph.[30]

As to protectable originality, Judge Zobel found that the only protectable expression that Sony might have copied was "the position of the individuals relative to the boundaries of the photo" and that this "limited sharing [was] not enough to establish substantial similarity and copyright infringement."[31]

For the work of photojournalists and nature photographers—including iconic images by Ansel Adams, Dorothea Lange, and Bill Cunningham—this means that the copyright in their work was or would have been "thin" and might effectively only prohibit mechanical reproduction of their works. And that makes a certain amount of sense: A photographer should be able to capture her own images of Yosemite's "Half Dome" or the moon over New Mexico villages without fear of infringing iconic Ansel Adams photographs (if those works were still under copyright).

But proper application of copyright law is also important in some very recent disputes about photographs.

Deep Fakes

Deep fakes are convincing digital replicas of known individuals doing and saying things they have never said or done. The deep fake problem exploded into the public consciousness around 2017 and is typically associated with porn and celebrities (almost always women) being convincingly inserted into hard-core pornographic videos.

To make a deep fake pornographic video, one needs a "face set"—a set of photographs of the face of the deep fake target. Such photo sets are readily available online for actors, politicians, and other public figures, meaning that the photographs were taken by scores of different photographers. But a "face set" of a private person could also be lifted from her Facebook page or Instagram account, or from finding the same person in the social media accounts of third persons. And it is possible to make an audiovisual deep fake from *one* image of the face. Those scenarios make a copyright claim *appear* much more viable. As Professors Robert Chesney and Danielle Citron write: "A copyright owner is the person who took a photograph. Thus, if a deep fake involves a photo that the victim took of herself, the victim might have a copyright claim against the creator of the deep fake. . . . The prospects for success, however, would be uncertain. The defendant will surely argue that the fake is a 'fair use' of the copyrighted material, intended for educational, artistic, or other expressive purposes. Then too, whether the fake is sufficiently transformed from the original so as to earn 'fair use' protection is a highly fact-specific inquiry, and we do not yet have a track record of courts grappling with such questions."[32]

This analysis jumps to fair use—as both lawyers and lay people are wont to do—without considering more fundamental copyright issues. Even assuming that all the photos were owned by the same person, ask yourself: *What* would the computer algorithm be *extracting* from *photograph* A, *photograph* B, *photograph* C, . . . *photograph* X to create a convincing composite of the face of the deep fake victim? Whatever data points are being extracted and used, they are almost certainly not the "original expression" in any of the photographs. What is being extracted are data points that establish how the face of the person *actually looks* (from different angles, with different expressions, under different lighting conditions). In other words, one could own the copyright in *all* the photographs used to make a deep fake "face set" and have no infringement claim.

At the same time, the deep fake video—pornographic or otherwise—will very likely be based on an existing video. In the case of the pornographic deep fake, the target person's face is inserted in the place of the porn actor's face to give the appearance that the target person engaged in the recorded sex act. In the case of a deep fake in which the person says things in an interview or speech that they did not say, typically the video recording of a real speech or talk of the target person is used as the basis to manipulate digitally their facial movements and substitute different audio—a different speech or statement. In these cases, there is near 100 percent mechanical reproduction of the underlying *video* and while there may not be much originality in most porn or in the video of political or actor interviews, there is enough to make the deep fake an infringement of the underlying video.

The Wonderful World of Selfies

In contrast to face sets used for deep fakes, proper application of copyright's originality standard to photographs should be good (or ok) news for selfies.

There is much debate over the ubiquitous photographing of our social lives brought on by smartphones and the digital, networked environment. Those who think of photography as an art form may feel "the casual way shots are taken and indiscriminately shared feels like a thinning and cheapening of the camera's purpose."[33] But for copyright as long as the "prolific preening and posting" is *expression*, it does not matter whether it is "watered-down art."[34] What are the expressive aspects of selfies? Obviously poses and facial expressions—the same as whether we are creating them ourselves or Napoleon Sarony is coaxing them out of a difficult Oscar Wilde.

As markers chronicling the whens and wheres of our fabulous lives, many if not most selfies do serve as what Sontag called "photograph-trophies" or Barthes termed "certificates of presence."[35] But the *expressive* aspect of selfies is only enhanced if Leah Ollman is right that "[t]he line between shooting the style of our lives and styling our lives for the shoot has become increasingly blurred."[36]

Photographs and Fair Use Claims

It is virtually impossible to discuss copyright in the US without talking about "fair use," a judge-created exception to copyright liability that was codified into American law in 1976. Fair use allows for unauthorized uses of copyrighted works pursuant to a four-factor test with an emphasis on uses for education, research, commentary, criticism, and the like.

Beginning with the Supreme Court's 1994 *Campbell v. Acuff Rose Music, Inc.* decision, court determinations of fair use have increasingly depended on whether or not the defendant's use of the copyrighted work was "transformative." According to *Campbell*, a defendant's work will be transformative if it "adds something new, with a further purpose or different character, altering the first with new expression, meaning, or message."[37] By about 2010, commentators had come to the view that "the transformative use paradigm, as adopted in *Campbell v. Acuff-Rose* overwhelmingly drives fair use analysis in the courts."[38] The apparent dominance of the transformative use analysis has been picked up by lay observers. For example, a 2018 commentary on the Artsy. com website (mis)described fair use as "an exception to copyright law reserved for the original transformative use of copyrighted works (though courts weigh other factors in determining fair use as well)."[39]

In *Campbell*, the defendant had engaged in a "new expression"—literally a rap version of a 1964 Roy Orbison song—but it is the "further purpose" or "new meaning" versions of transformative use that have had the most traction with courts. As one commentator noted in 2008, "[i]n assessing transformativeness, the courts generally emphasize the transformativeness of the defendant's purpose in using the underlying work, rather than any transformation (or lack thereof) by the defendant of the content of the underlying work."[40]

It is probably fair to say that this doctrinal development poses more risk to photojournalists and other commercial photographers than to any other group of creative professionals for the simple reason that the downstream user who finds a photograph and embeds that photograph as an illustration in a newspaper story, blog post, promotional brochure, or tweet will *always* be able to claim a different "purpose" or new "meaning" as compared to the photographer who took the photo for its beauty, the information it conveys, or some combination thereof. For example, Getty Images advertises that it offers "[p]owerful imagery and video that can brilliantly convey any concept,"[41] but that implies that the images may be used to convey concepts that were completely absent from the photographer's thinking, i.e. that every Getty Image client's use can be "transformative."

An example of this problem is a 2019 litigation in Montana, *Peterman v. Republican National Committee*.[42] Erika Peterman had been hired by the Montana Democratic Party (MDP) to take photographs of Democratic congressional candidate and singer-songwriter Rob Quist. Peterman edited the photos and sent them to MDP; both MDP and the Quist campaign posted them to their respective Facebook pages. The Republican National Committee (RNC) downloaded a high-resolution version of the photo from Facebook and used it in a mailer attacking Quist—an action that the court ultimately found to be fair use. The RNC's minimal physical alterations of the photo were not what made it "sufficiently transformative." Instead, it was the RNC's *use* that was transformative: "[t]he mailer uses Quist's musicianship to criticize his candidacy, subverting the [original] purpose and function" of the photograph. In the context of the mailer, "the image takes on a new meaning."[43]

Obviously, a fair use doctrine that allows unauthorized uses of any photograph as long as "the image takes on a new meaning" would be a blow to effective copyright protection for photographers. The good news is that appellate courts have increasingly understood the problem, reining in lower courts' use of the transformative use doctrine as applied to photographs and thereby enforcing copyrights in photographs when they are reproduced whole.

What may be the first of these cases was the 2011 *Murphy v. Millennium Radio Group*[44] decision, in which a photographer, Murphy, was hired by *New Jersey Monthly* (*NJM*) to take a photo of two radio show hosts for an article naming them in the "Best of New Jersey" issue. An employee of the radio station scanned the photo and used it on the radio station's website, referring to the hosts' "Best of New Jersey" award. The district court found that this use was transformative, but the Third Circuit disagreed:

> The Image was originally created to illustrate a *NJM* article informing the public about Carton and Rossi's "best of" award; the Station Defendants themselves state they "used [the Image]... to report to their viewers the newsworthy fact of [Carton and Rossi's] receipt of the magazine's award." Although they claim that the difference is significant, there is, in fact, no meaningful distinction between the purpose and character of *NJM*'s use of the Image and the Station Defendants' use on the WKXW website.[45]

This sort of word game about a defendant's "purpose" was also present in the Ninth Circuit's 2012 *Monge v. Maya* litigation, where the plaintiffs were Noelia Lorenzo Monge, a Latina pop music singer, and Jorge Reynoso, a well-known Latin music producer. The couple had married discreetly in 2007, but several photos of their wedding evening were eventually published by "TV NOTAS" in a story about the clandestine wedding with some text and captions accompanying each photo. Monge and Reynoso sued for copyright infringement. As in *Murphy*, the district court granted summary judgment to the defendant on the grounds of fair use, reasoning that "[t]he photographs were used not in their original context as documentation of Plaintiff's wedding night but as confirmation of the accompanying text challenging Plaintiff's repeated public denials of the marriage."[46] Again, the court of appeals reversed, concluding that the defendant "did not transform the photos into a new work, as in *Campbell*" and had "left the inherent character of the images unchanged."[47] The court reasoned that, while there had been some "further purpose," that change in purpose was insufficient to establish more than marginal transformation.[48]

That same year *Balsley v. LFP, Inc.* concerned a set of photos of Catherine Balsley, a news reporter for an Ohio CBS affiliate, who had participated, perhaps too enthusiastically, in a wet T-shirt contest while on vacation.[49] Photos taken by another bar patron, including some of Balsley dancing nude, appeared online in May 2003. Balsley lost her news reporting job shortly thereafter. Balsley and her husband found the photographer and bought the copyright to the photos "so that they would have the legal means of ending the photographs' dissemination."[50]

Despite these efforts, some of the photos were published in the February 2006 issue of *Hustler* magazine as that month's "Hot News Babe." The sole issue at trial was *Hustler*'s claim of fair use, a defense rejected by the jury. As in *Monge*, the photo of Balsley appearing in *Hustler* "was unaltered other than for minor cropping and was merely reprinted in a different medium." The appellate panel upheld the jury's verdict against Hustler, holding that *Hustler* "did not add any creative message" and that the magazine's "use of the photograph was the same as the [photographer]'s original use—to shock, arouse, and amuse."[51]

Last in this suite of appellate decisions protecting photographers is the 2019 *Brammer v. Violent Hues* litigation concerning a photograph of a lively Washington, D.C. neighborhood "Adams Morgan at Night," taken by commercial photographer Russell Bramer. Violent Hues lifted the photo from Brammer's Flickr account and used it without attribution on a website promoting the Northern Virginia International Film and Music Festival. The district court granted summary judgment for Violent Hues on fair use, reasoning that the photographer's stated purpose "in capturing and publishing the [photo] was promotional and expressive,"[52] while "Violent Hues' stated purpose 'in using the [photo] was informational: to provide festival attendees with information regarding the local area.'"

The court of appeals disagreed. While recognizing that whole-cloth reproduction of a copyrighted work *can* sometimes be genuinely transformative, the appellate court found that the unauthorized use of Brammer's photograph was not transformative:

> Violent Hues used the Photo expressly for its content—that is, to depict Adams Morgan . . . . Violent Hues' sole claim to transformation is that its secondary use of the Photo provided film festival attendees with "information" regarding Adams Morgan. But such a use does not necessarily create a new function or meaning that expands human thought; if this were so, virtually all illustrative uses of photography would qualify as transformative.[53]

Here, we have it: Undisciplined use of "new meaning" in transformative use analysis would be debilitating to copyright in photography. It would be mere word play to say that some photos have been transformed from "documentation of [a].. wedding night" to "confirmation of . . . text" stating that a couple got married. Fortunately, federal courts of appeal have caught onto the problem of how the formulation of "transformative" use affects photographs and their reasoning should, with time, take stronger hold in the lower courts.

Conclusion

Proper application of copyright law to photography requires nuance, subtlety, and some legerdemain about "originality" that usually accrues to the benefit of photographers. But that does not mean that every photograph is protected by copyright, and the copyright protection in a photograph will vary, with the strongest protection reserved for "when a photographer orchestrates the situation that is photographed, rather than simply photographing a ready-made scene or thing."[54] With the latter, photographers can expect protection from mechanical reproduction but not from *re-creation* of their images. That is the rough answer that copyright provides as it grapples with what Kracauer called "a medium which is neither imitation nor art in the traditional sense."

Notes

1 Burrow-Giles Lithographic Co. v. Sarony, 111 U.S. 53 (1884).
2 Statement and Brief for Plaintiff in Error at 5, Burrow-Giles Lithographic Co. v. Sarony, 111 U.S. 53 (1884) [hereinafter Burrow-Giles Brief].
3 Burrow-Giles Brief at 9, 18–19.
4 Sarony, 111 U.S. at 56.
5 Burrow-Giles Brief at 5.
6 Beaumont Newhall, *The History of Photography* (New York: The Museum of Modern Art, revised & enlarged ed., 1982), 71.
7 Sarony, 111 U.S. at 60 (quoting unpublished lower court decision). The courts may have actually overstated Sarony's array of decisions, as Oscar Wilde came in his lecture attire and may himself have been responsible for the "calculated pose." Maria Morris Hambourg et al., *In the Waking Dream: Photography's First Century* (New York: Museum of Modern Art, 1992), 340.
8 Sarony, 111 U.S. at 60.
9 *Id.* at 59. But the court also said that "[o]n the question as thus stated we decide nothing." *Id.* So technically, as Nimmer says, "[T]he Court expressly declined to rule on the question whether 'the ordinary production of a photograph' necessarily exhibits sufficient originality to claim copyright." Melville B. Nimmer and David Nimmer, *Nimmer on Copyright* (New York: M. Bender, 2014), Vol. 1 § 2.08[E][1].
10 Leigh v. Warner Bros., 10 F. Supp. 2d 1371, 1376 (S.D. Ga. 1998), *aff'd in part, rev'd in part sub nom.* Leigh v. Warner Bros., 212 F.3d 1210 (11th Cir. 2000).
11 Roger v. Koons, 960 F.2d 301, 307 (2d Cir. 1992).
12 Hugh Laddie, Peter Prescott, and Mary Vitoria, *The Modern Law of Copyright and Design*, § 4.57 (London: Butterworths, 3rd ed., 2000).
13 Marco v. Accent Publ'g Co., 969 F.2d 1547, 1551–52 (3d Cir. 1992).
14 Latimer v. Roaring Toyz, Inc., 601 F.3d 1224, 1230 (11th Cir. 2010).
15 See Bleistein v. Donaldson Lithographing Co., 188 U.S. 239, 251 (1903).
16 The same hesitancy of courts to make such judgments has been noted in French copyright law. *See* André Lucas and Henri-Jacques Lucas, *Traité de la propriété littéraire & artistique* (1994), § 128 at 138. ("And it is certain that fear to put forth a value judgment inclines the courts to behave indulgently."/"Et il est certain que la crainte d'émettre un jugement de valeur incline les tribunaux à l'indulgence.")
17 Ets-Hokin v. Skyy Spirits, Inc., 225 F.3d 1068, 1074–75 (9th Cir. 2000).
18 Under German law, works of photography ("Lichtbildwerke") are photographs with a sufficient level of originality and are subject to the regular copyright term, while all other photographs ("Lichtbilder") get more limited protection. Urheberrechtsgesetz [UrhG] [Copyright Law], September 9, 1965, Bundesgesetzblatt, Teil I [BGBL. I], as amended, § 2 Para. 1 and § 72 Para. 3. Norway provides a similar two-tier system of protection. Lov om opphavsrett til åndsverk [Copyright Act] 12 mai 1961 No. 2 § 1 [Act No. 2 of 12 May 1961 Relating to Copyright in Literary, Scientific and Artistic Works, etc., with Subsequent Amendments], Latest of 22 December 2006 (in force 1 January 2007), accessed May 12, 2020, http://bat8.inria.fr/~lang/orphan/documents/europe/norway/norwegian_copyright_act-20061222. html. In Italy, the relevant law is Legge 22 aprile 1941, n.633 § 87 [Law No. 633 of April 22, 1941 for the

Protection of Copyright & Neighboring Rights, World Intellectual Property Organisation] (February 10, 2012), http://www.wipo.int/wipolex/en/text.jsp?file_id=128275#JD_IT099E_A87.

19 Laddie et al., *The Modern Law of Copyright and Design*, § 4.57 at 229.

20 Jewelers' Circular Pub. Co. v. Keystone Pub. Co., 274 F. 932, 934 (S.D.N.Y. 1921), *aff'd sub nom.* Jeweler's Circular Pub. Co. v. Keystone Pub. Co., 281 F. 83 (2d Cir. 1922). Learned Hand's reasoning in this case was almost certainly wrong in other aspects.

21 Bridgeman Art Library, Ltd. v. Corel Corp., 36 F. Supp. 2d 191 (S.D.N.Y. 1999).

22 *Id.* at 197.

23 Nimmer, *Nimmer on Copyright,* § 2.08[E][2]. For a parallel discussion and conclusion in relation to medical and scientific imaging, see generally Cindy Alberts Carson, "Laser Bones: Copyright Issues Raised by the Use of Information Technology in Archaeology," *Harvard Journal of Law and Technology* 10, no. 2 (1997), 281; Eva E. Subotnik, "Originality Proxies: Toward a Theory of Copyright and Creativity," *Brooklyn Law Review* 76, no. 4 (2011), 1514.

24 "Google Street View," Wikipedia, accessed October 6, 2019, https://en.wikipedia.org/wiki/Google_Street_View.

25 See generally Feist Publ'ns, Inc. v. Rural Tel. Serv. Co., 499 U.S. 340, 352–55 (1991) (explaining "sweat of the brow" doctrine as it developed in the US copyright law up until 1991); Abraham Drassinower, "Sweat of the Brow, Creativity, and Authorship: On Originality in Canadian Copyright Law," *University of Ottawa Law & Technology Journal* 1 (2003): 107 (discussing Canada's move away from a pure sweat of the brow doctrine).

26 Susan Sontag, *On Photography* (London: Penguin Books Ltd, 1977), 133. This follows from Sontag's view that "[L]ike every mass art form, photography is not practiced by most people as an art." Sontag, *On Photography,* 8.

27 "Support: Terra Metrics and Google Earth," TerraMetrics, last modified April 2, 2012, http://www.truearth.com/support/faqs_content_google.htm.

28 "Earth — The Blue Marble," NASA, accessed May 11, 2020, http://visibleearth.nasa.gov/view.php?id=54388.

29 Harney v. Sony Pictures Television, Inc., 98 U.S.P.Q.2d 1755 (D. Mass. 2011).

30 *Id.* at 1756.

31 *Id.*

32 Robert Chesney and Danielle Citron, "Deep Fakes: A Looming Challenge for Privacy, Democracy, and National Security," *California Law Review* 107, no. 1753 (2019).

33 Leah Ollman, "Reframing the Reality of Selfies," *Los Angeles Times*, August 11, 2019 at F7.

34 *Id.*

35 Roland Barthes, *Camera Lucida: Reflections on Photography,* translated by Richard Howard (New York: Hill and Wang, 1981), 87.

36 Ollman, "Reframing."

37 Campbell v. Acuff-Rose Music, Inc., 510 U.S. 569, 579 (1994).

38 Neil Weinstock Netanel, "Making Sense of Fair Use," *Lewis and Clark Law Review* 15, no. 3 (2011): 715.

39 Isaac Kaplan, "5 Lawsuits That Could Reshape the Art World in 2018," Artsy.com, January 1, 2018, https://www.artsy.net/article/artsy-editorial-5-lawsuits-reshape-art-2018 (describing artist Richard Prince as "the king of copyright infringement cases" and saying he "often wins these cases by asserting fair use – that is, his use of artwork created by others falls under an exception to copyright law reserved for the original transformative use of copyrighted works (though courts weigh other factors in determining fair use as well)").

40 R. Anthony Reese, "Transformativeness and the Derivative Work Right," *Columbia Journal of Law and the Arts* 31 (2008): 484–85. In the more blunt words of another scholar, "exact copying plus transformative *purpose* has a stunningly good fair use record in recent cases." See also Rebecca Tushnet, "Content, Purpose, or Both?" *University of Washington Law Review* 90 (2015): 876.

41 http://www.gettyimages.com/articles/travel/the-bizarrely-violent-sport-of-calcio-storico.

42 Peterman v. Republican Nat'l Comm., 369 F. Supp. 3d 1053 (D. Mont. 2019).

43 *Id.* at 1061.

44 Murphy v. Millennium Radio Grp., LLC, 650 F.3d 295 (3d Cir. 2011).

45 *Id.* at 306.

46 Monge v. Maya Magazines, Inc., 96 U.S.P.Q.2d 1678 (C.D. Cal. September 30, 2010), *rev'd,* 688 F.3d 1164 (9th Cir. 2012).

47 Monge v. Maya Magazines, Inc., 688 F.3d 1164, 1176 (9th Cir. 2012). *Id.* at 1175 ("[T]here was no real transformation of the photos themselves.").

48 *Id.* at 1176. The majority felt that that "difference in purpose is not quite the same thing as transformation, and Campbell instructs that transformativeness is the critical inquiry under this factor."
49 Balsley v. LFP, Inc., 691 F.3d 747, 755 (6th Cir. 2012).
50 *Id.*.
51 *Id.* at 759.
52 Brammer v. Violent Hues Prods., LLC, 922 F.3d 255, 263 n.3 (4th Cir. 2019).
53 *Id.* at 264.
54 LaChapelle v. Fenty, 812 F. Supp. 2d 434, 441 (S.D.N.Y. July 2011).

3.3

COPYRIGHT CONCERNS FOR VISUAL JOURNALISTS

Mickey H. Osterreicher

Visual journalists are being squeezed on all sides. From First Amendment challenges to their right to photograph and record in public to copyright issues regarding fair use to the use of drones for newsgathering, there is a growing perception by users of such images that anything found on the internet is there for the taking without the need for permission, credit, or compensation.

Monkey Selfies and Drones

Copyright questions of authorship and copyrightability regarding "selfie" photographs taken by a monkey were flying around a few years ago, but the US Copyright Office ultimately grounded the issue by noting as an example in its 2017 *Compendium of U.S. Copyright Office Practices* that "[a] photograph taken by a monkey" was a work the Office "will not register" as it falls into the classification of "works produced by nature, animals, or plants."[1] But what of images made using a drone-borne camera? Before getting to that question, it might be helpful to look at the history of aerial photography leading to these most recent drone-made works.

In 1783, an untethered hot-air balloon rose into the skies over Paris carrying two passengers in the first successful manned flight.[2] In 1826, the first permanent photograph was taken in France.[3] More than thirty years later, the two technologies came together in the world's first known aerial photograph, also shot over France in 1858 from a tethered hot-air balloon.[4] Given the state of the art at that time, the enterprising photographer also required a complete darkroom be taken aloft in the basket of the balloon to accomplish that feat.[5] Since then, citizens and journalists have used all sorts of devices in order to capture a bird's-eye view of the ground below.

In 1860, James Black, an aspiring photographer, accomplished a similar achievement when he took to the air over Boston in Samuel King's hot-air balloon the "Queen of the Air" to capture the first aerial photographs made in America.[6] Oliver Wendall Holmes, Sr., a Harvard professor, wrote about the photo in the 1863 edition of *The Atlantic Monthly*, proclaiming, "Boston, as the eagle and wild goose see it [later to become the title of the photo], is a very different object from the same place as the solid citizen looks up at its eaves and chimneys. As a first attempt it is on the whole a remarkable success; but its greatest interest is in showing what we may hope to see accomplished in the same direction."[7]

That "direction" has far exceeded what anyone could have envisioned. Aerial vehicles as well as photographic technology have experienced nothing short of a revolution. What has not changed is man's desire to see the world below from above. Camera-equipped small (weighing less than 55 pounds) Unmanned Aerial Systems (sUAS), better known as "drones," may well be considered the great prodigy of the Kodak Brownie, which in 1888 allowed almost anyone to take photographs that previously required costly and cumbersome equipment, long exposures, and often the controlled seclusion only found in a photography studio.

The use of remotely controlled aircraft is not new. People have been flying such devices since the 1940s. What is new is the convergence of several technological developments such as smaller batteries, global positioning systems (GPS), high-definition (HD) cameras, and miniaturized electric motors to make drones not only accessible, but affordable. With the proliferation of these aerial camera platforms have come concerns about safety, ethics, and privacy accompanied by legislative, regulatory, and legal issues. Currently, in the US, people may fly drones under a few different regulatory schemes, including commercial use, recreational use, and public safety/government use.[8]

While legislation, regulations, and case law regarding drones are slowly evolving, one issue still to be addressed is the copyright of works made using such devices.

The application of copyright law to the images made using drones should be the same (for now) as they are for any other type of photography/videography made from the ground or under the water. The intellectual property rights regarding images and video recordings captured by drones should also be subject to written agreements between the creator/copyright holder and the customer in the same way as they are for any other visual works, but given the nascent drone industry and the overriding concerns about privacy and airspace issues, some common licensing language and rights may be overlooked.

Drone pilots usually work as independent contractors, but some are on staff at news organizations or work for companies contracting with those media companies. The copyright of drone-captured images will be determined by the drone pilot's employment status, that is, whether it was a work made for hire or under a licensing agreement. Another complicating factor may be whether the drone pilot-in-command took the image or whether it was taken by a visual observer or another person in charge of the photographic mission. Much like a photographer using assistants, who sometimes actually push the shutter button, while the photographer directs the shoot, it will be important to have those issues addressed in writing before any drone shoot.

Just as with any licensing agreement for images, it is crucial that the terms of use and scope of the license be clearly spelled out. It is just as important that anyone contracting for drone use makes sure that whoever they are working with has the proper licenses, waivers, registration, and insurance and is not a "fly by night" (pun intended) operation.

Some other copyright questions that may come into play should images be infringed (as they most certainly will be) are questions of copyrightability, authorship, and fair use. Like the "monkey selfies," drone images are sometimes seen as the ultimate "selfie" especially when drones are equipped with "Follow Me" technology that allows the drone to be programmed to automatically follow a person or object, keeping it in the frame no matter where the drone is flown. As with images made on the ground, a drone photographer must consider camera type, lens selection, operative ISO, color or black and white imagery, framing, and time of day, but also aerial platform used, speed/hover, altitude, angle, and camera/drone moves/axis (for video). Just as in cases involving photography, it will be necessary to articulate any complaint for copyright infringement with specificity as to the creative processes behind the image in order to counter claims and defenses that the images in question were made automatically by the drone itself, thus possibly lacking authorship or copyrightability.

Fair Use

Because hundreds of millions of images are uploaded on the internet daily, it is not surprising that so many of those are infringed with impunity, especially because there are a great number of people who believe that the World Wide Web is the "public domain" and anything found there is free for the taking. Increasingly, there seems to exist a mob mentality of entitlement to those images, with anyone objecting to the use of an image without permission, credit, or compensation being labeled a "troll." Additionally, we have seen infringers defend infringement claims by asserting defenses that the infringed images lacked the requisite "creativity" to receive copyright protection.

One such case was decided in the US District Court for the District of Colorado, pitting a professional wedding photographer in Brooklyn, New York, against a group of political organizations in Colorado who were promoting "family values" and were alleged to be encouraging discrimination against lesbian, gay, bisexual, and transgender people.[9] Without permission, the Colorado organizations, in a political mailer, used an engagement photo taken in New York by the photographer of a same-sex couple. The photographer sued for copyright infringement (the couple also sued for unlawful appropriation of their personalities and likeness, which are not dealt with here) and the defendants asserted a claim of fair use. In its decision, the Court went through the fair use analysis and found that with regard to the "purpose and character of the use," "while use for nonprofit educational purposes is valid under this factor, Public Advocate's use of the photo is not the type of 'education' contemplated by the . . . statute's drafters relates to schooling, not mailers circulated during an election."

The defendants also asserted that their use of the photo was "highly transformative" but the court disagreed, finding that the defendants did nothing to the lifted portion of the photo, save for removing the bottom portion of [the couple's] legs . . . and superimposed it on a mailer. "While the Defendants placed the lifted portion in a different background and placed a caption on the mailer, such actions cannot be characterized as 'highly transformative.'"

In determining the first fair use factor, the nature of the copyrighted work, the Court noted that the more creative a work is, the more protection it should be accorded from copying, and the more informational or functional the plaintiff's work, the broader the scope of the fair use defense. Because the plaintiffs properly and with specificity alleged "numerous facts regarding [the photographer's] creative touch on the photo e.g., choosing the exact pose, camera angle, focal length of lens, aperture, shutter speed, lighting, and the photo's color," and because "[i]nspection of the photo reveals that it is more creative than informational or functional and that [the photographer] as a professional wedding photographer, took special care in taking the photo and making sure it depicted the appropriate tone for the occasion" the Court stated that this factor did not favor fair use.

With regard to the third factor, the amount and substantiality of the portion used in relation to the copyrighted work as a whole, the Court found that while the defendants were correct in arguing that they only used about 20 percent of the work, that 20 percent was "the focal point, the most important portion of the photo: Edwards and Privitere [the couple] holding hands and kissing"; thus, the "quantity of a taking does not necessarily determine the quality of the taking." Quoting Judge Learned Hand that "no plagiarist can excuse the wrong by showing how much of his work he did not pirate,"[10] the Court found that the third factor also did not favor fair use.

Finally, when considering the fourth factor, the effect of the use upon the potential market for or value of the copyrighted work, the Court noted the requirement "to consider not only the extent of market harm caused by the particular actions of the alleged infringer, but also whether the unrestricted and widespread conduct engaged in by the defendant . . . would result in a substantially adverse impact on the potential market for the original." This inquiry "must take account not only of the harm to the original but also to the market for derivative works" and that "this factor, more than any other factor, is evidence driven." Here, the Court declined to "speculate on the photo's market and potential market," believing "that would be improper."

Balancing all the factors together, the Court found "that the plaintiffs had stated a plausible copyright infringement claim under the Copyright Act" and denied the defendants' motion to dismiss the copyright infringement claim based on the fair use doctrine. In a sad but cautionary postscript, the court awarded the photographer a mere $2,501 judgment to cover costs related to her claim because the work was not registered prior to the infringement.

As seen earlier, if a claim is alleged with the required specificity regarding the "range of creative choices available in selecting and arranging the photo's elements," examining aspects like "lighting, camera angle, depth of field, and selection of foreground and background elements,"[11] there will be a greater likelihood that a court will find the plaintiff has met his or her burden. But even in cases where the image passes the copyrightability threshold, courts may wrongly decide the fair use question.

Brammer v. Violent Hues, LLC is a recent case where the lower court not only got all four fair use factors wrong, but then added insult to injury by finding that the infringers used the photo "in good faith."[12] This case began when Violent Hues Production, LLC, a film festival organizer, used a professional time-lapse night photo on its website to promote a festival. The photographer, Russell Brammer, then sued for copyright infringement, with Violent Hues claiming a fair use defense. The district court agreed with the defendant, and granted summary judgment, dismissing the claim. The US Court of Appeals for the Fourth Circuit resoundingly reversed and remanded that dismissal, finding that under the four-factor test for fair use, the use was not transformative, was commercial as well as creative (rather than factual), and harmed Brammer's potential market for the work. The Fourth Circuit also went on to find that the lower court erred in its "good faith" determination, first because "good faith" is not a proper part of a fair use analysis, but more overly because the belief by the defendant that "the Photo was freely available" runs counter to the fact "that all contemporary photographs are presumptively under copyright [under] 17 U.S.C. § 302(a)."

Explaining fair use, the Fourth Court aptly noted:

> The fair use affirmative defense exists to advance copyright's purpose of "promot[ing] the Progress of Science and useful Arts." U.S. Const. art. I, § 8, cl. 8; *see also Campbell v. Acuff-Rose Music, Inc.*, 510 U.S. 569, 575 (1994). The defense does so by allowing "others to build freely upon the ideas and information conveyed by a work." *Feist Publ'ns, Inc. v. Rural Tel. Serv. Co.*, 499 U.S. 340, 350 (1991). **But fair use "is not designed to protect lazy appropriators**. Its goal instead is to facilitate a class of uses that would not be possible if users always had to negotiate with copyright proprietors." *Kienitz v. Sconnie Nation LLC*, 766 F.3d 756, 759 (7th Cir. 2014).[13]

But just as we saw in *Brammer*, lower courts often get fair use wrong in cases that do not involve photographs or small, individual creators. *Dr. Seuss Enterprises v. ComicMix LLC* is now on appeal to the US Court of Appeals for the Ninth Circuit.[14] In *ComicMix*, the district court granted summary judgment to the defendants, finding that the "mash-up" of Dr. Seuss's *Oh, the Places You'll Go!* with elements from *Star Trek* into *Oh, the Places You'll Boldly Go!* constituted fair use because it copied no more of the original work than was necessary to accomplish their purpose, was highly transformative, and "the harm to Plaintiff's market remain[ed] speculative." This ruling came even though twice before, the same court had denied the defendant's motion to dismiss the copyright infringement claim under fair use.

More troubling was the fact that the *Boldly* creator testified that he did "slavishly copy" not only Seuss's illustration style, but also his composition, coloring, and almost all the rest of the expressive elements of Seuss's original work. Additionally, "the Court declined to find that 'Boldly' is a parody" nor a work of commentary about the original, but rather a different use of Seuss's expressive elements, which, in most cases, would be seen as a derivative work protected under the exclusive right of the copyright owner to produce such works.

What may be of some comfort is that the Ninth Circuit has previously ruled on a similar case also involving a Dr. Seuss book with a more favorable result along with establishing controlling precedent. The appeal in *Dr. Seuss Enterprises, L.P. v. Penguin Books USA, Inc.* involved another alleged "parody" or "mash-up" entitled *The Cat NOT in the Hat*.[15] In that book, the O.J. Simpson murder trial was revisited in rhyming Dr. Seuss style. Not only did the Ninth Circuit "conclude that the district court's finding that Seuss showed a likelihood of success on the merits of the copyright claim was not clearly erroneous," the court also affirmed a preliminary injunction against distribution of the book (a much higher legal standard to meet). In doing so, the Court found that the use was not transformative and was not a parody because while "broadly mimic[ing] Dr. Seuss' characteristic style, it does not hold *his style* up to ridicule." The Court also found that there was "no effort to create a transformative work with 'new expression, meaning, or message'" and the creative, imaginative, and original nature of the plaintiff's work weighed against fair use. Additionally, the Court held that the defendant copied substantial portions of the "highly expressive core" of the plaintiff's work. Finally, because the Court found that the use was non-transformative and commercial, it concluded "that market substitution is at least more certain, and market harm may be more readily inferred." Many copyright experts believe that this holding should have been recognized and followed by the *Boldly* trial court which is expected to be rectified by the Ninth Circuit on appeal.

In another case involving a fair use defense, a photographer, Jonathan Otto, took a photo on his iPhone of President Trump at a private wedding, which was subsequently published by several media outlets. In that case, *Otto v. Hearst Communications, Inc.*, the trial court found that the use by Hearst was not "fair use" and that "[i]t would be antithetical to the purposes of copyright protection to allow media companies to steal personal images and benefit from the fair use defense by simply inserting the photo in an article which only recites factual information—much of which can be gleaned from the photograph itself."[16] The court went on to say "[s]tealing a copyrighted photograph to illustrate a news article, without adding new understanding or meaning to the work, does not transform its purpose—regardless of whether that photograph was created for commercial or personal use."[17]

While the court granted the plaintiff's motion for partial summary judgment on the issues of Hearst's liability for copyright infringement and Hearst's assertion of its affirmative defenses and denied Hearst's motion for partial summary judgment on both the issues of fair use and willfulness, that victory was short-lived when, after a one-day bench trial, the same judge awarded Mr. Otto only $750 (the lowest possible statutory damages award).

Registration and Implied Copyright

While it is true that the US Copyright law confers exclusive rights upon the author of a work as soon as the work is created, there was a question (as well as a split between the courts of appeals) as to whether a copyright owner may file an infringement suit upon application to register the copyright in the work or whether the owner must wait until the Register of Copyrights has acted on that application. In March 2019, the US Supreme Court issued a unanimous opinion in *Fourth Estate Public Benefit Corp. v. Wall-Street.com*, deciding that question by holding that registration occurs, and a copyright claimant may commence an infringement suit, once the US Copyright Office formally registers a copyright and not before.[18]

That opinion had direct implications in a recent case in which Gigi Hadid, a model and popular social media celebrity, was sued by a photographer who alleged that she infringed his copyrighted photo of her when she posted it to Instagram without his permission.[19] In defense of her action, Hadid's lawyers argued that "Ms. Hadid's reposting of the photograph on her personal Instagram page was fair use and consistent with an implied license, and therefore not actionable."[20]

It is not necessary to elaborate on the defendant's four-factor fair use analysis, as it is much a repetition of the same justifications used by most accused infringers. What is more interesting to note is her claim "that Ms. Hadid had an implied license permitting her to repost the photograph on Instagram"[21] because "[s]he stopped to permit the photographer to take her picture and, by posing, contributed to the photograph's protectable elements. And in that moment, the photographer elected to take a photograph, which was indisputably made more valuable through Ms. Hadid's participation in its creation. In other words, only as a result of the mutual actions of Ms. Hadid and the photographer was a photograph of a smiling Ms. Hadid even possible."[22]

The judge never reached the merits or the novel arguments but instead dismissed the case under *Fourth Estate* because the plaintiff failed to formally register his copyright with the US Copyright Office before commencing this case.

Conclusion

As illustrated in the above cases, many of the issues, including market harm; stating allegations in complaints with specificity to help ensure an affirmative ruling on creativity, copyrightability, and authorship; and prompt and timely registration will be crucial in the furtherance of copyright protection as we move into new areas of visual imagery such as selfies and images made using a drone. Until those types of cases become commonplace, with well-established case law, visual journalists will need to remain vigilant and willing to defend their rights against those who believe that they can infringe the work of creators with impunity.

Notes

1 U.S. Copyright Office, Library of Congress, *Compendium of U.S. Copyright Office Practices*, § 313.2 (3rd ed. 2014), https://www.copyright.gov/comp3.
2 Tim Sharp, "The First Hot-Air Balloon, The Greatest Moments in Flight," Space.com, published April 9, 2019, http://www.space.com/16595-montgolfiers-first-balloon-flight.html.
3 "World's First Photograph," Milestones in Photography, National Geographic, https://www.national geographic.com/photography/photos/milestones-photography/#/1459.jpg.
4 "History of Aerial Photography," Professional Aerial Photographers Association, http://www.papainter national.org/history.asp.
5 "History of Aerial Photography."
6 James Wallace Black, "Boston, as the Eagle and the Wild Goose See It," The Met Collection, The Metropolitan Museum of Art, http://www.metmuseum.org/Collections/search-the-collections/283189.
7 Oliver Wendell Holmes, "Doings of the Sunbeam," *Atlantic Monthly* 12, no. 69 (1863), http://www.gutenberg.org/files/15016/15016-h/15016-h.htm#sunbeam.
8 "Unmanned Aircraft Systems (UAS)," Federal Aviation Administration, last modified April 30, 2020, https://www.faa.gov/uas.
9 Hill v. Pub. Advocate of the United States, 35 F. Supp. 3d 1347 (D. Colo. 2014).
10 Sheldon v. Metro-Goldwyn Pictures Corp., 81 F.3d 49, 56 (2d Cir. 1936), *cert. denied*, 298 U.S. 669 (1936).
11 Rentmeester v. Nike, Inc., 883 F.3d 1111, 1120–21 (9th Cir. 2018).
12 Brammer v. Violent Hues Prods., LLC, 922 F.3d 255, 266 (4th Cir. 2019).
13 *Brammer,* 922 F.3d at 262 (emphasis added).
14 Dr. Seuss Enters., L.P. v. ComicMix LLC, 372 F. Supp. 3d 1101 (S.D. Cal. 2019).
15 Dr. Seuss Enters., L.P. v. Penguin Books USA, Inc., 109 F.3d 1394 (9th Cir. 1997).
16 Otto v. Hearst Commc'ns, Inc., 345 F. Supp. 3d 412, 428 (S.D.N.Y. 2018).
17 *Otto,* 345 F. Supp. 3d at 419.
18 Fourth Estate Pub. Benefit Corp. v. Wall-Street.com, LLC, 139 S. Ct. 881 (2019).
19 XClusive-Lee, Inc. v. Hadid, No. 19-CV-520-PKC-CLP, 2019 WL 3281013 (E.D.N.Y. July 18, 2019).
20 Memorandum of Law in Support of Defendant's Motion to Dismiss at 7, XClusive-Lee, Inc. v. Hadid, 2019 WL 3281013 (E.D.N.Y. 2019) (No. 19 Civ. 520).
21 XClusive-Lee, Inc., 2019 WL 3281013 at 12.
22 *Id.* at 13.

3.4

SOCIAL MEDIA

Use It and Lose It?

Joseph T. Baio

When the ground first shook under him, Daniel Morel's friend thought it was funny. Morel's photograph taken at that moment caught his friend in a shallow squat, elbows thrust out, laughing but a bit puzzled. It turned out that this was no laughing matter.

Over the next forty-five minutes, Morel, a professional photojournalist from Haiti, walked the familiar but radically transformed streets of Port-au-Prince and recorded the immediate aftermath of what may be the greatest natural disaster of our time: the 7.0-magnitude earthquake that devastated Haiti on January 12, 2010, killing perhaps 250,000 or more adults and children. By the time he got to the badly damaged remains of his father's former bakery, Morel had taken more than 300 photographs that captured the chaos, devastation, loss of life, and heroic acts of rescue that followed the initial quake, an event that lasted fewer than thirty seconds.

When he reached the tenuous safety of his hotel, Morel downloaded the pictures to his computer and did a tight edit, culling what he thought were the fifteen best pictures to tell the story of what he had witnessed. He uploaded those pictures to Twitter, identifying himself as the creator of the works and letting potential users know how they could reach him if they wanted to license his works for a fee.[1] He then hunkered down for a restless night of aftershocks, relying on intermittent power from generators that would have to last for who knew how long.

Within hours after Morel posted his work, another Twitter user posted the images under his name. Agence France-Presse (AFP) and its partner, Getty Images, downloaded eight of the pictures (stripped of their metadata), with a misidentified author, and began transmitting the images, including their own source credit lines, to more than a thousand subscribers and licensees, all without permission from or payment to Morel. The next day, while Morel was still in Haiti documenting the aftermath, the wrongfully credited images appeared on the front pages and electronic versions of newspapers and magazines worldwide, on countless websites, and on major international networks, many of which acquired the pictures from AFP or Getty Images.[2]

Almost three years later, and after numerous legal skirmishes between Morel and his well-heeled opponents (one of which, AFP, actually started the legal proceedings *by suing Morel*), a federal jury in the Southern District of New York awarded Morel $1,220,000 in statutory damages for defendants' copyright infringements and violations of the Digital Millennium Copyright Act (DMCA).[3] With a mixture of persistence, courage, skill, and good fortune, Morel was able to vindicate some of his legal rights in the works he created despite having transmitted them over social media. Most are not so fortunate.

This chapter discusses the legal hazards that creators of copyright-protected materials face when they post their visual works on the internet, particularly on social media. It also identifies the legal protections under the US copyright laws that are available to content creators who post their works on social media, and the significant, sometimes overwhelming, legal and factual barriers they must overcome to preserve and advance their legal rights in the works they create and disseminate.

To Post or Not to Post: That Is the (First) Question

The starting point for content creators is whether to post work on any social network at all. The act of posting anything on publicly available electronic platforms exposes the work to unauthorized but ultimately "fair use"[4] and outright piracy, irrespective of the author's adoption of pre-publication protections, the Terms of Service (TOS) of the internet platform that is used by the author to transmit the work, and the rights granted copyright owners to control the use and to exclusively exploit the commercial potential of their creations. It is estimated that as many as 2.5 billion images (or 85 percent of those posted) are used without a license every day.[5] If the potential for negative impacts from posting—whether economic, reputational, or emotional—exceeds the expected gains, the author might rationally decide not to post, given the high likelihood of misappropriation.

The fact is, in most cases, the financial and non-monetary costs of suing a defendant for copyright infringement for misappropriating images from social media—particularly for a single image or a few pictures—will dwarf any reasonably possible recovery, let alone the actual amounts eventually recovered by litigants. Still, content creators can take steps, both before transmitting images and after their work is wrongfully exploited, to protect their work, halt, or at least impede, further misappropriations, and recover damages from infringers.

Pre-Posting Protections: What Can You Do to Protect the Work You Created?

If the decision is made to post, there are many tools the author can use to increase the chances that the transmitted work will not be misappropriated and to achieve the full protection of the law. No approach is foolproof, however, and some come with a cost. The tools include (particularly for works with a visual component): adding a copyright notice, DMCA badge, watermark, or transparent file overlay; reducing the resolution, size, and quality of the posted work; impairing the viewer's ability to right-click or otherwise copy the work; and registering for copyright.

As described elsewhere in this book, the author's copyright exists at the moment of creation (when the expression of the idea is fixed in a tangible medium), independent of any copyright notice affixed to the work or registration with the Copyright Office.[6] Adding a copyright notice, however, shows viewers that the author knows the work is protected, and can remove from infringers' defenses the argument that they were innocent—that is, that they did not know the work had copyright protection. Timely registration gives the author the ability to seek statutory damages, which are recoverable even if the plaintiff cannot prove actual damages.[7]

Many of the other techniques impair the visual quality of the image, discouraging copying but also negatively affecting the intended recipients' experience and enjoyment. In addition, technological advances continue to enable determined infringers to overcome or reverse any self-help methods used by authors. It is therefore not surprising that the vast majority of items sent through social media have no pre-publication protections embedded in the uploaded images.

Posting on Social Media: The Terms of Service (TOS) May Determine Your Rights in Any Posted Content

Joining the pantheon of *Great Lies Told By Good People* is this: "I have read and agreed to the Terms of Service for this site."

Fortunately, the declarant is not under oath when affirming this falsehood with a single, thoughtless click. Unfortunately, the "small print" that is not read (or is not understood even if read) can substantially impair or eliminate the ability of a content creator to prevent others from downloading or exploiting protected content. Clicker beware!

In his case against AFP and Getty Images, Morel was saved, in part, by Twitter's existing TOS,[8] which provided:

- *You retain your rights to any Content you submit, post, or display on or through the Services.*
- *By submitting . . . Content on or through the Services, you grant us a worldwide, non-exclusive, royalty-free license (with the right to sublicense) to use, copy, reproduce, process, adapt, modify, publish, transmit, display, and distribute such Content in any and all media.*
- *You agree that this license includes the right for Twitter to make such Content available to other companies, organizations, or individuals who partner with Twitter.*
- *Such additional uses by Twitter, or other companies, organizations, or individuals who partner with Twitter, may be made with no compensation paid to you with respect to the Content that you submit.*

Based on these terms, the Court rejected the argument that AFP—a Twitter user—secured a license to publish and commercially exploit the images that Morel uploaded on Twitter. As the Court noted, the TOS expressly recognized and preserved Morel's retention of rights in his own content, and AFP was neither a sublicensee, partner, nor third-party beneficiary of the rights of Twitter.[9]

Social media companies' TOS likely will determine the extent to which a content creator legally can limit the use of, and retain the exclusive ability to commercially benefit from, works that are transmitted over social networks. That reality alone means that publishing work on any social media, through any intermediary, or on any third-party website is fraught with peril for a number of reasons.

First, the extent to which companies' TOS recognize and preserve the rights of content providers varies widely, ranging from very protective to practically confiscatory. A number of online watchdogs and services keep track of and rate the TOS policies of major social networks and transmitters of content, providing authors a useful tool to cut through the sometimes impenetrable legalese and help them evaluate what they are giving up.[10] Second, the TOS of media companies frequently grant themselves the right to use, commercially exploit, and sublicense uploaded content without any compensation to the author, even when the terms purport to preserve the ownership rights of the author. Uploaders can find the rug pulled out from under them if the media company uses such terms to sublicense its rights to the "infringing" user. Third, companies frequently reserve the right unilaterally to amend their TOS at any time and for any reason. For example, Twitter amended its TOS as of January 1, 2020. The new terms arguably would have stripped Morel of his ability to successfully prosecute his lawsuit against AFP and Getty Images. The current Twitter terms now include the following:

> *This license authorizes us to make your Content available to the rest of the world **and to let others do the same**. You agree that this license includes the right for Twitter to provide, promote, and improve the Services and to make Content submitted to or through the Services available to other companies, organizations or individuals for the syndication, broadcast, distribution, Retweet, promotion or publication of such Content on other media and services, subject to our terms and conditions for such Content use.* (Emphasis added).

Although the breadth of this new provision has not been tested in any court, a Twitter user may point to it to argue that claimants like Morel and others have given up their rights to prevent *any* Twitter customer from using uploaded work in any way the customer sees fit. Fourth, with rare exceptions, the US courts typically enforce companies' TOS, even when they include jargon-heavy and buried terms.

A recent federal district court decision highlights some of the evolving legal pitfalls awaiting content producers who upload their work to social media. In *Sinclair v. Ziff Davis, LLC,*[11] Stephanie Sinclair, a Pulitzer-prize-winning photojournalist and Instagram user, sued Mashable, a media and entertainment platform, and its parent company, Ziff Davis, for copyright infringement after Mashable posted one of Sinclair's copyrighted photographs on its website. In reaching her decision, Judge Kimba M. Wood took the parties on a serpentine journey through Instagram's interconnected TOS, Platform Policy and Privacy Policy, the "public" status of Sinclair's Instagram account, the technical process that Mashable used to access and display the copyrighted work, and the rights that the respective parties acquired or granted on the path to litigation. At the end of the road, Judge Wood held that Mashable used the photograph pursuant to a valid sublicense from Instagram, so its use of the image did not infringe Sinclair's copyright.[12]

The basic facts are straightforward. Initially, Mashable offered Sinclair fifty dollars to use her photograph to accompany its online article about women photographers. When she refused, Mashable promptly accessed the same image that Sinclair had posted on Instagram and included a copy of the photograph along with the article without paying Sinclair anything. The lawsuit followed.

The Court began its documentary analysis with Instagram's TOS, which Sinclair conceded was binding on her. The TOS granted Instagram "a non-exclusive, fully paid and royalty-free, transferable, sub-licensable, worldwide license to the Content . . . [posted] on or through [Instagram], subject to [Instagram's] Privacy Policy." The Privacy Policy, embodied in a separate document, allowed users to designate their accounts as "private" or "public." Sinclair had selected the "public" setting, which rendered her content searchable under the Privacy Policy and subject to use by others via Instagram's "application programming interface," or "API." Under Instagram's Platform Policy—yet another document—API enables users to "embed" publicly posted content on their websites. "Embedding" allows a website coder to incorporate content that is located on a third-party's server into the coder's website, where the image can be seen by those who visit the website. Mashable used Instagram's API to embed Sinclair's publicly posted image on Instagram, which image was included in the article on women photographers.[13]

Judge Wood rejected every argument raised by Sinclair to support her claim, including her contention that the sublicense was invalid because it was created by a series of highly complex, arcane, convoluted, and interconnected documents. While the court agreed that "Instagram could certainly make its user agreements more concise and accessible," Judge Wood noted that the law does not require anyone to do so. Complaint dismissed and case closed (for now).

The *Sinclair* case, while limited to its facts, should trouble any content creator who wants to reach a large audience through social media and still maintain control over the use of that content. Like any Instagram user, Sinclair could have selected the "private" setting to preserve her legal rights, but that would have severely limited her viewing audience. And while it is true that Judge Wood's decision turned on Mashable's use of the "Embed" feature, "copying" technology is constantly evolving, and media companies and others retain the rights to grant sublicenses without compensation to authors and to amend their policies at will. Who can say where and when the next copyright-killing trap door will be found?

Your Works Have Been Pirated: What Can You Do to Pursue Your Rights and Be Compensated?

Without Going to Court

The most likely, less costly, and least painful way to obtain some measure of justice against online infringers is to take action before, and perhaps instead of, starting a lawsuit. This approach can take a number of forms that can be pursued with or without the benefit of a lawyer:

Cease and Desist Demand

If the author or creator finds anyone using the work without permission on their website or otherwise, the author can send cease and desist letters to each infringer. The letters should be as specific as possible about the work's creation, the author's ownership, and the infringing use discovered. The letter can include a demand for money or an invitation to begin settlement discussions, noting that the next step will be the filing of a lawsuit if the infringer ignores the demand. Failure to comply with the demand can lead to a finding that the infringers acted "willfully," subjecting them to greater damages.

DMCA Takedown Notice

If a content creator discovers her work appearing without permission on sites run by internet service providers (ISPs), such as Facebook, Instagram, and YouTube, the author can demand in writing that the ISPs expeditiously remove, or disable access to, the work.[14] To be effective, the sender of the notice must be the owner of the work and include additional information spelled out in the statute. If the recipient of the notice meets the requirements of the statute and takes down the content promptly, the recipient may be able to rely on the statutory safe harbor and avoid money damages. Most ISPs in the US will honor a valid notice.

Negotiated Resolution

An early monetary settlement may be possible, depending in large part on the infringer's attitude, belief in its right to use the work, financial wherewithal, and appetite for potential litigation. Settlements take two to tango, however, and a content creator with exaggerated notions of the value of the work can end the prospects for settlement, even if the infringer is prepared to cough up some money.

The Terrors and Pleasures of Litigation

Copyright litigation is complex and time-consuming, and the costs of litigating a copyright lawsuit in federal court can easily exceed the amount recovered by a successful plaintiff. *Otto v. Hearst Communications, Inc.*[15] illustrates some of the many barriers litigants must overcome, even when there is no question that the work at issue is protected by copyright law and the defendant is an infringer without a legitimate defense.

Jonathan Otto, the plaintiff, was not a professional photographer; he called himself "a guy with a cell phone." In June, 2017, he was attending a wedding held at Trump National Golf Course when President Trump made a surprise appearance during the reception. Otto took a not-so-artful snapshot of the President clasping hands with the bride. Otto texted the image to another guest at the wedding, but did not send it through any social media himself. The next morning, Otto discovered that the image had gone viral, having been posted on Instagram by a family member of the bride. The image appeared on several media outlets, including Esquire.com, operated by Hearst Communications. The article to which the photo was attached was entitled, "President Trump is the Ultimate Wedding Crasher."

Judge Gregory H. Woods described what happened next:

> Perhaps recognizing a lucrative business opportunity, Otto retained counsel the following day and quickly filed a copyright in the image. Otto brought this action, among several others against various media publishers, alleging that his copyright in the photograph had been infringed.[16]

Hearst raised a gaggle of defenses against the cell phone picture taker, including: The company's publication was non-infringing or protected by the "fair use" doctrine; Otto waived his rights, consented to the use, or granted an implied license to others when he texted it to the wedding guest without restriction; and Otto released his claim by virtue of his conduct.

In a thirty-one-page decision, Judge Woods dismissed all the affirmative defenses and ruled on summary judgment that Otto owned a valid and enforceable copyright in the picture. Hearst actually copied and published the work, thereby infringing upon Otto's exclusive right to control the reproduction and use of his photograph. Victory for the amateur picture taker!

The Judge's decision, however, did not end the matter. There still had to be a trial to determine whether Hearst's infringement was "willful" and what damages Otto was entitled to receive as a result of that infringement.[17] A non-jury trial was held on July 15, 2019. Four days later, Judge Woods read his decision from the bench.[18] It was not good for the amateur photographer.

The Judge noted that Otto, as plaintiff, had the burden of proof with respect to both issues that were tried. Interweaving the facts presented with established law, Judge Woods first held that Otto did not prove that Hearst acted "willfully"—that is: (1) with actual awareness of its infringing activity; or (2) with "reckless disregard" for, or "willful blindness" as to, Otto's copyright.[19]

In reaching that conclusion, the Court considered, among other things, Hearst's low incident of alleged infringement compared to the large number of images the company published on a monthly basis, the extent of its copyright compliance training for employees, and the availability of expert lawyers and senior editors for consultation, supporting the notion that Hearst generally and thoughtfully considered the rights of third-party content suppliers. The Court also recited witness testimony (to the extent it was offered) about the actions taken by the employees who decided to include the image along with the article, finding it credible and proof of the absence of bad faith.

The Court's finding that Hearst did not act willfully had a very significant impact on Otto's claim for damages. A plaintiff in a Copyright Act case must eventually elect either: (1) the actual damages suffered by the author plus the infringer's non-duplicative profits resulting from the infringement; or (2) "statutory damages," which are established ranges per work depending on the relative culpability of the infringer. The statutory amount for a wholly innocent infringer[20] can be as low as $200 per work and as high as $30,000 per work, while the range for a willful infringer starts at $30,000 and caps out at $150,000 per work.[21] Infringers whose conduct falls between the two extremes—as Judge Woods found in this case—face statutory damages as low as $750 to as much as $30,000 per work.[22]

Unsurprisingly, Otto argued for the maximum amount or close to it, while Hearst claimed that nothing above the minimum was justifiable under the facts and law. In the oral ruling, which covered thirty-four transcript pages, the Court awarded Otto $750, the smallest amount permissible under the law.

The starting point for Judge Woods was the six-part test established in *Bryant v. Media Right Products, Inc.*[23] Under *Bryant,* the fact-finder should consider: "The infringer's state of mind;

(2) the expenses saved, and profits earned, by the infringer; (3) the revenue lost by the copyright holder; (4) the deterrent effect on the infringer and third parties; (5) the infringer's cooperation in providing evidence concerning the value of the infringing material; and (6) the conduct and attitude of the parties."

The Court had already held that the defendant's state of mind was not "willful." Judge Woods also found that the fifth and sixth factors—which are quite vague—were neutral on the facts presented and were given no weight in the Court's determination of a proper statutory damages amount. Judge Woods then considered the second and third factors, finding that the only revenue lost by Otto and expense saved by Hearst was the amount of the reasonable license fee that Hearst did not pay to Otto. At trial, two experts testified about the amount of that reasonable fee; both were hired by Hearst. Otto offered no witness or separate evidence on the subject.

The experts, whom the Court found credible, testified about (1) the lack of uniqueness "high quality" in Otto's snapshot; (2) the standard licensing fees that Hearst paid for the use of a single "celebrity" photograph on Esquire.com from 2015 to 2017 ($125 before any discount); and (3) the fees typically negotiated by other large media companies for images like Otto's photographs ($25 to $50). Given the ad-based business plan of Esquire.com, the Judge also found that the most revenue Hearst might have realized from the ads that ran alongside the article was $148.99.[24]

Otto's counsel argued that the image should be valued at $4,000, before adding any multiplier to deter infringers, because there was evidence that Hearst was willing to pay that amount for a particular commissioned image. Judge Woods, finding this argument "wholly implausible," counted off the various things that Otto's snapshot was not: It was not commissioned, not a professional photograph, not well-composed, not unique because other wedding guests took similar photographs, and not used exclusively by Hearst. Stating the obvious, he wrote that not all photographs are worth the same amount. The Duchess of Sussex can expect to receive more for a staged photo of her child, the Judge noted, than new parents could expect for an iPhone snap of their bundle of joy. Otto was no Duchess of Sussex.

Finally, the Court considered the deterrent effect of the award on Hearst and third parties, noting that statutory awards are not merely compensatory, but are also meant to discourage wrongful conduct.[25] The Court also recognized that the defendant's size and financial assets are highly relevant to arriving at an appropriate statutory damages award. Still, because he found a lack of evidence that Hearst generally disregarded the rights of copyright owners, Judge Woods concluded that a large statutory damages award was not necessary to deter Hearst against future infringement.

Otto also argued that there is a broad need for general deterrence against infringers based on an alleged "flooding" of courts with copyright infringement cases. Judge Woods rejected the argument finding no evidence demonstrating a deluge of filings.

After evaluating all of the *Bryant* factors, the Court concluded that the reasonable license fee for Otto's work was $100. The Judge noted that courts in the Second Circuit commonly award statutory damages of between three and five times the reasonable license fee where the defendant's conduct—like Hearst's—was neither willful nor innocent. Finding that a multiplier greater than 7.5 would be excessive, the Court awarded plaintiff statutory damages of $750, the minimum this "successful" litigant could recover under the law.

On the surface, Morel "won" and Otto "lost" (so far) their cases, even though they both owned the copyright to their work, used social media to transmit their work, had media giants infringe their copyrights, and were awarded statutory damages. Plus, they were both in the "right" place at the "right" time when their respective events occurred.

There also were major differences between the two, however, as there always will be among litigants. Morel was a professional photojournalist with decades of experience, while Otto was a wedding guest with a cell phone. Morel sought and received a jury trial and Otto went for a bench trial. The Haitian earthquake was a historically significant event, and Morel was one of the only professional photographers on the ground who immediately jumped into the fray and took iconic, prize-winning photographs of the earliest moments of the disaster.[26] Otto haphazardly photographed an insignificant though mildly amusing moment that happened to match up nicely with a soap bubble of an article that could have used any number of snapshots taken by the many guests who attended the twenty-four or so weddings that the President had habitually crashed on Trump properties.

But the final judgment in a case rarely tells the whole story about who won and who lost. Before diving deeper into that issue, there is another critical factor to consider before evaluating whether, as a practical matter, when you post it, you lose it: the legal costs that will be incurred by content providers hoping to vindicate their legal rights in federal courts.

Do the Infringers Have to Pay Your Legal Fees If You Win?

Unlike in other common-law countries, the general rule in the US is that the losing party in a litigation does not pay the legal fees of the winner. In the absence of an express fee-shifting provision applicable to a particular claim or defense, each party in a US litigation must bear its own legal costs and major expenses. The Copyright Act, as well as other statutory provisions protecting intellectual property, includes such a fee-shifting provision. Section 505 states:

> In any civil action under this title, the court in its discretion may allow the recovery of full costs by or against any party other than the United States or an officer thereof. Except as otherwise provided by this title, the court may also award a reasonable attorney's fee to the prevailing party as part of the costs.

The statute gives little guidance as to how the trial court is to determine who the prevailing party is in all cases and what that party must show in order to recoup its legal fees. The federal courts, including the Supreme Court of the United States, have helped clarify the applicable standards.

A prevailing party is one who "[s]ecures a judgment on the merits or a court-ordered consent decree."[27] In *AFP v. Morel*, the Court evaluated Morel's request for legal fees and held that Morel was unquestionably the prevailing party in light of his substantial recovery at trial. The plaintiff in *Otto v. Hearst* asserted in his pending request for attorney's fees that he is the prevailing party because he secured a judgment awarding damages, small though it was.

In two decisions delivered twenty-two years apart, the Supreme Court identified the factors a trial judge should weigh in deciding whether to award attorney's fees to the prevailing party under Section 505. In *Fogerty v. Fantasy, Inc.*,[28] the Court held that a district court should not award fees as a matter of course but should make a more particularized, case-by-case assessment designed to further the goals of the Copyright Act. Prevailing parties must be treated the same way; defendants should be encouraged to litigate meritorious defenses to the same extent that plaintiffs are encouraged to litigate valid infringement claims.

The Court then identified several non-exclusive factors to be considered, including "frivolousness, motivation, objective unreasonableness and the need in particular circumstances to advance considerations of compensation and deterrence."[29] These factors are themselves quite vague and overlap somewhat with those that a fact-finder should consider in assessing the appropriate level of statutory damages. After letting the lower courts wrestle with the factors for a couple of decades, and finding a split in the way those courts were evaluating whether to award attorney's fees,[30] the Supreme Court revisited the issue in *Kirtsaeng v. John Wiley & Sons*.[31]

Writing for a unanimous Court, Justice Elena. Kagan noted that a number of courts in the Second Circuit had given too much weight to the reasonableness of a losing party's litigating positions, a factor that is important in evaluating whether to award attorney's fees but one that should not be dispositive of the issue. Instead, the Court held, district court judges should give weight to *all* the factors identified in *Fogerty*. The Court once again offered little guidance, however, as to what those other factors actually encompass and how they should be weighed.[32]

Morel's request for attorney's fees, which was decided a year before the *Kirtsaeng* opinion, was denied.[33] Finding that "Morel fought a fair fight and won," Judge Nathan noted that this was a close case on the merits. Following Second Circuit precedents, Judge Nathan started with the objective reasonableness of the defendants' litigation positions, stating that it was the prominent factor to be considered. The Court found that the legal positions advanced by the defendants were objectively reasonable, particularly those addressing novel issues that could help further define the contours of copyright law in the digital age.

While the Court considered the "David versus Goliath(s)" aspects of the case, the Court found that the size of Morel's award provided both adequate compensation to him and remedy enough to discourage the media giants from infringing in the future. The other factors were either neutral or in the defendants' favor, in the Court's view.

In January 2020, the Court denied Otto's request in part because it found that Otto forced litigation in pursuit of "an unjustifiably inflated claim," and it did not believe that Hearst needed a "high statutory damages award" to deter it against future infringement.[34]

What Is the Answer under Current Law to the Question: "Social Media: Use It and Lose It?"

If the past is any predictor of the future, then the vast majority of people who post original content on social media will lose all control over what they post, if not legally then surely as a practical matter. Most will not care. Most social media users who post selfies or photos of their friends and relatives at gatherings (or everything they eat and drink in a day), videos of their beloved cats or cute pet tricks, or recordings of the lullabies they sing to their precious babies, to name just a few popular posting categories, likely do not want to control the use of their content and are delighted if it goes "viral." Some will feel differently, particularly if the acquirer uses it without permission and for a commercial benefit. So what should the latter consider before taking legal action against infringers?

Assuming the content is protectable under US copyright laws and the user cannot successfully assert a "fair use" defense,[35] potential copyright holders should consider and evaluate the following before deciding to press his claims in federal court:

The Number of Works Misappropriated

In general, the more works that are misappropriated, the greater the potential for a larger recovery, particularly if the author eventually accepts statutory damages. As already noted, the recovery caps for statutory damages limit the potential for an award for each work. Single-work litigations, therefore, can be a risky proposition, as Otto and many other determined plaintiffs have found.

But a claim that seeks recoveries for a lot of works can fail just as easily as an unsuccessful effort to collect for a single picture. In *Zuma Press, Inc. v. Getty Images (US), Inc.*,[36] the plaintiff claimed that Getty Images infringed the plaintiff's copyright in 47,048 images by displaying them and offering to license them. Getty Images had complied with Zuma's takedown notice after earning less than $100 in licensing fees. Zuma nevertheless sued for copyright infringement and under Section 1202 of the DMCA for intentionally altering the copyright attribution information contained in the images, hoping no doubt for a windfall in statutory damages.

The Court ended Zuma's quest on summary judgment. The Court found that the undisputed facts showed that Zuma actually caused Getty to confuse Zuma's images with those that Getty had been authorized to use. Zuma created this confusion by engaging in an elaborate program of zig-zagging licenses, transfers of rights, and the commingling of images, all with the intent to deceive Getty Images. The Court barred the plaintiff's copyright claims under the equitable estoppel defense and dismissed the DMCA claims because Zuma failed to show that the defendant acted with the requisite intent to falsify copyright management information.

Conversely, the infringement of a single image can yield a big award if, for example, the content creator can successfully prove significant actual damages. In *Davidson v. United States*,[37] the sculptor of a replica of the Statue of Liberty that was planted in front of a Las Vegas casino sued the US, acting through the US Postal Service, for infringing his copyright by using a cropped version of a photograph of the face of his replica on billions of postage stamps.

The Court found that Davidson's replica, which altered Lady Liberty's face by adding elements of his grandmother's features, was copyright-protected, and that the Postal Service's use of a cropped photograph of the Las Vegas knockoff constituted copyright infringement. After walking through a blizzard of expert testimony, the Court awarded Davidson damages in the amount of $3,554,946.95, plus interest, despite the fact that the Postal Service offered testimony that it had never paid any license fee in excess of $5,000. A very nice payday for an artist who received a net amount of under $200,000 to construct and deliver the whole structure.

The Number and Identity of the Infringers and the Relevant Jurisdiction

Sometimes, like in *Davidson*, there is only one infringer; in other cases, like *Morel* and *Otto*, there are many. When more than one infringer is involved, the author may be able to secure settlements (most of which are not public) and win judgments from each infringer for each work that was misappropriated.[38] Under Section 504(c)(1) of the Copyright Act, however, an aggrieved party is only entitled to *one statutory award per work* against infringers who are jointly and severally liable. The statute provides:

> Except as provided by clause (2) of this subsection, the copyright owner may elect . . . an award of statutory damages for all infringements involved in the action, with respect to any one work, for which any one infringer is liable individually, or for which any two or more infringers are liable jointly and severally, in a sum of not less than $750 or more than $30,000 as the court considers just.

Litigants are "jointly and severally liable" for infringement of a copyright when they "participate in, exercise control over, or benefit from an infringement."[39] Various federal jurisdictions, however, interpret the "one award per work" very differently, and the different interpretations can have a monumental impact on the size of a potential statutory award.[40]

In *Arista Records LLC v. Lime Group LLC*,[41] for example, several record companies successfully sued an online file-sharing service, LimeWire, and its owner for secondary copyright infringement.[42] Plaintiffs argued that they were not limited to one award per work, but rather were entitled to a separate statutory award from LimeWire for each infringement of each song by its many users. If one hundred different users each downloaded the same individual recording through LimeWire's software, the record industry claimed that it was entitled to one hundred statutory awards against the defendants for the infringements of that single song because the individual users, who acted independently from one another, were not jointly and severally liable with each other, even though LimeWire was jointly and severally liable with each infringer.

Although plaintiffs identified approximately 10,000 individual songs that had been infringed, they claimed that LimeWire's legion of users were responsible for an estimated 500,000 illegal downloads of those songs. Based on their theory, the plaintiffs claimed that they were therefore entitled to 500,000 statutory awards against LimeWire and its founder. In effect, the record companies argued that they were entitled to a maximum statutory recovery of $75 trillion, more than the annual GDP of the world.[43] Following the canon that courts should avoid endorsing statutory interpretations that would lead to absurd results, District Court Judge Kimba Wood rejected the plaintiffs' theory and held that the correct interpretation of the statute limited plaintiffs to a single statutory damages award per work infringed, regardless of how many individual LimeWire users infringed a particular song.[44]

The *LimeWire* Court expressly rejected the ruling by the Ninth Circuit Court of Appeals in *Columbia Pictures Television v. Krypton Broad. of Birmingham, Inc.*[45] There, the defendant owned a corporation that, in turn, owned three television stations that contributed to the copyright infringements of several television shows by the three different television stations (who were also joined as defendants).[46] Because the three stations were not jointly and severally liable with each other, the stations' owner was liable for three statutory awards for each show that was infringed. Citing other precedents, Judge Wood concluded that the reasoning in *Columbia Pictures* did not apply to situations involving large numbers of infringements, like in *LimeWire*.

The Ninth Circuit has had the last word on the subject (so far). In *Friedman v. Live Nation Merchandise, Inc.*,[47] a case involving one defendant that was responsible for 104 downstream infringements, the Court rejected the principal rationale for the decision in *LimeWire*: that the statute makes no sense when a case involves a massive number of downstream infringements. Such reasoning, the Court noted, "would mean reading the statute in two different ways depending on how many down-the-line violations there were. And it would require us to come up with some definition of the number of violations required to invoke the exception, without any apparent basis for doing so."[48]

The *Friedman* Court still found a way to limit plaintiff's recovery to a single statutory award per work, while claiming to follow the statutory language and the precedent established in *Columbia Pictures*. The Court noted that the statute provides for one statutory award per work "*for all infringements involved in the action*."[49] Downstream infringements, irrespective of their number, cannot be "involved in the action" unless the alleged infringers responsible for those infringements are joined as defendants in the case and are found to be liable as infringers. None were joined in *Friedman*.

For a potential plaintiff with a copyright infringement claim against a solvent defendant responsible for identifiable downstream infringers who can be added as defendants, heading west seems to be the way to go, even if the downstream users are judgment-proof. But the law on this point, like so many statutory and common-law provisions involving internet activity and copyright law, is unsettled and evolving. Perhaps Congress or the Supreme Court someday will give potential litigants a clearer roadmap.

What It Will Cost v. What Reasonably Can Be Expected as Damages

Before embarking on a litigation "adventure," aggrieved authors should consider what it may cost to pursue a copyright suit measured against the realistic damages they can receive at the end of what may be a very long and winding road. While a significant dollar recovery is possible against a moneyed infringer who has cashed in on the content maker's work, such an infringer can put up a ferocious and costly defense if so inclined. The *Morel* case, for example, involved extensive discovery and depositions, over fifteen pre-trial and post-trial motions, an eight-day trial, and considerable post-trial maneuvers. Although his recovery was substantial, Morel's trial counsel racked up $2.5 million in attorney time, none of which was recovered from AFP and Getty Images.[50]

In light of the costs to litigate, many users who transmit their content on social media will "lose it" as a practical matter, even if the law gives them rights they cannot afford to pursue. An alternate tribunal, however, may eventually be created where smaller copyright claims can be resolved in an efficient and effective way.[51] Time will tell.

Notes

1 At the time, Twitter users could add images through Twitpic, an affiliate of Twitter. Morel used Twitpic to upload his pictures, which were transmitted on Twitter in full resolution without a watermark.

2 "Of the Haiti Earthquake," Time video, accessed April 29, 2020, http://content.time.com/time/video/player/0,32068,746598186001_2041945,00.html (Morel explains how he documented the devastating earthquake in Haiti).

3 See Agence France Presse v. Morel, 934 F. Supp. 2d 547 (S.D.N.Y. 2013) (upholding the jury's damages awards). The author was lead trial counsel for Morel.

4 See J. Hughes, "Gorgeous Photograph, Limited Copyright," *infra* at chap. 4 for a discussion of the fair use doctrine.

5 "Copytrack Global Infringement Report 2019," Copytrack, March 2019, accessed April 29, 2020, https://www.copytrack.com/wp-content/uploads/2019/04/190328_Global_Infringement_Report_2019_EN_Online.pdf.

6 In a 2019 decision, however, the Supreme Court held that, with few exceptions, an author cannot sue for copyright infringement in federal court until the Copyright Office has registered the work, a process that could take as long as a year or more after an application is filed. Fourth Estate Pub. Benefit Corp. v. Wall-Street.com, 139 S. Ct. 881 (2019).

7 If registration is made prior to an infringement or for published work, within three months after publication of the work, statutory damages and attorneys' fees may be recovered by the copyright owner. If not, only an award of actual damages suffered by the owner and additional profits made by the infringer may be recovered.

8 Terms of Service go by a variety of names, including Terms and Conditions, Rights and Obligation of Users, and Terms, Conditions, and Privacy Policies, among other labels. They provide the "rules of the road" for users of social media, electronic media, and other customer-interactive sites. A user typically **must** accept the terms in order to use the providers' services.

9 Agence France Presse v. Morel, 934 F. Supp. 2d 547 (S.D.N.Y. 2013).

10 See, e.g., "Terms of Service Didn't Read," accessed April 29, 2020, https://tosdr.org/index.html.

11 Sinclair v. Ziff Davis, LLC, No. 18-CV-790-KMW, 2020 WL 1847841 (S.D.N.Y. April 13, 2020).

12 *Id*. at *2.

13 *Id*. at *3–4. A detailed explanation of the embedding process can be found in Goldman v. Breitbart News Network, LLC, 302 F. Supp. 3d 585, 587 (S.D.N.Y. 2018). In Goldman, the Court found that embedding an image constitutes "display" that is capable of infringing a copyright in the image. *Id*. at 596 (holding that embedding constitutes display but noting the possible viability of license as a defense).

14 17 U.S.C. § 512.

15 Otto v. Hearst Communications, Inc., 345 F. Supp. 3d 412 (S.D.N.Y. 2018).

16 *Otto*, 345 F. Supp. 3d at 419.

17 As frequently happens after a court resolves some but not all issues on summary judgment, the parties renewed settlement discussions. During the negotiations, the Magistrate Judge apparently urged the plaintiff not to be greedy, because the damages to be awarded for the infringement of a single image by a non-professional could be quite small, even if the plaintiff opted for statutory damages. The settlement negotiations concluded unsuccessfully.

18 Transcript of Oral Decision, Otto v. Hearst Communications, 17 Civ. 4712 (S.D.N.Y. 2019), medialaw.org/images/07.24.19otto.pdf.

19 *Id*. (citing Section 502(c) of the Copyright Act; Island Software & Computer Serv., Inc. v. Microsoft Corp., 413 F.3d 257, 263 (2d Cir. 2005) (plaintiff can show "willfulness" through circumstantial evidence); Global-Tech Appliances, Inc. v. SEB S.A., 563 U.S. 754, 769–70 (2011) (defining "recklessness" and "willful blindness")).

20 Defendants who can show that they were "not aware and had no reason to believe" that they were infringing copyright may have the damages reduced to "not less than" $200 per work. 17 U.S.C. § 504(c)(2). Defendants bear the burden of proof as to their innocence.

21 The claimant bears the burden to prove that the infringer acted willfully.

22 The jury awarded Morel the maximum statutory damages available under the Copyright Act: $150,000 for each work that defendants infringed, or $1,200,000 for the eight works misappropriated. He received and collected an award of an additional $20,000 as statutory damages under the Digital Millennium

Copyright Act as a result of defendants' mischaracterization or alteration of the credit attribution for the eight images.

23 603 F.3d 135, 144 (2d Cir. 2010).

24 The decision does not reveal the specific evidence the Court relied on and the calculation made to reach this very precise number.

25 Citing Yurman Design, Inc. v. PAJ, Inc., 262 F.3d 101, 113–14 (2d Cir. 2001).

26 Morel won First Prize in the Spot News Stories category and Second Prize for Spot News Singles in the 2011 World Press Photo Competition for his iconic images of the Haiti earthquake aftermath. He won these awards while his case was pending in the federal district court. Some of his photographs can be viewed (but not legally copied) here: https://www.worldpressphoto.org/collection/photo/2011/30240/12/2011-Morel-Morel-SNS1-LL.

27 Buckhannon Bd. & Care Home, Inc. v. W. Va. Dep't of Health & Human Res., 532 U.S. 598, 600 (2001).

28 Fogerty v. Fantasy, Inc., 510 U.S. 517 (1994).

29 *Id.* at 534 n.19.

30 The Court compared the decisions in Matthew Bender & Co. v. W. Pub. Co., 240 F. 3d 116, 122 (2d Cir. 2001) (giving substantial weight to objective reasonableness), with, e.g., Bond v. Blum, 317 F. 3d 385, 397–398 (4th Cir. 2003) (endorsing a totality-of-the-circumstances approach, without according special significance to any factor), and with, e.g., Hogan Sys., Inc. v. Cybersource Int'l, Inc., 158 F. 3d 319, 325 (5th Cir 1998), *abrogated by* Kirtsaeng v. John Wiley & Sons, Inc., 136 S. Ct. 1979 (2016) (presuming that a prevailing party receives fees).

31 568 U.S. 519 (2016).

32 The Supreme Court also ruled that the "costs" that are recoverable by a successful copyright litigant are limited to those set out in 28 U.S.C. §§ 1821, 1920. Rimini Street, Inc. v. Oracle USA, Inc., 139 S. Ct. 873 (2019).

33 Transcript of Memorandum & Order, Agence France Presse v. Morel, 10 Civ. 2730 (S.D.N.Y. 2015), https://blogs.nppa.org/advocacy/files/2014/01/AFP-v-Morel-attorneys-fees-03-23-15.pdf.

34 Otto v. Hearst Commc'ns, Inc., No. 1:17-CV-4712-GHW, 2020 WL 377479 (S.D.N.Y. January 23, 2020), *reconsideration denied*, No. 1:17-CV-4712-GHW, 2020 WL 1033355 (S.D.N.Y. March 3, 2020).

35 See J. Hughes, chap. 4, *Gorgeous Photograph, Limited Copyright.*

36 349 F. Supp. 3d 369 (S.D.N.Y. 2018).

37 138 Fed. Cl. 159 (2018), https://ecf.cofc.uscourts.gov/cgi-bin/show_public_doc?2013cv0942-136-0.

38 Morel settled out of court with a number of media outlets, including ABC, CBS, CNN, and The Washington Post. *See* Agence France Presse v. Morel, No. 10-CV-2730-AJN, 2015 WL 4154072 (S.D.N.Y. July 9, 2015), https://casetext.com/case/presse-v-morel-3, 22. Otto also sued at least four other entities that allegedly infringed his picture and settled at least one claim for $9,500. *See* Opinion & Order, Otto v. Hearst Commc'ns, Inc., No. 1:17-CV-4712-GHW (S.D.N.Y. March 5, 2019) (Cott, Mag. J.).

39 Bouchat v. Champion Prods., Inc., 327 F. Supp. 2d 537, 547 (D. Md. 2003) (quoting Sygma Photo News, Inc. v. High Soc'y Magazine, Inc., 778 F.2d 89, 92 (2d Cir. 1985)).

40 Timothy L. Warnock, "One Work, Three Infringers: Calculating the Correct Number of Separate Awards of Statutory Damages in a Copyright Infringement Action," *Vanderbilt Journal of Entertainment & Technology Law* 14 (Winter 2012), http://www.jetlaw.org/wp-content/journal-pdfs/Warnock.pdf.

41 Arista Records LLC v. Lime Gr'p. LLC, 784 F. Supp. 2d 313 (S.D.N.Y. 2011). The author of this chapter was the lead trial lawyer for LimeWire in the damages phase of the suit brought in the Southern District Court of New York.

42 Entities or persons may be liable for secondary or contributory copyright infringement if, with knowledge of the infringing activity, they induce, cause, or materially contribute to the infringing conduct of another. The Court found that defendants had induced multiple users of the LimeWire online file-sharing program ("LimeWire") to infringe Plaintiffs' copyrights. See *Arista*, 784 F. Supp. 2d. at 315.

43 The statutory maximum of 500,000 infringing downloads × $150,000 = $75 trillion. Had plaintiff's theory been accepted, the *statutory minimum* of $750 for willful infringement would have resulted in an immediate award of $37.5 billion against the defendants.

44 *Arista*, 784 F. Supp. 2d. at 315–16.

45 Columbia Pictures Television v. Krypton Broad. of Birmingham, Inc. 106 F.3d 284 (9th Cir. 1997), *rev'd on other grounds sub nom*, Feltner v. Columbia Pictures Television, Inc., 523 U.S. 340 (1998).

46 *Id.* at 288.

47 Friedman v. Live Nation Merch., Inc. 833 F.3d 1180 (9th Cir. 2016).

48 *Id.* at 1191.

49 17 U.S.C. § 504(c)(1) (emphasis added).

50 Morel's agreement with his trial counsel was to pay 15% of his recovery in legal fees, so Morel collected the bulk of his award and his various settlements with other infringers.

51 The Copyright Alternative in Small-Claims Enforcement Act of 2019 (the CASE Act) is a proposed US law that would provide a new means for copyright owners to file infringement claims and for content users to seek validating declaratory relief, among other expedited remedies. Copyright Alternative in Small-Claims Enforcement Act of 2019, §1504(c)(1), H.R. 2426, 116th Cong. (2019–2020), introduced in House May 1, 2019; see also "CASE Act," Wikipedia, last modified April 26, 2020, https://en.wikipedia .org/wiki/CASE_Act.

3.5

LANDMARK CASE

Rentmeester v. Nike, Inc., 883 F.3d 1111 (9th Cir. 2018)

In 1984, a photographer named Jacobus Rentmeester instructed University of North Carolina basketball player Michael Jordan to perform a *grand jeté*, a ballet move in which the dancer leaps forward and extends her legs in opposite directions. Jordan executed the move, and the resulting photograph depicted the young athlete soaring toward a basketball hoop—one foot pointed forward, the other back, with an outstretched hand palming a basketball, seemingly lifting him toward the basket. Shortly after Rentmeester's photograph appeared in *Life* magazine, Nike got in touch with him to acquire color transparencies of the photo as the company had recently entered into a partnership with Jordan. Rentmeester was receptive and provided Nike with a limited license to use the transparencies solely for slide presentations.

In 1984 or 1985, Nike commissioned its own photograph of Jordan. Nike's photograph clearly traced its inspiration back to Rentmeester's work as Nike's photo also depicts Jordan leaping toward a basketball hoop, with legs diametrically spread and a basketball held in an outstretched hand. The photograph is also outdoors, and Jordan is captured at dusk. However, Nike's photograph features several obvious differences from Rentmeester's photo. For one, Jordan, now a rookie on the Chicago Bulls, is shot against the Chicago skyline—in Rentmeester's version, Jordan is captured on a sparse patch of grass. In Nike's photo, Jordan is wearing a different outfit, viewed closer to the camera, stretching his other arm backward, and seen closer to the hoop. While Jordan's legs are similarly angled in both photographs, Rentmeester's photo has one foot at four-o'clock and the other nearly at nine, whereas Nike's photograph features Jordan's feet at five and at eight. In Rentmeester's photo, Jordan's left leg is slightly bent, whereas both legs in Nike's photo are entirely straight. These distinctions may seem minor, but thirty years and several billion dollars later, they would inform the Ninth Circuit's decision as to whether Nike's photograph infringed on Rentmeester's work.

Rentmeester saw the photograph in 1985, threatened to sue, and Nike agreed to pay him $15,000 to continue using the photograph on posters and billboards for two years. In 1987, Nike created the iconic "Jumpman" logo, which features a black silhouette of Jordan taken from Nike's earlier photograph. In 2015, Rentmeester sued Nike, claiming that both the Jumpman logo and the Nike photograph that it was based on infringed upon the copyright in his 1984 photo. Nike filed a motion to dismiss, which the district court granted. Rentmeester appealed, and the Ninth Circuit agreed to hear the case.

The Ninth Circuit affirmed the lower court decision, holding that Nike's photograph was not substantially similar to Rentmeester's. A successful copyright infringement suit requires two steps: First, the plaintiff must show that she owns a valid copyright in the underlying work; next, the plaintiff must establish that the defendant copied protected elements of the underlying work. Rentmeester did not have any problem clearing the first hurdle—the photo is clearly copyrightable, and Rentmeester has been the sole owner of the photograph's copyright since its creation in 1984. The bulk of the court's analysis focused on this second requirement, which Rentmeester failed to overcome.

The crux of this analysis was whether Nike's photograph was "substantially similar" to Rentmeester's photo. Even though Rentmeester has plausibly alleged copying, the query into infringement turns on whether Nike copied enough of the protected expression from Rentmeester's photo to establish unlawful appropriation. In order to do this, Rentmeester must establish that Nike's photograph was "substantially similar" to his. The Ninth Circuit explained that copyright protection must be approached in the context of each work as a whole—individual elements such as pose, lighting, and subject matter are not copyrightable in isolation.

Applying this reasoning to the two photographs, the court concluded that "just as Rentmeester made a series of creative choices in the selection and arrangement of the elements in this photograph, so too Nike's photographer made his own distinct choices in that regard." These two distinct sets of choices produced two images that were different "in more than just minor details." According to the court, Rentmeester's copyright "does not confer a monopoly" on the "general 'idea' or 'concept'" of Michael Jordan performing a *grand jeté*. While the pose in this context is highly original, Nike did not replicate the details of the photo. The court focused on the difference in "position of each of [Jordan's] limbs," reasoning that those differences are significant because "they affect the visual impact of the images." Similarly, the court points to the inclusion of the Chicago skyline, the positioning of the basketball hoop, the absence of a grassy knoll, and the "arrangement of the elements" in Nike's photo as further evidence that the two works were not substantially similar. As a result, the court holds that neither Nike's photograph nor the Jumpman logo infringes on the copyright in Rentmeester's 1984 photograph of Michael Jordan.

Ultimately, the place of visual art in the twenty-first-century copyright law is better understood not through a landmark case, but through a landmark issue. *Rentmeester* exists in the evolving, controversial, and deeply relevant area of appropriation art. Indeed, *Rentmeester*, along with other prominent appropriation art decisions like *Cariou v. Prince*, represents a seesawing between content creators and creative appropriators that is amplified by the digital age. These cases raise important questions about the character and elements of art and visual creative expression. What elements are entitled to legal protection, when are these elements entitled to such protections, and when can the slew of observers and potential appropriators use the work for their own creative purposes? *Rentmeester* does not attempt to answer this question, but it suggests an inclination toward permitting appropriation in close disputes between lucrative, multinational brands and photographers suing for infringement of older photographs.

Sinclair v. Ziff Davis, LLC, No. 18-CV-790 (KMW), 2020 WL 1847841 (S.D.N.Y. Apr. 13, 2020)

On September 22, 2015, Stephanie Sinclair, a professional photographer, publicly shared her copyrighted photograph "Child, Bride, Mother/Child Marriage in Guatemala" on her public Instagram page, which was viewable by anyone with an internet connection. Media and entertainment platform Mashable made an offer to license the photograph from Sinclair for use in an online article entitled "10 female photojournalists with their lenses on social justice." Sinclair rejected Mashable's offer, but Mashable proceeded to use Instagram's application programming interface (API) to embed Sinclair's original Instagram post in its article. The embed frame of Sinclair's Instagram post, as it appeared in the Mashable article, was hosted on Instagram's servers, linked back to Sinclair's Instagram page, and included the photograph, Sinclair's original caption, and the date of the original post. The Mashable article specifically discussed Sinclair and her work above the embed.

Sinclair filed suit against both Mashable and its parent company, Ziff Davis, LLC, for copyright infringement. Mashable moved to dismiss the case, arguing that Instagram's integrated agreements (i.e. its Platform Policy, Terms of Use, and Privacy Policy) clearly granted it a sublicense to display the photograph. Indeed, the Terms of Use stated that, by posting content to Instagram, the user "grant[s] to Instagram a non-exclusive, fully paid and royalty-free, transferable, sub-licensable, worldwide license to the Content that you post on or through [Instagram], subject to [Instagram's] Privacy Policy." Pursuant to Instagram's Privacy Policy, users can revoke Instagram's sub-licensable right by designating the content at issue as "private."

Judge Kimba Wood of the US District Court for the Southern District of New York sided with Mashable, ruling that Instagram's agreements permit publishers to embed content publicly posted on Instagram. Because Sinclair posted the photograph publicly, Judge Wood opined, "Plaintiff made her choice. This Court cannot release her from the agreement she made."

While the Court conceded that Instagram's integrated agreements could be more concise and accessible, it declined to accept Sinclair's contention that the agreements were unenforceable because they were purportedly "circular," "incomprehensible," and "contradictory."

Judge Wood also touched upon a dilemma faced by professional photographers: deciding whether to remain in "private mode" on one of the most popular public photo-sharing platforms in the world, or to promote and share work publicly. On the one hand, sharing content publicly allows widespread exposure and can be effectively used to market and promote one's work. Indeed, many photographers use Instagram as a digital portfolio, showcasing their works to the masses. On the other hand, if sharing content publicly grants a valid sublicense to publishers of digital content, the licensing value of such content may be diminished.

This holding sent shock waves throughout the creative community as rights holders were forced to rethink how they make their works available to the public. Alternatively, for publishers and media entities, the decision permitted the use of publicly available content, provided that the publisher used the embed API that linked directly back to the Instagram account user's full Instagram page. On April 27, 2020, Sinclair filed a motion for reconsideration, which is pending as of the date of this writing.

As with the *Goldman* case (discussed in Chapter 8), the *Sinclair* holding does not create a per se rule with respect to the practice of embedding. In *Goldman*, the photographer never posted to Twitter but rather shared his image of Tom Brady in a private Snapchat, with one friend capturing a screen grab and further distributing it on the Twitter platform. Twitter's terms, unlike Instagram's, do not grant publishers a sublicense to embed using the Twitter environment. Users of content should note that the Instagram Privacy Policy requires the user to obtain consent before using content in an ad.

PART IV

Fine Art

Introduction

It seems apt to define "fine art" as it is in the title of Part IV. The various definitions embrace the idea that fine art is work by artists who create purely for aesthetic, intellectual, or creative expression and that the art has no practical use. (Some early definitions included the requirement that work was not commissioned, but that would exclude great works of art, such as the Sistine Chapel or *David* by Michelangelo and even works by contemporary artists.) Historically, fine art encompassed painting, drawing, sculpture, music (think: classical), and poetry. While categories are often problematic, as you read through the chapters in Part IV, it is important to have a general definition to understand that, while all fine art is visual, not all visual art is fine art, and the issues that fine artists face include not only copyright but gallery-artist contracts, authorship issues, and moral rights questions.

The first chapter, "The Art Collector's Burden: Guiding a Collection Through the Thicket of Copyright Law," by Judith Prowda, guides the collector through the thicket, explaining why in the global and online expansion of the art market, copyright should be foremost on the minds of the private collector as she acquires art, even though it seldom is. She explains the common misconceptions beginning with the belief that the collector owns the copyright in the work purchased, absent an agreement so stating. Not owning the copyright means the collector cannot reproduce the work, even online without the artist's consent. She discusses work for hire and the pitfalls of joint copyright, and presents her take on when appropriation art is or should be fair use through the lens of the key case *Cariou v. Prince,* and how that determination impacts the rights a collector has to display work publicly and the value of the work. Finally, she discusses moral rights, the Visual Artists Rights Act (VARA), and key issues that have arisen, including disavowal of authorship and what qualifies as "works of recognized stature." She discusses disavowal through cases brought by notable artist Cady Noland against collector(s) who "conserved" (or negligently restored) her work and then displayed the conserved piece without Noland's permission. Prowda raises the question of whether collectors should be allowed to be indemnified when an artwork loses value "due to frivolous VARA" claims.

In the second chapter, "Protection of Street Art: Has VARA Finally Found its Métier," William T. McGrath also examines if VARA—which has failed to live up to expectations in the first twenty years—has finally emerged as an effective way to protect the street (graffiti) artists whose work was illegally destroyed in the 5Pointz case. He first explains the meaning of moral rights, how the US version, VARA, came to be enacted, and how ineffective it has been in preserving art and protecting the reputations of artists because the statute is narrow and courts seem inclined to embrace defenses and exceptions. VARA worked in the significant 5Pointz litigation that involved a large warehouse, known as 5Pointz, which became the home of one of the largest collections of graffiti (aerosol art), including high-end works by internationally recognized artists. The owner wanted to demolish the building, the artists sued under VARA, and eventually prevailed, obtaining maximum statutory damages for the willful destruction of their work. McGrath notes that the legal significance will be long-lasting—not all art hangs in museums; temporary work has emerged as a major category of contemporary art; and this kind of art is not excluded from VARA protection.

The third and fourth chapters extend the inquiry into appropriation art, taking different points of view on when appropriation art should be considered a fair use. In "Appropriation Art: Creating by Taking," Daniel Brooks distinguishes appropriation of commonplace objects by artists such as Marcel Duchamp, Pablo Picasso, and Georges Braque from that of post-modern artists such as Jeff Koons and Richard Prince who take artworks with an existing copyright. He questions the current court trend that favors "transformativeness"—first discussed in an article by Judge Pierre Leval—as the most important factor to consider when finding that a use is fair. While a transformativeness analysis may work for other genres, Brooks argues that it is problematic when applied to appropriation art because (1) it makes the determination dependent on the subjective aesthetic views of judges, (2) it denigrates the right of a copyright holder to authorize a derivative work because all appropriation art is a derivative work, and (3) it ignores the complexity of balancing all four factors of fair use in favor of only one. He suggests that copyright and creativity are better served by asking whether the appropriation of copyrighted work was necessary regardless of the degree of transformativeness.

John Koegel, in "Appropriation Art: Creating by Using," argues that appropriation art has a long and distinguished history and that its very nature—the taking of something—rightly challenges ideas of ownership and authorship and the meaning of artistic "creation." He notes that, as artists moved from utilitarian objects and began recontextualizing works with existing copyrights, law clashed with art, and as appropriation artists became highly successful, lawsuits ensued. He discusses the high-profile lawsuits against famous appropriation artists such as Andy Warhol, Jeff Koons, and Richard Prince who prevailed in some, but not all of their cases. The different outcomes highlight the complexity of using the fair use doctrine—which is somewhat subjective—for artwork that employs prior art as part of its expression, not necessarily to comment on the source material itself, but rather to comment on cultural issues. He postulates that copyright law should support appropriation art because rarely is the original copyright holder harmed by the secondary use; using copyright law to squelch appropriation art ignores the law's fundamental purpose—to benefit the public; and that copyright law was never meant to function like patent law that bars any use of the subject matter covered by the patent.

Part IV ends with an interview with Alex Branczik of Sotheby's who presided over what has become the most extraordinary performance piece in art auction history—the shredding of Banksy's *Girl with Balloon* recreated as *Love is in the Bin*. Branczik discusses, generally, the idea of authorship as a line of inquiry that artists have been mining since the early twentieth century, and how those explorations underscore the rich genre of contemporary appropriation art. He suggests that Banksy's genius was in employing the medium of the auction as the stage upon which to create *the* performative piece of the twenty-first century—where a new piece did not rise from the ashes, but rather from the shredder.

4.1

THE ART COLLECTOR'S BURDEN

Guiding a Collection through the Thicket of Copyright Laws

Judith B. Prowda[*]

Introduction

Copyright may not be foremost on the mind of most collectors when they are acquiring works. Before purchasing, a prudent collector will exercise due diligence related to a number of essential categories, including authenticity, provenance, title, condition, and fair market value.[1] Since the art market is not transparent, research into each of these categories is essential in managing risk.[2] It is rare, however, for a collector to consider questions related to copyright until they arise.

This chapter will focus on some of the most prominent copyright issues that collectors will encounter about works they own, from everyday questions relating to managing their collection, to highly complex problems that affect the artist who created the work, as well as the reputation and value of the collection. Discussion of recent (and ongoing) landmark cases provides context for some of the most pressing issues at the intersection of copyright and art.

This chapter was written with the private collector in mind, but the issues may apply more broadly. Also, since the focus is primarily on the US copyright law, collectors in other parts of the world should inform themselves of copyright laws in their jurisdiction.

Copyright Ownership

Ownership of the Artwork vs. the Underlying Copyright

One of the most common misconceptions collectors hold is the belief that they own the copyright to the works they are purchasing. This is rarely the case, however.

The 1976 US Copyright Act explicitly states that the right to the physical object is distinct from the copyright. When an artwork is sold, ownership of the copyright remains with its owner (typically the artist) unless it has been transferred in a signed writing (which almost never happens). Typically, an artist's dealer will inform the collector that the copyright in the work remains with the artist only after the sale. While the issue of copyright ownership is unlikely to arise after a work is sold, buyers should beware: Copyright vests, if at all, at the moment of an artwork's creation (as long as it satisfies certain requirements for copyrightability), and for works created on or after January 1, 1978, lasts for an additional seventy years after the artist's death. As such, copyright may be an artist's most valuable asset.

Without ownership of the copyright, the collector may not create greeting cards, publish a book depicting the copyright-protected work, post an image of the work online, or permit a film director to include a copyright-protected work in a film, even fleetingly,[3] without first obtaining express written permission from the artist (unless such work is in the public domain) because doing so would violate one or more of the artist's bundle of exclusive rights.[4] Unless the collector and artist have agreed otherwise in writing, the artist is free to license the image to third parties on an exclusive or non-exclusive basis.

However, a collector does not need to obtain the artist's permission before selling or displaying works from his collection: The first sale doctrine provides that the owner of a particular lawfully made copy or any person authorized by the owner may, without the authority of the artist, sell or otherwise dispose of that copy.

Therefore, a collector who has acquired a work from a party with legitimate ownership may sell it to another without violating the artist's exclusive right to distribute. The first sale doctrine also provides that a lawful owner of a copy may display it to viewers present in the place where the work is located (e.g. residence, museum, or gallery), but not online without the consent of the artist. The collector may, however, display an image of a work online for the purpose of facilitating a discrete sale of the object she owns.[5] This reproduction qualifies as fair use (discussed below) because it "in no way 'displac[es] the need for the original work'" but instead serves a "fundamentally different purpose and promote[s] the development of a robust legal secondary market" in support of the first sale.[6] As such, the reproduction is consistent with the purpose of copyright law.

Works for Hire: Works Prepared by an Employee Within the Scope of Their Employment and Special Commissions

Generally, the artist is considered the author of an artwork for the purposes of copyright ownership unless the work is a "work made for hire." The 1976 Act defines a work made for hire as either (1) a work prepared by an employee within the scope of his or her employment; or (2) a work specially ordered or commissioned for use in one of the nine enumerated categories listed in section 101 of the Copyright Act and parties agree in writing that the work shall be considered a work made for hire.[7] Since works of visual art are not included in the list of nine categories, they would not qualify as works for hire unless an employer-employee relationship was established.

To illustrate the first example (a work prepared by an employee within the scope of his or her employment), an artist creating works of visual art for an animation company would be acting within the scope of his or her employment, therefore creating works made for hire. Accordingly, the artist's employer is considered the author for the purposes of copyright and copyright initially vests in the employer, not the artist. If desired, the employer could transfer the copyright to the artist in a signed writing.

However, if an artwork is specially ordered or commissioned, the copyright would vest in the artist, not the hiring party, because visual art is not one of the nine categories of works for hire listed in section 101 of the Copyright Act. To prove that the artwork was a work made for hire, an employer-employee relationship would need to be established. Significant factors "in virtually every situation" include the hiring party's right to control the manner and means by which the product is accomplished; the skill required; the provision of employee benefits; the tax treatment of the hired party; and whether the hiring party has the right to assign additional projects to the hired party.[8]

Moral rights, however, discussed in greater detail below only vest in the content's creator. Moral rights are further distinct in that they can be waived by the artist in a signed writing, but they may not be transferred, in writing or otherwise.

Joint Authorship

If the work is a joint work[9] created by two or more authors, the collector needs to only obtain written permission from one of the joint authors to license the work, unless the collector seeks an exclusive license. This is because each joint author is a "tenant in common," that is, a co-owner of an equal, undivided interest in the whole work, regardless of the extent of the contribution, unless the joint authors have agreed otherwise in a signed writing.

Therefore, under the US copyright law, a joint author can unilaterally license the work on a non-exclusive basis, including to someone other than the owner of the work. An exclusive license requires the approval of all of the co-authors. If the license is non-exclusive, one or more of the joint authors may grant the same rights to different third parties. So, for example, each joint author may license their right to reproduce to one or more persons, and their right to create derivative works to another person or persons, without giving notice to the owner of the work.

Copyright Infringement and Fair Use

Perhaps one of the most hotly contested debates in copyright is to what degree an artist may use the copyrighted material of another artist to create new works. The digital age complicates the issue by providing artists with new tools that make it easier than ever to appropriate another's content. If a court rules that such an appropriation is a violation of the original artist's copyright, how could this determination affect the owner of the infringing work?

Cariou v. Prince

As it happens, a lot. In a high-profile case involving the internationally known appropriation artist Richard Prince, the US Court of Appeals for the Second Circuit largely reversed a New York district court's ruling that Prince had infringed on registered copyrights of photographs taken by Patrick Cariou, a professional photographer.[10]

In 2000, Cariou, who had spent years living among Rastafarians in Jamaica, published a book, entitled *Yes Rasta*, that included portraits of individuals and images of the Jamaican landscape. To create a series of paintings, entitled *Canal Zone* (2007–08), Prince used forty-one images from Cariou's book, which he scanned, enlarged, cropped, and covered with heavy brush strokes and various other painterly elements. The portions of *Yes Rasta* photographs and the amount of each Prince painting they constituted varied from piece to piece. In all, Prince included images from *Yes Rasta* in thirty paintings.

Prince first exhibited his works in St. Barts, and then at one of the Gagosian Gallery's locations in Manhattan in late 2008, where several were sold for prices ranging between $400,000 and $2,430,000. When Cariou learned of the show, he sued Prince, as well as Gagosian Gallery and its owner, Larry Gagosian, for copyright infringement. The defendants asserted a fair use defense and moved for summary judgment.

Fair Use Factors

A fair use determination considers four factors:

1 the purpose and character of the use, including whether such use is of a commercial nature or is for nonprofit educational purposes;
2 the nature of the copyrighted work;

3 the amount and substantiality of the portion used in relation to the copyrighted work as a whole; and

4 the effect of the use upon the potential market for, or value of, the copyrighted work.[11]

District Court Decision

Upon finding the four fair use factors weighed in favor of plaintiff, the District Court for the Southern District of New York granted Cariou's motion for summary judgment. The court's analysis included all four fair use factors, but the key holding in the case—and the most damaging for the defendants—was the district court's analysis of the first fair use factor: purpose and character of the use. In a departure from precedent, the district court found that a work would be considered transformative only if it in some way commented on the original work or the broader culture. Prince himself testified that he did not intend to comment on any aspect of Cariou's work. Hence, the district court concluded that the *Canal Zone* series was not transformative, and that this factor weighed against a finding of fair use.

The district court's drastic ruling not only awarded damages, but also granted sweeping injunctive relief to Cariou, ordering the defendants to "deliver up for impounding, destruction, or other disposition, as [Cariou] determines, all infringing copies of the [p]hotographs, including the [p]aintings and unsold copies of the *Canal Zone* exhibition book, in their possession."[12] At oral argument before the Second Circuit on appeal, Cariou indicated that he opposed the destruction of any of the works of art that were the subject of this litigation. The court agreed, and specifically Judge Parker of the Second Circuit panel observed that destruction "seems like something that would appeal to the Huns or the Taliban."

Second Circuit Decision

A divided Second Circuit reversed in part, vacated in part, and remanded, concluding that twenty-five of Prince's thirty artworks before the court made fair use of Cariou's copyrighted photographs and that neither Gagosian nor the gallery was liable as vicarious or contributory infringers with respect to those works. The remaining five works were remanded back to the district court to decide whether those works impermissibly infringed Cariou's copyright, applying the proper standard—how Prince's artworks may "reasonably be perceived" in order to assess their "transformative nature." What is critical is how the work in question appears to the "reasonable observer," stated the appellate court, "not simply what an artist might say about a particular piece or body of work."[13]

If the district court once again found infringement (with respect to the five remanded works), warned the Second Circuit, the destruction of the works as a remedy would be "improper and against the public interest." The appellate court also instructed the district court to determine whether the Gagosian defendants should be held liable, directly or secondarily, as a consequence of their actions with regard to those works.

The Second Circuit, like the district court, analyzed all four fair use factors, but gave the most weight to the first and fourth factors.

While the Second Circuit decision did not make fair use cases any more predictable than its precedents,[14] the court confirmed the importance of transformativeness in the first fair use factor. After closely comparing each of Prince's allegedly infringing paintings with Cariou's photographs, the court concluded that twenty-five of the Prince works "manifest[ed] an entirely different aesthetic from Cariou's photographs." While Cariou presented "serene and deliberately composed portraits and landscape photographs depict[ing] the natural beauty of Rastafarians and their surrounding environs," Prince's offered "crude and jarring works" that were "hectic and provocative." The remaining five works presented "closer questions" and the appellate court could not say with certainty whether they transformed the original works by adding "a new expression, meaning, or message."

The fact that Prince created his works for the commercial art market was not of great significance in the analysis of the first factor due to the transformative nature of the work.

With respect to the potential market analysis in the fourth fair use factor, the concern is not "whether the use suppresses or even destroys the market for the original work or its potential derivatives, but whether the secondary use *usurps* the market of the original work." The court reasoned that the audiences for the two artists were very different and therefore Prince did not usurp the market for Cariou's pictures with his paintings.

The "ultimate test of fair use," stated the court, quoting the US Constitution, "is whether the copyright law's goal of 'promot[ing] the Progress of Science and the useful Arts' . . . would be better served by allowing the use rather than preventing it." The determination of fair use is an "open-ended and context-sensitive inquiry."

Eventually, the parties settled.

★ ★ ★

But what if the parties had *not* settled and the district court had found the remanded works to be infringing and the Gagosian defendants were liable, directly or secondarily, for copyright infringement? If those works had already been sold to collectors (whose ownership of the works would not have been disturbed), then presumably, the collectors (and third parties, such as galleries and museums) would not be allowed to display them publicly, because doing so could infringe on Cariou's exclusive right to display. It is foreseeable that the value of infringing works would likewise be affected and would prove difficult to resell. Perhaps Gagosian would refund collectors their purchase price, but would have been under no legal obligation to do so, absent a contractual requirement. *Caveat emptor!*

Moral Rights

In recent years, collectors have been involved in a number of lawsuits regarding the moral rights of artists that affect the value and control of works in their collection. An understanding of moral rights is especially important for collectors of contemporary art.

Moral rights are non-economic rights in creative works that exist independent of an artist's copyright. The term is derived from the French term *droit moral,* and is viewed as personal and spiritual in nature, stemming from the notion that art embodies the creation of the artist, who injects some of their spirit into the art during the creative process.[15] Compared to the expansive moral rights laws in European civil law countries, especially France, where moral rights can apply to a wide range of creative works, moral rights in the US exist under very narrow circumstances.

The federal moral rights statute in the US, the Visual Artists Rights Act (VARA), was enacted in December 1990, effectively amending the US Copyright Act of 1976. Moral rights protection of visual artworks also exists at the state level in some jurisdictions.

VARA recognizes two moral rights only: attribution and integrity. The moral right of attribution allows an author of a work of visual art (defined below) to claim authorship of that work, to prevent the use of their name as the author of any work of visual art which they did not create, and to prevent the use of their name as the author of a work of visual art that is distorted, modified, or mutilated that would be prejudicial to their honor or reputation.

The moral rights of attribution and integrity grant an author of a work of visual art the right "to prevent any intentional distortion, mutilation, or other modification of that work which would be prejudicial to their honor or reputation." The integrity right also prevents any destruction of a work of "recognized stature." The statute states that "any intentional or grossly negligent destruction of that work is a violation of that right." The term "recognized stature," which is not defined in the statute, is the subject of a landmark case, referred to as 5Pointz, discussed below (ongoing as of this writing).

As its name implies, VARA narrowly applies to visual works of art only. The statute defines "a work of visual art" as "a painting, drawing, print, or sculpture" that exists in a single copy or in a signed and numbered limited edition of no more than 200 copies, or "a still photographic image produced for exhibition purposes only" that also exists in a single copy or in a signed and numbered limited edition of no more than 200 copies. VARA protection does not extend to works for hire, works of applied art, or promotional or advertising works.

Also specifically excluded under VARA is the "modification of a work of art which is a result of the passage of time or the inherent nature of the materials." While seemingly intuitive, this language has created an awkward set of obligations for art collectors. An outdoor sculpture that naturally develops a patina as a result of exposure does not violate VARA, but failure to maintain an artwork, which results in the work's destruction or prejudice to the artist's honor, would constitute a violation. Further complicating the matter, restoration efforts that result in a grossly negligent modification of a work could also be considered a violation. In extreme cases, an artist might go so far as to disclaim authorship of an artwork because subsequent conservation, or lack thereof, has become prejudicial to his or her honor and reputation.

The Cady Noland Cases

Right of Attribution: Cady Noland's Disavowal of Authorship in "Cowboys Milking"

Invoking her VARA right to disclaim authorship, the artist Cady Noland asserted that her 1990 aluminum print, entitled *Cowboys Milking*, had been modified or damaged subsequent to her authorship after viewing the work during a Sotheby's auction preview only three days before the November 10, 2011 sale.[16] The work had been consigned to Sotheby's by the New York gallery Mark Jancou Fine Art Ltd. Noland claimed that her honor and reputation would be prejudiced if the print were offered for sale with her name associated with it, in violation of her VARA rights. She disclaimed authorship of the work under 17 U.S.C. § 106A, and demanded that Sotheby's withdraw it from auction "in light of the material and detrimental changes to the work that have occurred since its creation."

Following a rapid series of unsuccessful negotiations between Sotheby's and Jancou, during which it was revealed that the conservator was able to reduce the damage but that "[s]ome deformations . . . [would] always be noticeable," Sotheby's withdrew the piece from auction.

Jancou promptly sued Sotheby's and Noland for $26 million in a New York state court, alleging (1) breach of contract, and (2) breach of fiduciary duties. The parties cross-moved for summary judgment. Putting the VARA arguments to the side, the court found that the consignment agreement between Jancou and Sotheby's gave Sotheby's the right to withdraw the print from auction "if in [its] sole judgment" there were doubts as to attribution and granted summary judgment to Sotheby's, dismissing the plaintiff's contract claim.

Similarly, the court granted summary judgment to Sotheby's dismissing the plaintiff's breach of fiduciary duties claim, reasoning that Sotheby's exercised its honest judgment to withdraw the work from auction based on doubt as to the print's attribution. The case was affirmed on appeal, without the appellate court determining the merits of Noland's VARA claim.[17]

This case illustrates the relatively wide leeway an auction house has to remove a piece from sale under the terms of the consignment agreement between the parties, as long as the auction house does not act in bad faith.[18] It is also a cautionary tale to collectors that artists have the final word as to whether their work is authentic in the eyes of the market, regardless of whether or not VARA technically permits a disclaimer. A work may be rendered instantly worthless because the artist declares it so. Notably, French artist Balthasar Klossowski de Rola (Balthus) (1908–2001) famously repudiated authorship in his drawing *Colette de Profil* (c. 1954), belonging to his ex-wife, presumably out of personal animus.[19] The court acknowledged that the artist's repudiation, whether true or not, rendered the work "unsalable."

Likewise, *Cowboys Milking* (1990) by Cady Noland, which was listed in the printed auction catalog with an estimate of $250,000 to $350,000, immediately became *Cowboys Milking* (1990), *formerly* attributed to Cady Noland, with a negligible market value.[20]

There had been a good reason to be optimistic. The prior evening, Noland's 1989 *Oozewald* hammered down at $6.6 million (well above its $2 million to $3 million estimate), setting a new record for the highest price ever paid for an artwork by a living female artist.

It is also conceivable that an artist's disavowal of a work may increase, rather than decrease, its value. In 2017, Richard Prince disclaimed authorship of a work from his Instagram series, owned by Ivanka Trump, as an act of protest against her father, then President-elect Donald J. Trump.[21] The work, which she purchased for $36,000, shows an Instagram post of Ms. Trump getting her hair done. Prince announced his disavowal of the work in a series of tweets, echoing Mr. Trump's rhetoric by calling his own work "fake," and returned the purchase price to Ms. Trump. How this eventually plays out in the marketplace is anyone's guess.

Right of Integrity and the Restoration Exception?: Cady Noland's Disavowal of Authorship in Log Cabin Blank with Screw Eyes and Café Door

In another highly publicized case involving disavowal of authorship, in July 2017, Noland sued two Berlin galleries (Galerie Michael Janssen and KOW), one of the gallerists (Michael Janssen), and a German collector (Wilhelm Schürmann) in connection with the display and attempted sale of what Noland alleges to have been an unauthorized copy of her sculpture, titled *Log Cabin Blank with Screw Eyes and Café Door* (*Log Cabin*) in violation of her right to integrity under VARA.[22] Coincidentally, Noland created *Log Cabin* in 1990, the same year as *Cowboys Milking*.

The aptly titled work resembles the front façade of a log cabin in size and structure, with a door-shaped opening, two window-shaped openings, and a triangular-shaped top, measuring approximately 12 feet high, 18 feet long, and 5½ to 6 feet wide. It was fabricated with wooden logs and other components that Noland ordered to her specifications from Master Log Homes in Darby, Montana, a company that manufactures log cabin homes and offers a range of prefabricated options. Two American flags are an integral part of the work.

Noland claimed copyright ownership in *Log Cabin*. However, the US Copyright Office denied her original registration in July 2017 and two requests for reconsideration in September 2017 and May 2018, thereby exhausting her copyright registration application review before the US Copyright Office.

Log Cabin Exhibited and Sold to Collector in Germany in 1990

Schürmann purchased *Log Cabin* in 1990, shortly after its creation, from Galerie Max Hetzler in Germany, and subsequently exhibited the work at various locations in Germany, including through a ten-year loan to the Suermondt-Ludwig Museum in Aachen. With Noland's permission, the Aachen museum displayed the work outdoors. Sometime after June 1, 1991 (the effective date of VARA), Schürmann obtained Noland's consent to stain the wood a darker color.[23] Noland later alleged that this newly stained work comprised a derivative work, as defined in section 101 of the Copyright Act, thus qualifying for separate copyright and/or VARA rights recognition.

In displaying the work outdoors, the Aachen museum placed the work directly on the ground without a protective foundation, causing some of the wood to rot and deteriorate. After consulting with a conservator, Schürmann and the defendant, KOW, replaced all of the original wooden components, intending to preserve the work.[24] The replacement wooden components were ordered from the same Montana company Noland had used to create the original work in or around 1990, and were shipped to Germany pre-cut, using Noland's original blueprints or plans.[25] In 2011, KOW exhibited the restored work in its show *Cady Noland/Santiago Sierra*. Noland requested that an image of *Log Cabin* be removed from KOW's website because she objected to her work being exhibited in context with that of *Sierra*, but was apparently unaware of the conservation at that time.[26]

Log Cabin Sold to Ohio Collector in 2014

Sometime later, Schürmann and KOW recruited Galerie Janssen to help sell the work. Michael Janssen, owner of Galerie Michael Janssen, exhibited the work in his gallery in Berlin. Janssen worked with intermediaries in the US—Marissa Newman Projects, LLC, a New York gallery, and Brett Shaheen, a dealer in Ohio.

Eventually, Janssen identified an American collector and art patron, Scott C. Mueller, who was willing to buy the work for $1.4 million. The contract of sale included a New York choice-of-law provision and delivery to the buyer in Ohio. Because of Noland's previous disavowal of *Cowboys Milking*, Mueller was advised to include a detailed twelve-month buyback provision in the contract of sale, stating that if Noland "refuses to acknowledge or approve of the legitimacy of the Work," or "seeks to disassociate her name from the Work," or "claims that her moral rights under the Visual Artists Rights Act or other similar legislation have been violated," the buyer elects to have Janssen buy back the work.[27]

Pursuant to the agreement, Mueller wired the full purchase price of $1.4 million to Janssen in July 2014.

Noland Disavows Refurbished Log Cabin, Triggering Buyback Provision

Prior to delivery, Mueller's Ohio dealer and advisor Brett Shaheen, with Janssen's permission, informed Noland by fax on July 18, 2014 that *Log Cabin* had been purchased by a "private Cleveland-based collector," and further explained that work had been conserved. Noland immediately fired back, angrily denouncing the work in a handwritten note faxed to Mueller, declaring, "This is not an artwork," and objecting to the fact that the sculpture was "repaired by a conservator [sic] BUT THE ARTIST WASN'T CONSULTED." Noland requested Shaheen to tell Mueller "that any effort to display or sell the sculpture must include notice that the piece was remade without the artist's consent, that it now consists of unoriginal materials, and that she does not approve of the work."[28]

By fax letter to Noland dated July 21, 2014, Mueller identified himself as the purchaser of *Log Cabin* and noted that his goal was to donate the piece to the Cleveland Museum of Art. However, because of Noland's reaction, he planned on "returning the piece" to the seller.[29] Through Shaheen, Mueller informed Newman and Janssen that the parties should proceed to unwind the deal and initiate the buyback provision in the contract of sale. Mueller requested a full refund of $1.4 million.

Janssen Galerie eventually returned $600,000 of the $1.4 million purchase price to Mueller. Mueller sued Janssen Galerie, Schürmann, and Newman to recover the $800,000 balance. A federal district court found in favor of Newman with respect to her commission, as she never signed the agreement between the Janssen Galerie and Mueller, owed no fiduciary duty to Mueller, and was not unjustly enriched. The court dismissed the action against Schürmann without prejudice. Galerie Michael Janssen was never served with process and the action was eventually dismissed.

Noland's Claims Against Janssen et al.

Noland filed a separate action against Janssen, Schurman, and KOW alleging that the defendants violated her moral rights under VARA when they negligently restored her work without her consent.[30] In particular, Noland stated that "[T]he collector who loaned *Log Cabin* to a German museum was 'either negligent or indifferent to the work' and 'failed . . . to protect the work from rot, deterioration and exposure to the elements.'"[31] In Noland's view, the refurbished *Log Cabin* is "a distorted, mutilated or otherwise modified copy of her original [s]culpture, and . . . she has the right to prevent the use of her name as the author of [the refurbished *Log Cabin*], which she believes is prejudicial to her honor or reputation."[32]

Further, Noland claimed that "the marketing of the refurbished *Log Cabin* in the United States, and the distribution of photographs and/or plans of the refurbished work in New York, Ohio or elsewhere in the United States was a violation of her rights under VARA."[33] While VARA—embodied in section 106A of the Copyright Act—does not create additional causes of action for infringement of a copyright holder's exclusive section 106 rights, construing Noland's complaint in the light most favorable to the artist, the third amended complaint can be understood to have asserted additional claims based on the defendants' alleged (1) "copying" of *Log Cabin* by replacing all of its wooden components, (2) display of the restored version of the work, and (3) distribution of unauthorized reproductions of the work in the form of photographs of the construction and/or the original plan documents.[34] With respect to the first of these alleged copyright infringements, Noland's pleading explained: "by discarding the rotting logs and wooden elements that made up the cabin's facade and replacing them with new ones, the conservator essentially destroyed the original work and created an unauthorized reproduction."[35] The artist's attorney declared, "Wood can be restored, even rotting wood . . . [but] [t]his is a forgery."[36]

Noland's earlier complaints had been dismissed for failure to state a claim, when in March 2019, she was granted leave to replead one last time.[37] She filed her third amended complaint on March 29, 2019, seeking (1) damages and relief for defendants' violation of her moral rights under VARA and under copyright with respect to *Log Cabin*, (2) a declaration that *Log Cabin* was sufficiently original to warrant copyright registration, and (3) an injunction prohibiting the importation of *Log Cabin* and photographs and plans of the work into the US as a work attributed to Noland.

In May 2019, the defendants filed a motion to dismiss the suit, asserting that Noland failed to make a legitimate claim under VARA because (1) the work was not subject to copyright protection (hence, not eligible for VARA protection as a matter of law); (2) the work predated VARA's effective date (hence, not eligible for VARA protection as a separate and independent matter of law); and (3) the restoration of the work to Noland's original specifications was not a "distortion," as alleged by Noland. The defendants further argued that the staining of the pre-VARA work after VARA's effective date could not possibly amount to the creation of a derivative work that was retroactively protected under VARA.

Finally, the defendants argued that even if the work were copyrightable, (1) physically replacing components thereof as part of a restoration effort did not effect a "reproduction," but rather was an appropriate exercise of the owner's rights under the first sale doctrine, and (2) reproducing and/or displaying an image of the work as part of an effort to facilitate the sale of the actual object owned by Schürmann would be fair use in support of the owner's first sale right under section 109 of the Copyright Act.

June 1, 2020 Southern District of New York Ruling

Ruling in favor of Janssen, the district court granted Janssen's motion to dismiss Noland's third amended complaint.[38] Reaffirming its earlier holding of March 8, 2019, the district court reasoned that the alleged purchase of the wood in Montana was not a predicate act because it was not independently an act of copyright infringement. The court further reiterated that the first sale doctrine applied to the sale of the refurbished work. Following a detailed analysis of the four fair use factors, the court determined that the photographs and plans disseminated in connection with the sale of the refurbished work constituted fair use, thereby dismissing Noland's copyright infringement claims.

Finally, the court ruled that Noland could not grandfather in her preexisting sculpture, created pre-VARA, observing that Schürmann, not Noland, was the author and the moral rights holder of the derivative stained cabin. Thus, the court dismissed Noland's moral rights claims under VARA. Noland did not exercise her right to file an appeal before the Second Circuit.

Fortunately for Mueller, the governing contract of sale included a buyback provision, requiring the seller to indemnify the buyer in the event the artist objected to the restoration of the work (even though a dispute arose over repayment anyway); however, Mueller represents only a subsequent or downstream purchaser. One wonders whether the contract governing the acquisition of the work by its *original* purchaser, Schürmann, from Galerie Max Hetzler in 1990 included any provisions governing the purchaser's restoration of the artwork, the artist's obligations in connection with such restoration, or the purchaser's right to rescind the agreement in the event the artist disclaimed the work. Accordingly, the case provides important guidance for collectors acquiring works from living artists whose participation or approval may be desired over the future "life" of the work.

One commentator proposes a change in the law, such that indemnification would be a remedy available to collectors whose artwork loses value due to a frivolous VARA claim made by the artist, such as, for example, pronouncing standard conservation or normal, minor wear and tear as "mutilation."[39] The amount of the indemnification would be the current fair market value of the conserved work. Some might argue that artists need to safeguard what few rights they have, while others may take the view that an indemnification is proper in rare circumstances where works of living artists are of sufficient value to warrant litigation. This commentator also contemplates that a contractual provision between the artist and collector at the primary market stage would reduce the likelihood of a future dispute from occurring in the first place with respect to conservation.[40]

Noland v. Janssen is important to collectors because it settles questions about what they may or may not do with the art they own. The case also underscores the challenges inherent in asserting copyrights internationally. Since the restoration of Log Cabin occurred outside the US, it could not serve as a basis for liability in a US court. The court further held that purchasing replacement logs from a Montana supplier was insufficient as a predicate act to the restoration abroad because it was itself not an independent violation of copyright. Moreover, since the original work predated the effective date of VARA, it did not qualify for protection under the statute. Importantly, the case reaffirms a line of cases that permits the use of photographs in marketing materials to facilitate the sale of the work.

The case also leaves difficult questions unanswered. Specifically, the court does not rule on whether the restoration performed on *Log Cabin* was tantamount to creating an infringing work and whether it might constitute mutilation or destruction actionable under VARA. Collectors may still wonder about questions that were not addressed in *Noland v. Janssen*. For example, if a work is intended to be exhibited outdoors, and deteriorates due to its contact with the natural elements, would this modification be an exception under VARA as "a result of the passage of time or the inherent nature of the materials"? May an artist disclaim authorship in such a work? Would a collector be liable under VARA if they follow the advice of a responsible conservator in restoring a damaged work? When does a conserved work cease to be "original"?[41] How do moral rights apply to conceptual works and works comprised of fragile materials that degrade over time? Perhaps future courts will have an opportunity to consider these complex issues.

Right of Integrity: 5Pointz, Works of "Recognized Stature," and Assessment of Statutory Damages

In a highly significant case concerning works by aerosol artists, a New York federal court interpreted the meaning of "recognized stature" of works of art, a term which is not defined under VARA. Aside from addressing "recognized stature," the court also established a benchmark for plaintiff culpability by assessing the maximum amount of statutory damages available. The final outcome of this case, which was decided by a unanimous Second Circuit in favor of the plaintiff artists in February 2020, affirming a New York district court, is expected to have far-reaching consequences beyond the category of aerosol art. In July 2020, the defendants filed a petition for a writ of certiorari before the US Supreme Court, which is pending as of this writing.

Background

For over a decade, aerosol artists, led by curator Jonathan Cohen ("Meres One"), were permitted to paint the façade of a derelict factory complex in Long Island City, transforming it into the world famous 5Pointz, aka the Institute of Higher Burnin' or 5Pointz Aerosol Art Center. The property owner Jerry Wolkoff had purchased the 200,000 square foot industrial complex in 1971, with the idea that he would eventually develop the property. The artists were always aware that the building would one day be torn down but the parties did not sign a contract.

What ultimately became 5Pointz originated in the early 1990s as Phun Factory, a place where artists could legally paint on the walls of a dilapidated water meter factory owned by Wolkoff. During those years, there was no control over the artists who painted on the walls or the quality of the work, which was generally viewed by the public as graffiti. The neighborhood was crime-infested.

Then, in 2002, Wolkoff put Cohen in charge. Cohen and several other artists rented studio space in the warehouse buildings and collectively strove to improve conditions. Wolkoff recognized the merit of the work and approved of Cohen's role as a volunteer curator. Cohen abided by Wolkoff's three restrictions—"no pornography, no religious content, and nothing political," and established his own set of norms for the creation and curation of the art.

The neighborhood crime rate dropped and the 5Pointz site became a major attraction, drawing thousands of daily visitors, including school groups, tourists, and weddings and was used as a site for television, music video, and film production.

By 2010, the neighborhood surrounding 5Pointz had become increasingly valuable and Wolkoff decided it was time to redevelop the site into high-rise residential towers. When plans to demolish the property and develop the residential project later emerged, and the New York City Landmarks Commission denied protection, a group of the artists, including Cohen, the named plaintiff, filed suit on October 10, 2013, seeking preliminary injunctive relief and alleging that the proposed destruction of the art would amount to a violation of VARA.[42]

Cohen I[43]

Following a hearing before Judge Frederic Block in 2013, the court issued an order denying the plaintiffs preliminary injunctive relief and stated that "a written opinion would soon be issued." The court recognized the tension between the rights of artists under VARA and the rights of property owners, cautioning that "defendants are exposed to potentially significant monetary damages if it is ultimately determined after trial that the plaintiffs' works were of 'recognized stature'" under VARA.

During the eight-day period that it took the court to issue its written opinion, Wolkoff destroyed almost all the plaintiffs' paintings by whitewashing them in the dead of night without warning and barring the artists access to their works.[44] By failing to give the artists ninety days' written notice to remove and salvage their works integrated into a building, defendants violated section 113(d) of the Copyright Act. This willfully destructive act would eventually prove fatal to the defendants' case and weigh heavily in the court's ultimate assessment of statutory damages.

Thus, the court in *Cohen I* held that the plaintiffs' works are protected under VARA as works of "visual art," and that under 17 U.S.C. § 106A(a)(3)(B), VARA "gives the 'author of visual art the right to sue to prevent the destruction of [the] work if it is one of "recognized stature."'" VARA also permits the artist to seek monetary damages under 17 U.S.C. § 106A(a)(3)(A) if the work is distorted, mutilated, or otherwise modified to the prejudice of the artist's honor or reputation.

Jury Trial

A three-week jury trial was held in October 2017. Each of the twenty-one plaintiff-artists testified. In addition, on behalf of the plaintiffs, three experts testified as to quality and recognized stature, appraisal value, and removability of the works. Two fact witnesses testified as to the artistic importance of the works and the importance of 5Pointz as a culturally significant site.

Wolkoff was the primary witness for the defendants. Two experts also testified for the defendants on recognized stature and appraisal value.

Just prior to summations, the plaintiffs—with the defendants' consent—waived their jury rights. The court would consider the jury's verdict to be advisory and make independent findings of fact and conclusions of law. The advisory jury's input was particularly appropriate in cases involving community-based standards such as this. Here, the jurors were asked to assess whether each destroyed work was of recognized stature and/or whether it was mutilated, distorted, or otherwise modified to the prejudice of the artist's honor or reputation by the whitewashing.

Cohen II[45]

In his final decision, handed down on February 12, 2018, and spanning 100 pages with color reproduction of all artworks in dispute, Judge Block found the defendants liable for forty-five of forty-nine works of art of recognized stature, stating that "given the abject nature of Wolkoff's willful conduct, the Court awards the maximum statutory damages under VARA for each of the 45 works of art wrongfully and willfully destroyed . . . ." The defendants' arguments that the plaintiffs knew that the building would eventually be demolished and that outdoor aerosol art is ephemeral by nature were unavailing. As the court noted, VARA draws no distinction between temporary and non-temporary works on the side of a building, particularly when all that makes such a work temporary is the building owner's expressed intention to remove or destroy it.

Accordingly, Judge Block ordered Wolkoff to pay the twenty-one artist-plaintiffs the maximum amount of enhanced damages of $150,000 per act of infringement, for a total of $6.75 million ($150,000 for each of the forty-five works in question).

The court was guided by the analysis of recognized stature in *Cohen I*, which referenced *Carter v. Helmsley-Spear, Inc.*, the seminal case interpreting the phrase "recognized stature," to require a two-tiered showing (1) that the artwork has stature—that is, is perceived as meritorious, and (2) that the stature is recognized by art experts, other members of the art world, or some cross-section of society. Since the *Carter* court reversed on appeal, finding the work in question was a work made for hire and therefore did not qualify for VARA protection, it did not have the occasion to put its formulation to the test. But it urged other courts to "use common sense and generally accepted standards of the artistic community in determining whether a particular work" is a work of recognized stature since "[a]rtists may work in a variety of media, and may use a number of materials in creating their works."[46]

Cohen II applied the common sense approach urged by *Carter*,[47] relying on the plethora of exhibits and credible testimony, "that even under the most restrictive of evidentiary standards almost all of the plaintiffs' works easily qualify as works of recognized stature." This conclusion was supported by Wolkoff's faith in Cohen's meticulous selection of "a handful of works from the thousands at 5Pointz for permanence and prominence on long-standing walls that spanned multiple stories and were visible to millions on the passing trains." Referred to by the court as the "jewels" of 5Pointz, these works were considered "outstanding examples of the aerosol craft by the 5Pointz community, the larger art community and the public." The court also accorded great weight to the testimony of the plaintiffs' expert, Renée Vara, as to the quality and recognized stature of the works, and to the impressive professional achievements of the artists.

In assessing damages, the court concluded that actual damages were not appropriate because "plaintiffs failed to establish a reliable market value for their works." Statutory damages, however, were particularly appropriate where actual damages are difficult to calculate. Here, the court has the discretion to award between $750 and $30,000 per act of infringement, unless the infringement was committed willfully, in which case the award may be as high as $150,000 per act of infringement. The court's message was pointed: Wolkoff's conduct was "the epitome of willfulness." Instead of giving the artists ninety days to try to preserve their works (which the plaintiffs' conservation expert testified was feasible in many cases), he acted "precipitously" in whitewashing the works, knowing that the artists had invoked their rights under VARA. This was "an act of pure pique and revenge for the nerve of the plaintiffs to sue to attempt to prevent the destruction of their art." The timing of Wolkoff's whitewashing—ten months before receiving permits to demolish the building—was troubling for the court. In assessing the maximum statutory damages, the court explained, "If not for Wolkoff's insolence, these damages would not have been assessed." This act not only deprived the artists the opportunity to salvage their works, but also the public, "which would undoubtedly have thronged to say its goodbyes and gaze at the formidable works of aerosol art for the last time. It would have been a wonderful tribute for the artists that they richly deserved."

Second Circuit Decision[48]

On appeal, the Second Circuit unanimously affirmed the district court, holding that the artwork created by appellees was protected by VARA and that Wolkoff's violation of the statute was willful. The appellate court further held that the damages awarded involved no abuse of discretion.

Recognized Stature

Critically, the court provided some guidance on the fluid meaning of "recognized stature," opining that the high quality, status, or caliber is its stature, and the acknowledgment of that stature by a relevant community speaks to its recognition.[49] Artistic quality, the court acknowledged, will often be the most important component of stature. A "relevant community" will generally include "art historians, critics, museum curators, gallerists, other artists, and other art experts."[50] Therefore, except for the rare case when an artist or work is so prominent that the issue of recognized stature is not questioned, this inquiry will generally require expert testimony, an approach which ensures that the court's personal opinion does not factor into the court's analysis. In sum, the court found that Judge Block had not clearly erred in concluding that most of the plaintiffs' works satisfied the criteria for recognized stature.

The Second Circuit also rejected Wolkoff's argument that temporary works could not achieve recognized stature, concluding that there was "nothing in VARA that excludes temporary artwork from attaining recognized stature." To adopt an additional requirement not included by Congress would "upset the balance achieved by the legislature."[51] As an example of a temporary work that achieved recognized stature, the court referenced *The Gates* by Christo and Jeanne-Claude, a 2005 installation of 7,503 orange-draped gates in Central Park. This site-specific work lasted only two weeks but received significant critical acclaim and attention, not just from the art world, but also from the general public. In addition, the court hypothesized that a Banksy painting at 5Pointz would possess recognized stature, even if temporary, noting that Banksy's *Girl With Balloon* self-destructed after selling at Sotheby's for $1.4 million in 2018. Some industry experts have speculated that the prank may have even increased the market value for the work.[52] Only time will tell.

The court next rejected Wolkoff's argument that the recognition should be evaluated as of the date of the whitewashing, not the date of the trial, finding that the artistic merit of the works, as assessed by an expert after their destruction, can be probative of their merit pre-destruction. The court had no objection to testimony by Cohen, an aerosol artist himself, about his curatorial process, which involved Cohen's review of an artist's portfolio and plan, as evidence of stature.

Finally, the Second Circuit concluded that the site of a work is relevant to its recognition and stature, noting that the "[a]ppearance at a major site—*e.g.,* the Louvre or the Prado—ensures that a work will be recognized, that is, seen and appreciated by the public and the art community."[53] Inclusion in a curated site such as 5Pointz suggests that a work is meritorious, especially if the curator is distinguished, noted the court, finding that Judge Block did not err in his consideration of the 5Pointz site as some evidence of recognized stature.

Willfulness

The Second Circuit also agreed that Wolkoff's act of whitewashing the site evinced a deliberate choice to violate VARA rather than to follow the ninety-day statutory notice procedures. Moreover, Wolkoff's testimony that he "would make the same decision today"[54] further underscored his willfulness.

Most troubling to both Judge Block and the appellate court was Wolkoff's decision to whitewash the art without giving the artists time to photograph or to recover their works, and without any reason to believe that the artists would attempt to illegally salvage their work.[55]

Based on the record, the Second Circuit found that the Judge Block could conclude that Wolkoff acted willfully and was liable for enhanced statutory damages.

Statutory Damages Award Not an Abuse of Discretion

Finally, the Second Circuit addressed Wolkoff's challenge to the amount of the statutory damages awarded—$6.75 million—the maximum amount allowed. The high court noted that district courts enjoy wide discretion in setting statutory damages, and found no abuse of that discretion.

Citing the six factors relevant to a determination of statutory damages, the court concluded that "Wolkoff rings the bell on each relevant factor." Those six, drawn from copyright law, are "(1) the infringer's state of mind; (2) the expenses saved, and profits earned, by the infringer; (3) the revenue lost by the copyright holder; (4) the deterrent effect on the infringer and third parties; (5) the infringer's cooperation in providing evidence concerning the value of the infringing material; and (6) the conduct and attitude of the parties."[56]

In particular, the court noted that Wolkoff, a sophisticated real estate developer, was "willing to run the risk of being held liable for substantial statutory damages rather than to jeopardize his multimillion dollar luxury condo project." Moreover, he whitewashed the artworks without any genuine business need to do so, in a "sloppy, half-hearted" way that left the works partially visible under "cheap" white paint, and these "mutilated" works stood for months between whitewashing and the buildings' eventual demolition.[57]

The court also considered testimony from the artists themselves about the significance of 5Pointz to their careers and how the loss of 5Pointz precluded future opportunities and acclaim. The court ruled that while the artists' loss was difficult to quantify, that did not mean there was no loss.

The Second Circuit concluded that the maximum statutory award would deter Wolkoff, as well as other building owners, from committing future violations of VARA. Specifically, such damages would encourage building owners to negotiate in good faith with artists whose works are incorporated into structures and to abide by the ninety-day notice provision set forth in VARA regarding when incorporated art can be removed without destruction or other modification.

The final factor—the conduct and attitude of the parties—also cut in favor of the maximum statutory award. The court observed that Wolkoff made serious misrepresentations at the preliminary injunction phase by testifying that he stood to lose millions of dollars in credits and possibly the entire project if he could not demolish the site within a few months, only to later change his testimony that there was at most a "possibility" that the delay would have caused him financial loss. Subsequently, the truth emerged that he had not even applied for a demolition permit until four months after the demolition had occurred and that he suffered no loss for the delay. The artists, in contrast, had fully complied with the law.

Takeaway of 5Pointz for Collectors

5Pointz is important for several reasons. First, it clarifies the meaning of "works of recognized stature" under VARA, adopting a common sense approach that includes recognition within a particular artistic community, media attention, and professional achievements of the artist, rather than an unduly restrictive interpretation that is "more akin to a masterpiece standard." As the district court noted, "If not a single one of these works meet the recognized stature standard, it is hard to imagine works that would, short of Caravaggio or Rembrandt."

Second, temporary works are eligible for VARA protection (as long as they generally satisfy the requirements for copyright, i.e. subject matter, originality, and fixation). This could be significant to street artists in future cases.

Third, even if a work is not of "recognized stature," VARA also protects works from "intentional distortion, mutilation or other modification . . . [that] would be prejudicial to [the artist's] honor or reputation." A court would consider "whether such alteration would cause injury or damage to the plaintiffs' good name, public esteem or reputation in the artistic community." This question was moot in *Cohen II* because the court was already awarding the maximum amount of statutory damages per infringement.

Fourth, proving actual damages in all copyright cases is challenging for plaintiffs, not just VARA cases. Here, the willfulness of destruction and the attitude of the owner were critical factors in determining damages. Even though the facts in this case were particularly egregious—"simply, as the district court put it, an 'act of pure pique and revenge,'"—it is worth noting that the Second Circuit affirmed an award of enhanced statutory damages when actual damages could not be proven.

Fifth, a more collaborative, interest-based, negotiation between the artist and property owner, especially in the early stages of the conflict, may save the property owner liability under VARA, and possibly avoid the need for litigation altogether. As the district court noted, "Of course, all this could have been easily avoided with a written waiver of the artists' VARA rights up front."[58]

Therefore, it is advisable for the parties to negotiate and sign a contract even before undertaking a project. This would ensure that both sides understand their rights and responsibilities and can reach an agreement that is fair, balanced, and workable.

Conclusion

Given the global and online expansion of the art market and the growing collector base worldwide, knowledge of copyright as it relates to art is immensely beneficial.

Certain issues are relatively straightforward, such as the principles that ownership of a work is not ownership of the copyright in the work and that problems related to publishing images of copyright-protected works in a collection can be avoided by obtaining permission from the artist.

Other potential complex issues with uncertain outcomes if litigated, such as copyright infringement/fair use and moral rights, are best addressed at the acquisition stage by contract, especially with respect to high-priced art. While many collectors acquire art as a lifelong passion, not for investment purposes, they still do not want their work to diminish in value and importance as a result of the loss of art market acceptance or an adverse court ruling.

Collecting art can be immensely rewarding and highly stressful at the same time. Copyright concerns are often overlooked, even after purchase, and, in reality, most deals are sealed with no more than an exchange of payment for the work, an invoice, and a handshake. Hopefully, this guide through the thicket of copyright will help to avoid potential risk and ease the art collector's burden.

Acknowledgment

★ The author gratefully acknowledges Megan E. Noh, Esq., Partner, Pryor Cashman, for her valuable insight and comments on earlier drafts of this chapter, and Lawrence P. Keating, student at Fordham Law School, for his excellent research assistance.

Notes

1 *See Art Transaction Due Diligence Toolkit*, Responsible Art Market (RAM), accessed December 29, 2019, http://responsibleartmarket.org/guidelines/art-transaction-due-diligence-toolkit.
2 Mary Rozell, *The Art Collector's Handbook: The Definitive Guide to Acquiring and Owning Art* (Lund Humphries, 2020), 45–57.
3 *See* Ringgold v. Black Entm't Television, Inc., 126 F.3d 70, 77 (2d Cir. 1997) (holding that a poster depicting an original work by the artist was exhibited on a television program as part of the background set, in nine separate shots for a total air time of only 26.75 seconds, was not a *de minimis* use; notably, the court found that the poster was being used for a decorative purpose, precisely the same purpose for which the artist Faith Ringgold created the original work); see also Cartoon Network LP, LLLP v. CSC Holdings, Inc., 536 F. 3d 121, 127–128 (2d Cir. 2008) (finding that a work that exists for only 1.2 seconds

is of merely transitory duration but noting with approval cases holding that a work "embodied . . . for at least several minutes" is of more than transitory duration).

4 17 U.S.C. § 106 (2018). A copyright holder's bundle of exclusive rights includes the rights to reproduce, prepare derivative works, distribute copies, perform, and display, as well as the right to perform by means of digital audio transmission as applied to sound recordings.

5 Stern v. Lavender, 319 F. Supp. 3d 650, 681 (S.D.N.Y. 2018) (citing Rosen v. eBay, Inc., No. 13-CV-6801-MWF-Ex 2015 US Dist. LEXIS 49999 (C.D. Cal. January 16, 2015)). This rationale should apply equally in the auction house/gallery space, online, and in print.

6 *Id.* at 683 (citing *Rosen*, 2015 US Dist. LEXIS 49999).

7 17 U.S.C. § 101. The nine enumerated categories of works made for hire are a contribution to a collective work, a part of a motion picture or other audiovisual work, a translation, a supplementary work (to another author's work, such as a foreword, chart, or table), a compilation, an instructional text, a test, answer material for a test, and an atlas.

8 See, e.g., Aymes v. Bonelli, 980 F.2d 857, 861 (2d Cir. 1992); Cmty. for Creative Non-Violence v. Reid, 490 U.S. 730 (1989).

9 The US Copyright Act of 1976 defines joint work as "a work prepared by two or more authors with the intention that their contributions be merged into *inseparable or interdependent* parts of a unitary whole." §101 (emphasis added). A writing is not required to establish the existence of a joint work. For an in-depth discussion on joint works, see Chapter 1.

10 Cariou v. Prince, 714 F.3d 694 (2d Cir. 2013).

11 17 U.S.C. § 107.

12 *Cariou*, 714 F.3d at 704 (quoting Cariou v. Prince, 784 F. Supp. 2d 337 at 355.).

13 *Id.* at 707. The Second Circuit rejected the district court's standard that Prince's work "must comment on Cariou, on Cariou's photos, or on aspects of popular culture closely associated with Cariou or his photos." *Id.* at 698 (internal quotations omitted).

14 Precedential fair use cases include Rogers v. Koons, 960 F.2d 301 (2d Cir. 1992); Campbell v. Acuff-Rose Music, Inc., 510 U.S. 569 (1994); and Blanch v. Koons, 467 F.3d 244 (2d Cir. 2006), among others.

15 Carter v. Helmsley-Spear, Inc., 71 F.3d 77, 81 (2d Cir. 1995).

16 Mark Jancou Fine Art Ltd. v. Sotheby's, Inc., 2012 N.Y. Misc. LEXIS 6059 (November 13, 2012), *aff'd*, 2013 N.Y. App. Div. LEXIS 4814 (June 27, 2013).

17 Mark Jancou Fine Art Ltd. v. Sotheby's, Inc., 967 N.Y.S.2d 648 (2013).

18 *See* Isaac Kaplan, "Why Are Artworks Pulled from Auction?" *Artsy* July 13, 2017, https://www.artsy.net/article/artsy-editorial-artworks-pulled-auction.

19 Arnold Herstand & Co. v. Gallery: Gertrude Stein, Inc., 626 N.Y.S.2d 74, 83 (N.Y. App. Div. 1995).

20 Amy Adler, "Cowboys Milking, Formerly Attributed to Cady Noland," *Brooklyn Rail*, March 2016, https://brooklynrail.org/2016/03/criticspage/cowboys-milking-formerly-attributed-to-cady-noland.

21 Randy Kennedy, "Richard Prince, Protesting Trump, Returns Art Payment," *New York Times* January 12, 2017, https://www.nytimes.com/2017/01/12/arts/design/richard-prince-protesting-trump-returns-art-payment.html; Benjamin Sutton, "Richard Prince Disowns His Ivanka Trump Portrait, Possibly Increasing Its Value," *Hyperallergic*, January 13, 2017, https://hyperallergic.com/351403/richard-prince-disowns-his-ivanka-trump-portrait-possibly-increasing-its-value.

22 Noland's original 2017 lawsuit included New York art advisor and dealer Chris d'Amelio as a defendant. Noland voluntarily dismissed her claims against Chris D'Amelio on May 22, 2018, without prejudice and without costs. Third Amended Complaint & Demand for Trial by Jury, at ¶ 51, Noland v. Janssen, 2019 US Dist. LEXIS 37781, (S.D.N.Y. March 8, 2019) (No. 17-CV-05452-JPO) (hereafter *TAC*).

23 Whether the work was stained for "purely aesthetic reasons," as Noland testifies, Affidavit of Plaintiff, Cady Noland in Opposition to Defendants' Motion to Dismiss, August 3, 2018, ¶¶ 9–10, or "to protect it from the elements" as explained by Shaheen, Letter from Shaheen to Noland, July 18, 2014 (faxed July 21, 2014), was not made clear.

24 *Id.; See* Eileen Kinsella, "Cady Noland Disowns $1.4 Million Log Cabin Artwork Sparking Collector Lawsuit," *ArtnetNews*, June 25, 2015, https://news.artnet.com/market/cady-nolandlog-cabin-lawsuit-311283. A conservation report prepared by KOW stated, "the only way to ensure the long-term viability/existence of the artwork would be to replace the rotting logs with new ones."

25 *TAC*, ¶ 31.

26 Complaint, Exhibit A at 11, Mueller v. Michael Janssen Gallery Pte. Ltd., 225 F. Supp. 3d 201 (S.D.N.Y. 2016) (No. 15-CV-04827).

27 *Id.* at *4.

28 Complaint, Exhibit A at *5, *Mueller*, 225 F. Supp. 3d 201 (No. 15-CV-4827).

29 *TAC*, at ¶ 55; Fax from Mueller to Noland, July 21, 2014. The work had not yet been shipped to Mueller (or even to the US) at that time.

30 17 U.S.C. § 106A(a) (1990): ("[T]he author of a work of visual art . . . (3) . . . shall have the right - (A) to prevent any intentional distortion, mutilation, or other modification of that work which would be prejudicial to his or her honor or reputation, and any intentional distortion, mutilation, or modification of that work is a violation of that right, and (B) to prevent any destruction of a work of recognized stature, and any intentional or grossly negligent destruction of that work is a violation of that right.")
Note that Noland does not allege in any of her complaints that the conservation undertaken at Defendants' behest was "intentionally" or "grossly" negligent.

31 Julia Halperin and Eileen Kinsella, "Cady Noland Sues Three Galleries for Copyright Infringement Over Disavowed Log Cabin Sculpture," *ArtnetNews*, July 21, 2017, https://news.artnet.com/artworld/cady-noland-copyright-infringement-log-cabin-1030649; see also Complaint, *Noland*, 2019 US Dist. LEXIS 37781 (S.D.N.Y. March 8, 2019) (No. 17-CV-5452-JPO).

32 *TAC*, at ¶ 64.

33 *Id.*

34 Complaint at 8, *Noland*, 2019 US Dist. LEXIS 37781, (S.D.N.Y. March 8, 2019) (No. 1:17-cv-05452-JPO).

35 *Id.*

36 Halperin and Kinsella, "Cady Noland."

37 *Noland*, 2019 US Dist. LEXIS 37781 at *13. The case is further complicated by complex procedural issues. Here, the court dismissed Noland's moral rights and copyright infringement claims under the US and German laws due to territorial limitations of the US Copyright Act, finding that she did not successfully plead a qualifying "domestic predicate act [that] was itself and act of infringement in violation of the copyright laws." Since "[t]he US Copyright Act does not have extraterritorial application," and all the alleged relevant conduct occurred abroad, Noland's alleged federal copyright claims were not actionable. The court declined in its discretion to exercise supplemental jurisdiction over the remaining claims under German copyright law. Since the court had not previously reached the merits of the defendants' two prior motions to dismiss, Noland was granted a final leave to replead.

38 Noland v. Janssen, 2020 U.S. Dist. LEXIS 95454 (June 1, 2020).

39 Sinclaire Marber, "They Can't Take that Away from Me: An Indemnification Solution to Unmerited VARA Claims," *Columbia Journal of Law & the Arts* 41 (Winter 2018).

40 Sinclaire Marber, E-mail to Judith B. Prowda, December 1, 2019, on file with the author.

41 *See* Elena Goukassian, "Art Gets Damaged All the Time. Here's How It Gets Back to the Market," *Artsy*, July 24, 2018, https://www.artsy.net/article/artsy-editorial-art-damaged-time-market.

42 Angy Altamirano, "Artists File Suit to Keep 5Pointz," *QNS*, October 16, 2013, https://qns.com/story/2013/10/16/artists-file-suit-to-keep-5pointz; *Cohen*, 320 F. Supp. 3d at 434.

43 Cohen v. G & M Realty L.P., 988 F. Supp. 2d 212 (E.D.N.Y. 2013) (hereafter *Cohen I*).

44 Cara Buckley and Marc Santora, "Night Falls, and 5Pointz, a Graffiti Mecca, Is Whited Out in Queens," *New York Times*, November 19, 2013, https://www.nytimes.com/2013/11/20/nyregion/5pointz-a-graffiti-mecca-in-queens-is-wiped-clean-overnight.html.

45 Cohen v. G & M Realty L.P., 320 F. Supp. 3d 421, 447 n.22 (E.D.N.Y. 2018), *aff'd sub nom.* Castillo v. G&M Realty L.P., 950 F.3d 155 (2d Cir. 2020), *as amended* (February 21, 2020) (hereafter *Cohen II*).

46 *Id.* (citing Carter v. Helmsley-Spear, Inc., 71 F.3d 77, 83–85 (2d Cir. 1995)).

47 *Id.* at 438 (citing Christopher J. Robinson, "The 'Recognized Stature' Standard in the Visual Artists Rights Act," *Fordham Law Review* 68 (2000): 1968). "By setting the standard too high, courts risk the destruction of the unrecognized masterwork; by setting it too low, courts risk alienating those . . . whose legitimate property interests are curtailed."

48 Castillo v. G&M Realty L.P., 950 F.3d 155, 162 (2d Cir. 2020), *as amended* (February 21, 2020).

49 *Id.* at 166.

50 *Id.* at 166.

51 *Id.* at 167.

52 Nate Freeman, "Is That Banksy Worth More Now That It's Shredded? We Asked the Experts," *Artsy*, October 10, 2018, https://www.artsy.net/article/artsy-editorial-banksy-worth-shredded-asked-experts.

53 *Castillo*, at 170.

54 *Id.* at 172.

55 *Id.* at 171.

56 *Id.* at 171–72.

57 *Id.* at 172.

58 *Cohen II*, 447 n.22. Whether the artists would have agreed to waive their moral rights will never be known, but an open discussion on the issue may have prompted some of the artists to document and/or preserve their work before it was too late.

4.2

Protection of Street Art
Has VARA Finally Found Its Métier?

William T. McGrath

In 1990, when Congress enacted the Visual Artists Rights Act (VARA), the US recognized formally for the first time the concept of "moral rights" for visual artists. Though European countries have protected these rights (known as "droit moral") since the nineteenth century, the US had always been reluctant to embrace any authorial rights that transcended the rights provided by traditional copyright law. With the passage of VARA, visual artists in the US suddenly enjoyed a new set of rights that purported to protect their reputations and the artistic works themselves. In the parlance of moral rights, these are the rights of "attribution" and "integrity."

The legislative history of VARA contains sentiments that would warm the heart of any visual artist. The House Report states: "the theory of moral rights is that they result in a climate of artistic worth and honor that encourages the author in the arduous act of creation." The Report notes that visual arts protected by VARA "meet a special societal need" and that "it is paramount to the integrity of our culture that we preserve the integrity of our artworks . . . ." The safeguards of VARA would "enhance our cultural heritage."[1]

For at least the first two decades after its enactment, however, VARA failed to live up to these lofty expectations. In the early years, cases were infrequent and dealt with a miscellany of types of works. It was hard to find a pattern of protection for artists and their works. Despite its potential importance in the world of visual arts, VARA had failed to find a niche where its impact could be felt and its primary goals achieved. It was hard to see that VARA served any particular purpose.

More recently, with the burgeoning interest in street art, especially urban murals, VARA may have found its métier. Murals and other works of urban art are important contributions to society. Since they are by nature easily accessible and vulnerable to depredation of various types, VARA's goal of preservation of significant works of visual art takes on a major role.

The Nature of Street Art

It is neither my intent nor desire to define the term "street art." It is not necessary for me to do so—you know it when you see it. But I do want to be clear about the type of art I will be focusing on in this chapter and the terminology I will be using when referring to that art.

Street art is a broad term that encompasses many different styles of art and different methods of creation. Street art is in publicly viewed spaces, on buildings, streets, or other structures. Some street art is created with permission, and some is created illegally. While street art often has stylistic similarities to graffiti, most discussions of street art distinguish it from graffiti. Graffiti tends to be word-based, and is usually an act of personal branding. Graffiti is generally considered to be illegal. Street art, in contrast, tends to be image-based. It often has a political, social, or cultural message, though sometimes it is simply decorative. Much street art is in the nature of painting applied to an exterior wall of a building or other structure, and can be considered a mural. Street art is frequently created with permission or is commissioned by a property owner, but not always. Whether VARA can or should protect unsanctioned street art is a topic best saved for another day, so I will address only street murals that have been created with approval.

Street art is often painted or stenciled. Some forms of street art are "aerosol art," using spray paint. But sculptural works could also be categorized as street art if placed on or near a public street or plaza. One might say that the *Fearless Girl* sculpture by Kristen Visbal, a commissioned work originally placed in the plaza down the street from the New York Stock Exchange and staring down the "Charging Bull" statue in the same plaza, could be labeled street art.

I use the terms street art or urban art in this essay, but I am writing only about a specific subset of street art, namely, street art murals, which I sometimes refer to synonymously as urban murals. The works I am writing about are typically on the exterior walls of a building and thus pit the interests of an artist against the interests of a building owner or municipality.

Our inquiry is to investigate whether VARA, which has been largely ineffectual in protecting artists' rights since its inception, will emerge as an effective mode of protecting street art as it proliferates in modern culture.

The Nature of Moral Rights

While VARA is part of the US Copyright Act, the rights granted to artists under VARA are quite different from rights under copyright. Copyright protects a broad array of original works of authorship, such as literary works, motion pictures, music, architectural works, and, of course, most types of artwork. The copyright owner has exclusive control over certain uses of the copyrighted work, including reproduction, publication, public performance, and display. Because these exclusive rights can be sold or licensed to others, they are referred to as "economic" rights.

Moral rights, in contrast, are "personal" rights. As one court succinctly put it, moral rights are "rights inhering in the artist's personality, transcending property and contract rights and existing independently of the artist's economic interests in his work."[2] For example, if an artist sells her copyright in an oil painting, her economic interests, such as the right to allow reproduction of the work, are extinguished, but her personal rights over the integrity and attribution of the painting remain in force. An important early VARA case characterized these moral rights as "rights of a spiritual, non-economic and personal nature that . . . spring from a belief that an artist in the process of creation injects his spirit into the work, and that the artist's personality, as well as the integrity of the work, should therefore be protected and preserved."[3]

How did Congress suddenly get inspired to protect moral rights after more than a century of ignoring such rights? In fact, it was the nation's economic interests that spurred legislation to protect the personal interests of artists. In 1886, a group composed mostly of European nations entered a multilateral copyright treaty called the Berne Convention. Over time, most developed nations joined the Berne Convention, with the notable exception of the US, which disdained it for over a century. But by the 1980s, as global trade increased, membership in the Berne Convention became imperative for the US. Yet, there were some significant impediments to the US joining the Berne Convention. One of these was that the treaty required every member nation to recognize, to some extent, an artist's moral rights. The US joined the Berne Convention in 1989 and shortly thereafter enacted VARA.

While this moral rights legislation meets the minimum requirement for accession to the Berne Convention, we shall see that the US still did not wholeheartedly embrace the European model of robust protection of moral rights, but rather took a narrow approach in the legislation. Though it provided a basic level of moral rights protection, Congress did not want to interfere significantly with the distribution and marketing of works protected by copyright. In other words, art is important, but let's not go crazy.

Works Protected by VARA

The narrow scope of VARA is seen in Congress's decision to protect only certain limited categories of works of visual art. Notably, the statute does not protect motion pictures, literary works, music, or architecture. The definition of "works of visual art" in the statute does not include the entire array of pictorial, graphic, and sculptural works protected by copyright. Works of visual art include only two types of artistic works. The first type is a "painting, drawing, print, or sculpture, existing in a single copy, or in a limited edition of 200 copies or fewer, signed and consecutively numbered by the author . . . ." The second type of protected work of visual art consists of still photographic images "produced for exhibition purposes only," signed and in limited numbered editions.[4]

Many types of art are not included. The statute specifically excludes posters, applied art, motion pictures, books, merchandise, advertising, magazines, or electronic publications. Also excluded are all works made for hire. In addition, in order to constitute a work of visual art, the work must be copyrightable.

Rights Provided by VARA

VARA provides two types of rights to visual artists: the right of attribution and the right of integrity. The right of attribution is the right of an artist to be recognized by name as the author of her work or to publish anonymously or pseudonymously. It also includes the right to prevent the artist's work from being attributed to another and to prevent the use of the artist's name on work created by others.[5] This right has only infrequently been invoked in VARA litigation.

More important for our purposes is the artist's right of integrity. There are two types of integrity rights in the statute. First is the right to prevent any distortion, mutilation, or modification of the work of visual art, but only if it is intentional and would be prejudicial to the artist's honor or reputation. The concept of prejudice to one's honor or reputation has been described as "inherently murky."[6] One of the leading cases discussing prejudice under VARA explained that an artist's honor or reputation would be harmed if the modified artwork "present[ed] to viewers an artistic vision materially different from that intended by [the artist]."[7]

The integrity right also provides a right to prevent destruction of a protected work. This right exists only if the work is "of recognized stature," and if the destruction is intentional or grossly negligent. To complicate matters, the statute does not include any definition of "recognized stature." Cases that have interpreted this phrase have not been able to provide any significant clarity as to whether a work has recognized stature. Courts typically recite broad subjective standards such as requiring the work to have "merit" or "intrinsic worth" (i.e. stature) and insisting that this stature must be recognized by experts, the art community, or some cross section of society. In *Carter I*, the court postulated a large gray area for the standard by commenting that "a plaintiff need not demonstrate that his or her artwork is equal in stature to that created by artists such as Picasso, Chagall, or Giacometti." At the other end of the spectrum, VARA would not support a lawsuit over "the destruction of a five-year-old's fingerpainting by her class mate."[8] The court did add an important point that the recognized stature requirement must be interpreted in a manner that would maintain the preservative purpose of VARA.

Is VARA Effective in Protecting Art and Artists?

The early decades of VARA litigation were, at best, disappointing to visual artists. In cases where an artist sought to prevent or be compensated for the modification or destruction of a work, courts routinely found some reason why VARA did not apply to the dispute at hand. VARA seemed ill-suited to address the integrity problems most often encountered by artists.

Examples abound. In *Kelley v. Chicago Park District*,[9] VARA was not applicable to prevent destruction of a wildflower garden installed in Chicago's Grant Park by a well-known landscape artist because the court ruled that wildflowers, as living, ever-changing objects of nature, were neither "fixed" in form nor "authored" by the artist, and thus were not copyrightable. In *Cheffins v. Stewart*,[10] a court found that a mobile replica of a Spanish galleon that achieved notoriety at the Burning Man festival was not within the scope of VARA protection because it was "applied art" (i.e. utilitarian in nature), which is excluded for the definition of works of visual art. In *Pollara v. Seymour*,[11] a painted banner was held to be promotional material and thus not protected. In *Carter II*, the court found that the sculpture was made for hire, and thus not within the definition of a work of visual art. In *Lilley v. Stout*,[12] the photographs at issue were not protected because they had not been produced for exhibition purposes only. In *Kleinman v. City of San Marcos*,[13] a colorfully painted junked automobile adorned with the phrase "make love, not war" used as a planter on the property of a retail novelty store was found to be promotional. The statute also declines protection for modifications resulting from the passage of time or the nature of the materials, or as a result of conservation or the manner of public presentation.[14]

The case *Phillips v Pembroke Real Estate Inc.*[15] is another important illustration of how courts have not been receptive to VARA in the context of art in public spaces. The case involved the question whether VARA protects against the removal of "site-specific" art. The artist, David Phillips, is a nationally recognized sculptor who works primarily with stone and bronze forms that he integrates into local environments. Under a commission, Phillips created an integrated work consisting of a variety of sculptural and design elements organized along the diagonal axis of Eastport Park in Boston. The works consisted of stone walls, large pieces of granite, and bronze sculptural elements. Phillips's sculpture was "site-specific" in the sense that each individual piece was designed specifically for, and derived meaning from, its location within the park. After a period of time, the proprietor of the park decided to move the sculptures to an entirely different location outside the park. Phillips sued, claiming that removal of the sculptures would constitute destruction of the work.

The court ruled that VARA does not apply at all to site-specific art. It held that VARA is intended to cover only art that is not permanently affixed or integrated in such a way that the mere act of moving it would destroy it. The court was concerned that protection for site-specific art would "dramatically affect real property interests and laws," and that it would entail "a radical consequence for owners of land." Not all courts, however, have agreed with the categorical approach of the *Phillips* case. *Kelley v Chicago Park District*, the case in which the court held that a living garden was not copyrightable, questioned the holding of *Phillips*. The *Kelley* court noted that nothing in the definition of "work of visual art" implicitly or explicitly excludes this form of art from moral rights protection. The court also noted that site-specific art is not *necessarily* destroyed if moved.

All this is not to say that artists were never successful in pressing VARA claims in the past. Occasional cases have resulted in rulings favorable to the artist, such as *Martin v. City of Indianapolis*,[16] where the artist recovered damages for destruction of a sculptural work. There have also been some notable settlements in VARA litigation. Mural artist Kent Twitchell sued the US government and other defendants for painting over his six-story mural *Ed Ruscha Monument* in Los Angeles.[17] The case settled for $1.1 million. The successful cases, however, have been few and far between, and have been significantly outnumbered by the failed attempts to invoke the integrity rights of VARA.

These examples—and there are more—raise the question of whether VARA has been effective in achieving the goals of preserving art and protecting the reputations of artists. Is VARA nothing more than an ineffectual, token statute that facilitated the US entry to the Berne Convention?

Admittedly, the statute is narrow in its coverage and courts have exhibited a willingness to embrace a variety of defenses and exceptions. It may be that the cases brought by artists in the early decades of the law were not the best vehicles to set the course for the development of artists' rights. Some cases presented radical untested theories, such as *Kelley*'s argument that a wildflower garden the size of a football field could be considered a "painting" or "sculpture" under copyright law and met the requirements of fixation and authorship that are preconditions to all copyright subject matter. One can fashion arguments to support copyright in such a work of landscape art, but it would be forging new terrain in copyright law. The court's conservative approach to the issue does not shock the conscience. Some cases, such as *Lilley v. Stout*, sought protection for works that clearly did not meet the definition of a work of visual art. Others involved works that were more about marketing and promotion than about the moral rights of artists.

But urban murals are an emerging form of popular art for which VARA may provide effective protection. To be sure, street murals still face significant impediments to obtaining VARA protection, but the fundamental means for vindicating the interests of mural artists are in place and may grow stronger as these murals receive greater acceptance as a legitimate art form.

The Emergence of Urban Murals

There is nothing new about murals. Paintings graced cave walls in Lascaux, France, 20,000 years ago. There were wall paintings in Pompeii in 79 A.D., and Renaissance frescoes by Raphael and others filled the rooms of the Villa of Agostino Chigi in Rome.[18] Destruction of murals is not new either. A mural by Diego Rivera commissioned for Rockefeller Center in 1932 was later chiseled off the wall by the Rockefellers when Rivera refused to remove an image of Vladimir Lenin.[19]

There has, however, been a perceptible increase in the appearance and appreciation of urban murals as a form of public art, not only in the US, but in cities around the world. They are found not only in major art centers like New York, Chicago, and Los Angeles. Captivating murals adorn buildings in Philadelphia (a "mural mecca"),[20] Jersey City (home to a spectacular mural of David Bowie),[21] and Detroit (e.g. Katherine Craig's *The Illuminated Mural*),[22] to name just a few. In recent years, VARA litigation has been filed over destruction or threatened destruction of street murals in Pittsburgh, Memphis, Los Angeles, and Normal, Illinois.[23] The popularity of this art form is not surprising. Urban murals often have a vibrancy, scale, and immediacy that are hard to replicate in other art forms.

Urban Murals Legitimized in the 5Pointz Litigation

Long Island City is a neighborhood located on the western tip of Queens, at the terminus point of the Queensborough Bridge. It is along the line of IRT Flushing Line 7 Train. Once home to many factories and commercial sites, it was rezoned in 2001 as a residential neighborhood and has undergone significant gentrification. It has served as home to such notables as Patrick "Battle Axe" Gleason and Metta World Peace.

It was also the home of a place known as 5Pointz, a compound of twelve dilapidated warehouse buildings that, beginning in the early 2000s, became the repository of the largest collection of aerosol art in the US.[24] Prior to that, the exterior walls of the buildings, owned by a developer named Gerald Wolkoff, had become a place for unsightly graffiti. An aerosol artist named

Jonathan Cohen approached Wolkoff with a proposal that would make Cohen the curator of the space, with authority to decide who would be allowed to paint, on what walls, and what works could be overpainted.

Under Cohen's artistic management, 5Pointz evolved into a canvas for "high-end works by internationally recognized aerosol artists."[25] The site had high visibility, including exposure to millions of commuters on the 7 train, and became extremely popular. It became a site for fashion shoots, movie scenes, and outdoor concerts (DJ Kool Herc performed for 4,000 fans). It was listed in guide books as "a New York must see." Wolkoff, himself, appreciated the transformation of his property, describing the art as "beautiful." But, as the neighborhood became more residential, Wolkoff decided to develop the property for two large apartment complexes, which would require demolition of the buildings.

Cohen and other artists filed a VARA suit in 2013 in federal court in Brooklyn to prevent the destruction of the art. The case was assigned to Judge Frederic Block. Judge Block was a small-town lawyer for over thirty years before being named a federal judge, and has since served on the bench for over twenty-five years. He is also an author of several books and is known to speak his mind.

From the outset, Judge Block appreciated the significance of the case, writing that this was the first time a court had to decide "whether the work of an exterior aerosol artist—given its general ephemeral nature—is worthy of any protection under the law."

The first stage of the case was a hearing on Cohen's request for a preliminary injunction to prevent the destruction of the buildings until a full trial could be held. In ruling on a preliminary injunction, a court must consider several factors: Is the plaintiff likely to prevail when the full trial is conducted? What are the respective hardships each party would suffer from an adverse ruling? What is in the best interest of the public? Can the plaintiff be adequately compensated in some other way if no injunction is allowed?

The judge's affinity for the artists' claims is apparent in his initial written opinion, where he quotes Picasso's belief that "the purpose of art is washing the dust of daily life off our souls." According to Judge Block, Picasso "surely would have supported applying VARA to protect the works of the modern aerosol artist." The judge added that "our souls owe a debt of gratitude to the plaintiffs for having brought the dusty walls of [Wolkoff's] buildings to life."

Despite these sentiments, the judge ruled "regrettably" that he would not enjoin the demolition of the buildings. He felt that other factors outweighed the harm to the artists, such as Wolkoff's interests as a property owner, the city's refusal to designate the property as a landmark, and the benefit to the public from adding new housing to the market, including some affordable housing units. He also felt that if the artists proved their case at the trial, money damages could provide an adequate remedy.

At the conclusion of the injunction hearing, Judge Block denied the requested injunction, and indicated that a written opinion would be issued soon. Wolkoff, unwilling to wait for the opinion, had the paintings whitewashed at night without notifying the artists or giving them an opportunity to return to the site to salvage or photograph their works.

The judge was none too pleased with this. In the concluding paragraphs of his written opinion, the judge noted that although Wolkoff had defeated the artists' request to enjoin destruction of the buildings, Wolkoff was exposed to "potentially significant monetary damages," since VARA protects even temporary works from destruction.[26] The court added a final cautionary note: If Wolkoff were to make abundant space available at the planned apartment complex for exterior art and allow Cohen to continue as a curator, it could be propitious. In his own way, the judge was hoping to preserve the spirit of 5Pointz if not its original art. The judge wrote, "For sure, the Court would look kindly on such largesse when it might be required to consider the issue of monetary damages; and 5Pointz, as reincarnated, would live."

After four more years of collecting evidence, taking expert witness depositions, and preparing for trial, a three-week trial took place in late 2017. Two months later, Judge Block issued his ruling on the merits of the case: He determined that forty-five out of the forty-nine works in the suit were protected under VARA, and that Wolkoff's destruction of those works was willful. The court awarded the maximum amount of statutory damages—$150,000 for each of the protected works, for a total of $6.75 million.

Wolkoff appealed and in 2020 the federal court of appeals in New York City affirmed Judge Block's ruling in every respect.

The Impact of the 5Pointz Case

The court opinions in the 5Pointz litigation addressed several legal issues of great practical importance to the viability of any VARA claims for the destruction of urban murals.

First, the most important aspect of the 5Pointz case is the recognition that not all art hangs in museums, or, more precisely, that some street art venues become an "outdoor museum," as one of the artists testified. The court of appeals, citing Banksy and Christo as examples, rejected Wolkoff's argument that the murals at 5Pointz did not deserve to be protected under VARA, commenting that "in recent years, 'street art,' much of which is 'temporary,' has emerged as a major category of contemporary art."[27] Judge Block likewise praised the aerosol artworks, observing that they reflected "striking technical and artistic mastery and vision worthy of display in prominent museums if not on the walls of 5Pointz."[28]

Second, it will often be the case that urban murals are created in a context that might be seen as "not permanent," and Wolkoff argued as much. Importantly, Judge Block ruled that street art is not excluded from VARA protection merely as a result of the temporary nature of the art, and the court of appeals upheld that ruling. Any painting on the exterior of a building is necessarily temporary if the artist is not the owner of the building. Buildings are sold; buildings deteriorate; buildings are demolished. As Heraclitus said, "change is the only constant in life."

The 5Pointz rulings, however, clarify that whatever is or is not known about the duration of the artwork due to the vicissitudes of the building does not deprive the artist of protection under VARA. Judge Block found that "there is no legal support for the proposition that temporary works do not come within VARA's embrace." The statute does not categorize artworks as permanent or temporary. It identifies specifically which types of artworks are excluded from protection, and "temporary" or "ephemeral" artworks are not on the list.

Even a scenario in which a building owner tells an artist before the creation of a mural that the building will be destroyed at some future date does not disqualify it from protection. VARA accounts for this possibility and provides a way for building owners to handle the problem without liability. The solution is simple: procure a written waiver. If the artwork is incorporated into a building and cannot be removed without destroying the art (as would be the case with most exterior building murals), VARA allows the building owner to avoid liability by entering a written waiver agreement, signed by the parties, that specifies that the installation of the work may be subject to destruction.[29]

If the artwork is one that can be safely removed without destruction, the building owner needs to only provide the artist with ninety days' notice of the planned demolition and allow the artist to remove the work or pay for its removal.[30] In the 5Pointz case, Wolkoff had done none of this.

Third, the 5Pointz case debunked the notion that only highbrow art can be protected by VARA. The "recognized stature" requirement of VARA plays an important gatekeeping function required to balance the competing interests of artists and property owners. Congress did not intend VARA to protect every work of visual art from destruction—to do so would unduly encumber the rights of property owners. To warrant preservation, recognized stature is required. 5Pointz teaches us that art need not be traditional or venerable to have stature. It need not be created by artists whose works are discussed in art history classes. It need not be oil painting on canvas. It can be fifty feet in height. It can be created with spray paint.

The court of appeals did not attempt to precisely define the highly subjective phrase "recognized stature," but it did add some contour to the efforts of prior courts. It stated that a work is of recognized stature "when it is one of high quality, status, or caliber that has been acknowledged as such by a relevant community." The court explained that the most important component of stature will generally be artistic quality.

Judges, however, are typically loath to say whether any work of visual art has artistic quality, thanks to a century-old admonition from Supreme Court Justice Oliver Wendell Holmes. In a case involving copyright in an illustrated circus poster, Justice Holmes wisely noted that "it would be a dangerous undertaking for persons trained only to the law to constitute themselves final judges of the worth of pictorial illustrations." The problem he perceived was that some works of genius would not be appreciated. "Their very novelty would make them repulsive until the public had learned the new language in which their author spoke."[31] So it is with street art.

If judges are not suited to dictate what art is meritorious, how is the jury to be guided? Past cases have looked not only to art experts and other members of the artistic community, but also to recognition by "some cross-section of society." In the same vein, the court of appeals in the 5Pointz case said that recognized stature could be established by "substantial evidence of non-expert recognition."[32] The import of this is that an immensely popular street mural painted by a group of local artists in the small town of Normal, Illinois, might achieve recognized stature, even though unknown to art historians or art market elites. Its iconic status in central Illinois justifies its protection under VARA.

Judge Block found the testimony of Wolkoff's expert on the issue of stature to be flawed because she used an unduly restrictive measure "that was more akin to a masterpiece standard" in assessing recognized stature.[33] Even art by unknown artists can achieve recognized stature.

Finally, when an artist's right of integrity clashes with a building owner's right of dominion over his property, courts will understandably be reluctant to permanently enjoin the destruction or allow the art to diminish the value of the property. This is evident from Judge Block's refusal to prevent the destruction of 5Pointz, despite his obvious appreciation of the art. He realized, however, that while the goal of preservation could not be achieved, there was another avenue to recognize the artist's rights, namely monetary compensation. It might not be the perfect solution, but it can help salve the artist's wounds.

The salve the court used was an award of "statutory damages." An artist who prevails in a VARA claim is entitled to recover damages under one of two approaches. She can recover either actual damages or, alternatively, she can request statutory damages for each work that has been violated.

Actual damages are typically based on the lost market value of the work. Statutory damages, in contrast, may be awarded by a court in its discretion according to a monetary range set forth in the Copyright Act. The range is from $750 to $30,000 per work for non-willful infringement. For willful infringements, the range increases substantially up to $150,000 per work. Statutory damages are particularly appropriate when actual damages are difficult to calculate.

Judge Block declined to award any actual damages to the artists, finding that the methodology of their appraisal witness for valuing the works was flawed. Instead, the judge awarded the maximum amount of willful statutory damages to each prevailing artist, totaling $6.75 million.

Statutory damages are intended not only to compensate a plaintiff, but also to deter reprehensible conduct. When Wolkoff challenged the court's finding of willfulness, Judge Block wrote that he was "appalled" at Wolkoff's conduct in the litigation, which included not just the premature whitewashing incident, but also Wolkoff's "material misrepresentation" that misled the court to believe that the destruction of the buildings was imminent, when in fact Wolkoff had not even yet applied for a demolition permit. Judge Block stated that, but for Wolkoff's misrepresentation of the urgency, he would have granted the artist's request for a preliminary injunction "until such time as the buildings were demolished." This would have allowed the public to "say its goodbyes" to 5Pointz and would have been "a wonderful tribute for the artists."[34] The message is that when demolition is unavoidable, every day of additional life for a work of recognized stature, even aerosol art, is treasured.

Conclusion

Though the original art at 5Pointz has been lost, the case provides a legacy of legal principles that will fortify sanctioned street artists in their efforts to protect their works from callous destruction or mutilation. The court's paeans to the works at 5Pointz will undoubtedly influence future courts to take street art seriously and provide additional heft to artists in the balancing of their artistic interests against the commercial interests of property owners. Frederic Block has made many important rulings in his career on the bench, but only in this one has he enabled VARA, at long last, to find its métier.

Notes

1 H.R. Rep. No. 101-514, at 6 (1990).
2 Kelley v. Chicago Park Dist., 635 F.3d 290, 296 (7th Cir. 2011).
3 Carter v. Helmsley-Spear, Inc., 71 F.3d 77, 81 (2d Cir. 1995) (hereafter *Carter II*).
4 17 U.S.C. §101 (2018).
5 *Carter II*, 71 F.3d at 81.
6 Cohen v. G & M Realty L.P., 320 F. Supp. 3d 421, 441 (E.D.N.Y. 2018), *aff'd sub nom.* Castillo v. G&M Realty L.P., 950 F.3d 155 (2d Cir. 2020), *as amended* (February 21, 2020).
7 Carter v. Helmsley-Spear, Inc., 861 F. Supp. 303, 324 (S.D.N.Y. 1994), *aff'd in part, vacated in part, rev'd in part*, 71 F.3d 77 (2d Cir. 1995) (hereafter *Carter I*).
8 *Carter I*, 861 F. Supp. at 325 (internal quotations omitted).
9 Kelley v. Chicago Park Dist., 635 F.3d 290 (7th Cir. 2011).
10 Cheffins v. Stewart, 825 F.3d 588 (9th Cir. 2016).
11 Pollara v. Seymour, 344 F.3d 265 (2d Cir. 2003).
12 Lilley v. Stout, 384 F. Supp. 2d 83 (D.D.C. 2005).
13 Kleinman v. City of San Marcos, 597 F.3d 323 (5th Cir. 2010).
14 17 U.S.C. § 106A(c).
15 Phillips v. Pembroke Real Estate, Inc., 459 F.3d 128 (1st Cir. 2006).
16 Martin v. City of Indianapolis, 192 F.3d 608 (7th Cir. 1999).
17 The mural was destroyed in 2008, but can still be viewed online. See Paige Pfleger, "What Right Do Muralists Have to the Buildings They Paint On?" *NPR*, June 27, 2015, https://www.npr.org/2015/06/27/417204222/what-right-do-muralists-have-to-the-buildings-they-paint-on.
18 Mary Quinlan-McGrath, "The Astrological Vault of the Villa Farnesina: Agostino Chigi's Rising Sign," *Journal of the Warburg and Courtauld Institutes* 47 (1984): 91–105.
19 Allison Keyes, "Destroyed by Rockefellers, Mural Trespassed on Political Vision," *NPR*, March 9, 2014, https://www.npr.org/2014/03/09/287745199/destroyed-by-rockefellers-mural-trespassed-on-political-vision.
20 Images available online. See Lauren Silverman, "On Philly's Walls, Murals Painted with Brotherly Love," *NPR*, August 23, 2010, https://www.npr.org/templates/story/story.php?storyId=129281658.
21 Image available online. Matthew McCann, "David Bowie Mural," Dronestagram, http://www.drone-stagr.am/david-bowie-mural.
22 Image available online. Pleger, "What Right Do Muralists Have," https://www.npr.org/2015/06/27/417204222/what-right-do-muralists-have-to-the-buildings-they-paint-on.
23 Holbrook v. City of Pittsburgh, No. 18-CV-539-RCM (W.D. Pa. September 16, 2019); see also Grace Ha, "Pennsylvania District Court to Rule on Whether Street-Artists VARA Plaintiff Must Plead Facts Supporting 'Recognized Stature' of the Work," Hughes Hubbard & Reed (blog), May 14, 2019, https://www.

hhrartlaw.com/2019/05/pennsylvania-district-court-to-rule-on-whether-street-artist-vara-plaintiff-must-plead-facts-supporting-recognized-statureof-the-work/#_ftnref1. Complaint, Binczyk et al v. City of Memphis, No. 18-CV-2280 (W.D. Tenn. filed April 25, 2018); see also "Artists Sue City of Memphis Over Controversial Murals That Were Painted Over," *Local Memphis ABC 24*, April 26, 2018, https://www.localmemphis.com/article/news/local/artists-sue-city-of-memphis-over-controversial-murals-that-were-painted-over/522-d80ba853-2764-4aa0-ba60-d40f48973201. Complaint, Thrasher v. Siegel, No. 17-CV-3047 (C.D. Cal. filed April 24, 2017), https://www.courthousenews.com/wp-content/uploads/2017/04/Bukowski.pdf. Baird v. Town of Normal, No. 19-CV-1141, 2020 WL 234622 (C. D. Ill. January 15, 2020); see also Kelsey Watznauer, "Artists Sue Normal, Developer Ahead of Uptown Mural's Destruction," *Pantagraph*, April 27, 2019, https://www.pantagraph.com/news/local/govt-and-politics/artists-sue-normal-developer-ahead-of-uptown-mural-s-destruction/article_5becd162-4da9-5ff2-ab8b-ce2f21cf1ed4.html.

24 Cohen v. G & M Realty L.P., 988 F. Supp. 2d 212, 214 (E.D.N.Y. 2013).
25 *Id*. at 219.
26 *Id*. at 227.
27 Castillo v. G&M Realty L.P., 950 F.3d 155, 167 (2d Cir. 2020).
28 Cohen v. G & M Realty, L.P., 320 F. Supp. 3d 421, 431 (E.D.N.Y. 2018).
29 17 U.S.C § 113(d)(1)(B).
30 17 U.S.C § 113(d)(2)(B).
31 Bleistein v. Donaldson Lithographing Co., 188 U.S. 239, 251 (1903).
32 Castillo v. G&M Realty L.P., No. 18-CV-498 at 15 (2d Cir. 2020).
33 Cohen v. G & M Realty L.P., 320 F. Supp. 3d 421, 439 (E.D.N.Y. 2018).
34 Cohen v. G&M Realty L.P., No. 13-CV-5612-FB-RLM, 2018 WL 2973385, at *6 (E.D.N.Y. June 13, 2018).

4.3

APPROPRIATION ART
Creating by Taking

Daniel J. Brooks

Introduction

A familiar saying, attributed both to Pablo Picasso and to T.S. Eliot (and, therefore, probably apocryphal), asserts, "Good artists borrow, great artists steal." Whatever its provenance, the saying accurately reflects an important strand in art history. The tradition of appropriating objects or artworks created by others is widespread: from collages of wine labels by Picasso and Georges Braque to the use of found objects ("readymades"), such as snow shovels and urinals, by Marcel Duchamp to Andy Warhol's iconic appropriation of symbols of popular culture, including Campbell Soup cans, Brillo boxes, and Marilyn Monroe, to post-modern appropriation artists, such as Sherrie Levine, Barbara Kruger, Jeff Koons, and Richard Prince, who, by appropriating other artists' works as their own, implicitly question concepts of originality and ownership.[1] When the appropriated element incorporated into a new work—rather than being a commonplace object—is itself an artwork protected by the copyright laws, the copyright owner's rights and the appropriator's fair use defense to copyright infringement are implicated, placing limitations on the artist's right to create a new work by taking from another artist.

In his seminal opinion first delineating the fair use defense in this country, in a case involving an abridgment of a book containing the writings of George Washington, Justice Story famously stated: "There must be real, substantial condensation of the materials, and intellectual labor and judgment bestowed thereon; and not merely the facile use of the scissors; or extracts of the essential parts, constituting the chief value of the original work."[2] Scissors have been supplanted by digital means of appropriation, but it remains true that fair use requires more than mindless and unnecessary extraction of protected expression, justified only by the happenstance that, regardless of the availability of alternatives in the public domain or the economic harm to the copyright owner, the appropriator found, liked, and was easily able to reproduce the original copyrighted work and incorporate it into a new work. Guidance on the constraints that should apply to appropriation artists may be found in the statutory codification of the fair use doctrine and in the cases interpreting the fair use defense to copyright infringement.

Background on Fair Use Analysis

The common-law fair use doctrine was codified in § 107 of the Copyright Act of 1976. The preamble to §107 contains examples of secondary uses that had been found to be fair uses, and then lists four non-exclusive factors distilled from common-law cases, which must be explored in assessing the fair use defense:

> [T]he fair use of a copyrighted work . . . for purposes such as criticism, comment, news reporting, teaching (including multiple copies for classroom use), scholarship, or research, is not an infringement of copyright. In determining whether the use made of a work in any particular case is a fair use the factors to be considered shall include -
>
> 1 the purpose and character of the use, including whether such use is of a commercial nature or is for nonprofit educational purposes;
> 2 the nature of the copyrighted work;
> 3 the amount and substantiality of the portion used in relation to the copyrighted work as a whole; and
> 4 the effect of the use upon the potential market for or value of the copyrighted work.[3]

Unless an artist always has *carte blanche* to steal another artist's work, the fair use doctrine must require some justification for unauthorized appropriation. Often, bona fide justifications for taking someone else's work correlate with the examples set forth in the preamble to § 107. For instance, as Justice Story put it, "no one can doubt that a reviewer may fairly cite largely from the original work, if his design be really and truly to use the passages for the purposes of fair and reasonable criticism."[4] Book reviewers engaged in criticism do not need an author's consent before copying from the book being reviewed because "[q]uite apart from the impairment of freedom of expression that would result from giving a copyright holder control over public criticism of his work, to deem such quotation an infringement would greatly reduce the credibility of book reviews, to the detriment of copyright owners as a group . . . ."[5]

Similarly, it was fair use to use a clip from John Lennon's iconic song, *Imagine*, envisioning a world without religion, in a film juxtaposing marching soldiers and an image of Stalin, in order to make a political comment arguing that secular utopian views are naïve and ultimately result in dictatorship.[6] In a case involving news reporting as fair use, an existing controversy regarding whether it was appropriate for Miss Puerto Rico Universe to have posed for nude modeling photographs justified publication of the photos because they "were the story" and "[i]t would have been much more difficult to explain the controversy without reproducing" the newsworthy photos.[7]

Teaching and scholarship often qualify for fair use treatment because "the administrative costs of finding and obtaining consent from copyright holders would frustrate many academic uses."[8] An internet search engine that facilitates research by copying website images has been justified as fair use because it "transforms the image into a pointer directing a user to a source of information."[9] Finally, parody, a form of criticism and comment, is often accorded protection as fair use because: "Parody's humor, or in any event its comment, necessarily springs from recognizable allusion to its object through distorted imitation. Its art lies in the tension between a known original and its parodic twin. When parody takes aim at a particular original work, the parody must be able to 'conjure up' at least enough of that original to make the object of its critical wit recognizable."[10]

To be sure, fair use is not strictly limited to the purposes (criticism, comment, news reporting, teaching, scholarship, and research) identified in the preamble to § 107.[11] The Supreme Court has made clear, however, that while the preambular examples are "illustrative and not limitative," analysis of the first fair use factor, "the purpose and character of the use, including whether such use is of a commercial nature or is for nonprofit educational purposes," may "be guided by the examples given in the preamble to § 107 . . . ."[12]

The Concept of Transformativeness

The goal of incentivizing creativity and innovation by giving copyright holders exclusive rights to their works has long coexisted with the recognition that, "[i]n truth, in literature, in science and in art, there are, and can be, few, if any, things, which, in an abstract sense, are strictly new and original throughout. Every book in literature, science and art, borrows, and must necessarily borrow, and use much which was well known and used before."[13] The fair use doctrine attempts to accommodate the tension between protecting creators of original works and allowing others to express themselves by reference to copyrighted works (i.e. allowing them to make unauthorized copies of portions of those works), by "permit[ting] courts to avoid rigid application of the copyright statute when, on occasion, it would stifle the very creativity which that law is designed to foster."[14]

The question of when copying is justified (and fair use) was addressed in an influential article by then-District Judge Pierre N. Leval, who wrote that the first fair use factor (the purpose and character of the use) "raises the question of justification[,]" which, in turn, depends "primarily on whether, and to what extent, the challenged use is transformative."[15] Elaborating on transformativeness, Judge Leval stated: "[t]he use must be productive and must employ the quoted matter in a different manner or for a different purpose from the original. A quotation of copyrighted material that merely repackages or republishes the original is unlikely to pass the test; in Justice Story's words, it would merely 'supersede the objects' of the original."[16] In *Campbell v. Acuff-Rose*, the Supreme Court adopted Judge Leval's reasoning on the "purpose and character" prong of the first fair use factor, stating that the "central purpose of this investigation is to see, in Justice Story's words, whether the new work merely 'supersede[s] the objects' of the original creation . . . or instead adds something new, with a further purpose or different character, altering the first with new expression, meaning, or message; it asks, in other words, whether and to what extent the new work is 'transformative.'"[17] Emphasizing the importance of the transformative use standard, the Supreme Court stated: "Although such transformative use is not absolutely necessary for a finding of fair use, the goal of copyright, to promote science and the arts, is generally furthered by the creation of transformative works. Such works thus lie at the heart of the fair use doctrine's guarantee of breathing space within the confines of copyright."[18]

Problems with Transformativeness as Applied to Appropriation Art

Although conceived of as a way of analyzing the first fair use factor (the purpose and character of the use, including whether such use is of a commercial nature or is for nonprofit educational purposes), the transformativeness test has come to dominate analysis of all four fair use factors. As to the first fair use factor, while a commercial purpose normally militates against fair use, the Supreme Court held in *Campbell* that "the more transformative the new work, the less will be the significance of other factors, like commercialism, that may weigh against a finding of fair use."[19] As to the second fair use factor (the nature of the copyrighted work), while recognizing that certain creative works "are closer to the core of intended copyright protection than others, with the consequence that fair use is more difficult to establish when the former works are copied[,]" the Supreme Court held in *Campbell* that in the case of a transformative parody, this factor was entitled to little weight because "parodies almost invariably copy publicly known, expressive works."[20] Subsequent cases, including appropriation art cases, have effectively eliminated (or at least sharply discounted) the second fair use factor, even when parody is not involved, as long as the "creative work of art is being used for a transformative purpose."[21] As for the third fair use factor (the amount and substantiality of the portion used in relation to the copyrighted work as a whole), even wholesale copying, with little alteration, by an appropriation artist has been found not to weigh against fair use because the secondary use "must be [permitted] to conjure up at least enough of the original to fulfill its transformative purpose."[22] Finally, the fourth fair use factor (the effect of the use upon the potential market for or value of the copyrighted work) has also been subordinated to the transformativeness test: Market harm is only cognizable when the secondary use completely "usurps" the market for the original work, which is highly unlikely if the secondary use is transformative, and, therefore, presumably aimed at a different audience than the original.[23]

Placing such inordinate weight, in the assessment of all four fair use factors, on whether a secondary work of art is "transformative" (a term not found in the codification of fair use in §107 of the Copyright Act) makes the determination of fair use dependent on the subjective aesthetic views of judges acting as art critics, a task for which they are unsuited. As Justice Holmes remarked: "[I]t would be a dangerous undertaking for persons trained only to the law to constitute themselves final judges of the worth of [a work], outside of the narrowest and most obvious limits."[24] As a leading authority on copyright has put it, applications of the transformative use standard have been "conclusory—they appear to label a use 'not transformative' as a shorthand for 'not fair,' and correlatively 'transformative' for 'fair.' Such a strategy empties the term of meaning—for the 'transformative' moniker to guide, rather than follow, the fair use analysis, it must amount to more than a conclusory label."[25] Finding fair use whenever, in the subjective opinion of the judge or judges assigned to the case, the secondary work is deemed to be "transformative" results in "the transformative use standard . . . becom[ing] all things to all people."[26]

Another problem arising from the expansive use of the transformativeness standard is the denigration of one of the important exclusive rights conferred upon copyright owners: the right to create or authorize others to create "derivative works."[27] In contrast to the statutory fair use provision found in §107, which never employs the word "transformative," the statutory definition of a derivative work is "a work based upon one or more preexisting works, such as a translation, musical arrangement, dramatization, fictionalization, motion picture version, sound recording, art reproduction, abridgment, condensation, or any other form in which a work may be recast, transformed, or adapted."[28] Because the creation of a derivative work requires the permission of the copyright owner of the original preexisting copyrighted work, the expansive application of the transformative use doctrine "necessarily implie[s] a narrow conception of the derivative right . . . ."[29] One court has warned that the high-water mark in transformativeness based on perceived aesthetic alterations of original artistic works in secondary works of appropriation art threatens to eviscerate §106(2)'s derivative work right: "To say that a new use transforms the work is precisely to say that it is derivative and thus, one might suppose, protected under §106(2). *Cariou* and its predecessors in the Second Circuit do not explain how every 'transformative use' can be 'fair use' without extinguishing the author's rights under § 106(2)."[30]

Restoring Meaning to All Four Fair Use Factors by Not Focusing Exclusively on Transformativeness

If an appropriator invariably had to pay for a license in order to copy original works, many types of creative works—often tracking the preambular examples in §107—would be stymied. A reviewer could not pay an author because such a payment would undermine the credibility of the review; a parodist would likely be unable to obtain a license from someone whose work she desires to ridicule; a scholar would be unable to afford to pay royalties to every author of a work she desires to cite; a search engine would be unable to locate and pay each owner of every snippet of information it wishes to use as a pointer to enable others to conduct research on the internet. These unauthorized uses should be accommodated, whether or not they are transformative, by focusing on the purpose and character of the secondary use, including its commercial or nonprofit nature, as instructed by the first fair use factor. In accordance with the second and third fair use factors (the nature of the copyrighted work and the amount of the copying), the copying of expressive material, especially if it exceeds the secondary user's purpose, should also be taken into account, whether or not the secondary work is transformative. While certain transformative works, notably parodies, need to "conjure up" recognizable portions of well-known original works, the same is not necessarily true of all transformative works, such as works of art that incorporate other visual images for their aesthetic appeal.

Cognizable harm under the fourth fair use factor should not be limited to the complete usurpation of the original author's market. An unauthorized transformative use, targeted to a different market or audience, can, nevertheless, cause brand name fatigue and dissuade potential licensees from licensing the original for other, unrelated uses.[31] Instead, the focus should be on whether the appropriation of the specific image was necessary. An artist seeking to incorporate a copyrighted visual image (such as a photograph) into a work of appropriation art will often be able to obtain a public domain equivalent for free or a stock photograph for a modest royalty. Unnecessarily taking, instead, a copyrighted photograph drives down the price "to the cost of copying, leaving nothing to cover the cost of creating the work."[32] This would not only harm photographers, whose works are subject to widespread misappropriation which is exceedingly difficult to police, and who are dependent upon a functioning licensing market in order to earn a livelihood, but also secondary users because "killing the proverbial goose that laid the golden egg"[33] would deprive them of usable raw materials for their derivative works.

Conclusion

Creativity will be maximized, consistently with the goal of the copyright laws, by adjusting a standard that predominantly emphasizes transformativeness to focus, instead, on whether the appropriation of copyrighted materials was necessary and, therefore, justified, regardless of whether the original work was transformed.

Notes

1 *See* E. Kenly Ames, "Beyond *Rogers v. Koons*: A Fair Use Standard for Appropriation," *Columbia Law Review* 93, no. 6 (1993): 1477.
2 Folsom v. Marsh, 9 F. Cas. 342, 345 (No. 4,901) (C.C.D. Mass. 1841).
3 17 U.S.C. § 107 (2018).
4 Folsom, 9 F. Cas. at 344.
5 Ty, Inc. v. Publ'ns Int'l Ltd., 292 F.3d 512, 517 (7th Cir. 2002).
6 Lennon v. Premise Media Corp., 556 F. Supp. 2d 310, 322–23 (S.D.N.Y. 2008).
7 Núñez v. Carribean Int'l News Corp., 235 F.3d 18, 22 (1st Cir. 2000).
8 Kienitz v. Sconnie Nation LLC, 766 F.3d 756, 759 (7th Cir. 2014).
9 Perfect 10, Inc. v. Amazon.com, Inc., 508 F.3d 1146, 1165 (9th Cir. 2007).
10 Campbell v. Acuff-Rose Music, Inc., 510 U.S. 569, 587–88 (1994) (citation omitted).
11 Cariou v. Prince, 714 F.3d 694, 706 (2d Cir. 2013).
12 Campbell, 510 U.S. at 578–79.
13 *Id.* at 575 (quoting Emerson v. Davies, 8 F. Cas. 615, 619 (No. 4,436) (C.C.D. Mass. 1845)).
14 Stewart v. Abend, 495 U.S. 207, 236 (1990).
15 Pierre N. Leval, "Toward a Fair Use Standard," *Harvard Law Review* 103 (March 1990): 111.
16 Leval, "Toward," 1111.
17 Campbell, 510 U.S. at 579.
18 *Id.*
19 *Id.*
20 *Id.* at 586.
21 Cariou, 714 F.3d at 710.
22 *Id.* at 710 (internal quotations and emphasis omitted).

23 Cariou, at 708–09; see also Authors Guild v. Google, Inc., 804 F.3d 202, 224 (2d Cir. 2015) (Leval, J.) (cognizable harm under the fourth fair use factor requires the secondary use to completely supplant and substitute for the original work; "the possibility, or even the probability or certainty, of some loss of sales does not suffice to make the copy an effectively competing substitute that would tilt the weighty fourth factor in favor of the rights holder in the original").

24 Bleistein v. Donaldson Lithographing Co., 188 U.S. 239, 251 (1903).

25 Melville B. Nimmer and David Nimmer, *Nimmer on Copyright* (New York: M. Bender, 2014), Vol. 4 § 13.05[A][1][b], 13–170.

26 Nimmer, *Nimmer on Copyright* (citation omitted).

27 17 U.S.C. § 106(2).

28 17 U.S.C. § 101.

29 Paul Goldstein, *Goldstein on Copyright*, 3rd ed. (New York: Aspen 2014), Vol. 2, § 12.2.2.1(c), at 12:37, 1238 n.78.7.

30 Kienitz, 766 F.3d at 758.

31 See Henley v. DeVore, 733 F. Supp. 2d 1144, 1163 (C.D. Cal. 2010).

32 William M. Landes, "Copyright, Borrowed Images, and Appropriation Art: An Economic Approach," *George Mason Law Review* 9, no. 1 (2000): 18–19.

33 Cambridge Univ. Press v. Patton, 769 F.3d 1232, 1258 (11th Cir. 2014).

4.4

APPROPRIATION ART

Creating by Using

John Koegel

A term has been applied to certain works of art that noticeably depict a preexisting image or object: appropriation art. In these works, the artist uses certain source material as a significant component of his or her work. Indeed, sometimes the work is entirely a representation of the source material. Some artists create artworks based entirely on their imagination, while others create art that depicts something the artist sees. Throughout the history of art, artists have been offering their "take" on something they are looking at (some aspect of their landscape). Artists then interpret or reflect that landscape. In doing so, they provide a focus on some portion of the world they encounter that the viewer is then invited to consider. Appropriation art is an evolving form of realism in which the artist presents an object or image exactly as it exists, sometimes by itself but oftentimes with other objects or images that have never been combined in the same way.

The purest form of appropriation is a new work that simply replicates a source. These works are presented by some artists to engender an inquiry and discussion of what authorship or originality means. The re-creation of a prior work (and clearly identified to be a re-creation and not the source itself) is recognized to be an exploration of these subjects. Other artists replicate existing images or objects to invite a reflection on the image or object (i.e. the viewer is encouraged to think differently about the image or object and what the image or object means to society at large). When the presentation of source material is combined with other sources or modified in some way, it is generally understood that the artist is making a comment on the source material and thus an invitation to think about the source material in one or more different ways. Using a source in a visual work of art is not the same as plagiarism because the source material is not viewed to have come from the imagination of the artist. It is normally clear that the image is taken from somewhere. The viewer is supposed to engage in a thoughtful reaction to the reality that is being represented in a different context and by that appropriation alone, the viewer is engaged to reflect on the source material in a new way.

Most scholars/historians trace the beginning of appropriation art to the beginning of the twentieth century with artists such as, and most notably, Pablo Picasso and Georges Braque. These collagists and others combined bits of existing material, often newsprint or photographs, sometimes adding additional elements of their own, thereby creating an artwork whose whole is more meaningful than the sum of its parts. The importance behind collage was to challenge the dogma that art must spring entirely from the creativity of the artist. Collage shifted the focus of artistic creation toward a recognition of the artist as one who might juxtapose existing elements in ways that would draw new meanings from those recognizable elements. Collage was then adapted by artists in a movement referred to as Dada. The most well-known Dada artist was Marcel Duchamp who called his artworks "ready-mades." He selected existing objects which he simply exhibited as artworks. This act of simply changing the context and the presentation of a utilitarian object to function as an aesthetic or conceptual object was a startling appropriation that had an enormous impact on viewers and on subsequent artists influenced by his dramatic idea.

Beginning in the mid-1950s and running solidly through the 1960s, the Pop Art movement evolved. This movement involved the use of existing imagery from mass culture principally from advertising, photography, comic strips, and other mass media sources. Jasper Johns was a major Pop artist beginning with his paintings of the American flag (1955). Johns was also inspired to incorporate real objects into sculptural renditions such as a pair of painted bronze Ballantine ale cans (1960). A close friend and compatriot of Johns, Robert Rauschenberg also appropriated objects and images in most of his 1950s collage works. Following closely in these footsteps was Roy Lichtenstein, who began making paintings of cartoon characters and exact copies of segments from comic strips in 1960. He produced a prodigious body of this work throughout his highly celebrated career. Claes Oldenburg, a compatriot of Lichtenstein, appropriated three-dimensional objects by simply changing the materials from which they were made. Other notable examples of Pop artists taking images from advertising and mass media culture are James Rosenquist, Tom Wesselmann, and Larry Rivers.

Andy Warhol stood astride this group but eventually overtook all of them in recognition and importance. One of the most celebrated American artists of the twentieth century, he was perhaps the most prominent figure in the Pop Art movement of the 1950s and 1960s, when he championed the practice of presenting everyday items such as Campbell's soup cans, Brillo pads, and portraits of famous people. He sought to address a consumer society and mass media culture that he saw as idolizing fame and fashion. So his oeuvre (which is enormous) consists largely of works that significantly utilize an existing image.

The appropriation of existing images or objects can also be found in the works of many contemporary artists. Some prominent examples are Barbara Kruger, who combines black and white images taken from advertising and other media with pungently confrontational assertions overlaid in red and white typeface; Haim Steinbach, who displays several disparate objects on a shelf; Christian Marclay, who most famously created a single video work entirely consisting of short segments from motion pictures; Elaine Sturtevant, who made inexact "repetitions" of contemporary Pop artists such as Warhol, Johns, Lichtenstein, and Haring; and Louise Lawler, who photographs the works of other artists and presents these photographs as works that she created. Artists most known by the title of "appropriation" are Sherrie Levine, Richard Prince, and Jeff Koons. Each of these artists has created well-known works that simply replicate an existing image. Levine appropriated exact copies of famous photographs by photographers such as Edward Weston or Walker Evans. For Prince and Koons, the appropriation was exact copies of advertisements. In each instance, the work was identified as being a work of art by Levine, Prince, or Koons. In each instance, it is clear that the artist is making a reproduction of the source material. The legal issue that arises is whether the owner of the source material has any right to prevent or claim compensation from Levine, Prince, or Koons when they produce, display, and sell any of these appropriated reproductions.

As appropriation has become more commonplace, lawsuits (and claims) against artists from the owners of source material have increased. It is not surprising that most of these lawsuits are directed at artists who have achieved significant economic success for their artwork. So it is equally not surprising that Jeff Koons, one of the more successful and hence highly visible appropriation artists, has been a frequent target of copyright infringement litigation based on works he created using existing copyrighted works.

Inspired by the groundbreaking efforts of Marcel Duchamp, Koons, from the onset, looked to the world of ordinary objects as his landscape. Among his earliest works were plastic inflatables manufactured for children. By simply displaying these in an art gallery setting, Koons sought to have those commonplace items seen and understood quite differently—the same artistic concept pursued by Duchamp. Koons followed this group of works with a series in 1980 entitled *The New* where he presented objects such as vacuum cleaners encased in plexiglass. In his next series of works in 1985, Koons moved from simply re-presenting an inflatable object to casting the inflatable object in some other material. This next group, entitled *Equilibrium*, presented ordinary objects cast in bronze—an aqua lung, a snorkel, and a lifeboat. In 1986, in a series entitled *Luxury and Degradation*, Koons presented objects—a travel bar, a Baccarat crystal set, or a simple pail cast in stainless steel along with paintings of billboard advertisements for certain liquor brands. Koons saw this group of work as commenting on the pretensions of the middle class, which Koons viewed as superficial. Following a 1986 group of statuary works (also cast in stainless steel) that included his most famous work, *Rabbit*, Koons produced a series of large sculptures, some made of porcelain and others poly-chromed wood, along with several elaborate mirrors. The title for this 1988 group of twenty works was *Banality*. Rather than just transfer found objects into another medium, Koons collaged or spliced together different images into a newly forged grouping, thereby creating a dialogue among the characters or objects in the group. To date, six of the sixteen sculptures in the series have been subjected to lawsuits from copyright owners of artwork he appropriated. The first lawsuit was in 1989 by Californian photographer Art Rogers who contended that Koons had made unauthorized use of a photograph printed on a mass produced, commercially distributed note card.[1] Koons did not dispute that he used the black and white photographic note card as a source for his sculpture, *String of Puppies*. However, he pointed to the differences between the photograph and the sculpture, which he argued created an entirely different, distinct artistic expression. For example, he changed the medium from a two-dimensional photograph to a three-dimensional sculpture which was 42 × 62 inches as opposed to 5 × 7 inches. All of the figures were painted, flowers were added, and the puppies were painted blue with white dots on their noses turning this sculpture from any real depiction to an unreal one. Basically, Koons converted (transformed) a commercial greeting card with an idyllic photograph of a loving couple holding their prize-winning German Shepherd puppies set against a warm pastoral background into a large-scale sculptural work of art depicting two eerie, vacuous-looking people sitting on a bench holding eight absurdly colored, cartoonish dogs. On the basis of these differences, Koons claimed fair use, likening the use to a parody of the generic image that the photographer had commercially distributed. The district court and the court of appeals ruled that the differences were not meaningful under existing applicable law, and Koons violated the photographer's exclusive right to authorize a derivative work. In analyzing the fair use factors, the courts found (against evidence to the contrary) that the photographer suffered market injury solely because Koons sold his sculpture for a substantial profit.[2]

Koons faced three additional lawsuits for other works in this series around the same time as the *Rogers* lawsuit. The first was brought by the publisher of the famous comic strip Garfield. The most prominent and well-known character was the dog, Odie, which was regularly featured in this comic strip since its inception in 1978.[3] Koons created a three-dimensional version of Odie and collaged it with another cartoon character and a basket containing a toy bumblebee. Like *String of Puppies*, this sculpture, entitled *Wild Boy and Puppy*, was a large and unquestionably distinct work of art. Nevertheless, the court decided to simply follow the court of appeals in the *Rogers* lawsuit by holding that the Koons use was an infringement of the cartoonist rights and not a fair use. The court said that the commercial nature of Koons's work not only resolved the question of the purpose and character of the sculpture, but also created a presumption of economic injury. The court also refused to view the use of Odie as a form of parody since Koons was not clearly poking fun at this particular cartoon character, but rather at society in general.[4]

The next lawsuit against a *Banality* series sculpture was brought by a photographer who created a photograph of two young boys pushing a pig, which was commercially distributed on birthday cards and note cards. Koons used this subject of the boys and the pig to create a sculpture entitled *Ushering in Banality* that not only changed the size, medium, and colors, but also included other components to create a cluster of characters considerably different from the photograph. Relying on the decision in the Rogers case, the court declined to conduct any fair use analysis and simply ruled that the Rogers decision foreclosed, as a matter of law, any asserted defense of fair use.[5]

The next case against a *Banality* series sculpture was brought by the motion picture distributor, MGM-Pathe, which owned the rights to the animated character, Pink Panther. In that sculpture, Koons combined the Pink Panther with a model taken from a photograph in *Penthouse* magazine. That lawsuit was held in abeyance pending the result of the *Rogers* case and was then eventually settled.[6]

Recently, two other *Banality* series sculptures have been challenged through the courts in France (hence judged under the French copyright law). One was brought by a photographer who licensed a photograph of two naked children in 1975 for a postcard which Koons used to produce a sculpture entitled *Naked*.[7] The other challenge was brought by an art director for a 1985 advertisement for a line of clothes (*Naf Naf*), which Koons used as a source for a sculpture entitled *Fait d'Hiver*.[8] The courts in both of these cases ruled against Koons, finding his sculptural works to be infringements.

Notwithstanding all of these court decisions against Koons for his 1988 *Banality* sculptures, Koons did prevail against a challenge brought in 2003 by a photographer who was commissioned by a fashion magazine to shoot a series of photographs for an article on metallic makeup.[9] The challenged work, *Silk Sandals*, was one of seven monumental paintings created in 2000, in which Koons collaged fragments from a number of widely published mass media sources. The painting at issue (which was 10' × 14' and entitled *Niagra*) combined eight images culled from widely distributed publications and through this combination, Koons altered the content, orientation, scale, and medium of all of these published images, thereby creating a comment on the objects depicted. The district court found that Koons's use of a portion of the source photograph was transformational and that Koons's painting was not a substitute for the photograph and therefore not competitive with the image. The court of appeals affirmed this finding of fair use, observing that Koons's purpose in using the photograph was sharply different from the photographer's goal in creating it.[10] The court applied 1994 guidance from the Supreme Court's *Campbell v. Acuff Rose*[11] decision to recognize that, when a source is used as raw material in furtherance of a distinct, creative, or communicative purpose, the use is transformative. The court noted that Koons had a genuine creative rationale for using the image in the photograph and that there would be no reason to question his artistic purpose. The court also observed that there was no deleterious effect on the potential for or value of the source photograph and that simply asserting the loss of some license fee is not market injury. Finally, the court made an important comment on the purpose of copyright indicating that the ultimate test of fair use is whether copyright's goal of promoting progress in the arts is better served by allowing a challenged use than by preventing it. Recognizing that the public exhibition of art is properly considered to have value that benefits the broader public interest, the Second Circuit found Koons's use to be in furtherance of that goal.

Another Koons work was challenged recently by a photographer who, in 1986, was hired to take a photograph for a liquor ad (Gordon's Gin).[12] This advertisement was unquestionably part of the landscape in 1986 when it appeared on many billboards. And the billboard advertisement contained more than just the creativity of the photographer. Since Koons was addressing this product through his artwork, this piece stands out as one of his significant works of appropriation art.

Richard Prince is another high-profile, extremely successful appropriation artist who has faced multiple lawsuits alleging copyright infringement. For decades, Prince has found inspiration in objects from contemporary media and popular culture. He uses the term "rephotography" for his technique of reproducing these images to be exhibited in a completely different context (namely, as a work of art in an art gallery or museum). In doing so, he seeks to present the image for reconsideration by the viewer. In 2008, Prince exhibited thirty paintings and collages in an exhibition entitled *Canal Zone*. He made these works by using black and white photographs of Rastafarians taken by Patrick Cariou, a photographer who published these works in 2000 in a book about Rastafarians. The district court granted summary judgment in favor of the photographer but the court of appeals reversed in part, holding that twenty-five of the thirty works were clearly protected by fair use.[13] The other five works, which were not found to be fair use as a matter of law, were said to involve "relatively minimal alterations" and were remanded to the district court for further factual consideration. The court of appeals gave substantial weight to the question of whether the Prince works "transformed" the source material, adopting an "objective viewer test" to determine whether the challenged works would appear to a reasonable viewer to have new aesthetics and thereby seen to be a new expression. Analyzing the works as a reasonable observer, the court found differences that fundamentally altered the photographs in terms of composition, presentation, scale, color palette, and medium. These changes were sufficient to render twenty-five of the thirty challenged works to be transformative as a matter of law. The other important factor—effect of the challenged use on the potential market for/or value of the source material—was also found to weigh in favor of Prince since the target audience for black and white prints and the collage art was distinctly different and therefore Prince's use could not be seen as usurping any market that the photographer might have pursued. The other fair use factors were given minimal weight due to the finding that the photographs were sufficiently transformed.[14]

In 2014, Prince created a series of works based on photographs found through the internet on Instagram. Returning to an earlier (and initial) interest in pure "rephotography," he selected certain photographs of people for a group of works that he entitled *New Portraits*. In each instance, he revised and/or created some text in the same format as the text would appear on an Instagram posting and then produced a large-scale (5' × 6') photo-realistic painting. Thirty-seven of these new portraits were exhibited in 2014 at the Gagosian Gallery in New York and twenty-six were exhibited in 2015 at the Tokyo gallery of Blum & Poe. Two photographers sued Prince for using their Instagram images—one, a photograph of a Rastafarian smoking a joint taken in 1986 and, the other, an image of musician Kim Gordon in 2014. Each asserted that the predominant aesthetic feature in each Prince painting simply exploited the creative virtues of the underlying photographs and potentially usurped a market for photographic prints that these photographers could target with derivative works of their own. So far, the court to which these cases have been assigned has said that the question of sufficient transformation and the question of market impact do not unquestionably favor a finding of fair use as a matter of law, denying Prince's motion to dismiss the claim. So any determination of fair use requires some evaluation of additional, factual information permitting the case to continue.[15]

Warhol was also the subject of several lawsuits. In 1966, he was sued by a photographer (Patricia Caulfield) whose photograph of poppies Warhol found in a photography magazine. Warhol enlarged the image and had it silk-screened onto canvases that were then painted in bright, often unrealistic colors. The resulting series (entitled *Flowers*) were displayed in the Leo Castelli Gallery in 1974. Warhol was also sued by a photojournalist, Charles Moore, whose 1963 photograph of police dogs attacking protesters in Birmingham, Alabama, was published in *Life* magazine. Warhol overlaid colors and multiplied the images to create a series of large paintings, which he entitled *Race Riot*. Even though both adaptations were arguably transformative, Warhol elected to settle with these photographers.

Then, in 1996, Warhol was sued by *Time* magazine and photographer Henri Daumann. In November 1963, *Time* published a memorial edition on the life of John F. Kennedy, which included a number of photographs taken during his funeral. Warhol took a small portion of one photograph that included the face of Jackie Kennedy under a veil and produced sixteen paintings of various colors. Like the earlier cases, this lawsuit was settled.[16]

Currently, a group of Warhol paintings created in 1984 is being challenged by photographer Lynn Goldsmith who, in 1981, took a portrait photograph of the musician, Prince Rogers Nelson, commonly known as "Prince." Warhol created sixteen paintings of Prince in various colors, consistent with many of his other celebrity portrait paintings. In comparing the two works, the court noted that the Goldsmith black and white photograph includes not only Prince's face, but also much of his torso and seeks to depict Prince as a vulnerable person. In contrast, Warhol's paintings used only the face and significantly altered many of the realistic features in the photograph. The district court ruled that Warhol's use qualified as a fair use, principally on the observation that the paintings were transformative since they presented a different aesthetic and had a different character than the photograph. This determination was also based on the finding that the paintings were not market substitutes for copies of the photograph and therefore the photographer's market for her photographs had not been usurped.[17]

Not only well-known artists are sued for infringement based on appropriating existing works.

In 1999, the artist Thomas Forsythe was sued by Mattel (the manufacturer of Barbie dolls) for his series of seventy-eight photographs in which he depicted Barbie dolls in various absurd and often sexualized positions.[18] The district court found that Forsythe's use of Barbie was fair use and not infringing because the purpose was to criticize and comment on the idealized beauty depicted by Barbie. Moreover, his works could not be seen as affecting any market demand for Barbie dolls. The court of appeals affirmed this outcome.[19]

In 2001, Mattel also sued the artist Susanne Pitt claiming that her use of a Barbie doll, which was physically altered and clothed in sadomasochistic attire and presented as a work of art, violated its copyright rights.[20] The district court likewise concluded that potential harm to Mattel's market was unlikely to be affected and that Pitts's use of the doll was "patently transformative."[21]

In 2009, a poster created for the Obama campaign for President by Shepard Fairey was challenged by the Associated Press, which claimed copyright in a 2006 photograph of Obama that was taken at a press conference by one of its freelance photographers. While Fairey did use the photograph, and while the facial features and pose of the subject were the same, Fairey made a number of significant additions which made his work noticeably altered and different from the photograph. Prior to the commencement of the lawsuit, Fairey altered evidence by attempting to delete images from his computer's hard drive, and misrepresented the source photograph he used to the court. The case was set for trial when the parties settled as Judge Hellerstein indicated that he would not grant summary judgment for either party. Consequently, there was no verdict about whether Fairey's use was fair and privileged.

In 2012, a Pop artist named Thierry Guetta was sued by a photographer for using a 1977 photograph of the musician Sid Vicious.[22] In this case, the district court recognized the elements added by Guetta in his painting but found that the overall effect did not render the painting sufficiently transformative since the court could not see any new meaning added to the photograph. Accordingly, the court found that the painting infringed the photograph.

In 2014, the artist Elizabeth Peyton was sued by the same photographer, Dennis Morris, for several 1994 drawings in which she used certain 1977 photographs of the musician John Lydon as a source.[23] All of the drawings are artistic renderings and lack the same character as the photographs which were used. No court determination was ever made since this lawsuit was settled through mediation.

In 2012, a political action group, which produced a posterized rendering of a photograph of the mayor of Madison, Wisconsin, on T-shirts and tank tops with the phrase "sorry for partying," was sued by the photographer who took the photograph used as the source.[24] The district court found the use to be fair, viewing it to be both transformative and parodic. The district court further found that the artistic use could not substitute for and did produce any demand for the photograph. The court of appeals rejected the transformative test but affirmed this determination principally on the ground that the artistic use had no perceptible market effect on the photograph.

In 1988, the artist David Salle was sued by photographer Ken Heyman for infringing a 1964 photograph of the art collector Robert Scull in his dining room, published in a 1965 book on Pop Art. Salle used the photograph in 1982 to create an enormous backdrop, part of a set design for an opera.[25] That backdrop was photographed by a friend of Salles, and this photograph appeared in a monograph published by Vintage Books. Heyman sued Salle and the other photographer. Salle was also sued in 1984 for a large-scale painting that was prominently featured in an exhibition at the Leo Castelli Gallery.[26] One relatively minor portion of the painting contained a drawing that was published in a 1982 book by two artists who remarkably had simply traced a Pulitzer Prize-winning photograph of the assassination of Jack Ruby. Both of these lawsuits were withdrawn following informal criticism by the judges who would have eventually ruled on these claims.

In 2000, artist Barbara Kruger was sued by photographer Thomas Hoepker for using a photograph of a background as source for one of her iconic works.[27] The lawsuit was dismissed without any finding on the subject of copyright infringement.

The most important fair use case to date was not about art; it involved two songs. In 1994, the US Supreme Court decided the case *Campbell v. Acuff-Rose Music*.[28] Regardless of the medium, this case greatly changed the calculus for determining whether a commercial work of art that utilizes existing artwork as source material will be within the protection of the fair use exception. The Supreme Court observed that the primary objective of copyright law is to balance the benefit to the public and the exclusive rights of authors when transformative works are created. The opinion elevated the importance of an inquiry into whether the challenged work was transformative of the source material. The court observed: "Such works thus lie at the heart of the fair use doctrine's guarantee of breathing space within the confines of copyright . . . and the more transformative the new work, the less will be the significance of other factors, like commercialism, that may weigh against a finding of fair use."[29] The court also sought to eliminate the use of any presumptions in evaluating a fair use defense and especially the presumption that was applied in the earlier Koons cases that a commercial use would be presumptively unfair.

As a result of *Campbell* and court decisions which have followed *Campbell*, the most important consideration in determining whether a use of preexisting material will be fair and privileged is whether the challenged work "transforms" the source material. Through subsequent court decisions, a number of guidelines have been articulated for reaching this determination. Among them, most notably are the following: (i) whether the challenged work alters the source material with some new meaning or some new message; (ii) whether the challenged work employs some new aesthetic to the source material and hence whether there are aesthetic differences between the two works; (iii) whether the challenged work has a different purpose or different character than the source; (iv) whether, conversely, the challenged work merely supersedes the purpose of the source or simply serves as a substitute for the source; and (v) whether the challenged work should be viewed as enriching to society (i.e. whether the public benefited by having the challenged work). Any or all of these are currently the questions to be applied by a court or trier of fact in reaching this important initial determination. As it now stands, this one determination will greatly (indeed, almost decisively) impact the outcome. The more a challenged work transforms the source, the more the challenged work should qualify as fair use. A challenged work that presents little or no transformation will most likely be viewed as unfair.

The other important assessment is whether there is some detrimental market effect on the owner of the source material (since copyright law offers authors the expectation of economic return as an incentive to create new works). A number of different guidelines have similarly been articulated for reaching this determination. Among them, most notably are the following: (i) whether the challenged use usurps some traditional, reasonable, or likely to be developed market for the source material; (ii) whether the target audience of the two works is the same; (iii) whether potential purchasers would likely opt to acquire the challenged work instead of the source material; (iv) whether there is any evidence that the monetary value of the source has decreased as a result of the challenged use; and (v) whether unrestricted and widespread uses of the challenged work beyond whatever it has actually occurred would potentially result in an adverse impact on the market for the source material. Prior to the *Campbell* decision, this consideration (market effect) was supposed to have the greatest impact on assessment of fair use. But in light of *Campbell* and the importance of giving latitude to different or transformative new works, the weight of this consideration has been significantly diminished.

By increasing the weight of the transformation assessment (the first fair use factor), the court reduced the weight of the other three statutory factors to a point where, currently, the second and third factors (the nature of the source material and the amount of the source used) have little or no bearing on the fair use determination.

While the decisions since *Campbell* have shed much of the precedential weight of *Rogers v. Koons*, one detrimental and erroneous remark by the district court has not been adequately debunked: "in Copyright law, the medium is not the message." Since a change in the medium of some source changes the context of that source, and since that, in turn, changes the viewers' perception of the source, as far as visual art is concerned, a change in medium is significantly transformative.

Copyright law (through the application of the fair use privilege) with few exceptions should support appropriation art. While enormous changes have taken place over the 231 years since the adoption of the US Constitution, the constitutional purpose and authority for any copyright law (and the rights granted to authors by the law) entirely supports a robust allowance for appropriation art. The authority to offer authors the right to control and benefit from their creative contributions is based on a succinct purpose, which is the promotion of "progress" in the various endeavors that copyright law encourages.[30] Accordingly, Congress has been empowered to fashion copyright laws for this stated, ultimate purpose. As evidenced by the approach of the founders of the Constitution who were the framers of the first copyright law, the primary and ultimate beneficiary of the limited copyright right is supposed to be the general public. This can be seen and recognized in the first Copyright Act which was codified two years after the Constitution was adopted. In the initial Copyright Act, in order to hold a copyright right, the author had to take three steps: (1) record a claim of copyright; (2) publish that claim; and (3) deposit a copy of the work with the federal government. Twelve years later (1802), an additional requirement was added: formal notice imprinted on the work itself. In addition, the first copyright term was fourteen years, thought to be enough time to achieve an economic return on the endeavor. While a renewal term of fourteen years could be obtained, it was only possible if the author was still alive and if the author took some affirmative action (i.e. filing a renewal claim if the author seriously wanted to hold onto the right). So at the time when copyright was closer to its foundation, this limited copyright monopoly was available to an author only when the author presented the work to the public, only when the author demonstrated that having the right meant something to him/her, and only when the author informed the public that he/she was the author and that he/she claimed copyright rights to a particular work and then only for a short period of time (closely tied to the author). Even though Congress has greatly expanded the ability to own a copyright right (eliminating all formalities) and even though that term has now been extended to seventy years beyond the life of the author, the fundamental purpose or basis for copyright remains—to encourage distribution of creative activity to the public for the benefit of the public. While the creator has and should have the ability to reap economic opportunities that may have served as an incentive, those opportunities should be limited to those that are traditional, reasonable, or likely to be developed. The copyright right should not be like a patent that bars any use of the subject matter covered by the patent. Rather, it should be treated as a right to pursue compensation through those forms of exploitation that the existing marketplace offers since those marketplace opportunities represent the existing incentive to create and publish.

A work of art containing source material that serves a different function from that source material should be recognized invariably to be a distinctly different artistic expression for a distinctly different audience (or market) and thereby privileged under copyright law.

Notes

1 Complaint, Rogers v. Koons, 751 F. Supp. 474 (S.D.N.Y. filed October 11, 1989) (No. 89-CV-6707).
2 Rogers v. Koons, 751 F. Supp. 474 (S.D.N.Y. 1990), *amended on reargument*, 777 F. Supp. 1 (S.D.N.Y. 1991), and *aff'd* 960 F.2d 301 (2d Cir. 1992); see also Rogers v. Koons, 960 F.2d 301 (2d Cir. 1992).
3 United Feature Syndicate, Inc. v. Koons, 817 F. Supp. 370 (S.D.N.Y. 1993).
4 *Id.* at 383–85.
5 Campbell v. Koons, No. 91-CV-6055-RO, 1993 WL 97381, at *3 (S.D.N.Y. April 1, 1993).
6 MGM-PATHE Communications Co. v. Koons, No. 91-CV-04852-DNE (S.D.N.Y. 1991).
7 Cour d'appel [CA] [regional court of appeal] Paris, civ., December 17, 2019, 17/09695; see also Eleanor Rosati, "Paris Court of Appeal Confirms that Koons's 'Naked' Sculpture Infringes Copyright in 'Enfants' Photograph, Rejecting Freedom of the Arts and Parody Defences," *IPKat*, December 23, 2019, https://www.artforum.com/news/jeff-koons-loses-appeal-in-copyright-case-over-naked-sculpture-81685.
8 Naomi Rea, "Jeff Koons Is Found Guilty of Plagiarism in Paris and Ordered to Pay $168,000 to the Creator of an Ad He Appropriated," *Artnet News*, November 9, 2018, https://news.artnet.com/art-world/jeff-koons-plagiarism-lawsuit-1354876.
9 Blanch v. Koons, 467 F.3d 244 (2d Cir. 2006).
10 *Id.* at 252–53.
11 Campbell v. Acuff-Rose Music, Inc., 510 U.S. 569 (1994).
12 Complaint, Gray v. Koons, No. 15-CV-09727 (S.D.N.Y. December 14, 2015).
13 Cariou v. Prince, 784 F. Supp. 2d 337 (S.D.N.Y. 2011), *judgment rev'd in part, vacated in part*, 714 F.3d 694 (2d Cir. 2013); see also Cariou v. Prince 714 F.3d 694 (2d Cir. 2013).
14 Cariou, 714 F.3d at 705–11.
15 Graham v. Prince, 265 F. Supp. 3d 366, 385–86 (S.D.N.Y. 2017); Complaint, McNatt v. Prince, No. 16-CV-08896 (S.D.N.Y. filed November 16, 2016).
16 Dauman v. Andy Warhol Found. for Visual Arts, Inc., No. 96-CV-9219-TPG, 1997 WL 337488 (S.D.N.Y. June 19, 1997).
17 Andy Warhol Found. for the Visual Arts, Inc. v. Goldsmith, 382 F. Supp. 3d 312, 330–31 (S.D.N.Y. 2019).
18 Mattel, Inc v. Walking Mountain Prods., No. 99-CV-8543 (C.D. Cal. 1999).
19 Mattel, Inc v. Walking Mountain Prods., 353 F. 3d 792 (9th Cir. 2003).
20 Mattel, Inc. v. Pitt, No. 01-CV-1864-LTS-AJP, 2001 WL 1155153 (S.D.N.Y. October 1, 2001).
21 Mattel, Inc. v. Pitt, 229 F. Supp. 2d 315, 322 (S.D.N.Y. 2002).
22 Morris v. Guetta, No. 12-CV-0684-JAK, 2013 WL 440127 (C.D. Cal. February 4, 2013).
23 Complaint, Morris v. Target Corp., No. 14-CV-4010 (C.D. Cal. filed May 26, 2014).
24 Kienitz v. Sconnie Nation LLC, 965 F. Supp. 2d 1042, 1054 (W.D. Wis. 2013), *aff'd*, 766 F.3d 756 (7th Cir. 2014).
25 Heyman v. Salle, 743 F. Supp. 190 (S.D.N.Y. 1989).
26 Cockrell and Oberg v. Salle and Leo Castelli Gallery (84-CV-5291) (S.D.N.Y. 1984).
27 Hoepker v. Kruger, 200 F. Supp. 2d 340 (S.D.N.Y. 2002).
28 Campbell v. Acuff-Rose Music, 510 U.S. 569 (1994).
29 *Id.* at 579 (internal citations omitted).
30 U.S. Const. art. 1, § 8, cl. 8.

4.5

AUTHORSHIP AND AUTHENTICITY

Banksy

Interview with Alex Branczik

Alex Branczik (AB) is a Senior Director and Head of Contemporary Art, Europe, at Sotheby's London. He was closely involved in the sales of major collections, including the Collection of Jean-Yves Mock and the groundbreaking Bear Witness single-owner sale. He drove the transformation of Sotheby's October Contemporary Art sales from mid-season events into high-profile auctions, which included the sale of Gerhard Richter's *Abstraktes Bild* from the collection of Eric Clapton for £21.3 million—at the time, the record for any work by a living artist. He also oversaw the sale of Zeng Fanzhi's *The Last Supper* for HK$180.4 million, which, at the time, set a new auction record for any work by a Chinese contemporary artist.

Michelle Bogre (MB) interviewed him on the phone on October 18, 2019. This interview has been edited for clarity and length.

MB: Do you think that the ideas about authorship have changed in the twenty-first century?

AB: The idea of authorship has been a line of inquiry for artists to mine for centuries. We are looking here at Duchamp's urinal,[1] to the Robert Rauschenberg's erased[2] Willem de Kooning drawing, to the contemporary notion that it does not matter whether artists paint their own paintings. Jeff Koons does not paint his own paintings; he hires studios to do them. Does that mean it is not a work by Koons? No it does not. I think authorship has continued to be a ripe avenue for exploration into the twenty-first century.

MB: The idea of authorship has changed even more for photography, I think, as photographers appropriate work by taking images off of Google, for example.

AB: Did Richard Prince not do that in the 1980s?

MB: Prince appropriated work for sure, but he usually appropriated copyrighted work and then claimed a copyright in the work he created. These photographers are taking satellite images, which may not have a copyright and then claiming a copyright in the work they create from that image. So maybe what has changed is the availability of sources from which to appropriate.

AB: Let's consider Richard Prince's joke paintings.[3] He was interested in painting jokes because they are authorless, part of the shared narrative of who we are in the society we live in. You never pin an author to a joke. The trajectory of what constitutes authorship started much earlier in the twentieth century and now we no longer think that artists have to completely create the image for it to be their artwork. That was shocking in the 1980s, for example, with Richard Prince and Glenn Brown, the British painter, who had numerous court cases with Chris Foss, the science fiction illustrator, because Glenn appropriated his images. That was shocking then, but it does not seem shocking now.

MB: You are right. Let's take the Jeff Koons sculptures of the puppies made from the Art Rogers photograph. Koons never claimed he made the sculptures. He hired artisans in Italy to do that.

AB: Totally. Koons employed the best craftsman or industrial professionals because he wanted the work to be perfect.

MB: Today we accept that authorship lies as much in the idea as the hand of the artist on the work itself. Let's talk about Banksy's *Love is in the Bin*. When I looked at the video,[4] it struck me that the actual shredding was a wonderful performative piece. So, does *Love is in the Bin* now have two types of authorship: the performative shredding event and the renamed half-shredded piece? Or was the video just an ephemeral performance? How would you look at that?

AB: I said at the time, and I still believe that it was a genius piece of performance art. It plays to the very core of the art market and the auction room. I also am convinced that the shredder stopped exactly where Banksy designed it to stop. If the painting had shredded all the way through and ended up in a pile on the floor that would have not have been a good photograph to circulate around to the world media It would just have been an empty frame, so there is no doubt in my mind that the artwork titled *Love is in the Bin* is exactly the piece that Banksy intended it to be. I cannot say it is for sure; you would have to speak to Banksy, but that is my conviction. When I said that publicly shortly after the auction, sure enough the next day or a couple of days later, Banksy published another video, which ended with the piece shredding entirely, and the line: "In rehearsals, it worked every time." He is an artist who has been a master of the visual image and of reducing complicated matters like Brexit, the art market, or the value of art, into a simple shareable iconic image. I think the picture of the half-shredded painting is now an iconic image, which is the essence of what Banksy does. Everywhere I go, people know that image. It was on view in Stuttgart in the Staatsgalerie, hung next to a Monet. The Banksy is behind protective glass; the Monet is not.

MB: Yes, it strikes me that if he had intended it to shred all the way through, it would have. Half-shredded now, it hangs, it has a frame. So should the act of authorship include the placement of the shredder?

AB: The act of authorship was not the placement of the shredder; it was the whole concept of the work. The original artwork, *Girl with Balloon*, that was shredded was an original Banksy. We were given a certificate by Pest Control—the Banksy authentication body—which gave us a full date and ownership history of *Girl with Balloon*, created in the weeks leading up to the auction. So, it was a Banksy painting that was being shredded, but the work was not complete, I suppose, until the hammer fell on that night in October in the Sotheby's showroom, and shortly after, he named it *Love is in the Bin*. I said at the time that he did not destroy a work of art; he created one. He used the medium of the auction as the stage upon which to create the performance and the new piece.

MB: You have resale rights in the UK, so Banksy shares in the resale of *Love is in the Bin*? Will the notoriety help that?

AB: We have resale rights, but they are capped at 12,000 euros so it is more like a royalty. So if there is a benefit to Banksy, it was that it was such a successful performance that it has contributed to an increase in price for his other works. For example, we sold another painting by Banksy two weeks ago for 10 million pounds.

MB: I thought it was brilliant, but to get back to something you said, you mentioned that *Girl with Balloon* was authenticated by Pest Control, but then was that a valid authentication if Banksy intended to create the new piece? What's going on in the art world with authentications? I know that some authentication bodies or foundations—Warhol, Roy Lichtenstein, Keith Haring, and Noguchi—have stopped authenticating works because of too much litigation. What happens when artworks are not authenticated?

AB: That started a while ago and has been more of a case in the US than in Europe. Authentication services started with good intentions: someone trying to catalogue the entire production of an artist and to look after the artist's estate. But when you have an Andy Warhol or Jean-Michel Basquiat, whose paintings are worth millions, the legal ramifications of saying that something is or is not by the artist can become so expensive that it becomes prohibitive for these well-intentioned bodies to exist. If you tell someone their painting is not by Warhol, you may well get slapped with a lawsuit, which will cost a lot of money to deal with, whether you are right or wrong. For Banksy, there is probably a greater need for an authenticating process because he makes street art that he does not want to be sold, and he makes work that is made to be sold. He does not want bits of his street art to be taken down to benefit an individual rather than the general public. So, he needs an authentication process that does not so much determine if a work is by Banksy as it determines whether it is a Banksy that can be sold or one that cannot. One of the great things about Banksy is that you do not have to be wealthy to enjoy his work. You can walk around the corner and have the delight of seeing an unexpected mural on a wall, or you can buy limited edition prints, which are priced at a fraction of the value of unique artworks.

Notes

1 Jon Mann, "How Duchamp's Urinal Changed Art Forever," *Artsy*, May 9, 2017, https://www.artsy.net/article/artsy-editorial-duchamps-urinal-changed-art-forever.
2 Zuzanna Stanska, "The Story How Robert Rauschenberg 'Erased de Kooning,'" *Daily Art Magazine*, August 1, 2017, https://www.dailyartmagazine.com/story-robert-rauschenberg-erased-de-kooning.
3 "Paintings," Richard Prince, accessed May 19, 2020, http://www.richardprince.com/paintings/monochromatic-jokes.
4 See ZCZ Films, "Banksy: Love Is in the Bin," YouTube video, uploaded October 30, 2018, 3:31, https://www.youtube.com/watch?v=OgUvznznbCuc (originally titled *Girl with Balloon*, the half-shredded work was retitled *Love is in the Bin*).

4.6

LANDMARK CASE

Mass. Museum of Contemporary Art Found., Inc. v. Buchel, 593 F.3d 38 (1st Cir. 2010)

Christoph Büchel is a Swiss artist known for provocative, large-scale art installations. In 2006, Büchel and the Massachusetts Museum of Contemporary Art (MASS MoCA) reached an agreement regarding a project entitled "Training Ground for Democracy." MASS MoCA would exhibit this project, which Büchel envisioned as "essentially a village, . . . contain[ing] several major architectural and structural elements integrated into a whole, through which a visitor could walk (and climb)." *Mass. Museum of Contemporary Art Found., Inc. v. Buchel*, 593 F.3d 38, 43 (1st Cir. 2010). Visitors would essentially role-play a sort of military training and would "train" to participate in all the activities that collectively constitute modern democracy, in all its flaws and contradictions. As one may expect, this would be the largest project in MASS MoCA's history.

Unfortunately, the parties never formalized most elements of their relationship, even though this project would require plenty of time, money, labor, and space. The museum and the artist never executed any written instrument addressing the financing of the project, nor did they enter into any written agreements addressing the artist's rights under the Visual Artists Rights Act (VARA) or the creative liberties that the museum may take when dealing with unclear directions. The only significant matter that the parties expressly signed off on was that Büchel would own the copyright in the exhibition once it was completed.

Over the course of the exhibition's development, the artist and the museum found themselves increasingly at odds. The museum was frustrated by what they perceived to be the artist's lack of concrete directions, unreasonable financial and logistical demands, and obstinacy regarding the details of the projects. However, the artist felt that the museum was compromising his artistic integrity and ignoring his instructions. In particular, the museum and the artist frequently (and unsurprisingly) argued about the budget, with the museum attempting to minimize costs and the artist steadfast in his demands that his artistic vision be fully realized. As the disagreements hardened and the room for compromise dwindled, the museum announced that it was cancelling "Training Ground," and instead opening a new exhibit entitled *Made at MASS MoCA*, which would explore the unique challenges inherent to complex collaborative projects between artists and institutions. Due to space constraints, the exhibition would need to include some of the areas where the unfinished "Training Ground" project was kept. In order to restrict viewing of this unfinished project, the museum covered it in yellow tarpaulin.

The museum sued Büchel a day before it announced *Made at MASS MoCA*. The museum asserted that it was entitled to present the unfinished constructions and materials of "Training Ground" to the public, and sought relief clarifying that it was entitled to do so under VARA. Büchel responded with five counterclaims. The two most important ones were the first and second, which sought an injunction under VARA prohibiting the museum from publicly displaying his unfinished work, and VARA damages stemming from the museum's alleged distortion and modification of his art, respectively. The federal district court ruled in favor of the museum, determining that VARA did not preclude the museum from displaying the incomplete project. Likewise, the court denied Büchel's requests for injunctive relief and damages under VARA.

Hearing the case on appeal, the First Circuit was more receptive toward Büchel's claim that there existed genuine issues of material fact that require a rejection of the museum's motion for summary judgment. The First Circuit found that a reasonable jury could find that Büchel was entitled to relief under VARA in relation to the museum's continuing work on "Training Ground" over his objections, but determined that Büchel could not survive the museum's motion for summary judgment on his distortion claim. The First Circuit first addressed whether VARA applied to unfinished works. The court focused on the "fixation" requirement for copyright protection under the Copyright Act, and read VARA in accordance with the definition of "fixation" under section 101 of the Copyright Act. Accordingly, the court found that VARA does in fact protect unfinished works, as long as those works (1) would qualify for copyright protection had they been completed, and (2) were fixed. Applying this analysis to the case at hand, the First Circuit found that Büchel's unfinished project was subject to VARA protection.

The court then moved to the museum's motion for summary judgment on Büchel's claim that the museum's continuing work on the exhibition violated his VARA rights. According to the court, the factual record allowed inferences that museum staff members ignored the artist's instructions and intentionally modified "Training Ground" in ways in which he did not approve. The alterations also seem to have adversely affected the artist's reputation, as various publications wrote about the chaos surrounding the development of Büchel's installation. Ultimately, the record includes information that cuts both in favor of the artist in the museum, but viewing the facts in a light most favorable to the party facing summary judgment dismissal (i.e. Büchel) compelled the court to reject the museum's motion for summary judgment on this matter. Then, in upholding the museum's motion for summary judgment on Büchel's distortion claim, the First Circuit noted that the museum's covering of the unfinished artwork could not reasonably constitute distortion under VARA. The court reached this conclusion despite the fact that the unfinished project was still highly recognizable under the tarpaulin. The court remarked that to conclude otherwise would mean that covering a finished artwork before its formal opening would give rise to a distortion claim, which would be excessive. The First Circuit also pointed to the existence of a separate moral right: the right of disclosure. Given that the drafters of VARA chose not to protect this right, Büchel's claim that the museum's inadvertent display of his unfinished project constituted illicit alteration must fall.

VARA is a relatively new addition to the Copyright Act, and any decisions addressing its application will likely hold significant precedential value for future disputes. The First Circuit's decision is important for several reasons, one of which is that it clarifies that unfinished works are entitled to VARA protection, provided that they are fixed and would otherwise receive copyright protection had they been completed. This reasoning could extend to other areas of visual art, such as street art. Nevertheless, disputes over the scope of VARA will continue, and decisions such as this offer valuable insight into how courts may address this novel area of copyright law.

Cariou v. Prince, 714 F.3d 694 (2d Cir. 2013)

In 2000, photographer Patrick Cariou published a book of portrait and landscape photographs entitled *Yes Rasta* taken throughout six years living among Jamaican Rastafarians. The book featured Cariou's black-and-white photographs portraying the community amidst its natural surroundings. In 2007, an exhibition called *Canal Zone* by Richard Prince, famed appropriation artist, premiered in Saint Barthélemy, subsequently moving to New York. The exhibition included thirty-five of Cariou's images across twenty-nine artworks, enlarged, tinted, and altered by Prince such that the images appeared variously in collage format, with "lozenges"—blue circular shapes—over the subjects' facial features, or with other additions, such as a guitar pasted onto a subject's body. Some of these altered images were subsequently sold.

This case addressed the ensuing dispute, as Cariou sued Prince for copyright infringement in the Southern District of New York based on Prince's unlicensed use of his work. Cariou asserted that he had lost business as a result of Prince's appropriation, considering that a New York City gallery owner had approached Cariou regarding an exhibit but, subsequently, mistakenly believed that Cariou and Prince had been in collaboration and lost interest, believing that a second "Rasta show" would not prove lucrative. In his defense, Prince argued fair use, which the Southern District rejected, but which, on appeal, the Second Circuit found, overturning the district court's ruling.

The Second Circuit conducted its own fair use analysis, addressing and giving special weight to the first factor—the purpose and character of the use—and considering the transformative nature of Prince's works. Here, the court considered whether Prince's versions had "merely supersede[d] the objects of the original creation, or [had] instead add[ed] something new, with a further purpose or different character . . . ." *Cariou v. Prince*, 714 F.3d 694 (2d Cir. 2013) (quoting *Campbell v. Acuff-Rose Music, Inc.*, 510 U.S. 569, 579 (1994)). The Second Circuit corrected what it deemed a mistake by the district court, which had mandated that secondary works "comment on, relate to the historical context of, or critically refer back to the original works" in order to qualify for fair use. *Id.* at 707 (quoting *Cariou*, 784 F. Supp. 2d 337, 348 (S.D.N.Y. 2011)). The Second Circuit clarified that while many types of fair use, such as satire and parody, *do* by nature reference an original work, such reference is not a legal requirement, and secondary works that do not comment on the original may indeed be transformative; altering the original with "new expression, meaning, or message" is enough. *Id.* (quoting *Campbell*, 510 U.S. at 579).

Based on this clarification, the Second Circuit deemed all but five of the Prince artworks to be transformative, owing to their employment of "an entirely different . . . hectic and provocative" aesthetic as compared to Cariou's photographs. *Id.* Although Prince had not himself claimed that his use was transformative, the court stressed that the critical finding is how a work appears to a reasonable observer, not merely what the artist says. To cap off its first factor analysis, the court addressed the commercial nature of the use, but, in typical fashion, dismissed the use's commerciality as largely irrelevant, considering the transformativeness.

The court proceeded to a factor four analysis, considering the effect of the secondary use on the potential market value for the original work. Here, the court emphasized the "significant differences" not only between Prince and Cariou's work but also between their intended audiences. Again rejecting the district court's analysis—which had held that Prince's work had unfairly damaged the market for Cariou's, as evidenced by the fact that Cariou had missed out on the gallery exhibition—the Second Circuit stressed that the emphasis should have been on whether Prince's secondary use had *usurped* the market for the original, not whether it had suppressed or destroyed it. Usurpation, stated the Second Circuit, only arises "where the infringer's target audience and the nature of the infringing content is the same as the original." *Id.* at 709. Because the artists' audiences did not overlap and because the court found no evidence that Cariou would ever develop his work in the manner of Prince's artworks, the court found that factor four favored Prince. *Id.*

The court quickly dispatched the second factor, the nature of the copyrighted work: Although Cariou's work was creative, Prince's work had been transformative, mitigating any influence this factor may have had. As to the third factor—the amount and substantiality of the portion used— the court again disagreed with the Southern District, which had held that Prince had taken more of Cariou's work than necessary. Instead, the Second Circuit noted that the law does *not* require that the secondary artist takes no more than necessary but, rather, requires some consideration of the quality of the materials taken and their importance to the work. Considering that many of Prince's works used Cariou's photographs in whole, sometimes failing to alter, i.e. transform, them much, the court did refrain from determinations on five artworks and sent them back to the district court for further analysis. The parties ultimately settled the remaining dispute.

A notable recent appropriation art case in the line of well-known predecessors *Rogers v. Koons* and *Blanch v. Koons*, *Cariou* addresses complicated questions over where to draw the line between art and infringement, considering that appropriation artworks are sometimes nearly identical to their originals, relying on viewers' conceptualizations to deem them new works. Appropriation art also risks inciting tension between the artistic community and the legal one, as judges may walk the line between personal taste and impartiality, differentiating art as "low" or "high" value. Or, as copyright scholar William Patry and other *Cariou* critics conceive, courts may give appropriation artists an unjustified green light to use others' works merely because of their popularity and fame. Meanwhile, courts like the Seventh Circuit, in *Kienitz v. Sconnie Nation LLC*, have concerns that *Cariou*'s emphasis on transformative use does not follow section 107 and risks overriding section 106(2)'s protection of derivative works. *See* 766 F.3d 756, 758 (7th Cir. 2014). Others question *Cariou*'s willingness to make fair use transformative judgments on behalf of a "reasonable observer," essentially fast-tracking the fair use inquiry.

Notably, Prince was taken to court in 2017's *Graham v. Prince* over additional Rastafarian appropriation, this time for having taken a screenshot of an Instagram upload of a photographer's image and adding graphics and comments. *See* 265 F. Supp. 3d 366 (S.D.N.Y. 2017). Prince again wielded a fair use defense via a motion to dismiss, which the court dismissed on procedural grounds, stating that it was too early to conduct such a fact-sensitive inquiry. Recognizing *Cariou* as "essentially a prequel" to this action and citing its "objective viewer test" regarding new works' transformativeness, the *Graham* court declined to apply the Second Circuit's "reasonable viewer" test out of hand, stating that viewing the two works side-by-side did not make it clear that Prince's was aesthetically different enough to pass. With *Graham* in mind, it will be interesting to see how subsequent courts, particularly in the Second Circuit, continue to regard *Cariou* and what lasting effects it may have on courts' amenability to appropriation art.

PART V

Music

Introduction

The business of music is a dynamic and changing field because, of all the creative forms, music may be the most universal. The music we listen to when we are young forms our ideas and ideals. We bond over music as we mold our self-identities and autonomy, so we are invested in it. We are fans. Music adapts to the times and tells the tales of a generation. Typically, parents hate the music their children listen to because it is not as "good" as the music they listened to. Today, with digital technology that allows free access to almost all music, music is everywhere. If not directly pumped into our ears via wireless earbuds, it wafts over the air in restaurants, bars, clothing stores, and even sometimes in elevators. The very ubiquitousness also makes us feel that having free access to music is our right, notwithstanding that music copyright is among the most complicated of all the arts. As a result, music copyright holders may be the most impacted by digital technology and the internet. To address this reality, Congress passed the Orrin G. Hatch-Bob Goodlatte Music Modernization Act (MMA), one of the most significant pieces of copyright legislation in decades. It is actually three laws, the MMA, the CLASSICS Act, and the Allocation for Music Producers (AMP), and the intent is to update current laws to reflect modern consumer preferences and changes in the music marketplace. The MMA addresses changes in the process for obtaining a compulsory license for the digital performance of a work (downloaded or streamed), from a song-by-song basis to a blanket license; it creates a process for the use of orphan works, and it changes the rate setting standard used by Copyright Royalty Judges from policy-oriented to an open-market standard. The CLASSICS Act extends federal copyright protections to pre-February 15, 1972, sound recordings, and the AMP codifies the process by which music producers receive royalties via SoundExchange for public performances of their works per Section 114 of the Copyright Act of 1976. The law is too new to know if it will live up to its expectations. These chapters discuss sections of this Act and the state of the music industry that underscored the need for these changes.

In the first chapter, "A Remix Compulsory Licensing Regime for Music Mashups," Peter S. Menell looks at how copyright law is ill-equipped to respond to music mashups, which he calls the "defining musical genre" of the early twenty-first century. Mashups, which consist entirely of sampled musical sources, some a mere few seconds (almost all with existing copyrights), have collided with copyright law since the rise of rap and hip-hop. Coming from twentieth-century thinking, mashup artists were considered massive infringers (mashups can contain up to 60 samples), triggering lawsuits and settlements. Menell posits that this approach fails because it stifles creativity and drives both musicians and listeners underground, generating a disdain for the copyright law regime. Neither fair use nor licensing (how would a mashup artist afford to license 60 samples that might comprise a song?) addresses the realities of this genre. To revitalize both the law and the music, he suggests a Remix Compulsory Licensing Act (RCLA) that would be simple, efficient, nondiscriminatory, and fair by providing digital clearance for remix requests. Not only would this generate revenue for existing copyright holders, it would supercharge creativity and channel remix artists and their fans into authorized distribution platforms.

In his interview, "Sampling: Using Recordings as Musical Instruments," Cameron Mizell continues this look at music and sampling with a frank discussion about the challenges and joys of being a professional musician in this age of digital files and downloads. He believes that music is both thriving and challenging today. In spite of the fact that Congress added streaming services to the statutory rate scheme, musicians only make micro-pennies. He discusses how musicians need to generate varied revenue streams and discusses the dangers of the holding in *Williams v Gaye*, known colloquially as the "Blurred Lines" case that held that the "vibe" of the song could be substantially similar and hence, infringing. (This case is discussed in more detail in the Landmark Case section at the end of Part V.)

Bill Stafford dives even deeper into how music is so embedded in our minds that it can be in our subconscious, in "Subconscious Copying: From George Harrison to Sam Smith, a Song Gets in Your Head and Winds up in a New Song." Songs, more than other art forms, may be unintentionally infringed, he writes, because of the role that our subconscious minds play. He quotes noted neurologist Oliver Sacks' comment that the music we hear in our formative years may be engraved on our brains for the rest of our lives. Further complicating this imprinting is a condition known as cryptomnesia, whereby we might recall something but believe it to be a new idea, when, in fact, it is a retrieved memory. Since copyright is a strict liability law (the intent of the infringer is not relevant), a musician who writes a new song based on a buried memory may still be guilty of infringement, as occurred in the case *Bright Tunes Music Corp. v Harrisongs Music, Ltd.*, where George Harrison was in fact found guilty of "subconscious copying." The issues musicians face today are further complicated because music has its own tonal gravity—expected movement of scales, chords, and rhythms. Almost all Western music is built on the major pentatonic scale, essentially five notes and four chord choices. Stafford suggests that the current trend of copyright litigation transforms copyright into a bludgeon that will stifle creativity. When there are 97 million songs in existence and new songs being written every day, someone will surely infringe something, often without knowing it. The law, he argues, must adapt to recognize nuances for music that was subconsciously copied so that musicians are not found guilty of copyright infringement.

In "Why Music Should Not Be Free: The Battle for Survival," award-winning songwriters and composer friends and colleagues, Phil Galdston and David Wolfert, riff on the profession and practice of music and how it has changed in the digital age. They both are highly critical of the trend toward "fair use" in musical genres such as mashups, with Wolfert calling it a "bogus" concept. Music should not be free, like air and water, and using music without paying for it, or without permission, is theft. Both are skeptical that songwriters will benefit from the MMA, and encourage all musicians both to learn about copyright and to join professional advocacy groups such as MusicAnswers, a group of more than 3,800 songwriters, composers, performers, and producers that seek to protect and reclaim traditional rights meliorated in this digital age.

In "Music, Deposit Copies, and Unanswered Questions After Skidmore v. Led Zepplin," Bob Clarida shifts focus from the questionable ruling in the "Blurred Lines" case to the more esoteric question of whether or not the scope of copyright protection in a pre-1978 musical composition should be determined solely by the content of the deposit copy on file with the Copyright Office as held in Skidmore v. Led Zeppelin. (The Ninth Circuit affirmed after *en banc* review.) The issue, as Clarida lays out in detail, is that if the Copyright Office only accepts deposit copies in written form (musical notation) but those deposit copies are materially incomplete (different) relative to the recorded version, how can a composer show infringement or other material elements of original authorship? The question is even more salient considering that most jurors cannot read musical notations, and aren't allowed to base their findings of substantial similarity on recordings. Clarida asserts in his conclusion that the Zeppelin holding goes too far and takes the law in the wrong direction because it gives significance to a 1909-era formality, rather than a twenty-first-century world.

Part V ends with an interview with singer-songwriter Jonathan Coulton, who might be the only songwriter to include on his personal website ideas from the Creative Commons, Free Culture, and the Copyleft movement. Coulton presents the fresh idea that songwriters and musicians can actually do better if they make some of their music free to their listeners because this eventually builds a devoted (and paying) audience. For him, these aren't theoretical ideas; it is how he transitioned from his career in software coding to that of a professional musician. He discusses computer-based third-party solutions to enable independent creators to find other revenue streams, including ways, for example, to partner with streaming services such as Spotify to create mini-platforms within their platform to directly connect to fans. Finally, he too finds the idea of protecting the "feel" of a song to be "highly problematic."

5.1

A REMIX COMPULSORY LICENSING REGIME FOR MUSIC MASHUPS*

Peter S. Menell

Introduction

Spurred by advances in digital technologies, music mashups emerged as a defining musical genre in the early twenty-first century, reshaping content industries and the broader culture. Digital technology and file-sharing platforms enabled creators to reach vast audiences without the high share of proceeds demanded by traditional record labels, publishers, and distributors. Creators seeking to earn a living in the creative arts faced new challenges in this environment. The very technologies that liberated them from the shackles of the old intermediaries made it ever more difficult to achieve an adequate return on their investments in training, time, expense, and opportunity cost to produce art. Aggressive copyright enforcement, which was rarely a problem in the pre-internet age, took center stage in the twenty-first century, especially for independent creators.[1]

A just, effective, and forward-looking copyright system would ideally channel internet-age creators and consumers into well-functioning digital-content marketplaces. Such a system must come to grips with the reality that a growing segment of the population does not view traditional markets for copyrighted works as the only means to access creative works. To many, participation in markets for copyrighted works is voluntary; it is more about convenience and fairness than compliance with the rule of law. Thus, trends in technology, social dynamics, and moral conscience have eroded copyright protection. Heavy-handed responses by copyright owners—such as mass litigation campaigns, efforts to ramp up enforcement tools, and troll litigation—have alienated consumers, judges, and legislators and spurred work-arounds that lead new generations away from authorized digital-content marketplaces and copyright-based creative careers.

Notwithstanding the decline of the copyright system's public approval rating,[2] the core social, economic, and moral foundations on which copyright was built have not been rendered obsolete by technological advance. To a large extent, what many creators want and need has remained the same: freedom to create and fair compensation based on the popularity of their art. And what many consumers want has also largely remained the same: easy access to creative original art at a fair price. These two forces create the conditions for copyright to provide a critical engine of creative and free expression in the digital age. For the copyright system to remain vital, copyright reform must channel post-Napster creators and consumers into a balanced marketplace, not alienate them. This chapter explores why and how to transition the copyright system to the internet age through the lens of music mashups, a salient art form that has a particular cultural and social significance.

Music Mashup Culture

Popular music exerts strong biological,[3] social, and cultural force on every generation and has long been among the most important formative copyright experiences for many young people during the past half-century. New musical genres differentiate generations and play a critical, formative role in each generation's values, self-identity, autonomy, and creative development.

In the late twentieth century, rap and hip-hop genres paved the way for music mashups, which rely entirely on sampled sources to construct musical collages. Coinciding with the emergence of bootleg websites at the turn of the new millennium, music mashups emerged as a distinct genre which involved superimposing a vocal track from one recording onto the instrumental track of another.[4] While well known to most younger music fans, the mashup genre is less familiar to older generations, a gap that can be attributed in part to the effects of copyright law.

Music mashups are as different as the artists who create them. Some combine an entire instrumental track from one recording with the entire vocal track of another recording. Others break the vocal tracks into samples, superimpose a variety of recordings, or use an eclectic collage technique weaving multiple samples—as many as thirty, and sometimes more—into a seamless mashup composition. The mashup genre went viral with the 2004 release of Danger Mouse's *The Grey Album,* combining Jay-Z's *The Black Album* with The Beatles' *The White Album.* Although Danger Mouse released only 3,000 physical copies of the album and never intended to sell the album commercially, due in part to concerns about copyright infringement, the album unwittingly became an overnight digital sensation. After EMI, the owner of The Beatles' sound recordings issued cease and desist letters to file-sharing sites hosting *The Grey Album,* music activists mounted "Grey Tuesday," a twenty-four-hour online protest promoting distribution of the album. Approximately 170 websites went "grey" on February 24, 2004—muting the appearance of their home page while hosting copies of the album—leading to 100,000 downloads of the album on that day. The album would garner favorable reviews from numerous critics as well as Best Album of 2004 honors from *Entertainment Weekly.* Later that year, MTV introduced "Ultimate Mashups," a series mashing together pairs of well-known recording artists.

Artists such as Gregg Gillis, who performs under the stage name Girl Talk, created marvelous meandering compositions by interweaving genres and samples entirely from existing recordings. A typical Girl Talk composition, such as "Play Your Part (Pt. 1)," squeezed nearly thirty samples into five frenetic minutes. Listeners were quickly hooked by the dynamism, playfulness, and intrigue of Girl Talk and other mashup artists.

As popular as they were, mashups raised copyright questions that had no clear answers. Embedded within some of Girl Talk's mashups are extended excerpts from popular copyrighted sound recordings, such as a ninety-second piano track from "Layla"[5] in "Down for the Count,"[6] with a rap vocal track superimposed. Under the Sixth Circuit's questionable *Bridgeport* decision,[7] even a minuscule sample would be vulnerable. In contrast, the Second Circuit developed a body of case law offering a viable fair use defense for works considered "transformative" for collage-style works and works used for a different purpose.[8]

Fair use analysis does not offer certainty however, as it is nuanced, case-specific, and often subjective—in the eye, or more aptly, ear of the beholder. Gillis does not appear to be commenting on or parodying the "Layla" track—considerations that would favor his use—but rather using it for its distinctive musical qualities as well as for commercial purposes. And while the "Layla" piano track provides an exquisite backdrop for B.o.B's "Haterz Everywhere,"[9] it is not at all clear that this appropriation qualifies as fair use under current case law. Gillis' sample of Beyonce's "Single Ladies (Put a Ring on It)" in "That's Right" is even more cavalier. The section beginning at 2:44 and running for seventy seconds appropriates the heart of Beyonce's hit song with relatively little embellishment.[10]

Among fans, the appreciation for Girl Talk's mashups owed as much or more to the creative contributions of the underlying composers and recording artists as it did to Gillis' creativity in mashing them together. Although Gillis has ample compositional talent, the system lacks a workable method for allocating the fruits of his borrowing. To enable Gillis to commercialize these collages without according any value to the creators of the appropriated works seems questionable. It could be equally problematic if each underlying copyright owner could exercise veto power over mashups, because then few, if any, mashups would be created and those that are would be far less interesting or overtly parodic. The transaction costs alone would be prohibitive for most of Girl Talk's intensive musical collages.[11] Assuming the transaction cost hurdle could be surmounted, it seems unlikely that Rick Springfield would be inclined to have "Jessie's Girl" juxtaposed with a rap song celebrating oral sex. So neither extreme mashup carte blanche nor copyright owner veto power is able to achieve the proper balance.

Legal uncertainty surrounding this new art form stunts and distorts its development and breeds contempt for the copyright system. The constraints and uncertainties surrounding copyright law, including the amorphous boundaries of the fair use doctrine, have pushed the mashup genre significantly underground. Much of this work is available through streaming services that operate under the radar or in a state of legal and commercial limbo. Mashup artists, many of whom work as live performance DJs in dance clubs, distribute recordings of these works through unlicensed channels primarily to promote their live performance gigs. Major record labels have largely steered clear of signing and releasing mashup artists out of concern for copyright liability and friction with their conventional artists.

Most mashup music has been pushed into viral marketing and distribution through mashup artist websites and file-sharing platforms such as SoundCloud, the leading mashup hub. While many of the mashup websites initially operated without substantial interference from owners of the sampled works, that changed when the recording industry sought to monetize their catalog, and post-Napster generations became a greater share of the marketplace. For example, in June 2014, Kaskade, a popular mashup artist and DJ, was the subject of dozens of takedown notices submitted to SoundCloud.[12]

While the distribution channels for mashups are largely user-uploaded and noncommercial (in the sense that listeners do not pay for access), some unlicensed mashups are available on YouTube, iTunes, Spotify, and Amazon, although their availability is limited and unpredictable. With regard to YouTube, it is unclear whether mashup artists have been able to derive much, if any, revenue through advertising monetization because to benefit, artists must own all the "necessary rights to commercially use all visuals and audio elements."[13] Uploaders who violate these rules are subject to takedown notices and may have their YouTube channels removed. The YouTube Content ID system rules also allow YouTube to divert the advertising revenue to the copyright claimant under certain circumstances.

While YouTube's Content ID system represents an innovative solution to screening uploaded content, the lack of a sophisticated mechanism for dividing mashup advertising revenue among the multiple creative influences (including the mashup artists) limits the ability of this new creative force of mashup artists from profiting directly from others' enjoyment of their mashups. Other considerations, such as self-expression and promotion for live performances, provide indirect rewards for posting mashups. Given liability and platform concerns, many mashup artists have taken a more cautious approach, keeping their works off of websites that charge for downloads, characterizing their works as experimental, and offering to remove mashups at the request of copyright owners of embedded works.

Copyright concerns have played a significant, but not particularly constructive role in the emergence and evolution of the mashup genre. While the protest over *The Grey Album* catapulted mashup music onto the cultural radar, lingering concerns about copyright exposure have continued to limit the full blossoming of the genre. Legal uncertainty has important ramifications for the development of the music mashup genre as well as for the larger creative and copyright ecosystems. The current circumstances push the growing community of music mashup artists and fans outside of the copyright system and content marketplace. They also limit the ability of new generations of creators to test their talent and pursue financially sustainable careers.

A copyright system that fails to understand, accept, and embrace these formative and social processes sacrifices relevance among younger artists and fans. Growing distrust among this demographic will make the copyright system progressively less acceptable to a growing proportion of society. Since digital and internet technologies provide easy access to unauthorized sources of copyrighted works, failure to accommodate new and popular art forms such as mashups encourages "work-arounds" to copyright markets, alienates post-Napster generations (and increasingly those who grew up in the era in which copyright markets were obligatory) from copyright markets, and confronts judges responsible for adjudicating copyright disputes with difficult choices, as reflected in the file-sharing and internet safe harbor cases.

By extending a compulsory license to mashup artists, Congress can invigorate the copyright system and channel new generations of consumers and creators into well-functioning online marketplaces for digital content. By augmenting the cover license, which has been in place for more than a century, with digital technologies for identifying and tracking usage of preexisting copyright works, a remix compulsory license would provide a calibrated mechanism for enabling both mashup artists and owners of sampled works to profit equitably from the public's enjoyment of the resulting collages.

Such a regime would remove the dark cloud constraining and distorting the mashup genre. It would not supplant fair use, but rather sidestep its amorphous contours in those situations in which mashup artists choose to operate within the compulsory license regime. Others would be free to test the limits of fair use, but it seems likely that an increasing number of mashup artists would prefer to avoid legal uncertainty, and see the virtue in sharing the proceeds of their success with those whom they sample. Opening up a compulsory license channel would stimulate copyright markets and expand the range of works available across a range of platforms—from YouTube to Spotify, iTunes, and SoundCloud. Consumers would see greater reason to participate in these markets, thereby further stimulating the creative arts.

This policy innovation would also signal that Congress seeks to embrace new creators and their fans through adapting copyright to the realities of the internet age. By moving copyright away from control toward calibrated compensation, Congress would recognize that remix artists and consumers play a vital role in the era of configurable culture,[14] foster norms that channel modern creators and consumers into markets for copyrighted works, and begin the process of building intergenerational bridges.

Copyright General Framework

The US copyright law protects two principal components of musical creativity: musical compositions (often referred to as the "circle c," based on the © symbol for copyright notice) and sound recordings of musical compositions (often referred to as the "circle p," based on the symbol for notice of copyright in a phonogram). Subject to various limitations and exceptions such as the fair use doctrine and the "cover" license, the Copyright Act grants composers and recording artists the exclusive rights to reproduce, adapt, and distribute copyrighted works. In addition, it grants composers the exclusive right to publicly perform their works.

A mashup artist infringes the right to reproduce by copying a copyrighted musical composition or sound recording. This involves two components: (1) factual copying, resulting in (2) substantial similarity of protected expression. The first component is easily proven where a preexisting sound recording is sampled. The presence of a copyrighted sound recording in a mashup artist's work will suffice.

A more difficult question is whether the use of the sample appropriates "substantial" amounts of the protected expression. Under the *de minimis* use doctrine, which essentially means that the courts will not concern themselves with trifles, courts will generally excuse very small amounts of copying because they cause too little harm to justify providing a remedy. The applicability of this doctrine to digital sampling, however, was cast in doubt in a controversial 2005 case, [15] which found a two-second sample to be infringing.

Where the *de minimis use* doctrine does not apply, courts apply a multifaceted test to determine whether the amount of protected expression appropriated would be considered substantial by an ordinary observer. The court must first dissect the plaintiff's copyrighted work to filter out the unprotected elements, such as ideas and unoriginal expression. It then determines whether the defendant's work is 'substantially similar' to the protected expression, a notoriously vague standard.

A copyright owner need not prove that all or nearly all of the copyrighted work has been appropriated to establish infringement. The legislative history explaining the infringement standard provides that "a copyrighted work would be infringed by reproducing it *in whole or in any substantial part,* and by duplicating it exactly or by imitation or simulation. Wide departures or variations from the copyrighted work would still be an infringement as long as the author's 'expression' rather than merely the author's 'ideas' are taken."[16]

Thus, courts have held that even a small amount of the original can be an infringement if it is qualitatively significant. Determining the threshold for infringement is particularly difficult when a defendant has copied distinct literal elements of the plaintiff's work and incorporated them into a larger work of her own. This class of cases has been referred to as fragmented literal similarity.[17]

If copyright infringement is found, the defendant can escape liability by establishing that the use falls under the fair use doctrine. Although fair use is considered critical to copyright law's fundamental purpose of promoting the progress of knowledge and learning, its availability to insulate copying is very difficult to predict, making legal advice inherently speculative. As a result, those seeking to build on the work of others cannot typically achieve complete certainty as to the legality of their use short of obtaining a license.

Federal copyright law also imposes liability upon those who publicly perform musical compositions without authorization, but does not impose liability on the public performance of sound recordings. Consequently, to perform a track publicly, a user must obtain a license from the owner(s) of the copyright in the musical composition but not the owner(s) of the copyright in the sound recording.

Copyright liability can extend beyond the mashup artist to record labels and websites that reproduce and distribute an infringing work. Internet service providers such as SoundCloud and YouTube, however, are immune from liability for storing infringing files at the direction of a user so long as they meet several procedural threshold requirements, and (1) do not have actual or constructive knowledge of the location of specific infringing files residing on their system, or (2) fail to expeditiously remove such files upon becoming aware of their location.[18]

Copyright law's robust and highly discretionary infringement remedies compound the uncertainties surrounding its limiting doctrines. As a result, cumulative creators must be extremely cautious in their use of copyrighted works. Even a small transgression can trigger injunctive relief barring distribution of the infringing work as well as substantial monetary damages. For works that are registered prior to infringement, copyright owners can seek either actual damages and disgorgement of profits, or statutory damages, which range from $750 to $30,000 per infringed work and can be increased up to $150,000 per infringed work, at the court's discretion, in the case of willful infringement. This regime exposes mashup artists and the websites that distribute their works to enormous potential liability. Girl Talk "samples" twenty to thirty separate musical compositions and sound recordings, up to sixty copyrighted works in total, in a single mashup composition.[19] By so doing, Gillis exposes himself to liability for sixty times the statutory damage range since most of the music that he samples are popular works released by major record labels, which routinely register their releases with the Copyright Office. Thus, the potential liability is staggering. While it is unlikely that a court would award millions of dollars of damages in a case such as this, just the minimum statutory damage award rises above $10,000 per mashup composition.

Although no case has yet confronted the intensive sampling found in Girl Talk's works, a number of cases dating back to the early rap and hip-hop era found liability for unlicensed use of samples. With the advent of digital-sampling devices in the 1980s, a new breed of musical creators with extensive knowledge of beats, precise turntable dexterity, and training in recording technology—as opposed to musical instruments—emerged. As hip-hop moved beyond the dance clubs to commercial recordings, issues of copyright infringement followed. Traditional musicians and recording industry executives were not amused by what they viewed as "groove robbing,"[20] and it was not long before copyright owners threatened and ultimately pursued copyright infringement lawsuits.

In a notable early dispute, which ultimately settled, Jimmy Castor sued the Beastie Boys and their record label Def Jam over their use of a small sample (less than two seconds) on their break-through debut album *Licensed to Ill*.[21] In another early controversy, the 1960s pop group The Turtles sued De La Soul over its use of their 1960 hit: You Showed Me, resulting in what was reported to be a $1.7 million settlement.

The first litigated sampling case reinforced artists' and hip-hop labels' worst fears about copyright liability. On his third album, *I Need a Haircut*, Biz Markie's rap song "Alone Again" sampled Irish pop singer Gilbert O'Sullivan's hit recording "Alone Again (Naturally)."[22] O'Sullivan's publisher sued for copyright infringement, prompting the court to grant Markie's wish for a haircut. It is never a good sign when a judge begins the opinion by quoting the Ten Commandments. The first sentence of *Grand Upright Music v. Warner Brothers Records* states, "Thou shalt not steal." The court's analysis of copyright infringement did not delve deeper than establishing that the plaintiff owned the copyrights in both the musical composition and the sound recording, and that Biz Markie sampled the recording. The decision neither evaluated whether the sampling constituted substantial similarity of protected expression nor considered whether it qualified for fair use. Instead, the court focused on the fact that the defendants had been denied a license, treating the failure to clear the rights as a proof of infringement. The opinion assumed, without analysis, that a license is required for any sampling of sound recordings, labeling the defendants' behavior as "callous disregard for the law." Judge Duffy concluded the opinion by ordering an injunction as well as "sterner measures," referring the matter to the US Attorney for consideration of criminal prosecution. Biz Markie learned his lesson: His next album was entitled *All Samples Cleared!*

In 1993, another district court applied the substantial similarity framework to a digital-sampling case.[23] In evaluating the defendants' motion for summary judgment, the court rejected the defendants' assertion that a finding of substantial similarity for infringement requires similarity of the songs in their entirety such that a lay listener would "confuse one work for the other." Applying the "fragmented literal similarity" framework, the court focused on "whether the segment in question constituted a substantial portion of the plaintiff's work, not whether it constituted a substantial portion of the defendant's work." The court found that the bridge section, which contains the words "ooh . . . move . . . free your body," was taken. It also found that a distinctive keyboard riff, which functions as both a rhythm and melody, included in the last several minutes of the plaintiff's song, was also sampled and incorporated into the defendants' work. The court denied the defendants' motion for summary judgment, rejecting the contention that a series of "oohs," "moves," and "free your body" were too clichéd or lacking in expressive qualities to attract copyright protection.

In 1994, the Supreme Court considered whether "Oh Hairy Woman," the rap group 2 Live Crew's parody of Roy Orbison's classic hit, "Oh Pretty Woman," was fair use.[24] 2 Live Crew had contacted Acuff-Rose Music, the copyright proprietor, and offered compensation and attribution, but Acuff-Rose declined their offer. Undaunted, they proceeded with their version, which both sampled the original sound recording and altered some of the lyrics, prompting Acuff-Rose to sue. Applying the fair use doctrine, the district court concluded that 2 Live Crew's parodic version qualified for fair use, even though its commercial purpose cut against such a finding. On appeal, the Sixth Circuit reversed, emphasizing that the "blatantly commercial purpose" of the use and the appropriation of the heart of the song prevented a finding that the use was fair.

In a wide-ranging opinion that substantially liberalized the fair use doctrine, a unanimous Supreme Court recognized the transformativeness of the parodic use as a substantial factor in assessing fair use eliminated any presumption that commercial use established market harm, thereby widening the berth for parodies. The court also eliminated any inference that seeking permission weighed against fair use. Based on these considerations, the court reversed the Sixth Circuit and remanded the case for further fact-finding with regard to the market effect factor. The case settled without further judicial consideration of the fair use balance.

A decade later, the Sixth Circuit squarely addressed digital samples of sound recordings, ruling that the Copyright Act bars application of the *de minimis* use doctrine in this class of works, with the implication that even the copying of a single note could constitute copyright infringement.[25] The Ninth Circuit has since rejected that interpretation,[26] holding that the "de minimis" exception applies to sound recording infringement actions, just as it applies to all other copyright infringement actions.

A line of cases emanating from the Second Circuit since 2006 suggests a more sympathetic attitude toward "transformative" use of preexisting copyrighted works through the fair use doctrine.[27] Although none of these cases involved musical works, they all involved literal appropriation of fragments in collage art or even the entirety of prior works in developing new visual works. The cases draw heavily on Judge Leval's seminal law review article on transformativeness[28] as well as the Supreme Court's invocation of that consideration in the *Campbell* case. These trends would seem to provide greater leeway for music mashups to avoid copyright liability. Some cases, however, cut in the other direction. In *Kienitz v. Sconnie Nation, LLC,*[29] Judge Easterbrook expressed skepticism of the Second Circuit approach in *Cariou* because to rely on "transformative" as the most important part of a fair use analysis could not only replace the list of factors in § 107 of the Copyright Act, but also override the exclusive right to prepare derivative works set forth in § 106(2) of the Act.

Several recent music cases suggest a relaxation of infringement standards and broadening of fair use in music copyright cases.[30] Nonetheless, the application of these rules to music mashups remains uncertain, creating substantial exposure for mashup artists and online platforms distributing unlicensed mashups.

Rap/Hip-Hop's Rocky Road to Constrained Copyright Legitimacy

The wide media coverage of the early sampling lawsuits, reportedly large settlements to copyright owners, and early, cramped judicial decisions brought an end to the era of unauthorized sampling and "the golden age of sampling."[31] The record industry imposed tight reins on rap and hip-hop artists; unless samples were cleared, labels would not release the new projects. Although the Supreme Court's *Campbell* decision opened the door to a fair use defense, few labels wanted, and few artists dared, to test those limits. This is understandable as copyright litigation is time-consuming, expensive, distracting, and risky. But the reality of the licensing era meant constrained experimentation, higher entry costs (if an artist did not have a major label and a good attorney, it was difficult to get licensing requests answered), and many creative compromises. Remix artists had to develop the capacity for self-censorship.

There are a number of problems inherent in this licensing regime: There is no standardized price list for samples; licensors often want to hear how their works are going to be used; and complex licensing terms and monitoring arrangements have to be established. The creative arts and complex accounting systems do not mix well. As a result, creative freedom took a large hit. In addition, rap and hip-hop artists increasingly found themselves getting the short end of the stick. The licensors—major publishers and record labels with extensive knowledge and negotiating experience—have tremendous leverage, especially in dealing with new entrants. To have a chance at a fair deal, remix artists would need experienced (and hence expensive) legal talent, often beyond the reach of upstarts.

Licensing costs often proved prohibitive, especially for those seeking to license multiple popular works. Remixes containing more than a few samples become less and less economically valuable to the remix artist. Estimates of the costs of licensing underlying works for some of the early rap hits (before rap artists (and their labels) worried about copyright infringement)—such as those released by the Beastie Boys—would run into the $10 million to $15 million range based on the standard fees that emerged in the industry.[32] The total clearance fees of the sampled works, therefore, could swamp the total revenue available, even on a highly successful product.

Beyond the exorbitant cost, licensing multiple samples would also exact a toll in the personal costs of loss of creative output and emotional stress in working out the deals. Perhaps most significantly, there is a high likelihood that some of the underlying samples could never be cleared because the copyright owners would refuse to license the work for any fee.

Bridging the Divide: The Case for a Remix Compulsory License

A cramped interpretation of fair use confronts mashup creators with the choice of either bearing exorbitant transaction costs and constraints on their artistic freedom for those works that cannot feasibly be cleared, or running the risk of crushing liability. Even if many of these uses are ostensibly "tolerated," such a regime unduly chills mashup creativity and distribution. By contrast, a broad interpretation of fair use potentially deprives the authors of sampled works of a fair share of the social value of their works. And without a clear resolution of this interpretive issue, everyone bears the costs of legal uncertainty.

Rather than tinker with the inherently vague, constitutionally based, and politically charged fair use doctrine, there is much to be gained by opening up an alternative path for mashup music that insulates artists and distribution platforms from undue legal liability while encouraging low transaction costs and fair pricing of samples. A predictable, feasible alternative to relying on the fair use doctrine is the establishment of a proportional compulsory license for mashup music. The elimination of statutory damages for mashup works would further insulate these productive uses without unduly exposing copyrighted works to piracy. The increasing shift to digital distribution platforms for music in conjunction with advancing technologies for monetizing and dividing revenues makes such a regime feasible. These augmentations to copyright law would liberate new generations of creators as well as old dogs who can learn new tricks to pursue their passions, increase the value of older catalog works through revenue sharing and increased exposure, expand the catalog of and reduce the costs associated with online content distribution, break down anticompetitive forces, and build wider support for authorized content markets.

Given the transaction costs and creative compromises inherent in an arms-length licensing regime and the inherent unpredictability, subjectivity, and cost of the fair use safety valve, the search for a stable platform for remix art lies in a system for easily and cheaply preclearing uses coupled with sharing of the revenues from the remixed works. As music enjoyment increasingly shifts toward streaming and online access, capturing a substantial share of the value and distributing it equitably becomes ever more feasible. Furthermore, such a regime holds the promise of attracting new generations of artists and fans into a vibrant, authorized content ecosystem. As such ecosystems grow, the piracy problem abates. Just as the television broadcasters are opening up authorized online channels for televised content to entice cord-cutters, the music industries would benefit over the long run by opening up music markets to the full range of music mashups.

The "Cover" License as a Model for Opening up the Remix Marketplace

The "cover" license provides an instructive model for developing such a system. For reasons that are no longer salient, Congress established the nation's first compulsory license as part of the 1909 Copyright Act that allowed for mechanical royalties in Section 1(e).[33]

This provision authorized anyone to sell piano rolls of musical compositions that had been released for a statutory fee of two cents per copy. With the emergence of the sound recording industry over the next several decades, the compulsory mechanical license morphed into a mechanism for recording artists to record their own versions of previously released musical compositions—what we call a "cover." The omnibus Copyright Act of 1976 updated the law and authorized the compulsory license for phonorecords.[34]

There are, however, limits on the use of the underlying musical composition. The "compulsory license includes the privilege of making a musical arrangement of the work to the extent necessary to conform it to the style or manner of interpretation of the performance involved, but the arrangement shall not change the basic melody or fundamental character of the work." Furthermore, the compulsory license applies only to nondramatic musical works.

The statutory rate for the cover license has gradually risen over the past century. It now stands at 9.1 cents per composition or contestants' recorded performances on or 1.75 cents per minute of playing time or fraction thereof, whichever is greater. Although the statute sets forth procedures for obtaining the compulsory license, most cover licenses are negotiated directly between the copyright owners and the licensees in the shadow of this regime to avoid the Copyright Office's burdensome procedures, such as monthly accounting. The statutory license rate provides a maximum effective limit on those negotiations.

As a result, recording artists have enjoyed substantial freedom to record and distribute their own versions of musical compositions, resulting in many of the more memorable sound recordings such as the Jimi Hendrix version of Bob Dylan's "All Along the Watchtower." Bob Dylan has remarked that the Hendrix cover "overwhelmed" him.[35]

The cover license has produced a vast number of remarkable sound recordings, as well as some truly regrettable, but innocuous, releases. The cover license enables young musicians to develop and showcase their skill using popular songs. It provides a convenient mechanism for record labels to test markets. Television music reality shows, such as *American Idol* and *The Voice*, have relied upon this provision of the copyright law to promote sales of contestants on iTunes and other digital platforms. The resulting sales benefit the musical composers as well as the recording artists, with relatively few resources wasted on transactions or risk of holdup. Thus, the cover license promotes cumulative creativity, expressive freedom, and compensation while minimizing transaction costs. Its built-in metering—basing the compensation on sales—provides versatility and simple accounting.

There have been, however, complaints about the cover license not keeping up with inflation, underpricing some works, and impinging on composers' ability to control the use of their works. Nonetheless, the cover license has done much to support young musicians, promote experimentation, reduce uncertainty, ease the transition to digital download platforms, and expose musicians and the public to a diversity of styles.

Designing a Remix Compulsory License

The cover license has succeeded because of its standardized features and low barrier to entry. It provides those interested in covering a previously released musical composition with a preset pricing mechanism that does not require any initial outlay. If the cover attracts demand, then both the owner of the copyright in the underlying musical composition and the cover artist will see significant value. If it is a market flop, no one is worse for the wear. The division of the value is proportional to market value. The fact that it is available to anyone invites new forms of creativity and avoids the composer's endorsement.

The keys to the success of the cover license are that it is simple, efficient, nondiscriminatory, and ostensibly fair. A remix compulsory license would stretch the cover license along several dimensions. It would authorize much greater opportunity for alteration. In fact, the motivation for most remixes is to create something substantially new. To the extent that a remix does so, it finds further cover under fair use considerations. Furthermore, a remix compulsory license must deal with a much more complicated revenue-sharing formula. But the end goal tracks the cover license model. It offers remixers a balanced, low-cost, preclearance institution.

A remix compulsory license could work as follows. A remix artist would assemble an outline for the new work. Using an internet portal, the time usage of each selection would be coded and submitted through a standardized Copyright Office remix registration form along with the registration fee and a deposit copy. The composition and sound recording list would establish the division of value among the various musical composition owners, sound recording owners, and the remix artist. The Copyright Office would review the submission for compliance with applicable regulations and, assuming compliance, issue a digital registration certificate containing registration information, ownership shares, and the location where revenues for each of the contributors would be sent. This digital clearance file could then be provided to distribution channels as a way of insulating them from copyright liability for distributing the work and providing the necessary information-channeling revenue to owners of underlying copyrights.

This mechanism would automate the clearance process, avoid the problems of gaining permission from copyright owners, and afford remix artists with a relatively straightforward, inviting, and voluntary on-ramp to the music marketplace. If the project succeeds, then all contributors would see some return. The underlying works would receive revenue streams without putting forth any additional effort. The precise splits as well as a variety of other operational details would need to be determined. It is not difficult to imagine a variety of eligibility requirements and revenue splits. For example, the license could be available for nondramatic remixes meeting a modest threshold of originality, splitting revenue three ways equally among the musical composition owners, sound recording owners, and the remix artist, and proportionally based on the time usage.

The best plan, however, would result from a multi-stakeholder process involving all affected communities. As a guide to the process, the following outlines the principal issues to be worked out: (1) eligibility requirements, (2) revenue sharing, (3) administrative process, (4) features and limitations, and (5) possible extensions.

Eligibility Requirements

A core rationale for a Remix Compulsory License Act (RCLA) is to address the high transaction costs associated with intensive remixes. Therefore, there is some justification for limiting the compulsory license to those projects involving a relatively large number or high intensity of samples. A low-intensity threshold could displace the existing sample market for less intensive remixes, although it may be beneficial due to delay and transaction cost problems plaguing the rap and hip-hop genres. Alternatively, a high threshold could distort remix art by pushing remix artists to intensity levels beyond what they believe is artistically optimal. A balance is necessary to deter mere bootlegs of previously released tracks. Just as copyright law demands a higher level of derivative originality for derivative works to garner protection, RCLA might also need to demand more than trivial adaptation.

Revenue Sharing

A key difficulty is figuring out a method to split money in a mashup of dozens of samples. This is obviously one of the most sensitive aspects of the RCLA regime and raises deep philosophical and economic questions. The performance rights organizations—ASCAP, BMI, and SESAC—deal with analogous issues in the division of their royalty pools.[36] The point of the exercise would be to develop neutral principles for division of the fruits of both original and derivative creativity. Alternatively, economists might ask how society could reward useful labor or maximize the social welfare from alternative distributional rules.

Any revenue-sharing plan should seek to minimize transaction costs, including the costs of dispute resolution. A costly division rule could well defeat the primary purpose of facilitating the remix art form. Thus, the revenue-sharing system should be clear, modular, and objective. These considerations point strongly toward using a time-based metric for measuring relative contribution of samples for dividing value. It also favors dividing value among classes of contributors—composer, recording artist, and remixer—on a fixed focal point, ex ante basis such as an equal three-way division. It is possible to imagine more sophisticated algorithms, such as factoring in the intensity of the remix or the market popularity of the sampled works, but such approaches create substantial complexity.

A time-based metric has the virtue of accounting for the significance of the sampled work to the remix composition—longer samples earn a higher percentage of the pie—and of integrating the market success of the sampled works. Remixers would undoubtedly be influenced by the popularity of works within the culture. Hence, we would expect better-known works to be sampled more heavily, thereby increasing their share of the overall remix pie.

Another important issue relates to the minimum eligibility quantum. It might be appropriate to choose a *de minimis* level of usage for revenue sharing. For example, samples of less than two seconds could be categorically exempt. Certain sounds of even that length, however, might be sufficiently iconic to merit recognition, but stretching the rules beyond copyright limits would make the regime less workable.

Finally, it will also be important to develop some rules for ensuring that revenue sharing is not distorted by the inclusion of long, barely imperceptible samples. A remixer might be able to skew the division or revenue toward his or her own work by including long, imperceptible samples.

Administrative Process

To achieve its goal of reducing transaction costs and welcoming remix artists into authorized distribution of their works, RCLA must establish an efficient and inexpensive online process for registering works and administering royalty payments.[37] Developing this infrastructure would complement the broader call for modernizing copyright registration, developing comprehensive and up-to-date databases, and facilitating notice.[38] The availability of royalty payments for remixes would encourage musical composition and sound recording owners to register their works.

The choice of institution to administer RCLA parallels contemporary discussions about how best to modernize copyright registration. RCLA could potentially be handled through the Copyright Office, a quasi-public agency (such as SoundExchange), or private collectives (such as ASCAP). Like existing collectives, a portion of the revenue collected could be used to cover administrative costs. This could include the costs of dispute resolution, which would depend on the complexity of the eligibility requirements and revenue-sharing algorithm.

Additional Features and Limitations

The interplay of RCLA with other copyright rules would greatly influence its political viability and efficacy.

Like the § 115 compulsory license, RCLA would operate as a safe harbor for use of copyrighted works. In this way, it would augment the fair use doctrine but not supplant fair use. Such a rule would interfere with First Amendment protections.

It would also be important to limit the types of uses eligible for the compulsory license. In order to avoid false endorsements and interference with the advertising marketplace, the compulsory remix license ought not to be used for advertisements, subject to fair use or express license. An argument can also be made that the compulsory remix license could not be used for political campaigns, but such remixes could well be permissible based on fair use. There would also be issues surrounding synchronization (television, motion pictures, and video games) and dramatic work licensing.

RCLA should expressly disclaim that sampled composers and recording artists have consented to their works being remixed. Such artists might welcome such uses, but given the compulsory nature of the licensing regime, it would be important to insulate the sampled authors and recording artists from any implication that they have endorsed the work unless they so choose.

The threat of substantial statutory damages poses a significant risk for many remix artists. The uncertainty surrounding the application of the fair use doctrine to remix art exacerbates this concern. Given that all remix work has some transformative quality, there is good reason to remove or at least cap the level of statutory damages available for remixed music. Statutory damages would not be available against remixers or those who distribute remixed works on the grounds that these works are not piratical but presumptively productive (even if they do not qualify for fair use).

Possible Extensions

The music mashup genre is the leading wedge of an expanding range of remix art throughout the culture. It potentially provides a useful template for other forms of remix art. For example, it could be adapted for dividing revenue for video mosaics of the music videos used in conjunction with audio remixes. Like music mashups, such music video mashups have proliferated, raising similar concerns about how fair use applies and the transaction costs of gaining permission. The RCLA framework could be tailored to this novel art form. Music mashup artists as well as video producers, music composers, and recording artists should all share in the resulting video mosaic. As digital technology expands the ability for artists to remix prior creations and for a wider range of creators to reach broad audiences without traditional publishing gatekeepers, we are witnessing substantial battles over forms of remix art such as appropriation art and fan fiction. Compulsory licensing is not necessarily the right solution for all of these contexts. Nonetheless, it opens the policy toolbox for tailoring distinctive regimes to new challenges.

Additional Benefits of a Remix Compulsory License

The remix compulsory license would greatly expand the marketplace for remix creativity and the motivation to undertake such projects. As such, it would promote freedom of expression. Such a regime would also greatly reduce the overhead costs of remix art as well as expand compensation for a broad range of composers, recording artists, music publishers, and record labels. Furthermore, this policy would provide several significant ancillary benefits to the copyright system.

RCLA would enrich the availability of source material for mashup artists by motivating copyright owners to make tracks available for reuse. Remix artists depend critically on the availability of high-quality source materials, especially the stems from which multitrack recordings are compiled. Although some master recording proprietors release such material, availability has been limited. A more robust system for expanding and sharing revenue from remix art would encourage more record labels and recording artists to share stems and other subcomponents that could expand the supply of raw materials for remix projects.

Perhaps the greatest long-term benefit of a remix compulsory license would be in channeling remix artists and their fans into authorized distribution platforms. As more of this work becomes available on streaming and download services and as remix artists affirmatively promote revenue-generating distribution channels, more fans will be attracted to these sources. This legitimation of remix content will also lower administrative costs for distribution channels, such as YouTube, Spotify, and iTunes, and will broaden their catalogs. As more consumers join these services, the piracy problem will abate. There is no need to download and stream illegally if users can listen to the music they want through a fairly priced and fully authorized channel. This would erode the corrosive effects of a gap between norms and law, thereby improving the acceptability of copyright markets more generally. Just as Netflix, Hulu, and Amazon Prime have brought cord-cutters and downloaders into the marketplace, fully stocked remix subscription services can do the same.

Part of the challenge of licensing samples is the difficulty in identifying rights holders. Scholars have lamented the lack of formalities as undermining efficient resource development. A remix compulsory license system would spur the development of comprehensive, easily searchable music rights registries by encouraging rights holders to ensure that the most accurate and current data is available for claiming revenue. Furthermore, a compulsory system would encourage software entrepreneurs to develop convenient databases and related tools for remix artists to more easily compile their registration forms.

Notwithstanding the disintermediation that the internet has made possible, major record labels still command tremendous control over competition and revenue sharing through their ownership of a vast legacy catalog. No online service can achieve economic viability without licenses to a substantial portion of the legacy collection. Through this power, the major record labels have structured online royalties in such a way that not only their own artists, but also independent artists, cannot derive a fair share of streaming revenues. They also extend this power through their control over licensing samples of many classic works. In addition to streamlining sample licensing, a remix compulsory license would open up the marketplace to all-comers on a fair, reasonable, and non-discriminatory basis. This would remove the entry barriers faced by younger artists, those without formal legal representation, and those without record labels. Although it would reduce the market power of the major players, a remix compulsory license could very well increase their licensing revenues by spurring a vast expansion in remix art, opening authorized online distribution channels to these works, and welcoming a vast influx of artists and fans to commercial streaming, download, and advertising-based music services.

Objections and Responses

Proposals to provide a compulsory license for remixes have already provoked objections from a variety of stakeholders. Composers and recording artists have objected to the loss of control such a system would entail. Some copyright scholars have expressed concern about the effects of licensing systems on the scope of fair use.

Like any complex system for allocating rights, a remix compulsory license system could be gamed to skew the distribution of value among claimants. The eligibility requirements and revenue-sharing algorithm will inevitably be somewhat over- and underinclusive. Many of those issues could be addressed through the design of the revenue-sharing model. Simpler systems are more transparent, but less sophisticated, while more complex algorithms could hide abuses. RCLA system would need to be carefully monitored in order to ensure that it did not skew revenue sharing in unanticipated and undesirable ways. Adjustments to the system could be made through transparent rulemaking processes.

Various scholars have resisted compulsory licensing systems on the grounds that free markets are better able to allocate resources and less prone to rent seeking and other distortions introduced by government-based resource allocation systems. With over two decades of experience, there has been ample opportunity to see if the market can produce effective alternatives and little has emerged. A remix compulsory license would draw remix artists and their fans into authorized markets. The expanded velocity of activity would greatly expand overall market performance.

Fair Use

The establishment of a convenient and effective compulsory license for mashups could affect the scope of fair use. In assessing the potential market for copyrighted works under the fourth fair use factor, courts consider the availability of licensing channels. A comprehensive compulsory licensing regime could lead courts to narrow the scope for fair use in evaluating sampling of sound recordings. It is critical, however, to distinguish between economic uses and political, parodic, and other free-speech uses.

The need for fair use in cases of economic uses would be alleviated by the ease and low cost of the compulsory license. If this pathway is widely used, the problem that fair use seeks to resolve largely solves itself. Moreover, the elimination of statutory damages for mashups would curtail both the motivation to bring infringement actions and the adverse effects of enforcement actions on mashup artists. With regard to speech-motivated uses, the Supreme Court's decision in *Campbell*, in conjunction with the growing recognition of First Amendment dimensions of copyright law, should continue to provide a relatively wide berth for parodies, commentary, and political uses. Furthermore, Congress can bolster protection for freedom of speech by expressly stating that the compulsory license does not alter the traditional fair use privilege.

Moral Rights

It is not difficult to imagine that Rick Springfield might not appreciate Girl Talk weaving a rap song about oral sex between verses of his hit recording "Jessie's Girl."[39] It could be personally offensive to him as well as his fan base. Several commenters to the recent copyright studies raised impassioned moral criticisms of music remixes.[40] They strongly criticized how unauthorized remixes deprive original composers and recording artists of control over the use of their works, impair the integrity of their works, unjustly enrich remixers, and falsely associate the original composers and recording artists with offensive messages. Some commenters invoked private property metaphors reminiscent of Blackstone's exclusive dominion view of private property.

Yet, it is in precisely these areas where the First Amendment has the most force. As the Supreme Court noted in *Campbell*, parody will often offend the work or artist being used and, hence, is much less likely to be authorized by the target. The First Amendment comes down strongly on the side of preventing censorship, even of hate speech. Thus, even if composers and recording artists could decline consent because a use is offensive to the author or fans, that basis for asserting copyright infringement would support the fair use doctrine as a parody or social commentary.

A plausible argument can be made, however, that a compulsory license for mashups legitimates such offensive art. It should be noted that the same argument applies to parodic fair use cases as well as First Amendment protections. But neither fair use law nor the First Amendment requires that a compulsory license be extended. They affirmatively authorize such offensive uses. A compulsory license creates a somewhat distinct imprimatur by commoditizing the offensive use. In addition, it potentially removes the risk of copyright infringement, although that depends, of course, on the breadth of fair use.

Perhaps the best approach to alleviating this morality-free expression dilemma would be for Congress to disclaim that composers and recording artists whose works are remixed reflect these creators' endorsement of the remixed work absent express approval. Such a norm would be understood from the context, but the legislative statement could have some expressive significance. Beyond controlling hate speech, the broader desire for authors to control use of their works for artistic integrity reasons runs counter to the broad cultural freedom that has developed in the US. In contrast to its European counterparts, the US has long resisted strong moral rights protection. While the US grudgingly added moral rights protections for works of visual art as part of its accession to the Berne Convention, it has not made any such efforts in the musical arts realm. And although the desire to control how one's expressive works are used can have social value, it comes at the expense of free expression.

By releasing artistic works into the marketplace and public discourse, creators open themselves to comment as well as ridicule. That is an implicit part of the social contract in a free society. Efforts to regulate such speech inherently involve the government privileging some speech over other speech, a dangerously slippery slope. The protest movements and traditions in American society over the past century reinforce the importance of respecting everyone's right to speech, even if it offends.

These values have particular force in the music domain. Through its ability to combine poetry with rhythm and melody, music can be especially powerful in delivering messages and promoting freedom. This freedom is especially important to new generations and marginalized communities. It played a particularly important role in the development of the modern music industry, which flourished in the protest songs of the 1960s and has profited handsomely as new genres have emerged.

It is ironic, therefore, that some rock 'n' roll icons, who themselves benefitted from broad artistic freedom, have stepped forward to object to their art being remixed without their exclusive control. The past decade has shown that the remix art movement cannot be stopped in the internet age; it can only be channeled in ways that can empower the next generation while breathing new life into the works of those who came before. A remix compulsory license would broaden expressive freedom while sharing the expanded revenues with those whose works were sampled. To stand in the way of mashup art is futile. Steven Tyler cannot effectively prevent Girl Talk and other remix artists from using his and Aerosmith's catalog. He can only limit their distribution through authorized services, which ultimately will counterproductively steer fans of Aerosmith and remixed Aerosmith into unauthorized channels. This is more likely to reduce the flourishing of art than it is to protect his reputation or financial well-being.

Bridging Fair Use's Binary Divide

As scholars have recognized, the fair use doctrine often creates a polarizing binary choice between exclusive control and free, uncompensated use of preexisting works of authorship. Although the Supreme Court's 2006 decision in *eBay, Inc. v. MercExchange, LLC* opened up the potential for awarding ongoing royalties as opposed to injunctive relief in intellectual property cases,[41] the availability of such remedies is risky. Such risks have pushed the rap and hip-hop genres into a costly and restrictive licensing marketplace to the detriment of creativity and economic opportunity for many artists. Mashup artists have avoided that path, but find themselves without effective access to authorized online markets for their work and live under a looming cloud of potential liability and arbitrary takedowns of their works.

The rap and hip-hop experience suggests that many scholars place far too much faith in fair use (it is too costly and risky to use) and too little attention on the values of compensating those whose work is used. The binary choice is a falsely polarizing one between control and free.[42] Fair compensation furthers copyright law's utilitarian goals as well as basic moral values. In fact, many remix artists support compensating those whose works upon which they build their own, but given the prohibitive transaction costs involved, are forced to either forgo distributing their art in recorded form or run the risk of massive copyright liability. A carefully calibrated remix compulsory license offers a constructive, practical path for re-equilibrating copyright protection for the internet age.

The point here is not to diminish the critical importance of fair use to a productive and free culture. Rather, it is to suggest that society can better pursue expressive creativity and free expression—and relieve pressure on the fair use doctrine—by offering sensible, low transaction cost, and balanced compulsory licenses. Remix artists remain free to roll the fair use dice. But as we saw with the cover license, a compulsory license can open up a valuable complementary pressure-release valve for creative free expression without adversely affecting the fair use doctrine.

Conclusion

In the real world of transaction costs, subjective legal standards, and market power, no solution to the mashup problem will achieve perfection across all dimensions. The appropriate inquiry is whether an allocation mechanism achieves the best overall resolution of the trade-offs among authors' rights, cumulative creativity, freedom of expression, and overall functioning of the copyright system. On balance, a remix compulsory license regime offers a constructive path for supporting a charismatic new genre, engaging post-Napster generations, and channeling disaffected music fans into authorized markets. In so doing, it promises to raise the overall social welfare and compensation of both legacy and new artists.

In many respects, the debate over remix music mirrors a recurrent generational divide over youth's desire for freedom and older generations' resistance, as represented in Steven Stills's timeless protest anthem "For What It's Worth," brilliantly reinterpreted (through licensed sampling) in Public Enemy's "He Got Game".

> There's battle lines being drawn
> Nobody's right if everybody's wrong
> Young people speakin' their minds
> Getting so much resistance from behind
> It's time we stop
> Hey, what's that sound?
> Everybody look, what's going down?[43]

Although Stills had much larger social and political concerns on his mind, his words resonate in the contemporary debate over music mashups. Copyright should not stand in the way of young people "speakin' their minds." Its reform can play a role in motivating and sustaining the careers of the next generation of Steven Stills and those, like Public Enemy, who personalize, engage, and remix that art. Robust pathways for cumulative creativity, free speech, low transaction cost, and fair compensation licensing point the way.

Acknowledgment

★   This essay remixes Peter S. Menell, "Adapting Copyright Law for the Mashup Generation," *University of Pennsylvania Law Review* 164 (2016).

Notes

1 See Peter S. Menell, "Envisioning Copyright Law's Digital Future," *New York Law School Law Review* 46 (2002–2003): 63.

2 See Peter S. Menell, "This American Copyright Life: Reflections on Re-equilibrating Copyright for the Internet Age," *Journal Copyright Society U.S.A.* 61 (2014): 244–69. 42nd Brace Lecture.

3 See, e.g., Daniel J. Levitin, *The World in Six Songs: How The Musical Brain Created Human Nature* (Dutton, 2008) (exploring how songs about six subjects—friendship, joy, comfort, knowledge, religion, and love—have shaped human development); Daniel J. Levitin, *This Is Your Brain on Music: The Science of a Human Obsession* (Plume/Penguin, 2006), 85 ("[T]he emotions we experience in response to music involve structures deep in the primitive, reptilian regions of the cerebellar vermis, and the amygdala-the heart of emotional processing in the cortex.").

4 Roberta Cruger, "The Mash-Up Revolution," *Salon*, August 10, 2003, accessed May 14, 2020, http://www.salon.com/2003/08/09/mashups_cruger [http://perma.cc/PP4G-CFBH].

5 *See* Layla, Last.fm, accessed May 14, 2020, http://www.last.fm/music/Derek+and+the+Dominos/_/Layla/+wiki [http://perma.cc/T5LP-ZJ2A] (characterizing Layla as "among the greatest rock songs of all time" and "one of rock music's definitive love songs, featuring an unmistakable guitar figure, played by Eric Clapton and Duane Allman, and a piano coda that comprises the second half of the song").

6 Girl Talk, "Down for the Count," track 8 on *All Day*, Illegal Art, 2010.

7 *See* Bridgeport Music, Inc. v. Dimension Films, 410 F.3d 792, 798 (6th Cir. 2005) (finding a two-second sample to be infringing); but see VMG Salsoul, LLC v. Ciccone, 824 F.3d 871, 874 (9th Cir. 2016) (rejecting *Bridgeport Music's* interpretation of the Copyright Act).

8 *See* Cariou v. Prince, 714 F.3d 694, 705–06 (2d Cir. 2013) (finding fair use in part because the artwork "manifest[ed] an entirely different aesthetic . . . ."); Blanch v. Koons, 467 F.3d 244, 252 (2d Cir. 2006) (finding fair use when the defendant's "purposes in using [the plaintiff's] image are sharply different from [the plaintiff's] goals in creating it"); Bill Graham Archives v. Dorling Kindersley, Ltd., 448 F.3d 605, 609 (2d Cir. 2006) (finding fair use because the defendants used the concert posters as "historical artifacts").

9 B.o.B, "Haterz Everywhere (Feat. Rich Boy)," on Eastside, Atlantic Records, 2007.

10 "Direct Sample of Vocals/Lyrics'," WhoSampled, accessed May 14, 2020, reference to Girl Talk "That's Right" sample of Beyonce's "Single Ladies (Put a Ring on It)," https://www.whosampled.com/sample/70977/Girl-Talk-That%27s-Right-Beyoncé-Single-Ladies-(Put-a-Ring-on-It), [http://perma.cc/6RXC-MM7Y] (providing a side-by-side comparison of "Single Ladies" and "That's Right").

11 See Kembrew McLeod and Peter DiCola, *Creative License: The Law and Culture of Digital Sampling* (Duke University Press, 2011), 165–66 (detailing the high transaction costs associated with clearing samples).

12 See thisisadynasty, "brb . . . Deleting SoundCloud.," *Kaskade* (blog), *Tumblr*, accessed May 14, 2020, https://thisisadynasty.tumblr.com/post/87945465547/brbdeleting-soundcloud [http ://perma.cc/-KX3T -46SP] (posting a screenshot of a notice from SoundCloud to take down mashups).

13 "What Kind of Content Can I Monetize?" YouTube, accessed May 14, 2020, https://support.google.com/youtube/answer/2490020?hl=en [http://perma.cc/E588-6KJX].

14 Cf. Aram Sinnreich, *Mashed Up: Music, Technology, and the Rise of Configurable Culture* (University of Massachusetts Press, 2010), 194–95, 208 (arguing that the rise of configurable culture, typified by mash-ups, suggests a "paradigmatic change" in cultural production and the need for "a new set of [cultural] institutions to serve [the people's] needs").

15 See Bridgeport Music v. Dimension Films, 410 F.3d 792 (6th Cir. 2005).

16 H.R Rep. No. 94-1476, at 61 (1976) (emphasis added).

17 *See* Melville B. Nimmer and David Nimmer, *Nimmer on Copyright* (New York: M. Bender, 2014), Vol. 4 § 13.03[A][2] (defining fragmented literal similarity as when "no more than a line, or a paragraph, or a page or chapter of the copyrighted work has been appropriated").

18 See 17 U.S.C. § 512(c) (2018); Viacom Int'l, Inc. v. YouTube, Inc., 676 F.3d 19, 32 (2d Cir. 2012) (holding that a service provider can only be held liable for copyright infringement if it has "actual knowledge or awareness of facts or circumstances that indicate specific and identifiable instances of infringement").

19 Mark J. Butler, *Playing with Something That Runs: Technology, Improvisation, and Composition in DJ and Laptop Performance* (Oxford University Press, 2014), 234. The total number of copyrighted works potentially infringed is double the number of songs sampled because there are generally two copyrights in every track (the musical composition and the sound recording).

20 Richard Harrington, "The Groove Robbers' Judgment: Order on 'Sampling' Songs May Be Rap Landmark," *Washington Post*, December 25, 1991, https://www.washingtonpost.com/archive/

lifestyle/1991/12/25/the-groove-robbers-judgement/50cfcf66-b3b5-485e-81ae-eb3c75edf7ca; see also McLeod and DiCola, *Creative License*, 62–63.

21 See McLeod and DiCola, 131 (detailing the high transaction costs associated with clearing samples); see also Terence McArdle, "Jimmy Castor Dead at 71; '70s Songs Became Popular Among Sampling Hip-Hop Artists," *Washington Post*, January 19, 2012, https://www.washingtonpost.com/entertainment/music/jimmy-castor-dead-at-71-70s-songs-became-popular-among-sampling-hip-hop-artists/2012/01/19/gIQAbbkCBQ_story.html (quoting a 2004 interview in which Castor commented: "Hip-hop has been fairly good to me. . . . In the beginning it wasn't, when people like the Beastie Boys just raped my music. C'mon man, as L.L. Cool J said to me one day, 'That's like taking someone's vintage car out of the driveway and just driving it away!' When they pay, I love it.").

22 Grand Upright Music, Ltd. v. Warner Bros. Records, Inc., 780 F. Supp. 182, 183 (S.D.N.Y. 1991).

23 *See* Jarvis v. A & M Records, 827 F. Supp. 282, 289–90 (D.N.J. 1993) (acknowledging that factual copying of a sound recording is not sufficient to establish infringement, but rejecting the defendants' stricter test for substantial similarity).

24 Campbell v. Acuff-Rose Music, Inc., 510 U.S. 569 (1994).

25 Bridgeport Music, Inc. v. Dimension Films, 410 F.3d 792, 800–01 (6th Cir. 2005). *Bridgeport* involved a two-second sample looped on a lower pitch and extended to about 16-seconds in a rap song.

26 VMG Salsoul, LLC v. Ciccone, 824 F.3d 871, 874 (9th Cir. 2016).

27 See, e.g., Cariou v. Prince, 714 F.3d 694, 706 (2d Cir. 2013) (reasoning that use of a copyrighted work was fair because the artwork "manifest[ed] an entirely different aesthetic"); Blanch v. Koons, 467 F.3d 244, 252 (2d Cir. 2006) (holding that use was fair since the defendant's "purposes in using [the plaintiff's] image are sharply different from [the plaintiff's] goals in creating it" and this "confirms the transformative nature of the use"); Bill Graham Archives v. Dorling Kindersley Ltd., 448 F.3d 605, 609 (2d Cir. 2006) (finding fair use because the defendants used the concert posters as "historical artifacts").

28 See Pierre N. Leval, "Toward a Fair Use Standard," *Harvard Law Review* 103 (1990): 1111 (arguing that a fair use analysis "turns primarily on whether, and to what extent, the challenged use is transformative").

29 Kienitz v. Sconnie Nation, LLC, 766 F.3d 756, 758 (7th Cir. 2014).

30 See Skidmore as Tr. for Randy Craig Wolfe Trust v. Zeppelin, 952 F.3d 1051 (9th Cir. 2020); Gray v. Perry, No. 2:15-CV-5642-CAS-JCx, 2020 WL 1275221 (C.D. Cal. March 16, 2020); Estate of Smith v. Graham, 799 F. App'x 36 (2d Cir. 2020) (summary order).

31 *See* McLeod and DiCola, *Creative License*, 19–32 (identifying *Grand Upright Music* as ending the era of the "Wild West" in unauthorized sampling).

32 McLeod and DiCola, 203–05.

33 Section 1(e) provided that:

> [A]s a condition of extending the copyright control to mechanical reproductions, that whenever the owner of a musical copyright has used or permitted or knowingly acquiesced in the use of the copyrighted work upon the parts of instruments serving to reproduce mechanically the musical work, any other person may make similar use of the copyrighted work upon the payment to the copyright proprietor of a royalty of two cents on each such part manufactured, to be paid by the manufacturer thereof.

34 When phonorecords of a nondramatic musical work have been distributed to the public in the US under the authority of the copyright owner, any other person, including those who make phonorecords . . . may, by complying with the provisions of this section, obtain a compulsory license to make and distribute phonorecords of the work.

35 See John Dolen, "A Midnight Chat with Dylan," *South Florida Sun Sentinel*, September 28, 1995, accessed May 14, 2020, https://www.sun-sentinel.com/news/fl-xpm-1995-09-28-9509270260-story.html [http://perma.cc/VKR3-8GXW].

36 See *Music Licensing Practices of Performing Rights Societies: Hearing Before the Subcomm. on Intellectual Prop. & Judicial Admin. of the H. Comm. on the Judiciary,* 103rd Cong. 26–31 (1994) (statement of Morton Gould, President Emeritus, American Society of Composers, Authors and Publishers (ASCAP)) (describing ASCAP's licensing practices).

37 Hannah Karp, "Turning a Profit From Music Mashups," *Wall Street Journal*, March 6, 2015, https://www.wsj.com/articles/turning-a-profit-from-music-mashups-1425687517 [http://perma.cc/8S7W-ANA9] (noting that Dubset Media, Inc. has developed technology to track how much of each song is used in mashups).

38 See generally Peter S. Menell, "Economic Analysis of Copyright Notice: Tracing and Scope in the Digital Age," *Boston University Law Review* 96 (2016); Christopher Sprigman, "Reform(aliz)ing Copyright,"

Stanford Law Review 57 (2004) (arguing for changes to copyright procedures, not substantive rights, to address modern concerns surrounding the copyright laws).

39 "Jessie's Girl" a ballad about a young man's love for his best friend's girlfriend, see Rick Springfield, "Jessie's Girl," track 2 on *Working Class Dog*, RCA Records, 1981. The song topped the Billboard Hot 100 in 1981. "The Hot 100-1981 Archive," Billboard, https://www.billboard.com/archive/charts/1981/hot-100 [http://perma.cc/HA7K-VJRZ].

40 Dina LaPolt and Steven Tyler to Commerce Committee, Task Force, US Patent and Trademark Office, February 10, 2014, *Comment Letter on Department of Commerce's Green Paper on Copyright Policy, Creativity, and Innovation in the Digital Economy*, http://www.ntia.doc.gov/files/ntia/lapolt_and_tyler_comment_paper_ 02-10-14.pdf [http://perma.cc/2WS7-Q9MP] (characterizing mashups as "derivative works" and suggesting approval is a right artists possess).

41 eBay Inc. v. MercExchange, L.L.C., 547 U.S. 388, 391 (2006) (holding in a patent infringement case, that courts have equitable discretion to grant relief).

42 Jane Ginsburg's work recognizes this flaw. See Jane C. Ginsburg, "Fair Use for Free, or Permitted-But-Paid?" *Berkeley Technology Law Journal* 29 (2014): 1386. ("[T]he copyright law should distinguish new distributions from new works, and should confine (free) 'fair use' to the latter. . . . [M]any distribution uses formerly deemed 'fair' [should] be 'permitted-but-paid,' and be subject to a statutory framework for license negotiations"); see also Alex Kozinski and Christopher Newman, "What's So Fair about Fair Use?" *Journal of the Copyright Society of the USA* 46 (1999): 515. ("[W]e have inefficient hold outs, in the form of authors who use their exclusive right to prevent the creation of valuable derivative works. A piece of land can't serve both as your living room and Trump Towers, but a piece of intellectual property suffers from no such limitations." Peter S. Menell and Ben Depoorter, "Using Fee Shifting to Promote Fair Use and Fair Licensing," *California Law Review* 102 (2014): 69–71.)

43 Buffalo Springfield, "For What It's Worth," track 1 on *Buffalo Springfield*, Atco, 1967.

5.2

SAMPLING

Using Recordings as Musical Instruments

Interview with Cameron Mizell

Cameron Mizell (CM) is a Brooklyn-based professional musician, teacher, artist, and industry consultant. He has worked on both sides of the business—with Verve Records and as a label manager at Destiny Records. In 2008, with Dave Hahn, he founded Musician Wages, a website that offered music industry advice geared toward the working musician. Musician Wages closed in 2014. In 2019, to accompany his new album of guitar duets, he released a book of sheet music and original watercolors, also available as high-quality fine art prints.

Michelle Bogre (MB) interviewed Cameron Mizell on December 4, 2018 in New York City. This interview was edited for length and clarity.

MB: What is the state of the music business today? You are both a consultant and a working musician, so you come at it from both perspectives.

CM: The music industry is thriving in some ways because music is more accessible and consumed everywhere. I get up every morning and the first thing I do is turn on a Bluetooth speaker and start streaming music. People are listening to music more frequently because it is so easy to do. It is also easier to make music. And for people who want to learn music, there are a lot of resources online. For example, I have students from all over the country that I teach over Skype. So in that way, I think that there is more music being made and consumed in an easier fashion than in past decades. However, from a business perspective, it is incredibly challenging because it is a lot harder to make money from music. There are fewer places to perform professionally. The pay for local gigs has been stagnant for decades so there has not been much of a raise for musicians.

MB: Can musicians still make money from recordings?

CM: That has completely bottomed out. For example, about ten years ago I had a number of recordings out of two of my own albums. And then I had recorded some albums with some other people that were collaborations, so we would share the revenue from those. I was making about $1,000 a month, simply from iTunes. There was this brief period of a level playing field where an independent artist such as myself had the ability to have my music available in the same format right next to major label artists. And if I positioned myself smartly, people would discover my music and buy it. That revenue supported me recording more music and also supported me playing my music and paying my band. So, overall, my business was growing. But once legal streaming came to the US that changed. Downloads started to decrease. And it did not bounce back. This morning I got a payment of $44 for maybe a month of streaming, compared to the $1,000 I was making from iTunes downloads, when I had fewer recordings out there. Streaming really pays so little now that I do not think of it as money that I can rely on.

MB: So streaming changed everything?

CM: In a sense. The music industry pressured Congress to change the statutory rate for streaming services. Since Napster came out in 1999, the industry has been trying to figure out what to do. The truth is, the rate at which laws change is micromovement compared to how fast technology develops. What ends up happening is music starts getting used in a way that has not necessarily been properly anticipated and there is no way to license it. When YouTube launched, there was no compulsory rate for music in videos. People were using music in their videos but not legally paying for that use. Then when Google bought YouTube it seemed like there might be some compensation for the musicians or composers. What ended up happening, though, was YouTube came to an agreement with major labels, figuring that people were going to upload this stuff anyway, that created ad revenue to be shared with the content owners. But the truth is it is not very much money.

MB: Is the onus on you to monitor the plays? Do ASCAP or BMI not do that for you?

CM: In some ways, yes, but it should not have to be that way. I am registered with BMI. Whenever I perform live, I log in and submit my set list so that BMI then will pay me for playing my music in a venue. Otherwise I do not get paid. I know my music is getting played. It is on the radio. It is being played in cafes, and I should get paid, but I do not know how the algorithms work. I do not think I ever get paid for my music being streamed in cafes. The way that they figure who to pay is typically based on what is most popular because whatever is the most popular must be being played the most.

MB: So their algorithm is kind of outdated?

CM: It is top-heavy. In all fairness, it has to be incredibly difficult to sort that out, but I do not think it would be impossible. Data analytics ought to be more accurate. This is not to say that the people who are getting a lot of the money do not deserve to be earning money for their music being played, but perhaps all the revenue that is being collected is not being distributed as fairly as it could.

MB: What are the different ways that technology has changed the business? What do musicians do if they are only performing artists?

CM: I work with musicians who are solely performing artists. One of the things Musician Wages really focused on was the musician business. One way we discussed performing musicians' careers on the site was by drawing a line between playing your original music and playing music somebody else wrote. It is harder to make money only playing your own music. If you play other people's music, there are more opportunities to make money. When I play my own music, even though my band are my friends, I still want to pay them at least as much as I would charge to play a gig. So whether or not I make money from performing my music, I am still paying my band at the risk of losing money. Also the opportunities to get paid playing your original music just at a club or restaurant are actually pretty low. Most places do not pay that much unless you can guarantee a sizable paying audience. In contrast, playing in a cover band or wedding band, you are playing somebody else's music. When I am the sideman, I negotiate my rate so the artist or band leader is paying me whether they are making money or not. However, playing other people's music, being a reliable sideman, takes a certain amount of skill and is valuable to artists and band leaders.

Now there are other ways to make money. If you are a recording artist and signed to a label, you have probably gotten some money as an advance, which is typically just like a fee for being in the studio. These days at least, you know, that is harder. It used to be that you might get $50,000 or something, to essentially spend a year or half a year making an album. That does not happen so much anymore. There are also licensing opportunities. You can still make money if you get your music into a film or television series. And also if you have got production chops and a home studio, you can actually record music at home on a much smaller budget.

MB: Does copyright protect music today or does it impede it? Are there things that you cannot do because of the way copyright is aggressively enforced today?

CM: It is pretty easy to accidentally write somebody else's song so you will see these copyright lawsuits and sometimes it can be for something that is very simple. Tom Petty won a case against Sam Smith[1] for what some people would say is just a similar little scale. How do you copyright a scale? But that scale was a hook in our collective musical consciousness.

MB: That is an interesting statement. How much music is in our collective consciousness so that anyone who taps into that risks a lawsuit? Is that an abuse of copyright, do you think?

CM: Yes, I think so. There does need to be protection for intellectual property, obviously. I am making a lot of that. But one of the recent lawsuits that worries me was the Marvin Gaye estate suing Robin Thicke and Pharrell, for, what was that? "Blurred Lines?" I love that that is what the song was called. They essentially said that the vibe of the new recording was too similar to Gaye's "Got To Give It Up." Marvin Gaye has passed away, but the other musician that was on it—I think there were just two musicians that made that particular recording—the other guy was like, "No, it is not alike." He said it was not the same. And people transcribed the parts and demonstrated musically that they were two separate songs. You cannot really say that they are the same thing, musically.

If you put the two pieces of music in front of me, I would say first, they are in different keys. The way that the rhythm is subdivided is different. I would say they certainly are two different songs, but Marvin Gaye's estate won. It all came down to the fact that the producers of "Blurred Lines" said that they used that song as inspiration. That is really disturbing because artists often use other work as inspiration or a framework to create something. You have to study the masters to hone your own skill set. You listen to songs and maybe you like the key shifts in the song, and then you will write something that does the same thing but it is a totally different type of song.

I will take a song, like a song by Gershwin. It is thirty-two bars long. And I maybe take the phrases, I break it down to the framework, but I remove the content, and then I fill it in with my own content. I think that it is often about context, and context is very important. If you take a Beatles song, and you take the chorus, but you turn it into a heavy metal song or something, you could maybe say they are the same three notes, but the context is totally different.

MB: Was copyright ever intended to protect context?

CM: I took a class in college and then got interested in the history of hip-hop just from a musicology perspective, and hip-hop uses a lot of sampling. A sample in the most basic sense is just taking another recording as it is and doing your own thing over it. That is obviously copyrighted material, but then there are people like J Dilla, and he just will take the sounds and recontextualize them in a way that is mind-blowing. While he is using something that somebody else recorded, he is creating a context that gives it a whole new life.

MB: Under the fair use doctrine, that could fall under transformative.

CM: Yes, there is a spectrum, right? I think people have a difficult time seeing where things fall and that is why we have a lot of big lawsuits.

MB: Is copyright too long today?

CM: Maybe. Copyright lasting the life of the artist is one thing, but if something is valuable to the public, there ought to be something to allow that to just become part of our collective intellectual property. We want people to be able to learn—maybe some songs that are challenging. I simplify songs for my students all the time just to teach them. What if you want to have a high school jazz band perform a song but you need to make a high school level arrangement? There is a ton of licensing stuff that happens with that arrangement or adaptation. It is very difficult to sort out but, at the same time, musicians need to be protected. I have a friend who wrote an Indie rock song, but she also sings in a professional choir, and the choir director wrote an arrangement of her pop song for Chanticleer, which is a world renowned men's choir. They performed it everywhere and the arrangement was published. And now all these recordings are popping up of local choirs doing her song and she is not getting paid for it. You want people to perform the song, but at the same time, she deserves something. She cannot do much about it. She could write letters or sue them, but you can spend your life doing that and not making art.

MB: Think about Mozart or Bach—that was the day of patronage, not copyright. An artist was supported and paid for what they did, and did not expect to then be able to live off of it whenever it was performed. We have shifted it now, but copyright is almost consuming itself.

CM: Yes it is.

MB: A lot of teachers tell students to never ever sell their copyrights. That is a noble aspiration but not realistic today. Artists and musicians entering the market today will have to sell copyrights sometimes.

CM: Work made for hire is just sometimes the way you have to make a living. We also work together a lot today. I am cowriting stuff all the time, and I essentially just have an agreement when I sit down with somebody that we are splitting everything 50/50. It does not matter how much or what each of us writes. We sit together and influence each other.

MB: The one little idea might take the song from good to great. You cannot quantify that.

CM: You really cannot. I do not want to put all my effort and argument into deciding who did what. I just want to keep making more art. It is unfortunate sometimes when maybe you have one thing that really takes off, but then nothing else ever does that well so you could have made more money off the one piece.

MB: Do you think about copyright issues when you write? Do copyright lawsuits live in the periphery of your brain?

CM: I do not know because I think that the way that I am creating now is at the highest level that it has been. I am constantly learning, but sometimes copyright crops up. I was writing a song with some people and after sharing it with some Dominican musician friends, they sent me a link to a salsa song that I had never heard, but it was basically the song we just wrote. I knew there were ways to fix that, but everyone does not have that skill set. Chuck Close said something like: Professionals do not wait for inspiration, they just to get to work. And that is the thing—I sit down every day and write or draw, or whatever, just do something creative. And then the true art happens in the editing process. I ask myself how I can make it my own, or how can I avoid copyright pitfalls. So it does affect the process, but more in the editing process. I try not to blatantly break copyright law, but at the same time, I try not to let it impede my creative process. Fixating on copyright can be damaging to just making art, but of course we do have to protect our work.

MB: How does streaming impact you? Music copyrights are more complicated than those in the visual arts.

CM: Yes they are. We have the writer copyrights, the performance rights, and the sound recording, for example. Streaming is a huge issue in the music world. There are people making a ton of money off of streaming, but it is not the musicians.

MB: The finances of those companies are not very transparent.

CM: If you go to a music conference, there is always a panel with somebody from Spotify. And, I swear, every time that person leaves the panel early because everybody bombards them with questions about how much money Spotify makes. Musicians have a case for being upset about the way it all works. Everyone thinks that being a musician is so great because we love what we are doing.

MB: Loving what you do does not pay the rent.

CM: When Metallica sued Napster, everybody hated them for it. Well they were right; they were 100 percent correct. They predicted what was going to happen. You cannot go into a grocery store and say, "I like this apple so much, I'm just going to take it." You do not get to do that.

MB: So for young musicians, do they just have to find multiple revenue streams? Is that the reality of the twenty-first century?

CM: The reality is that, if you want to be a musician, to be famous, and to write hit songs, well, good luck. I have no advice for you. I do not have the five secrets to the music industry. Being successful is more about developing the attitude and the professionalism of being a musician so that you have valuable skills that people will pay for. Some of that has to do with recording. Some of that has to do with other elements like being prepared for a rehearsal, knowing how to behave at a gig, and knowing how to go about your life in general. That includes figuring out multiple streams of revenue. In the past, I recorded a number of Christmas albums under a couple pseudonyms and the music was played a lot, and February would roll around, and that payment would come through. It used to pay rent money, but now it only pays beer money even though it is being listened to more now than it was ten years ago.

MB: Would you make another one, or is it not worth it?

CM: I would not do it now. I just recorded another album with another guitarist. We love the way we made the music. We recorded it in Austin, Texas, because that is where the label is based. The guitars resonate, and it sounds beautiful, but we really are not expecting to make money on this album even though I think people are really going to like it.

MB: So what is the solution to the streaming phenomenon?

CM: Congress needs to create a statutory rate for streaming rather than leaving it to the free market. They take all the subscriber revenue and all the advertising revenue, and they split that up amongst all of the streams and then divide it up and pay it out that way. But because of the lack of transparency, I do not know that I am getting paid the same as somebody who signed to a major label who has negotiated a special rate with Spotify.

MB: Maybe the payment of streaming should not be a free market.

CM: I am a member of the local New York musician's union. The union is advocating for some of these changes for streaming and they have got a little bit more leverage. So I think that is important. Politicians understand that Amazon is a monopoly and they need to do something about it, well they need to do something about the music business too. Everyone talks about, say the coal industry, or the struggles of blue collar workers. Who talks about how many musicians in their 50s or 60s who have lost their jobs are struggling to have a career? I am not saying that change is not inevitable, but there are people making a lot of money from technology, from making an app to make music accessible, without thinking about the musicians. Music is a finite resource, even though we do not think about that. If musicians cannot make a living, they will stop making music.

MB: That is a very interesting observation.

CM: Gillian Welch has a song called "Everything is Free." It is great. There is a line in there that is something like, she is just going to sit at home and write love songs and, if you want to hear them, you can write them yourself. The other thing that hurts the music profession are the talent shows, like *American Idol*. The talent performing does not get paid but the show generates a lot of money for the producers.

It is hard to just make art today like, say, Frank Zappa did in the 1960s. It is almost impossible to just make a bunch of records that might be niche records, but they are taking art in different directions and encouraging new things to happen. If we are just basically writing the same song over and over again, because it tends to be a hit song, we are not promoting art. We are promoting a kind of emotional manipulation through art. We need to find a way to support making challenging art again. And, of course, people who are working on the fringe are not necessarily going to make as much money and maybe will not be appreciated until someone looks back at their body of work or whatever. But if people are not doing that, we are hurting art. The whole purpose of art is to create empathy and let us feel things through another person's perspective. We hear a song about something like heartbreak or joy or whatever, and it is maybe something that we have never experienced ourselves, but, through the music, we can feel something. That can be very useful in social movements; songs can bring together people and move hearts and minds. However, the craft of writing and playing songs that make an emotional impact takes a lot of work, a lot of failure, and a lot of time to develop a voice. Somehow, artists need to support themselves along the way.

Note

1 Tom Petty and Sam Smith settled a copyright dispute over the likeness of Smith's three-time-nominated "Stay With Me" and Petty's "I Won't Back Down" by giving Petty cowriting credit and 25 percent share of royalties, even though Smith maintained that the similarities were a complete coincidence because he had never heard Petty's song.

5.3

SUBCONSCIOUS COPYING

From George Harrison to Sam Smith, a Song Gets in Your Head and Winds Up in a New Song

William Stafford

In psychology, the subconscious is the part of the mind that is not currently in focal awareness. Philosophers such as Descartes have described subconscious mental processes for centuries, and cognitive psychologists have determined that implicit memories influence a person's behavior, even though they are not aware of their influence.[1] While mental health professionals have unlocked many of the mysteries of our subconscious thoughts, the application of such regarding the protection of an author's creative works has been left largely to the interpretation of the courts. Under the Copyright Act, the owner of a copyrighted work has the exclusive right to reproduce, create derivative works, distribute, perform, or display that work.[2] If that work is used without permission, it is generally considered to be infringing upon the copyright owner's rights. The estimated cost to the US economy of copyright infringement and piracy is more than $12 billion annually.[3] Infringers may invoke defenses such as the doctrine of fair use, an exemption to the US copyright law that allows copyrighted works to be used for educational purposes, news reporting, and other informational context without payment or permission. They may also claim that their music was an independently created work that just happens to sound similar. But what if they indeed did use elements of the copyright owner's music without realizing they had done so? After all, we are exposed to music at a very early age: from lullabies, musical toys, radio, and television to jingles in stores and theme songs at events. According to neurologist Oliver Sacks, "What is heard during one's early years may be 'engraved' on the brain for the rest of one's life. Our auditory systems, our nervous systems, are indeed exquisitely tuned for music."[4]

This complex question involves a condition known as cryptomnesia, which occurs when a forgotten memory returns without being recognized, and is believed to be something new and original. It is a type of memory bias whereby a person may falsely recall an idea, engage in inadvertent plagiarism or infringement, and experience the memory as if it were a new inspiration. Cryptomnesia presented a challenge to the courts when the legal scrutiny focused on musical works. This gave rise to the legal doctrine of subconscious copying, which applies to the usage of melodic, harmonic, and textual information that was archived in a part of the mind not currently in focal awareness. Although this doctrine was intended as a means in which a creator may protect his or her copyrighted works, it does not always fit cleanly over the music itself. Musicians embrace inspiration, and often place great importance on their influences. Many techniques and styles are handed down through generations and are typically rooted in tradition. Entire genres of music have been built upon similar sounds, harmonies, and rhythms. These creatively connected practices further cloud the certainty under which a work may be considered to have been subconsciously copied. And while it is difficult to imagine a jury fully delving into a defendant's mind to analyze this opaque concept, the law is clear that subconscious copying is copyright infringement. Unless it is not, such as the aforementioned original work that just happened to sound similar. The history of how the courts have determined this difference is fascinating, especially considering that relatively few cases involving subconscious copying were ever litigated. It stands to reason that the number of such cases will increase considerably as music is made more instantly accessible. The door is gradually opening to the likelihood that subconscious copying may happen more frequently, as the compositional elements of popular music have not changed to the extent that access and availability have increased in this digital age.

Music has its own tonal gravity based on our expectation of how it moves and resolves. But how as a society did we decide to favor certain patterns of scales, chords, and rhythms over others? In part, our acceptance of certain sounds is based on the overall formal and tonal practices developed in Western music tracing back to the 1800s.[5] This is "popular" music. The music that drives commerce, builds careers, and is most listened to by the populous society in the US and abroad. At a fundamental level, Western popular music has adapted to and become limited by what is pleasing to the ear.[6] Our culture has gravitated toward familiar sounds that are composed using rules and practices with a surprisingly limited scope. To begin with, there are only a total of twelve notes available from which to choose. These notes make up a chromatic scale when played in sequence, and are not usable together for popular music, as they have no tonal center. The intrinsic feel of a tonal center is important, because a melody stopping on a tone that our ears feel should have resolved can evoke a feeling of incomplete thought. To many listeners, this amounts to discomfort for not being given the satisfaction of finality or "coming home." From the twelve available notes, only a specific pattern of seven of those notes sound good together, comprising the major scale. And out of those seven notes, only five of them sound good together no matter which order you play them. Thus, most of the music you have heard in your life was written on five notes called the major pentatonic scale. The chords that accompany the melody of those five notes are even more limited, as there are basically four choices: The **I** (tonic, based on the first major scale note); **IV** (sub-dominant, based on the fourth major scale note); **V** (dominant, based on the fifth major scale note); and **vi** (submediant, based on the sixth major scale note). In fact, these four chord patterns are so formulaic that you can mash up some of the biggest pop hits of the last sixty years, put them against the same chords, and get away with it sounding good.[7]

Regarding meter and form, nearly all popular music is in 4/4 time (beats per measure), following either a verse/chorus or rondo form in the manner that musical ideas and variations are presented. By means of comparison, writers of literary works have an almost unlimited range of words to use, and visual artists have innumerable colors and many types of media in which to render their works. The composer of popular music is basically limited to five notes, four chords, two forms, and one meter. These limitations are factors that should be taken into consideration when determining the possibility of a composer either copying subconsciously or independently creating a similar sounding work.

The subconscious copying doctrine originated with the Honorable Learned Hand, a judge and judicial philosopher who presided over the case *Fred Fisher, Inc. v. Dillingham* in 1924.[8] The defendant was found guilty of infringement even though he was given the benefit of the doubt about being "unconscious" of ever copying the work. Being established in opera helped his claim, as many thought it would have made little sense for him to gamble his reputation on deliberate piracy. Explaining the doctrine, Judge Learned Hand stated that copyright infringement did not rely on the defendant's "good faith," and because there was no other way to explain the extreme likeness between the two compositions, it must have followed that the defendant copied subconsciously and "invaded the author's rights."[9] As monumental as this doctrine may have seemed at the time, it has only been applied a few times since Judge Hand's decision to actually establish copyright infringement.

One of the most notable applications occurred in the 1976 case *Bright Tunes Music Corp. v. Harrisongs Music, Ltd.*[10] The artist George Harrison wrote the iconic gospel-rock song "My Sweet Lord," but was found to have actually written nearly a complete replica of a hit song from six years earlier called "He's So Fine" by the Chiffons. Since Harrison was able to recount in detail how he wrote "My Sweet Lord" with gospel artist Billy Preston, and offer descriptions of his guitar strums and organically improvised usages of "Hallelujah" from classical repertoire, his assertion that he did not intentionally copy the Chiffons's song was viewed as credible. While this may have preserved his integrity in some circles, it did not clear him of liability. Judge Richard Owen said in his conclusion to the proceedings:

> Did Harrison deliberately use the music of He's So Fine? I do not believe he did so deliberately. Nevertheless, it is clear that My Sweet Lord is the very same song as He's So Fine with different words, and Harrison had access to He's So Fine. This is, under the law, infringement of copyright, and is no less so even though subconsciously accomplished.[11]

Harrison paid $587,000 in damages as a result of this verdict. "Access" is a key word in this and many music copyright cases. Even if a song is deemed substantially similar to a prior work, it does not necessarily prove that the second author in fact copied the music. In order to win an infringement suit, an author must prove that the alleged infringer had *access* to the copyrighted work, so that copying *could* have taken place.[12]

The following chart shows that most defendants in the past forty years prevailed in music cases because they were not proven to have had access to the original work:[13]

Reasons for Decisions in Favor of Defendants in Music Cases from 1978 to Jan. 2018

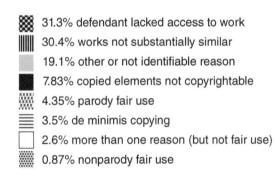

- 31.3% defendant lacked access to work
- 30.4% works not substantially similar
- 19.1% other or not identifiable reason
- 7.83% copied elements not copyrightable
- 4.35% parody fair use
- 3.5% de minimis copying
- 2.6% more than one reason (but not fair use)
- 0.87% nonparody fair use

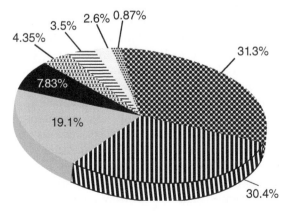

Musicians who subconsciously copy works might contest the access issue based on the fact that they have no recollection of actually accessing the original work. The degree of access would then be largely determined by how widely the work was disseminated and how likely it was that the defendant was exposed to it. It is reasonable to imagine this chart looking very different in the years ahead, given the immense exposure and access afforded to anyone possessing a cell phone or a computer with internet access.

The headlines light up when a court ruling is issued involving celebrity artists, copyright, and huge monetary awards. However, the majority of disputes alleging copyright infringement are settled privately or through mediators outside of the court. Aside from the expense, many claimants are discouraged from litigating due to the uncertainty of the outcome. Music claims by nature may lend themselves to more subjective bias than disputes involving defined boundaries, such as physical territory or manufactured goods. The human brain interprets music primarily through the ear and in a much different way than it does other mediums, such as film or literature. Concert pianist and author Natasha Spender has opined that music is "one of the most highly organized in respect of perceptual and motor activities that occur in sequence, each individual component occupying a very small interval of time."[14] That small interval of time is indicative of how quickly we hear and interpret music as a continuous thread of data. The same is not true when studying two paintings side by side, with the luxury of time and simultaneous visual comparison. Complicating matters further, various studies using positron emission tomography (PET) scans of the brain have shown that the hemispheres in which rhythm, timbre, and pitch are processed vary from person to person. And within those variances, an anomaly, such as tone deafness, might also affect the aural fact finding and ultimate ruling in a case. With so many unknowns, it would seem logical for a greater number of future disputes involving substantial similarities and possible subconscious copying to be settled privately. One such case was the recent settlement between the recording artists Tom Petty and Sam Smith. In April 2014, Smith released a very successful song he cowrote entitled "Stay With Me." Petty, a celebrated multi-platinum writer and performer, believed that Smith's song was substantially similar to his 1989 hit "Won't Back Down." Although Smith stated that he was not familiar with "Won't Back Down," he acknowledged the similarity following a comparison of both compositions, calling it a "complete coincidence." The matter was settled amicably with Petty being credited with a 25 percent share as a cowriter on "Stay With Me." We will never know for certain whether Smith created that two-phrase sequence of five notes independently or if he had heard the popular song and subconsciously retrieved that catchy melody from a memory he did not know he had. Mr. Petty, pleased with the efficiency and outcome of the settlement, described the episode as a "musical accident."[15]

Two weeks after the settlement of "Stay With Me," the decision of another claim became one of the most high-profile and controversial copyright cases in decades. The plaintiff was the family of the late soul legend Marvin Gaye, who contended that Pharrell Williams, along with Robin Thicke and rapper TI (Clifford Harris Jr.), copied Gaye's 1977 hit "Got To Give It Up" with their very popular song "Blurred Lines." During his testimony, Thick sang to the jury a medley of songs that included U2's "With Or Without You," Alphaville's "Forever Young," Bob Marley's "No Woman, No Cry," Michael Jackson's "Man In The Mirror," and the Beatles' "Let It Be" to demonstrate that songs with little in common can be seamlessly stitched together and that tracks often contain commonplace musical elements. It was an entertaining example of the interchangeable nature of the aforementioned five notes, four chords, two forms, and one meter. As the lead writer and producer, Pharrell Williams gave evidence that Marvin Gaye and 1970s soul were part of the musical milieu in which he grew up. When the lead attorney asked Williams if he felt that "Blurred Lines" captured the feel of the era in which Gaye recorded, he responded "Feel. Not infringed." The musicologist for the Gaye family had studied the sheet music and sound recordings of the two works, and identified eight "substantially similar" features which "surpass the realm of generic coincidence."[16] The court sided in favor of the Gaye family, and levied an impressive award of $7.4 million in damages (later revised down to $5.3 million plus 50 percent of all future music publishing revenue). Many musicians and outside music experts disagreed with this ruling, and there were numerous magazine and newspaper articles describing how this decision could have a chilling effect on the future of songwriting. Some opinions included this case as an example of how copyright law was out of touch with the way music is produced today. The outcome of this case appeared to blur the line between inspiration and copyright infringement more than ever.

According to the music metadata company Gracenotes, there are over 97 million songs in existence as of this writing. To get a sense of that, 97 million minutes would equal 184 years. New songs are being written and recorded every day, and the limited guidelines informing music composition are still largely in use. This vast trove of popular music is expanding exponentially, and new compositions do not leave the affected realm of copyright until seventy years after the death of the last surviving author. Music that does enter into the public domain is free for anyone to use; however, that affects very little of today's popular music. Earlier copyright protection is still in effect for ninety-five years after the date of first publication, so the songs entering the public domain now are from 1924. This cumulative volume, combined with the instantaneous access of digitally distributed music, allows more people more access to music than at any other time in history. Based on these metrics, it is logical to assume that instances of subconscious copying will increase. If subconscious copiers are held liable for copyright infringement in increasing numbers, the risk of creating music may discourage some authors and composers from engaging in their craft. Although such a risk would ostensibly be beyond the control of someone who is unaware of any subconscious influence, the doubt and uncertainty alone could affect their creative output. Any suppression of creativity would be at odds with the premise of the Constitution to incentivize creators "to promote the progress of Science and Useful Arts."[17] Technically, as each year goes by, the occurrences of true originality are diminishing. One might question how this movement of true originality toward the endangered species list may be addressed in the years to come. "How many five-note phrases are left?" Laws may eventually adapt to recognize nuances in liability for music that is determined to have been subconsciously copied. Perhaps it might even become a defense one day, as musical "borrowing" grows more prevalent and accepted. A more radical reaction could be the expansion of the music itself, the social acceptance of extra elements to breathe possibilities into new music being truly original. This type of musical evolution would be akin to aural Darwinism. Consider that Middle Eastern music is based on a twenty-four-note scale, with new tones halfway in-between the twelve tones used in our Western popular music yielding twenty-four intervals of a quarter tone each.[18] As much as those quarter-step tones may sound foreign and out of tune to a Western ear, they are socially accepted and in common use by nearly 10 percent of the world's population. While some of the foundations of music composition are based on math and physics, it appears that the majority of these rules have been decided by societies who agree on what they find appealing. Tastes may change; however history demonstrates that our creative drive and need to express ourselves through music is innate and durable. We may not always be certain of where that song in our head came from, but it is a safe bet that the music we consume lives in our minds and the media from which we access it.

Notes

1 Christopher B. Jaeger, "'Does That Sound Familiar?' Creators' Liability for Unconscious Copyright Infringement," *Vanderbilt Law Review* 61, no. 6 (2008): 1915.
2 17 U.S.C. § 106 (2018).
3 Stephen E. Siwek, "The True Cost of Sound Recording Piracy to the U.S. Economy," *Institute for Policy Innovation* (2007): i.
4 Oliver Sacks, *Musicophilia* (New York: Vintage Books, Random House, 2008).

5 Joseph M. Santiago, "The 'Blurred Lines' of Copyright Law: Setting a New Standard for Copyright Infringement in Music," *Brooklyn Law Review* 83, no. 1 (2017): 305.
6 Santiago, "Blurred Lines," 305.
7 Sky Stack, "Why All Music Is Unoriginal" *Medium* (blog), May 15, 2017, https://medium.com/@skykstack/why-all-music-is-unoriginal-e154d524e7a2.
8 Fred Fisher, Inc. v. Dillingham 298 F. 145, 147 (S.D.N.Y. 1924).
9 Rebecca Skirpan, "An Argument That Independent Creation Is as Likely as Subconscious Copying in Music Infringement Cases," *Law School Student Scholarship* 112 (2013) https://scholarship.shu.edu/student_scholarship/112.
10 Bright Tunes Music Corp. v. Harrisongs Music, Ltd., 420 F. Supp. 177 (S.D.N.Y. 1976), *aff'd sub nom.* ABKCO Music, Inc. v. Harrisongs Music, Ltd., 722 F.2d 988 (2d Cir. 1983).
11 *Bright Tunes,* 420 F. Supp. 177 at 180–81.
12 Edward Samuels, *The Illustrated Story of Copyright* (New York: Thomas Dunne Books, an imprint of St. Martin's Press, 2000).
13 Edward Lee, "Fair Use Avoidance in Music Cases," *Boston College Law Review* 59, no. 6 (2018): 1903, https://lawdigitalcommons.bc.edu/bclr/vol59/iss6/2.
14 Natasha Spender, "The Neuropsychology of Music: Apropos 'Music and the Brain,'" *The Musical Times* 119, no. 1626 (August 1978): 676–78.
15 Rick Sanders, "The Lines of Copyright Infringement Have Always Been Blurred," Aaron Sanders PLLC, March 12, 2015, https://www.aaronsanderslaw.com/the-lines-of-copyright-infringement-have-always-been-blurred.
16 Ben Challis, "Blurred Lines: The Difference between Inspiration and Appropriation," *WIPO Magazine*, September 2015, https://www.wipo.int/wipo_magazine/en/2015/05/article_0008.html
17 U.S. Const. art. I, § 8, cl. 8.
18 Joseph Pacholczyk, "Arab Music, §1, 5: Art Music after 1900," in *The New Grove Dictionary of Music & Musicians,* ed. Stanley Sadie (London: Macmillan Publishers Limited, 1980).

5.4

WHY MUSIC SHOULD NOT BE FREE

The Battle for Survival

Interview with Phil Galdston and David Wolfert

Phil Galdston (PG) is a songwriter, producer, and music publisher. More than 130 million copies of his songs and productions have appeared on more than 80 million records worldwide. "Save the Best For Last," recorded by Vanessa Williams and cowritten with Jon Lind and Wendy Waldman, is undoubtedly his best-known song. It simultaneously topped Billboard's charts for three weeks and was nominated for a GRAMMY as Song of the Year. He is a music professor, director of songwriting, and faculty songwriter-in-residence at New York University (NYU)'s Steinhardt School. He is also one of the founders of MusicAnswers, a rapidly growing organization of more than 3,800 songwriters, composers, performers, and producers seeking to protect and preserve rights in the digital age.

David Wolfert (DW) is a GRAMMY and EMMY-nominated songwriter, composer, orchestrator, and producer who has worked in all areas of music, including film, records, advertising, and television. As a music activist, he regularly advocates on behalf of musicians and songwriters, including through MusicAnswers, of which he is a co-founder. He is also an adjunct professor at NYU, where he teaches both undergraduates and graduates.

Michelle Bogre (MB) interviewed them together on August 26, 2019 in New York City. This interview has been edited for length and clarity.

MB: There is a lot of pessimism about the music business today. Copyright does not necessarily seem to work for the way people use music. Let's talk about copyright and music in the twenty-first century. How does it work or how does it not work? How should it work? What are the issues?

DW: The key issue, and I think by far the most important issue is that unlike most other art forms, a piece of music has a bifurcated copyright path. The song itself, which is typically called the underlying musical work, is a copyrightable entity, as is the recording, which is not the song but is everything else: the performance, the production, and the arrangement. This served songwriters really well when a song was written at a piano, or on a guitar or in one's head, and it was the three elements of music: melody, harmony, and rhythm. It was a tune. It had chords, it had words, and that was a copyrightable entity. And then if you were lucky and good, the song was brought to a studio where it was given an arrangement. And it was recorded and that became the second entity. The way that music is written now is a different process, especially in the pop field. Often the arrangement is created before the song is written because it is generated on someone's laptop, or sometimes even the band will write an entire song without what we consider traditional song elements —melody and lyrics—so the two copyrights, the two arts, if you will, have become conflated in the way music is made and also in the way that music is understood. Many years ago, if you asked a student what they liked about a song, they might have said they liked the words or the melody. Now, they will say they like the beat or the groove, and while rhythm can often be important, it is not part of the traditional song copyright.

PG: Well, a beat is not copyrightable.

DW: It is only copyrightable in the context of the recording.

MB: But you cannot get a copyright just for the drum performance.

PG: Bo Diddley tried to copyright a drum beat and he was turned down. He sued many people.

DW: On the other hand, there have been lawsuits over (a clapping rhythm). I think the point is that it has become complicated to understand the way the law is written, even for the intelligent and well-read creative person, and how we are protected and may be alleged to have infringed: by a decision made by a jury who are not professionals. If professionals cannot get their handle on the law, then certainly lay people cannot. Just consider the number of really high-profile cases recently, which most musicians and songwriters think were erroneously decided. My own view is that the law needs to address the means of distribution and everything else that has changed. The law needs to address or restore the bifurcation in an understandable way or figure something else out to give us protection. The law has to grow or change to reflect new production techniques. If I write words and music to a track that someone else has written, and the track gets sued as part of a song copyright, then I am liable, which to me is kind of ridiculous. But it is definitely the law today.

MB: So how does that work? How is the track a separate copyright; that is, how is it separate from the composition?

DW: The track is now often considered part of the composition and the person who writes the track is frequently given a 50 percent writer's credit. In fact, in some circles, writing the melody and lyrics is often called the "top line" as if it is kind of insignificant. In fact, in the vast majority of songs, those contributions are the most memorable and most responsible for a song's success.

PG: And top line writers are frequently compensated at a lower level. I think that perhaps, for the purposes of this discussion, at the conceptual level of the copyright in music, you have some key elements that even very knowledgeable and experienced songwriters do not understand. First, what is a copyright in a new musical composition? It is when the participants in the creation of that work agree to codify their contributions in that work. It is that simple. And the law says that the number of people who agree to have their contribution codified will divide the copyright equally until and unless they decide otherwise. They have the right to decide otherwise, but they usually do not. For example, you have Jerry Wexler, the great music executive and producer saying to Gerry Goffin and Carole King, "I need a song for Aretha Franklin and I have a great title, 'Natural Woman,'" and for that title, as I understand it, he received 20 percent of the copyright. If you flash forward into the twenty-first century, you can look at an extreme example: Kanye West's first hit "Through The Wire," was a sped-up version of Chaka Khan's recording of a song written by David Foster, Tom Keane, and Cynthia Weil. Kanye made a really ill-advised business move. He created his rap, he made his record, he turned it into the record company, and then the record company gave him the standard form, which required him to clear the sample. In other words, he had to secure permission to use the master *and* to add his contribution to the song. If you look at the credits, there is no Kanye West songwriting credit because, as I understand it, Foster, Kean, and Weil declined to give him credit.

But you asked the global question, "What is copyright?" I do not think you can find more than one in 10,000 music creators who understand copyright. They think it is the same thing as owning this phone, but they are wrong. And because they do not understand, they do not accept the idea that copyright has a term limit. Marilyn Bergman, a great lyricist, and former president of ASCAP, always argued for copyright with few limits, closer to property rights. I am not going to argue against that. I am here to say that those who are using copyrights to make money tend to understand the concept and the limits of copyright. So I think we have to start with that. Society is telling you that there is value in your attempt to create a work. And if you create the work, it will convey to you protection of that work for a period of time—which has changed many over the years—and you will control that copyright.

MB: MusicAnswers is an activist group. Does it advocate for a longer duration?

PG: We advocate for music professionals. The key juncture in this discussion, and what we say at MusicAnswers is, "You need to know that the moment you write something, it is yours." The standard technique we use in teaching about this at NYU is to stand in front of a group of young songwriters and say, "So tell us how the rights of a song are divided." And most of them say that there is a writer's right and a publishing right. There's only one problem: There is no a publishing right. There is only a writer's right. Many people will say that legal tradition and precedent conveys a publishing right and that, for example, that has been the tradition for the 107 years that ASCAP has been in existence. Others will strongly—even violently—disagree. But the history of ASCAP is interesting: The founders of ASCAP were twelve legendary writers who wanted to make ASCAP an organization of writers and publishers. They offered to give the publishers 25 percent of the performing rights. The publishers refused. They offered them 33 percent. The publishers refused, so the writers caved and offered 50 percent. So there is a 50/50 split. That is why David and I publish a lot of our own songs. Beyond these details, so many songwriters do not understand the bifurcated copyright—that in the composition and the recording—that David spoke of. It is crucial that we educate people. Even my children, who are now 35 and 32, sometimes conflate the song and the record. So maybe we need new language.

DW: Why music creators do not grasp the concept of copyright is complicated because even though there are two separate copyrights, there are virtually unlimited royalty streams. In other words, ASCAP, which does not own anything, pays you; your publisher, which may or may not own anything, pays you; and you get paid differently for different types of streams and usage. You also get licensing fees. It is an enormous amount to absorb for a person who is trying to learn about the world and also trying to learn how to write songs. And also, new means of delivery are being invented every week. For a young songwriter, the very concept of copyright gets lost in all of that.

MB: It is interesting that you say that. Is it also because songwriters think that because they are protected by ASCAP or BMI, that they do not have to understand the business?

DW: It is not true that BMI and ASCAP fully protect songwriters. That is not their job or role. They only monitor a very minuscule part of your rights, if you are a writer. In fact, in this current marketplace, you are liable to make more money off licensing fees, which ASCAP and BMI cannot touch, than royalties. And under the new Music Modernization Act (MMA) if there is an interactive stream, the money is now bypassing ASCAP and BMI. I learned some of this late. I was a grown man with two children who had earned a living in various forms of music since I was 17. ASCAP asked me to be an expert witness in federal court for a mammoth $110 million copyright case. They took me into prep with their lawyers and their outside counsel for four days and I realized there were hundreds of things that I did not know, and I had been successfully managing my own affairs for years.

PG: Well, that is an interesting point because there were two seminal events in my education. I thought I knew this stuff pretty well, but when I was invited by Marilyn Bergman to appear at a panel, at the end of the day, I said to the chief counsel of ASCAP, "You cannot send people like me into these events so uninformed." I thought that I was pretty well informed, but I just got scorched because I did not know anything. And then I was asked by the National Music Publishers Association to be one of the songwriter witnesses in what are known as the CRB (Copyright Royalty Board) hearings. These hearings are convened when the users of music—record companies, for example—and the owners or the administrators of the rights to the music cannot agree on the rate users will pay owners per records sold, so it goes to a three-judge tribunal. When it came time for me to be deposed, one of the lawyers for Warner Brothers Records said to me, "Such and such a song that you wrote has earned many millions of dollars. Is that correct?" I said it was. He said, "And I understand that there is a tape of you writing most of that song with one of your collaborators and that tape is around 30 minutes long." And I said, "That is true." He said, "Well, is that not a pretty good payday? Thirty minutes work for millions of dollars?" I said, "Well, you did not ask me how long it took us to write this song." So he asked me how long. I said, "Thirty-eight years," because that is how old I was when I wrote the song. And this is what we try to teach students. This is the point of copyright: Songwriting is an art form from which you receive not one penny until or unless the song sells or gets streamed or generates any revenue from the various streams. I wrote maybe 400 or 500 songs before I had my first hit. This is why copyright is a valid concept. Some other countries pay money or provide a form of patronage to artists. That is not how it is done here. We take a risk.

MB: I used to teach copyright to art and design students. The first thing I would ask was who in the room, other than me, had not downloaded a song for free. Usually, not a single hand went up. So I would tell them that they had all infringed the copyright of a songwriter. They would say, "Oh, no it is different. It's music." And I would tell them that it was not different.

PG: I want to go back to how copyright works in the twenty-first century. David explained the variety of revenue streams, which seem to be ever-expanding, even if some are just tributaries of original ones. I think what is particularly important is that, if you start with this idea that this song is yours until and unless you do anything, then most of the structures that have existed over the past 107 years are kind of irrelevant. Is it irrelevant to the greatest degree of success one could enjoy? No, because it is still a marketplace out there. So, you can get Taylor Swift on Sirius X and whatever piece she has given up, that makes some sense. But a lot of the rest of it is certainly open to question yet. We talk about the conflation of who is representing who. The reason we hem and haw about BMI and ASCAP is because BMI is owned by terrestrial radio stations, and ASCAP, at this point, is controlled mostly by the major publishers, who are owned by multinationals. Yes, there are twelve writers on the ASCAP board, but those twelve writers do not stay on the ASCAP board for thirty years, as have some publishers. Every day they show up to represent songwriters is a day they are not writing music, which is their best chance to get paid. That is not true of the publishers. They are getting paid by their employers, regardless. I just want to make sure that people understand that, once you own the copyright, there are a lot of options here that did not exist before, and many of the traditional ones may not be as relevant as they once were.

DW: So let me follow up on that. Music copyright covers a lot more than a song. I am a composer, as well. The copyright and the authorship of most of your favorite movie and television shows do not contain the writer's name anyway because they are done under a work-for-hire contract. That makes a mockery of the original concept of copyright, and it also complicates royalty streams. For instance, you have to negotiate your right to collect your "writer's share" of the performance royalties even though you are not legally a writer; it does not matter that you work twenty-four hours a day, six months in a row on the music—you are not legally the writer. So work-for-hire changes how the royalty streams work. For movie and television composers, neighboring rights are becoming some of the primary sources of income, which are not covered by any law anywhere that I am aware of and are not collected properly in America.

PG: You are right. This is a point we make all the time. People think that because you are a work-for-hire writer, you are in the identical boat as with all other writers. But you are actually not, certainly not in the area we are discussing; you took the coin in advance in exchange for your copyrights. If we go back to why we are in this situation and what copyright means in the twenty-first century, the truth is that the creators of music have been punished for the success of the art form to which we have contributed. We are punished for its popularity and ubiquity. Today, when you walk into a store, it is all music. Marketers figured out that music sets the tone for everything. I would guess that retail outlets use Pandora and other streaming services more per capita than anybody else. People think—they have been encouraged to think—that music is like water or air so they don't think they should have to pay for it. When I first started becoming active in this arena, I would say, if there was a break in the gasoline line leading to any gas station and everybody was coming down and filling up their tank for free, the police would be there in two seconds. How come nobody is there to stop the theft of our work? And it is theft. Flat out theft. It is not piracy. Piracy sounds cool; swashbuckling guys or Robin Hood.

MB: Is copyright too long today in light of decisions like the "Blurred Lines" case (Williams v. Gaye, 895 F.3d 1106 (9th Cir. 2018)) which now protects the "mood and feel"? If copyright is seventy years, plus life of the author, and we have decisions that protect mood and feel, will that not stifle creativity and contribute to the "theft" of music?

DW: I do not believe that the issue in the Gaye case has much, if anything, to do with the length of copyright. The fundamental problem with that case is that it is a highly questionable decision. So a related issue is how do you prevent this type of decision from happening? And it just happened again to Katy Perry.[1]

PG: Yes, but eventually we hope this case will be overturned or, at minimum, not replicated. Maybe copyright cases of this kind should not be decided by juries or they should be decided by juries of our true peers who understand music.

MB: Partly, the answer lies in the Constitution, which gives Congress the right to make laws to protect copyright for a limited time, not forever.

DW: In terms of the length of copyright, I had my greatest success when I was well into my forties from a song called "I Believe in You and Me," that I wrote when I was barely into my thirties. If you build a building and put your sweat and your blood into it, you can leave it to your children, who can leave it to their children, who may leave it to their children. That is the nature of property and copyright is how the law recognizes creative work as property. Why should the songs that I write have less of a life? Let's say for the sake of argument that Whitney Houston did not find my song fifteen years after it was written, but seventy-five years after it was written, which is not out of the question. My heirs would have much less time to benefit from its success. Why is that fair?

MB: Do cases like these not put a chill on songwriting, particularly considering the length of copyright?

PG: They have, already. Many writers of note are running their latest songs by musicologists before they are released. They are putting the melodies into the big computer and searching through a database of thirty to fifty thousand songs to see if there are similarities. The other reason these decisions are so bad, is that if Bo Diddley could not get a copyright on what we call the Bo Diddley rhythm, we have to ask why could he not? Because it is not what is known as "unique expression." And that is also true of these two cases. The groove and that mood that the jury said infringed is not that unique.

DW: The substance of what was considered infringed is not notated. In other words, it is not music by any traditional definition of the word. It is something for sure, but it is not music and it is not a song. But I want to go back to your question, because as I understand it, that principle of copyright and the reason it is different in America than it is in the rest of the world, which recognizes moral rights, is that the American concept of copyright seeks to balance commerce with creativity. That is its intent: To encourage people to create and the reason it is limited is because it allows society to benefit from people's creations.

MB: Was it not its original purpose to balance knowledge and creativity, not commerce? The idea was that we needed to share knowledge, and to do that, we had to give creators some protected time, but that time had to be limited because if it does not get into the public domain, then the public does not benefit. Now it has become an economic principle because we view copyright as economic and Europe does not.

DW: We also view knowledge as economic. We commodify it, particularly today when knowledge is readily accessible at any moment from these little devices (our smartphones). Maybe it begs a reexamination as a result of that.

MB: I am very torn on the duration. I think it is a little long. But I also make the same argument you make in my class when someone says it should be shorter. I am like, why? Why can my heirs not profit from my work for a much longer time?

DW: That is an issue. Another issue that we face today is technology—the fact that music is so readily available is a huge factor, but also how music is created. Before the advent of hip-hop, the idea of taking someone else's record and using it as the underpinning for your record was unthinkable. You might inadvertently or subconsciously steal someone's melody, but you would never deliberately play that record and sing on top of it. The design of digital audio workstations, which is where 99.9 percent of music is created these days makes it super easy. I can take anything, change its tempo, change its key, and probably use it in ways previously unimaginable. So the whole concept of fair use in music is skewed. It is not as easily quantifiable as it is, like in a Jeff Koons decision or the Shephard Fairey Obama Hope poster. In music, someone says they only used one note of the base note, but it is my bass note. Who are you to decide that what you have done to my bass note is transformative? The fact that that music has morphed into a different technology blurs the lines even before, if you will forgive the reference.

PG: I am sitting here listening and reflecting on something that we have never really connected before. David began by talking about the bifurcated copyright. Then we talked about the conflation of the terms "song" and "record" once hip-hop and more accessible recording platforms took hold. I always recoil when someone listens to a demo of one of my songs, and says, "I love that record" because it is not the record they are hearing, it is the song. We have talked about the different industry structures at work, how some of them are irrelevant, but what we did not really talk about is how they drive the market and the creation of music. For example, for twenty years or so, consumers and critics have lamented the state of pop music. And if you talk to professionals, particularly those who lived and worked in the field fifteen or twenty years ago, they will say that there were a couple of things that really damaged the the quality of much of popular music. The most important one was that performers or their support teams realized there was more money to be made if they could own a part of the copyright in the composition. If Brian Hyland had written "Sealed With A Kiss," or if he could have put his name on it, he would still be making royalties like your husband is. But he did not and he could not. When performers started demanding a share of the copyright, or they signed publishing deals that required that they had to share in the copyright of a certain percentage of the songs on their albums, things began to decline. If the quality of the song did not decline, the writer's rights diminished, which has an effect on the quality of the songs.

MB: It changed the idea of authorship.

DW: When I was 27 years old, arguably one of the most successful recording artists in the world liked one of my songs and said, "I have to have a quarter of the writing credit." What is a 27-year-old going to do? I said yes, but I had never heard of something like that. It comes down to the concept of authorship as you said. When ten people have their name on a song, it is likely that one of them did nothing but pick up the dry cleaning, but it is also likely that one of those people just programmed the drums.

PG: I once heard Duke Fakir of The Four Tops talk about a situation where he was in around the studio and Holland, Dozier, Holland, the great writing team that created many of Motown's biggest hits, came in with the latest song that they were going to record. The writers were talking and one of them said to the other, "You know, I just got a new Cadillac." Duke said, "How did you get the money to do that?" And they said, "From our airplay royalties." Duke and his partners said, "What are airplay royalties?" And the writers explained that whenever their songs were played on the air they made money. And Duke asked, "How come we, the people who are singing these songs, do not make any of that money?" Well, the fact that performers did not make money in North America was a contributing factor to driving them to want to share in the writer's royalty. That started the change in notions of authorship. Today, the competition is even stiffer. You have a very narrow pipeline, so the companies who are the gatekeepers as to which records get made, play an undue role in whose name goes on the song. That is one reason you can end up with ten people sharing the songwriting credit. In their judgment, it is not about nurturing talent or developing the art form. It is about making a hit. The companies that publish the songs and the labels that release the records of those songs, which are often part of the same overarching corporation, are getting their piece regardless of how many writers share the writer's credit. It is the writers who get hurt. It does shift the idea of authorship.

MB: We alluded to fair use in music as being skewed. Can you explain?

DW: I think it is a bogus concept. Theft is theft. You take my wallet, take a dollar out, and give me back my wallet, you have still stolen from me.

MB: So you do not think there should be any fair use in music?

DW: As it applies to commercial and artistic uses, I do not. I cannot have a conversation about this with art professors, curators, or artists, some of whom are close friends of mine, because once the conversation turns to what is now called "appropriation," I shut down. I do not believe that there is such a thing. If you want to appropriate my work, you call me up, you ask me, and we come to a deal. It is likely if you are just taking a bass note, I will say, okay, it is yours. But the idea that someone can appropriate my creation or anybody's creation and decide at what granular level it is transformative, I find that abhorrent. I am the person who put my soul and my years of training into my art, and, and I am being told that, well, that is not important enough, and someone can just use it without acknowledging me, without paying me, even without asking, I have a problem with that.

PG: But, sometimes there can be carve outs. ASCAP got into this terrible public relations situation with the Girl Scouts. My view is that if you are at summer camp and you are singing our songs, that should be fine. I am perfectly happy with that. I am not okay with instances where commercial business entities are generating revenue from the use of our work. What do you lose by being humane, generous, and humble about this? What do you lose by asking? If you think you are losing something, how are you going to feel when somebody does it to you?

DW: I want to go back to technology for a second because what has happened in the visual arts, is the same thing that happened to music, starting with the first sample. Now it is exacerbated by the fact that everything is so readily available online. I can see the *Mona Lisa* right now if I want to, I can take a screenshot, I can print it out and I can have my own version of the *Mona Lisa*. Technology has affected all art forms in that way.

PG: I like your idea that it is not ownership, it is authorship, because I really think that is true. In this discussion, we have looked at two extremes and we have looked at what is in between, what it really means to try to create and have a life and how society should respect that and what it means to be at the other end. And it has been a maddening process all these years to watch these protections get knocked down and to feel at the same time that the practitioners of the art forms that can be copyrightable are not nurtured by society or by business. Too many music publishers today think their job is to sell music, not to sell the best music or to encourage the creation of the best music. They seem to be primarily interested in producing what sells, which tends in their view to be what sold yesterday.

DW: I just want to push back a hair on that. I do not want to come off as saying that all music sucks. Obviously, the definition of what is good is subjective. There are some wonderful songs being written now. There are some wonderful records being made now. It is just that the marketplace and the protections for the people who create music are not in place.

MB: Does the fact that the means of production can now be in my house, or in my bedroom— does that give young musicians even greater opportunity because they can cut out the middleman?

DW: We always say that music has never been more popular. It has never been more available. And the opportunity to make it has never been easier. It is just that people are not getting paid for it.

PG: Unless you are going to fight for your rights, unless you know what they are and you fight for them and work within a community to fight for them, all the ease and the convenience of making music is going to take the value of the work down the tubes, or at the least, it is going to be diminished. Songwriting will be so unimportant. Our rights and our royalties have always been at the bottom of the economic food chain; we are fighting now to make sure they do not go even lower, when they actually should be going higher because music is so important. Let me make one other point about this. David started this discussion by talking about the division of rights from an economic point of view. I have had this conversation with several really important people who write, record, and perform. I ask them how good their record deal is. I say, "You are a legacy artist. You are someone who made a lot of money doing this, who made a lot of money for the people who released your music. How good is your deal?" They will say, "It is really good." I will say, "Do not tell me the numbers, but please tell me how good do you think it is? Are you at the upper level of royalty rates?" They will say they are at the upper level. But then I will ask what percentage of the profits they think they are getting? They usually do not know and that is the problem. We only look at what we think the maximum royalty rate we can get is in the current marketplace, instead of looking at what piece of the whole pie we are getting.

DW: The problem with the fact that the means of distribution are expanding all the time is that you have to couple it with expectations. I cannot tell you how many of my young students will tell me they are going to release a record on YouTube or put it on Spotify. But their expectation of success is so low that if 250 people click on their record, they are ecstatic. That is a result of what we can only assume was very careful calculation by certain important players on the user side of the marketplace to lower the expectations that my generation had. As songwriters, we were able to make a living, support a family, and put our children through college. Zero percent of people starting out expect that today. They are happy if people like their music.

MB: So why do you think so many students come here to study music and songwriting?

DW: Because songwriters are not made, they are born. That is the only explanation I have. For example, I cannot go two or three days without writing. I really start to turn into a creepy person. Our experience is that those who decide to take the more academic route are doing so because they share that drive—that obsession—and find this environment productive.

PG: You have to divide this between graduates and undergraduates. So what is the difference? When NYU asked me to start the songwriting program, I said, "Sure, but I would like to begin with graduate students." And they asked me why. I said it was because I only wanted to work with people who were committed. So when they asked me to start the undergraduate program, I said yes, but I thought we had to have a high level of truth in advertising because I knew parents would be wondering how much money their child could make when they graduate. And I felt we had to be realistic. We had to let students and parents know that the music business is not a meritocracy and it does not have an institutionalized path to success, as it exists, for example, in the law or business or medicine. We will teach you the tools and inform you about your rights and the way the business works. But there is no simple template for a successful career writing songs. Do not come here if that is foremost in your mind.

DW: It is so much harder today for our students because the industry does not really nurture talent anymore. It is very much true that in the American musical tradition—I am sure it is true in all the art forms—there were people whose expertise was recognizing talent. That is what they were taught to do. They managed their investment in talent based on what they thought the future was. The hit song that I had in 1996 was a result of a publishing deal that I signed in 1970. The person whose office I went into when I was 20 year old and played my honestly crappy little song had expertise in recognizing talent and they made their money back many times over, twenty-six years later. That part of the business has disappeared. I was lucky because when I was young, and eager, and a sponge, I was exposed to experienced people who would agree to write with me. I was educated in my craft, not out of the goodness of anybody's heart, but because they figured that if they made this investment enough times, sooner or later, some people would pay off big. The only place in America now that you can find that kind of community for a songwriter is in institutions like this. Especially since the technology has driven people back to the bedrooms to make their music, how do you learn? You cannot watch a YouTube video to learn how to be a songwriter. You need to find community. So that is why a lot of people come here to find people like them and to find people whose advice will make them a better songwriter.

PG: The sense of community is so important.

DW: I have to read this into the record. Two days ago I got this email from a 16-year-old who attended our songwriting camp at NYU. " Hello . . . I just wanted to thank you all so much again for the amazing and valuable opportunity you gave me, as well as everyone else in our workshop, to learn and truly embrace the art of songwriting. I feel that I have changed so much as a person as well as a writer and I definitely made lifelong connections with so many unique artistic people . . . . I am really happy to say that I have been songwriting nonstop. All of your advice and knowledge has guided me and inspired me as I write. I cannot thank you enough."

MB: You have mentioned streaming. It only pays micro-pennies. If that is the future, what does that mean for songwriting?

DW: The short answer to your question is that it is part of the diminished expectations. If you are just a pure songwriter, and not a performer, it is hard to make a living.

PG: We are still debating this internally. So David referred to a conscious attempt by people who put together these platforms to gut copyright, and even if that was not the goal, the by-product is to diminish the value of copyright. So how did this happen? In part because when these streaming businesses started, the hedge fund investors did not worry about how to pay the copyright holders. I think this is something we have to fight for in the future. The vertically integrated companies like Universal, Warner, and Sony are making staggering sums of money because they have eliminated the cost of manufacturing and distribution. They have reduced to almost nothing the costs of promotion because they only have to deal with a couple of streaming platforms. So how come music creators are not demanding to be paid more? We should be getting more. I think that is the future fight.

MB: Are the streaming rates not set like statutory rates are?

DW: The rates that a record company charges for use of their copyrights or those they administer are guided by individual agreements. The rates that the performing rights organizations charge for streaming are subject to the consent decree, and what the consent decree says, and this is where it gets really complicated, is that if you are Spotify, a website, a radio station, or a TV station and you want to use ASCAP's music—which encompasses millions and millions of copyrights, including mine and Phil's—all you have to do to use the music ASCAP represents is to apply for a license. You do not have to agree on a price. You do not even have to tell ASCAP what you will use it for. Then ASCAP calls and negotiates a price. ASCAP is constrained by the consent decree in many ways. One of them is that when the dispute cannot be resolved, it automatically goes to federal court. Until the MMA it all went to the same courtroom and the same judge. Now it does not. One of the rules of evidence governed by the consent decree is that you could not introduce what anybody else was getting paid. So the fact that the record company is making generally fifteen times what the songwriter gets at a minimum was never introduced in federal court because it could not have been. And not only that, but the publishers also are allowed to make their own deals with the streaming services. Many times, they are owned by the same people. So the publishers, because they are not constrained by consent decree, can go and they can make a direct license deal that includes a multimillion dollar advance, which is not payable to their artists. One thing the MMA does allegedly is to create a path by which an interactive stream will now be considered a mechanical royalty that will be set by some board somewhere that allegedly is going to be higher. There are other things it does, but not one songwriter has made a penny more because of the MMA; at least, not yet.

MB: So do we need more activist groups like MusicAnswers?

PG: Well, our view is that we do not think we need more groups, we just need more people to belong to those, like MusicAnswers, that have a proven record of fighting the good fight in an intelligent way. We started with the idea of saving the performance rights organizations (PROs) because we could see how they were imperiled. That still remains a cornerstone, but we are not exactly sure what role the PROs will play in the future. Some of that is of their own determination. For example, the ASCAP board endorsed the MMA before the MMA's language was finalized. We argued quietly against that step. That said, when we started MusicAnswers, we realized that the job was to unite writers, performers, and producers. And our theory was, and remains, that the interests that bind us are greater than the interests that divide us.

DW: Yes, I think we need to increase our membership to include as many music creators whose livelihood and rights are concerned. But I also think that the issues we face are not specific to music. I think that the devaluation of the creative act is a societal ill. It is maybe too late to fix it, but we need to try. We need to educate people that it is important to factor in the cost of creativity—I hate the word "content"—when they are drafting their business plans. I know this is grandiose, but we would like very much to partner with groups that are doing the same things for other art forms. Also, there is a huge responsibility on the part of the education system in America especially at a business school level, to instill a sense of morality and to redefine what stealing is.

MB: That is a very good point. We should not just be addressing this in art and design schools, but in business schools too, that it is almost immoral to devalue creativity.

DW: Yes, today the young entrepreneur is not equipped to ask about the creative person. It is not in his or her vocabulary. It should be.

PG: Let's look at this another way. So, tomorrow, you are a streaming service, and you are going into the hedge fund, and you are presenting your business plan. You mostly have to deal with executive salaries, and you need them to be competitive. And then, you have the cost of content. Which of those two costs can be cut? Content. We are going the wrong way. We are going back to the time when musicians were the least well paid on any gig. So, I always tell my students that, if they do not wake up every day wanting to make music or write songs, then they should find another profession. Because you have to deal with the reality that this is a very demanding, very challenging road. The reward must start with the value to you of creating the work. That said, as we, and others, have asked, how can you have a life in music if you cannot make a living at it? As we see it, this is a battle for the survival of those who choose to pursue the art and craft of music creation.

Note

1 Gray v. Perry, No. 15-CV-5642-CAS-JCx, 2020 WL 1275221 (C.D. Cal. Mar. 16, 2020). A federal jury previously found that Perry's song "Dark Horse" copied a Christian rap song and that she must pay nearly $2.8 million in damages because of similarities in the rhythm. Most musicologists disagree because the similarities use basic derivative descending minor scale in a basic rhythm common in many trap beats. They note that the songs are in different keys, have different beats per minute and different melodies. Fortunately, the court agreed and, on Perry's motion for judgment as a matter of law, vacated the jury verdict on liability and damages.

5.5

MUSIC, DEPOSIT COPIES, AND UNANSWERED QUESTIONS AFTER *SKIDMORE V. LED ZEPPELIN*

*Bob Clarida**

. . . really makes me wonder . . .

Jimmy Page and Robert Plant, "Stairway to Heaven" (1973)

Introduction

The Ninth Circuit's two most high-profile music infringement cases in years, *Williams v. Gaye* (*Gaye*)[1] and *Skidmore v. Led Zeppelin* (*Zeppelin*),[2] have generated a number of headlines, to put it mildly. Many suggest that these decisions lend legitimacy to weak infringement actions, i.e. claims based on a similarity of "feel" (in *Gaye*) or on commonplace musical elements, like minor-key arpeggios over descending chromatic lines (in *Zeppelin),* and will thus open the floodgates to more such claims.

Time will tell whether the levee's going to break, as Zeppelin once sang. But even if these similarity determinations were controversial, at least they were made by juries after comparing two specific songs. They did not therefore result in many rulings on broad principles of law that will be binding on future courts faced with different songs embodying different alleged similarities.

One potentially consequential ruling of law for future litigants, however—and one that has generated far fewer headlines—is the Ninth Circuit's holding in *Zeppelin* that the scope of copyright in an unpublished pre-1978 musical composition is determined solely by the content of the deposit copy on file with the Copyright Office for that work.[3] I will call this the "*Zeppelin* Holding," and as used by the *Zeppelin* court, consistent with the 1909 Act, the term "unpublished" includes compositions made available in sound recording form, but not sheet music, at the time of the copyright registration. *Gaye* had made a similar ruling at the summary judgment stage, limiting the scope of copyright in Marvin Gaye's "Got to Give It Up" to the elements shown in, or reasonably implied by, the deposit copy.[4] *Gaye* prevailed at trial nonetheless. The plaintiff in *Zeppelin* did not, hence the appeal that resulted in the *Zeppelin* Holding. As of this writing, the Ninth Circuit has affirmed after *en banc* review (a full court review) of the *Zeppelin* decision, and plaintiff's counsel has filed a petition for *certiorari* with the U.S. Supreme Court. Because there is no clear split of authority between the Ninth Circuit and other Circuits on this issue, it is somewhat unlikely that the Supreme Court would agree to hear the case.

Some background: For music copyright registrations filed before the current Copyright Act took effect in 1978, the Copyright Office only accepted deposit copies in written form, which generally consisted of musical notation in conventional five-line staff format ("Notation"), frequently including lyrics and chord symbols, like this:

This exclusive reliance on Notation leads to the problem that both *Gaye* and *Zeppelin* confronted, essentially for the first time: If the scope of the copyright in a musical work is limited to the details that were incorporated into the Notation submitted to the Copyright Office, and those details are materially incomplete, relative to the recorded version of the work, it might be impossible for the composer to show an infringement of *other* significant elements of original authorship contained in the recorded version of the registered composition, no matter how direct and flagrant the defendant's copying of those other elements. There is a disconnect, in other words, between the music known and beloved by the public (and allegedly copied by the defendant) in its recorded form, and the notated music a court is willing to protect against infringement.

Because of this disconnect, if a deposit copy omits details that an infringer copies without authorization—and we will see some examples below of songs that are vulnerable to such a fate—is it the Ninth Circuit's position that such infringement can never be actionable, because the copied elements are not in the Notation? Or is it potentially actionable if the plaintiff satisfies whatever administrative requirements the Copyright Office currently deems necessary? What are those requirements?

And what if the plaintiff *does not* satisfy them—can a court decide they are not mandatory anyway? After all, until the Supreme Court's recent *Fourth Estate* ruling,[5] a number of courts, including the Ninth Circuit, contended that a plaintiff need not obtain the issuance or refusal of a registration from the Copyright Office before commencing an infringement suit, even though the plain language of the statute and the Copyright Office stated otherwise. As that controversy demonstrates, courts are under no obligation to defer to the Copyright Office on registration issues in the context of litigation, so why should they defer—or should they not—with respect to the relationship between deposit copies and copyright scope? Just because the Copyright Office says that registered musical composition "X" consists of no more than the Notation on deposit for such work, must that be the end of the discussion in court? Is there a plausible argument to the contrary? A practical work-around? That is the subject of this essay.

Full disclosure: I was not a juror in *Zeppelin* so my opinion does not count, but I personally agree with the jury verdict: no infringement. Yet, I still find the *Zeppelin* Holding unfortunate for many reasons, and not just because it could leave some significant authorship unprotected. More fundamentally, it seems to proceed from and reinforce the flawed premise that the Notation originally deposited for a musical composition *is* the work of authorship, just as the text of a printed book fully represents the literary authorship of that book. However, unlike literary authorship, jurors are seldom able to read the Notation for themselves, and the *Zeppelin* Holding all but requires courts to deny jurors the opportunity to hear the composer's own recording of the song at issue for purposes of determining similarity.

So, as happened in *Gaye* and *Zeppelin*, jurors in an infringement trial do not base their similarity findings on the recording of the plaintiff's song that the defendant allegedly heard and from which it allegedly copied, but on a twice-removed legal fiction: third-party courtroom performances and explanations of the Notation. The *Zeppelin* Holding tells jurors, in effect, "the music is only what is written in special symbols you cannot read, which the composers did not actually write down and the defendant did not ever see, but which will be explained and performed for you by trained expert witnesses who are being paid to come to different conclusions about it." This strikes me as less than ideal. No wonder the court in *Gaye* held the very contents of the deposit copy to be a fact issue for the jury. Are the contents of a deposit of a literary work an issue of fact for the jury? Does it not just say what it says?

The *Zeppelin* Holding also puts courts in a difficult position if they allow the jury to hear a recording of the plaintiff's song for some purposes—as the Ninth Circuit in *Zeppelin* instructed the district court to do on remand for purposes of showing access—but then rely on a curative instruction telling jurors to unring the bell and make the substantial similarity comparison based only on the Notation, as if that were possible.

The original decision of Congress and the Copyright Office to permit only written deposits for musical compositions in 1909, left in place for almost seventy years as recorded music came to dominate both the production and consumption of commercial music, has therefore given rise to non-trivial complications for infringement litigation in the twenty-first century, with questionable offsetting benefits. It is entirely understandable that the Copyright Office, *circa* 1909, would have relied solely on Notation to define the scope of copyright in a musical composition. Most music was sold in sheet music form, to be played on home pianos, so the Notation would likely have been quite representative of most works, and in any case, the Copyright Office probably did not have much equipment on hand to evaluate the musical authorship embodied in piano rolls, wax cylinders, and the like, even if it had wanted to. And as *Zeppelin* points out, at the time of the 1909 Act there was the still-fresh legal controversy about what constituted a "writing" or a "copy" of a musical composition after the 1908 decision in *White-Smith v. Apollo*,[6] a problem that was avoided by requiring Notation as a deposit.

But in my view, this history is not a very persuasive argument for continuing to interpret the scope of such copyrights so narrowly *in the courts* now that the statute and the Copyright Office have embraced a less formalistic view. The 1909 Act did not require judicial deference to Copyright Office determinations of copyrightability or registrability, any more than the current Act does. In the years from 1909 to 1978, the Copyright Office took a number of positions about what it would accept as deposit copies for certain types of works, for its own good reasons, but it is not the Copyright Office's role, nor was it in 1909, to define the outside limit of protectable authorship in a composition, when that issue has been raised in litigation. The Copyright Office's role is and has always been to determine whether *the material deposited* is copyrightable. It is certainly not to relegate any other *undeposited* authorship to the public domain. If such authorship is not covered by an existing deposit copy, it should at least be protectable going forward, in my view, as unpublished/*un*registered authorship always was at common law before 1978, and still is today for all non-US works, whose owners can sue without ever having registered.[7]

In sum, Notation may have served a pragmatic administrative purpose for registering copyright in musical compositions under the 1909 Act, but I contend that other admissible evidence as to copyright scope should not be precluded in a present-day litigation, if such evidence is available. The original deposit copy should not be an irreparable "gotcha" technicality. After all, under the current Act, even the "facts stated in the certificate" are at best entitled to a rebuttable presumption of truth in a court proceeding[8]; the Act gives the contents of the deposit copy no prima facie weight at all, let alone dispositive weight. Why then should the "facts stated" in the *deposit copy* impose an irrebuttable evidentiary limit in court, either today or under the 1909 Act? This is fundamentally an evidence question, it seems to me, namely, "what did the plaintiff compose and what did the defendant copy?" When viewed as such, the answer is clear in Rule 102 of the Federal Rules of Evidence: "These rules should be construed so as to administer every proceeding fairly, eliminate unjustifiable expense and delay . . . to the end of ascertaining the truth and securing a just determination."

I submit that the *Zeppelin* Holding conflicts with these principles. The scope of copyright in a work registered under the 1909 Act should, in my view, be determined in each case by the totality of admissible evidence in that case, not resolved solely by the Copyright Office's past or present practices regarding acceptable deposit copies. Speaking only for myself, I think that would be a fairer, more truthful, less legally fictitious way to litigate music infringement disputes. But until that revolution comes, how can a composer protect elements of his or her work that are not present in the Notation, elements perhaps known to millions but legally invisible?

Definition: Undeposited Authorship

It is demonstrably true that many musical compositions, as released to the public, embody far more authorship than does the corresponding Notation deposited to register those compositions. An unduly alarmist but well-researched piece of legal journalism by Vernon Silver in Bloomberg Businessweek, discussing the *Led Zeppelin* case in June 2019,[9] lays out some fascinating documentation of this phenomenon, including a photo, credited to the Library of Congress, showing the original deposit copies of "Stairway to Heaven," "Hotel California," and "Born to Run," which lack many well-known features of these works. Among other discrepancies, the photo shows that the original deposit copies for "Stairway to Heaven," "Hotel California," and "Born to Run" all omit the famous guitar intros of those songs, and begin with the vocal melody:

Courtesy Library of Congress

Contrast these deposit copies with the Notation in the deposit copy for the Rolling Stones classic "(I Can't Get No) Satisfaction," which clearly includes (a slightly inaccurate?) form of the guitar introduction:

For present purposes, I will refer to all the musical material that is audible on the composer's publicly released recording of a song, but not visible in the Notation, as the "Undeposited Authorship" of that song. It might take the form of an instantly recognizable instrumental introduction, as in some of the above works, or a guitar solo, vocal backgrounds,[10] a bass line, an extra verse, or any other element of the song's composition or arrangement. To distinguish elements of Undeposited Authorship in a composition or arrangement from the "Form SR" authorship embodied in a corresponding sound recording, I propose, for purposes of this essay, that Undeposited Authorship consists only of elements that can in principle be shown with reasonable accuracy in conventional five-line staff music notation. So, the nasal timbre of a singer's voice, the amount of reverb on the drums, etc., should not be considered as Undeposited Authorship or at least not Undeposited Authorship of the *composition* at issue. If such features are present in the deposit copy submitted with the registration of a post-1972 sound recording, of course, they are not undeposited at all, but they also cannot be infringed by an independent fixation of similar sounds, which Undeposited Authorship, as defined here, could be.

Reasonable minds may differ in particular cases about whether such musical elements should be considered part of the registered composition, or instead part of an arrangement of that composition, i.e. a derivative work; whether they are owned by the composer of the registered work or by someone else; whether they are original enough to pass muster under *Feist*;[11] whether they are scènes à faire, etc. Those details may turn out to prevent a given plaintiff from prevailing on an infringement claim over unauthorized use of a particular piece of Undeposited Authorship, provided that some future court somewhere actually permits such a claim to proceed. My point is only that it should be allowed to proceed. If it is, I now turn to some of the registration questions, ownership questions, and damages questions that the *Zeppelin* Holding has left for future courts to resolve.

Registration Questions

As the Copyright Act states, and the Supreme Court recently confirmed in its *Fourth Estate* decision, no infringement action may commence with respect to any US work that has not been registered with the Copyright Office, unless registration has been formally refused.[12] Under the *Zeppelin* Holding, Undeposited Authorship could therefore not be included within the scope of an infringement action for a US work without some further steps by the composer; after *Fourth Estate*, it seems likely that the Copyright Office must either grant or refuse registration, and if the latter happens, the court must affirmatively overrule the views of the Copyright Office to allow the suit to proceed despite the refusal to register. I see three possible approaches for a plaintiff seeking to protect Undeposited Authorship: (1) persuade the court to consider the original Notation as "identifying material" for a registered but partly undeposited work; (2) file a supplementary registration seeking to add the Undeposited Authorship to the existing deposit copy; and (3) file a completely new registration to cover only the Undeposited Authorship. The first two approaches would probably be doomed, barring a court's utter disregard for the Copyright Office, but I believe the third is appropriate and indeed may already have been successful, at least at the registration stage. Indeed, in the *en banc* argument of *Zeppelin* on September 23, 2019, the Justice Department advocate for the Copyright Office's position affirmatively endorsed this third approach, as did the Copyright Office's *amicus* curiae brief in that proceeding. Case No. 16-56287, Dkt. entry 125, at 19 (9th Cir., filed August 15, 2019).

But back to square one: The composer could ask the court (perhaps after a refusal by the Copyright Office) to consider the Notation in the original deposit copy of a musical composition to be a form of "identifying material," sufficient to support a registration for the work but not dispositive as to the scope of that registration when challenged in litigation. The current Act provides for such deposits in § 408(c),[13] and the use of such identifying material has been implemented in the regulations in 37 C.F.R. § 202.21.[14]

For decades, this approach has been a standard practice for registering and litigating over computer software, for which the Copyright Office requires a deposit of only a few token pages of the source code (which might run to many thousands of pages in total). In such cases, the remainder of the code is fully protected by the registered copyright in the work, despite the fact that it has never been deposited with the Copyright Office; it is Undeposited Authorship, but because it is software that raises no eyebrows. At trial, the plaintiff must simply come forward with competent evidence about what the complete work is, and is not prevented from doing so.

How about under the 1909 Act? Like the current Act, it also required the deposit of a "complete copy" for unpublished works,[15] but did not prevent the Copyright Office from accepting identifying material instead.[16] So there is no statutory impediment to protecting Undeposited Authorship in this manner—which is more than can be said for the so-called "application approach" to § 411 rejected by the Supreme Court in *Fourth Estate*—but the Copyright Office just has to agree to do it, as it has done for software but not for pre-1978 unpublished musical works.

The Copyright Office cannot realistically be expected to start now. There is little chance, I believe, that a court could be persuaded to adopt this "identifying material" theory absent extremely compelling circumstances. Merely saving the original registration date to preserve the composer's right to attorneys' fees and statutory damages would probably not be reason enough for any court to indulge in the retroactive legal fiction that the original deposit copy of a work was really just identifying material for a more fully elaborated work. Of course, courts under the *Zeppelin* Holding indulge in the retroactive legal fiction that the Notation is and always was a "complete copy" of the registered work, but that legal fiction can at least plausibly be laid at the feet of the composer whose team submitted the deposit copy, and is thus arguably in no position to complain if it is incomplete.

Failing the above, a second option might seem to be for composers to file supplementary registrations with the Copyright Office to augment the original Notation of a given composition with demonstrably contemporaneous sound recordings, transcriptions, or other evidence that could present a more complete embodiment of the works they actually created and sold. An attempted supplementary registration would also quite likely be rejected by the Copyright Office under the rules set forth in its current Compendium, which states that supplementary registration cannot correct errors or omissions in the deposit copy.[17] Again, however, § 411(a) of the statute could permit an applicant for supplementary registration to file an application to "supplement" the deposit copy, receive a refusal from the Copyright Office, and then bring suit following the rejection. That would put plaintiffs at a disadvantage in litigation, no doubt, but it is no worse than the absolute bar to bringing suit that the *Zeppelin* Holding seems to impose, particularly if the Undeposited Authorship is a key part of the claimed infringement.

Even if successful, the supplementary registration approach would not allow the composer to maintain the original filing date,[18] as many composers no doubt would seek to do in order to preserve eligibility for statutory damages and attorneys' fees when suing after the commencement of an infringement. But a suit that can "only" yield actual damages (and likely an injunction) for the infringement of Undeposited Authorship—but not statutory damages and attorney's fees—is still a better outcome than the same plaintiff could achieve under the *Zeppelin* Holding.

Finally, if the courts or the Copyright Office prove unwilling to accept either the identifying material option or the supplementary registration option, as they probably would, and if the courts refuse to credit claims brought after a Copyright Office refusal, there should at least be no reason that a composer cannot file a new, fresh, second application to cover previously Undeposited Authorship in an existing composition, supported by a sound recording deposit. Perhaps the new registration could be called an "arrangement" of the originally registered composition, to avoid ambiguity about what it covers, and it could specifically disclaim the previously registered Notation and claim authorship only in the Undeposited Authorship. The Copyright Office will not generally accept a second basic registration for a work that has already been registered,[19] but that should not matter because one premise of the *Zeppelin* Holding is that the Undeposited Authorship was never registered.

It appears that the Copyright Office has already accepted such belated "arrangement" filings. To cite one example, a second "arrangement" registration was filed in 1988 for the 1968 Rolling Stones composition "Sympathy for the Devil." Here is the online record of that registration:

Sympathy for the Devil

Type of Work	Music
Registration Number/Date:	PA0000386748 / 1988-08-19
Title	Sympathy for the Devil.
Appears in	<u>Beggars banquet. London PS 539, [19--]. 1 sound disc : 33 1/3 rpm, stereo.; 12 in. side 1, band 1</u>
Publisher Number	London PS 539
Notes	Written by Mick Jagger and Keith Richards.
Performer	Performed by the Rolling Stones.
Copyright Claimant	Abkco Music, Inc.
Date of Creation	1968
Date of Publication	1978-01-01
Authorship on Application	words, music & arr.: Mick Jagger & Keith Richards.
Previous Registration	Prev. reg. 1968, EU75421.
Basis of Claim	New Matter: "arrangement and revised melodic line."
Copyright Note	C.O. correspondence.

First, note that this is a Form PA registration, not Form SR; the type of work is "music"; and the "new matter" authorship claim is for "arrangement and revised melodic line." It is *not* therefore a registration of the sound recording, despite the reference to "Beggars Banquet . . . 1 sound disc; 33/13 rpm, stereo.; 12 in. side 1 band 1," which appears to be a description of the deposit copy. "Beggar's Banquet" is in any case a pre-1972 sound recording, which the Copyright Office would not have registered at the time of this filing in 1988.

In fact, despite the recent passage of the Compensating Legacy Artists for their Songs, Service, and Important Contributions to Society Act (CLASSICS Act), it is still not possible to register copyright in pre-1972 sound recordings. The CLASSICS Act states explicitly that section 412 does not apply to pre-1972 recordings, although they may be identified to the Copyright Office for purposes of entitling the owners *of the recordings* to claim statutory damages and attorneys' fees, if the owners provide certain information about the recordings (but significantly, no deposit copy).[20] It is therefore now possible to sue in federal court for unauthorized use of an unregistered pre-1972 sound recording as to which no deposit copy has ever been submitted to the Copyright Office but, under the *Zeppelin* Holding, the composer of the undeposited musical authorship embodied on that recording is still out of luck, at least in the Ninth Circuit. By what logic? None, just an accident of history.

But back to "Sympathy for the Devil," Reg. No. PA386748: The Rolling Stones are listed as performers, which is probably gratuitous because there is no claim for "performance" author-ship; and Jagger and Richards are credited with "words, music & arr[angement]." The previous registration of the song from 1968 is duly acknowledged, and the creation date of this new "arrangement," "written by" Jagger/Richards, is listed as 1968. It certainly appears that this registration covers the (previously) Undeposited Authorship from the 1968 "Sympathy for the Devil," *as recorded*, though without further digging in the archives of the Copyright Office, and especially without reviewing the correspondence between the filer and the Copyright Office that is reflected in the registration record, it is impossible to say with certainty.

But whatever the details of this 1988 registration, whether the deposit was a sound recording or a notated transcription, new filings of this kind could prove extremely useful for composers whose works are poorly represented by the Notation originally filed to represent them in the Copyright Office. These new filings would not give composers the benefit of the original filing date, which would seem to be impossible without changes to Copyright Office practice, but they face no bright-line obstacles in the statute, the Compendium, or the federal regulations, and indeed the Copyright Office appears to have granted such registrations with full knowledge of their relationship to prior registrations for the "same" work. And as Jagger/Richards may have done with this later filing for "Sympathy for the Devil," composers could make prophylactic filings of this kind to register their previously Undeposited Authorship in particular works prior to any infringement. This would lock in their eligibility for statutory damages and attorney's fees against post-registration infringers, just as pre-1972 sound recording owners can now do under the CLASSICS Act (*without* even submitting a deposit copy). If the foregoing is correct, the *Zeppelin* Holding does not establish a permanent bar to protecting Undeposited Authorship, but merely puts it in a category of authorship that has not *yet* been deposited.

Ownership and Damages Questions

Ownership

Finally, assuming a composer can find some way to sue over the unauthorized use of Undeposited Authorship, significant questions of ownership might arise: Who owns the Undeposited Authorship? The facts will in some cases render the question moot. If Bruce Springsteen single-handedly (or even two-handedly) created the "Born to Run" guitar intro riff, and he is the author of the song as originally registered, recognizing this element of Undeposited Authorship will only expand the scope of authorship he can protect. This might be the best case for recognizing Undeposited Authorship, because it would raise few, if any, ancillary issues.[21]

In other cases, where the author of the Undeposited Authorship is not already credited as a composer of the song, existing doctrines and industry practices should be able to prevent litigation chaos in all but exceptional circumstances. For authorship created by producers, arrangers, or session musicians—think Luther Vandross on "Young Americans,"[22] ownership will likely have been resolved by contract and will probably vest in the record label or music publisher. Where there are no contracts, as sometimes there were not, the pre-1978 "instance and expense" test for determining work-made-for-hire status[23] will vest ownership in the parties, again mostly labels and publishers, who paid to have the authorship created.

Those labels and publishers could in many instances be expected to cooperate with the named composers, to the extent needed to pursue a claim efficiently. Where such cooperation proves impossible, courts could require the joinder of any holdout owners under § 501 of the current Act, and the copyright owners could work out their own disputes as to allocation of any damages award, as is common today in cases involving songs with multiple unrelated authors. These are manageable allocation problems, hardly reason to impose the drastic remedy of the *Zeppelin* Holding—complete preclusion of protection—on the copyright owner.

For authorship created by other members of the composer's own group—think George and Ringo on any Lennon/McCartney song—the "dominant author" doctrine,[24] the *Thomson v. Larson* standard for determining joint authorship intent,[25] and the three-year statute of limitations for challenging authorship status[26] could make it very difficult for authors other than "dominant" authors to assert sole or joint authorship in a belated infringement claim concerning Undeposited Authorship against a third party.

If such group members are not joint authors of the song, though, what status do they and their contributions have? This question was left hanging by the Second Circuit in *Thomson v. Larson*, where the plaintiff, a dramaturg, contributed as much as 9 percent of the dialog of the hit Broadway show *Rent*, but was held not to be a joint author because the evidence failed to show a mutual *intent* for joint authorship on the part of all contributors. The matter settled before the court determined the extent of Thomson's rights to her non-jointly authored contributions in *Rent*, but it does not seem unreasonable to argue that Thomson/George/Ringo might be held to have granted, by their conduct, a non-exclusive license to the dominant author to make use of their contributions.[27]

Damages

The judicial recognition of Undeposited Authorship in an infringement case could affect the total amount of a damages award based on the infringer's profits, as in *Zeppelin* and *Gaye*, to the extent the Undeposited Authorship increased the allocation of an infringer's profits attributable to the infringement, and it could also present issues of allocation between and among the cocreators of the infringed work. As noted earlier, courts frequently make such determinations already, and doing so to recognize Undeposited Authorship should not be any reason for courts to shy away from giving *all* creators their due when their authorship has been infringed.

It does not seem likely that statutory damages would be affected much, if at all. In the unlikely event that a court allowed a plaintiff to fold both the original Notation and the Undeposited Authorship into a single registration, there would be no change in the availability or potential amount of statutory damages for that one registration. If a plaintiff filed a second, freestanding registration for the Undeposited Authorship under the rubric of an "arrangement," as with the "Sympathy for the Devil" example, the second registration would likely be untimely under § 411, and would thus provide no basis for a second statutory damages award. Even if the "arrangement" registration were filed prior to the defendant's infringement, however, entitling the plaintiff to seek a second statutory damages award for infringement of this "other" work, courts could and should apply the principle that the mere existence of multiple registrations does not require multiple statutory damages awards, where the separately registered works were not separately exploited, and had no separate "copyright life."[28] In a situation like "Sympathy For the Devil," where the so-called "arrangement" is simply the form in which the originally registered work was released to the public, the case for applying this principle should, in my view, be compelling. Indeed, it may often be the case that the Notation in the lead sheet has had no separate copyright life, at least relative to the sound recording of that song.

Conclusion

This chapter does not purport to present an exhaustive list of questions raised by the *Zeppelin* Holding. Others include: How, if at all, does the *Zeppelin* Holding apply to limit the scope of copyright in non-US works restored under General Agreement on Tariffs and Trade (GATT), § 104A? Or non-US works in general, as to which registration is not a prerequisite under § 411? Should the author of a pre-1978 non-US musical work have *less* protection by virtue of having registered it? How much deference should courts give to the Copyright Office's internal policies and regulations regarding other registration matters? Is a final refusal of an attempted *supplementary* registration covering Undeposited Authorship even sufficient to permit suit under § 411(a)? Will courts outside the Ninth Circuit find the *Zeppelin* Holding persuasive? And what will remain of the *Zeppelin* Holding, even in the Ninth Circuit, after And what will remain of the *Zeppelin* Holding, even in the Ninth Circuit, if the US Supreme Court chooses to grant *certiorari*?

I believe the *Zeppelin* Holding goes too far. It takes the law in exactly the wrong direction by giving dispositive significance to a 1909-era formality that US law has not recognized in over forty years, and most other countries never did because they did not have copyright registration regimes. For most songs, the Notation is not the whole truth. The *Zeppelin* Holding says that there is no other truth. It really makes me wonder.

Acknowledgement

★ Partner, Reitler Kailas & Rosenblatt LLC. I am grateful to my friend, fellow musician, and colleague Tom Kjellberg of Cowan Liebowitz & Latman for his many wise observations as I tried unsuccessfully to enlist him to be a coauthor of this essay. He talked me off of several glittery doctrinal stairways that I was too eager to climb. If it were possible to become a joint author by advising a colleague what not to include, he would certainly qualify.

Notes

1 Williams v. Gaye, 885 F.3d 1150 (9th Cir. 2018).
2 Skidmore as Tr. For Randy Craig Wolfe Tr. v. Led Zeppelin, 905 F.3d 1116 (9th Cir. 2018), *reh'g en banc granted sub nom.* Skidmore as Tr. for Randy Craig Wolfe Tr. v. Zeppelin, 925 F.3d 999 (9th Cir. 2019), and *on reh'g en banc sub nom.* Skidmore as Tr. for Randy Craig Wolfe tr. v. Zeppelin, 952 F.3d 1051 (9th Cir. 2020).
3 Zeppelin, 905 F.3d at 1134 ("Given that copyright protection under the 1909 Act did not attach until either publication or registration, we conclude that for unpublished works the deposit copy defines the scope of the copyright").
4 Gaye, 885 F.3d at 1169 ("The experts' quarrel over what was in the deposit copy was a factual dispute for the jury to decide").
5 Fourth Estate Pub. Benefit Corp. v. Wallstreet.com, LLC, 139 S. Ct. 881 (2019).
6 White-Smith Music Pub. Co. v. Apollo Co., 209 U.S. 1 (1908).
7 17 U.S.C. § 411(a) (2018) ("[N]o civil action for infringement of the copyright in any *United States work* shall be instituted until preregistration or registration of the copyright claim has been made in accordance with this title" (emphasis added)).
8 17 U.S.C. § 410(c).
9 Vernon Silver, "Rock Riff Rip-Off: The Legal Loophole That May Leave Some of Rock's Greatest Riffs Up for Grabs," June 20, 2019, https://www.bloomberg.com/features/2019-classic-rock-riffs-loophole. Silver may endear himself to copyright lawyers everywhere with lines like "I kid you not, a visit to the card-catalog room of the U.S. Copyright Office can be deeply moving." As I hope to show below, however, Silver errs to the extent that he believes that an unregistered work, or unregistered elements of a registered work, might be "up for grabs."
10 Legendary soul singer Luther Vandross reportedly created the background vocal arrangements behind the melody of David Bowie's 1975 hit "Young Americans." See, e.g., Mashaun D. Simon, "'Plastic Soul': David Bowie's Legacy and Impact on Black Artists," *NBC News,* updated January 11, 2016, https://www.nbcnews.com/news/nbcblk/plastic-soul-david-bowie-s-legacy-impact-black-artists-n494241. Are Vandross' contributions included in the deposit copy of the Bowie song? In my view, it should not matter, if a third party infringes them.
11 Feist Publ'ns., Inc. v. Rural Tel. Serv. Co., Inc., 499 US 340 (1991).
12 17 U.S.C. § 411(a); *see also Fourth Estate,* 139 S. Ct. at 888.
13 17 U.S.C. § 408(c).
14 37 C.F.R. § 202.21.
15 Copyright Act of 1909, Pub. L. 60–349, 35 Stat. 1075, 1080, https://www.copyright.gov/history/1909act.pdf.
16 See, e.g., U.S. Copyright Office, *Compendium of U.S. Copyright Office Practices,* §§ 5.2.1(II.d.), (II.c.) (special relief from deposit requirements for some unpublished works).
17 U.S. Copyright Office, *Compendium of U.S. Copyright Office Practices,* § 1802.7(D) (3d ed. 2017), https://www.copyright.gov/comp3. This rule extends to errors or omissions in registrations for pre-1978 works. See 37 C.F.R. § 202.6(d)(6) (2017).
18 U.S. Copyright Office, *Compendium,* 1802.7(D) (copyright owner cannot alter deposit copies, only information on certificates); 37 C.F.R. § 202.6(d)(4)(ii); also 37 C.F.R. § 202.6(d)(6) (copyright owner cannot alter basic registrations issued under prior Copyright Act).
19 See, e.g., U.S. Copyright Office, Library of Congress, *Circular 2: Copyright Registration,* revised October 2019, https://www.copyright.gov/circs/circ02.pdf.
20 "[A]n award of statutory damages or of attorneys' fees . . . may be made with respect to an unauthorized use of a [pre-1972] sound recording . . . only if [] the rights owner has filed with the Copyright Office a

schedule that specifies the title, artist, and rights owner of the sound recording." See 17 U.S.C. § 1401(f) (5)(A)(i) (emphasis added).

21 There is abundant online commentary to the effect that Miami Steve Van Zandt contributed to the creation of the opening guitar riff in "Born To Run," notwithstanding Springsteen's composition of the song on piano, but that is an issue for the two creators to decide *inter se*. Provided Springsteen was at least *an* author of the riff, he could bring suit for infringement.

22 Simon, "Plastic Soul."

23 See, e.g., Playboy Enters., Inc. v. Dumas, 53 F.3d 549, 554 (2d Cir. 1995).

24 See generally Aalmuhammad v. Lee, 202 F.3d 1227 (9th Cir. 2000).

25 See generally Thomson v. Larson, 147 F.3d 195 (2d Cir. 1998).

26 Zuill v. Shanahan, 80 F.3d 1366, 1369–1371 (9th Cir. 1996), *as amended* 1996 U.S. App. LEXIS 14516 (June 14, 1996).

27 Effects Assocs. v. Cohen, 908 F.2d 555 (9th Cir. 1990) (elements of implied license).

28 See, e.g., Lee Middleton Original Dolls, Inc. v. Seymour Mann. Inc., 299 F. Supp. 2d 892, 898–99 (E.D. Wisc. 2005) (no separate statutory awards where plaintiff separately registered sculptures of a collectible doll's head, right hand, left hand, right foot, and left foot, because plaintiff did not sell parts separately (citing Walt Disney Co. v. Powell, 897 F.2d 565 (D.C. Cir. 1990) (no "separate copyright life" for various separately registered poses of Mickey and Minnie Mouse))).

5.6

CO-AUTHORSHIP

A Little Help Can Lead to a Big Headache

Interview with Jonathan Coulton

Jonathan Coulton (JC) is a singer-songwriter based in Gowanus, Brooklyn. He is known for his eclectic catalog of masterful songwriting on subjects from zombies and mad scientists to sad parents and dissatisfied software engineers. He has written songs for *The Good Fight* and *Braindead* television series as well as the *Portal* video games. He is the house musician for the NPR show *Ask Me Another* and the host and namesake of the annual Jonathan Coulton (JoCo) Cruise. His songs have been described as "equally funny and profound, full of wordplay that kept tilting, fast, into deeper emotion."

Michelle Bogre (MB) interviewed him on August 26, 2019 in New York City. This interview was edited for length and clarity.

MB: On your website, you talk about hearing Larry Lessig speak about Creative Commons. I never read a creative person's website that talks about Larry Lessig and Creative Commons. So, tell me a little bit about how you came to rethink copyright.

JC: Well, before I was a professional musician, I was a frustrated amateur musician and I wrote software for a living. I always wanted to be a professional singer-songwriter but could not really figure out how to break into the business, and I knew that the songs I was writing were kind of quirky, so there was not a place on the radio for me. I understood all of those challenges and I just did not really know how to crack it, and I also was interested in technology and the internet. Somewhere around 2003 to 2004 I was invited to perform at a conference called PopTech because somebody had seen a song that I did about a robot uprising in the future and they thought it was funny and they thought my music would speak to the PopTech attendees. So I went, performed my music, and one of the speakers was Lawrence Lessig. He gave his famous black and white PowerPoint presentation about Creative Commons. Listening to him was the first time I had ever thought to think about copyright the way he does. I remember leaving that talk and feeling like my head was on fire. I realized that copyright law was completely out of step with how we actually use media in the digital age and that we were going to have to rethink copyright. I thought it was exciting—that the idea of Creative Commons was a way to not only plant a flag in terms of what you believed, but also presented a way to allow certain uses of your intellectual property that actually benefited you.

So, when I thought about myself, I thought: "I have these songs that nobody's going to play on the radio, but a lot of people would play on their podcasts." This was the age of self-published everything, blogs were a big thing, MP3s were relatively new, and technology provided a small, portable, but high-quality digital format that you could sell, trade, and share. So I had this vision of this universe of little bits of intellectual property floating around getting passed along by people.

I could say in advance, "I give you permission to make a new thing using my intellectual property as long as it is noncommercial, and as long as you put the same license on it." It was just a very beautiful idea of what art and culture could be and it fit the world of self-publishing tools and digital media allowing us to make things, bouncing off of the things that other people make, everything building on top of itself. We could finally fulfill this beautiful dream of a more open culture and Creative Commons was the hack that allowed us to tweak existing copyright law in a way that more clearly aligned with how we had demonstrated we wanted to use media and culture.

MB: Do you think that being a software coder influenced your thinking?

JC: I think so. I have always been interested in the intersection of art and technology, and specifically music and computers. I followed with great interest the technological trends that were happening around the music business, so I paid attention to file sharing and when MP3 players came along another little light bulb went off in my head. I think I was primed to think about things differently. I had technical knowledge of how the internet worked, and how HTML worked, so I understood how copyright was out of step with digital technologies because, anytime you listen to a digital file, you are making a copy of it, and you are breaking the law and obviously that is not what we intend. As a software designer you want the technology that you are making to support the needs and desires of the user. It became clear to me that the law was in the way of the technology.

MB: You did a project called "Thing a Week." Was that your first foray into testing whether you could get an audience or get them to pay for a download of your music?

JC: As a part-time professional musician, I had some exposure to audiences and, between talks at PopTech, I posted some of my songs to my website, which I had never thought to do before. I put them up for free, and I used the conference chat room to let people know they had been posted. I got a good response and that was exciting. It was part of the reason that I decided to quit my software job and try to make a living as a musician. The "Thing a Week" was very calculated. It was: "Let's pretend this is my job and I have to do this, so I am going to force myself to record a new song every week and see how that feels." I wanted to leverage the power of file sharing and burgeoning social media and podcasting and give each song away. It was set up initially as a blog/podcast, so it was an RSS feed that you could subscribe to. Every week there would be a post on Friday about the song or my travails in making or writing it and if you were subscribed, the MP3 would just flow into your podcast feed. I am not sure if the feed is still available. I have not checked in a while.

I wanted to see if it would work and how much attention I could get, and then if I could turn that attention into making a living. I figured the worst thing that could happen was that one of my songs would become a runaway internet viral hit but I would not get paid a dollar. From where I was standing, that did not seem like a terrible thing. It actually felt like a good place to start.

MB: So it was a branding and marketing experiment?

JC: I do not know if I initially thought of it as a marketing and branding strategy, but it definitely became that. I became aware that "free culture" and "copy left" were ideas that had a lot of followers and that it even was a brand to say that I was interested in that, so I certainly pushed that angle. I was also interested in ways to encourage people to create things, so I would often call for help. For example, if I did not want to do a guitar solo, I would call for people to send me solos, and I would put them in my song. For one song, I had everybody send me the sound of a handclap, and I put them all together. There was a synergy of the medium, message, and content where I was writing these nerdy songs, distributing them in this nerdy way, and I was talking about all of that nerdy copyright stuff. So, it was a lucky confluence of things.

MB: When did you start getting paid? How did you transition that totally free giving music away to making money from music?

JC: It evolved over the course of that year. A moment ago, when I said that the worst thing that could happen is that one of my songs could become famous and I would not get paid a dime, well that is actually what happened. Song Number Four was a cover of Sir Mix-a-Lot's "Baby Got Back." It went bananas and got passed around and linked and somebody called me and said that that was playing on the radio station somewhere. It was a very exciting and also panicky twenty-four hours because it was so early in the process that I realized I had been in such a rush to publish that I had not set up a way for people to give me money, even if they wanted. I also had not thought about protecting myself against a direct link to the MP3. I noticed that a lot of people were just linking directly to the MP3 and not to my blog post, which meant that they were hearing the song but they did not know who it was by. It was a wake-up call. So I rushed to create a way to allow people to buy a song for a dollar. Some people would pay me and some people would get it for free. I did not keep very accurate records of this, but I have a vague recollection of how the year went. I tried a couple of other things: I put up a donation button; I tried a pay-what-you-will scheme. The donations did not work as well as having a free version and a for-sale version. At the end of the year, when I had fifty-two songs, I bundled them into albums—four collections of thirteen each, titled by the seasons of the year. I eventually made CDs and started selling those CDs through CD Baby. I also started to do live shows, which is a whole other story of ramping that up and figuring out how that worked. I remember that somewhere about halfway through the year, there was a month where I had earned enough money to pay the babysitter who was taking care of my child while I was in the office pretending to have a job. That felt like a huge success. I was very proud at that moment even though I was just barely treading water in terms of this experiment. My wife and I had decided that, if it was a complete failure, I would just go to another company and get another software job.

MB: I noticed that you recently did a cover of 1970s songs, which I thought was an interesting idea. You set up a Kickstarter to raise $20,000, but raised $150,000. That was quite a success.

JC: It was a phenomenal success. I had fronted all the recording costs myself up front but by the time that Kickstarter was over and before the album was released, it had paid for itself and earned some profit.

MB: You are also releasing a vinyl? Why did you do that? How has the market responded to that traditional medium?

JC: A couple of years ago I got a turntable again and really loved it. I forgot how great it is to put on a record. It is a big physical artifact, which is such a rare thing these days. So the last couple of albums I have done, I hired a professional designer and made a very expensive physical package. When you are selling a thing as ethereal as music, you need to figure out where the places are that people will spend money and then make sure it is possible for those people to spend their money. There are a lot of places in all the possible revenue streams for a song where people either do not have to spend money or only minimal amounts of money. It is just the way things have worked out. So it has always been the case that we had to find the places where we could actually earn money by making something valuable to the people who want it. For me, recently, that has been through Kickstarter and specifically through vinyl.

MB: How does the sale of vinyls compare to the sale of the other formats?

JC: Over the years the buckets that make up my income have varied greatly and I definitely feel the changes. It is easy for me to feel the market effect because I know how many extra CDs are sitting in my basement right now, and how much I earn from digital sales each month. Hardly anybody buys directly from me anymore. That has been supplanted by the other digital stores. I do pay attention to that. There was a time when people bought MP3s but streaming services really destroyed that market. Everybody was afraid of file sharing, but we should have been afraid of streaming services. I do not need to tell you this, but obviously the royalty structure for streaming services is not great, especially for independent artists. It is best for record companies who are still taking large slices from their artists' work. I do not have a record label so I am in the lower tier because I am independent. So streaming revenue has not replaced the revenue that I used to get from selling MP3s and CDs.

MB: What do you think the model is going to be for independent songwriters today with streaming? You entered the profession when people were still willing to pay a dollar for a download. What is it going to look like going forward? Do you need to perform? What if you are not a recording artist?

JC: If I had to guess, I would say that the trend certainly indicates that we are heading toward a place where the music itself is a loss leader. We are already there in many ways. People are going to have to come up with ancillary revenue streams, which is disheartening on the one hand, but on the other hand, there were large stretches of human existence where you could not sell music at all. Commerce was not part of music. If you were a composer, you maybe had one patron. But mostly you wrote songs because you liked to, and maybe somebody would throw some pennies into your hat while you were playing. Being a songwriter, earning money writing songs, that is a blip on the radar as far as human history is concerned. I allow for the idea that this blip is ending and that we are going to be in a place where music is largely free. But I am encouraged by the many third-party solutions that have sprung up to try to enable independent creators to find other revenue streams. It is going to be different for everybody. If you are the kind of musician that can do live performances, that will certainly be an important part of your revenue. If you are the kind of musician who writes music that is very current and useful in a commercial sense, you will get placements on television shows and in commercials and that will be a big part of it.

The other part of free culture that I was excited for when it was first starting was this idea of micropayments and tracking ownership and automating all these small uses of music. We are starting to see it, but it is a mess. I mean, the YouTube Content ID stuff is too cumbersome to use. Because I make money elsewhere, I can leave that money on the table. I tried to engage with YouTube Content ID for a while and it was just confusing people, but I think it is an important idea. I hope that we continue in that direction and that people succeed in making the process more fluid. YouTube was always one of those gray areas for me where somebody would post a vacation video and use one of my songs. That is fine for me. I think that is a totally fair and reasonable use of my music and I am thrilled that they are exposing it. But I am also aware that there is a big corporation who is hosting that video and who is making money off of that video—maybe not directly if there are no ads, but certainly indirectly by having a large library of content. So there is definitely some commerce happening there and I believe it would be fair for musicians to get a piece of it. I hope that we will get better at having a technological solution that allows people to be paid for small uses of their music. I think that the person with a vacation video would be happy if a few cents went to me if they did not have to think about it or sign up for an account. This is the blockchain idea. We will see if that helps. The impediment is there is still a lot of companies trying to be middlemen and trying to control that.

MB: Then the law really needs to change if streaming is becoming the method by which most people receive most of their music.

JC: I do not know what a fair royalty rate would be, because streaming music is not the same as buying music. Musicians are complaining all the time that they got 100,000 streams but very little money, and I understand and share that frustration. But how much are 100,000 streams worth? I do not know the answer and we do not have a price for someone listening to a song once. You should not get a dollar every time somebody streams your song. How many times do they have to listen before it is the same as having bought it?

Also, those companies are still propped up by a lot of investment, so they are not fully functioning as profitable companies. Apple is using Apple Music to sell iPhones, basically. Amazon's content is largely a loss leader for the rest of Amazon's business. Same with Google. I do not know if Spotify is profitable yet.

MB: I think their bookkeeping is a bit arcane and certainly not transparent. They may well be making money. They say they are not, but then they would not be attracting so much investment.

JC: I still believe increased transparency and more technology can solve these problems, even things out and make things more fair for creators. But obviously we need some legislation and once again, the technology curve is so far ahead of the legal curve that it is very hard to imagine how it will work out.

MB: It is an interesting idea that technology holds the key to identify, credit, and somehow reimburse creators for creating. The question is: How will it be tracked? Who tracks it?

JC: I think that so many times when a musician is not getting paid, it is because of transactional friction. That is what I learned when I had "Baby Got Back" available for free. People would have gladly given me a dollar, but I made it impossible for them to give me that dollar. I think people really are willing to pay for things, and if you make it a clear transaction, and you say: "Look, you are supporting me by paying me for this. It costs me money to make this stuff. I need to make a living and feed my family." People really do respond. There is a threshold of fandom past which people are more than happy to give you money for the things that you create. I am hopeful that technology and the legal system will continue to reduce the friction of those transactions.

MB: Do you still follow copyright decisions about music? What do you think about the Blurred Lines[1] case and the criticism that the court now protects the "feel" of a song?

JC: I think it is highly problematic. Depending on the style of music, I think it is a really dangerous precedent to have set. You know the arrangement of my "Baby Got Back" was used by the show *Glee* and put up by them on iTunes. I pursued the idea of suing them but Fox was signaling that they were not going to give an inch. An attorney friend of mine said, "You can do this and probably you will extract something from them, but this will be your job for three years." I decided I did not want that to be my job for the next three years, so I dropped it. I felt as though I had humiliated them enough through social media. And while our lawyers were talking to each other, I released the same song in the style of *Glee*. They were mad about that. At that point, I felt I had won in the court of public opinion. They looked like bad guys.

MB: I want to go back to the idea that, going forward, we need to connect the end user more directly to the creator because if we do that people will be more willing to pay—maybe because music is more personal than other art forms. Music also benefits from a statutory licensing scheme. I have always thought that if there was a statutory licensing scheme for photography, there would be less infringement because, say, bloggers would pay a reasonable amount of money to use a photograph, if they did not have to negotiate every single use.

JC: The compulsory license to do a cover song is such a great thing for everybody. There is no negotiation. You do not have to talk to a lawyer; you do not have to get permission. You just do it. And you know exactly what it is going to cost. But there is a whole economy of transactions that are not happening because the law and technology are not there.

MB: So are you optimistic about the music industry or about making a living as a musician?

JC: I am but it is easy for me to say because it works for me. I was very much in the right place at the right time. I thought that anyone could do it, but looking back, I realized that I had certain privileged positions that I did not recognize and that really were a special circumstance for me: the kind of music that I did; my background; the fact that I am a straight, white male—all these contributed to the fact that it worked out for me. There is no recipe that is going to work out for everybody. I still make albums. I tour a lot less than I used to because I am older and less hungry. I also have a fan cruise that I do, which has become a big part of the money that I make.

Together with three business partners, we run the Jonathan Coulton cruise. We are on our tenth year and we will have 2,000 passengers. Obviously that is a revenue source that not everybody has access to.

I am not saying anything really groundbreaking here, but I think that there is now a real potential to have more of a middle class existence in the music business. This used to be more of either you had to be a huge hit or you tried for a long time and then nothing happened and you could not make it work. I think it is now more possible for an independent musician to make a living. I know a few musicians who most people have never heard of, who work hard and write a lot of stuff, and release a lot of stuff and tour a lot. I do not know whether they are getting rich, but it seems like that is what they do to sustain themselves. I think that is a new part of the music economy—people who are not famous, but still make a living. There have always been some of those people, but I think it is more possible to do now. I am optimistic that this trend is going to continue.

MB: Interesting point. In the "old days" there were stars and successful songwriters who made a lot of money. Either you made it big or you quit the profession. Maybe that is what is changing now.

JC: We still do have a hit-based economy but maybe it is harder to measure what constitutes a hit. You still see people who have breakout songs and breakout albums and who become rich overnight from that, but I think there are a lot more people—and I have never seen data on this so I do not know for sure—but anecdotally, there are a lot more people in that middle area who are not famous who do not have hits, but who are still chugging away.

MB: It may actually be true and partly driven by the technology that enables you to be an independent musician working out of your apartment producing the quality that used to only be possible if you had the money to rent a studio.

JC: It is much cheaper now to make the music, to record the music, and to distribute it.

MB: So maybe that is how technology will change in the twenty-first century—enabling more people to be creative and make a living, not get super rich, but make a living maybe that is the new model. It is a transition even though we do not fully understand how it is going to work.

JC: We do not have a lot of control over where it goes. One of the things that I took from that first Lessig talk was that you can make all the laws you want, but consumer behavior will demonstrate how it should go. We are all downloading music illegally, so clearly something is wrong with the laws that are in place. When massive amounts of people are behaving in a certain way, I think we are signaling that is what we want to happen. When everyone was bemoaning the file sharing threat in those early days, I was unsympathetic in part because I did not have a viable business to lose but also, it was like, "Guys, it really feels like you are whining about a thing you also do. I have no doubt you have downloaded music for free." In the end, I believe if you enable people to act on their innate fairness, they will be fair.

MB: What do you think should change to help musicians?

JC: I wish that companies like Spotify would partner with us. I get paid however many micro-pennies for each stream, but another way that Spotify could compensate me is by giving me access to the data they have, allow me access to those users, and allow me to make my own mini-platform inside their platform to engage directly with my fans and sell my merchandise through them and sell my vinyl through them. But that is not how they are thinking right now. If they would do that, they would not have so many musicians angry at them because that data is more valuable to musicians now than it has been in the past. I think that would also help the cultural shift that we are undergoing—this idea that people already do not think that it is wrong to download a song, especially if they have already bought it before. I totally get that. I think there is a huge cultural shift, and the law is out of step with it. The technology is trying to get us there, but these companies still have a very linear, mono-focused way of thinking about the business.

Note

1 Williams v. Gaye, 895 F.3d 1106 (9th Cir. 2018). In this case, Marvin Gaye's estate won a multi-million-dollar judgment against Robin Thicke and Pharrell Williams over their song "Blurred Lines," which the Gaye estate claimed infringed Gaye's 1977 hit "Got to Give it Up." The decision was widely criticized because, according to dissenting Judge Jacqueline Nguyen, it "accomplish[ed] what no one has before: copyright a musical style."

5.7

LANDMARK CASE

Williams v. Gaye, 895 F.3d 1106 (9th Cir. 2018)

Robin Thicke and Pharrell Williams's "Blurred Lines" was the top-selling single in the world in 2013. The song was obviously a hit, but it attracted controversy on multiple fronts. Some listeners were upset by the song's lyrics, which they read as misogynistic and encouraging harmful perceptions of consent. Another line of criticism centered on the song's catchy melody and eventually snowballed into a copyright infringement lawsuit. Indeed, Marvin Gaye's estate argued that the song infringed on Gaye's 1976 hit "Got To Give It Up" and alleged copyright infringement not just against Thicke, Williams, and their record company but also against Clifford Harris, Jr. (commonly known as the rapper T.I.), who had separately written and recorded a verse that was subsequently added to "Blurred Lines." The dispute garnered tremendous attention, with musicians, critics, industry professionals, and copyright scholars falling on both sides. The case went to trial, musicologists were brought in, and the jury awarded the Gaye estate $7.3 million in actual damages and infringer's profits from both Williams and Thicke.

Williams and Thicke asked the district court for judgment as a matter of law and for a new trial, which the court denied. Eventually, the district court lowered the amount awarded to the Gaye estate to $3.2 million in actual damages, while also mandating that the Gaye estate receive 50 percent in future royalty revenues from Williams, Thicke, and Harris in conjunction with "Blurred Lines." Both sides appealed. The "Blurred Lines" parties appealed the denial of their motions for summary judgment and a new trial and the decision to hold Harris liable for infringement, while the Gaye estate appealed the district court's decision not to award them attorneys' fees and costs.

The Ninth Circuit heard the appeal, and issued a decision largely on procedural grounds. However, the procedural issues seem less important to a discussion of the merits of the Gaye estate's copyright infringement claim, so they will be touched upon briefly, with greater focus given to both the majority's discussion of the jury's verdict and the merit-focused dissent. The Ninth Circuit accepted the district court's conclusion that there existed issues of material fact, and thus refused to overturn the district court's denial of Williams and Thicke's motion for summary judgment. These issues of material fact involved disputes between both sides' musicologists about the similarity of the songs' signature phrases, hooks, bass lines, keyboard chords, harmonic structures, and vocal melodies. Ultimately, the Ninth Circuit adopted a lenient standard of review that looked at whether there was an absolute absence of evidence to support the jury's verdict. Finding that there was not such an absence, the Ninth Circuit accepted the district court's analysis of the merits. However, the Ninth Circuit overturned the district court's decision to hold T.I. liable for damages.

In assessing whether "Blurred Lines" infringed on "Got To Give It Up," the district court relied on the substantial similarity test for copyright infringement. Copyright infringement requires that the defendant copied from the plaintiff, and this may be established both through circumstantial and direct evidence. In the absence of direct evidence, proof of infringement shifts to a review of evidence that the defendant had access to the work, and that the works are substantially similar. Both Williams and Thicke admit that they were inspired by Gaye's song, so access in this case is not disputed. Instead, the case turned on the two-part test for substantial similarity.

The two-part test for substantial similarity includes both an extrinsic and intrinsic component. The extrinsic test is objective, and considers whether the two works share similarities that may be measured by external, objective criteria. This is where the musicologists came in, breaking down each song into its musical building blocks, and then comparing the pieces. Unlike the extrinsic test, the intrinsic test is subjective, and revolves around the ordinary, reasonable listener's reaction to the two tracks. This test turns on whether such a listener would find the overall concept of feel of the works to be substantially similar. The court made sure to note that substantial similarity is a holistic test, meaning that such similarity may be found in a combination of individually unprotectable elements in a disputed work.

For the extrinsic test, the musicologist for the Gaye estate pointed to the similarities in the two songs' bass lines, signature phrases, and hooks before ultimately opining that nearly every bar of "Blurred Lines" contained something that was similar to "Got To Give It Up." The Gaye estate also brought in a professor of African American music, who played three "mash-ups" she created to show the melodic and harmonic similarities of the two songs. This professor concluded that the two songs shared structural similarities on a sectional and phrasing level. Meanwhile, Williams and Thicke's musicologist disputed the opinions of the Gaye estate's experts, instead arguing that the songs were not substantially similar. The dissenting judge in the Ninth Circuit's three-judge panel echoed this point in a blistering dissent. In this, Judge Nguyen argued that the Gaye estate's musicologist "cherry-picked brief snippets" of the songs to issue overly broad conclusions. *Williams v. Gaye*, 895 F.3d 1106, 1138 (9th Cir. 2018). Judge Nguyen accused the majority of allowing the Gaye estate to "copyright a musical style" and said that the similarities of the works as a whole "aren't even perceptible, let alone substantial." *Id.* at 1142. Ultimately, the dissent concluded that there are in fact no genuine issues of material fact; that Williams and Thicke are entitled to summary judgment under the extrinsic test; and that the Gaye estate should now worry that their same reasoning may be used to dispute the copyrights in some of their own music, which also borrowed from previous artists. The majority countered by arguing that the dissent ignored the procedural matters to jump straight to the merits and that it was not in a position to issue a post-trial judgment as a matter of law.

Williams v. Gaye is one of a slew of recent high-profile decisions addressing copyright infringement claims against popular songs. Many of these decisions result in multi-million dollar jury verdicts against the contemporary appropriator. These decisions always invite robust commentary and debate, given the nature of musical appropriation. A popular song is not like a photograph or a book: Musicians do not start on a blank canvas or page but heavily rely on existing melodies, chord progressions, and subject matter when creating their own songs. Some amount of appropriation is inevitable, but how much constitutes infringement? Some observers worry that decisions such as this stifle creative freedom on the part of working musicians, while others point to the seemingly endless, uncompensated, unauthorized musical appropriation currently occurring in the digital era. In short, the Ninth Circuit's decision raises many questions, answers few, and reflects an enduring problem area in modern copyright law.

PART VI

Video Games and Virtual Worlds

Introduction

Video games are reported to be the largest growing industry worldwide, with no signs of slowing down. Modern video games are the quintessential art form of the twenty-first century and have evolved dramatically from the early days of crude animations with simple game scenarios to elaborate and beautiful virtual worlds, complete with realistic CGI actors who can perform feats not possible in any other medium. Video games offer gamers an interactive, multiplayer storytelling experience where the gamer is not merely a passive observer but becomes immersed in the virtual world, taking part in the outcome with a community of worldwide Hollywood stars, athletes, musicians, and others who can appear ageless in games; gamers can create multiple avatars based on their favorite heroes, create their own environments, and choose endless outcomes in the story decision tree. With its realistic depiction of environments, objects, and people, video games encompass many forms of intellectual property, intersecting copyright, trademark, rights of publicity, privacy, gaming, and many other laws and regulations. The chapters in Part VI touch on the intersection of video games and the law, and some of the legal challenges that the video gaming industry faces in creating more realistic works that will only increase as virtual reality moves into augmented reality.

In Chapter 6.1, "Video Games and Virtual Worlds: Recreating the World and Fighting a Dragon In It," Chrissie Scelsi examines the intersection of state right of publicity laws with federal copyright and examines the challenges this complexity creates for the video industry. No other industry allows for the creation of immersive worlds that may replicate many of the features of the real world with such authenticity. She examines the legal challenges that specific authentic properties raise with subjects such as people, buildings, and vehicles, and discusses specific issues involving celebrities, tattoos, and mural art. Scelsi traces the history of publicity and trademark law and focuses on some recent case issues involving "emotes," or dance moves, and the separate challenges raised with esports.

In "Virtual Property & Virtual Currency," Brandon J. Huffman looks at the world of video games and examines what property rights the gamer has in creating unique virtual worlds complete with structures, landscapes, and people, including the rights in unique properties that are often offered for sale within these games, and the transactions fueled by virtual currency. He examines the differences and similarities in the law regulating real properties and virtual properties, looking at copyright, trademark, publicity, as well as other regulatory issues, including money laundering. He also discusses virtual currency, an important component of many successful games that rely on in-app or in-game purchases, as well as consumer protection, gambling, and lottery laws. Huffman reminds us that the laws involving games are complex, and he provides a good check list of issues that any game company or attorney should be aware of as well as practical advice on some standard terms and conditions that should be included in any game's terms of service. In Chapter 6.3, "Press 'X' To Open: Pandora's Loot Box," Caroline Womack focuses on issues unique to video games, specifically gambling issues in luck-based games. This chapter focuses on "loot boxes," which are digital crates that contain random in-game rewards that appeal to children and adult players. Womack looks at whether this game device should be regulated under gambling laws and describes the different rules regulating games of chance and games of skill. Finally, she looks at this issue of gambling on a global perspective.

6.1

VIDEO GAMES AND VIRTUAL WORLDS

Recreating the World and Fighting a Dragon in It

Chrissie Scelsi

Homer: "Wait, so this is a play based on a YouTube of kids playing a video game?"
Marge: "That's right."
Homer: "Tsk, it's about time."[1]

The intersection of the law of the right of publicity and copyright arguably presents some of the most intriguing issues as well as challenges in current legal practice. This is especially true when it comes to video games and immersive entertainment, which not only includes the opportunity to present massive fantasy worlds, but also the ability to recreate the real world in virtual forms in unprecedented detail. The advent of platforms like YouTube and Twitch has created an additional layer of content creation on which players can broadcast themselves playing games, where the games depicting reality become part of a different depiction of reality, which could even feature virtual or augmented reality. Further, the explosive growth of smartphone technology means that anyone can be an author, or, thanks to the cameras in everyone's pockets, become a star or an extra in someone else's video or meme. Authorship will become more complicated as artificial intelligence (AI) technologies develop because AI's very metaset of layers of content presents interesting issues at the intersection of the right of publicity and copyright law. This reality can blur not only the lines between copyright and right of publicity law, but also privacy. This chapter explores some of these challenges.

Challenges Depicting Reality: People

Depicting people may be the most complex aspect of developing a video game when considering copyright and right of publicity laws. When depicting people, game developers must consider the rights to the person's physical appearance, the sound of his or her voice, signature apparel or instruments, and even holograms. Perhaps the best example is *Beatles: Rock Band*,[2] which, like others in the *Rock Band* series, allows players to simulate playing rock music by using game controllers shaped like musical instruments. The Beatles' extensive career meant that the licensing process included not only the band members and their music, but also their instruments, clothing, venues, friends, producers, and the studio chatter during recording sessions. In addition, advances in technology like holograms that can go on tour well after a celebrity's death[3] now present even more challenging estate planning issues for entertainers and their families—not to mention their attorneys—in crafting estate plans that cover as many of the potential bases as possible, given current technology, as well as licensing their name and likeness for new technologies and how new technology might mesh with the intentions of the client, particularly from an ethical standpoint.

History of Right of Publicity Cases in Games

Perhaps the most challenging part of depicting people in games is that the law of right of publicity is state law, and at times can read like a who's who of which states had famous residents die there. The state laws vary as to whether a right exists at all, whether it extends after a person's death, and for how long. Some state laws only cover people who died domiciled in that particular state, while other states' laws cover people regardless of whether they were domiciled in the state at the time of their death. For example, Hawaii passed a right of publicity law that covers the name and likeness of the deceased person, whether they are domiciled in the state or not, for a term of seventy years. Whether the courts will restrict the broad jurisdictional reach is too early to tell. Indiana similarly has a statute that tries to avoid choice of law review, but courts often read the domicile requirement regardless.[4]

Who owns rights of publicity can be problematic and a common tension in the gaming world. Most publishers encourage players to create user-generated content to drive interest in their games, and also include a license to use such content in their end-user license agreements (EULA) and terms of service (TOS). As will be discussed later in this essay, the interests of the parties can come into conflict when it comes to the question of who owns what rights to esports teams and their players.

One of the earlier cases involving right of publicity in video games was the case of *Pesina v. Midway Manufacturing Corp.*,[5] in which a martial artist, Daniel Pesina, alleged that the martial arts movements of a character in the game *Mortal Kombat* violated his right of publicity. Even though Pesina had previously had his movements videotaped so that they could be incorporated into games, the court found that he could not show that his image was recognizable in the game, because it had been so extensively changed that the public would not recognize him. This concept of transformative use has been important in a number of video game cases. A similar question was at issue in the case of *Kirby v. Sega*,[6] in which artist Lady Miss Kier alleged that her likeness had been appropriated for the Ulala character in the game *Space Channel 5*. Ultimately, the court found that even though the character had similarities to Lady Miss Kier, the areas where they differed were sufficient enough to warrant protection under the First Amendment protection and defeat her claim.[7]

Perhaps nowhere was the question of transformative use more relevant than in the case of *No Doubt v. Activision*, where the band sued the publisher over its depiction in the game *Band Hero*,[8] even though the band members had approval rights in the contract over how their respective names and likenesses would be depicted in the game. The band members sued when they discovered that their game avatars could be unlocked and made to sing other artists' songs—most notably, that Gwen Stefani's avatar could be unlocked and made to sing the Rolling Stones' song "Honky Tonk Women." This case also presents an interesting ethical point for attorneys advising on such licensing deals, as Activision noted in its answer to the band's complaint that it had "experienced representation," advised them on the deal, and they should not have been surprised by the existence of the unlocking feature, as it is common in games. To this author, this points to the duty of competence not only on staying up on the law, but also the functionalities of technologies for which clients' content is being licensed. While the case ultimately settled, the lower court rejected the transformative use defense, finding that the band members' depictions were not transformative, as they were illustrated doing exactly what they do in real life—a decision that was upheld by the California Court of Appeals. The transformative use question continues to persist in recent cases such as those brought by Lindsay Lohan and mob wife Karen Gravano, who sued

Rockstar Games over allegedly violating their rights of publicity in the game *Grand Theft Auto*. Those cases were found not to be violations on grounds similar to those articulated in *Pesina and Kirby*, in that the characters were generic and not sufficiently recognizable so as to violate the right of publicity.

Depicting reality without violating the rights of publicity of the people involved is also challenging in the world of college sports games. While the National Collegiate Athletic Association (NCAA) had been licensing the names and logos of schools for use in video games, it did not allow student athletes' names or likenesses to be similarly licensed, citing its rules about players not being able to make money off of their names and likenesses. A thicket of cases were brought by former college players (on behalf of a putative class) against Electronic Arts (EA) over alleged violations of players' rights of publicity in EA's *NCAA Football* and *Madden NFL* games, including *Hart v. Elec. Arts, Inc.*[9] and *In re NCAA Student-Athlete Name & Likeness Licensing Litig. (Keller)*,[10] which both involved the use of the likeness of former college quarterbacks along with certain biographical information. Though, like the *No Doubt* case, the depiction of athletes in the *Hart* and *Keller* cases was found to be too close to the athletes' actions in reality and not transformative enough to warrant First Amendment protection. A similar case, *Brown v. Electronic Arts, Inc.*, involving EA's use of the likeness of a former NFL player, concerned a false endorsement claim under the Lanham Act, rather than a right of publicity claim, and was decided on narrow grounds using the *Rogers* test rather than the transformative use test.[11] Still, the court dismissed Brown's claims on First Amendment grounds. Even though the court in *Keller* cited *Brown*, it seemed hesitant to fully extend the transformative use test to right of publicity cases, as "the right of publicity protects the *celebrity*, not the *consumer*."[12]

The question of right of publicity for student athletes has come full circle in 2020, as the NCAA appears to have reversed course and finally stopped prohibiting players from profiting from the use of their names and likenesses.[13] This raises questions as to whether the hugely popular NCAA video games published by EA that were sued out of existence in 2011 may return in the future.

Ironically, when the former college player cases settled in 2014, the NCAA announced that it would grant players receiving funds from the NCAA a special waiver allowing them to receive the monetary awards. Current thinking in the legal community is that it would be far too complicated for the game companies to try to go back and license the likenesses of players who played while the game was out of commission, particularly given that there is no union to assist with that process, so the publishers would have to negotiate such licenses with each individual player.

Tattoo Cases

Another interesting litigation trend in the gaming space is the depiction of tattoos on the avatars of professional basketball players in 2K Games.[14] In *Solid Oak Sketches v. 2K Games*,[15] the tattoo artists alleged that the avatar depictions infringed their copyright in the underlying tattoo designs. The court ruled in favor of 2K Games, finding *de minimus* use because, in the game, the tattoos appeared very small and hard to see, as the players are moving quickly. The court also noted that the artists had granted an implied license to the tattoo artwork, as they had to be aware at the time that the tattoo was inked that the players were famous, and likely to be appearing in public, on television, and in other forms of media. The court further noted that the depiction of the tattoos was not transformative because they appeared as they did in real life, and thus were an incidental part of the game. The court's analysis went on to conclude that the game developers had to copy the entire work to realistically depict it in the game, and that no realistic market exists for the tattoos on their own in the game.

Emote Dance Cases

The intersection of the right of publicity and copyright law has been the most prominent in the lawsuits that have been filed over alleged violations of these rights in emotes (dances) in the game *Fortnite*. Emotes are a cosmetic feature of the game where players can select short dances for their avatar to perform. Rapper 2 Milly, *The Fresh Prince of Bel-Air* star Alfonso Ribeiro, and the Instagram celebrity known as the "Backpack Kid" filed the first dance move lawsuits in 2018 against Epic Games, Inc. (Epic), alleging copyright infringement over the alleged use of dance moves in the *Fortnite* emotes.[16] Ribeiro also sued publisher Take-Two Interactive over the alleged similar use of the "Carlton Dance" in the game *NBA 2K*.[17] Despite Copyright Office policy that states that a simple set of basic dance moves is not sufficient to be registered, and that the steps are instead building blocks on which new works can be built,[18] counsel for Ribeiro and 2 Milly attempted to register both dances with the Office. Both registrations were rejected by the Copyright Office on the grounds that allowing such short sets of steps to be registered would inhibit the creation of new works. After this rejection, the copyright infringement lawsuits were withdrawn, and the attorney stated that the suits would be refiled in California, alleging violations of the state right of publicity law.

These lawsuits not only point out the complexity of the intersection of copyright and right of publicity, but also the complexities that can exist when delving into who truly owns these dances at issue. As the attorneys for Take-Two noted, the "Carlton Dance" moves first appeared when Ribeiro starred on the television show *The Fresh Prince of Bel-Air*, which was produced by NBC, and featured a copyright notice identifying the network as the owner of the show. The issue of ownership and originality is further complicated by Ribeiro's own accounts about the dance; he had stated in a TMZ interview[19] that he "stole" the moves from actress Courtney Cox's dance in the Bruce Springsteen music video for the song "Dancing in the Dark," as well as comedian Eddie Murphy's dance in a comedy special. Ribeiro has since walked this statement back, and said that he used the word "stole" in a joking manner rather than a legal sense, but its impact on the question of ownership is not helpful for his copyright claim that he is the creator and owner of the dance moves. It is not as clear as to whether it would be as devastating to a right of publicity claim. Also, the dance is more readily associated with his character than the actor himself, which complicates the issue as it has in other similar right of publicity and copyright claims in the game space.

Other similar dance move suits that present interesting wrinkles are those filed by Russell "Backpack Kid" Horning and the mother of "Orange Shirt Kid."[20] The dance at issue in the "Backpack Kid" case is known as the "floss," which made the dancer a viral sensation after he performed it as part of Katy Perry's appearance on *Saturday Night Live*. Unique to his claim was that he had successfully registered his dance move with the Copyright Office, had performed the dance at a number of Epic events, and had even initially said that he was happy that the floss appeared in *Fortnite*. The fact that Epic was monetizing the emotes without giving credit to the person who made it famous seems to be driving these claims. It is interesting to note that similar claims have not been brought against Energizer Holdings, Inc., which has a television ad campaign in which robots are clearly seen doing the "floss" dance. The suit[21] brought by the mother of the *Fortnite* player known to the community as "Orange Shirt Kid" also raises interesting issues, namely that the dance was submitted to Epic as part of a game-related contest. Orange Shirt Kid did not win the contest, but his dance eventually was added after the player community started a campaign to get Epic to include it in the game. The contest rules granted Epic use of the materials that were submitted, though this is not mentioned in the player's complaint. Again, a lack of credit and the fact that the company was monetizing the emotes seem to drive these lawsuits. The plaintiff noted that the emote sold by Epic was named "Orange Justice" instead of "Orange Shirt Kid," and that the shirt for a player's avatar still featured the same catchphrase as the one worn by her son without giving him credit or asking his consent. The attorney for the plaintiffs was able to obtain a registration for Orange Shirt Kid's dance (like Backpack Kid) though the impact of that registration is unclear as the lawsuits are still pending.

Perhaps the most interesting development in the emote lawsuits was a recent preemptive move by Epic Games, which filed a complaint for a declaratory judgment of non-infringement against Matthew Geiler, better known on the Internet as "Dancing Pumpkin Man."[22] Geiler and his company allege that the copyright and trademark rights to the character in the video that made him famous have been infringed by the "Pump It Up" emote featured in *Fortnite*. The complaint questions what elements of a character can be deemed protectable. The "Dancing Pumpkin Man" video features a man dressed in a plain black unitard and a jack-o'-lantern decoration mask dancing in front of a graveyard scene. Epic notes that neither the unitard nor mask was made by Geiler. Comparatively, the Pump It Up emote allows an avatar to transform its head into a jack-o'-lantern face with "green flames pouring from the eyes, nose and mouth, a broad, grinning mouth, a long, prominent stem that curves, and dark striations delineating the segments of the pumpkin giving it a yellow-and-orange design."[23] Epic lists other examples of jack-o'-lantern head characters in popular culture as evidence that the concept of a dancing pumpkin man is not unique to Geiler's video, or the first to do so.[24] The complaint further illuminates differences between the video and the game experience, including the fact that the pace of the video is moderate, while the pace of the game is fast, the music in the video is not featured in the game emote, and the background in the video is static, while the game play is interactive.

Unlike most of the previously discussed lawsuits, there is a license in play. According to the complaint, Epic entered into a license with the defendant to use the "Dancing Pumpkin Man" video in *Fortnite*. Epic noted that the license agreement with Geiler includes, as many other licenses do, language stating that the "agreement constitutes the entire understanding between the parties" and that Geiler commented on the Facebook post announcing the Pump It Up emote, "Luckily they did a licensing deal with me ahead of time!," as evidence of an admission that the license conveyed all of the rights that the defendant is trying to now claim.[25] Geiler claims that the emote infringes the character's likeness, which he felt was not included in the existing license. This case, depending on its outcome, may force Epic to change its licensing strategy. Either way, this dispute demonstrates the importance of ensuring that a license is as clear as possible about what rights are being granted, particularly in areas where this can become unclear, such as the space in the Venn diagram between copyright and right of publicity.

Right of Publicity and Esports

This complex, blurred line is perhaps no more evident than in the realm of esports. Created as a marketing tool for video games, esports have blossomed into large-scale leagues for games like *League of Legends* and *Overwatch*, with thousands of people attending live events and even more viewers watching online and through traditional broadcast television. In these leagues, the game publisher holds all the cards, because it owns the intellectual property rights to the game, the league, and how both are presented to the world. As such, it is in the publisher's interest to try to obtain the rights to as many aspects of the league as possible. However, for players and potentially their teams, it is in their best interest to scale back these attempts to a more realistic scope. This tension between the parties creates interesting negotiating positions, as the publisher's esports agreement may ask for the rights to the player's image and likeness in perpetuity. From the player's perspective, this can seem like a massive overreach, as she could change teams, leagues, or even games in the span of a few months or years, leaving the player in an untenable position in terms of her rights of publicity going forward.

This tension can also extend to the employment context, as game publishers are often engaging players who stream or play the game professionally, or hiring them on as employees. This becomes complicated because the company's employment agreement may technically grant it the intellectual property rights to the content created by the contractor or employee, but may leave the right of publicity of that individual in flux. Such a situation may work in the standard streaming context, but not when the employee's likeness is incorporated into the game itself, or ancillary merchandise, particularly when the relationship ends but the publisher wants to continue to use the content until a replacement can be found. This may call for the publisher to obtain a separate release from the contractor or employee asking for the additional rights to her name and likeness for a period of time after the engagement ends. If the publisher has to remove the person's likeness from the game, it may have to carefully draft patch notes in order to help with the process of removing the avatar without drawing too much attention to the removal.

Similar concerns can arise when a high-profile streamer or esports player runs afoul of the publisher's content program rules, or esports league regulations. Being banned can affect the ability of the player to monetize his or her content, cost him or her league winnings, and create outrage in the game's community of fans. Such situations have garnered major coverage as of late, often portraying the publisher as the villain despite the fact that it has all the rights to administer its content creation program or esports league as it sees fit. A prominent recent example involves Blizzard—the publisher of *Hearthstone*—banning player Chung Ng Wai, a.k.a. Blitzchung, and fining him the amount of his prize winnings after he spoke out in favor of protestors in Hong Kong during an interview after a professional event.[26] This move caused outrage in the gaming community, as well as among some of the company's employees, who staged a walkout in protest of the ban. Blizzard found itself in a sticky situation trying to balance the rights of players to freely express themselves against its business interests, as one of its investors is Chinese gaming giant Tencent, and the company earns a significant amount of revenue from gaming in the Chinese market. Interestingly, the NBA found itself in similar territory when Houston Rockets General Manager Daryl Morey tweeted a pro-Hong Kong message, which prompted the Chinese Basketball Association and Tencent, which is the NBA's rights holder in China, to announce that they would cut ties with the Rockets and not air the NBA's preseason games that were being played in China. This turn of events led the NBA Commissioner to issue a statement similarly trying to show that the league respects the free speech of its coaches, executives, and players, but also apologizing for offending its friends and fans in China. This move was not entirely surprising, as the NBA's television deal with Tencent is reportedly worth $1.5 billion. As these examples demonstrate, much as the issues around copyright and right of publicity in esports can be complex in and of themselves, so too can the web of business interests that may drive different parties to seek to obtain and control.

Challenges Depicting Reality: Buildings

The ability of video games and immersive entertainment to create breathtaking virtual landscapes creates myriad licensing and legal issues for game developers and publishers because, sometimes, even having the license to an image or song may not be enough if there are other third-party rights embedded in the work. These issues arise in depicting both inanimate and animate elements of the real world. For example, some buildings, such as the Great Pyramids and the Eiffel Tower at night, require developers to obtain a license to feature them on film or in a game, despite the fact that the copyright to the architectural works is in the public domain, and the EU Copyright Directive allows photos of public buildings or buildings visible from a public place under the freedom of panorama. (Belgium, France, and Italy have not instituted this Directive as it applies to architectural works.) In addition, the Societe d'Exploitation de la Tour Eiffel, which manages the

Eiffel Tower, added the lighting design that is visible at night recently enough that it is a protected artistic work under French law and requires a license to depict it for commercial purposes.

In addition to licenses, creating a realistic virtual version of an existing building can also require extensive research into the history of and how the building was constructed. When the digital versions are accurate, they can become a resource, as noted by headlines after the tragic fire at Paris's Notre-Dame Cathedral that cited the game *Assassin's Creed Unity* as an "unlikely source" that could help provide resources for the reconstruction effort. While this may have seen like an "unlikely" source of information to reporters, anyone who plays the game can see the extensive work that went into creating a virtual version of the cathedral that players can see, climb on, and explore. Ubisoft historian Maxime Durand noted in interviews after the fire that he has spent four years working on the game,[27] which is set during the French Revolution, and level artist Caroline Miousse said that she spent two years and probably 80 percent of her time building the virtual model of the cathedral.[28] However, even this extensive research may not be as helpful as some have hoped, because of technological differences between when the game was developed and what is available today. As Durand noted, the "reality is that photogrammetry—the ability to scan monuments—was technology that we added later in the 'Assassin's Creed' franchise," and that "back then we really relied on pictures—photos, videos of—modern day Notre-Dame."[29] An interesting wrinkle developed when the matter of the cathedral's iconic spires came up. The spires had not yet been added as the building would have appeared in the time period of the game, but the publisher worried that players would not recognize the cathedral without them, and opted to err on the side of making the building recognizable rather than historically accurate.

Challenges in Depicting Reality: Vehicles

Just as creating depictions of inanimate objects can quickly become a complex issue of licensing and research, so too can depicting the animate aspects of life. Vehicles have been a vexing area, as there can be not only issues of copyright, but also trademark and trade dress. This was first raised in a lawsuit between EA and the makers of Bell helicopters[30] over whether the depiction of the vehicles in the game *Battlefield 3* was protected under the First Amendment. EA sought a ruling that the depiction would be protected, so it would not need a license. The suit was largely seen as testing the limitations of the Supreme Court's 2011 ruling that video games were protected works of free expression under the First Amendment.[31] EA and Bell ultimately settled out of court in 2013, which left a void of uncertainty for game developers looking to depict military vehicles. In 2020, game developers have more clarity from a case brought by AM General LLC against Activision Blizzard for trademark and trade dress infringement over its depiction of Humvee vehicles in the *Call of Duty* game series.[32] The Court granted Activision Blizzard's motion for summary judgment, and examined the claims under the prongs of the *Rogers* test,[33] which include artistic relevance, and whether the use of the work is misleading as to its source. In evaluating the *Polaroid* factors[34] for determining whether the use is misleading, the court found mostly in favor of Activision Blizzard based on consumer sophistication and lack of actual confusion. The court noted that only 16 percent of players were confused as to the association between Activision Blizzard and AMG from the depiction of Humvee vehicles, which is not significant enough evidence of actual confusion to outweigh the First Amendment interests in the case. The court pulled no punches on the issue of consumer sophistication, stating:

> One problem for Plaintiff on this point is that the purchasers of Humvees—that is, some 50 militaries from around the world, including the U.S. Armed Forces—are not buying *Call of Duty* games, and vice versa. Thus, there is no risk whatsoever that someone will buy the wrong product by accident out of sheer confusion about who built or distributed the product.

Indeed, the court in *Louis Vuitton* noted that "moviegoers are sophisticated enough to know that the mere presence of a brand name in a film, especially one that is briefly and intermittently shown, does not indicate that the brand sponsored the movie." There is no reason to believe that video game players are any less astute.[35]

While this ruling, which involves trademark rather than copyright or right of publicity, is largely relevant only in the US, and is likely to be appealed, it provides some case law on point as to the interplay of the First Amendment and intellectual property, and some guidance on what factors game developers need to keep in mind when trying to depict real-world vehicles.

Conclusion

In creating authentic, immersive worlds, filled with cultural icons from the music, entertainment, and sports industries, video game companies must navigate complex intellectual property issues involving every object or person that the company creates in this environment as well as what a gamer is able to create. Various copyright, trademark, trade dress, and publicity rights attach to certain buildings, street art, tattoos, cars, bikes, and other objects. People can be identifiable not only by their features but by certain attributes. Celebrities, musicians, and athletes consider themselves as brands and are aware of their licensing value, looking for hints of recognizable features in popular games. Having an understanding of the basis for all these various laws, that have similarities yet distinct legal differences, is essential for anyone practicing in this area to clearly know the boundaries of what can and cannot be created without a license.

Notes

1 *The Simpsons*, season 31, episode 6, "Marge the Lumberjill," directed by Rob Oliver, written by Ryan Koh, aired on November 10, 2019, on FOX, https://www.fox.com/watch/376e7a6a0565c6d8a5b27432 617dfc08.
2 Jeff Howe, "The Beatles Make the Leap to Rock Band," *Wired*, August 12, 2009, accessed May 14, 2020, https://www.wired.com/2009/08/mf-rockband.
3 Mark Binelli, "Old Musicians Never Die. They Just Become Holograms," *New York Times Magazine*, January 7, 2020, https://nyti.ms/35xwRlq.
4 See, e.g., Shaw Family Archives Ltd. v. CMG Worldwide, Inc., 486 F. Supp. 2d 309, 314 (S.D.N.Y. 2007).
5 Pesina v. Midway Mfg. Co., 948 F. Supp. 40 (N.D. Ill. 1996).
6 Kirby v. Sega of Am., Inc., 144 Cal. App. 4th 47 (2006).
7 See id. at 56. ("Although Ulala dons assorted costumes in the game, she is seen most often with her hair in short, high pigtails, wearing an orange cropped-top bearing the numeral '5' and orange miniskirt, orange gloves and boots with stiletto heels, a blue ray-gun holster strapped to her thigh, and a blue headset and jetpack . . . . Kirby, as the record reflects, is found more frequently in form-fitting body suits, with her hair shaped into a page-boy flip, held back with a head band.")
8 No Doubt v. Activision Publ'g Inc., 192 Cal. App. 4th 1018 (2011).
9 Hart v. Elec. Arts, Inc., 717 F.3d 141 (3d Cir. 2013).
10 In re NCAA Student-Athlete Name & Likeness Licensing Litig. (Keller), 724 F.3d 1268 (9th Cir. 2013).
11 Brown v. Elec. Arts, Inc., 724 F.3d 1235, 1248 (9th Cir. 2013).
12 *NCAA*, 724 F.3d at 1281. The Rogers test, which was created to balance trademark and similar rights protected by the Lanham Act against First Amendment rights, is a two-prong test that considers (1) whether the trademark or identifying material has artistic relevance to the underlying work, and (2) whether the trademark or identifying material explicitly misleads as to the source or the content of the work. Brown, 724 F.3d at 1239. The transformative use test, however, which balances the First Amendment and the right of publicity, considers whether the work in question adds significant creative elements so as to be transformed into something more than a celebrity likeness or imitation. *NCAA*, 724 F.3d at 1273.

13 Colin Dwyer, "NCAA Plans to Allow College Athletes to Get Paid for Use of Their Names, Images," *NPR*, October 29, 2019, https://www.npr.org/2019/10/29/774439078/ncaa-starts-process-to-allow-compensation-for-college-athletes.
14 The 2K games include 2K14, 2K15, and 2K16, respectively.
15 Solid Oak Sketches, LLC v. 2K Games, Inc., No. 16-CV-724-LTS-SDA, 2020 WL 1467394 (S.D.N.Y March 26, 2020).
16 Complaint, Ferguson v. Epic Games, Inc., No. 18-CV-10110-CJC-RAO (C.D. Cal. December 5, 2018); Complaint, Ribeiro v. Epic Games, Inc., No. 18-CV-10412, 2018 WL 6655966 (C.D. Cal. December 17, 2018).
17 Complaint, Ribeiro v. Take-Two Interactive Software, Inc., No. 18-CV-10417-RGK (C.D. Cal. December 17, 2018).
18 U.S. Copyright Office, Library of Congress, *Circular 52: Copyright Registration of Choreography and Pantomime*, revised September 2017, 3, https://www.copyright.gov/circs/circ52.pdf.
19 "Alfonso Ribeiro Confessed He Stole Carlton Dance . . . Fortnite Suit Screwed?" *TMZ*, December 18, 2018, https://www.tmz.com/2018/12/18/alfonso-ribeiro-stole-carlton-dance-courteney-cox-eddie-murphy-fortnite-lawsuit.
20 Complaint, McCumbers v. Epic Games, Inc., No. 19-CV-00260-CJC (C.D. Cal. January 11, 2019); Complaint, Redd v. Epic Games, Inc., No. 18-CV-10444 (December 17, 2018).
21 Complaint, Epic Games, Inc. v. Sick Picnic Media, LLC, No. 19-CV-11215-PGG (December 6, 2019).
22 Haydn Taylor, "Epic Games Files Preemptive Lawsuit against Dancing Pumpkin Man," *GamesIndustry.biz*, December 10, 2019, https://www.gamesindustry.biz/articles/2019-12-10-epic-games-files-preemptive-lawsuit-against-dancing-pumpkin-man.
23 Epic Games, Inc., No. 19-CV-11215-PGG.
24 *Id*.
25 *Id*.
26 Patrick Lum, "'No Regrets': Hong Kong Hearthstone Gamer Banned over Pro-Democracy Support," *Guardian*, October 8, 2019, https://www.theguardian.com/sport/2019/oct/08/blitzchung-hearthstone-blizzard-banned-hong-kong-protests.
27 Ben Gilbert, "The Effort to Rebuild Notre-Dame Cathedral Could Get Help from an Unlikely Source: A Video Game," *Business Insider*, April 16, 2019, https://www.businessinsider.com/notre-dame-cathedral-assassins-creed-2019-4.
28 Gilbert, "The Effort to Rebuild."
29 Ben Gilbert, "As France Rebuilds Notre-Dame Cathedral, the French Studio Behind 'Assassin's Creed' Is Offering Up Its 'Over 5,000 Hours' of Research on the 800 Year-Old Monument," *Business Insider France*, April 18, 2019, https://www.businessinsider.fr/us/notre-dame-fire-assassins-creed-maxime-durand-ubisoft-interview-2019-4.
30 Elec. Arts v. Textron Inc., No. 12-C-00118-WHA, 2012 WL 3042668 (N.D. Cal. July 25, 2012).
31 Brown v. Entm't Merchants Ass'n, 564 U.S. 786 (2011).
32 AM Gen. LLC v. Activision Blizzard, Inc., No. 17-CV-8644-GBD-JLC, 2020 WL 1547838 (S.D.N.Y. March 31, 2020).
33 *Id*. at *4–6.
34 *Id*. at *6–10.
35 *Id*. at *10 (internal citations omitted).

6.2

VIRTUAL PROPERTY AND VIRTUAL CURRENCY

Brandon J. Huffman

Introduction

When I was younger, I spent hours online with my friends playing action RPGs and repeating the bosses over and over in an effort to find rare items.[1] I also spent hours designing custom items, architecture, and cities for little virtual people to live (and die) in. Looking back, it is interesting to wonder: what rights did I have in any of the items I found or created?

Today, many games have shifted to allow players to buy rare items. Or to buy in-game currency to exchange for other items in the game. What rights do players today have? How are these purchases regulated? What risks do developers and publishers face by including these kinds of transactions? This chapter will attempt to answer these questions and others.

What Is Virtual Property?

Virtual property could mean a lot of things. It could be a person's digital creations in a cloud-based platform for creation. For example, I am writing this chapter in Google Docs, a platform for word processing in the cloud. Virtual property could be a person's avatar's belongings in an in-game environment such as Thunderfury, Blessed Blade of the Windseeker, the level 80 legendary sword in *World of Warcraft*, a massively multiplayer online role-playing game.

The focus of this chapter is on digital belongings—the digital goods and digital money that players acquire (or create) in digital worlds. A discussion of these items necessarily involves the discussion of the code underlying them. I will also make a distinction between these items and those (like this chapter) created by tools actually intended to be used for creation.

All of the same property—and infinitely more—that exists in the real world can exist in the virtual world. Players in a virtual world may be able to obtain legendary swords, create fashionable looks for in-game characters, build houses, sell motorcycles, and a myriad of other things.

But, in a virtual world, the rights are different.

Virtual Currency

In many games, players can use real-world money to purchase virtual tokens, gems, karma, beads, mana, life, or other measurable in-game resources. These resources can generally be exchanged for other in-game virtual property, additional game features like another game mode, extended story, or consumable items in the game.

As a point of clarification: In this essay, "virtual currency" refers to currency within video games, rather than cryptocurrencies based on blockchain technology like BitCoin, Ethereum, and others. While it is possible that an in-game virtual currency could be tied to a blockchain ledger or a cryptocurrency, the multitude of issues this would raise are beyond the scope of this essay.

Property Rights

Traditional Property

Traditional property rights are often described by law professors as a "bundle of sticks." While it is debatable whether this is a useful analogy,[2] it is one that every lawyer in the US heard in law school. The crux of it is that the owner of property—traditional property—actually possesses a certain bundle of independent rights related to the property. For example, in the case of real property (land), these rights include the right to control access to, and development on, the land, certain rights to adjacent, subjacent or traversing water, and so on. In the case of personal property, rights are usually more focused on the rights of possession and alienability (the ability to sell or transfer ownership of the item).

In thinking about these rights, it can be helpful to think about the exploitation of property. How does a person make money from "ownership"? In the context of real property, this sometimes takes the form of a lease (rental) of the property or a license, which is a limited right to be on the property and use it in certain ways. The simplest form of exploitation of property is the sale of it. If you own a boat, you can sell that boat for profit.[3]

Intellectual Property

The creator of digital assets in a virtual environment may also have certain intellectual property rights. The overview of these rights provided below is an oversimplification— more information on what intellectual property rights exist in creations, brands, and personas is provided elsewhere in this book. When these exist in a virtual world, they are, by default, no different.

Copyright

For example, the creator of a fashionable design for a character in an online game may have a protectable copyright interest in that design.[4] The creator of an art piece to hang on the walls of a virtual gallery may have a copyright interest in that work.

Copying another's creations, whether those creations are in the real or digital world, may be infringement. When environments in the real world are captured (whether by video, photogrammetry, or recreation), creators need to be careful not to infringe on the copyrights of visual artists, sculptors, and other artists whose work may appear in the real world. This is true even where those works may be in public spaces.

Trademark

Trademarks protect commercial identifiers. For example, a person who creates an online store or sells items in a virtual world for real-life currency could have a protected trademark interest in either their brand identifiers or their products' names in the virtual world.

These rights can also originate in the real world and be introduced to the virtual world. When real-world goods or environments are captured to be included in a virtual world, like cars, weapons, and ammunition, there may be implications for the real-life trademark owners.

Likewise, when working to make virtual worlds that appear to be perfect replicas of real-world spaces, developers and artists must be careful not to infringe on the trademark interests of real-world businesses.[5]

Whether an accurate capturing of a real-world mark on the item it identifies is an infringement of the trademark rights is a question that depends heavily on the specific facts. Some uses may be fair use. But where a mark is featured in a way that suggests endorsement, or is applied to a virtual item that is not the actual real-life product, a defense against an allegation of infringement could be harder to find.

Publicity

The right of publicity is an outgrowth of an individual's right of privacy, which varies from state to state. The basic premise is that an individual has a right to control the exploitation of her own image or likeness. Commercial exploitation of a person's image, likeness, persona, or similar personal identifier could be a violation of the individual's right of publicity, even if it only happens in the virtual environment. For example, inclusion of a particular athlete or celebrity in a virtual world could result in litigation (and has).[6]

A Note about Patents

In the context of virtual worlds, patents are most likely to come up in the context of design patents, which protect the unique visual qualities of a manufactured item. Capturing that design and incorporating it into a virtual world could be patent infringement (in addition to potential copyright, trademark, or trade dress infringement).

Regulations

Beyond the sort of existential discussion of what "property" means, there are practical, real-world regulations that affect purveyors of virtual worlds.

Money Laundering Concerns

In early 2019, *The Independent* reported that criminals were using the in-game currency V-bucks in the game *Fortnite* to launder money.[7] This was just the latest in a series of stories, including popular games published by Valve, Microsoft, and others.

To understand this issue and the regulations that apply, it is important to first understand what money laundering is: Money laundering is the process of taking money from criminal or other nefarious activity and channeling it through some other vehicle so that it comes out the other side "clean." This is done to hide the fact of the crime or to evade taxes. Following the path of money is a tried and true method for finding criminals and proving their crimes.[8] Video games and other apps with in-game currency or transferrable items can become a conduit for money laundering.

The US Treasury Financial Crimes Enforcement Network (FinCEN) has released guidance on how anti-money laundering (AML) regulations apply to virtual currencies in 2013 and 2019.[9] This guidance explained that exchangers and administrators could be subject to the Bank Secrecy Act, an AML statute with many requirements potentially too cumbersome for smaller companies to comply (especially video game companies without a ton of financial experience). The guidance explains:

> An *exchanger* is a person engaged as a business in the exchange of virtual currency for real currency, funds, or other virtual currency, while an *administrator* is a person engaged as a business

in issuing (putting into circulation) a virtual currency, and who has the authority to redeem (to withdraw from circulation) such virtual currency. A *user* is "a person that obtains virtual currency to purchase goods or services" on the user's own behalf.

While exchangers and administrators can be "transmitters" subject to the regulations, users generally would not be. The guidance goes on to discuss different business models, anonymization, and processing that could be potentially problematic.

When video game companies are pursuing new business models involving virtual currencies or virtual goods, they should, at minimum, make themselves aware of the Bank Secrecy Act and the FinCEN guidance to determine whether or not they are subject to the regulations. As games tend to be at the forefront of exploring new economic models (often in order to keep their prices low to encourage user adoption or reduce friction in user acquisition), FinCEN is definitely paying attention.

If subject to these regulations, the company will need to adopt a written AML policy and a process for identifying its customers. As companies are also working to reduce the amount of data they collect from customers in light of new privacy laws like the California Consumer Privacy Act and the European Union's General Data Protection Regulation, adopting these policies may require additional thought.

Gift Cards

Another financial regulation that may apply to virtual goods and currency relates to the legal treatment of gift cards. The Credit Card Accountability Responsibility and Disclosure Act of 2009[10] (the CARD Act, because Congress loves a punny acronym) and the regulations put forth under its authority[11] apply to gift certificates, prepaid cards, and other stored value in the form of a card, code, or other device.

How does this apply to games? Imagine a consumer purchases a certain charm for a virtual necklace for their avatar. He buys the trinket, say, with a credit card from the company's website, but what he actually receives is a code to redeem in game for the charm. Until that is redeemed, it is, simply, a gift certificate subject to the CARD Act. This is a somewhat obvious example, but more convoluted or digital versions of the same process would also be subject to the CARD Act. The CARD Act specifically does *not* require any physical card. Redemption of purchased virtual goods should be instantaneous and result in a license to use the virtual item (more on that below).

The CARD Act imposes a multitude of requirements. But key among them are terms around how stored value may expire and what notices must be provided to consumers. The law prohibits companies from charging certain dormancy fees and setting expirations of less than five years on actively used cards, and imposes strict definitions on what is considered an actively used card. It requires clear and conspicuous notice of information about the terms and conditions governing the card. The notice must be made prior to purchase, in a form that can be retained by the individual and readily understandable by consumers.

Notably, the CARD Act is the floor. State laws can impose more restrictive conditions. California, for example, has nearly prohibited expiration of gift cards and the imposition of service fees.[12] California also requires that if there is less than $10 in stored value, it must be redeemable in cash.

Game developers and publishers need to be careful when introducing any stored values and especially careful if implementing virtual wallets or direct currency purchases in games.

Consumer Protection, Gambling, and Lottery Laws

Consumer protection laws, both at the federal and at the state levels, are designed to ensure that consumers are not duped, abused, or taken advantage of. In most instances, the simplest way to comply is to disclose to customers, before they purchase something, what they are getting and what their rights are, and not try to hide details, swindle users, or engage in any kind of fraud.

In some cases, though, concealing what is being purchased goes hand in hand with the monetization practice. The classic, non-digital version of this is a pack of collectible cards (baseball cards are the simplest reference). The digital implementation of this is a loot box, or loot crate, where a consumer purchases a digital container without knowing the contents. The contents are virtual goods. In both the digital and the real-world examples, the objects received may have varying values (real or perceived) or quality.

The Federal Trade Commission (FTC) held a workshop in August 2019 to discuss the implementation and treatment of loot boxes.[13] During that event, the FTC heard from industry representatives, watchdog groups, and others. Much of the discussion centered on level-setting: answering questions about what loot boxes are and how they are implemented. There was less discussion around the specifics of whether or how to regulate them, but the direction of the questions certainly pointed to that as a possibility in the future. Regulations have been implemented in much of Europe and Asia already.

A question often posed by commentators and others in the games industry is "are loot boxes gambling?" This question is very difficult to answer as every state has its own definition of gambling. The simplest formulation of this definition, though, is an activity that includes three elements: chance, prize, and consideration. "Chance" means that there is an element (how much of an element varies) of randomness, outside of the user's or player's control. "Prize" means a thing of value (though even that simple definition is inherently complicated by whether the value is real or perceived, whether a digital item that cannot be transferred or sold can have value, or whether something like continued play time is a prize). "Consideration" means that the user buys the chance either with cash or by giving up something else (there are debates around whether a "like" on social media, consenting to provide user data, and other minor acts can constitute consideration).

This is the same question that has to be asked when a company, games or otherwise, is running a promotional contest or a sweepstakes. If it fails to abide by the laws and regulations in place, it could be running an illegal lottery or be in violation of a state's gambling laws.

In terms of loot boxes, though, I believe this question misses the mark. The appropriate question is more akin to "is this practice fair to consumers?" I believe this is where the FTC is headed.

For some historical context, in 2017, the FTC settled its complaint against Trevor "TmarTn" Martin and Thomas "Syndicate" Cassell, two social media influencers who promoted and endorsed an online gambling service CS:GO Lotto.[14] *Counter-Strike: Global Offensive* (CS:GO) is a game created by Valve. In the game, players could obtain "skins," which would allow cosmetic changes to their avatars. Third-party sites allowed players and viewers of *CS:GO*, which gained popularity as an esport, to bet skins on the outcome of particular matches. Winners would receive both the return of the skins they bet, and skins from the losers. TmarTn and Syndicate promoted one such site, CS:GO Lotto, but failed to disclose their relationship with the site—essentially misleading consumers who viewed their content.

This was a situation that, quite literally, involved gambling. But the FTC's action mainly focused on the lack of disclosure—the lack of consumer protection—not gambling.

The FTC's primary mission is, after all, "protecting America's consumers." Many in the industry have already committed to better disclosures and information for consumers around loot boxes, which could alleviate the need for regulation.[15]

Terms of Use/Terms of Service

In 2006, Marc Bragg tested the boundaries of virtual property rights when he sued Linden Research, Inc.[16] Bragg had created a character in the online world of *Second Life*, a role-playing game created by Linden. When Bragg discovered a way to acquire land in the virtual world at lower-than-market prices, Linden kicked him out and removed his account. He sued. While the case was ultimately settled, it became clear that the crucial facts and the core of the debate would have been around one thing: the Linden terms of service and the contract they formed between Linden and Bragg.

Terms of service, terms of use, user agreements, or other such agreements lay out for users the contract they enter into by using a software product, including games.

Intellectual Property

Well-drafted terms of service can make clear who owns what. As a starting point, they will state that the platform or the purveyor of the digital world owns the world itself and the software underlying it. They will typically make clear that anything created in the world is not owned by the creator or, in the limited situations where it is, that the creator is giving the platform a license to use the creation on and in connection with the platform.

For example, the *Second Life* terms and conditions include a section entitled "Content Licenses and Intellectual Property Rights," which includes the following subsections:

1.1. Linden Lab owns Intellectual Property Rights in Second Life.
1.2. Linden Lab grants you certain licenses to access and use Second Life while you are in compliance with the Agreements.
1.3. You also grant Linden Lab and other users of Second Life a license to use in snapshots and machinima your Content that is displayed in publicly accessible areas of the Second Life.
1.4. You shall be responsible for restricting access to Content for which you do not wish to grant a User Content License.
1.5. You may grant certain Content licenses to other users through the Second Life permissions system.
1.6. You agree to respect the Intellectual Property Rights of other users, Linden Lab, and third parties.[17]

These headers are a bit more explanatory than typical, but give a good idea of the types of rights, grants, and licenses that digital world operators are likely to include in their terms.

To protect the platform holder from potential lawsuits for copyright infringement based on the actions of the users, a safe harbor exists under the Digital Millennium Copyright Act (DMCA).[18] By adhering to certain requirements, platform holders ensure that any lawsuit for copyright infringement based on user-generated content in their virtual world is properly brought against their users, not the platform holder.

DMCA requirements include providing a notice and takedown process whereby content holders can notify the platform (in a very specific way) and have allegedly infringing content removed by the platform. The platform notifies the user who created or posted the content on the platform, and that the user has the ability to submit a counter-notification to the platform that denies the infringement, provides certain information about herself, and consents to jurisdiction in federal court in case the rights holder wants to sue.

The platform holder also has to have a repeat infringer policy so that someone who repeatedly receives takedowns can be banned. While not a virtual environment, perhaps the most well-known repeat infringer policy is the YouTube Strike system.[19]

Prohibit Transfers

Game developers and publishers should prohibit transfers of virtual goods and currency from user to user to the extent possible in their virtual worlds. When transfers from one user to another are permitted, technical measures should sometimes be implemented so that the item is actually returned to the platform holder, and then reissued to the other user.

Limiting peer-to-peer transfer of virtual goods can limit concerns about money laundering.

Any time limitations are placed on user-to-user transfer, those limitations should be clearly spelled out in the terms. For example, King Games, the company behind *Candy Crush* and other casual games, includes in its terms of use:

> You agree that Virtual Money, Virtual Goods and/or Subscriptions are not transferrable to anyone else and you will not transfer or attempt to transfer any Virtual Money, Virtual Goods and/or Subscriptions to anyone else.[20]

Likewise, operators should take care to avoid transfers on third-party exchanges and ban users who violate that policy. This can help curb both money laundering and betting on third-party sites.

Prohibit Cashing Out

A virtual world host should not allow users who buy virtual goods or currency to exchange them for cash. Especially if transfers are allowed, prohibiting cashing out reduces concerns about money laundering and helps create an argument that any chance mechanics are not gambling as there is no real "prize."

For example, Blizzard provides the following language in its End User License Agreement:

> As an active Account holder, you may participate in the Blizzard Balance service ("Blizzard Balance"). Blizzard Balance can only be used to obtain certain products and services offered by Blizzard; it has no cash value. . . . Regardless of how it is acquired, Blizzard Balance is non-transferable to another person or Account, does not accrue interest, is not insured by the Federal Deposit Insurance Corporation (FDIC), and, unless otherwise required by law or permitted by this Agreement, is not redeemable or refundable for any sum of money or monetary value from Blizzard at any time. . . . Blizzard Balance is not a bank account. And, while you can register and play on multiple Accounts, you are not allowed to have more than three (3) Accounts with Blizzard Balance.[21]

Note that, here, transfers are also prohibited. And Blizzard has taken special care to exempt out of the no-cash-out policy "unless otherwise required by law or permitted by this Agreement." As mentioned earlier, some states require small amounts held in gift cards to be redeemable. It could be this provision is intended to deal with that kind of requirement.

Do Not Store Value; License

A platform provider can seek to avoid gift card regulations and limit claims of property ownership by specifically spelling out that, when a customer purchases virtual items or currency, what they actually receive is a license (a limited right to use) those items. Again, looking to Blizzard for an example:

> Blizzard grants you a limited license to acquire, use, and redeem Blizzard Balance pursuant to the terms of this Agreement. . . .
> Blizzard Balance does not constitute or confer upon you any personal property right.[22]

Similarly, CCP hf., the company behind *Eve Online*, a massively multiplayer space combat simulator, includes in its End User License Agreement:

> You have no interest in the value of your time spent playing the Game, for example, by the building up of the experience level of your character and the items your character accumulates during your time playing the Game. Your Account, and all attributes of your Account, including all corporations, actions, groups, titles, and characters, and all objects, currency, and items acquired, developed, or delivered by or to characters as a result of play through your Accounts, are the sole and exclusive property of CCP, including any and all copyrights and intellectual property rights in or to any and all of the same, all of which are hereby expressly reserved.[23]

These terms have been especially relevant for *Eve Online*, where battles between players have led to estimated losses exceeding a million dollars in a single battle.[24] To be clear, that is the virtual destruction of virtual property for which users paid real-world cash exceeding a million dollars.

Allow for Shutting Down

Terms of service should, if possible, explain when and how the game will shut down. Setting expectations around elimination of virtual goods will reduce friction with players. Often, the decision to shut down a game will not be made until much later. When this happens, as much advance notice should be given as possible.

Compare: Tools

If you are reading this far, you might be wondering how the rules apply to software that is specifically marketed as a tool for creators. Even Photoshop, to some extent, creates a virtual environment in which you can work and create things.

The answer is that it still comes back to the contract. For example, every Adobe product has specific terms around the ownership of content. Here is the example from Photoshop itself:

   4.1 Content. "Content" means any material, such as audio files, video files, electronic documents, or images, that you upload and import into the Services or Software in connection with your use of the Services.
   4.2 Ownership. You retain all rights and ownership of your Content. We do not claim any ownership rights to your Content.[25]

But what about tools that exist in virtual reality or other environments? Same answer. The contract is king.

For example, Tilt Brush is an artistic tool that allows drawing and painting in three dimensions in a virtual reality environment. Tilt Brush has two different licenses, a regular license and a commercial license.[26] Both allow users to create, but the regular license has some restrictions on what users can use their own creations for (for example, film and television use depicting active use of the product requires formal permission).

This is also true when tools are open source. Open source is often misunderstood. An open source tool is one that does not prohibit others from using the software code (usually, using the code behind software to make your own software would be copyright infringement). Here, again, the details of the license are key. Some open source licenses may restrict the ability of creators to profit off their creations, but many open source tools—most even—would not. Typically, the licenses associated with these tools are more about the tools themselves without as much attention to the works created using them, but users should still carefully read the terms.

Conclusion

If it has not been made clear, the law surrounding virtual property is complicated. In all this text, I never addressed tax laws, state inheritance laws, international issues, or any number of other legal hurdles. Each of the laws mentioned is long and often riddled with jargon and cross-references, and nuances that can fill thousands of pages of law review articles.

For users, the next time you buy a skin, gems, or a loot box, or start creating your masterpiece in virtual reality, this chapter should be a reminder to find out what you are agreeing to. Developers should be mindful of this complexity when including virtual property or virtual currency in a game or digital world.

Notes

1 I still spend a lot of time playing games, but now they are mostly single-player.
2 Denise R. Johnson, "Reflections on the Bundle of Rights," *Vermont Law Review* 32 (Winter 2007): 247.
3 The boat is more likely to be sold at a loss. I am told that the best days with a boat are the day you buy it and the day you sell it.
4 Whether the design is protectable in the real world is another issue. Star Athletica, LLC. v. Varsity Brands, Inc., 137 S. Ct. 1002 (2017). Presumably, a design would need to rise to the level of real-life protectability before it could be considered protectable in the virtual world.
5 See, for example, The Hollywood Sign, accessed May 13, 2020, https://hollywoodsign.org.
6 For example, video game developers have been sued by college athletes, professional wrestlers, professional basketball players, dancers, hip-hop artists, and Lindsay Lohan for alleged right of publicity violations.
7 Anthony Cuthbertson, "How Children Playing Fortnite Are Helping to Fuel Organised Crime," *Independent*, January 13, 2019, https://www.independent.co.uk/news/fortnite-v-bucks-discount-price-money-dark-web-money-laundering-crime-a8717941.html.
8 Even Al Capone, perhaps the most infamous gangster in American history, was ultimately sentenced based on a guilty plea to tax evasion charges. See "Al Capone," Famous Cases & Criminals, FBI, accessed May 13, 2020, https://www.fbi.gov/history/famous-cases/al-capone.
9 Financial Crimes Enforcement Network, *Application of FinCEN's Regulations to Persons Administering, Exchanging, or Using Virtual Currencies*, FIN-2013-G001, March 18, 2013, https://www.fincen.gov/sites/default/files/shared/FIN-2013-G001.pdf; Financial Crimes Enforcement Network, *Application of FinCEN's Regulations to Certain Business Models Involving Convertible Virtual Currencies*, FIN-2019-G001, May 9, 2019, https://www.fincen.gov/sites/default/files/2019-05/FinCEN%20Guidance%20CVC%20FINAL%20508.pdf.
10 Credit Card Accountability Responsibility and Disclosure Act of 2009, Pub. L. No. 111-24, 123 Stat. 1734 (2009), https://www.ftc.gov/sites/default/files/documents/statutes/credit-card-accountability-responsibility-and-disclosure-act-2009-credit-card-act/credit-card-pub-l-111-24_0.pdf.
11 Federal Deposit Insurance Corporation, Consumer Financial Protection Bureau, *Selected Regulations*, last modified October 31, 2016, https://www.fdic.gov/regulations/laws/rules/6500-580.html.
12 State of California Department of Consumer Affairs, *FAQs and Tips on Gift Certificates and Gift Cards: Legal Guide S-11*, December 2010, https://www.dca.ca.gov/publications/legal_guides/s_11.shtml.
13 Federal Trade Commission, *Inside the Game: Unlocking the Consumer Issues Surrounding Loot Boxes*, accessed May 13, 2020, https://www.ftc.gov/news-events/events-calendar/inside-game-unlocking-consumer-issues-surrounding-loot-boxes.
14 Federal Trade Commission, *CSGO Lotto Owners Settle FTC's First-Ever Complaint against Individual Social Media Influencers*, September 7, 2017, https://www.ftc.gov/news-events/press-releases/2017/09/csgo-lotto-owners-settle-ftcs-first-ever-complaint-against.
15 Entertainment Software Association, *Video Game Industry Commitments to Further Inform Consumer Purchases*, accessed May 13, 2020, https://www.theesa.com/perspectives/video-game-industry-commitments-to-further-inform-consumer-purchases.
16 Bragg v. Linden Research, Inc., 487 F. Supp. 2d 593, 595 (E.D. Pa. 2007).
17 "Second Life Terms and Conditions," Linden Lab, accessed May 13, 2020, https://www.lindenlab.com/legal/second-life-terms-and-conditions.
18 17 U.S.C. § 512 (2018).

19 "Copyright Strike Basics," YouTube Help, YouTube, accessed May 13, 2020, https://support.google
    .com/youtube/answer/2814000.
20 "King Games – Terms of Use," King, last modified September 26, 2019, https://king.com/
    termsAndConditions.
21 "Blizzard End User License Agreement," Blizzard, last modified June 1, 2018, https://www.blizzard
    .com/en-us/legal/fba4d00f-c7e4-4883-b8b9-1b4500a402ea/blizzard-end-user-license-agreement.
22 "Blizzard End User License Agreement."
23 "Eve Online – End User License Agreement," Eve Online, Updated May 24, 2018, https://community
    .eveonline.com/support/policies/eve-eula-en.
24 Lee Yancey, "EVE Online: 15 Best Battles That Shaped the Game's Epic History," April 17, 2019,
    https://www.denofgeek.com/us/games/eve-online/280213/eve-online-best-battles.
25 "Adobe General Terms of Use," Adobe, March 16, 2020, https://www.adobe.com/legal/terms.html.
    That emphasis is in the original. They make this point very clear.
26 "Tilt Brush License and Brand Guidelines," Tilt Brush Help, accessed May 13, 2020, https://support
    .google.com/tiltbrush/answer/7203483?hl=en.

6.3

PRESS "X" TO OPEN

Pandora's Loot Box

Caroline Womack Carroll

"I have a bit of a problem," wrote Cadence. "A gambling problem." Cadence started playing *Path of Exile* in early 2012. At the time, the game was a safe way for Cadence to manage a multiyear-long gambling addiction. It satisfied the persistent desire to pursue the thrill of a luck-based game without pulling out a credit card, and it provided the satisfaction of taking a chance.

The safe haven provided by the excitement of *Path of Exile* was no longer so safe, however, when the game introduced "mystery boxes" in 2017. Mystery boxes, also known as "loot boxes," are digital "boxes" or "crates" which contain randomized in-game rewards. Loot boxes can be purchased by the player or earned through completion of in-game requirements. The user is only made aware of what the box contains once the loot box is activated in the form of "opening" or "unlocking" it. This action of "opening" the digital box reveals the content therein. Loot boxes can contain anything, including in-game currency, cosmetic character skins, power-up items, or avatars.

It only took one day, some extra in-game currency, and a bit of disposable income for Cadence to feel the pressure. "I kept getting duplicates," Cadence wrote. "So I needed more boxes. Oh hey, there's more supporter packs I can buy, and get more out of my money. And more duplicates.. More boxes. More duplicates. More boxes... When your brain works like mine, you can't stop."[1]

Cadence isn't alone. While the developers of *Path of Exile* were sympathetic enough to disable Cadence's ability to purchase mystery boxes, many are not so lucky. In fact, it is possible that many players are not aware of exactly *why* loot boxes are so satisfying. For Cadence, loot boxes were more than just a fun way to get new in-game content; rather, they served as a trigger which reignited a serious underlying gambling addiction.

Loot boxes are one of the most powerful financial forces in the video game industry to date, as evidenced by the drastic rise of loot box availability in video games over the past ten years. "Industry analysts predict that loot boxes will drive a large proportion of the revenue generated in the $230 billion video game economy by 2022. Gamers are already projected to spend approximately $30 billion on loot boxes this year alone, with this figure rising to $50 billion over the next four years."[2] Unsurprisingly, the frequency of loot box features in video games has increased from a mere 4 percent in 2010 to 71 percent as of November 2019.[3] A multitude of popular video games that appeal to a wide age range of audiences contain loot boxes, including *Overwatch*, *Player Unknown Battlegrounds*, and *Dota 2*.

This chapter seeks to further understand the impact of loot boxes on children and adults alike while tackling a serious outstanding question: whether loot boxes are gambling and, if so, whether they should be regulated as such. The first section begins with a brief overview of how gambling law is generally applied in US jurisdictions. The second section will then apply such analysis to loot boxes in an effort to determine whether the activity of purchasing and opening loot boxes falls under the legal definition of gambling. The chapter will then conclude with an informative overview of how loot boxes have been regulated in other countries and in the US.

Gambling Law in the US: A General Overview

In order to understand whether loot boxes can (or should) be legally recognized as gambling, it is pivotal to first know the legal definition of gambling in the US. One of the aspects of gaming law that makes such evaluation so difficult, however, is that the law governing what activities constitute gambling varies depending on the jurisdiction in which such activity takes place. While such variation is naturally bound to result in complexity when scholars attempt to partake in a broad evaluation of the legality of such activities, there is a general consensus that three elements must be present in an activity in order for it to be considered gambling: (1) consideration; (2) chance; and (3) a prize of value.[4]

Consideration

The legal field defines consideration as a benefit bargained for and received by each party to a transaction.[5] It is predominantly relevant in the field of contract law, as it is required in order for an agreement to be enforceable in the eyes of a court.[6]

While a discussion on the evolution and history of the legal concept of consideration warrants its own essay, there are two relevant theories of understanding consideration in the context of gaming law: valuable consideration and contract consideration.[7] The *valuable consideration* theory, which is the most common view adopted by US jurisdictions, merely requires that the participant parts with something of value to participate in a prize event.[8] Alternatively, the *contract consideration* theory is a much lower standard which does not require the participant to part with anything of value.[9] Instead, there must only be some sort of detriment or inconvenience to the participant in order to satisfy the element of consideration in this circumstance.[10]

Chance

The element of chance is certainly one of the more complicated elements in the context of the US gambling law, as jurisdictions vary in the manner and method of interpreting whether a game is one of skill or chance for the purpose of satisfying this element. Determining whether a game is one of skill or chance is most prevalent when there is a question as to whether the game in question fits into the definition of a "game of chance" as defined by the applicable jurisdiction's gambling law, especially when such law prohibits taking part in broadly defined "games of chance."

A majority of jurisdictions have adopted the *predominant factor test* to aid in determining whether a game is one of skill or chance. This test requires the court to determine whether chance or skill is the dominant factor in determining the outcome of the game.[11] For example, a card game such as blackjack or poker depends partially on skill, of course, but also depends on the element of chance in the sense that some players may draw better cards than others.[12] In a jurisdiction that follows the predominant factor test, the court would be tasked with determining what exactly is the dominant factor of the game.

A smaller number of jurisdictions have adopted the more strict *material element test*, which deems any game in which chance plays a material role to be one of chance.[13] An older and more subjective test adopted by some jurisdictions, known as the *gambling instinct test*, deems that a game is one of chance if it appeals to one's gambling instinct.[14] Strict jurisdictions may adhere to the *any chance* test, which deems that the presence of (quite literally) *any* element of chance in the determination of the game's outcome is conclusory as to the nature of the entire game, regardless of any skill that may be associated therewith.[15]

While there are various methods implemented in determining whether an activity may be categorized as one of skill or chance, there are instances in which this determination may not be a prevailing issue. Games that merely require the player to pull a lever, for example, are not likely to be subject to these tests because there is no question as to whether the act of pulling such lever requires any "skill." Overall, games that *do not* require the player to exhibit *any* skill are likely to be considered games of chance in almost all jurisdictions, unless otherwise explicitly sanctioned by statute or otherwise.

Prize of Value

The prize of value element is satisfied by the participant's receipt of something of *value* and, for the most part, is relatively easy to identify. "In general, a prize is deemed to be present in an event when a participant can win something of marketable value in excess of the amount paid to enter. For example, on a modern slot machine, players may risk $1.00 for the chance at winning a prize worth thousands of dollars (even if the machine often pays back nothing or less than the amount wagered on most plays)."[16]

But in a world where the definition of "marketable value" is ever-changing, what does this truly mean? The digital marketplace has brought to light a new requirement to redefine the nature of such value for the purpose of conducting a gaming analysis, especially in a world where children and adults alike are eager to obtain in-game content to enhance a game-play experience.

Overall, there is not a clear consensus as to whether digital in-game prizes, such as avatars and cosmetic skins, have "marketable value." The 2018 Ninth Circuit case of *Kater v. Churchill Downs Inc.*, however, provides insight as to how the law and interpretation thereof may seek to adapt to such a marketplace.[17] Therein, the court determined that the "virtual chips" which permitted users to play Big Fish Casino's virtual casino game were a "thing of value" under Washington law, despite Big Fish Casino's insistence otherwise.[18] Particularly, the court found that the chips granted the user the *privilege* of playing the game beyond a mere enhancement thereto, which gave the chips value regardless of their supposed lack of out-of-game value.[19]

The *Kater* holding is not a promise that courts and legislators will be inspired to adopt the view that in-game currency and other digital items have a marketable value for the purpose of determining whether such activity is gambling. Rather, this holding is a clear sign that the definition of "value" in the eyes of the consumer is changing into something more than just a tangible item or currency. While the Washington law is admittedly broad as to the definition of a "thing of value" for the purpose of determining whether the activities in question constitute gambling, the court's determination that a digital item which cannot be legitimately traded in or cashed out has value may inspire other interpretations in light of the ever-changing consumer desires.

Loot Boxes: Are They Gambling?

While a general, simple answer to the question of whether loot boxes are gambling cannot be provided in light of the variation in gaming law across jurisdictions, it is certainly possible to apply the foregoing elements of gambling activities to the act of purchasing and opening loot boxes. Overall, in light of the analysis set forth, there is a high possibility that obtaining, through purchase or otherwise, and opening loot boxes may be considered an gambling activity subject to state and federal regulation.

Consideration

There are various ways players may obtain loot boxes. Depending on the game, the player may be given the opportunity to pay for loot boxes with in-game currency earned through game-play events without spending any real-world currency. Alternatively, players may also have the option to purchase in-game currency *or* loot boxes themselves with real-world currency.

In Blizzard's *Overwatch*, for example, players may purchase two loot boxes, each of which contains up to four items, for $1.99.[20] Blizzard gives players the option of purchasing up to fifty loot boxes at once at a lower cost of $39.99.[21] Players do not *need* to purchase loot boxes, however, and may automatically earn a small number of loot boxes through in-game events and special offers.[22]

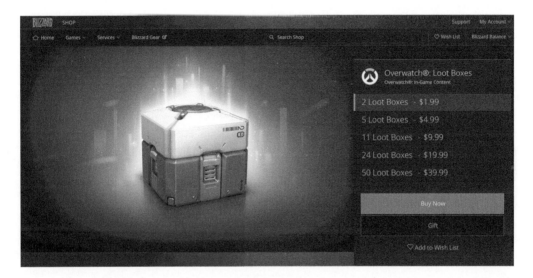

The consideration element is assuredly satisfied in the context of obtaining and opening loot boxes. Most obviously, the player, in return for payment, can receive the loot box in exchange for real-world currency. Even in the event that a player does not exchange real-world money for loot boxes (and, rather, earns them through playing the game itself), the player may satisfy the lower bar of contractual consideration in the sense that the player has expended time and energy in playing the game for prolonged periods of time or, even more simply, logging in. Should the player not have earned the loot boxes for these efforts, it is possible that they would not have logged in at all. While the latter circumstance is obviously the less prominent example, the exchange of real-world currency for in-game loot boxes clearly satisfies the first required element of consideration.

Chance

Unlike many cases in the context of gambling and gaming law, the element of chance is one of the easier elements to evaluate in this circumstance. While a game itself may be challenging, the act of purchasing and opening a loot box does not require any skill.

In *Overwatch,* for example, the player is only required to press and hold a single button in order to open the loot box.[23] Similarly, *League of Legends* players only have to click a single "Open" button in order to reveal the contents of in-game loot boxes called "Hextech Chests."[24] Furthermore, the quality and nature of the content inside of the loot boxes are not related to the skill exhibited by the player in the game. Accordingly, in light of the fact that the contents of loot boxes are predominantly influenced by chance, the act of opening loot boxes satisfies this element.

Prize of Value

The issue of whether the prize of value element is satisfied in this context is complicated by the fact that many in-game items available in loot boxes may not *technically* have real-world value. While it is possible that future legal interpretation of "value" in this context may be influenced by *Kater* as described earlier, the varied nature of gambling legislation across jurisdictions in the US makes application of the Ninth Circuit's perspective in the *Kater* case somewhat arbitrary. However, players have assigned more than just personal value to the items they have obtained through loot boxes; many digital items obtained through loot boxes actually *do* have real-world value despite the fact that the nature of assigning such value may be in violation of the game's terms of service.

UnrankedSmurfs.com is just one example of a website that sells *League of Legends* accounts despite the contractual prohibitions on such behavior.[25] UnrankedSmurfs lists several user accounts "for sale," and such accounts are valued at a certain dollar amount depending on the in-game content available thereon. Much of the content on these accounts is obtained by opening large numbers of loot boxes at different times during which the content is made available by the game developer.[26] An account that has a large amount of exclusive content can be sold for hundreds of dollars.[27]

The developers of *League of Legends* and games similar thereto may not have intended to assign such value to in-game content distributed through loot boxes. Regardless, it is likely that a court presented with the question of whether in-game content has value in this context will take heed of the fact that users have recognized and assigned such monetary value despite the developer's intentions. It is likely that the activity of purchasing and opening loot boxes could satisfy the prize of value element of gambling in light of the fact that users have assigned value to in-game content obtained through loot boxes.

The Global Perspective

While it is apparent that the acts of obtaining and opening loot boxes are likely to be gambling for the purpose of determining whether such activity is subject to legal regulation, the impact of loot boxes on consumers in the video game industry goes far beyond a mere law-centric analysis. With so many games containing loot boxes that are marketed toward, sold to, and beloved by individuals as young as mere preteens, there is a serious concern that children are being exposed to, and may develop, severe gambling problems as they mature.[28] A 2019 study conducted by students at Australia's Deakin University determined that "[m]any of the characteristics of loot boxes are commonly associated with gambling" and that there is an obvious, serious link between the amount of money that players spend on loot boxes and the severity of their problem gambling.[29] Dr. Aaron Drummond of Massey University's School of Psychology analyzed twenty-two popular video games containing loot boxes and concluded that "loot boxes present a number of striking similarities to real-world gambling."[30] Another study published in peer-reviewed journal *Addicted Behaviors* by scientists at the University of British Columbia's Centre of Gambling Research consisted of interviews of 144 adult gamers and 113 undergraduates about their use of loot boxes.[31] The study similarly determined that engagement with loot boxes "is correlated with gambling beliefs and problematic gambling [behavior] in adult gamers."[32]

The global concern about the influence and effects of loot boxes has skyrocketed in recent years. The Chinese government was among the first to take action in response to concerns raised regarding loot boxes in 2017 when it began requiring game developers to disclose the odds of item drops from loot boxes.[33] Such action has since been supported by leading platform providers on which game developers rely, including Sony, Microsoft, and Nintendo.[34] This regulation has since been followed by the Chinese government's efforts to put a daily cap on the number of loot boxes that may be purchased by individual players.[35]

In 2018, the Netherlands Gaming Authority released its results of *Study into loot boxes: A treasure or a burden?* in response to concerns raised by parents, players, and addiction specialists.[36] The study revealed that four out of the ten loot boxes assessed by the Authority contravened Dutch gaming law and could, indeed, result in increased chances of gambling addiction in young adults as a result of the audience's vulnerability.[37] The study resulted in action being taken against such games by Dutch officials, who threatened to sanction popular game developers such as Valve if these practices were not modified.[38] Shortly thereafter, the Belgian Gaming Commission followed suit in ruling that loot boxes in games such as *FIFA 18*, *Overwatch*, and *Counter Strike: Global Offensive* were games of chance in the purview of regulation pursuant to Belgian gaming law.[39] Various other powerful decision-making authorities, including the United Kingdom's House of Commons,[40] the Swedish government,[41] and South Korea's Fair Trade Commission,[42] have made efforts to launch investigations or otherwise if possible regulate loot box gambling within the associated nations. Other countries, conversely, have been apprehensive to take a stand as to whether loot boxes should be considered gambling.[43]

As for the US, there has evidently been little movement in genuine efforts to regulate loot boxes. The Entertainment Software Rating Board (ESRB)[44] made its stance on loot boxes clear in 2017: "While there's an element of chance in these mechanics, the player is always guaranteed to receive in-game content (even if the player unfortunately receives something they don't want). We think of it as a similar principle to collectible card games: Sometimes you'll open a pack and get a brand-new holographic card you've had your eye on for a while. But other times you'll end up with a pack of cards you already have."[45] The ESRB responded to initial criticism on this subject in early 2018 by agreeing to label games that included loot boxes with a general "In-Game Purchases" label.[46] Further criticism led the ESRB to announce changes to their labeling procedure in April 2020.[47] While the label still states that the game includes "In-Game Purchases," the modified version incorporates additional text reading, "(Includes Random Items)," displayed underneath the original notice.[48]

While efforts to regulate loot boxes in the US have not been as obvious, it is important to recognize that several state senators have taken action in an effort to make changes to the industry. In 2018, Hawaii law makers attempted to introduce legislation that would require game developers to disclose the odds of goods available in loot boxes and restrict the sale of games containing such loot boxes to minors.[49] Unfortunately, however, these bills failed to advance.[50] Republican Senator Josh Howley of Missouri similarly proposed the Protecting Children from Abusive Games Bill in 2019,[51] while major media outlets such as NPR have taken notice of the need for such legislation.[52]

Conclusion

Loot boxes are not only becoming part of standard game play; they are becoming part of the lives of millions of children and adults alike who partake in video games every day from what *appears* to be the safety of their own homes.

Notes

1 CadenceLikesVGs, "Thanks, GGG, for Disabling Your Biggest Moneymaker For Me," Path of Exile Forum, Reddit, January 2019, https://old.reddit.com/r/pathofexile/comments/a88w1p/thanks_ggg_for _disabling_your_biggest_moneymaker; Makena Kelly, "How Loot Boxes Hooked Gamers and Left Regulators Spinning," *Verge*, February 19, 2019, https://www.theverge.com/2019/2/19/18226852/ loot-boxes-gaming-regulation-gambling-free-to-play.

2 David Zendle and Paul Cairns, "Video Game Loot Boxes are Linked to Problem Gambling: Results of a Large-Scale Survey," *Plos One* 13 (November 2018): 11, https://doi.org/10.1371/journal. pone.0206767 (citing "In-Game Gambling – The Next Cash Cow for Publishers," *Juniper Research*, April 2018, https://www.juniperresearch.com/document-library/white-papers/in-game-gambling-~-the -next-cash-cow).

3 Mattha Busby, "Loot Boxes Increasingly Common in Video Games Despite Addiction Concerns," *Guardian*, November 22, 2019, https://www.theguardian.com/games/2019/nov/22/loot-boxes-increasingly-common-in-video-games-despite-addiction-concerns (citing David Zendle, Nick Ballou, and Rachel Meyer, "The Changing Face of Desktop Video Game Monetization: An Exploration of Trends in Loot Boxes, Play to Win, and Cosmetic Microtransactions in the Most-Played Steam Games of 2010–2019," *PsyArXiv Preprints*, November 1, 2019, https://psyarxiv.com/u35kt).

4 1 Gaming Law & Practice § 2.02 (2019) citing Stepnes v. Ritschel, 663 F.3d 952, 958 (8th Cir. 2011) ("In most of the United States, non-specific gambling is generally defined as an event where someone risks something of value in the hopes of winning a valuable prize based on the outcome of an uncertain event. Breaking this down into the core elements, the previous general definition can be expressed by stating 'illegal gambling consists of three elements: consideration, chance, and a prize'.")

5 See *Black's Law Dictionary*. 11th ed. Thomson West, 2019.

6 Restatement (Second) of Contracts § 81 (1979).

7 1 Gaming Law & Practice § 2.02 (2019).

8 1 Gaming Law & Practice § 2.02.

9 1 Gaming Law & Practice § 2.02.

10 State ex rel. Schillberg v. Safeway Stores, Inc., 450 P.2d 949, 955 (Wash. 1969) (Under our constitution and lottery statute, therefore, one need not part with something of value, tangible or intangible, to supply the essential consideration for a lottery. He may, in order to secure a chance to win a prize awarded purely by lot or chance, supply the consideration by his conduct or forbearance which vouchsafes a gain or benefit to the promoter of the scheme. The benefit or gain moving to the one need not be the same as the detriment to the other. Consideration for a lottery may be both gain and detriment or one without the other.).

11 California is an example of one of the many states that has adopted the dominant factor test. See People ex rel. Green v. Grewal, 352 P.3d 275, 284 (Cal. 2015) (citing Hotel Emps. & Rest. Emps. Int'l Union v. Davis, 981 P.2d 990, 996 (Cal. 1999). ("[Under California gambling law,] '[c]hance' means that winning and losing depend on luck and fortune rather than, or at least more than, judgment and skill."). "Since customers playing defendants' computer sweepstakes games can exert no influence over the outcome of their sweepstakes entries by means of skill, judgment or how well they play the game, it follows that we are dealing with systems that are based on chance or luck." *Green*, 352 P.3d at 284.

12 While skill is certainly involved in games such as Poker and Blackjack, similar card games have been determined to be games of chance under the predominant factor test. See, e.g., Three Kings Holdings, L.L.C. v. Six, 255 P.3d 1218, 1220 (Kan. Ct. App. 2011); Idaho v. Coeur d'Alene Tribe, 49 F. Supp. 3d 751, 757 (D. Idaho 2014) ("As one court has observed, 'No amount of skill can change a deuce into an ace' and concluding that Texas Hold 'em is a game of chance (quoting Joker Club, L.L.C. v. Hardin, 183 N.C. App. 92, 643 S.E. 2d 626, 630 (N.C. Ct. App. 2007)). "Or, put another way, '[a] player may be skilled at playing the odds but he is still playing the odds.'" *Idaho*, 49 F. Supp. 3d at 757 (quoting Alabama ex rel. Tyson v. Ted's Game Enters., 893 So. 2d 355, 375 (Ala. Civ. App. 2002)).

13 See generally United States v. Gotti, 459 F.3d 296 (2d Cir. 2006) (holding that chance played a material role in determining the outcome of a mechanical poker game called "Joker Poker" and was therefore gambling under New York law).

14 Commonwealth v. Plissner, 4 N.E.2d 241, 245 (Mass. 1936). "It should be noted that there are no court opinions using the Gambling Instinct Test within the last 35 years; however, the older court opinions are still good law and there will always be a risk in certain states with regard to the Gambling Instinct Test." 1 Gaming Law & Practice § 2.02 (2019).

15 See Idaho v. Coeur d'Alene Tribe, 49 F. Supp. 3d at 757 "[The defendant's argument that a player's skill would predominate in a game of Texas Hold'em tournament] might gain traction if Idaho had defined contests of chance to mean games where the outcome depended *mostly*—or to 'a material degree'—upon chance. If that were the case, the Court would probably need to further analyze the game to determine whether chance or skill predominates. But Idaho law does not leave room for this sort of an inquiry.".

16 1 Gaming Law & Practice § 2.02.

17 Kater v. Churchill Downs Inc., 886 F.3d 784 (9th Cir. 2018).

18 *Id*. at 786–88.

19 *Id*. at 787.

20 "Overwatch®: Loot Boxes," Battle.Net, accessed May 13, 2020, https://us.shop.battle.net/en-us/product/overwatch-loot-box.

21 "Overwatch Loot Boxes."

22 See, e.g., Andrew Reiner, "Overwatch Once Again Gives All Players Five Free Holiday Loot Boxes," *Gameinformer*, December 24, 2019, https://www.gameinformer.com/2019/12/24/overwatch-once-again-gives-all-players-five-free-holiday-loot-boxes.

23 See, e.g., TmarTn2, "x60 OVERWATCH LOOT BOX OPENING!" May 25, 2016, YouTube, https://www.youtube.com/watch?v=gPkK9I1HiuY.

24 Redmercy, "$500+ HEXTECH CHESTS OPENING – League of Legends," April 4, 2016, YouTube, https://www.youtube.com/watch?v=qtzppiBT8rM.

25 "Buy League of Legends Account," Unranked Smurfs, accessed May 13, 2020, https://www.unrankedsmurfs.com.

26 It is relevant to note that some of the content made available on these accounts may have also been purchased with in-game currency at some point during the exclusivity period while *also* being obtainable through loot boxes. Regardless of how the content was functionally obtained (through in-game purchases or through randomized loot boxes), it is important to note that the content *can* be earned through randomized loot boxes and has been assigned a real-world value. In the context of traditional gambling, for example, one can purchase as many poker chips as they would like. In determining whether those poker chips have value, it is not relevant to determine *how* they were obtained.

27 See, e.g., "North America League of Legends Acccount: NEO PAX SIVIR AND PAX SIVIR," Unranked Smurfs, accessed May 13, 2020, https://www.unrankedsmurfs.com/league-of-legends/buy-skins/Xomo3mLN-neo-pax-sivir-and-pax-sivir.

28 Massey University, "Videogame Loot Boxes Similar to Gambling," Medical Xpress, June 19, 2018, https://medicalxpress.com/news/2018-06-videogame-loot-similar-gambling.html. ("Research investigating the exposure of adolescents to simulated gambling suggests that risks such as peer pressure and a dilution of monetary value through the exchange of real currency for virtual currency might facilitate migration to monetary forms of gambling."). Furthermore, it is relevant to note that there are often no options available to players (or parents of players) who wish to disable the loot box function altogether. For people like Cadence, this is certainly an issue; specifically, individuals who wish to avoid the temptation of purchasing or opening loot boxes entirely may not be able to do so. The fact that loot boxes can be earned even without making such a purchase may serve to be especially tempting or dangerous to an individual who is recovering from or still struggling with a gambling addiction which may be triggered by the very act of opening a loot box.

29 Zendle and Cairns, "Video Game Loot Boxes."

30 Massey University, "Videogame Loot Boxes."

31 See Gabriel A. Brooks and Luke Clark, "Associations between Loot Box Use, Problematic Gaming and Gambling, and Gambling-Related Cognitions," *Addictive Behaviors* 96 (September 2019): 26–34, https://doi.org/10.1016/j.addbeh.2019.04.009.

32 Brooks and Clark, "Associations."

33 Chaim Gartenberg, "China's New Law Forces Dota, League of Legends, and Other Games to Reveal Odds of Scoring Good Loot," *Verge*, May 2, 2017, https://www.theverge.com/2017/5/2/15517962/china-new-law-dota-league-of-legends-odds-loot-box-random.

34 Brendan Sinclair, "Nintendo, Sony, Microsoft to Require Loot Box Odds Disclosure," *GamesIndustry.biz*, August 7, 2019, https://www.gamesindustry.biz/articles/2019-08-07-nintendo-sony-microsoft-to-require-loot-box-odds-disclosure.

35 Josh Ye, "China Wants to Limit the Number of Loot Boxes Players Can Buy," *Abacus*, August 15, 2019, https://www.abacusnews.com/digital-life/china-wants-limit-number-loot-boxes-players-can-buy/article/3022774.

36 Netherlands Gambling Authority, "Study Into Loot Boxes: A Treasure or a Burden?" April 10, 2018, 2, https://kansspelautoriteit.nl/english/loot-boxes.

37 Netherlands, "Study," 3–4.

38 See Matt Davidson, "The Netherlands Determines Some Loot Boxes Are Gambling," *IGN*, updated September 6, 2018, https://uk.ign.com/articles/2018/04/20/the-netherlands-determines-some-loot-boxes-are-gambling; Shabana Arif, "The Netherlands Starts Enforcing Its Loot Box Ban," *IGN*, updated June 20, 2018, https://www.ign.com/articles/2018/06/20/the-netherlands-starts-enforcing-its-loot-box-ban.

39 Koen Geens, Deputy Prime Minister, Minister of Justice and Minister of Foreign Affairs, "Loot boxen in drie videogames in strijd met kansspelwetgeving," [Loot Boxes in Three Video Games in

Violation of Gambling Legislation], Press Release, April 25, 2018, https://www.koengeens.be/news/2018/04/25/loot-boxen-in-drie-videogames-in-strijd-met-kansspelwetgeving.

40 Alex Hern and Rob Davies, "Video Game Loot Boxes Should be Classed as Gambling, Says Commons," *Guardian*, September 12, 2019, https://www.theguardian.com/games/2019/sep/12/video-game-loot-boxes-should-be-classed-as-gambling-says-commons.

41 "Swedish Government May Consider New Loot Box Restrictions," iGaming Business, October 29, 2019, https://www.igamingbusiness.com/news/swedish-government-may-consider-new-loot-box-restrictions.

42 Zarmena Khan, "South Korea Is the Latest Country to Launch an Investigation into Loot Boxes and Microtransactions," Playstation Lifestyle, April 20, 2019, https://www.playstationlifestyle.net/2019/04/20/south-korea-addresses-loot-box-controversy.

43 *See* Taylor Wessing, "Recent Developments in France: The Position of the French Regulator Regarding Loot Boxes," Lexology, July 30, 2019, https://www.lexology.com/library/detail.aspx?g=a4802197-8e8e-4387-8b4f-a39e0884a005 ("The only hypothesis identified by the ARJEL [the French Authority for Regulation of Online Games] in which video games including loot boxes fall into the category of gambling is that where 'the player has the possibility to resell in real currency prizes won in the form of virtual objects or game levels, either on the site of the game itself, or on a dedicated site,' since there is in this case an expectation of money gain. For instance, the ARJEL raises the case of virtual objects (swords, shields or magic armors) won during participation in video game competitions which can be transferred for a fee on platforms. Thus, although the cases in which loot boxes can be qualified as gambling within the meaning of French law are marginal, the ARJEL points out that each situation requires a specific examination by its services.").

44 The ESRB is the self-regulatory organization tasked with providing age-appropriate ratings for a majority of the video games released in North America. "About ESRB," ESRB, accessed May 13, 2020, https://www.esrb.org/about.

45 Jason Schreier, "ESRB Says it Doesn't See Loot Boxes as Gambling," Kotaku, October 11, 2017, https://kotaku.com/esrb-says-it-doesnt-see-loot-boxes-as-gambling-1819363091.

46 Paul Tassi, "The ESRB Is Being Willfully Obtuse about Loot Boxes, and Will Never Be Any Help," *Forbes*, February 28, 2018, https://www.forbes.com/sites/insertcoin/2018/02/28/the-esrb-is-being-willfully-obtuse-about-loot-boxes-and-will-never-be-any-help/#c35c8206877a.

47 "Introducing a New Interactive Element: In-Game Purchases (Includes Random Items)," ESRB, April 13, 2020, https://www.esrb.org/blog/in-game-purchases-includes-random-items.

48 ESRB, "Introducing." ("We want to ensure that the new label covers all transactions with randomized elements. *In-Game Purchases (Includes Random Items)* accounts for loot boxes and all similar mechanics that offer random items in exchange for real-world currency or in-game currency that can be purchased with real money.").

49 Michael Brestovansky, "'Loot Box' Bills Fail to Advance," *Hawaii Tribune*, March 24, 2018, https://www.hawaiitribune-herald.com/2018/03/24/hawaii-news/loot-box-bills-fail-to-advance.

50 Brestovansky, "'Loot Box' Bills."

51 "Loot Boxes Should be Banned, Says US Senator," *BBC News*, May 9, 2019, https://www.bbc.com/news/technology-48214293; A Bill to Regulate Certain Pay-to-Win Microtransactions and Sales of Loot Boxes in Interactive Digital Entertainment Products, and For Other Purposes, S.1629, 116th Cong. (2019–2020), https://www.congress.gov/bill/116th-congress/senate-bill/1629/text.

52 Ben Johnson, "Loot Boxes Are a Lucrative Game of Chance, But Are They Gambling?" *NPR: All Things Considered*, October 10, 2019, https://www.npr.org/2019/10/10/769044790/loot-boxes-are-a-lucrative-game-of-chance-but-are-they-gambling.

6.4

LANDMARK CASE

Hart v. Elec. Arts, Inc., 717 F.3d 141 (3d Cir. 2013)

Ryan Hart was a football player who led the 2002–2005 Rutgers University NCAA Men's Division I Football team as its quarterback. As a collegiate athlete, Hart had to adhere to the National Collegiate Athletic Association's (NCAA) amateurism rules. These rules famously (and controversially) prohibit athletes from receiving pay while enrolled at a university and from permitting the use of their name or picture to directly promote the sale or use of any commercial product or service. Electronic Arts, Inc.'s (EA) highly successful *NCAA Football* video game series allows users to play against one another as various college football teams. Recent iterations of the game include more than one hundred virtual teams as well as a slew of in-game digital avatars that resemble their real-life counterparts and share their vital and biographical information. This case centers on the 2006 iteration, *NCAA Football 2006*, in which Rutgers's quarterback contained various features that linked him to Hart. The avatar was 6'2" and 197 pounds, and physically resembled the real-life Hart. The digital quarterback wore number thirteen, which was also Hart's number. Moreover, the avatar shared Hart's home state, home town, and class year.

Frustrated by the fact that EA was profiting off of his likeness without his permission, Hart filed suit against EA in state court alleging, among other things, violation of his right of publicity. EA removed the case to federal district court, which dismissed most of Hart's claims. Hart then filed his second amended complaint, which alleged a right of publicity violation on the grounds that EA (1) replicated his likeness in its *NCAA* series, and (2) used his image to promote the game, particularly in regard to an in-game clip that included actual footage from a Rutgers University football game. EA responded with a motion to dismiss, conceding that although it had violated Hart's right of publicity, it was nevertheless entitled to dismissal or summary judgment on First Amendment grounds. The district court granted EA's motion for summary judgment, and Hart appealed. The Third Circuit then agreed to hear the case.

The Third Circuit began its analysis by noting that video games are entitled to the full force of First Amendment protection. However, New Jersey also recognizes a right of publicity that is intended to safeguard an individual's interest in protecting the commercial use and value of their identity. This case therefore turned on a balancing test between the principles underlying the First Amendment and those underlying the right of publicity. The court proceeded to review the various right of publicity tests adopted across the US, and dismissed all but one for the purposes of this dispute. The predominant use test was adopted in Missouri, which considers whether the predominant purpose of the use of another's identity was expressive or commercial. If expressive, it is valid; if commercial, it is not. The Third Circuit dismissed this test as arbitrary, in that it asks judges to function as art critics. The court then moved on to the *Rogers* test, which was adopted in the Second Circuit but is mostly relevant to trademark-like right of publicity cases, which is not the issue here.

Instead, the court adopted the transformative use test, as it was laid out in California. Borrowing the concept of "transformativeness" from fair use in copyright law, the transformative use test inquires whether the use of an individual's identity "adds something new, with a further purpose or different character, altering the first with new expression, meaning or message." *Campbell v. Acuff-Rose, Inc.*, 510 U.S. 569, 579 (1994). The Third Circuit pointed to the use of the transformative use test in other right of publicity cases involving video games. For example, in *No Doubt v. Activision Publishing, Inc.*, a California court found that the use of unmodifiable avatars that were digital recreations of real-life musicians violated the musicians' right of publicity. 122 Cal. Rptr. 3d 397, 410 (2011). Even though literal reproductions of celebrities may still be "transformative," depending on the context into which the celebrity is placed, placing digital avatars in a context where they perform the same sort of activity that the real-life musician performs supports a right of publicity violation. *Id.*

Applying the transformative use test to the facts at hand, the Third Circuit found that *NCAA Football* did not sufficiently transform Hart's identity to overcome a right of publicity violation. Identity refers to both Hart's likeness and his biographical information, and the combination of the two of these had not been sufficiently transformed. For one, the digital avatar resembled Hart in hair color, hair style, skin tone, and accessories. As noted earlier, the avatar and the real-life player shared the same physical build and shirt number. Moreover, the context in which the avatar was placed favored a right of publicity violation. The court wrote that "the digital Ryan Hart does what the actual Ryan Hart did while at Rutgers: he plays college football, in digital recreations of college football stadiums, filled with all the trapping of a college football game." *Hart v. Electronic Arts, Inc.*, 717 F.3d 141, 166 (3d Cir. 2013). To this end, EA's appropriation of Hart's identity mirrored that of Activision in the *No Doubt* case.

The primary difference between this case and *No Doubt* is the presence of in-game customization of avatar appearance. In fact, this was the dispositive feature in the district court's decision to sustain EA's motion for summary judgment. However, the Third Circuit found that the mere presence of avatar customization was insufficient to overcome a right of publicity violation. The court warned that ruling otherwise would lead to "cynical abuse," because "if the mere presence of the feature were enough, video game companies would commit the most blatant acts of misappropriation only to absolve themselves by including a feature that allows users to modify the digital likeness." *Id.* at 167. Moreover, Hart's likeness is the default position, and tweaking his appearance (users could not change his biography) may even constitute the sorts of "trivial" variations that the transformative use test intends to protect against. *Id.* at 168. As a result, the Third Circuit concluded that EA's use of Hart's identity in its video game series did not sufficiently transform Hart's identity to overcome a right of publicity claim.

A slew of video game genres benefit from using the identities of real people, and this case illustrates one of the primary legal hurdles that companies creating such games must clear. The transformative use test also offers a valuable glimpse into how various areas of intellectual property law dovetail with one another. The right of publicity and copyright both aim to protect intellectual property: Copyright safeguards ownership of creative works, while the right of publicity targets property as an extension of one's identity (Hart's identity stemmed from his football accomplishments, which are the product of time, skill, and labor). The use of a prominent copyright concept in a different area of intellectual property law may even suggest that such borrowing may become more commonplace over time.

PART VII

Fashion

Introduction

Fashion designers encounter challenges when they try to rely on copyright law to protect their fashion designs because, strictly speaking, fashion design has never been protected by the US Copyright Act even though more than 100 bills to protect it have been introduced since 1914. (None have passed.) Garments are not protected in the US because they are considered "useful articles" and outside the scope of copyright. (Fashion "design" refers to the actual cut and assembly of the garment, not the drawings or sketches the designer makes, or the fabric from which the garment is constructed, which may be protected.) The Copyright Act, in § 101, excludes useful articles from copyright protection unless an article incorporates pictorial, graphic, or sculptural features that can be identified separately and exist independently of the "utilitarian aspects of the article." Consequently, it is generally not against the law to copy the precise construction of a garment, and because of this, key segments of the garment industry are based on making inexpensive knock-offs of more expensive designer fashions. This exception to copyright protection is specific to US law. The European Union, for example, provides copyright protection for fashion design (although of shorter duration than for other copyright protection) if the design is "new" and possesses "individual character."

Although fashion design is not protected, original fabric patterns (even lace or the decorative weave of a sweater) can be protected, if the pattern displays even a minimal level of originality. In the past, courts have deemed a shaded polka dot textile pattern[1] and a rose-themed fabric pattern made from public domain elements[2] protectable because they were minimally original. However, because so much current fabric design incorporates public domain elements, easily found in this digital age, the current trend in the courts is to scrutinize the degree of originality in designs made from public domain elements or works from nature, and if copyright protection is granted at all, it is a "thin" and narrow copyright which provides protection only against very close or nearly identical copies. Recent cases have, however, protected appliqués of strawberries, daisies, hearts, tulips, and even leafy "fall" designs because the selection and arrangement evidenced minimal originality. Without copyright protection, fashion designers turn to other areas of intellectual property law for protection of their brand, such as trademark, trade dress, and even design patents. The chapters that follow explore the scope of protection available to designers, and the particular issues that designers face in the twenty-first century.

In "Buyer Beware: Copyright Issues in the Fashion Industry," authors Jeffrey Kobulnik and Michael Bernet of Brutzkus Gubner in Los Angeles detail how copyright law is being used (or, rather, misused) as an offensive tool to stifle creativity. Their chapter details how companies register fabric designs that contain non-protectable public domain elements and then use that copyright registration to bring actions against competitor companies that also used similar non-protectable elements or concepts in their fabric designs. This practice is becoming more common because many companies source designs overseas, with different copyright regimes. This chapter asserts that some textile companies' business models hinge on extracting settlements from lawsuits based on fabric designs containing non-protectable elements because it is often less expensive for the defendant to settle than to defend against even a frivolous suit. The authors suggest that these fabric design infringement suits are on the rise in the US (more than 5,000 per year), in part because the Copyright Office, unlike the US Patent and Trademark Office, which will search for "prior art" before issuing a patent, does not scrutinize fabric design registrations for copyrightability, nor does it maintain a searchable database of registered designs (or any other prior registrations).

"Hermes in Hermès: Searching for Boundaries in Non-Traditional Trademarks and Copyrights," by Olivera Medenica of Dunnington Bartholow & Miller, LLP, provides an overview of the colorful history of copyright and fashion design in the US, and even questions whether copyright protection is needed for an industry that generates 100 billion US dollars in revenue annually. This chapter explains how the perceived need for protection has grown as fashion moved into the mass market and digital technology allows designs to be pirated soon after they first appear on the runway. Even though design piracy was not so much a problem when fashion was the domain of the rich, in the early twentieth century, designers banded together and formed the Fashion Originators Guild to decrease design piracy and promote original designs. The Guild was effective at combating design piracy until 1941 when the Supreme Court held that it violated antitrust laws. No other group has been as effective at curbing piracy, so designers—from Hermès (Birkin bag), to Louis Vuitton (red sole on shoes), to Adidas (three stripes)—have turned to aggressive use of trademark and trade dress to protect their designs. Medenica examines the success of these alternate areas.

Finally, an interview with Barbara Kolsun, a Professor of Practice at Cardozo Law School, leading fashion industry lawyer, and author of seminal texts on fashion law, covers some of the key issues in fashion law today, including sustainability and managing the world of social media. In the interview, Kolsun discusses the *Star Athletica* case in which the Supreme Court decided that "chevron" designs on cheerleader uniforms were protected because they could be "separated," but Kolsun notes that although the case received a lot of attention, it only clarified existing law, rather than creating new precedent.[3] Finally, she makes the case that some sort of limited term copyright protection for fashion design would protect newer designers who do not have the funds to protect themselves from piracy.

Notes

1 Prince Group Inc. v. MTS Products, 967 F. Supp. 121 (S.D.N.Y. 1997).
2 Folio Impressions, Inc. v. Byer California, 752 F. Supp. 583 (S.D.N.Y. 1990).
3 Star Athletica, LLC v. Varsity Brands, Inc., 137 S. Ct. 1002 (2017).

7.1

BUYER BEWARE

Copyright Issues in the Fashion Industry

Jeffrey A. Kobulnick and Michael A. Bernet

Copyright law is meant to incentivize the creation of "original works of authorship" for a limited number of years. While that sounds good in principle, the reality is that, in the fashion industry, copyrights are being used offensively in a manner that actually stifles creativity.

There are many companies today in the textiles industry, as well as other industries, such as jewelry, that are registering designs with the US Copyright Office that contain non-protectable public domain elements and then using their registration certificates as swords against unsuspecting third parties who use similar non-protectable elements or concepts in their own designs. That is, some companies are attempting to augment the purpose of copyright law by claiming that it grants them the exclusive right to use certain common and unprotected design elements by including them within a larger work and then claiming rights to the individual non-protectable elements rather than the work as a whole. While copyright law does appropriately grant protection to "particular arrangements" of individual non-protectable elements, unjustifiable infringement claims are frequently made against sufficiently dissimilar works that are also largely comprised of arrangements of individual non-protectable elements, especially within the fashion industry.

Claims are also commonly made against designs appearing on garments that, while similar, are so common and/or simple that one might reasonably believe (and perhaps justifiably) that the designs are not even sufficiently "original" to qualify for protection in the first place (such as floral prints, animal skins, and geometric patterns), or at least the scope of their protection should be so incredibly narrow that practically only a "virtually identical" design should be considered infringement (which is actually the standard for infringement of designs that contain individually non-protectable elements). The reality, however, as discussed further below, is that the cost and risks of defending against infringement claims in the US are so high (not even counting the potential costs of investigation) that it typically makes more sense from a financial perspective to settle claims quickly, even in cases where both designs comprise basic arrangements of public domain elements and where the designs are less than virtually identical. Additionally, juries often overlook dissimilarities, public domain elements, and other factors (besides the artwork) that contributed to an ultimate customer's decision to purchase a certain garment, and inappropriately conclude that infringement occurred and award plaintiffs excessive monetary judgments.

The standard test for copyright infringement in the US is "substantial similarity." That test is very vague, practically undefined and unpredictable, as reasonable minds can and do differ about what exactly it means, or where the proverbial line should be drawn for different works that involve similar concepts. This is especially true for works, such as fabric designs, that consist of arrangements of common non-protectable elements, which are supposed to be filtered out of the infringement analysis by law. For that reason, defendants often settle infringement claims because leaving the substantial similarity analysis to an untrained jury (along with the duty to filter out non-protectable elements) is inherently risky, and could even be fatal for some textile design companies who are typically contractually required to indemnify their retailer customers. Oftentimes, juries simply just compare the overall similarity of two fabric designs immediately upon seeing them and make their conclusions rather quickly. They do not consider (or even have reason to know) that many of the design elements contained in the designs are already in the public domain. As such, public domain design elements should be filtered out of the analysis and/ or may be appropriate grounds for cancelling a copyright registration altogether since the heavy reliance on and inclusion of public domain elements may mean that the registered work is not even sufficiently original to warrant protection in the first place, or that its scope of protection should be incredibly narrow.

For the textiles companies who purchase or license their designs domestically, if they get hit with an infringement or indemnification claim, the textiles companies can usually make a claim for indemnification against their suppliers under the Uniform Commercial Code, or pursuant to their own contractual terms. But oftentimes, textiles companies purchase their designs or finished garments from overseas, including in open markets, where they may be unable to locate their suppliers, sue them, or enforce any judgment against them. Even if there are procedures for making international claims and enforcing judgments, it is often not worth the trouble from a financial perspective. In the end, it is typically a domestic textiles company that gets stuck holding the bag when an infringement claim is made.

To some, the answer to this problem may seem obvious: use only original artwork on your garments. Some companies do exactly that and create everything in-house from scratch. But for many companies in the fashion industry, there is a long tradition of designers taking preexisting works, whether by licensing protected ones or using public domain elements, and modifying the works in some way to create a new work, for example, by changing the colors, or adding or removing elements. There is a prevalent myth among designers that if they modify another's work by a certain amount, such as 30 percent, then it is not infringement. That myth, however, is 100 percent wrong. Any modification of any particular protected work is inevitably a "derivative work" and, therefore, an infringement if the use is unauthorized. While there are "fair use" defenses to creations of derivative works in copyright law, such as the second work being considered "transformative" of the first and therefore protected by free speech principles, those defenses are often unsuitable in cases involving fabric designs that merely consist of arrangements of geometric shapes and patterns.

Textiles companies often genuinely believe that their garments contain original artwork that is free from any claims of infringement, and do not realize that similar works or concepts are out there. Part of the problem is that the US Copyright Office database is not sufficiently searchable, so there is practically no way for fashion designers and their customers to know with reasonable certainty if another work exists that is potentially too similar to their own. Indeed, it is not possible to view images of designs registered with the Copyright Office. Further, the Copyright Office does not maintain a database of public domain elements, so designers typically must rely on their own intuition as to what design elements they believe may be common and free for all to use. The current model is flawed because the world cannot see (or hear) what an author has created when they search the Copyright Office's records; rather, they can currently only see the facts stated in a registration certificate. The Copyright Office's database needs to be more searchable so that textiles companies and distributors can actually search for preexisting designs with certain elements and evaluate the similarity of the designs appearing on their garments against registered ones before they sell, manufacture, or buy them from overseas.

Improving the searchability of the Copyright Office's database will also greatly assist those defending against unjustified infringement claims that are founded on fabric designs that consist of arrangements of non-protectable elements. There are many companies that are registering designs that contain public domain elements, which means that those registered designs may not actually be sufficiently "original" enough to warrant copyright protection, those registrations should be cancelled or at least limited in scope, and those limitations should be clearly explained in the certificates (e.g. by describing the public domain elements that they contain).

Part of the problem is also that the Copyright Office does not seem to seriously vet the originality of the designs that are submitted, or the inclusion of public domain elements in those designs, likely because the task of doing so would be overly burdensome and cost-prohibitive, given the current model. The Copyright Office's staff who are tasked with evaluating new copyright applications do not search and compare the Copyright Office's own records of prior registered designs against the designs contained in new applications—like the US Patent and Trademark Office is able to do with its records and applications—leaving the Copyright Office's staff to rely on an applicant's representations with respect to originality and effectively rubber-stamp applications. As a result, many fabric designs are registered every year that should instead be rejected because they consist of public domain elements, which may be virtually identical to preexisting designs. Further, as indicated earlier, well-intentioned designers and companies cannot see what is actually registered if they were to try to search for similar designs on the Copyright Office's online database. The companies (usually) are not trying to copy, but rather are trying to find inspiration. They should be able to take some steps to clear a design before manufacturing instead of just relying on the representations of their suppliers or (potentially uneducated) designers. Oftentimes, a designer will rely on the same or similar inspiration materials (whether in the public domain or not) as the plaintiffs claiming infringement. To help address these problems, the Copyright Office should not only improve the searchability of its online database, but should also develop software that can identify public domain elements in new applications, train its staff attorneys to evaluate new applications against current registrations, and perhaps even create a division that is specifically dedicated to evaluating textile designs.

Another part of the problem is that there is a strong presumption in litigation that if the Copyright Office has issued a registration certificate, it is valid. It is a black letter law that copyright registrations actually constitute only "prima facie" evidence of the validity of a copyright, but perhaps too much weight is being given to these registration certificates (because they are not seriously vetted during the application process), and it can be incredibly arduous and expensive to investigate originality claims as the courts place the burden of proof on defendants to disprove the validity of a copyright registration. As there is no centralized database of public domain elements, researching these issues can be like trying to find a needle in a haystack—a very old haystack that was created long before digital records existed. This often makes it very difficult for alleged infringers to exonerate themselves, even in cases where the registered work contains very common and basic public domain elements and should therefore never have been registered, or at least the scope of its protection should be narrowed.

The problem is also compounded by the scope of copyright protection being perhaps broader today than it was originally intended, as demonstrated by some relatively recent court decisions. In 1991, for example, the US Supreme Court in *Feist* said that "the requisite level of creativity" needed to obtain copyright protection "is extremely low; even a slight amount will suffice."[1] Even more recently, in 2012, the Ninth Circuit stated in *L.A. Printex* that "there are gazillions of ways" to arrange flowers and their components on fabric, and each of them is copyrightable.[2]

The bar is so low now to obtain a copyright registration, and seemingly extends to even the most basic arrangements of individually non-protectable elements, that some textiles companies are able to register just about anything, and then use those registration certificates as tickets to make infringement claims against designers (and their manufacturers and retailer customers) of garments bearing similar concepts (even though concepts are not protectable by copyright law, only particular expressions are).

The problem is also made worse by plaintiffs registering entire designs without disclosing the public domain elements (or already protected elements) in their applications, as they are supposed to do, which is considered fraud on the Copyright Office and is a basis for cancellation. It is also very expensive for alleged infringers to investigate let alone prevail against copyright claims. If a lawsuit has already been filed, a defendant can request discovery from the copyright claimant, but there is no guarantee that the claimant will be forthcoming about the public domain elements contained in the registered designs. It can be extremely difficult (and expensive) to research similar old public domain designs, and retaining expert witnesses may be necessary to help with this task. Oftentimes, both plaintiffs and defendants source their designs and/or design elements from overseas, which can make it even more difficult to investigate whether they include public domain elements. Defensive investigation efforts also are often hindered because there is currently no requirement for copyright claimants to produce the "deposit copies" of their works (what they submitted to the Copyright Office as part of their applications) when they file an infringement claim, although defendants will typically (and should) request copies during discovery as some plaintiffs base their infringement claims on portions of their registered works as opposed to the works as a whole (which may be improper as the Copyright Office approved of the entire design, not its individual components).

Before a lawsuit is ever filed, or even during a lawsuit, a defendant can obtain a deposit copy of a registered work from the Copyright Office on an expedited basis, but even that currently takes approximately three months and costs around $1,200. This time delay can, and often is, disastrous to textiles companies that are forced to expend a significant amount of money defending claims against themselves and their retailer customers, long before ever seeing the full deposit copy. To make things worse, some judges now schedule trials to commence within just a few months of a complaint being filed (often because their dockets are so overloaded and they want to pressure the parties to settle quickly), which means that a defendant may not even have sufficient time to conduct an investigation into the originality of the registered work after receiving the deposit copy. To help address this problem, the US Congress and/or the courts should require copyright plaintiffs to attach their full deposit copies to their complaints, or at least otherwise make them immediately available to the defendants at the time they are served with a lawsuit.

Textiles companies are typically contractually required to indemnify their retailers, who usually make the most profits. The designers and manufacturers typically have slim margins, but they (at least the domestic ones) are the ones on the hook for defending copyright infringement claims against themselves and their retailer customers (and there are often many in any single case) as well as paying for all of their attorneys' fees and court costs, even if they ultimately defeat the claim. Consequently, defending these types of lawsuits is very expensive, but that is part of the cost of doing business with retailers.

Additionally, once a fabric design company or manufacturer gets hit with an infringement claim, they often find themselves the target of even more claims because they are now on the plaintiff's (and their attorneys') radar and because the claims may be related to a common designer who regularly modified and/or borrowed from preexisting works. In the latter instance the designer did not realize he or she should not have borrowed from preexisting works and ended up creating many unauthorized derivative works over many years. To address this, textiles companies should regularly train their employees on copyright law principles, and have systems in place to help prevent infringement claims, including maintaining detailed records of how each fabric design was created, sourced, and/or modified. Maintaining these types of records will not only greatly help a textiles company exonerate itself when it gets hit with an infringement claim by demonstrating that it properly licensed its source materials and/or independently created its designs and elements, but these records will also greatly reduce the time and work needed to defend a claim (i.e. lower defense costs), and allow the companies (and their attorneys) to better evaluate the merits of new claims and put them in a better position to decide whether it makes more sense to settle or defend against such claims.

Sometimes, alleged infringers have insurance. When they do not have insurance, it is more expensive to defend and/or settle a claim. Even more, the ones that do have insurance are sometimes denied coverage, or do not actually have as much coverage as they thought. For example, many general commercial liability insurances plans do not cover copyright infringement claims unless they are phrased in terms of an "advertising injury." Further, unless there are highly unusual circumstances (i.e. "objectively unreasonable" conduct by a plaintiff or its attorneys), courts will generally not award attorneys' fees to a prevailing defendant. Domestic textiles companies that sourced infringing designs from overseas can request monetary contributions to any judgment or settlement payment (if those sources can even be found), but the overseas suppliers generally deny liability and refuse to contribute in any meaningful way. As previously mentioned, the domestic companies can try suing the overseas suppliers, but it is often futile or too costly of an effort.

The result is that companies facing copyright infringement lawsuits may be forced to close or seek bankruptcy protection, even when they did nothing wrong. Facing this reality, many alleged infringers choose to settle claims quickly rather than defend and potentially lose more money regardless of the merits of the case. To make matters even worse, many plaintiffs and their attorneys not only know this—they count on it. That is, there are some textiles companies (and law firms) that have become prolific filers of copyright infringement claims in the US based on fabric designs, including both warranted and unwarranted claims, because extracting large settlement payments has become part of their regular business model. Some attorneys in particular have become well known for their "sue and settle" method of litigation, demanding large settlement payments regardless of the merits of their clients' claims because they know (and will even brazenly articulate in the context of a protected settlement communication) that it is cheaper to settle than defend (even if the defendant wins). Some of these textiles companies are essentially professional plaintiffs, and it is likely that some of them make even more money annually from suing third parties for infringement than from producing designs and garments, which is supposed to be their core business.

Copyright infringement claims within the apparel industry have become increasingly common. Between 2007 and 2011, there were approximately 2,000 to 3,000 copyright infringement lawsuits filed each year in the US (although that number includes all copyright infringement cases, not just fabric design cases). Since 2012, that number has increased to between 3,000 and 5,000 lawsuits each year. Most of the fabric design infringement cases are filed by only a handful of plaintiffs and law firms. Most of the cases are also filed within only a handful of judicial districts where the same plaintiffs and law firms are located, namely in the Central District of California and the Southern District of New York. As a result, those districts (which are also among the busiest judicial districts in the US) are becoming seriously congested with these types of cases.

As detailed, fabric design infringement cases have become a major problem for unsuspecting textiles companies and the judicial system. There are several things that can and should be done to address this growing problem. First, textile design companies should make every effort to use only original designs. They should also train their design team to better understand copyright law, and what can and cannot be used as part of their "new" designs. They should also maintain detailed records of their source materials, and purchase and license designs and elements only from trustworthy sources (who they can actually locate, sue, and enforce a judgment against, if need be). In other words, while it may seem less expensive in the short term, ultimately it may not be a good idea to purchase designs from overseas sources.

Additionally, textiles companies should be sure to include indemnification agreements in all of their purchase orders, just in case they do get hit with a claim. If a company does get a claim, they should check to see if the claim may be covered by insurance, consider early settlement, and conduct an internal investigation into what happened in order to prevent repeat occurrences. Finally, the Copyright Office desperately needs to improve its online database to become more searchable, and claimants should be required by law to attach their full deposit copies to any infringement complaints. Until those measures are taken, we will likely continue to see an increase in the number of both warranted and unwarranted fabric design infringement claims that are filed each year.

Notes

1 Feist Publ'ns., Inc. v. Rural Tel. Serv. Co., Inc., 499 U.S. 340, 345 (1991).
2 L.A. Printex Indus., Inc. v. Aeropostale, Inc., 676 F.3d 841, 850–51 (9th Cir. 2012), as amended on denial of reh'g and reh'g en banc (June 12, 2012).

7.2

HERMES IN HERMÈS

Searching for Boundaries in Non-Traditional Trademarks and Copyrights

Olivera Medenica

The relationship between copyright and fashion design in the US has a colorful history that may seem unjust to those unfamiliar with the fundamental principles of copyright law. While French laws have provided intellectual property protection to fashion designs since the Industrial Revolution, the US has remained stalwart in its refusal to do the same. The fashion industry, creative as it is, has managed to make do with a patchwork of intellectual property laws not well suited for sartorial redress. Protecting a fashion design thus means navigating murky intellectual property and geographical boundaries where protection may seem as elusive as the missing buttons of a sarong. In an industry as cross-border-driven as fashion, the endless complexity of different intellectual property frameworks may seem almost impossible to navigate for the novice fashion designer seeking some level of certainty as to what can or cannot be protected.

Hermes and Hermès: Not So Simple

In Greek mythology, Hermes was one of the twelve Olympian gods who was known to be quick and cunning, moving between mortals and the divine, thus representative of boundaries and transitions. He was known as the Greek god of trade, eloquence, and the messenger of gods. Not unlike Hermes, fashion brands must learn to cunningly navigate between different worlds, judicial systems, and regulatory frameworks in attempting to register what may appear as a deceptively simple design. Some well-known brands have managed to do so successfully, while others have not.

French luxury brand Hermès, for example, was able to successfully register its famous "Birkin" handbag as a trademark with the US Patent and Trademark Office (USPTO). Its trade dress is defined by "(a) a distinctive three lobed flap design with keyhole shaped notches to fit around the base of the handle, (b) a dimpled triangular profile, (c) a closure which consists of two thin, horizontal straps designed to fit over the flap, with metal plates at their end that fit over a circular turn lock, (d) a padlock which fits through the center eye of the turn lock and (e) typically, a key fob affixed to a leather strap, one end of which is affixed to the bag by wrapping around the base of one end of the handle." Even the straps and hardware, which includes the turn lock and padlock, are the subject of a separate trade dress registration. Hermès was able to do so, however, because its Birkin bag has received considerable coverage in the press, including a stint on HBO's *Sex and the City*, and is generally well known to consumers. These are some of the essential factors that would warrant trade dress protection under the US law.

Conversely, while Hermès successfully secured protection for its design, other brands were unable to do so despite the fame of the product itself. For example, Cult Gaia sought trade dress

273

protection for its popular "Ark" bag, a structured handbag made of interlocking rigid strips arranged in a half-moon shape. The design shot to fame after it saturated fashionable circles on Instagram and became the hottest accessory of summer 2017. Given its fame, Jasmin Larian, Cult Gaia's owner, rightfully sought to capitalize on the bag's success and submitted a trademark application with the USPTO for the bag's three-dimensional design. The application, however, was preliminarily denied based upon functionality—a nonnegotiable ground for finding trade dress invalid. This determination was based upon the examiner's purported finding that Cult Gaia's design, which consists of a "half-moon shaped carrying-bag," is "merely an iteration or appropriation of a style of bag from the Japanese culture." In other words, if Cult Gaia were granted a trademark, it would according to the examiner, preclude others from designing vintage "generic Japanese lunch bag[s] common in fishing communities for decades."

For related reasons, when it comes to copyright, protecting such three-dimensional designs is even more difficult to obtain. This is because copyright protection is not available to apparel and accessories as they are deemed to be "useful items." While there may be significant exceptions to this rule, it is by far the most significant barrier to obtaining a copyright in fashion designs.

Protection of fashion designs is thus a complicated matter in the US. This essay will examine the boundaries between different intellectual property rights, and in particular, between copyright and trademark law. We examine the evolution of copyright law as it pertains to fashion design, and compare it with other traditional and non-traditional intellectual property rights. This essay will finish with a look at the latest case law applying these principles.

The Twentieth-Century Fashion Industry in the US

In the early twentieth century, the fashion industry in the US was vastly different from its modern counterpart. It certainly was not the thriving and robust industry that it is today, and was generally considered to be something only engaged in by the elite social class. Outside of this limited environment, apparel served a functional purpose and was bought for the limited purpose of replacing a worn item. Up until the 1930s, women's fashion magazines often presented illustrations for clothing patterns and women made their own clothes at home. Near the end of the Great Depression, however, the Roosevelt administration sought to standardize women's clothing, and American women were measured to formulate average sizing. This paved the way for mass production of clothing for the American market, which flourished as consumers' post-war purchasing power increased.

As a result, design piracy in the early twentieth century was not necessarily a mass market concern, but rather the concern of a select group of consumers fortunate enough to participate in the fashion industry. In other words, if any copying was taking place, it was limited and did not occur on a large, nationwide scale.

Nonetheless, design piracy concerns did exist, and fashion designers took matters into their own hands. In 1932, the Fashion Originator's Guild (the Guild) was established in the US by fashion industry insiders who manufactured, sold, and distributed women's garments, and in particular, dresses. The purpose of the Guild was to decrease design piracy and promote original designs among the US designers. Members of the Guild registered not only themselves, but their designs by submitting sketches to protect their creations. The Guild also employed "shoppers" to visit various stores of cooperating and non-cooperating retailers "for the purpose of examining their stocks, to determine and report as to whether they contain . . . copies of registered design."[1] Should the "shoppers" identify an infringement, the Guild possessed an elaborate system of trial and appellate tribunals to determine whether the garment was, in fact, an infringing design. The Guild was highly effective at combating design piracy, and during its tenure, more than 60 percent of women's apparel was designed by Guild members.

As all good things must come to an end, the Guild was eventually abolished by the US Supreme Court in 1941. In *Fashion Originators' Guild, Inc. v. FTC*, the Supreme Court held that the Guild's activities violated the Sherman and Clayton Anti-Trust Acts.[2] The Federal Trade Commission had issued a complaint against the Guild in 1936, held hearings, and ultimately found that it had engaged in a pattern of conduct that constitutes an unfair method of competition, thus requiring the Guild to cease its activities. The Guild appealed, which led to the Supreme Court's ruling. Portions of the Court's decision bear a striking resemblance to modern-day piracy concerns, and highlight the lack of intellectual property protection for fashion design extant then, and frankly, now:

> The garment manufacturers claim to be creators of original and distinctive designs of fashionable clothes for women, and the textile manufacturers claim to be creators of similar original fabric designs. After these designs enter the channels of trade, other manufacturers systematically make and sell copies of them, the copies usually selling at prices lower than the garments copied. Petitioners call this practice of copying unethical and immoral and give it the name of 'style piracy.' And although they admit that their 'original creations' are neither copyrighted nor patented, and indeed assert that neither existing legislation affords them no protection against copyists, they nevertheless urge that sale of copied designs constitutes an unfair trade practice and a tortious invasion of their rights.[3]

Since then, there has been no other US-based trade organization that has functioned as effectively as the Guild in combating design piracy. In 1962, the Council of Fashion Designers of America (CFDA) was founded to provide professional development support to American designers. While the CFDA is an established organization in the fashion industry, it does not police nor remove "style piracy" from stores.

Today's Fashion Industry and Piracy

Today, women's fashion is a $100 billion industry, and unfortunately, copying is rampant. There are a multitude of designs available in the marketplace for dresses, shoes, belts, and accessories, yet there is no all-encompassing right in the US that would protect such designs. Many designers invest a lot of time and money only to find their creations instantly replicated in knockoff designs and sold at significantly reduced or bargain basement prices. Some argue that this cycle benefits the fashion industry as a whole and pushes the fashion cycle forward to new creations. Others argue that offering knockoffs at such different price points does not impact a design house's income as the average consumer could not even afford the original design in the first place.

Conversely, some argue that protection is long overdue, and that creativity is wasted, and revenues lost, where design piracy is left rampant and unrestricted by any design right. The reason this debate has endured for so long is that copyright does not protect things that are functional. As discussed below, when examining what exactly a copyright is supposed to protect, it becomes self-evident that the fashion industry, and more specifically apparel, is an odd fit for intellectual property protection.

Copyright Protection for Fashion Designs

In the US, the Copyright Act does not protect fashion designs. As a three-dimensional item, fashion design would most appropriately fit under the category of "pictorial, graphic, or sculptural work" which includes two-dimensional and three-dimensional works of fine, graphic, and applied art, photographs, prints and art reproductions, maps, globes, charts, diagrams, models, and technical drawings, including architectural plans. Works of artistic craftsmanship are included "insofar as their form but not their mechanical or utilitarian aspects are concerned."[4] This is an important carve out, and governs the extent to which a pictorial, graphic, or sculptural work is subject to certain statutory limitations:

> the design of a useful article . . . shall be considered a pictorial, graphic, or sculptural work [and thus subject to copyright protection] only if, and only to the extent that, such design incorporates pictorial, graphic, or sculptural features that can be identified separately from, and are capable of existing independently of, the utilitarian aspects of the article.[5]

A "useful article" is defined as an "article having an intrinsic utilitarian function that is not merely to portray the appearance of the article or to convey information."[6] The Copyright Act thus grants limited protection to elements of a design that can be identified as separate from the "utilitarian aspect of the article." Given that the purpose of clothing or accessories is to cover the body, or carry things, this creates a bit of a problem when it comes to copyright protection.

The scope of these statutory provisions made the news in 2017 when the Supreme Court decided a case dealing with the copyrightability of cheerleading uniforms. In *Star Athletica, LLC v. Varsity Brands, Inc.*,[7] the Supreme Court answered a deceptively simple question that had puzzled many courts across the country: When is an artistic feature incorporated into the design of a useful article eligible for copyright protection? In this context, the analysis focused on an article of clothing. In other words, the Supreme Court examined whether there is any portion of a cheerleading uniform that is eligible for copyright protection despite the fact that the uniform has an inherently useful, or functional, purpose.

The parties in *Star Athletica* were competing businesses in the design and manufacturing of cheerleading uniforms. Plaintiff Varsity Brands argued that it hired designers who sketch unique designs for Varsity's cheerleading uniforms, and to protect these designs, it had registered hundreds of two-dimensional graphic designs with the Copyright Office, including the designs which were the subject of the lawsuit. After noticing Start Athletica's similar designs, Varsity filed a copyright infringement action claiming that *Star Athletica* copied Varsity's cheerleading uniform designs.

To "give effect to the clear meaning of the statute[] as written," the Court held that "a feature incorporated into the design of a useful article is eligible for copyright protection only if the feature (1) can be perceived as a two- or three-dimensional work of art separate from the useful article and (2) would qualify as a protectable pictorial, graphic, or sculptural work—either on its own or fixed in some other tangible medium of expression—if it were imagined separately from the useful article into which it is incorporated."[8] In other words, if there is a creative portion of the object that is not functional, then that creative portion may potentially benefit from copyright protection.

Applying this standard, the Court held that Varsity Brand's graphic designs—which consist of various geometric arrangements of different colors—could be imagined separately from the cheerleading uniform (i.e. the useful object) on which they were applied and thus were eligible for copyright protection. Put simply, the design itself can be imagined separately because, for example, it could have been painted on canvas. This is important because this hypothetical separation is a conceptual one, and not literal, as it does not matter whether the underlying useful article remains a fully functional article after the separation has taken place. Consider, for example, a lamp where the base is a sculpture, or a belt buckle where the buckle could similarly be deemed a piece of art. In those instances, physical separation is not possible; rather, the analysis is based on conceptual separability.

The *Star Athletica* decision is significant for the legal community because it creates one uniform legal standard, out of many, that addresses this particular issue. For the design community, however, there is not much that has changed as *Star Athletica* merely confirms the long-standing distinction between protectable works of art and non-protectable industrial design.

Indeed, when it comes to apparel, *Star Athletica* confirms that designs that have some form of print, pattern, or other pictorial design on the surface that can be conceptually separated from the underlying garment will benefit from copyright protection. However, if this expressive element is limited to the cut of a sleeve, drape of a dress, or the material used in the garment, then copyright protection would not apply. As much as it is celebrated as a breakthrough decision, *Star Athletica* does not do much in terms of extending copyright protection to fashion designs.

History of Legislative Attempts to Protect Fashion Designs

While the Guild was abolished in the 1930s, that has not stopped the CFDA's lobbying efforts to protect fashion design. Its members have been particularly vocal in combating design piracy and have supported numerous legislative attempts to secure copyright protection for fashion designs. Since 2006, there have been no less than six house bills proposed to amend Title 17 of the US Code (the Copyright Act). None of them has been successful.

The first of these bills, H.R. 5055, was introduced in 2006 by Representative Robert W. Goodlatte (R-Va.). The bill proposed to extend copyright protection to fashion design for a period of three years and would exclude from protection fashion designs that are embodied in a useful article that was made public by the designer or owner more than three months before the registration of the design. Both of these provisions reflect an understanding that trends arise and fade quickly. As a result, a shorter copyright term is sufficient to protect a fashion design, and the three-month window to register a design reflects an understanding that these designs must be registered promptly to benefit from protection. The bill also proposed the creation of a safe harbor where it would not be an infringement to sell or distribute a design if there were no reasonable grounds to know that protection was claimed for such design.

The bill, however, faced substantial opposition from legal experts claiming that copying is an integral and accepted part of the fashion industry. According to critics, an interference in the fashion marketplace would result in increased litigation and stifle creativity, thus resulting in less choice for consumers. Critics compared the US, where no protection is available, to foreign jurisdictions, where protection is available, and concluded that piracy is just as rampant in both regardless of the protection available to fashion designs.

Between 2007 and 2009, three additional bills were introduced, H.R. 2196, H.R. 2033, and H.R. 1957, which together are known as the Design Piracy Prohibition Act (DPPA). As with H.R. 5055, the DPPA sought to expand copyright protection to fashion designs for three years and included similar provisions as H.R. 5055. The DDPA, however, fared much the same way as H.R. 5055.

In 2011, the Innovative Design Protection and Piracy Prevention Act, or H.R. 2511, was also introduced to Congress, followed by S. 3523. Neither passed. Under H.R. 2511, when determining the originality of a garment, "the presence or absence of a particular color or colors or of a pictorial or graphic work imprinted shall not be considered in determining protection of a fashion design." While the bill was meant to be narrow, the latter clause would essentially broaden, not narrow, infringement claims when it pertains to clothing. S. 3523 proposed an amendment to the Copyright Act so that fashion designs would benefit from a three-year term of protection for original elements or arrangements of fashion designs that are the result of a designer's "own creative endeavor" and that "provide a unique, distinguishable, non-trivial and non-utilitarian variation over prior designs for similar types of articles." Critics however claimed that this would result in an increased cost to fashion designers to determine what is a "non-trivial and non-utilitarian variation."

American designers are thus left with no copyright protection for their fashion designs, despite considerable legislative efforts. While it significantly impedes protection, it does not leave fashion designers without recourse, as further discussed below.

An Alternative to Copyright: Trademark and Trade Dress

In the US, fashion designers rely heavily upon trademark and patent law to protect their designs. Each right, however, protects an aspect of the design but not necessarily the design as a whole.

A trademark, for example, protects any word, slogan, design, or combination thereof that identifies the source of the goods and distinguishes them from the goods and services of another party. This means, in the fashion context, that trademark law protects a designer's mark. Examples of a trademark are the interlocking "LV" for Louis Vuitton, or the Cs for Chanel, or the striped eagle for Giorgio Armani. These are distinctive logos that serve as a source identifier for the brand. In other words, when a consumer sees these brands, they expect a certain quality and product.

Trade dress, however, is a category of trademarks that also serves as a source identifier. Trade dress is the total image of a product, which may include features such as size, shape, color or color combinations, textures, or graphics. So, for example, the Birkin bag by Hermès, as discussed earlier, is a trade dress. So are the red soles of the Louboutin high heels, the "Stan Smith" or "Superstar" design of Adidas shoes, or the tasseled look of Aquazzura's "Wild Thing" high heel sandals. These are all distinctive marks that a consumer has come to recognize. For trade dress, however, a fashion designer must jump through a number of hoops to obtain the desired protection. She must show that (1) the design has acquired distinctiveness; and (2) the design is not functional. This means that the designer must show that the design is really well known and recognizable by consumers, and that the feature sought to be protected is not essential to the use or purpose of the article or does not affect the cost or quality of the article. In other words, it must not be functional.

These are not easy questions to answer, and often result in expensive litigation. For example, in *Christian Louboutin S.A. v. Yves Saint Laurent America Holding, Inc.*,[9] Louboutin had filed a trademark infringement suit against Yves Saint Laurent (YSL), claiming that the latter had infringed upon Louboutin's distinctive red sole design. Louboutin had previously obtained a federal trademark registration over its bright-red lacquered outsole. YSL came out with a collection of monochromatic footwear in various colors, including red. Louboutin thus argued that YSL's red monochrome shoe infringed upon his trademark.

YSL, however, sought to cancel Louboutin's trademark by claiming that Louboutin's red sole did not deserve protection because it serves the "functional" purpose of being aesthetically pleasing, or pretty. The Second Circuit, an appellate court based in New York, disagreed with YSL, ultimately ruling that color does not necessarily serve a functional purpose in fashion designs, and that Louboutin's red outsole had become so famous that it had acquired trademark rights. But the Court did not go so far as to state that YSL's shoe infringed on Louboutin's monochromatic shoe design. In other words, it was a very expensive and lengthy lawsuit to simply prove that Louboutin had a valid trademark. Not many start-up designers would have the funds to do the same.

The well-known brand, Adidas, also went to great lengths to protect its "Superstar" design which consists of a low-top sneaker shoe with a three-stripe logo, equidistant holes, toe cap, and tab on the back of the shoe. In 2008, the jury awarded Adidas $305 million in damages against Payless for selling similar looking sneakers with two or four stripes on the side of the shoe.[10] Payless unsuccessfully argued that the use of stripes serves as mere decoration, or ornamentation, and is not a source indicator (which is what trademarks must do to function as trademarks). The court ruled in favor of Adidas, although it ultimately reduced the award figure to $30,610,179, and Payless was left with a substantial fine to pay for it.

Adidas' branding strategy is quite remarkable, however, because it went on to develop this three-stripe brand well beyond its original placement on the side of sneakers. Indeed, Adidas has successfully expanded its three-stripe trademark registration to different garments, including jacket sleeves, athletic training suits, shorts, pants, T-shirts, and, of course, footwear. For apparel, the three diagonal stripes run the entire length of the garment, on sleeves or the sides of pant legs, in what would appear to be a decorative pattern. In doing so, Adidas has successfully secured protection of a design element merely because, over time, this design has come to be associated, in consumers' minds, as originating from Adidas. Adidas strategy, however, has in no small part been successful because it engages in a particularly aggressive litigation strategy, precluding others from using anything remotely resembling three stripes. Again, not something a nascent designer would have the means to do.

While trademark laws can be a powerful tool for design protection, it does not protect the design of a product as a whole. Even the Birkin bag's trade dress protects only limited aspects of the bag, and not the bag as a whole. Similarly, Adidas can only claim protection of the three stripes and not the garment as a whole. Most importantly, trademark laws favor brands that have strong logos, or a distinctive design that consumers can readily recognize. After all, rare are designers, like Louboutin, whose name is included in Beyoncé lyrics, or whose custom crystal-studded designs are regularly worn by the famed singer. This is not to say that lesser known brands cannot obtain trademark protection. On the contrary, they can. But as discussed earlier, *design* protection is another matter.

Despite this lack of protection, the fashion industry has managed to flourish, successfully relying upon porous intellectual property rights that fail to capture the essence of its designs. The future of copyright protection for fashion designs remains elusive as ever, given the lack of industry consensus as to whether protections are warranted in the first place. Perhaps there is hope for a "thin" or limited copyright that would protect fashion designs against identical copies or preclude derivative works from the scope of protection. But the question remains whether such protection would act as a sufficient or effective deterrent against knockoffs or copycats. While Hermes was known as the god of trade, he was also known to be a trickster and even a thief. Much like Hermes, the fashion industry does both, it trades and copies, in a commercial cycle frenetically powered by trends and new designs, managing to delicately balance aesthetics, functionality, and capitalism while capturing our imagination every new season.

Notes

1 Fashion Originators' Guild of Am. v. Fed. Trade Comm'n, 312 U.S. 457, 462 (1941).
2 *Id.*
3 *Id.* at 461.
4 17 U.S.C. § 101 (2018).
5 § 101.
6 § 101.
7 Star Athletica, L.L.C. v. Varsity Brands, Inc., 137 S. Ct. 1002 (2017).
8 *Id.* at 1007.
9 Christian Louboutin S.A. v. Yves Saint Laurent Am. Holdings, Inc., 696 F.3d 206 (2d Cir. 2012).
10 Adidas Am., Inc. v. Payless Shoesource, Inc., No. 01-CV-1655-KI, 2008 WL 4279812 (D. Or. Sept. 12, 2008).

7.3

IDEA/EXPRESSION DICHOTOMY

If the Belt Buckle Fits, You Can Copy It

Interview with Barbara Kolsun

Barbara Kolsun (BK), Professor of Practice and Director of the FAME Center at Cardozo Law School, is a leading fashion industry attorney and co-editor of the seminal texts on the subject, *The Business and Law of Fashion* (Carolina Academic Press, 1st Edition, 2020) and *Fashion Law – A Guide for Designers, Fashion Executives and Attorneys* (Bloomsbury, 2nd ed., 2014). and *The Business and Law of Fashion and Retail*, to be published by Carolina Press in 2020. Kolsun started the legal departments and was the first general counsel of Kate Spade, Stuart Weitzman, and Seven for All Mankind, and was assistant general counsel of Westpoint Stevens and Calvin Klein Jeans. While in private practice, her clients included Ralph Lauren and Tommy Hilfiger. Kolsun currently consults with fashion companies on various issues and was honored with lifetime achievement awards in 2015 by both the Luxury Law Summit in London and the World Trademark Forum at INTA. She has served as Chairman of the Board of the International Anticounterfeiting Coalition and has spoken and been published widely on fashion law around the world. Her experience as a professional singer and actress continues to motivate her fierce efforts to protect artists' and designers' intellectual property rights. She received her JD from Cardozo Law in 1982 and is a member of the Order of the Coif.

Michelle Bogre (MB) interviewed Kolsun in New York City on January 15, 2019. This interview has been edited for length and clarity.

MB: What are the key issues in fashion law these days?

BK: Well, for fashion and retail in general, sustainability, privacy, and managing the world of social media and the fact that advertising has changed so dramatically since Facebook, Google, Instagram and influencers and their social media platforms. Today what sells is what an influencer says or what an influencer shows. Of course, if they're paid influencers, they are subject to the rules and regulations of the Federal Trade Commission (FTC).

Another issue is the fact that US intellectual property law does not protect fashion like the law does in Europe. In the world of fashion, copyright protects jewelry designs, like those of David Yurman, assuming those designs are eventually registered, or things like lace or intricate fabric designs but not very much else. The *Star Athletica* case that the Supreme Court decided last year, which covered designs on cheerleader uniforms, clarifies copyright protection of fashion items.[1] Neither the cut nor the look or feel are protected.

Protection of fashion under US law is very different than it is in Europe because of culture. I don't believe that that will ever change. I think that we are a society of commerce and certainly the new generation of copyright lawyers has a broader view of copyright protection based on changes in technology. Another issue also related to social media is how people shop. So where are we going with retail? My short answer, considering the global pandemic, is Amazon and other online shopping. Finally, fashion designers have to deal with celebrities as ambassadors and influencers for fashion brands. The FAME (Fashion, Arts, Media & Entertainment Law) program at Cardozo was developed to teach lawyers how to counsel creative businesses.

MB: What did the *Star Athletica* case clarify that wasn't clear before? Did it define conceptual separability?

BK: As is often the case, the Supreme Court identified one test to determine the copyrightability of the stripes and chevron designs on cheerleader uniforms. The court was clear that copyright does not protect the cut or design of a garment. Despite numerous attempts to amend the US copyright law to add protection for fashion designs, the law remains unchanged. There's hardly a US fashion designer who doesn't also have a lower price line sold at Target, Kohl's, or Walmart. Designers want to make money and the way to make money is through more of a commercial enterprise. So even the designers themselves were ambivalent about a law that was too protective of fashion designs because they could be sued for being "inspired" by something else. It's very complicated.

The bottom line is we're not Europe.

MB: Explain the difference in the protection that Europe provides versus the United States.

BK: Generally, the European Union and its individual countries have copyright, trademark and patent protection, but they also have a separate scheme for fashion design protection that protects both registered designs and unregistered designs. I negotiated a settlement with a company in France that had copied one of my former brand's shoes, which would never have been protectable in the US under copyright or trade dress law. But in Europe under the design law scheme, it was protected and we were able to get the lower price company to pull the shoe off of the shelves and stop selling it. Europe just has a culture where design is revered. It is a big part of their economy and their identity. We don't come from the same place. We love fashion and New York is a fashion haven but we don't see the world the way they do.

I think we can conclude after all these unsuccessful attempts to make our law more like Europe's that we're just different and there's not a will to change the law.

MB: A commonly made argument here is that the industry doesn't need protection because it is thriving. So, what is the need? Why would we need to change the law?

BK: I think the point of better protection is to protect the original designs of newer designers who get knocked off and don't have the funds to protect themselves. On the other hand, if our law changed and we had a more robust design protection law, would those designers really be able to take advantage of that? Litigation is both time consuming and expensive.

MB: That's where a small claims copyright would be beneficial for fashion designers too.

BK: But you'd need a judge or a mediator who was a copyright expert. At least copyright has to be litigated in federal court where our judges are more experienced in intellectual property law and generally more knowledgeable about copyright, at least here, in the Southern District. For example, you read a case like Judge Denny Chin's decision in *Bill Diodato Photography, LLC v. Kate Spade, LLC*, 388 F. Supp. 2d 382 (S.D.N.Y. 2005), which is a well-reasoned analysis of that case.[2] I was the general counsel of Kate Spade at the time. It's a great case because you have a great judge who understands the law. The photographer lost because of the idea/expression dichotomy. The first thing I did when we got the cease and desist letter from him was to ask our interns to go online and see how many photographs they could find of women's feet underneath a toilet stall. And of course, there were dozens of them, and we included that as an exhibit in our summary judgment motion.

This goes back to your original question about protection of fashion. What is it you really want to protect? Is there anything I'm wearing that's protectable? Nothing except the trademark on my belt buckle, which says Calvin Klein. A trademark offers the best protection of all.

MB: Have your views changed about whether fashion deserves more protection?

BK: I've become less conservative in my views. I agree more with my younger colleagues here, who are much more open in terms of protection.

MB: Are there any other issues that young designers should consider?

BK: A big issue is eponymous brands. Every designer wants to name the brand after him or herself. When Stuart Weitzman names his brand after himself, when Kate Spade names her brand after herself, once you create that LLC, your name belongs to the LLC. And then once the LLC gets investors and gets sold as Stuart Weitzman and Kate Spade did to Tapestry, they don't own their name anymore and can't design under their names.

MB: Recently I was reading the Louis Vuitton versus My Other Bag case and I thought it was funny.[3] Are there a lot of fashion parody cases?

BK: I teach a whole class on parody. The important cases were brought by Louis Vuitton. My Other Bag is the most recent of their cases. In another case, Louis Vuitton sued Warner Brothers over a knockoff piece of luggage that a character referred to as "a Lewis Vuitton" in a scene in *The Hangover Part II*.[4] Louis Vuitton lost because the court found the use to be clearly a parody, and the scene only lasted twenty-five seconds.

MB: In fashion it seems as if the future copyright issues will involve technology, but beyond that there isn't much new on the horizon.

BK: As I said earlier, copyright protects jewelry, fabric designs, but not much else. Fashion also gets protection from design patents, trade dress, and trademark law. Thus, the wide use of logos and trademarks. However, photographs used in fashion advertising, videos, and the like are all protected by copyright.

MB: For photographers, trademarks as underlying rights in photographs are problematic. We have to teach students that they have copyright in the photograph, but not in any underlying rights that might be in the image.

BK: Well, I'm glad you brought that up, reminding students that the photographer is the copyright owner. I have to teach young designers that if you want to use a photograph of Kate Middleton on your website wearing your boots, you have to consider several issues, starting with who owns the copyright to the image. This is where their Copyright 101 class comes in handy because they have to analyze all the rights. And, there's so much use of photographs on websites. Photographs of celebrities wearing a brand's products require at least permission from the photographers, the models, and the celebrities.

MB: So it doesn't seem like we'll ever get fashion design protection in the United States, but it also seems like it doesn't matter.

BK: I agree.

MB: I think one of the main issues today with the rise of social media is that copyright law doesn't seem to always be in sync with how we use and share content on social media.

BK: Look at Instagram, and who owns those rights. I think that what our discussion comes down to is that the most pressing issue we really have to attend to is privacy. I mean that's just enormous with the influence of Google and Facebook. It hits us in the fashion world because of the way we pay for things, the mailing lists we're on, the sharing of data, and customer information. Once you give your email to a company you're on every other mailing list.

MB: What about counterfeiting? Is that a serious financial or economic issue for designers?

BK: I think counterfeiting is a huge problem. We've come a long way. Taobao, Amazon, and other online retailers have been pushed by brands telling them that if they want access to that brand's products then they have to clean up their counterfeit problem and they're working to do that.

MB: That can be a problem with all of the websites selling what is claimed to be designer merchandise. How do you control that or what does the law protect?

BK: Companies such as Amazon and eBay are working with the designers because the designers have put a lot of pressure on them to police their sites. eBay has a program that allows designers to report counterfeits, and it will remove those listings. Ultimately, it is the designer's responsibility to enforce its trademarks. The law is very clear on that after the Tiffany case against eBay[5] In lay terms, the case says that a company like eBay is doing what it can, but it is up to the designer to let them know what is on their site that is counterfeit and what has to be taken down. I think brands have to be clear on their own websites. I drafted this kind of language for brands I worked for that stated, "If you want to buy the real thing, you go to our stores, or you go to our authorized retailers."

Notes

1 Star Athletica L.L.C. v. Varsity Brands, Inc., 137 S. Ct. 1002 (2017).
2 (Ed. note. The case involved a photographer who sued Kate Spade, claiming that it infringed a photograph of a woman's feet, photographed from the outside of the toilet stall, in stylish colorful shoes, and a handbag resting on the floor.)
3 Louis Vuitton Malletier, S.A. v. My Other Bag, Inc., 156 F. Supp. 3d 425 (S.D.N.Y. 2016), *aff'd*, 674 F. App'x 16 (2d Cir. 2016).
4 Louis Vuitton Malletier, S.A. v. Warner Bros. Entm't Inc., 868 F. Supp. 2d 172 (S.D.N.Y. 2012).
5 Tiffany (NJ) Inc. v. eBay Inc., 600 F.3d 93 (2d Cir. 2010). (Ed. note: Tiffany sued eBay for contributory trademark infringement, trademark dilution, and false advertising, claiming that eBay facilitated and advertised counterfeit Tiffany jewelries on its online market website. The court ruled in favor of eBay, finding that for a service provider to be liable for trademark infringement, there must be a showing of an intentional incentive to infringe, or that service provider knew or should have known of the direct infringement and continued to provide the service.)

7.4

LANDMARK CASE

Star Athletica, LLC, v. Varsity Brands, Inc., 137 S.Ct. 1002 (2017)

When we think of copyright, we tend to think of "traditional" creative mediums: photography, literature, music, and sculpture. Clothing does not typically fit under this rubric, even though clothing design is a creative profession. Consumers choose clothes for aesthetic reasons, critics comment on the design of clothes, and high fashion enjoys the same sort of full-fledged artistic criticism that is aimed at films, books, and songs. For copyright purposes, clothing is not protected because it is considered to be a "useful article," defined as an article that possesses an intrinsic utilitarian purpose distinct from exhibiting the article's appearance or carrying information. The Copyright Act does extend protection to the design of a useful article if this design incorporates pictorial, graphic, or sculptural features that are capable of existing separately from the utilitarian elements of the article. If the useful article's design meets this "independent-existence requirement," then it is considered a pictorial, graphic, or sculptural work under the Copyright Act and consequently entitled to copyright protection. This is what the Supreme Court addressed in *Star Athletica*.

The dispute in *Star Athletica* centered on a copyright infringement lawsuit brought by a manufacturer of cheerleader uniforms against a competitor. Star Athletica created cheerleading uniforms with stripes, zigzags, and chevron patterns that were similar to those produced by Varsity Brands. The main difference between Star Athletica's uniforms and Varsity Brands' uniforms was the price; Start Athletica sold a cheaper product. Varsity Brands sued Star Athletica for copyright infringement. Star Athletica did not dispute that it based its designs on Varsity's but instead argued that clothing designs were not copyrightable because their aesthetic designs were inseparable from the uniforms' utilitarian purpose. The district court granted Star Athletica's motion for summary judgment, holding that the designs were conceptually and physically inseparable from the uniforms and were thus ineligible for copyright protection. The Sixth Circuit then reversed the lower court and concluded that the designs were in fact separately identifiable from the underlying utilitarian product and thus entitled to copyright protection. Star Athletica appealed, and the Supreme Court agreed to hear the case.

Writing for a 6-2 majority (with Justice Ginsburg separately concurring), Justice Thomas upheld the circuit court's decision. The court held that a feature incorporated into the design of a useful article is eligible for copyright protection only if it "(1) can be perceived as a two- or three-dimensional work of art separate from the useful article, and (2) would qualify as a protectable pictorial, graphic, or sculptural work—either on its own or fixed in some other tangible medium of expression—if it were imagined separately from the useful article into which it is incorporated." The court turned to the definition of "pictorial" and "graphic" in section 101 of the Copyright

Act, noting that those designs are inherently two-dimensional. Given that the Copyright Act protects pictorial, graphic, and sculptural designs present in the design of useful articles, the Act envisions that such designs may include two-dimensional features. While this aspect of the Copyright Act defeats Varsity Brands' argument that surface decorations on clothes are always separable because they are simply "on a useful article" rather than "designs of a useful article," Varsity Brands nevertheless prevailed on its copyright infringement claims because the cheerleader uniform designs are separable from the utilitarian functions of the clothing.

The court had no difficulty applying the "independent-existence requirement" to the uniforms in question. First, the court noted that the decorations on the uniforms could be identified as features having pictorial, graphic, or sculptural qualities. The chevron patterns, stripes, and zigzags all resulted in a distinctive design that could be identified separately from the underlying utilitarian purpose of the clothing. Next, the court noted that if those uniform designs were "separated and applied in another medium," they would fit into the definition of two-dimensional works of art under section 101 of the Copyright Act. The court stated that "imaginatively removing the decorations from the uniforms and applying them in another medium also would not replicate the uniform itself." Writing for the dissent, Justice Breyer argued that the designs were ineligible for copyright protection because, even if they were "imaginatively extracted," they would merely form a picture of a cheerleading uniform, which was the underlying useful article. The majority countered this argument by pointing out that the resemblance of a two-dimensional design extraction to the cheerleading uniform is not unlike how "two-dimensional fine art correlates to the shape of the canvas on which it is painted." The court reiterated that the only feature of the cheerleading uniforms subject to copyright protection was the two-dimensional art on the surface of the uniforms, and that Varsity Brands may only prohibit reproduction of this two-dimensional surface art. Varsity Brands may not, however, prohibit competitors from "manufacturing a cheerleading uniform that is identical in shape, cut, or dimensions to the uniforms at issue here." Ultimately, given that Star Athletica did in fact copy the two-dimensional surface art, Varsity Brands prevailed on the copyright infringement claim.

Clothing exists at a unique intersection of utility and creativity. This, in turn, expectedly results in a copyright status that is not like the traditional mediums of photography or music but is also distinct from fully utilitarian objects like plates and office desks. The Supreme Court's "independent-existence" test and the language of the Copyright Act recognizing pictorial, graphic, and sculptural designs in useful articles represents an attempt to fashion a clear, concrete test for articles that are part-creative and part-utilitarian. However, the court's decision divided fashion designers and copyright scholars, with some arguing that the decision appropriately recognized the creativity inherent to clothes design and others arguing that the decision created an ambiguous standard that may lead to inconsistent application and stifling of fashion trends in generic clothing. Whether the court's test will hold steady or get tweaked as the clothing industry responds to it is up in the air, but it will certainly prompt additional litigation about the scope and purpose of its application.

PART VIII

Technology

Introduction

Technology often moves at lightning speed, while policy and law move at more of a snail's pace, and this is clear when we examine the interplay of technology and copyright. We live in a world where creators and users are often the same and where we almost cannot imagine a day without "sharing" knowledge or artistic works that we find on our social media feeds even though that "sharing" often violates the letter of copyright law. The chapters in Part VIII present these issues.

Two authors explore whether the Digital Millennium Copyright Act (DMCA) has lived up to its promises. In "The DMCA Safe Harbor: User-Generated Content," Joseph C. Gratz offers an overview of the legislative struggle to protect both internet service providers (ISPs)—to ensure a robust and innovative internet—and the economic rights of copyright holders whose livelihoods are threatened when works are illegally shared rather than licensed. He explains how the DMCA's safe harbor provision, § 512(c), attempted to strike that balance. The DMCA has been criticized from almost every angle by almost every stakeholder, however, Gratz concludes that while far from perfect, the DMCA strikes a modest balance between expeditiously stopping harmful infringements while safeguarding against bad faith removals, allowing the internet to function.

In "DMCA Safe Harbor: Policy and Practice Divided," Chris Reed addresses how technology and policy have outpaced the law. He notes that the DMCA was intended to update the Copyright Act for the twenty-first century. However, because it was passed for a nascent internet culture, it never lived up to its potential and now is past its useful life, in part because recent court interpretations depart from what seems to have been Congress's intent. As did Gratz, Reed focuses on the safe harbor provision. He questions whether the notice and takedown system works as planned and suggests that the notice and takedown system works well for ISPs but not for content creators, upon whom it imposes an undue burden. It fails for copyright holders because: (1) it has been construed to mean (although actually not required) that a notice must be issued for each instance of infringing content, so copyright holders annually issue millions of notices; (2) platforms are slow to remove work because they insist on performing additional verifications that exceed what the law requires; and (3) some platforms insist on the right to make their own fair use analysis, also not required. Finally, noting that smaller, independent rights holders are harmed by the system—every hour spent issuing a takedown notices is an hour not spent creating work—he suggests ways to fix the system.

Scott Sholder questions whether copyright trolls are a solid business model or scourge of the intellectual property industry in "Copyright Trolls: When Copyright Litigation Becomes a Business

Model." He defines a copyright troll as a plaintiff (or, often, a plaintiff's lawyer) who engages in specific forms of predatory behavior using the legal system as a means to a financial end. Copyright trolls, modeling themselves after the success enjoyed by patent trolls, play a numbers game, targeting hundreds or thousands of defendants from whom they seek quick settlements priced just low enough that it is less expensive for the defendant to pay the troll rather than defend the (often specious) claim. He presents a history of the copyright troll business, beginning with Righthaven, which recruited copyright owners (principally, newspapers) to bring lawsuits by identifying possible cases of infringement and acquiring partial assignment of its clients' copyrights tailored precisely to the infringements identified. The model was so successful that porn trolls popped up, enticing people to download porn and then extorting them to settle. This was so egregious that several judges have in effect banned these sorts of copyright trolls from filing complaints in their courthouses. Today, copyright trolls are most associated with photographers and photo/video aggregators. This system will continue, he concludes, until the playing field is leveled by legislation such as the Copyright Alternative in Small-Claims Enforcement (CASE) Act.

The remaining two chapters explore the uncharted territory of artificial intelligence (AI). In "Virtual Reality: Blending the Real World with Copying," Kenneth Swezey and Elizabeth Altman present an extensive overview of how AI might eventually implicate authorship under the Copyright Act. The authors note that we need to understand some of the science and theory, because how AI works changes how it might intersect with copyright. So, speaking to our inner geeks, they begin with a lucid, deep scientific dive into what AI technology is. After explaining AI, the chapter presents four possible ways that AI might intersect with copyright: AI as author (the AI system itself is bestowed with authorship); programmer as author (more easily aligning with the current copyright regime); user as author (recognizing that computer-generated works will not exist without user input); or output as derivative work (playing off the programmer as author who then "licenses" users to create derivative works). The chapter concludes how it starts: the Copyright Act was written to be flexible enough to adapt to the technology of its time and the digital age is no exception—copyright law will eventually carve a niche for AI technology.

Finally, in "Artificial Intelligence and the Future of Literary Works," Mary Rasenberger explores the complex challenges that AI poses to copyright law and human creativity through the lens of book publishing because books have always been at the core of copyright protection. She focuses on generative AI systems, or those trained on data to create their own rules. She discusses the many ways that generative AI systems are already being used by *Bloomberg, The Washington Post,* and others to generate simple news stories, raising the questions of authorship of those stories. and who can be held responsible. She also explores the issues involved in creating AI systems, which, to function, must be trained on massive volumes of non-copyrightable data or copyrightable works. While courts have found this generally to be fair use, she questions the Google Books project because Google digitized 20 million books, not to save knowledge for the public good, but, as she asserts, to train its AI systems. Ultimately, she concludes that opt-out automated collective licensing systems may be the only workable solution for striking the balance between developments in AI research and application and the rights of creators whose works are used to train AI machines. She acknowledges that some copyright owners object to mandatory or opt-out extended collective licensing because they want to control the use of their works. In the end, while understandable, if this twentieth-century view of copyright ownership that, prevails, it may well spell the end of copyright protection in the coming years as mass use by AI systems becomes commonplace.

8.1

THE DMCA SAFE HARBOR

User-Generated Content

Joseph C. Gratz

Every technology that enhances creativity also provides opportunities for copyright infringement. How can we best strike the balance between encouraging the development of those new technologies that serve creators and ensuring that they will not do more harm to creators than good? And should we treat all kinds of creators, and all kinds of creativity, the same?

That is the central question at the intersection of copyright law and technology in the twenty-first century (as well as the twentieth and nineteenth centuries). One way in which US law tries to strike that balance is in section 512(c) of the Digital Millennium Copyright Act (DMCA). That law establishes a procedure by which copyright holders can provide notice to websites or other internet service providers who host infringing material provided by third parties requesting the removal of that material. So long as the service provider removes the material expeditiously and meets the DMCA's other requirements,[1] the service provider cannot be held liable for having hosted infringing material.

That is the essential bargain of the DMCA: Copyright holders identify material they believe to be infringing, and service providers receive a safe harbor if they remove that material expeditiously.

This does not comprehensively resolve every dispute: For example, the copyright holder can still sue the user who uploaded the material whether or not she sent a DMCA takedown notice, and the service provider can choose not to honor a particular notice, losing the protection of the safe harbor with respect to that particular piece of user-uploaded material. But in practice, the DMCA's procedures help to keep the peace between the rambunctious world of user-generated content and the economic priorities of creators.

The Takedown Notice

The DMCA sets forth a specific set of requirements that must be in every DMCA takedown notice. Many service providers offer forms that make it easier to fulfill these requirements, and using those forms often expedites the processing of takedown notices.

Every takedown notice must be signed by the copyright holder or her agent,[2] and must include:

- Identification of the copyrighted work (for example, by title, or by providing a link to an authorized copy);[3]
- Identification of the specific location where the service provider can find the material to be removed;[4]
- The sender's contact information;[5]
- "A statement that the complaining party has a good faith belief that use of the material in the manner complained of is not authorized by the copyright owner, its agent, or the law";[6] and

- "A statement that the information in the notification is accurate, and under penalty of perjury, that the complaining party is authorized to act on behalf of the owner of an exclusive right that is allegedly infringed."[7]

The point of these requirements is that enough information must be provided to allow the service provider to find the material in order to remove it, to allow the service provider to assess whether the claim is legitimate, and to ensure that takedown notices are sent only by the copyright holder or their designee. Third-party interlopers cannot send valid takedown notices; only the copyright holder (or her agent) can.

The sender of the notice must state their good-faith belief that the use of the material is not licensed, *and* that it is not authorized by law—for example, that it is not fair use. Courts have found that this means the sender of a notice must consider whether the use is fair use before determining whether to send the notice.[8]

After the service provider receives the notice, it must act "expeditiously" to remove the content identified in the notice in order to keep the safe harbor with respect to that content.[9] The law does not say what is and is not "expeditious," but a delay of a week has been found to be clearly "expeditious" in one particular case.[10] After removing the material, the service provider notifies the subscriber that the material was removed.[11]

The Counter-notification

If the user who uploaded the material believes that the material was not infringing, they may send a "counter-notification" to the service provider requesting that the material be put back. The counter-notification must be in writing (for example, via an email or a form provided by the service provider), must be signed by the user,[12] and must include:

- Identification of the material that was removed;[13]
- "A statement under penalty of perjury that the subscriber has a good faith belief that the material was removed or disabled as a result of mistake or misidentification of the material to be removed or disabled";[14]
- The subscriber's contact information; and
- A statement making sure that there is somewhere in the US where the sender of the notice can file a lawsuit against the subscriber.[15]

Some service providers provide forms to help with the submission of valid counter-notifications, but many do not.[16]

After the service provider receives the counter-notification, it provides a copy to the sender of the original notice.[17] Then, after ten business days, the material that was removed is replaced—unless the sender of the original notice notifies them that it has filed a lawsuit against the user.[18] Many users whose non-infringing material has been removed can be reluctant to send a counter-notification because they are concerned they may be sued—and even a weak lawsuit can be costly and unpleasant. For that reason, even blatantly abusive takedown notices frequently do not result in counter-notifications.

Repeat Infringers

In order to keep its DMCA safe harbor, every service provider must adopt and reasonably implement a policy for terminating the accounts of repeat infringers. This requirement is why sites keep track of how many instances of infringement have been reported with respect to a particular account. Many sites, for example, track how many "strikes" an account has received, and take action against accounts (either limiting their functionality or terminating them completely) after three or more "strikes."

The law provides substantial flexibility to service providers in dealing with repeat infringement, though, and does not require a "three strikes" policy. Instead, the law requires that every service provider "has adopted and reasonably implemented . . . a policy that provides for the termination in appropriate circumstances of subscribers and account holders of the service provider's system or network who are repeat infringers." The law does not say what "appropriate circumstances" are, though there must be at least *some* circumstances that would lead to the termination, and the policy must be implemented "reasonably."

Where the subscriber has sent a counter-notification in response to a particular DMCA notice, many sites do not take that notice into account as a "strike" for purposes of determining whether the subscriber is a repeat infringer.

Misrepresentations

Copyright holders are only allowed to send DMCA notices about material that they actually believe infringes their copyrights, is not licensed, and is not fair use. Subscribers are allowed to send counter-notifications only in response to DMCA notices that they actually believe resulted from a mistake. If either a DMCA notice or a counter-notification contained any statements that the sender knew to be incorrect, and those statements would have affected the way the DMCA notice was handled by the service provider, the sender of that notice or counter-notification can be sued for the damage caused by material being wrongfully taken down or wrongfully put back.[19]

Those lawsuits are relatively rare but are important to ensure that senders of notices and counter-notices are not abusing the system.

Criticisms of the DMCA

Copyright holders, uploaders of user-generated content, service providers, and free expression advocates all have criticized the DMCA from different angles.

Copyright holders have criticized the DMCA because it requires them to search for and identify infringements, and notify service providers of each infringement. Copyright holders would prefer a system in which service providers were required to search for copyright holders' material themselves. Service providers respond that there is no way to know what is or is not licensed or unlicensed but nonetheless tolerated by copyright holders, so specific identification by rights holders is necessary.

Service providers have criticized the DMCA because it provides few consequences for fraudulent or simply mistaken takedown notices. Service providers would prefer a system in which they could disregard notices sent by untrusted parties. Copyright holders respond that it is important for small and unsophisticated copyright holders to be able to take down infringements quickly, and there are relatively few malicious senders of DMCA notices.

Free expression advocates have criticized the DMCA because it incentivizes service providers to remove material in response to all DMCA notices, without an independent review of whether the claim of infringement is valid. In particular, the DMCA safe harbor might be denied to a service provider that did not remove material that the service provider believed in good faith constituted fair use, if a court later disagreed with the service provider's fair-use determination. This problem is especially acute where the material is being removed for reasons having nothing to do with the purposes of copyright, such as to avoid embarrassment.[20] Copyright holders respond that the counter-notification process adequately deals with invalid takedown notices. Free expression advocates respond that because the counter-notification process can be intimidating, even those who are engaging in what they strongly and correctly believe to be fair uses are reluctant to send a counter-notification.

Conclusion

While no framework for dealing with copyright infringement on the internet is perfect, the DMCA has important advantages: It stops harmful infringements expeditiously while employing some safeguards against fraudulent or bad-faith removals. Because it sets out the sequence of communications between copyright holder, service provider, and uploader, the DMCA streamlines removals and brings most disputes over copyrighted material uploaded online to an end quickly and efficiently.

Notes

1 In addition to taking down materials in response to valid DMCA notices, service providers must adopt and reasonably implement a repeat infringer policy, as discussed below, and must meet a number of other requirements, such as registration of their designated agent with the Copyright Office, which are beyond the scope of this essay.
2 17 U.S.C. § 512(c)(3)(A)(i) (2018).
3 17 U.S.C. § 512(c)(3)(A)(ii).
4 17 U.S.C. § 512(c)(3)(A)(iii).
5 17 U.S.C. § 512(c)(3)(A)(iv).
6 17 U.S.C. § 512(c)(3)(A)(v).
7 17 U.S.C. § 512(c)(3)(A)(vi).
8 Lenz v. Universal Music Corp., 815 F.3d 1145, 1151 (9th Cir. 2016).
9 17 U.S.C. § 512(c)(1)(C).
10 Long v. Dorset, 369 F. Supp. 3d 939, 947 (N.D. Cal. 2019) (finding a response delivered after five business days to satisfy the DMCA's requirements).
11 17 U.S.C. § 512(g)(2)(A).
12 17 U.S.C. § 512(g)(3)(A).
13 17 U.S.C. § 512(g)(3)(B).
14 17 U.S.C. § 512(g)(3)(C).
15 Specifically, "a statement that the subscriber consents to the jurisdiction of Federal District Court for the judicial district in which the address is located, or if the subscriber's address is outside of the United States, for any judicial district in which the service provider may be found, and that the subscriber will accept service of process from the person who provided notification under subsection (c)(1)(C) or an agent of such person." 17 U.S.C. § 512(g)(3)(D).
16 If the service provider does not provide their own form, you could use the following text: This is a counter notification under 17 U.S.C. § 512(g)(3). The material that was removed or to which access was disabled was located at [INSERT URL OR LOCATION]. Under penalty of perjury, I state that I have a good faith belief that the material was removed or disabled as a result of mistake or misidentification of the material to be removed or disabled. My name, address, and telephone number are [INSERT YOUR NAME, ADDRESS, AND PHONE NUMBER]. I consent to the jurisdiction of Federal District Court for the judicial district in which my address is located, or if my address is located outside the United States, I consent to the jurisdiction of the Federal District Court for any judicial district in which the service provider may be found. I will accept service of process from the person who provided the takedown notice or an agent of such person.
Signed, [YOUR NAME]
17 17 U.S.C. § 512(g)(2)(B).
18 17 U.S.C. § 512(g)(2)(C).
19 17 U.S.C. § 512(f).
20 See, e.g., Online Policy Grp. v. Diebold, Inc., 337 F. Supp. 2d 1195, 1205 (N.D. Cal. 2004) (company sent DMCA notice regarding internal company emails posted by critics of the company "to suppress publication of embarrassing content rather than as a shield to protect its intellectual property").

8.2

THE DMCA SAFE HARBOR
Policy and Practice Divided

Christopher S. Reed

Perhaps one of the greatest frustrations for copyright owners in the twenty-first century is that the same technology that has made it easier and less expensive to produce and distribute their creative works has also made it easier and less expensive to misappropriate them. Although Congress attempted to provide copyright owners with some redress, as is often the case, policy and technology have largely outpaced the law.

At the heart of copyright owners' frustrations is the way a 1998 law, the Digital Millennium Copyright Act (DMCA), has played out in practice. Broadly speaking, the DMCA was intended to update the Copyright Act for the digital age, but it was passed at the dawn of the commercial internet, long before anyone, including Congress, could have possibly imagined how the platform has become such a central part of our daily lives, and the epicenter of modern commerce. As a result, the process and practices set forth in the DMCA that made sense at the time they were conceived have now largely outlived their useful life. While rapid advancement in technology is partly to blame, recent court interpretations of some of the DMCA's central features have departed somewhat from Congress' original intent, creating a difficult climate for rights owners trying to enforce their rights on the modern internet.

A Brief Primer on the DMCA Safe Harbor

The DMCA was a sweeping piece of legislation, but the part that has caused the most heartburn for copyright owners is the safe harbor provision that effectively immunizes internet intermediaries such as online platforms for the copyright infringement perpetrated by their users, provided the platforms comply with certain obligations.

The provision was something of a grand bargain among stakeholders: the copyright owner community on the one hand, and the major internet companies on the other. Copyright owners were concerned (quite rightly, it turned out) that the internet would increase the speed with which copies of their digital works could be pirated across the internet. Because a digital copy of a work is almost always indistinguishable from a lawfully acquired original, the specter of piracy in the digital environment was far more pronounced than it was in the traditional physical-goods world.

Meanwhile, the internet companies were concerned that if they could be held liable for the infringing acts of their users (over which they had no control), the potential money damages awards could be crippling, since money damages for copyright infringement can be as high as $150,000 per work infringed. Given the volume of content being shuttled around the internet, the argument goes, the potential exposure for an internet platform could be staggering—so high that investors simply are not willing to take on the risk, thus stifling investment and innovation in the fledgling internet.

The safe harbor provision thus attempted to strike a balance between these two competing equities. Although its provisions are complex and nuanced, generally speaking, to avail itself of the safe harbor, an internet platform must remove allegedly infringing content from its platform "expeditiously" upon receiving a duly issued notification of claimed infringement by a copyright owner (often referred to as a "takedown notice"). The platform must provide a copy of the takedown notice to the user who uploaded the infringing content who may then issue a "counter notification," after which the platform must restore the content within a certain period of time, unless the rights owner notifies the platform that it has brought an infringement suit against the user.

Platforms must comply with a few other provisions as well, such as the requirement to designate an agent to receive takedown notices and filing that information with the Copyright Office as well as publicizing it online. Platforms must also maintain a repeat infringer policy that ultimately calls for the termination of service (in "appropriate circumstances") to its egregiously infringing users.

Perhaps most fundamentally, platforms that seek the protection of the safe harbor must not be aware of, or an active participant in, any infringement that takes place on its platform.

Notice and Takedown in Practice

Whether you believe that the notice and takedown system works depends on whether you are a copyright owner or an internet platform. The internet community believes that the system works well—something of an about-face for the industry, which originally decried the scheme because it would pose an undue burden on platforms that would stifle the development of the internet. Most copyright owners would say that the system we have today imposes an undue burden on them to actively police the internet for potential infringements in a way that goes well beyond what Congress intended.

Conceptually, the notice and takedown procedure seems like a reasonable balance between competing interests. Copyright owners must take certain steps to let the internet companies know about infringing conduct taking place on their platforms; in exchange for taking reasonable steps to quell that infringement, the internet companies are granted immunity from liability for the infringing conduct of its users. In practice, that balance has been upset.

The Perpetual Takedown-Repost Cycle

For copyright owners, the biggest failing of the notice and takedown procedure is that it has been construed to mean that a notice must be issued for every instance of infringing content, even if it has been taken down previously on the same platform. Although the letter of the law requires that copyright owners provide only a "representative list" of infringing works on a particular platform, the internet industry asserts, and a number of courts have agreed, that internet providers cannot be expected to remove material from their platforms unless copyright owners supply specific location information.

That interpretation of the legal requirements coupled with the speed at which content is posted and shared across the internet has resulted in what many refer to as "whack a mole"—the process of a copyright owner issuing a takedown notice for a particular piece of content, the platform removing it, and having it reappear nearly instantaneously, requiring another notice.

As a result, every year, copyright owners issue millions of notices. The Recording Industry Association of America says that it has sent more than 175 million notices since 2012,[1] while the Motion Picture Association of America reports that its members sent notices on just over 104 million unique URLs in 2015.[2] Google claims to have received over 4 billion notices.[3]

As Rep. Bob Goodlatte, former chairman of the House Judiciary Committee recently observed, "different groups point to the same statistics showing the mammoth amount of notices being sent today as proof of either the system is working as designed or the system not working as designed."[4] The tech sector bandies about the figure to show just how much it cares about copyright owners by removing so much infringing material. Copyright owners point to the same figures to argue that if the system worked, there would not be nearly as much infringing material online in the first place.

Internet Platforms' Responsiveness and Extra-Statutory Review Standards

Although the law requires that platforms remove infringing content "expeditiously," neither Congress nor the courts have offered much guidance on what that means. Courts have concluded that anything from a couple of days to a few weeks is consistent with the spirit of the statute; Google claims that it removes infringing URLs within six hours. As the music industry observed in a recent Copyright Office proceeding on the effectiveness of the DMCA, six hours can be "a particularly crucial window of time in the case of works that have not yet been commercially released."[5]

Perhaps one of the reasons certain of the platforms are so slow at removing content is because they insist on performing additional verifications on takedown notices that far exceed the scope of what is permitted under the notice and takedown provisions.

One platform recently required a representative of a corporate copyright owner to provide documentation to confirm that he was duly authorized to issue takedown notices. The law already requires that those issuing takedown notices certify, under penalty of perjury, that they are authorized to act on behalf of the copyright owner. Requiring additional documentation that exceeds the requirements of the DMCA imposes an undue burden on copyright owners and unnecessarily slows the takedown process.

Another example: Google asserts that it "may decline to remove URLs" submitted to it in a takedown notice if it "deduc[es] fair use."[6]

It is true that the law requires that copyright owners consider whether an uploader has a fair use defense before sending a takedown notice for a particular upload, but that does not vest in Google or any other platform the authority to make that finding on its own.

If a user receives a takedown notice for content that he or she believes is a fair use, the appropriate recourse is to issue a counter-notification, the procedure for which is clearly set forth in the law, and results in the restoration of content that was the subject of the notice unless the copyright owner files a copyright infringement suit against the uploader.

No Viable Recourse for Invalid Counter-Notices

Many in the internet community believe that the copyright owner community—particularly the big commercial owners, such as movie studios and record labels—are overzealous with issuing notices, resulting in bogus takedowns for user-uploaded content that should be considered fair use, or is otherwise authorized by law. Copyright owners have observed that given the volume of notices they issue, they receive surprisingly few counter-notices. For instance, the MPAA said that of the 104 million takedown notices its members issued in 2015, they received only 210 counter-notifications—far less than 1 percent.[7]

The content industry uses this and other similar statistics to support the claim that the system works as intended; the internet industry asserts that most people simply do not send counter-notices even when they are warranted, because the process is too intimidating and requires that users certify under penalty of perjury that the user has a good faith belief that the material was taken down by mistake.

Put simply, the counter-notice procedure puts most of the power in the hands of the user. All an uploader has to do is issue a counter-notice and the content is restored. To stop it, the copyright owner has to file suit against the uploader—a costly proposition that is almost always not going to make economic or business sense for the copyright owner.

Fixing the System

Perhaps the most critical and impactful improvement to the current notice and takedown system would be the imposition of a "takedown/staydown" requirement that would essentially require platforms to filter content upon upload and reject that which is known to be infringing. Some have expressed concern that such a system could be used as a form of censorship, if nefarious rights owners were to flag legal but nevertheless unflattering content—e.g. a negative review about a film—but others point out that such systems would have the same procedural safeguards that exist in the current regime.

YouTube's Content ID is an example of such a system. Content ID allows select rights owners to upload content directly into YouTube's system and have them match against future uploads. Copyright owners can then apply their own business rules to the uploads, ranging from blocking the content entirely, to allowing it to appear online, but capturing the revenue derived from advertising.

But make no mistake: Google did not invest $60 million on Content ID to benefit rights owners; it did it so that it could sell and profit from advertising sold on content claimed by rights owners. To do so on unclaimed, potentially unauthorized content would have subjected it to potentially crippling damages for copyright infringement since, as an active participant, it would not have had the protection of the DMCA's safe harbor.

Although Google created Content ID largely for its own business purposes, it is an important first step on the path to more effective online enforcement. The European Parliament recently passed a controversial directive that some say will essentially require such filtering. How the various EU member states implement the directive remains to be seen, but if companies are forced to implement filtering in the EU, it may make sense for them to implement the practice globally, thereby improving the enforcement climate for everyone.

Parting Thoughts

Perhaps the most troubling feature of the current notice and takedown regime is that smaller, independent rights owners are disproportionately harmed by it. The major rights owners such as the record labels, movie studios, and book publishers have the resources to hire staff or outside vendors whose principal function is to scour the internet looking for infringing copies. For independent creators, tracking infringing uses and issuing takedown notices can quickly become a full-time job, especially because in many cases, smaller rights owners do not have access to automated tools like Content ID.

Every hour that is spent issuing takedown notices is an hour that the independent creative professional is not putting into his or her craft. Eventually, that reallocation of time will result in less creative output, undermining the fundamental constitutional intent of copyright law: to promote the production of creative works for the public to enjoy.

The DMCA was intended to foster cooperation between industry stakeholders, namely the internet community on the one hand, and the copyright owner community on the other, by placing the burden of policing the internet in the hands of those best suited to address particular concerns. But instead of cooperation, the internet industry has sought at every turn—before Congress and in the courts of law and public opinion—to advance the most narrow reading of its obligations, threatening the end of days for the internet as we know it if the industry were to be held to any higher of a standard.

Recent events surrounding online privacy, data security, election interference, and the like have led some policy-makers to begin to question whether the internet companies should be subjected to more intense regulatory scrutiny. As that unfolds, it is possible that we will start to see the major platforms move away from their usual hardline stance against taking any responsibility for online infringement and begin to work more collaboratively with copyright owners to help foster an internet that works for everyone: creators, users, and the platforms that bring them together.

Notes

1 American Association of Independent Music et al., Joint Commentary, *In the Matter of: Section 512 Study: Notice and Request for Public Comment*, before the US Copyright Office, Library of Congress (March 31, 2016), 4, https://www.riaa.com/wp-content/uploads/2016/03/Music-Community-Submission-in-re-DMCA-512-FINAL-7559445.pdf (hereafter *Music Industry Comments*). This commentary, and the comments by the Motion Picture Association of America *infra* were offered in response to the Copyright Office's Notice and Request for Public Comment, 80 Fed. Reg. 81,862 (December 31, 2015), https://www.copyright.gov/fedreg/2015/80fr81862.pdf.

2 Motion Picture Association of America, Comments, *In the Matter of: Section 512 Study: Notice and Request for Public Comment*, before the US Copyright Office, Library of Congress (April 1, 2016), 2 (hereafter *MPAA Comments*).

3 "Content Delistings Due to Copyright," Transparency Report, Google, accessed May 15, 2020, https://transparencyreport.google.com/copyright/overview.

4 *Section 512 of Title 17 Hearing Before the Subcomm. On Courts, Intell. Prop. & the Internet of the Comm. On the Judiciary*, 113th Cong. 4 (2014) (statement of Rep. Bob Goodlatte, Chairman H. Comm. On the Judiciary).

5 *Music Industry Comments*, at 19.

6 Google, "Content Delistings Due to Copyright."

7 *MPAA Comments*, at 21.

8.3

COPYRIGHT TROLLS

When Copyright Litigation Becomes a Business Model

*Scott J. Sholder**

One of the most talked about topics in the modern digital world of copyrighted content is the phenomenon of copyright "trolls." To some, the term is pejorative and demonizes a specific legal service that many small businesses and individual artists see as valuable. To others, the term is a scarlet letter that should be sewn on the business suits of litigants and attorneys who exploit the high cost of copyright litigation in the US to turn a profit. Until Congress overhauls the 1976 Copyright Act or institutes an effective small-claims system for copyrights, the best we can do is understand the "who," "how," and "why" of the copyright troll movement.

Setting Boundaries

A key aspect of discussing the phenomenon of copyright "trolling" is making sure that the defined terms are clear. It is critical to establish, right up front, that not all copyright owners who sue to protect their rights are trolls; perhaps it is even safe to say that most are not. A copyright troll, in common parlance, is a specific breed of plaintiff (or, often, a plaintiff's lawyer)—one that engages in specific forms of predatory behavior using the legal system as a means to a financial end.

Distinguished federal judges presiding over what those jurists deem to be "troll" cases have said it best. Apropos to this essay, Judge Denise L. Cote of the US District Court for the Southern District of New York has stated that copyright trolls are litigants who "are more focused on the business of litigation than on selling a product or service or licensing their copyrights to third parties to sell a product or service."[1] Judge Cote's former colleague on the Manhattan district court bench (who now sits on the US Court of Appeals for the Second Circuit), Judge Richard J. Sullivan explained that "[a] copyright troll plays a numbers game in which it targets hundreds or thousands of defendants seeking quick settlements priced just low enough that it is less expensive for the defendant to pay the troll rather than defend the claim."[2] While recent trends in copyright trolling skew toward fewer than hundreds or thousands of defendants at a time, the "numbers game" is the same: pressure the defendant(s) to settle for less than the cost of litigation but for far more than the copyrighted property is worth.

In an empirical study regarding copyright trolls, Professor Matthew Sag of Loyola University Chicago School of Law aptly stated that the "unifying characteristic" of intellectual property trolls in general is that they are "systematic opportunists."[3] While the plaintiff or attorney on the receiving end of the "troll" label will inevitably state that he or she is standing up for creators or copyright owners who could not otherwise afford legal relief (which may, in some cases, be true), opportunism—not justice—is at the heart of the troll movement.

This essay will explore the origins of the copyright troll business model, discuss some noteworthy cases that set boundaries around, establish consequences for troll-like behavior, and address recent measures taken by the copyright defense bar to combat what that segment of the legal community deems to be abusive and inappropriate exploitation of the legal system.

"A Troll Is Born"

Copyright trolls learned their trade from patent trolls, who have been in the trolling business for far longer.[4] Patent trolls are intellectual property owners who register patents but do not practice them, and simply use their ownership status to sue practicing inventors and businesses for purported infringement when a new and potentially infringing technology is developed.[5] It is a lucrative business, and copyright owners and lawyers took notice nearly a decade ago.

Copyright trolling began in earnest with the advent of Righthaven and "porn trolls" like Prenda Law and Malibu Media.[6] In 2010 and 2011, Righthaven—a sort of clearinghouse for copyright infringement claims—began recruiting copyright owners (principally, newspapers) to bring lawsuits by identifying possible cases of infringement and acquiring partial assignment of its clients' copyrights tailored precisely to the infringements identified.[7] The model generated significant profits from a string of quick settlements.[8] Righthaven was done in, however, because it lacked standing, having only acquired the right to sue for certain infringements,[9] as one must be an author, owner, or exclusive licensee in order to have standing to sue for copyright infringement.[10] The Righthaven suits were dismissed, and the company became insolvent in late 2011.[11]

Copyright trolling's second wave involved a variety of "porn trolls." From 2011 to 2014, Prenda Law created sham entities to purchase copyrights to pornographic films, some of which they had filmed themselves.[12] They then uploaded the films to file-sharing websites to "lure" people to download them, filed copyright infringement cases against those people, and then threatened them with "enormous financial penalties and public embarrassment" unless they paid a $3,000 settlement fee.[13] Prenda Law attorneys made over $6 million through these "shame" settlements.[14] They were initially sanctioned for over $80,000 for fraud and extortion, and eventually were indicted on charges of fraud and money laundering; both Prenda lawyers have since pleaded guilty and have been sentenced to serve time in prison.[15]

Another porn troll is Malibu Media LLC, a producer of adult films who has filed more than 6,000 complaints since 2012.[16] Malibu Media's litigation strategy, like Prenda Law's, is to target internet users who distribute and download unauthorized copies of adult films using BitTorrent software and pursue monetary settlements from the users after filing "John Doe" lawsuits and threatening to expose the users' identities.[17] A new filer, adult film company Strike 3 Holdings LLC, seems to be taking the BitTorrent lawsuit baton from Malibu, with 229 lawsuits brought in 2017, 2,165 in 2018, and 1,089 as of July 2019.[18] However, the sharp practices continue, resulting in the recent sanctioning of the lawyer representing Strike 3 for failing to meet court deadlines in twenty-four separate cases.[19] Both Malibu and Strike 3 have been labeled "copyright trolls" by the courts,[20] and several judges have in effect banned these sort of copyright trolls from filing complaints in their courthouses, declaring that they "will not idly watch what is essentially an extortion scheme" in the form of Malibu Media and Strike 3 filings.[21]

Today's copyright trolls have broadened their horizons beyond pornography into audiovisual content in general, but they are most frequently associated with photographers and photo/video aggregators—self-styled licensing agencies who typically acquire a limited interest in photographers' copyrights (enough to have standing, such as an exclusive license) or receive a full assignment of a photographer's rights.[22] The types of photographs the aggregators collect range from paparazzi photographs of celebrities to nature photographs to "still-life" pictures of food used in advertising campaigns.

These plaintiffs retain, and are sometimes even actively recruited by, specialized law firms that deal exclusively with plaintiff-side copyright litigation. The most notorious firms include Liebowitz Law Firm and Higbee & Associates, but there are many more firms out there, and new copycats emerging regularly as attorneys of questionable scruples see dollar signs. Firms like these operate almost exclusively on a contingency fee basis.[23]

These lawyer-and-client teams typically partner with technologists who provide web-crawling and image-recognition software that scours the internet and finds new and old posts that match a database of collected photographs. The trolls' technological infrastructure has the capability of searching billions of websites for allegedly infringing content.[24] Once an image is flagged, some firms will pass the case to a "claims specialist"—a non-lawyer tasked with negotiating and collecting a settlement through often aggressive letter-writing campaigns and tactics driven by numbers as opposed to the law. Others, however, cut right to the chase and file lawsuits against accused infringers without demand letters, settlement negotiations, or takedown requests (even when takedown requests may be required by law prior to filing suit).

Statutory Damages and Too Many Mouths to Feed

The key motivator behind the copyright trolling strategy is the availability of statutory damages in the Copyright Act. Owners of copyrighted works registered in a timely manner in accordance with § 412 of the Copyright Act are entitled to opt to seek statutory damages—i.e. those damages set by the Copyright Act that do not require proof—as opposed to actual damages, like lost licensing revenue and a defendant's profits attributable to infringement. The Copyright Act sets statutory damages on a scale between $750 and $30,000 (or as low as $200 for "innocent infringement") and up to $150,000 for "willful infringement" per work infringed.[25] It is these facially intimidating numbers that provide the hook for copyright trolls to engage the practices that give them their name.

Imagine, as a non-lawyer or content neophyte, receiving a demand letter or complaint accusing you of copyright infringement and claiming you could be responsible for $150,000 in damages (plus attorney's fees) for the use of a single photograph. This is not an exaggeration; these types of demands are par for the course. As an individual, start-up, or small business, you may consider doing whatever it takes to avoid that nightmare scenario. When the "generous" opening settlement offer is in the low five figures, you may think you are getting off easy. Not so fast.

The nightmare scenario of $150,000 in damages for a single photo infringement is highly unlikely to ever become reality (and awards of attorneys' fees are in the court's discretion and are not awarded simply as a matter of course). While actual damages are tantamount to a reasonable licensing fee (or an infringer's profits), in photo/video cases, courts often use a multiple of a reasonable license fee as a benchmark for a statutory damages award, citing the multiplier as the needed sting of deterrence built into the statutory damages regime.[26] While courts and juries have discretion to set a higher damages award, it is a rare photo case that garners a six- or seven-figure damage amount.[27]

Pursuit of statutory damages could make otherwise inconsequential infringements very profitable—way beyond what even a multiple of a license fee would have garnered. It is here, more than anywhere else, that trolls "take advantage of asymmetric stakes and the high cost of litigation to extract settlements or licensing fees based on dubious claims."[28]

While statutory damages provide a perverse incentive for aggressive enforcement, even their unavailability sometimes does not deter a zealous troll. Oftentimes, in cases where only actual damages are available, and would range from less than $10 to several hundred dollars on the high end, trolls will still demand exponentially higher settlement fees. One of the reasons for demands of this magnitude—aside from perpetuating the trolling business model by leveraging the defendant's cost of litigation—is because there are many parties to pay even where a single image is involved.

First, there is the photographer. Second, there is the photo agency or aggregator (which sometimes may stand in the shoes of the photographer). Third, there is the lawyer, who takes a percentage of the recovery. Fourth, there is the technology provider that supplies the image-recognition software. Fifth, in cases that proceed to discovery, there are costs related to vendors such as court reporters and expert witnesses. With multiple splits, the proverbial juice must be worth the squeeze, hence why many trolls refuse to settle even the lowest-value cases for less than thousands of dollars.

Representative Cases

There are literally thousands of copyright troll cases clogging the dockets of the federal courts, with the highest concentration in the US District Courts for the Southern District of New York and the Central and Northern Districts of California.[29] The Liebowitz Law Firm alone has filed more than 1,500 cases since 2015, with over 1,300 of them venued in New York.[30] Because it would be impossible to provide a comprehensive overview of these cases in this essay, following are a few examples of recent cases that grabbed headlines.[31]

Trolling Can Backfire in Cases of Obvious Fair Use

Kanongataa v. Coed Media Group, LLC, No. 16 Civ. 7472 (LAK), Dkt. Nos. 27 & 46 (S.D.N.Y. Feb. 15, 2017): This case involved a plaintiff who streamed the birth of his son live on Facebook. Many news outlets reported on the bizarre occurrence, including NBC, ABC, Yahoo!, and pop culture website collegecandy.com, owned and operated by Coed Media, using very brief clips of the video (or in Coed's case, a screen grab). Plaintiff copyrighted the forty-five-minute video and, represented by the Liebowitz Law Firm, sued the various media companies who reported the story for copyright infringement.

On a motion to dismiss, the court held that news reporting uses were clearly fair use. In Coed's case, the court also held that the use of the screenshot was *de minimis* and therefore not infringing (this means a tiny fraction of the copyrighted work is not substantially similar as a matter of law). Coed's screen grab constituted a single frame of a forty-five-minute video—a fraction of a percent of the whole. The court awarded fees to the defendants, holding that "no reasonable lawyer with any familiarity with the law of copyright could have thought" that the plaintiff's case had merit.[32]

Sloppy Mass-Produced Litigation Doesn't Pay

Barcroft Media, Ltd. v. Coed Media Group, LLC, 297 F. Supp. 3d 339 (S.D.N.Y. Nov. 2, 2017): Two paparazzi photo agencies, represented by Sanders Law PLLC, sued Coed Media for using twelve of their images on various web properties without a license. After a bench trial, the court ruled against Coed Media on fair use and held it liable for infringement. However, the plaintiffs had demanded over $40,000 in damages, and the court only awarded $10,880, holding that the proper measure of damages is not a multiple of the highest license fee, or a multiple of the statutory minimum of $750 (as urged by plaintiffs), but rather what the defendant or a comparable party would have paid as a reasonable license fee multiplied by three or five, depending on the circumstances of the use. The court also declined to award Sanders Law PLLC's attorney's fees, finding Coed Media's defenses not objectively unreasonable, and the plaintiffs' litigation conduct abusive. The plaintiff's firm allegedly lost out on $180,000 in fees for less than $11,000 in damages.

An IP Address Alone May Not Be Enough to Support a Porn Troll Case

Strike 3 Holdings LLC v. John Doe subscriber assigned IP address 72.28.136.217, No. 1:19-cv-20761 (S.D. Fla. May 7, 2019): A Florida federal judge ruled that porn copyright cases cannot move forward based solely on an IP address, because the IP address does not constitute sufficient evidence identifying who actually illegally downloaded the copyrighted video. Typically, a porn troll plaintiff monitors IP addresses corresponding to downloads of their copyrighted films, files a lawsuit based on where an IP address is located, and then issues a subpoena to force the ISP to disclose the name of the subscriber to that IP address. Judge Ungaro explained that

> it is entirely possible that the IP address belongs to a coffee shop or open Wi-Fi network, which the alleged infringer briefly used on a visit to Miami. Even if the IP address were located within a residence in this district, the geolocation software cannot identify who has access to that residence's computer and who actually used it to infringe Plaintiff's copyright.

The court acknowledged that while some courts have determined that an IP address alone is sufficient to confirm venue, "several courts have found it troubling that the subscriber associated with a given IP address may not be the person responsible for conduct traceable to that IP address."[33]

Recent SDNY Cases Cracking Down on the Liebowitz Law Firm

Judges in the US District Court for the Southern District of New York are running short on patience when it comes to copyright trolls, particularly the Liebowitz Law Firm. Several decisions over the past two years have highlighted the growing tensions between the bench and copyright trolls. A few examples are as follows.

Cruz v. Am. Broad. Cos., No. 17-cv-8794 (LAK), Dkt. No. 7 (S.D.N.Y. Nov. 17, 2017): Judge Kaplan, *sua sponte*, upon the filing of a Liebowitz-signed complaint, ordered the plaintiff to post security for costs, including attorney's fees, as a condition of proceeding with the action. The judge noted that Liebowitz had filed 452 cases in the Southern District of New York in the last twelve months, including the *Kanongataa* matter, over which he had presided.

McDermott v. Monday Monday, LLC, No. 17CV9230 (DLC), 2018 WL 1033240 (S.D.N.Y. Feb. 22, 2018): The defendant filed a motion to dismiss for lack of personal jurisdiction and the plaintiff withdrew complaint without prejudice. Judge Cote explicitly labeled Liebowitz a "copyright troll" and noted that sanctions may be appropriate under the court's inherent power in cases of frivolous filings. While Judge Cote ultimately declined to award fees, she issued a warning to Liebowitz: "[i]f Mr. Liebowitz files any other action in this district against a defendant over whom there is no non-frivolous basis to find that there is personal jurisdiction, the outcome may be different."

Steeger v. JMS Cleaning Servs. LLC, No. 17 Civ. 8013 (DLC), 2018 WL 1136113 (S.D.N.Y. Feb. 28, 2018), *opinion vacated in part on reconsideration*, 2018 WL 1363497 (S.D.N.Y. Mar. 15, 2018): Less than a week after the *McDermott* ruling, Judge Cote issued an order to show cause as to why Liebowitz should not be sanctioned, resulting in his prompt dismissal of the case. She initially issued sanctions for $10,000 for Liebowitz's failure to notify the defendant of an initial pretrial conference, noting similar past practices, but later reduced sanctions to $2,000 and ordered Liebowitz to take extra ethics CLE classes.

Craig v. Universal Music Group, Inc. et al, No. 16-CV-5439 (JPO) (S.D.N.Y. Jul. 9, 2019): Judge Oetken issued sanctions against Liebowitz for over $98,000 for the attorney's bad-faith filing of a motion to disqualify one of the defendant's expert witnesses, noting that the motion contained "glaring deficiencies" and was "entirely meritless."

Rice v. NBCUniversal Media LLC, No. 1:19-cv-00447 (S.D.N.Y. Jul. 10, 2019): Judge Furman, noting that "there is a growing body of law in this district devoted to the question of whether and when to impose sanctions on Mr. Liebowitz alone," imposed sanctions of $8,745 on Liebowitz and his firm for their repeated failure to comply with court orders.

Berger v. Imagina Consulting, Inc., No. 18-CV-8956 (CS), 2019 WL 6695047, at *4 (S.D.N.Y. Nov. 1, 2019): Liebowitz was held in contempt of Court and sanctioned $500 per day that he failed to comply with the Court's orders. He was ordered to show cause on pain of "arrest by the United States Marshals Service" in connection with his misrepresentation about the date on which his grandfather passed away, which he used to justify missing a discovery conference but refused to provide documentation requested by the court. This misconduct was referred to the S.D.N.Y. Grievance Committee.

Usherson v. Bandshell Artist Management, 16-cv-6368 (JMF) (S.D.N.Y. June 26, 2020): Judge Furman sanctioned Liebowitz for misrepresenting the circumstances behind Liebowitz's and plaintiff's failure to appear at a mediation and his failure to ensure his client's works were registered prior to suing. Judge Furman issued a $103,517.49 sanction; required Liebowitz to serve the opinion and order on the plaintiff and all the firm's current clients; required Liebowitz to file the opinion and order on the docket of any of his firm's pending cases as well as any case filed within a year; and required Liebowitz to attach Copyright Office deposit copies to any complaint filed within a year. This matter was also referred to the S.D.N.Y. Grievance Committee.

What Can Be Done?

Apart from preventative measures aimed at reducing the risk of litigation,[34] the copyright defense bar has stepped up its game in the fight against the abusive litigation tactics of copyright trolls. There are many strategic plays that can keep copyright trolls at bay or increase a target's leverage in settlement negotiations and litigation.

A key threshold issue is whether the plaintiff's images were properly registered. The Supreme Court recently held that claimants may not file a copyright infringement suit until after their works are registered with the Copyright Office (as opposed to merely filing an application), a process which normally takes approximately seven months from the filing of the application.[35] A claimant can expedite the application process by paying an $800 fee, but that is a steep price and may deter some potential plaintiffs, and targets of troll claims should be on the lookout for this dispositive issue.[36]

Assuming the plaintiff has procured a registration, the next pressure point is on the timeliness of registration under § 412 of the Copyright Act (i.e. registration occurred before infringement or, if after, within three months of the work's first publication), absent which the plaintiff cannot opt for statutory damages or move to recover its attorney's fees. While the lack of statutory damages and attorney's fee-shifting is often not dispositive as noted earlier, it will take some of the sting out of a claim and can often move settlement negotiations to a more reasonable place.

Of course, if there is a clearly applicable defense to liability (such as statute of limitations, lack of personal jurisdiction, or in rarer cases, DMCA protection or fair use), explanation in writing of the shortcomings of the case and, if appropriate, a threat of sanctions under Rule 11 of the Federal Rules of Civil Procedure (which imposes penalties for filing frivolous claims) can sometimes force a plaintiff into submission. Of course, many defenses are fact-intensive, and trolls know this, so one should always be prepared for a debate particularly in the context of fair use.

An offer of judgment under Rule 68 of the Federal Rules of Civil Procedure can also be an effective tool in deterring copyright trolls. That rule says a defendant can offer a plaintiff an all-inclusive dollar-figure judgment in exchange for immediate resolution of the case.[37] If the plaintiff accepts, the case is over and judgment is entered on the public court docket.[38] The defendant gains leverage when the plaintiff rejects the offer of judgment or lets it lapse without response, because if the plaintiff secures a judgment that is less favorable than the offer of judgment would have been if accepted, the defendant is entitled to seek reimbursement of its costs from the time of the rejection of the offer forward.[39] The definition of "costs" under Rule 68 includes attorney's fees where the underlying statute allows for fee-shifting, as the Copyright Act does.[40] There is some dispute about whether a defendant can recoup its attorneys' fees under Rule 68 if it is found liable and is therefore not the "prevailing party" as contemplated by the Copyright Act's fee-shifting provision, but there is a case law to support the notion that even losing defendants can turn the fee-shifting tables on a plaintiff who rejected an offer of judgment.[41]

Another recent trend in repelling troll claims is to request that the court force the plaintiff to post a bond in order to proceed with the case. This tactic is particularly useful in very low-value cases (especially those brought by individual plaintiffs) especially where an offer of judgment has been rejected or has lapsed. Where, considering the cost of litigation, it would be unlikely for a plaintiff to be able to foot the bill for shifted fees (see *Kanongataa*),[42] it is prudent to ask the court to require security to allow the plaintiff to proceed with the case.[43] Courts have also held that plaintiffs who have a "record of non-compliance" with court orders may also be ordered to post a bond.[44]

There are also potential legislative solutions to the trolling problem. One, which was introduced into Congress to create a more cost-effective alternative for individual copyright owners than costly federal court litigation, may have a side effect of reducing troll activity. On May 1, 2019, the Copyright Alternative in Small-Claims Enforcement Act of 2019 ("CASE Act") was introduced in the House (H.R. 2426) and passed by an overwhelming vote and passed the Senate (S. 1273) Judiciary Committee, and is currently waiting to be brought to the floor for a full Senate vote.[45] A new version of a 2017 house bill that adds certain provisions to prevent copyright trolls from abusing the system (such as limited fee-shifting, dismissal of all frivolous claims by an abusive filer, and prohibiting abusive claimants from filing a new case for a year), the CASE Act seeks to create a voluntary copyright small-claims court (known as the Copyright Claims Board), which would fall under the auspices of the US Copyright Office and would provide an alternative forum for lower-value copyright claims, with a total cap on liability of $30,000 for any one proceeding and a limit on statutory damages of $15,000 per infringed work.[46] Unlike federal claims under the Copyright Act, representation by a lawyer would not be necessary,[47] and cases would also be handled through written submission and telephonic or web-based conferences.[48] An anticipated consequence of the CASE Act's small-claims option may be fewer overly aggressive claims for small dollar amounts clogging the federal court dockets and draining the resources of the recipients of such claims.

The ultimate legislative solution, of course, would be to eliminate or modify the Copyright Act's statutory damages provision, but this seems unlikely. Statutory damages have been around since 1976, and no proposed legislation to reform the Copyright Act—and there have been many—has even mentioned eliminating or reducing those damages despite some recommendations to reduce them.[49] Elimination or limitation of statutory damages also could have its own set of unintended consequences, for instance, removing the deterrence factor of steep presumed monetary liability and leaving plaintiffs largely uncompensated for infringements of their works.[50] Clearly, more study is necessary for such a drastic change to the law, but it would be a very effective way to curb copyright trolls' abusive practices.

Conclusion

Until major legislative reform takes place, or the CASE Act proves to be a suitable alternative to trolling (which is not a foregone conclusion), an ounce of prevention is worth a pound of cure, and the most effective form of preventing copyright claims is education about best practices in content licensing. Employees of traditional and digital media companies alike (even temps and interns) should be trained and instructed on what content they can and cannot use. Regardless of whether this education is provided internally or through outside counsel, the key points should be memorialized in written policies or employee manuals signed by all trainees. Using licensed content should be the default choice, whether through subscription services or directly from content owners. Another option is using Creative Commons licenses (available at www.creativecommons.org), which often allow for certain types of use without further permissions or license fees (although many do contain other conditions, all require attribution/credit to the copyright owner, and available images are not necessarily vetted prior to being made available). Contrary to popular belief, Google Images is not a collection of public domain or licensable images. Just because people think images on the internet or in social media are free, and just because many in the digital media industry use them as if they are free, does not make the so-called "right-click" license legally "right." When in doubt, consult in-house or outside counsel.

Today's climate of en masse, algorithm-based copyright litigation by contingency-fee law firms provides every incentive and virtually no downside to litigation for the millions of potential plaintiffs whose content makes its way online without authorization. Until the playing field is leveled via legislation, content users must look out for themselves, be proactive and diligent in their procurement of content, and use the available strategic litigation tools to stem the tide of copyright trolling.

Acknowledgment

* The author wishes to thank Nancy Wolff for the opportunity to contribute this essay and Rivka Teitelbaum for her invaluable assistance.

Notes

1 McDermott v. Monday Monday, LLC, No. 17-CV-9230-DLC, 2018 WL 1033240, at *3 n.4 (S.D.N.Y. February 22, 2018).
2 Creazioni Artistiche Musicali, S.r.l. v. Carlin America, Inc., No. 14-CV-9270-RJS, 2017 WL 3393850, at *4 (S.D.N.Y. August 4, 2017).
3 Matthew Sag, "Copyright Trolling, an Empirical Study," *Iowa Law Review* 100, no. 3 (2015): 1113.
4 Brian T. Yeh, "An Overview of the 'Patent Trolls' Debate," Congressional Research Service, April 16, 2013, https://fas.org/sgp/crs/misc/R42668.pdf.
5 "Patent Trolls," Electronic Frontier Foundation, https://www.eff.org/issues/resources-patent-troll -victims.
6 Connie Boutsikaris, "The Rise of Copyright Trolls" March 28, 2017, http://dunnerlaw.com/the-rise -of-copyright-trolls; "Pornography Copyright Trolls: Sword of Antipiracy or Abuse of Antiquated Law," McClanahan Powers, PLLC, May 15, 2015, https://www.mcplegal.com/insights/pornography-copyright -trolls.
7 David Kravets, "Newspaper Chain's New Business Plan: Copyright Suits," *Wired*, July 22, 2010, https:// www.wired.com/2010/07/copyright-trolling-for-dollars; see also Richard Esguerra, "Righthaven's Brand of Copyright Trolling," Electronic Frontier Foundation, September 2, 2010, https://www.eff .org/deeplinks/2010/09/righthavens-own-brand-copyright-trolling.
8 Ian Polonsky, "You Can't Go Home Again: The Righthaven Cases and Copyright Trolling on the Internet," *Columbia Journal of Law & the Arts* 36, no. 1 (Fall 2012): 80.
9 Polonsky, "You Can't Go Home Again," 87.
10 Silvers v. Sony Pictures Entm't, Inc., 402 F.3d 881, 884 (9th Cir. 2005); 17 U.S.C.A. § 501 (2018).
11 Polonsky, "You Can't Go Home Again," 90; National Telecommunications and Information Administration, United States Patent and Trademark Office, Department of Commerce, *Response to the Request for Comments on Department of Commerce Green Paper, Copyright Policy, Creativity, and Innovation in the Digital Economy*, by Andrew P. Bridges (2013), https://www.uspto.gov/sites/default/files/documents/Bridges _Comments.pdf.
12 Bonnie Eslinger, "Prenda Porn Troll Atty Cops to Copyright Fraud Scheme," *Law 360*, March 6, 2017, https://www.law360.com/articles/898898/prenda-porn-troll-atty-cops-to-copyright-fraud-scheme.
13 Eslinger, "Prenda Porn Troll"; United States v. Hansmeier et al., No. 0:16-CR-334-JNE-KMM, 2017 WL 3971874 (D. Minn. September 8, 2017).
14 Eslinger, "Prenda Porn Troll."
15 Bill Donahue, "Second Prenda 'Porn Troll' Attorney Sentenced to 5 Years," *Law 360*, July 9, 2019, https://www.law360.com/articles/1176607/second-prenda-porn-troll-attorney-sentenced-to-5-year; Bill Donahue, "Judge Calls Porn Troll a Fraud, Possible RICO Violator," *Law 360*, May 7, 2013,

https://www.law360.com/articles/439296/judge-calls-porn-troll-a-fraud-possible-rico-violator; Eslinger, "Prenda Porn Troll."

16 Owen Byrd, "Lex Machina Q4 2017 End of the Year Litigation Update," Lex Machina, January 16, 2018, https://lexmachina.com/lex-machina-q4-litigation-update (See Fig. 11); see also "Public Access to Court Electronic Records," Pacer, https://www.pacer.gov.

17 "Malibu Media: EFF Calls for Court Sanctions for Copyright Troll's Public Humiliation Tactic," Electronic Frontier Foundation, accessed May 18, 2020, https://www.eff.org/cases/malibu-media.

18 See Pacer, "Public Access to Court Electronic Records"; see also Bill Donahue, "As 'John Doe' Copyright Cases Spike, Judges Push Back," Law 360, May 17, 2019, https://www.law360.com/articles/1159798/as-john-doe-copyright-cases-spike-judges-push-back.

19 Roy Strom, "Judge Sanctions Fox Rothschild Partner in Porn Copyright Cases," *Law.com*, February 28, 2019, https://www.law.com/2019/02/28/judge-sanctions-fox-rothschild-partner-in-porn-copyright-cases.

20 Strike 3 Holdings, LLC v. Doe, 351 F. Supp. 3d 160, 161 (D.D.C. 2018); Malibu Media, LLC v. Ryan Ramsey, No. 14-CV-718 (S.D. Ohio May 26, 2015).

21 Malibu Media, LLC v. Doe, No. C 15-04441-WHA, 2016 WL 3383758, at *3 (N.D. Cal. June 20, 2016); see also Strike 3 Holdings, LLC v. Doe, 351 F. Supp. 3d at 166; Malibu Media, LLC v. John Does 1 through 10, 12-CV-3632-ODW, 2012 WL 5382304, at *3–4 (C.D. Cal. June 27, 2012); Mike Masnick, "Judge Alsup Threatens to Block Malibu Media From Any More Copyright Trolling in Northern California," *TechDirt*, May 15, 2017, https://www.techdirt.com/articles/20170512/18042637354/judge-alsup-threatens-to-block-malibu-media-any-more-copyright-trolling-northern-california.shtml.

22 See, e.g., Minden Pictures, Inc. v. John Wiley & Sons, Inc., 795 F.3d 997 (9th Cir. 2015); c.f. John Wiley & Sons, Inc. v. DRK Photo, 882 F.3d 394 (2d Cir. 2018), *cert. denied*, 139 S. Ct. 237 (2018).

23 Liebowitz Law Firm, PLLC, https://liebowitzlawfirm.com; Higbee & Associates, https://www.higbeeassociates.com.

24 Jeremy T. Walker, "Know the Law: Beware of Online Copyright Trolls," McLane Middleton, March 26, 2018 https://www.mclane.com/thought-leadership/know-the-law-beware-of-online-copyright-trolls?utm_source=Mondaq&utm_medium=syndication&utm_campaign=View-Original; Daniel Mazanec, "Online Image Infringement and the Statutory-Damages Threat," Law 360, February 20, 2018, https://www.law360.com/articles/1012274/online-image-infringement-and-the-statutory-damages-threat.

25 17 U.S.C. § 504.

26 Barcroft Media, Ltd. v. Coed Media Grp., LLC, 297 F. Supp. 3d 339, 356 (S.D.N.Y. 2017) (in order to "discourage wrongful conduct [and] provide reparation for injury . . . courts often impose as statutory damages a multiple of the applicable licensing fee a defendant would have paid but for the infringement") (internal quotations omitted); Erickson Prods., Inc. v. Only Websites, Inc., No. 12-CV-1693-PGG-KNF, 2016 WL 1337277, at *3 (S.D.N.Y. March 31, 2016) ("In willful copyright infringement cases, trebling the licensing fee is in line with the general approach taken by courts in calculating statutory damages.") (internal quotations and citations omitted); Sailor Music v. IML Corp., 867 F. Supp. 565, 570 (E.D. Mich. November 10, 1994) ("[C]ourts typically award three times the amount of a properly purchased license for each infringement."); see also Philpot v. L.M. Commc'ns II of S.C., Inc., 343 F. Supp. 3d 694, 702 (E.D. Ky. October 18, 2018), *rev'd and remanded on other grounds sub nom.* Philpot v. LM Commc'ns II of S.C., 776 F. App'x 906 (6th Cir. 2019); FameFlynet, Inc. v. Shoshanna Collection, LLC, 282 F. Supp. 3d 618, 627 (S.D.N.Y. 2017), *appeal withdrawn*, No. 18-633, 2018 WL 2740233 (2d Cir. March 20, 2018).

27 Mazanec, "Online Image Infringement."

28 Sag, "Copyright Trolling," 1113.

29 Data based on Westlaw Litigation Analytics.

30 Bill Donahue, "Fox Rothschild Is Fully Out of the Porn Copyright Biz," *Law 360*, July 18, 2019, https://www.law360.com/ip/articles/1179079/fox-rothschild-is-fully-out-of-the-porn-copyright-biz; data based on Westlaw Litigation Analytics.

31 The author's firm, Cowan, DeBaets, Abrahams & Sheppard LLP, represented the defendants in the first two case examples listed.

32 Kanongataa v. Am. Broad. Cos., No. 16-CV-7382-LAK, 2017 WL 2684067, at *2 (S.D.N.Y. June 21, 2017).

33 Malibu Media, LLC v. Doe, No. 13-365-PWG, 2014 WL 7188822, at *4 (D. Md. December 16, 2014); see also Elf-Man, LLC v. Cariveau, No. C 13-0507-RSL, 2014 WL 202096, at *2 (W.D. Wash. January 17, 2014) ("While it is possible that one or more of the named defendants was personally involved in the download, it is also possible that they simply failed to secure their connection against third-party interlopers."); AF Holdings LLC v. Rogers, No. 12-CV-1519-BTM-BLM, 2013 WL 358292, at *3

(S.D. Cal. January 29, 2013) ("Due to the risk of 'false positives,' an allegation that an IP address is registered to an individual is not sufficient in and of itself to support a claim that the individual is guilty of infringement."); Patrick Collins, Inc. v. Doe 1, 288 F.R.D. 233, 237–39 (E.D.N.Y. November 20, 2012) (finding an IP address insufficient to identify an infringer because "the actual device that performed the allegedly infringing activity could have been owned by a relative or guest of the account owner, or even an interloper without the knowledge of the owner").

34 See Scott J. Sholder, "CDAS's Copyright Photo/Video Claims Defense Checklist for Media Platforms," Cowan, DeBaets, Abrahams & Sheppard LLP, May 2, 2018, https://cdas.com/copyrightchecklist.

35 Fourth Estate Pub. Benefit Corp. v. Wall-Street.com, LLC, 139 S. Ct. 881 (2019).

36 *Id.* at 892 n.6.

37 Fed. R. Civ. P. 68.

38 The existence of a judgment can potentially be problematic if, for instance, the defendant is looking to raise capital or sell its business.

39 Fed. R. Civ. P. 68(d).

40 See Marek v. Chesny, 473 U.S. 1, 9, 105 S. Ct. 3012, 3016, 87 L. Ed. 2d 1 (1985) ("all costs properly awardable in an action are to be considered within the scope of Rule 68 "costs""); Jordan v. Time, Inc., 111 F.3d 102, 105 (11th Cir. 1997) ("Rule 68 "costs" include attorneys' fees when the underlying statute so prescribes. The Copyright Act so specifies); Wilson v. Nomura Sec. Int'l, Inc., 361 F.3d 86, 89 (2d Cir. 2004) ("Where the underlying statute defines 'costs' to include attorney's fees, therefore, such fees are 'costs' for purposes of Rule 68."); Baker v. Urban Outfitters, Inc., 431 F. Supp. 2d 351, 361 (S.D.N.Y. May 8, 2006), aff'd, 249 F. App'x 845 (2d Cir. 2007) ("The Copyright Act defines 'costs' to include attorney's fees.").

41 See Mango v. Democracy Now! Prods., Inc., No. 18-CV-10588-DLC, 2019 WL 3325842, at *4 (S.D.N.Y. July 24, 2019); Lee v. W Architecture & Landscape Architecture, LLC, No. 18-CV-5820-PKC-CLP, 2019 WL 2272757, at *4 (E.D.N.Y. May 28, 2019) ("[T]he notion of 'prevailing party' is not a factor in a Rule 68 analysis"); Baker, 431 F. Supp. 2d at 363 (defendant was awarded fees and costs pursuant to Rule 68 and § 505 of the Copyright Act where defendant's Rule 68 offer was rejected and the court ruled that plaintiff's damages were limited to an amount less than Rule 68 offer); Jordan v. Time, Inc., 111 F.3d 102, 105 (11th Cir. 1997) (holding that the plaintiff was required to pay the defendant's costs, including attorney's fees, incurred after the defendant made a Rule 68 offer, even where defendant was not the prevailing party); Lucas v. Wild Dunes Real Estate, Inc., 197 F.R.D. 172, 175–76 (D.S.C. August 31, 2000) (same).

42 Kanongataa, to date, has not paid a single cent of fees owed to the defendants in his ill-fated lawsuit.

43 See, e.g., Lee, 2019 WL 2272757, at *4 (requiring a plaintiff employed as a photographer, and Liebowitz Law Firm client, to post bond); Sadowski v. JSN Glob. Media, Inc., No. 18-CV-1392 (S.D.N.Y. July 12, 2018) (order requiring same); Tabak v. Idle Media, Inc., No. 17-CV- 8285-AT (S.D.N.Y. October 31, 2017) (same).

44 See, e.g., Lee, 2019 WL 2272757, at *2 (ordering the Liebowitz Law Firm to post a bond because of the "concern that if attorneys' fees are assessed against plaintiff, then plaintiff's counsel will voluntarily dismiss the case to avoid paying defendant any fees it may be owed"); see also Leibowitz v. Galore Media, Inc., No. 18-CV-2626-RA-HBP, 2018 WL 4519208, at *2 (S.D.N.Y. September 20, 2018). ("[I]mposition of the bond was justified by (1) the prospect that defendant could be entitled to costs under the Copyright Act and (2) [the Liebowitz Law Firm's] well-documented history of evading court orders in similar litigation in [S.D.N.Y. and E.D.N.Y.].").

45 See "Support the CASE Act: Copyright Small Claims," Copyright Alliance, accessed May 18, 2020, https://copyrightalliance.org/news-events/copyright-news-newsletters/copyright-small-claims; Daniel Sanchez, "Small Claims Copyright Court? Senate Judiciary Committee Approves the 2019 'CASE Act'," *Digital Music News*, July 19, 2019, https://www.digitalmusicnews.com/2019/07/19/case-act-2019-advances.

46 Keith Kupferschmid and Terrica Carrington, "The CASE Act: You Have Questions. We Have the Answers," *Copyright Alliance*, May 13, 2019, https://copyrightalliance.org/ca_post/the-case-act-you-have-questions-we-have-the-answers.

47 Kupferschmid and Carrington, "The CASE Act."

48 Kupferschmid and Carrington, "The CASE Act."

49 See David Kluft, "Highlights of Congressional Hearings on Copyright Remedies: Statutory Damages, Small Claims and Felonious Streaming," Trademark and Copyright Law Blog, August 12, 2014, https://www.trademarkandcopyrightlawblog.com/2014/08/highlights-of-congressional-hearings-on-copyright-remedies-statutory-damages-small-claims-and-felonious-streaming.

50 Pamela Samuelson and Tara Wheatland, "Statutory Damages in Copyright Law: A Remedy in Need of Reform," *William & Mary Law Review* 51 no. 2 (2009): 499–500.

8.4

VIRTUAL REALITY

Blending the Real World with Copying

Kenneth N. Swezey and Elizabeth Altman

Introduction

You have arrived home after a long day. You hang up your coat, kick off your shoes, and put on some music, the backdrop for the evening—right now you are in the mood for Bach, but later, you will switch on a jazz track or the Beatles. You sit down in the living room across from your television, which, powered down, displays the art screen saver you change every month or so; currently, you have chosen Rembrandt. You decide to unwind with a video game, and the painting gives way to a maze, which you career through, searching out the exit with a ruthless gang on your heels. Toward the evening's end, you are in for quieter fare and curl up in an armchair with your latest read, a novel you heard about after it received international fanfare. Before the night is through, you spend a few minutes corresponding with your lawyer, providing information on a parking ticket you recently received.

Do any of the milestones from this evening, from Bach to bed, appear out of place from the litany of ordinary events populating an otherwise quiet night in? Perhaps not, but yet, each and every part—the music, the artwork, the game, the novel, and yes, even the lawyer—could easily, and increasingly, have been "authored" by artificial intelligence (AI).

Throughout the past decade, the algorithmic capacities of AI have grown by leaps and bounds. Examples of AI-generated works could alone fill the pages of this book, and they include the novella you paged through,[1] as well as the Rembrandt on your screen.[2] AI systems' utilitarian prospects span medical diagnostics,[3] lawyering,[4] psychoanalysis, and investing, and AI has already been put to task to generate new Beatles' tunes, poetry, video games, news articles, contracts, recipes, and even pickup lines, and has shown early strides in mass transit and weaponry. AI is poised to touch upon and affect society beyond measure.

Indeed, increasingly capable and *autonomous* AI is poised to raise a host of hefty questions for the coming generation, first and foremost, and obviously, among them: Where is the line separating human versus machine? This philosophical "square one" necessarily begs the additional question, or, rather, *questions*, which stem from the arts, medicine, government, industry, and the law—the fields that AI will likely affect in years to come. This chapter will take up one such field, examining AI technology in the context of copyright law. Namely, how will the present copyright law embrace AI in terms of authorship, as artificial neural networks grow increasingly capable of generating creative works with minimal input, via processes that sometimes confound even their own programmers?

While there are numerous potential resolutions to this question, many of them ultimately run the route of "intellectual property thought experiment," an exercise in reimagining the law in the context and sweeping excitement of "the next big (technological) thing." However, it is important to remember that, at the end of the day, copyright and copyright law were built for the advent of new technology; Congress intended that the law retain enough statutory flexibility to withstand the needle-shifting technologies that inevitably move one era into another. Indeed, Congress has only passed new iterations of the US Copyright Act four times in the history of the US,[5] with the current 1976 Copyright Act patched for the present-day with just a handful of amendments.[6] As such, it is our contention that the Copyright Act, and the judges who interpret it, will be able to withstand, without undue overhaul, the onslaught of authorship questions that will be raised by AI technology. Whether this hardiness arises as a result of courts employing new or unique conceptualizations of what exactly AI-generated works are (for example, one could conceive of an AI algorithm *itself* as art, such that the algorithm would be considered the ultimate output, with any subsequent material it generates designated a derivative work) or whether it will require an expansion of existing doctrines, such as work made for hire (WMFH), it is our suggestion that copyright is better equipped to take on AI technology than one might otherwise presume; after all, the brave new world of AI was the brave new world of photography, radio, motion pictures, and computers, for generations before.

What is AI Technology, and How Does It Work?

Any discussion of the path that AI technology might chart within copyright law would do best to begin with at least a basic working knowledge of how AI operates, considering that it is the actual mechanics of AI giving rise to the questions that copyright currently faces.

What is AI? Short question, long answer. At the very least, scholars tend to agree that AI is hard to define, variously noting that "AI is a broad and nebulous field,"[7] that "[d]efining AI systems is not an easy task,"[8] and that "there does not yet appear to be any widely accepted definition of artificial intelligence even among experts in the field . . . ."[9]

Even so, various terms have begun entering the AI lexicon, signposts along the long and winding road of establishing a vocabulary to communicate a new—and evolving—technology. Foremost among them are "rules-based decision making," "machine learning," "neural networks," "weights," and "deep learning."

The terms operate somewhat akin to Russian nesting dolls. "Artificial Intelligence" is, itself, at the outermost layer, a broad umbrella encapsulating the methodologies that give rise to it. This "Artificial Intelligence" is conceivable as "any technique that enables computers to mimic human intelligence,"[10] such that the computers gain the ability to perform tasks dependent upon intelligent rationalization, decision-making, spontaneity, and communication.

First among the various techniques for building an AI is the rules-based decision-making process, wherein an AI system applies embedded "human-made rules to store, sort and manipulate data," accomplishing aims via an "IF-THEN" approach ("If X happens, then do Y") when faced with input data.[11] The rules within this programming trigger actions for the system to follow. Among modern-day AI methodologies, the circumscribed, logic-based nature of the rules-based process—especially as compared with neural networks' increasingly learning-based nature[12]—has led to disagreement as to whether rules-based systems truly even remain a branch of AI, or if, instead, AI requires that a machine be capable of autonomous "intelligence." Others distinguish between "machine learning" and "deep learning." Machine learning is the process whereby a computer learns to perform tasks by analyzing training examples. Deep learning, however, qualifies as a machine learning subset wherein a computer undertakes a similar task-oriented process but on a much larger scale, its algorithm "permit[ting its] software to train *itself* to perform tasks . . . by exposing multilayered neural networks to vast amounts of data."[13] Scholars align rules-based AI with the former camp and neural networks with the latter. Ultimately, however, semantics matter less than actually understanding the difference between the systems, namely that, as compared with neural networks, rules-based systems are incapable of thinking beyond their code.[14]

Autonomous "intelligence" has lately grown increasingly synonymous with neural networks. Neural networks were first proposed by researchers in the mid-1940s, enjoying a middling low-radar profile throughout the latter half of the twentieth century, only to grow exponentially in popularity as the go-to mechanism for engendering AI in the past decade. The term "neural" derives from the way that such networks mimic the biology of the human brain to achieve a learning outcome, with "perceptrons" duplicating the function of neurons, and containing sensory units, associator units, and response units. Such networks allow AI systems to replicate human problem-solving cognition by allowing them to "absorb[] and distribut[e] their information processing capacity to [these] groups of receptors."[15] Like neurons, perceptrons "find and create connections and similarities within the data they process."[16]

Essentially, neural networks "learn" information as they train for their particular applications, using that information to solve problems beyond the scope of their initial training. In the process of this "learning," however, neural networks have the potential to outpace their programmers' actual understanding of what and how they have learned. That is because of the way that neural networks process the information they are fed, via three programmed layers—an input layer, hidden layer, and an output layer. The process begins as neural networks receive relevant information data sets via their input layer, think "Top 100" songs, recipes from "Bon Appetit," or a collection of romantic lines from historic poetry or literature. These data sets then travel along the hidden layers residing in between the input and output layers.[17] Finally, the output layer produces its result—think, a new pop song, recipe, or pickup line.[18]

Within the input layer, associator units determine whether to transfer input data to subsequent perceptrons, making this determination based on random initial coefficients, or as they are called within the AI lexicon, "weights." These initial weights relate to the various relevant factors that support the ultimate task the network has been programmed to achieve, and they control whether and to what extent an associator unit will "amplify" or "dampen" the ability for data to travel throughout the network, conveyed as output signals to subsequent perceptrons.[19] After each completed round of input and output, the network measures its results, and repeats the process, varying the weights of each factor to better approximate the goal. In this way, the AI "assign[s] significance to inputs with regard to the task the algorithm is trying to learn," determining which ones are "more helpful [to] classifying [the] data without error."[20] Through numerous iterations of this intelligent trial and error training, the network will settle on a final set of weights that will best allow it to perform its task.

Because of the inherent internality of assigning weights, even where the input provided is otherwise controlled, "AI systems often remain black boxes: They may be able to correctly and consistently predict [or provide] a particular outcome . . . but they cannot explain the *reasons* for this conclusion."[21] An inventor

> will probably not know the final weights, and if he does, he will not know the significance of the weights for each component. Learning the final weights requires 'exhaustive experimental study' [in large part because] the weights [themselves] involve no human intervention. . . . If a network engineer opened up a network to examine the weights, their values would make no sense. The neural network has 'learned.' The network can now do something beyond its initial programming—something that its creator may have hoped it could do, but could never explain. Therein lie the intellectual property problems.[22]

Copyright Law's Authorship Requirement

Copyright law, the world over, protects the authors of creative works. The rationale for this protection may differ—the US, for example, has long heralded its copyright regime as a means of incentivizing further "Progress of Science and useful Arts,"[23] while European nations tend to justify copyright via a personhood rationale, recognizing that authors pour their personalities into their works and thus deserve continuing rights to them—but the general outcome is the same. Copyright affords authors a time-based monopoly[24] over their works, allowing them to benefit from the exclusive ownership of copyright's bundle of rights, specifically rights to reproduce, prepare derivative works, distribute, perform, display, and transmit.[25]

Copyright does not automatically attach to a work upon its creation, however. To merit its protections, in the US, for example, an author must have created an "original work[] of authorship fixed in a[] tangible medium of expression."[26] The phrase *"original* work" gives rise to copyright's originality requirement, which, while left undefined in the Copyright Act, has been expounded upon by the Supreme Court, which has specified that "the originality requirement is not particularly stringent" but nonetheless requires an author to "display some minimal level of creativity" in his or her work in order to receive protection for it.[27] While the majority of works pass this test, a "narrow category of works in which the creative spark is utterly lacking or so trivial as to be virtually nonexistent" will not; examples include telephone books organized by rote alphabetization[28] or simple lists of ingredients for a recipe.[29] Although a low bar, "[o]riginality remains the *sine qua non* of copyright; accordingly, copyright protection may extend only to those components of a work that are original to the author."[30]

Part and parcel to the originality requirement, copyright requires an act of *authorship.* "Authored" works are distinguished by the fact of being created versus discovered, as a person who merely discovers a fact will not be deemed an author. Furthermore, one cannot copyright a mere idea, even where the expression of the idea would be protectable.

With this primer, perhaps one of the more troublesome intersections between autonomous AI and copyright begins to materialize. AI is increasingly capable of generating creative works with minimal human intervention and increasingly does so by evolving *beyond* that initial intervention (i.e. accelerating its capacities, particularly in assigning weights, beyond that for which its original coding provided). As such, AI raises unique questions as to authorship and originality. Were AI technology merely another tool to facilitate human creativity, like computer technology has been—think a word processor for typing a novel, a phone app to record a song, or a Photoshop filter to vary the look of a photograph—it could seamlessly take its place among this list. But, where AI itself bears an increasingly autonomous creative role, in ways that its human programmers cannot always even understand, who, then, should the law consider the author of the final work?

Authorship, Originality, and AI

An inventor has every right to copyright an AI program itself, as the US Copyright Act has protected computer software within its definition of "literary works" since 1980.[31] However, where that software actually produces or contributes to the production of separate, subsequent works, "[t]he question of originality becomes much more difficult because [an] inventor [of an AI system] seeks a copyright for a work that he did not produce."[32] The question, in such cases, becomes what level of human creativity the law requires for copyright protection, now that a machine may conceivably be deemed an author or coauthor.

This is not the first time that courts have had to consider just how far copyright extends beyond human authorship. While many copyright regimes the world over do not explicitly require a human author as an element of originality, many such regimes, including that of the US', lack language specifically *protecting* works authored by non-humans, and, accordingly, courts have hesitated to award such copyrights. Instead, courts have heeded the suggestion underlying copyright case law that human authorship is implicit in originality.[33]

But, even if the level of human creativity required by copyright ends up barring an AI system from being seen as the "author" of its work, the authorship question will not yet have been resolved. Instead, it must settle on who, along the long line of individuals who may have played a part in bringing about the ultimate AI-generated work—all of whom may be necessary, from the programmer of the AI system to the ultimate user of the neural network, and from the person who has chosen the input data training set to the investor who financed the system's development—should be called "author."

To settle upon the appropriate person—or entity—to whom copyright should be awarded, it is helpful to consider various analogues within the history of copyright law that have likewise presented challenging questions surrounding originality and/or authorship, such as computer technology and human-alternative authorship. Where instructive, such precedent is examined throughout the following sections, which propose and explore the parties that could adopt the AI authorship mantle, including the AI itself, the programmer, or the user, or, instead, could involve no party, but, rather, a reconceptualization of what AI-generated works actually are. Further, we will consider the utility of adopting new ways to view AI output, either as a derivative work of the original AI system or a WMFH.

Approach 1: AI-as-Author

Should an AI system be considered the author of a work that it produces? This is not an entirely new question. For example, the National Commission on New Technological Uses of Copyrighted Works (CONTU) took up its predecessor in 1978, considering whether to extend protection to computer programs.[34] CONTU ultimately recommended that any new copyright laws permit copyright protection for computer programs "to the extent that they embody an author's original creation," a recommendation that Congress subsequently adopted by adding "computer program[s]" to section 101 of the Copyright Act.[35] However, with the fledgling state of deep learning technology at the time, CONTU ultimately punted on authorship, concluding that there was no reasonable basis to believe that computers played a part in producing the work they facilitated.

The Office of Technology Assessment (OTA) was also early to the fray, considering in 1986 whether the owner of a copyright in an *AI system* would be entitled to copyright in the system's output.[36] Acknowledging that AI is designed to produce "a pattern of output that would be considered intelligent if it were displayed by a human being," the OTA nonetheless similarly left unresolved the question of authorship.[37]

As AI technology has advanced to a state wherein authorship is worth readdressing, some parties have advocated for a straightforward, if questionable system to implement, wherein AI would own the copyright to its works. For example, in February 2017, the European Parliament proposed a legislative resolution intending to create a "specific legal status for robots in the long run," although this effort was ultimately abandoned.[38]

AI scholar and professor Shlomit Yanisky-Ravid, PhD, has opined that at least philosophically speaking, an AI system that creates an original piece of artwork technically does meet the criteria for copyright protection, the only exception being its status as a machine.[39] For instance, the Copyright Act states that "[c]opyright in a work protected under this title vests initially in the author"[40] with the Supreme Court merely expounding that an "author is the party who actually creates the work."[41] Emphasizing this generalized language, increasing factions propose a modern copyright regime that *would* recognize the legal status and rights of autonomous and spontaneously evolving AI systems.

Would it be irrational to grant AI systems ownership in the works they produce? This would not be the first time that courts have considered using a "legal fiction" to bestow personhood upon non-humans. However, when faced with this crossroads, the US courts have summarily refused to accord legal status to non-human entities, as far as copyright ownership is concerned.

In *Naruto v. Slater*, for example—or as it is known throughout intellectual property circles, "the monkey selfie case"—a monkey, through People for the Ethical Treatment of Animals (PETA), brought a copyright infringement action after having taken a selfie with an unattended camera, which the camera's owner subsequently commercially used.[42] Reviewing the events, the Ninth Circuit held that the monkey "and all animals, since they are not human [] lack[] statutory standing under the Copyright Act."[43] In other words, the Ninth Circuit did not believe that Naruto, a crested macaque, was a sufficient party to bring the case, regardless of the substance or merit of its suit. Turning to parallel case law related to cetaceans (namely, whales, dolphins, and porpoises that had, elsewhere, been invoked in a case involving habitat-damaging low-frequency sonar), the *Naruto* court maintained that "[i]f Congress and the President intended to take the extraordinary step of authorizing animals as well as people and legal entities to sue [on the animals' behalves], they could, and should, have said so plainly."[44]

Two decades prior, the Ninth Circuit fielded another authorship oddity in *Urantia Foundation v. Maaherra*, in which parties to an infringement dispute believed a book at issue to have been "authored by celestial beings" and merely transcribed by humans.[45] Noting that as a threshold matter in qualifying for copyright protection "a work must be original to the author," the Ninth Circuit concluded that "it is not creations of divine beings that the copyright laws were intended to protect, and that in this case some element of human creativity must have occurred in order for the Book to be copyrightable."[46] As such, the court determined that the human "scribes" in the case were at least partial authors, owing to their having, at minimum, organized and compiled the book's pages, even if the litigants did not so conceive themselves.

With these paradigms in mind, it would be difficult to reconcile affording artificial legal personhood to AI. Although AI systems are independent and artificial beings, with code that, once authored, is capable of autonomous development, no more can these systems enforce their rights than reap their benefits, especially considering that, like animals or "celestial" beings, they lack incentive to do either. Furthermore, as highlighted by *Naruto*, the statutory language of the Copyright Act includes a litany of human-centric language to persuade against non-human copyright ownership. Specifically, sections 101, 201, 203, and 304 address whether the "children" of an "author" can inherit certain rights under the Act, while section 203(a)(2)(A) contemplates the rights of an author's "widow" or "widower" in the event that the author is not survived by "children" or "grandchildren." As the *Naruto* court opined, these terms signify humanity by invoking various exclusively human establishments, such as marriage, descendance, and intestacy. Similarly, there is no indication that a court faced with issues of AI authorship would be any more inclined to leap into the potentially legislative waters of carving new territories of authorship than its counterparts who refrained from doing so, considering that, as in *Naruto*, Congress has not explicitly authorized AI systems to bring suit on their own behalves.

Further, even *should* Congress consider such authorization, it is unclear how a system enabling autonomous AIs would function. Ownership implementation hurdles would invariably abound and would draw into their uncharted (or unchartable) waters additional questions surrounding copyright duration, which in the US lasts for the *life* of the author plus an additional seventy years. Conceivably, an AI system is closer to immortal than otherwise; at what point would it yield ownership, or rather, *should* it?

Approach 2: Programmer-as-Author

If it would be unwieldy to award an AI system authorship, and thus ownership, of the copyrights for its generated works, perhaps that role would be more appropriately reserved for the inventor, or programmer, of the AI.[47]

The programmer-as-author approach would at least initially align with the current copyright regime, which affords copyrights to the authors of code and computerized software, but would extend ownership an extra step, to the person, or persons, who conceivably played the most necessary role in the process of the AI-generated work: generating the AI. Crediting human agency for the output of an AI system would track with the traditional view of computers as inert instrument[s], such as cameras or typewriters that function only via human activation, but in this programmer-as-author conceptualization, the programmer—rather than a third-party user—would own the program's output, in addition to the program. To function, this approach may require courts to reconfigure their conceptions of AI systems, necessitating a shift from viewing them as quasi-autonomous entities to instead conceiving of them as sophisticated—though not necessarily truly artificial—intelligence. Logically bolstering this shift is the sense that "the network would not have existed without the human effort put into designing its overall structure and topography, determining the component parts of the program, and deciding how to train the network."[48]

The approach is not without pitfalls, however. Although it may appear a seamless leap, courts have commonly dismissed computer programmers' attempts to assert ownership of their programs' output. In *Rearden LLC v. Walt Disney Co.*, for example, the company behind the facial performance capture software used in live-action Disney films *Beauty and the Beast* and *Deadpool* sued various film studios for infringement, alleging that the studios had used their technology without permission, and that as the programmers, they were the copyright owners of the files and images that their software had rendered.[49] Dismissing these claims, the court stressed that software owners' copyrights should only extend to program output where the program "does the lion's share of the work" and where the program's user plays only a "marginal" role in creating the output.[50] In this case, at least, the court determined that it would be inappropriate to so extend copyright, considering the users' significant contributions—namely, the film actors' facial expressions and movements—that had been inputted into the software.

However, the *Rearden* standard addresses computer software, not AI. If applied as formulated to AI, this standard would likely render *AI* programmers shoo-ins for copyright ownership, considering that AI systems typically *do* the lion's share of the work and users' input may often *be* marginal. While this standard may appropriately govern the processes of non-intelligent software, it may be lacking as to AI systems whose hallmark is creative autonomy. Though it may mediate questions of authorship as between the programmer and the user of an AI system, the standard does not fully approach either's claims against the actual AI.

The concerns raised by a programmer-as-author model tie to this push and pull between programmers and their AI, and whether programmers' contributions can actually meet the threshold for originality considering AI systems' increasing capacity for autonomously generating works. While courts could arguably resolve this contest by retooling their conceptions of originality to conceive of the inventor of a neural network as the author of the network *and* what it produces (and, for that matter, any such shift could arguably naturally occur, without explicit revision to the Copyright Act), it remains to be seen whether relying on a "conceptual shift as cure-all" would be asking too much, stretching a fiction about AI-output processes too far. However, this would not be the first time that the law has pointed out society's path at a technological crossroads, solidifying cultural philosophies and viewpoints in legal opinion so as to reiterate and advance those views. For example, bookending the Wright brothers first flight on December 17, 1903 was the legal presumption that a property owner owned "not just the surface of his land, but all the land below, down to the center of the earth, and all the space above, to 'an indefinite extent, upwards.'"[51] Although this view had prevailed both prior to and in the decades following flight, developing aviation technology increasingly undermined this presumption. "Common sense revolt[ed] at the idea" that the law could continue to toe the party line, pursuant to which flight—even at a reasonable distance—would constitute a taking of property without compensation in the event of disruption or interference.[52] Rather, the courts would retool property law concepts for "the modern world," as the Supreme Court recognized the folly of strictly abiding by a legal philosophy from a pre-flight one. Although the court's decision necessitated limiting property owners' rights to the air space above their land, without this intervention, owners would have been free to erect "no-fly zones" over their property or require airlines to license or purchase the air rights above their property, hindering aviation's development; the need and logistics of new technology had spoken, demanding "common sense." On the cusp of the AI-era, there is no reason to assume that the courts and law could not do what they have always done: revisit legal philosophies in a new light and base a modern approach to AI authorship on the common sense that someone, namely, some human, must own the output of autonomous but not sentient systems, and that this person would most naturally be the systems' programmers.

However, even such a "common sense" consensus leaves loose ends, ones beyond those already addressed. Critics grapple with the programmer-as-author approach so far as it fails to recognize the village that it takes to build an AI, to program it, to train it with input data, to provide it feedback signals for the development of its selection process, to own the system, and to operate it. Considering that all of these functions may indeed be executed by different persons or entities, and that the AI output owes itself to the fulfillment of each and every role, is it appropriate to elect the programmer to reap all the rewards, especially if she completes her role early in the chain reaction, removed from the output plan devised for the AI or the data input and selected (perhaps by the millions) for that plan's performance? Or, is the programmer, as the first driving force, the most obvious person to merit ownership? Would according him or her ownership fulfill the basic purpose of copyright itself: incentivizing the development of more creative works, in this case AI systems? Would the legal conceptual shift to programmer-as-author take copyright a step too far, singling out the AI programmer for spoils that other inventors of technology have never similarly hitherto enjoyed, considering that "the owner of a brush or a camera does not hold the rights over the painting or the photo produced by those objects[?]"[53]

With a litany of questions and a paucity of answers, perhaps it is enough to recognize that, at present, programmer-as-author fills in certain puzzle pieces even where it leaves others blank. At the very least, as compared to AI-as-author, this approach conceivably fosters a functional system of copyright rewards and responsibilities, considering that programmers have the wherewithal and incentive to assign copyright ownership, protect against infringement, and broker licenses, and are, in other words, capable of engaging with the myriad responsibilities and benefits that relate to ownership in a way that AI systems currently cannot.

Approach 3: User-as-Author

Another potential resolution of the AI authorship quandary would be to designate the user of an AI system as the author of its works. The utility in this approach comes from the fact that such systems usually require a significant amount of input, provided by the systems' user. User-as-author is not a new idea, with scholars having recognized the practicality of the approach early on in the age of computer technology:

> [T]here are several reasons it would make sense to designate the user of a generator program as the 'author' of its output, even when the user's contribution is minimal. For one thing, the

user will generally have already tithed to the owner of the program for rights to use it, either by purchase, lease, or license. This provides the programmer with some reward for the value of what he has created (that is, the program). It is not unfair in these circumstances to give some rights to a person who uses the work for its intended purpose of creating additional works.[54]

This approach also respects the fact that computer-generated works only exist because a user is the initial driving force motivated to engage the machinery.

Various courts have advocated for this approach, including in *Express Newspapers Plc v. Liverpool Daily Post & Echo Plc*,[55] which, albeit prior to the advent of AI, addressed ownership of a sequence of letters produced for a game by an automated process. There, the court reasoned that "the computer was no more than a tool" and that to deny copyright to the human creator who had used that tool "would be to suggest that, if you write your work with a pen, it is your pen which is the author of the work rather than the person who drives the pen."[56] With this consideration, the court deemed the user of a system that ultimately produced a computer-generated work to be its author.

Indeed, this conceptualization may best capture the actual process, or at least the present process, of users' experiences feeding and calibrating AI. Artist and technologist Ross Goodwin and filmmaker Oscar Sharp, for example, have shared their experience working with their AI system—which named itself "Benjamin"—on specific tasks, such as screenwriting.[57] Goodwin described the "one important lever" of creative control the human user or programmer retains when using an AI system, that is, over its "temperature" parameter, which determines the riskiness of the system's next-level predictions.[58] Goodwin and Sharp noted that they retain control over Benjamin's "temperature" to dial up or down Benjamin's creativity, and that in this way, the three of them write together now, developing poetry and movie dialogues.

Even so, this approach invites concerns. First, it is often difficult to distinguish *between* the user of a generative process and its programmer, so as to assign authorship, or coauthorship, appropriately. Second, this approach continues to fail to account for the AI's own agency in selecting, arranging, weighing, and ultimately creating its output, beyond whatever initial weights or temperatures its user assigns. And, as courts have already determined, where "an end-user's role in creating [computerized output] is marginal," such that "the [s]oftware does the lion's share of the work," a user's input "would fail to meet the minimum threshold of originality."[59] Even though authorship requires only a minimal level of originality, one must wonder—especially where the user has not exercised much agency in selecting the inputs to teach the system—if merely pressing a button on an AI system really surpasses that low bar.[60]

Approach 4: AI Output as Derivative Work

Another solution for determining the ownership of AI-generated works would be to consider them derivative works. This model would conceive of AI output as derivative of the AI software program, so that whoever owned the copyright in the algorithm—most likely the programmer— would also own the copyright in the output. In this way, this solution is essentially the programmer-as-author model, arriving at this result via an alternative legal framework.

Critics of this model point, again, to the increasing independence of AI systems that autonomously generate output as they evolve from their original inputs and weights. These are systems making choices independently of their underlying code. Similarly, this model also runs contrary to the "multiplayer" nature of AI; not only does AI-generated work depend as a cause in fact upon its software, but also upon the data sources it analyzes and the initial weights it is given as to right and wrong outputs, stages that typically involve different human actors. A rose by any other name would smell as sweet, and, here, regardless of calling an AI-generated work derivative or programmer-authored, the outcome still results in legal uncertainty.

Approach 5: AI Output as a Work Made for Hire (i.e. the User-as-Author)

The WMFH doctrine is another alternative for resolving the AI authorship question. Regardless of its application to the AI sphere, the WMFH doctrine "is an important and major exception" under copyright law "to the general rule that copyright protection properly rests with the one or the many who actually created the work"; under WMFH, authorship instead vests in "the employer and main contractor . . . even though they have not actually created" the work.[61] Via the WMFH doctrine, the employer, rather than the employee-creator, is responsible for and accounts for the actions of the creator, should his or her work ultimately be infringed or, alternatively, have caused harm.

Under an AI-focused WMFH framework, the law would essentially treat the user of an AI system as its employer, and therefore the "author-in-law" of any work it would produce.[62] The AI itself would operate akin to an employee or contractor working for the humans or firms engaged in its operation. This approach would treat the AI's users as its authors, and these users would both shoulder the accountability for and enjoy the benefits of the systems' productions.

The various benefits of this approach include, first, an avoidance of the problems attending the AI-as-author model, wherein the rights of copyright and the ability or incentive to profit from copyright ownership would vest, uselessly, in a machine, with no sense of accountability. The model also accounts for the fact that an AI system *is* actually the proximate creator of the work with the user of the system being the person or persons for whom the work was created.

Unsurprisingly, this model is also not without its drawbacks. Determining who the "employer" or "main contractor" is could be a confusing task; this role may seem naturally best suited for the user operating the AI system and directing its task, but it could also suit a user who otherwise buys and invests in the machine, without conducting the actual operation. Nonetheless, there would likely be room within this model for flexibility in toggling between either of these, or other, figures for the employer role, just as, in the traditional WMFH doctrine, courts have employed agency law to determine who qualifies as an "employee."

Conclusion: Copyright Law Is Built to Adapt to New Technologies

Copyright law, and indeed the law, is no stranger to advancement. Copyright has existed for nearly as long as the US, and has repeatedly seen and accommodated the rise of new technology. To facilitate this process, Congress has continued to make clear its intention for a flexible Copyright Act capable of growing with the technologies of the times, readily and without continual amendment.

As discussed, more than a handful of technologies have shifted the needle of society prior to AI and thus impacted the law, from flight and its implications for property law to photography and its impact on intellectual property.[63] AI technology may be the next era-shifting technology, poised to enter virtually every aspect of life, from the music on our stereos to the art on our walls. Will such circumstances require copyright to adjust, sit up, and take notice? Assuredly. Even so, the questions that AI will likely raise within copyright—first and foremost, surrounding authorship— are not insurmountable for the current copyright regime. Whether AI-generated works should be deemed works made for hire; derivative; or authored by the system's user, programmer, or even the AI itself, courts may always look to the tone of precedent, if not to the exact letter, put to technology from an increasingly technologically distant era. The current questions surrounding AI authorship may be best parsed by beginning with a "common sense" approach, weighing the pros and cons of each authorship framework against the importance of fostering evolving AI technology. Copyright law has seen technology come and go, and was, in fact, built for the ebb and flow. As AI technology settles into a common language and widespread application, there is every indication that copyright law will, once again, do what it does best, carving a niche for the technology within existing law and defining, even, our conception of the AI itself.

Notes

1 In 2016, the AI-generated "The Day a Computer Writes a Novel" reached the second round of the Nikkei Hoshi Shinichi Literary Award in Japan. A team of programmers at Japan's Future University Hakodate "selected words and sentences, and set parameters for construction before letting the AI 'write' the novel autonomously." Japanese science fiction novelist, Satoshi Hase, who reviewed the AI entries, found himself "surprised at the [body of] work," which he considered "well-structured novel[s]," notwithstanding some descriptive shortcomings. Chloe Olewitz, "A Japanese A.I. Program Just Wrote a Short Novel, and It Almost Won a Literary Prize," *Digital Trends*, March 23, 2016, https://www.digitaltrends.com/cool-tech/japanese-ai-writes-novel-passes-first-round-nationanl-literary-prize.

2 The Next Rembrandt, a program which, over eighteen months, analyzed 346 of the master's paintings and 150 gigabytes of digitally rendered graphics in order to create a new artwork, successfully learned and replicated Rembrandt's style. See, e.g., Shlomit Yanisky-Ravid, "Generating Rembrandt: Artificial Intelligence, Copyright, and Accountability in the 3a Era-the Human-Like Authors Are Already Here-A New Model," *Michigan State Law Review* 2017 (2017): 663; "A 'New' Rembrandt: From the Frontiers of AI and Not the Artist's Atelier," *NPR*, April 6, 2016, https://www.npr.org/sections/alltechconsidered/2016/04/06/473265273/a-new-rembrandt-from-the-frontiers-of-ai-and-not-the-artists-atelier. The artwork the AI generated was unveiled in Amsterdam in 2016 and is a portrait of a mustachioed and goateed middle-age man wearing a wide-brimmed hat, black shirt, and white collar.

3 For example, IBM's Watson correctly diagnosed a patient's rare disease within just ten minutes where it would have taken her doctors two weeks. See Nurfilzah Rohaidi, "IBM's Watson Detected Rare Leukemia in Just 10 Minutes," *Asian Scientist*, August 15, 2016, https://www.asianscientist.com/2016/08/topnews/ibm-watson-rare-leukemia-university-tokyo-artificial-intelligence.

4 Over the course of twenty-one months, a "lawyer bot," created by a Stanford University student, beat 160,000 parking tickets in London and New York, worth over $4 million. See, e.g., Samuel Gibbs, "Chatbot Lawyer Overturns 160,000 Parking Tickets in London and New York," *Guardian*, June 28, 2016, https://www.theguardian.com/technology/2016/jun/28/chatbot-ai-lawyer-donotpay-parking-tickets-london-new-york.

5 These iterations are the Copyright Acts of 1831, 1870, 1909, and 1976.

6 These include efforts at modernizing the US copyright regime, including bringing it closer in line with the global approach to moral rights and copyright formalities via the Berne Convention Implementation Act of 1988, as well as addressing digital rights management and copyright infringement issues in the Internet era, via 1998's Digital Millennium Copyright Act (DMCA).

7 Benjamin L. W. Sobel, "Artificial Intelligence's Fair Use Crisis," *Columbia Journal of Law & the Arts* 41 (2017): 58; see also Andres Guadamuz, "Artificial Intelligence and Copyright," *WIPO Magazine*, October 2017, wipo.int/wipo_magazine/en/2017/05/article_0003.html.

8 Yanisky-Ravid, "Generating Rembrandt," 673. Even John McCarthy, the originator of the term "Artificial Intelligence" failed to provide an independent definition.

9 Matthew U. Scherer, "Regulating Artificial Intelligence Systems: Risks, Challenges, Competencies, and Strategies," *Harvard Journal of Law & Technology* 29 (2016): 359.

10 Roger Parloff, "From 2016: Why Deep Learning Is Suddenly Changing Your Life," *Fortune* September 28, 2016, https://fortune.com/longform/ai-artificial-intelligence-deep-machine-learning.

11 "What Is a Rule-Based System? What Is it Not?" *ThinkAutomation*, accessed May 18, 2020, https://www.thinkautomation.com/eli5/what-is-a-rule-based-system-what-is-it-not; see also "AI Approaches Compared: Rule-Based Testing vs. Learning," *Tricentis*, accessed May 18, 2020, https://www.tricentis.com/artificial-intelligence-software-testing/ai-approaches-rule-based-testing-vs-learning.

12 Parloff, "From 2016."

13 Parloff, "From 2016"; see also Dani Deahl, "How AI-Generated Music Is Changing the Way Hits Are Made," *Verge*, August 31, 2018, theverge.com/2018/8/31/17777008/artificial-intelligence-taryn-southern-amper-music. ("Most of the[] [AI] systems [within the music industry] work by using deep learning networks, a type of AI that's reliant on analyzing large amounts of data" where you "feed the software tons of source material . . . which it then analyzes to find patterns.").

14 Paul Sciglar, "What Is Artificial Intelligence? Understanding 3 Basic AI Concepts," *Robotics Business Review*, April 19, 2018, https://www.roboticsbusinessreview.com/ai/3-basic-ai-concepts-explain -artificial-intelligence. Even though they may not be able to think beyond their code, rules-based systems still provide great functionality to human tasks—think Gmail's automatic e-mail filtering feature, Siri's assistance filling in your calendar, or the driver-assist feature in your car.

15 Yanisky-Ravid, "Generating Rembrandt," 675.

16 Yanisky-Ravid, 675.

17 "Hidden layers" are positioned in between the visible layers of the network, which explains the moniker, "hidden." In fact, "hidden layers" could be the key difference between mere "machine learning" and "deep learning" considering that the more hidden layers a system contains, the harder and more complex the problems it can tackle. Farhad Malik, "What Are Hidden Layers?" *Medium*, May 20, 2019, https://medium.com/fintechexplained/what-are-hidden-layers-4f54f7328263. In that sense, "deep learning," may technically be best defined as a system that has more than one hidden layer.

18 Janelle Shane documents her experiments facilitating "computer programs that try to invent human things," such as recipes and pickup lines on her blog, "AI Weirdness." See generally *AI Weirdness Blog*, accessed May 18, 2020, https://aiweirdness.com; see also "Chocolate Chicken Chicken Cake," the May 9, 2019 episode in the podcast *Sleepwalkers*, hosted by Oz Woloshyn and produced by iHeartRadio. Shane's foray into AI-generated recipes lent the episode its title, as, in addition to inventing protein-rich desserts, her AI instructed her to "fold water and roll it into cubes" and make use of ingredients such as "chopped whipped cream." Shane's growing canon of AI-generated pickup lines included the suave "You look like a thing and I love you," the geometric "You must be a triangle, cuz you're the only thing here," and the blunt "I don't know you."

19 Dana S. Rao, "Neural Networks: Here, There, and Everywhere—An Examination of Available Intellectual Property Protection for Neural Networks in Europe and the United States," *George Washington Journal of International Law and Economics* 30 (1996–1997): 511.

20 See "A Beginner's Guide to Neural Networks and Deep Learning," A.I. Wiki, accessed May 18, 2020, https://pathmind.com/wiki/neural-network; see also Shlomit Yanisky-Ravid & Sean K. Hallisey, "'Equality and Privacy by Design': A New Model of Artificial Intelligence Data Transparency Via Auditing, Certification, and Safe Harbor Regimes," *Fordham Urban Law Journal* 46 (April 2019): 439 ("Whereas an algorithm or formula creates outputs that derive from fixed weights attached to input variables, an AI system adjusts its weights according to the patterns it identifies from ideal outcomes chosen by the data provider."). For helpful visualizations of neural networks, see Anddy Cabrera, "Programming A Deep Neural Network From Scratch Using MQL Language," MQL5, January 26, 2019, https://www .mql5.com/en/blogs/post/724245.

21 Yanisky-Ravid & Hallisey, "Equality and Privacy by Design," 439.

22 Rao, "Neural Networks," 513.

23 See, e.g., Feist Publn's, Inc. v. Rural Tel. Serv. Co., 499 U.S. 340, 349–50 (1991) ("The primary objective of copyright is not to reward the labor of authors but '[t]o promote the Progress of Science and useful Arts.'"); see also Fogerty v. Fantasy, Inc., 510 U.S. 517, 527 (1994). ('[C]opyright law ultimately serves the purpose of enriching the general public through access to creative works...").

24 In the US, for individual authors, for example, the copyright term for this monopoly lasts for the life of the author plus seventy years after the author's death. 17 U.S.C. § 302 (2018).

25 17 U.S.C. § 106 ("Exclusive rights in copyrighted works").

26 17 U.S.C. § 102; see also, e.g., Prod. Contractors, Inc. v. WGN Cont'l Broad. Co., 622 F.Supp. 1500, 1502 (N.D. Ill. 1985) ("The two elements most essential in establishing the existence of a copyright are: (1) a work of authorship; and (2) fixation, i.e., fixed in a tangible medium of expression."). Considering how the Berne Convention and other international treaties have drawn the world's nation's independent regimes into greater alignment, many countries' copyright regimes, including the US' regime, mirror each other. For example, Great Britain's copyright law, formalized within the Copyright, Designs and Patents Act 1988 (CDPA), similarly provides protection where an individual creates work that "is original (not directly copied or adapted from an existing work), and exhibit[s] some degree of labour, skill or judgment in its creation." "Introduction to Copyright," UK Copyright Service, accessed May 18, 2020, https://www.copyrightservice.co.uk/copyright/copyright. For simplicity, the US laws will stand in as copyright *terra firma* for the ensuing discussion.

27 *Feist*, 499 U.S. at 355, 358–59.

28 *Id*. at 359.

29 See, e.g., Harrell v. St. John, 792 F. Supp. 2d 933, 943 (S.D. Miss. 2011) (holding that "a list of ingredients with very basic assembly or preparation instructions," is not protected under the Copyright Act).

30 *Feist*, 499 U.S. at 348.

31 "Although these 'programs' consist of numbers and not words, the Copyright Act protects literary works in any written form." Rao, "Neural Networks," 520 (citing 17 U.S.C. § 101's protection for "works . . . expressed in words, numbers, or other verbal or numerical symbols").

32 *Id.* at 537.

33 The historic *Burrow-Giles Lithographic Co. v. Sarony* decision, for example, states that photographs developed by cameras are copyrightable because the human input in deciding what populates the frame provides the requisite "intellectual invention." See 111 U.S. 53, 60 (1884).

34 See generally *National Commission on New Technological Uses of Copyrighted Works*, Final Report 2 (1978) (hereafter *CONTU Report*).

35 *CONTU Report*.

36 Office of Technology Assessment, U.S. Congress, *Intellectual Property Rights in an Age of Electronics and Information* (1986), 72.

37 *Intellectual Property Rights*, 72 (hereafter *Intellectual Property Rights*).

38 Jean-Marc Deltorn and Franck Macrez, Research Paper, "Authorship in the Age of Machine Learning and Artificial Intelligence," *Center for International Intellectual Property Studies* (2018): 91 n.55.

39 Yanisky-Ravid, "Generating Rembrandt," 685–87.

40 Yanisky-Ravid, 688 (citing 17 U.S.C. § 201(a)).

41 Yanisky-Ravid, 688 (quoting Community for Creative Non-Violence v. Reid, 490 U.S. 730, 737 (1989)).

42 Naruto v. Slater, 888 F.3d 418, 420 (9th Cir. 2018).

43 *Id.*

44 *Id.* at 425 (quoting Cetacean Cmty. v. Bush, 386 F.3d 1169, 1179 (9th Cir. 2004)).

45 Urantia Found. v. Maaherra, 114 F.3d 955, 956 (9th Cir. 1997).

46 *Id.* at 958 ("At the very least, for a worldly entity to be guilty of infringing a copyright, that entity must have copied something created by another worldly entity.").

47 Notably, the British Copyright, Designs, and Patents Act of 1988 takes this approach, affording copyright protection to the person responsible for the computer's creation. *See* Yanisky-Ravid, "Generating Rembrandt," 690 (citing Copyright, Designs & Patents Act 1988, c. 48 §§ 3, 9 (Eng.)).

48 Rao, "Neural Networks," 533.

49 *Rearden LLC v.* Walt Disney Co., 293 F. Supp. 3d 963, 967–71 (N.D. Cal. 2018).

50 *Id.* at 970–71.

51 Lawrence Lessig, *Free Culture: The Nature and Future of Creativity* 1 (2004), 3 (quoting St. George Tucker, *Blackstone's Commentaries* 3 (South Hackensack, NJ: Rothman Reprints, 1969), 18)).

52 See United States v. Causby, 328 U.S. 256, 260–61 (1946). In *Causby*, two farmers brought suit after the noise from low-flying military aircraft began startling and killing their chickens, which were flying into their henhouse walls in fright.

53 Yanisky-Ravid, "Generating Rembrandt," 695.

54 Pamela Samuelson, "Allocating Ownership Rights in Computer-Generated Works," *University of Pittsburgh Law Review* 47 (Summer 1986): 1203.

55 Express Newspapers Plc v Liverpool Daily Post & Echo Plc [1985] 3 All E.R. 680.

56 *Id.*

57 With Sharp and Goodwin's assistance inputting science fiction scripts, Benjamin authored a short science fiction film called *Sunspring*, famed as the first script likely written entirely by an AI system. "Oscar Sharp with Ross Goodwin & Benjamin," *Frankfurter Kunstverein*, accessed April 17, 2020, https://www. fkv.de/en/oscar-sharp-with-ross-goodwin-benjamin. The script itself was produced into a nine-minute film starring Thomas Middleditch, viewable at https://rossgoodwin.com.

58 See "Chocolate Chicken Chicken Cake."

59 Torah Soft Ltd. v. Drosnin, 136 F. Supp. 2d 276, 283 (S.D.N.Y. 2001). This case, cited for its holding by *Rearden*, referenced earlier, addressed ownership of the output of a computer program that searched for coded messages within the Hebrew Bible based on user-inputted search terms; this case originated the "lion's share" standard for output ownership, although in *Torah Soft*, the court determined that the software output was insufficiently original to merit copyright protection. *Id.* at 292.

60 Deltorn and Macrez, "Authorship in the Age of Machine Learning," 88. The analogy of a sound engineer tasked with pressing "record" during a music session comes to mind, and the fact that copyright recognizes the at least "minimal originality" behind this task. *See* Melville B. Nimmer and David

Nimmer, *Nimmer on Copyright*, Vol. 1 § 2.01[A][2] (2019). In fact, the leading copyright treatise, Nimmer on Copyright, conceives of the "minimal originality in selecting the particular sound to be recorded, at a particular point in time, with a particular sound volume, and physical distance and angle between microphone and subject" akin to the way that a photographer captures and processes light images. Where photography, even in this modern era of "point and click" camerawork, is deemed well worthy of copyright, and sound engineering is similarly deserving, perhaps there is room within the practice of AI button-pressing to discern originality.

61　Yanisky-Ravid, *Generating Rembrandt*, 711.

62　Annemarie Bridy, "Coding Creativity: Copyright and the Artificially Intelligent Author," *Stanford Technology Law Review* 5 (March 2012): 66.

63　In 1839, Louis Daguerre developed the daguerreotype, a system of capturing images on glass, which served as the precursor to photography. See Lessig, *Free Culture*, 31. By 1888, George Eastman had built upon this process, capturing images onto a "flexible, emulsion-coated paper film." Lessig, 31–32. Enter the courts. Cases at the time questioned whether "the photographer, amateur or professional, required permission before he could capture and print whatever image he wanted," weighing the extent to which a photographer was taking something of value from those whose portraits or scenery he or she shot, and if so, whether photographers should compensate landowners or individuals for capturing images otherwise in plain view. Lessig, 33. As with flight, the courts erred on the side of technological advancement, revisiting preexisting legal concepts in a way that would allow the new technology room to find its footing.

8.5

ARTIFICIAL INTELLIGENCE AND THE FUTURE OF LITERARY WORKS

Mary E. Rasenberger

Introduction

Copyright law and the copyright industries, including and especially book publishing, have already faced fundamental challenges in the digital age. But these challenges pale in comparison to those that lie ahead with the rise of artificial intelligence (AI) technologies. AI technologies could upend copyright law and the industries that rely on it in ways that will require entirely new approaches if copyright law is to continue to function as a means of incentivizing and rewarding new creation.

This chapter examines the complex challenges posed by AI to copyright law and the creative industries, and why profound shifts in how the copyright regime is perceived and exercised may be in order. I will focus on literary works as a way to ground the discussion since books have always been at the core of copyright protection. I conclude that opt-out automated collective licensing systems may be the only workable solution for striking the balance between developments in AI research and application and the rights of the creators whose works are used to train AI machines. As we speed toward a future where new expression can be generated in an instant by AI machines, and then subsequently digested and regenerated by other AI machines along ultimately untraceable paths, we need to proactively look for ways to ensure that copyright law continues to incentivize human creativity as intended by the framers of the Constitution.

Artificial Intelligence Defined

AI is a broad term that encompasses any "set of techniques aimed at approximating some aspect of human or animal cognition using machines."[1] In order to achieve human cognitive semblance, machines today are "trained" by being fed vast amounts of data. They read the data using "a cluster of statistical and programming techniques that give the computers the ability to 'learn' from exposure to data, without being explicitly programmed."[2] The process of reading (or ingesting) data, using statistical algorithms to detect patterns within the data, and making successful predictions about abstract queries is called "machine learning," and is integral to the development of AI.[3] As John Seabrook explained in his recent *New Yorker* article, "The Next World":

> There are two approaches to making a machine intelligent. Experts can teach the machine what they know, by imparting knowledge about a particular field and giving it rules to perform a set of functions; this method is sometimes termed knowledge-based. Or engineers can

design a machine that has the capacity to learn for itself, so that when it is trained with the right data it can figure out its own rules for how to accomplish a task. That process is at work in machine learning.[4]

This chapter focuses on "generative" AI systems that are trained by using data to create their own rules. Through machine learning, they can be trained to produce—or generate—expression that mimics a human-expressive activity.

Examples of generative use of AI include ING and Microsoft's "The Next Rembrandt," which used machine learning to create a 3D printed Rembrandt painting based on 168,263 Rembrandt painting fragments; the AI-generated *Portrait of Edmond de Belamy*, which fetched an astounding $432,500 at a 2018 auction; and OpenAI's "Musenet," an algorithm that can generate four-minute musical compositions. Computer scientists and machine learning enthusiasts have been experimenting with generating literary writing for decades, and a sci-fi novel written by a Japanese AI has even come close to winning a literary prize.

Many of the recent advancements in AI-generated creative works can be attributed to improvements in neural networks and the algorithms designed to recognize patterns in data that are loosely modeled on the human brain. More so than other forms of AI, these "generative" machines directly concern core copyright law issues because they appear to create copyrightable works, can potentially infringe works without direct human volitional actions, and generally are trained by ingesting large volumes of "data"—often in the form of copyrightable expression.

AI and Authorship

Ingestion of Literary Works by AI

One of the earliest major ingestion projects for machine learning was Google's mass digitization project for books: It scanned and created digital copies of millions of books from major academic libraries. Starting in 2002 until 2017, Google digitized more than 20 million books. Google was sued by groups of publishers and photographers and by the Authors Guild in *Authors Guild v. Google*.[5] In that case, Google advanced high-minded public benefit arguments to justify what would otherwise unquestionably be mass copyright infringement—indeed, the most staggering instance of it in history. Google argued that it was creating a new Library of Alexandria and that its search tool transformed the way readers and scholars would find books, "revealing stores of human knowledge that would otherwise be difficult or impossible to find,"[6] and enabled new fields of digital humanities research.[7] Hindsight proves that Google's main benefit from the digitization project was actually to acquire training data for its AI: mass quantities of written expression that could be fed into its AI systems to teach them to understand human language, to communicate, read, and write like humans. The massive benefit to its AI that Google obtained from the books was not disclosed in the litigation or recognized by the litigants; indeed, the settlement agreement permitted all internal, research, and "non-display" uses without compensation. Science historian George Dyson, who wrote about his visit to Google's headquarters in 2005, quotes a Google employee as saying, ominously, "we are not scanning all those books to be read by people. We are scanning them to be read by AI."[8]

Today, literary works are ingested by AI for any number of non-expressive uses, such as for scientific, medical, or academic inquiry. For instance, in his article "The New Legal Landscape for Text Mining and Machine Learning," Matthew Sag describes life-science researchers using text mining to "search across disparate disciplines and subfields to uncover previously unnoticed correlations or associations," such as the benefits of fish oil to sufferers of Raynaud's disease, and the identification of different molecules involved in Huntington's disease.[9] As Sag points out, in these cases, the breakthroughs enabled by text mining were not contained in the underlying works—rather, "they arose from recognizing the patterns between works."[10]

At the same time, books and articles are also being copied *en masse* by AI and being used to create new books and articles. The Hoshi Shinichi Award, a Japanese literary honor, expressly permits AI-written or -assisted books to enter the competition, and in 2016 the book *The Day a Computer Writes a Novel* was a finalist. It is the story of a computer program as it "realizes its capabilities as a writer and abandons its pre-programmed duties."[11] An AI machine "wrote" the novel after being trained by its designers on sentences, words, and structure that the designers wrote and chose. Based on the very specific parameters the designers provided, the computer used an algorithm to essentially remix a new novella out of the original piece.[12] This is a similar form of designer-driven AI "creation" to the renowned "Next Rembrandt" project, where the designers gave the AI machine the training, rules, and instructions to produce a physical (3D printer-generated) work of art that would "mimic the look of a genuine Rembrandt painting."[13]

In his *New Yorker* article "The Next Word," John Seabrook describes using an AI machine called GPT-2, developed by the company OpenAI, to write, in Escheresque fashion, an article in the style of *The New Yorker*. OpenAI describes GPT-2 as: "a large-scale unsupervised language model which generates coherent paragraphs of text, achieves state-of-the-art performance on many language modeling benchmarks, and performs rudimentary reading comprehension, machine translation, question answering, and summarization—all without task-specific training."[14]

For the experiment, OpenAI used a digital archive of all the magazine's nonfiction work since 2007, plus some classic pieces going back to the 1960s. "A human," Seabrook wrote, "would need almost two weeks of 24/7 reading to get through it all. . . . The AI computed the archive in under an hour."[15] Once trained, Seabrook gave it a prompt to recreate—Lillian Ross's famed 1950 profile of Ernest Hemingway, which begins at Hemingway's farm outside Havana, the Finca Vigia. The resulting language convincingly imitated the cadence and narrative rhythms of *The New Yorker*, but the substance of the sentences it produced was off. An initial AI-produced passage describes the writer walking up to Hemingway's gate and seeing: "a plump dog, that had been a common visitor to the Finca Vigia before the war, galloping up a path to the main building, with a tiny cow of the same name standing by her side. There was a puddle of red gravy in the front yard, and Hemingway sat down in a lawn chair."

A tiny cow standing next to a galloping dog? A puddle of what? Each time Seabrook instructed the AI machine to generate a new sentence, it did so based on the prior sentence rather than rely on just the instructions, and the further out it got, the whackier it got.

So far, none of this sounds like anything that will compete with real books. But as we have seen with *The Day a Computer Writes a Novel*, AI can already write so long as there is sufficient human involvement, and it will not be long before AI can write better books. Indeed, today there are books available on Amazon which appear to be written, at least in part, by computers. Kindle Direct Publishing (KDP), which is something like the wild west of publishing, allows anyone to "self-publish" anything that can be described as a "book"—"pages" of text or images with a cover—and to post those "books" and offer them for sale on Amazon's Kindle e-reader app. Such a porous marketplace is a natural habitat for scammers and pirates and others who try to take advantage of its algorithms to sell what might be cannot be characterized as anything other than as unreadable junk. We have seen examples of unreadable book summaries and test prep books that appear to have been created by AI machines cutting and pasting texts in a systematic way from the existing books, and even some romance novels created from cutting and pasting text from a number of other novels in a way that evades Amazon's digital fingerprint security measures. There are reports of books "written" by cutting and pasting from up to twenty different books.[16] Though there is no proof that these books are written with the assistance of AI, it is difficult to imagine the human who chooses to write a book entirely by cutting and pasting from twenty different books—a task that AI is more than capable of handling.

Not all AI technologies capable of generating text are being used by pirates and malicious actors. Many news organizations, including *Bloomberg*, *The Washington Post*, and others already use AI more successfully today by feeding the facts into templates to write very short, simple news stories, such as outcomes of local sports events and company earnings where the way the facts are expressed is formulaic.[17] Then, there are the AI tools that we are all starting to use in our writing with varying success, perhaps not recognizing them as AI: Google's Smart Compose and Apple's Auto-Correction to provide assistance with grammar, syntax, spelling, and finding the right word. AI already can improve or speed up writing by doing some of the grunt work, and that will only improve in the coming years. All in all, with computing power now improving by a factor of ten times a year, it is conceivable if not likely that AI will be writing sophisticated books and articles in the coming decade.

The Challenges to Copyright Law

AI impacts copyright law in several ways, introducing novel concepts that are either unclear under the current copyright framework or that the framework is not equipped to deal with. The proliferation of AI-generated works raises questions about authorship and attribution, ownership, responsibility for AI-caused infringement, and the use and ingestion of copyrighted works to train AI systems. We will look at these issues, in turn:

1   Are expressive works created by or with the assistance of AI copyrightable, and if so, who is the author and/or copyright owner of such works?
2   When an AI machine infringes copyrighted works, who can be held responsible?
3   Is it, or should it be, fair use to train AI machines by ingesting copyrighted works?

Are Expressive Works Created by or with the Assistance of AI Copyrightable, and if so, Who Is the Author and/or Copyright Owner of Such Works?

The US law provides copyright protection to "original works of authorship fixed in any tangible medium of expression." As a threshold matter, a work created by or with the assistance of AI must have authorship to be copyrightable, and this requires us to identify an author or authors. Much of the discussion around AI and copyright has focused on whether the AI machine that creates a work of original expression is the author of that work. Under existing copyright law, however, only humans and human-run corporations can be authors of copyrightable works. Copyrightable expression is, by definition, human. The intellectual property clause of the US Constitution empowers Congress to protect the exclusive rights of *authors and inventors* in their writings and discoveries;[18] and although the Constitution does not define authors and inventors as human beings or natural persons, it is clear from the context and the usage of these words at the time that the framers meant humans—not animals or paranormal or artificial beings.

A century of Supreme Court jurisprudence further validates the view that authorship is necessarily a product of a *human* intellect. In *Burrow-Giles Lithographic Co. v. Sarony*, the Supreme Court defined an author as someone "to whom anything owes its origin; originator; maker; one who completes a work of science or literature," and writing as the process "by which the ideas in the mind of the author are given visible expression."[19] Going further, in *Bleistein v. Donaldson*

Lithographing Co., the court tied copyrightable authorship to the uniqueness of the human creator's individual personality.[20] Even a "very modest grade of art," Justice Oliver Wendell Holmes, Jr. wrote in the opinion, "has in it something irreducible, which is one man's alone. That something he may copyright."[21]

The reason the copyright law protects only human authors is rooted in the constitutional purpose of incentivizing the progress of arts and sciences.[22] Forces of nature, machines, and works made by animals are not incentivized by copyright; and there are any number of policy reasons that we do not want to allow people to be able to claim ownership in, say, a beautiful rock or a bird's song.[23] AI machines, in spite of their anthropomorphic portrayals in works of fiction, also do not need incentives to create. It is the humans and human-run corporations who we want to incentivize with intellectual property rights, and the fact is that there is some human authorship in pretty much all AI-generated works today. At least for now, humans control AI machines and assert a great deal of control over the works they produce by making expressive choices in creating the rules, algorithms, processes, and tools that result in copyrightable authorship.

To the extent original expression is created solely by AI machines (though some scholars debate whether they are now capable of creating original expression), and is not attributable to human authorship, it is clear under current law that the expression would not be copyrightable. That is neither an unusual nor even a rare outcome under existing law. Copyright need not protect all types of expressive and artistic works; indeed, many works of art are not copyrightable; yet, they are no less artistic. Works of conceptual art, for instance, often lack original expression where the creativity is in the idea, not the expression. For instance, there is no original expression in Marcel Duchamp's seminal conceptual work *Fountain*, a urinal, signed "R. Mutt"—an ordinary object made into art by being put in a different context. Other creative works, such as Chapman Kelley's *Wildflower Works*, have been denied copyright protection for reasons of lack of fixation,[24] while works created by machines or animals, or attributed to deities, have always been excluded from copyright protection.[25]

Identifying the Author of Works Created by or with the Assistance of AI Technologies

If, then, an AI-generated work is to be copyrightable, it must have some identifiable human authorship. For works created by highly generative machines, one might conclude that, generally, there will be very little expression produced by AI that is copyrightable since so much of what is directly contributed by the people who design the AI machine—algorithms, processes, and instructions—arguably is not copyrightable or, at most, possesses thin copyright. But not so quick...

In their article, "Authors and Machines," Jane Ginsburg and Luke Ali Budiardjo provide a helpful framework for thinking about authorship of AI-generated works. They explain that authorship comprises two elements: (i) the conception of a work (the "creative spark" described by the Supreme Court in *Feist*[26]), and (ii) the execution—or fixation—of the conceived work.[27] The latter act of authorship can include the human supervision of the fixation, such as when a sculptor hires metal workers, provides precise instructions, and oversees the production. Ginsburg explains, "[t]he law attributes authorship to the 'mastermind,' whose detailed conception so controls [the work's] subsequent execution that the individuals carrying out the embodiment exercise no creative autonomy."[28]

Under this "mastermind" theory, an AI system following the detailed guidance of its users and/or programmers and under their authority would be an "amanuensis," and authorship in the work generated by the AI would be attributed to the human masterminds. In other words, when human programmers train AI by selecting and providing the training data and giving it specific directions to learn and render an expressive work, like the sculptor directing metalworkers, they are contributing authorship to AI's eventual output, even if they are not executing the work itself. The AI in this case is merely acting on the directions given to it by the programmer, as an amanuensis would. The copyright in the resulting work therefore belongs to the human programmers (or as a work made for hire for the corporate entity that employs them). Bruce Boyden, in his article "Emergent Works," provides a somewhat similar analysis. He argues that AI-generated works can be attributed to human authorship to the extent that the copyrightable expression was predicted by the designer.[29] Under this lens, to the extent that the AI designers could predict the outcome, they are the authors.

A good example of this sort of "amanuensis"-created AI work is the "Next Rembrandt" program that rendered an entirely new painting in the Dutch master's style.[30] There, a team of art historians and computer scientists decided the "what" and "how" of the output: selecting the paintings for training; programming algorithms that detected patterns within the models; and giving the AI the task to render something like the paintings it had learned from. The team behind the "Next Rembrandt" did not make creative choices for the AI (such as instructing it directly to use a certain color or figure), but arguably they gave it a sufficiently detailed conception of the work through the training data and instructions to be considered authors of the resulting painting. Similarly, in the case of the book *The Day a Computer Writes a Novel*, the designers provided the AI with sentences, words, and structure, and based on the specific parameters, the machine used an algorithm to essentially remix a new novella out of the material provided.[31] The AI system followed the detailed guidance provided to it, and could be deemed the amanuensis of the designers.

Others have argued that, where the AI is given less specific guidance and its output is less predictable, the humans providing the creative choices might be deemed coauthors with the AI machine, although the creative elements added by the AI machine would have no copyright. For instance, when Seabrook used GPT-2 for his article "The Next Word," he chose the training data and the prompt. The first few sentences generated by AI were arguably based on Seabrook's input, as well as the rules and learning that OpenAI embedded in GPT-2. In that sense, copyrightable coauthorship could be conferred on both Seabrook, who made the immediate creative choices as the AI's amanuensis, together with OpenAI programmers who designed the AI machine. But the more GPT-2 was left to write on its own, the less human, copyrightable authorship there was. In that case, it could be argued that Seabrook and OpenAI still had some coauthorship claim, but the better argument might be that the text entered the public domain, once it went beyond human direction and started writing based on its prior words. Indeed, no one would argue that we need copyright protection for such nonsensical text to incentivize its creation, but as AI writing improves, that will surely change. AI will generate more exploitable authorship, and those who own or control the AI may well try to assert copyright protection.

Some argue that AI machines presently are not capable of any original expression without human direction. There is indeed some truth in that—if you consider that the way machine learning generates new works is to ingest large volumes of existing data, find patterns per the instructions provided, and create new arrangements of data based on those patterns. For now, when creating expressive works at least, it appears that AI machines essentially create complex mash-ups like the Next Rembrandt. In that sense, they are derivative in its common parlance meaning. It is highly unlikely that an AI-generated work would be a "derivative work" of any particular work under the copyright law meaning of the term because an AI-created work will include elements of many different works and so will not be substantially similar to any one of the works ingested by the AI machine. Nevertheless, current AI machines do not add anything truly new; they generate new works through mechanical processes without adding any "creative spark" in the words of the Supreme Court.

AI technology is developing quickly, however, and it is conceivable that there will come a day when AI can add creativity in generating new works. And long before that, it will become difficult to determine what is human- or AI-created, and who authored what. Some will undoubtedly take advantage of that lack of transparency by unfairly asserting rights in non-copyrightable AI-generated works. We will need to develop clear, enforceable rules for transparency around the AI or AI-assisted creation of works and their copyrightability.

I suggest that one place to start is to look to the very purpose of copyright—its incentives. Whether or not an AI-generated work is attributable to humans under the amanuensis or predict-ability theories of authorship, there are no obvious policy reasons for bestowing copyright pro-tection to these essentially derivative (though non-infringing) AI-generated works. To the extent that AI development needs incentives, patent, trade secret, and other IP protections are available to developers to protect many of the elements they design for their AI machines. Extending copy-right to AI works that lack any *meaningful* human original authorship serves no purpose. Why would we want to protect look-alike Rembrandts, or look-alike Prince artwork for that matter? And to get back to literary works, likely the first of the creative businesses to be disrupted by AI, why would we want to protect romance novels, for instance, that are generated by AI's "reading" and mimicking the patterns of human-written romance novels? It surely will not advance litera-ture in any meaningful way.

But even more importantly, if we were to provide copyright protection to novels, poems, or other literary works generated by AI in this ingest, mash-up, and spit-out manner, the copyright incentives to protect the artistic and commercial values of *human-authored* works would decay. It would put the human-authored works that they are based on at a huge competitive disadvantage. AI will soon be able to produce these secondary works faster and cheaper than their human-authored counterparts; and humans will not be able to compete with that. The retort I often hear, as if the advance of technology is the end-all and be-all, is—"Well, writers, welcome to the club of those who will be put out of business by AI." Really? I generally respond to these 'usually young' people, "Do you not understand the importance of books? Of human culture? Do we really want to be a society that has AI-created culture?" Admittedly, I shudder at the thought of a world without human culture—not because I am so old-fashioned, but perhaps, because I am older, I understand, not just from the historical and anthropological perspectives gained from reading, but from the view of a life lived, just how important human culture is. The day we give over culture to AI is the day we, as humans, extinguish ourselves, because what makes us human is our ability to express ourselves. Since the dawn of humanity, we have collectively been trying to make sense of what it is to be human. No matter how well-trained, AI will never be able to reflect the experience of being human, to which all literature and art ultimately speak. AI-generated works, however, merely rehash, mash-up, and rework what they are fed; they do not understand or emote; they cannot bear witness.

As the Supreme Court has noted, copyright is "an engine of free expression."[32] Bestowing copyright on AI-generated works will ensure that the marketplace can no longer afford anything but, and copyright law will no longer function as our founders intended, to build free market-places where works of human intellect can be freely traded, and where human creators of expres-sive works can be paid for their creative labor.

Who Is Responsible When an AI Machine Infringes?

Authorship of AI-generated works is a fascinating topic, but AI-generated piracy is perhaps a nearer and more troubling prospect since, under current copyright law, it is possible that no one would have liability for the infringing conduct of an AI machine, including the enterprise that creates it or owns it.

Digital book piracy is already a major problem for authors and publishers, with new rogue foreign websites popping up constantly, sellers on Google Shopping, eBay, and LinkedIn's Slide Share offering innumerable illegal copies of ebooks, and unauthorized audio recordings of every major book readily available for listening on YouTube. Most authors could, if they knew where to look online, find vastly more pirated copies of their books than they could count. Today at least we can identify the hosts of the pirated content and even locate them in many cases. But what happens when there is no human or corporate entity which we can trace the infringement and hold accountable, or contact for help?

A potential obstacle to having a claim against any identifiable corporation or individual for an AI machine's unauthorized copying is the relatively new "volitional conduct" doctrine adopted by some circuits. It requires that the defendant volitionally engaged in the conduct that was the proximate cause of specific acts of infringement. It means that if the defendant operates technology that infringes, but does not click the button, pull the trigger, or otherwise direct the specific acts of infringement, it is not liable. If courts were to extend this line of cases to AI-directed infringement, where an AI machine is the proximate cause of the infringement, there would be no one to hold liable—it would create criminal-less crimes.

For example, in *Cartoon Network, LP v. CSC Holdings, Inc.*,[33] the Second Circuit held that Cablevision was not liable for direct infringement where its automated service performed television programming for its customers. Even though the Cablevision computers were playing the shows (i.e. engaging in a performance), the court found that Cablevision lacked the requisite volition since the customers were the proximate cause of each infringing performance when they clicked the buttons to record or play a particular show. The fact that it was Cablevision's system conducting the performances was held irrelevant to direct liability. Other courts have adopted this approach.[34]

This "volitional conduct" doctrine, if applied to AI, would presumably let the companies that developed or owned infringing AI machines off the hook for direct infringement, even if those AI systems infringed on a mass scale. The case law on secondary liability—which is lacking in bright-line rules, and requires the plaintiff to prove multiple factors—might not be of much assistance either. For instance, a court might apply the analysis in *Sony*[35] to find that the developers of an AI system built to infringe copyrights were not secondarily liable where the AI also had a "substantial non-infringing use."

This potential lack of accountability for infringement conducted by AI machines presents a serious challenge for copyright law, as it allows beneficiaries of copyright infringement—the owners of the technology aiding the infringement—to evade liability and leave rights holders without recourse. Down the road one can imagine AI systems that infringe for their own purposes. How will copyright owners stop them or receive any retribution from their infringement?

If copyright is to survive the AI age in any meaningful way, Congress and/or the courts will have to create rules for identifying the legal person or entities responsible. But, even then, ascribing human control to an AI machine's actions eventually might become so difficult that it will become impossible to hold humans or corporations responsible.

If I force myself to look into the future in a clear-eyed, unbiased way, the only effective means I can envision to protect copyrights online will be via sophisticated automated collective licensing systems that crawl the internet and are able to identify online displays, distributions, or streams of copyrighted works, and automatically charge the most proximate user or owner of the AI system a royalty every time a literary work is copied, distributed, publicly performed, or displayed by the AI actor. How to build a system is far beyond my knowledge base, but I am sure that there are those who already could build such a system today.

Is It Always Fair Use to Train AI Machines by Ingesting Large Volumes of Works?

As we have seen, machine learning methods involve the copying of mass volumes of non-copyrightable data or of copyrightable works. To date, courts have addressed the ingestion of mass copying of copyrighted works only in connection with search engines; and they have found the uses to be fair use in each of these cases.[36] It is argued by some that this means that *all* intermediate copying, or "data-mining" as it is often called, of copyrighted works for purposes of training AI should be fair use, or even that it is fair under the Second Circuit's logic in the *Authors Guild v. Google* decision. But it is not that simple.

After the amended settlement agreement was rejected by the district court in *Authors Guild v. Google*, the fair use case proceeded on the merits. As mentioned earlier, neither the district court nor the Second Circuit addressed Google's AI uses of the scanned books. There was nothing in the record about it because Google had no incentive to disclose how they intended to extract value from the data, and it was too early for those outside of the AI industry to grasp that enormous competitive value. The Second Circuit held that Google's mass copying was fair use because, under its understanding of the facts, the copying was conducted for what the court deemed a socially beneficial, fair use purpose—a book search engine that displayed snippets in connection with a particular search. The fact that the books were ingested to teach Google's computers to read and write natural human language was never addressed by the court; and to date, no case has squarely determined whether and under what circumstances the mass ingestion of copyrighted works for AI training is fair use. The court decided the case on very different grounds.

In some cases, ingestion of copyrighted works arguably should be fair use, such as the ingestion of data for training non-generative AI algorithms and processes to perform functions that do not result in expressive works. Using photographs to train self-driving vehicles, for instance, conceivably could be fair use. However, copying creative works to train AI machines to generate competing expressive works is likely not fair use, even under existing law. For all the reasons described in this chapter, it is hard to see how the unauthorized ingestion of copyrighted works to generate new creative works that will compete in the marketplace with the copied works will not ultimately harm the value of ingested human-created copyrighted works that the AI machines mimic in style and essence. The third factor would not favor a fair use finding, since entire works are copied, and for most literary works, the second factor should also weigh against fair use. A court could be misguided into finding that the use is transformative under current law, but that would be incorrect. Competing works that serve as a market replacement for the copied work by definition are not transformative.

I do not believe that we should leave these decisions to courts to decide on fair use grounds, however. Courts applying the fair use factors to a particular case will not get the full picture and so are not likely to find the right balance. The main problem is with the fourth factor. The copying of a particular work to train AI may not harm the market for that work, but in the aggregate it will cause harm to the overall markets for new works. Over time, the author is going to have a hard time getting paid for new work and the copyright ecosystem will break down. A court will not take that into consideration, especially if it analyzes the facts of the case under the fourth factor in isolation, as many courts have in recent years, despite the Supreme Court's instruction in *Campbell v. Acuff-Rose* to consider the harm to the value of the work if the infringing activity were "widespread and unrestricted."

Fair use litigation leaves important policy making in the hands of a few judges who decide cases based on a particular set of facts in front of them, and who do not have all the information they need to understand the long-term implications of their decisions, although those decisions do create rules for future behavior. An inconsistent litigation-driven approach to solving issues that have important consequences for entire industries is not at all practical or sound. We will need a better approach when it comes to AI.

The reason it is so important to address the copying of works that occurs during their ingestion by AI machines is that, when it comes to AI machines generating new works, that initial copying to train the AI generally will be the only recognizable act of infringement under current law. It is highly unlikely that an AI-generated output will infringe any particular ingested work. Although the output will contain a combination of elements taken from the works it was trained on, that output (as a whole) will not be substantially similar to any ingested work. At most, the output will mimic a style, which is not protected by copyright.

As such, if we permit all mass ingestion of copyrighted works for AI training purposes to result in the production of competing works, we are effectively giving the owners of the AI machines a subsidy and making a decision to allow AI to overtake human creation. As we move toward a future where AI will be omnipresent, it is important to be clear about our goals. If as a society we care about human-created artistic works, we need to ensure that we have policies that will protect the incentives for human creation.

James Grimmelmann, in his article "Copyright for Literate Robots," asks: "[W]ho decided it would be a good idea to give artificial intelligence researchers free rein over humanity's complete creative output? It is easy to see how bulk non-expressive copying promotes progress in artificial intelligence. It is much harder to articulate any kind of connection between such copying and the kind of research needed to guarantee that a superintelligence respects human goals."[37]

Writers today are cheap. Most authors earn so little now that writing is already becoming an unsustainable profession. A recent Authors Guild survey found that the median writing income for full-time authors in 2017 was just $20,300. But once an AI-writing machine is developed and writing, it will be able to produce works even more cheaply. Once the cost of a sophisticated AI-writing machine is amortized, the price of having it write and create other works will be nearly zero. Human writers will not be able to compete with that.

We are confronting serious policy issues about the future of creativity. Do we want humans or AI creating our literature and other arts? If we want to continue to incentivize human creation, we need to find a way to compensate authors. One of the reasons courts have permitted mass copying for search engines, I believe, is that they cannot envision how mass copying could be conducted under license. The idea of clearing millions of works one by one is daunting to say the least, and the transaction costs are ridiculously high. A levy or collective licensing system is usually considered the better solution where transaction costs are too high.[38] Rather than make all copying for AI purposes free and thereby discount the authors' interests, an automated collective licensing system would at least put some money back in authors' pockets, and go a way toward ensuring that the copyright incentives still function.

As we have seen, courts have sympathized with technology companies who conducted mass copying for functional purposes for the obvious reason that obtaining permissions on a work-by-work basis is highly impractical. The reasonable means then of enabling licenses for mass use for AI—which we do want to encourage—is collective licensing and preferably an extended collective license, where all works in a certain category (e.g. books or out-of-print books) for certain uses (e.g. AI machine learning) are covered unless the copyright owner opts out.

Some copyright owners have objected to the notion of mandatory or opt-out extended collective licensing because they want to control the use of their works. That is understandable under twentieth-century views of copyright ownership, but clinging onto absolute rights may well spell the end of copyright protection in the coming years as mass use by AI systems becomes commonplace. Already, courts have found mass ingestion and copying to be fair use, and without a reasonable and fair means to license works, they very well might extend fair use to all AI training.

Finding a way to compensate copyright owners for AI-related uses without clearing rights on a case-by-case basis will eventually become paramount. It will alleviate pressures on the creative industries and is preferable to allowing mass ingestion of works on a fair use basis, which in practice amounts to a free compulsory license.

The more sophisticated and self-generating AI becomes, the more sophisticated and complex automated licensing systems will need to be. They will need to crawl the internet for uses, locate the user, identify the owner, charge, and remit a small royalty. Some have suggested that blockchain technologies could be used to create such licensing systems. The technology and systems behind such a licensing system are far beyond my capabilities, but with the proper investment and minds involved should be imminently doable. Suffice it to say that it is in all our interests now to create computerized collective systems that will enable efficient licensing of intellectual property from the smallest consumer uses to the large-scale corporate uses.

Copyright law was created initially to ensure that book authors and the publishers who invested in them would be compensated for their work.[39] Books teach us, inspire us, and move us forward as a society. Yet they are especially vulnerable to arguments for open access and exceptions, especially fair use, precisely *because* of their educational and cultural importance. This is apparent, for instance, in the way courts in recent fair use cases have been easily swayed by arguments regarding the benefits of public access to books.[40] Without sophisticated collective licensing systems, copyright owners will not be compensated for AI uses of their works, even to train AI machines to create competing works. It will become too difficult to track, much less to compensate for AI uses of copyrighted works. Eventually, even the most talented writers and other creators may be unable to earn enough from their work to remain in their professions, and the value of human-created work will be profoundly diminished.

Notes

1 Ryan Calo, "Artificial Intelligence Policy: A Primer and Roadmap," *U.C. Davis Law Review* 51 (2017): 399, 404–05.
2 Matthew Sag, "The New Legal Landscape for Text Mining and Machine Learning," *Journal of the Copyright Society of the U.S.A* 66 (2019): 291, 299.
3 Karen Ho, *What is AI?*, MIT Tech. Rev., November 10, 2019 (available at https://www.technology review.com/2018/11/10/139137/is-this-ai-we-drew-you-a-flowchart-to-work-it-out/)
4 John Seabrook, "The Next Word," *The New Yorker*, October 14, 2019.
5 Scott Rosenberg, "How Google Book Search Got Lost," *Wired*, April 11, 2017, available at https://www.wired.com/2017/04/how-google-book-search-got-lost/.
6 Brief for Appellee, *Authors Guild v. Google*, 13–4829cv (2d Cir. 2014) at 22, available at https://www.authorsguild.org/wp-content/uploads/2014/12/2014-Jul-03-AGvGoogle-Google-Brief-on-Appeal.pdf.
7 *Id.*
8 George Dyson, "Turing's Cathedral," *Edge*, October 23, 2005, available at https://www.edge.org/conversation/george_dyson-turings-cathedral.
9 Sag, "The New Legal Landscape for Text Mining and Machine Learning."
10 *Id.* at 296.
11 Danny Lewis, "An AI-Written Novella Almost Won a Literary Prize," *Smithsonian Magazine*, March 28, 2016, available at https://www.smithsonianmag.com/smart-news/ai-written-novella-almost-won-literary-prize-180958577/.
12 *See id.*
13 Steve Schlackman, "Who Holds the Copyright in AI Created Art," *Art Law Journal*, April 22, 2018, available at https://alj.artrepreneur.com/the-next-rembrandt-who-holds-the-copyright-in-computer-generated-art/.
14 Open AI, https://openai.com/blog/better-language-models/ (last visited May 2, 2020).

15 John Seabrook, "The Next Word," *The New Yorker*, October 14, 2019.

16 *See* "Nora Roberts Takes a Stand against Digital Plagiarism," *AuthorsGuild.org*, April 29, 2019, available at https://www.authorsguild.org/industry-advocacy/nora-roberts-takes-a-stand-against-digital -plagiarism/.

17 Ron Schmeltzer, Forbes, August 23, 2019, available at https://www.forbes.com/sites/cognitiveworld/ 2019/08/23/ai-making-waves-in-news-and-journalism/#6e3817a87748

18 U.S. Const. art. 1, § 8, cl. 8.

19 Burrow-Giles Lithographic Co. v. Sarony, 111 U.S. 53, 58 (1884).

20 Bleistein v. Donaldson Lithographing Co.188 U.S. 239, 250 (1903).

21 *Id.*

22 U.S. CONST. art. 1, § 8, cl. 8.

23 Ginsburg & Budiardjo, *supra* note 3, at 448 ("[W]e should not assume that we need copyright-like protection to stimulate the production of authorless outputs. Absent an author, the premise underlying incentive justifications requires substantiation. One must inquire whether these outputs in fact need the impetus of exclusive rights, or if sufficient incentives already exist, for example higher up the chain, through copyright or patent protection of the software programs, patent protection of the specialized machinery to produce different kinds of outputs, and copyright protection of the database the software consults. Trade secrets and contracts may also play a role in securing the outputs.").

24 *See* Kelley v. Chicago Park District, 635 F.3d 290, 304 (7th Cir. 2011) ("A living garden like Wildflower Works is neither 'authored' nor 'fixed' in the senses required for copyright."); *see also* Agnieszka Kurant, "Phantom Capital, Hybrid Authorship, and Collective Intelligence," *Columbia Journal of Law & the Arts* 39 (2016): 371.

25 *See, e.g.,* Naruto v. Slater, No. 16-15469 (9th Cir. 2018), available at http://cdn.ca9.uscourts.gov/ datastore/opinions/2018/04/23/16-15469.pdf (holding that the Copyright Act does not authorize animals to file infringement suits); United States Copyright Office, The Compendium of U.S. Copyright Office Practices § 313.2 ("The Office will not register works produced by nature, animals, or plants. Likewise, the Office cannot register a work purportedly created by divine or supernatural beings, although the Office may register a work where the application or the deposit copy(ies) state that the work was inspired by a divine spirit.").

26 Feist Publ'ns v. Rural Tel. Serv. Co., 499 U.S. 340, 346 (1991).

27 Jane C. Ginsburg and Luke Ali Budiardjo, "Authors and Machines," *Berkeley Technology Law Journal* 3 (2019): 343.

28 *Id.* at 358.

29 Bruce E. Boyden, "Emergent Works," *Columbia Journal of Law & the Arts* 39 (2016): 377, 387.

30 Ginsburg, *supra* at 433, fn. 312.

31 *See* Danny Lewis, "An AI-Written Novella Almost Won a Literary Prize," *Smithsonian Magazine*, March 28, 2016, available at https://www.smithsonianmag.com/smart-news/ai-written-novella-almost -won-literary-prize-180958577/.

32 Harper & Row v. Nation Enterprises, 471 U.S. 539, 558 (1985).

33 Cartoon Network, LP v. CSC Holdings, Inc., 536 F. 3d 121 (2d Cir. 2008)

34 *See, e.g.,* Arista Records LLC v. UseNet.com, Inc., 633 F. Supp. 2d 124 (S.D.N.Y. 2009) (finding that defendants acting with the requisite volition to be rendered "active participants in the process of copyright infringement" where they were aware of infringing activity on their online bulletin boards, took active measures to create servers dedicated to mp3 files, and took active steps to exercise control over access to them); Perfect 10, Inc. v. Giganews, Inc., 847 F. 3d 657 (9th Cir. 2017) (finding that defendant did not act with the requisite volition where actions were limited to passively storing material at the direction of users in order to make that material available to other users upon request); Fox News Network, LLC v. TVEyes, Inc., 883 F.3d 169 (2d Cir. 2018).

35 Sony Corp. of America v. Universal City Studios, Inc., 464 U.S. 417 (1984); A&M Records, Inc. v. Napster, Inc., 239 F.3d 1004 (2001); MGM Studios, Inc. v. Grokster, Ltd., 545 U.S. 913 (2005).

36 *See, e.g.,* Authors Guild v. Hathitrust, 755 F.3d 87 (2d Cir. 2014) (finding full-text searches of scanned books to be fair use); Perfect 10, Inc. v. Amazon.com, Inc., 508 F.3d 1146 (9th Cir. 2007) (finding reproducing thumbnails to be fair use); Authors Guild v. Google, Inc., 804 F.3d 202 (2d Cir. 2015) (finding search function and limited display to be fair use); Fox News Network, LLC v. TVEyes, Inc. Nos. 15-3885, 15-3886 (2d Cir. February 27, 2018) (suggesting that the recording and database functions would qualify as fair use, but rejecting fair use on the grounds that service allowed users to view substantial segments of copyrighted transmissions in a way that could deprive Fox of licensing revenue).

37 James Grimmelman, "Copyright for Literate Robots," *Iowa Law Review* 101 (2016): 657, 678.

38 *See* 17 U.S.C. §§ 114, 115, and 117. ASCAP and BMI are private collecting societies for performances or musical compositions.

39 *See generally* Lyman Ray Patterson, *Copyright in Historical Perspective* (Vanderbilt University Press, Nashville Tennessee, 1968).

40 See, e.g., Cambridge Univ. Press v. Patton, 769 F.3d 1232, 1267 (11th Cir. 2014) ("At the same time, the use provides a broader public benefit—furthering the education of students at a public university.").

8.6

LANDMARK CASES

Perfect 10, Inc. v Amazon, Inc., 508 F.3d 1146 (9th Cir. 2007)

This case, in the Ninth Circuit, involves Perfect 10, Amazon, Inc., and Google, Inc. (a consolidated case based on several cases that Perfect 10 brought against search engines). Perfect 10 was an adult entertainment company that created and commercially distributed copyrighted photographs of nude models, which it offered on a paid-subscription website accessible via password. A number of independent, third-party website publishers placed images obtained from Perfect 10's subscription-only service on their sites. Google provided automated search engine software, or a "web crawler," which would obtain copies of public web pages and images to store in its search index. It also offered a blog host service called "Blogger," which allowed account holders to upload images from the web onto Google's server and post them on their blogs or via hyperlink. The web crawler included many of these third-party sites that contained the infringing images from Perfect 10.

As part of their image search service, Google provides thumbnail copies of images in response to search requests which are viewable by the user. A viewer can choose to click on the thumbnail image to be directed to the full-size image via a hypertext link. The full-size image is located on a third-party website but is "framed," so the image appears on the viewer's computer screen, without any of the other content from the originating website. Google did not store or physically transmit the full images, only the image thumbnails. Perfect 10 sued, believing that the linking and framing of full-size images constituted a direct infringement of its exclusive right to publicly display as well as to publicly distribute the full-size image, and the caching and display of the thumbnails represented direct copyright infringement as well. Consequently, Perfect 10 requested that Google be enjoined from framing websites that infringed its content and from creating and distributing thumbnails of its images. The lower court found that Google would only infringe Perfect 10's distribution and display rights if it hosted and physically transmitted the content itself—now known as the "server test"—rather than only providing an hyperlink instruction for the user's computer to fetch the infringing pages from servers not under its control.

When considering the display of the thumbnails, Google claimed that the display was a fair use; the lower court did not agree. On appeal, the Ninth Circuit agreed that infringement of the full-size images would only occur if Google hosted and transmitted a copy of the content itself, combining the display right with the right to make a reproduction, but it overturned the lower court's finding that displaying thumbnails was not fair use. It held that displaying thumbnails at a size of about 3 percent of the original size was "highly transformative" and that Google transformed the images from a use of entertainment and artistic expression to one of retrieving information, citing the similar case, *Kelly v. Arriba Soft Corp.*

335

Goldman v. Breitbart News Network, LLC, 302 F. Supp. 3d 585 (S.D.N.Y. 2018)

In July 2016, a man snapped a photograph of New England Patriots Quarterback Tom Brady and Boston Celtics general manager Danny Ainge on a street in East Hampton. He shared it on Snapchat and it quickly went viral on social media, fueling speculation that Brady was assisting the Celtics in recruiting basketball star Kevin Durant to Boston. Several media outlets and blogs picked up on this story, and used the photograph to illustrate their articles about the Brady/Durant story. The photographer did not license this photograph to these outlets, and eventually sued several of them for copyright infringement. Rather than copying the photograph on their own servers (along with the rest of the article), each of the news outlets instead embedded tweets containing the photos into their stories. This copyright infringement dispute turns on whether the act of embedding a photograph insulates a publisher against claims of infringing a photographer's exclusive display rights under the Copyright Act.

When a coder embeds an image, the image is incorporated onto the web page, but the image is still *stored* on a third-party server. Because the image is still stored on the third-party server, the defendants claimed that they were not displaying the image of Brady and Ainge, but were merely providing "instructions" for the user to access the third-party server where the image was held (even though the users can view the image in the article). As the court explained, the result of embedding is "a seamlessly integrated webpage, a mix of text and images, although the underlying images may be hosted in varying locations."

The location of the supposedly infringing material is important because of the "server test," which was adopted by the Ninth Circuit in *Perfect 10.* It states that publisher liability for infringement comes down to whether the infringing image is stored on the publisher's own server, or whether it is embedded or linked from a third-party server. The justification for the server test was that publications and search engines should not be liable for infringement that takes place on servers not under their control. In the case of Google (one of the defendants in *Perfect 10*), the company's engine simply instructs the user's computer to fetch the infringing pages from third-party servers. Google was not in the position to take down the infringing content from third-party sites. The server test was met with some controversy, with critics claiming that it cut against the text and purpose of the Copyright Act, and essentially created a loophole for media platforms to freely display copyrighted content on their pages. As a result, the server test's reception in other circuits has been mixed.

The Southern District of New York rejected the server test, both in its applicability to the facts at hand and its overall compatibility with the Copyright Act. The court flatly stated that, "the plain language of the Copyright Act, the legislative history undergirding its enactment, and subsequent Supreme Court jurisprudence provide no basis for a rule that allows the physical location or possession of an image to determine who may or may not have 'displayed' a work within the meaning of the Copyright Act."

The court noted that possession is not a requirement for infringement anywhere under the Copyright Act and that several sections of the statute address infringers that do not possess the copyrighted material. The court also pointed to the legislative history behind the Copyright Act, which reveals that its drafters intended copyright protection to include new, not-yet-developed technologies. This, combined with further evidence that Congress intended the display right to be read broad enough to capture each and every method by which the images can be displayed or picked up and conveyed, contributed to the court's renouncement of the server test.

Eschewing the server test overall, the Southern District still distinguished the server test from the present case. For one, the court found the defendants' argument that its use of the image merely constituted a set of "instructions" directing the users to the third-party site where it was stored unpersuasive because technical distinctions invisible to the user should not be the lynchpin on which copyright liability lies. However, the court focused on two primary distinctions between this case and *Perfect 10*: (1) the defendant in *Perfect 10* was a search engine rather than a media outlet, and (2) the user in *Perfect 10* actively decided to click on the image displayed. Media outlets, unlike search engines, are expected to exercise far closer control over what comes up on their website. By essentially forcing readers to view the image when they access the article, readers are unlike the users who have to consciously click on a thumbnail to access the image. Even though the court expressed skepticism about the server rule more generally, it nevertheless emphasized that the defendant outlets in this case were unlike the successful defendant search engines in *Perfect 10*.

The Southern District's decision (and the conflicting attitudes toward the server test across jurisdictions) reveals several tensions in modern copyright law. One tension, which is a common theme in all of these "landmark cases," centers on the challenges presented by the internet. Social media in particular is replete with instances of unauthorized reproduction and display of copyrighted works (particularly photographs), and the server test functioned as an attempt to create some sort of clear, simple rule for instances of potential infringement. The case also raised questions about the role of internet giants in shaping modern law. The Southern District distinguished Google and individual online media outlets on copyright grounds, but one can still speculate whether Google's size and obvious relevance to the internet ecosystem contributed to how the two cases turned out. Perhaps courts are careful not to risk inhibiting the growth of internet players like Google. However, the rise and (partial) fall of the server test ultimately points to the fact that the internet is not just a novel but a rapidly changing institution in modern life and that fashioning appropriate "rules" for it from pre-internet statutes is a big challenge. The server test represented an attempt to square this new landscape with the 1976 Copyright Act, but so does the shift away from the server test. We should expect more inconsistency; more back and forth; and more caveats, distinctions, and reiterations over time.

PART IX

Future Copyright

9.1

FUTURE OF COPYRIGHT

Several themes emerge when looking at the future of copyright in the twenty-first century. The role of fair use, written to encourage creation while still allowing the public some access to creative works (knowledge), stands out as a dominant feature of US copyright law. It has stood the test of time, remaining flexible in a changing world, but, when taken to the extreme, it has still affected the market for licensing revenue. What role will Internet Service Providers (ISPs) play in the future to ensure that the economic incentives provided to authors under copyright remain viable and are not swallowed up by unfettered infringements by internet users? Will there be new collective licensing models to compensate creators, such as book authors, for some of the online sharing or piracy that has become commonplace online? Will the termination provision provide authors with a real opportunity to renegotiate past grants of rights, or will the process be too complex for creators to navigate? Will the Digital Millennium Copyright Act (DMCA)'s safe harbor provision (§ 512(c))—to protect ISPs from damages for infringing work posted by users— be reviewed so the burden does not fall so heavily on creators, given the growth of the internet industry? Will a simplified and less costly copyright small claims tribunal finally be created by Congress and provide creators and small businesses with a venue for the low-value, high-volume infringements that plague many individual creators and vex publishers? If such a venue exists, how will that increase or decrease some of the current copyright litigation shops that bring a high volume of infringement claims in federal court? How will the Copyright Act address ownership and copyright protection for works created with the use of machines or drones, or through the assistance of artificial intelligence (AI)? How will the role of the Copyright Office in the twenty-first century change to address these issues? These are some of the questions addressed in the preceding chapters, representing varied points of view of copyright lawyers and creators from different fields.

Fair Use

As noted in many chapters, whether a court considers the use of another author's work "transformative" has become the dominant test for determining whether the second use qualifies as a fair use, and hence non-infringing. As noted in the chapters, this term evolved from a 1990 Harvard Law Review article on fair use by Judge Pierre Leval, who looked at forms of quoting and other productive uses of copyrighted works by subsequent users and suggested that, if the second use did not supplant the original, but was used for a different purpose, adding new meaning, it was transformative and the new use should be a fair use. That "transformativeness" phrase and other language from his article was relied upon and quoted in the seminal 1994 Supreme Court fair use case, *Campbell v. Acuff-Rose*, which determined that even a commercial work that parodied an existing song could qualify as a fair use. Prior to this case, the presumption was that if a use were commercial, and there was harm to any licensing market under the fourth fair use factor, the use would not qualify as a fair use.

As of this writing, the Supreme Court is about to hear oral arguments (remotely) on the first major fair use case in twenty-five years. This case pits two internet giants, Oracle and Google, against each other in a long-standing dispute (going back and forth for years within the various district and circuit courts) based on Google's taking of application programming interface (API) code from Oracle's popular Java script. APIs are, generally speaking, specifications that allow programs to communicate with each other, which they could not do without APIs. This case raises the question of whether an API is copyrightable, even though the underlying software code is (under literary works). Initially, Google prevailed; the court ruled that Oracle's Java APIs were not protected. The appellate court reversed the decision, which opened a fair use defense for Google, which Google then won, but that decision was reversed and is now before the Supreme Court. This decision could change how courts analyze the four factors as described in the statutory language of § 107. It is possible that the Supreme Court may provide more clarity on how the transformative nature of a work relates to the other statutory factors. This decision could again shift the dominance of the first factor—purpose of the use—and provide more weight to the potential harm to a future market in the fourth factor. Even though this case involves software, protected under copyright as a category of literary work, any decision—just as the *Campbell* decision did—is likely to shape fair use cases in all categories of copyrighted works. As a result, nearly sixty amicus briefs (friend of the court briefs that explain why the decision affects industries other than the parties involved) were filed in total on both sides, representing a widely diverse group of creators, computer scientists, and other stakeholders.

Section 512 Review

The DMCA, enacted in 1998, is more than twenty years old, crafted when the internet economy was in its infancy. Section 512, as part of the DMCA, was enacted to address online piracy and provide a system for online ISPs and copyright owners to work together to remove infringing content. Qualified ISPs were given immunity from monetary damages for copyright infringement in order to foster the growth of internet industries that might otherwise face staggering statutory damages for copyright infringement based on common practices and user conduct. Congress also knew that as technology advanced, so would online piracy. As a result, a statutory balance was struck such that compliant online service providers would qualify for immunity for ordinary internet activity if they adopted a policy to terminate repeat infringers and accommodate "standard technical measures" that identify or protect copyrighted works developed according to broad consensus between copyright owners and service providers.

The conduct that has generated the most litigation and dissatisfaction is § 512 (c), which addresses content uploaded at the direction of users. In order to maintain its safe harbor, an online service provider must maintain a compliant notice and takedown procedure by responding expeditiously to remove content claimed to be infringing upon receipt of a statutorily proper notice from a copyright owner. In addition to responding to takedown notices, online service providers must also act expeditiously to remove or disable access to material when they have "actual knowledge" of infringement or, in the absence of such actual knowledge, when they have "aware[ness] of facts or circumstances from which infringing activity is apparent." This "awareness'" of infringing activity standard often is referred to as "red flag" knowledge. Notwithstanding, § 512 did not require that online service providers monitor online activity or affirmatively seek information regarding users' activity except to the extent consistent with a standard technical measure. Last, to qualify for the safe harbors under § 512(c), an online service provider must not "receive a financial benefit directly attributable to the infringing activity, in a case in which the service provider has the right and ability to control such activity."

At the time of the DMCA, Congress anticipated that online service providers and copyright owners would cooperate to remove infringing content. However, rather than encouraging cooperation between ISPs and content owners in the removal of infringing content, courts have interpreted the knowledge standard in § 512(c) in a manner that discourages cooperation in large part to avoid losing immunity by curating or having too much knowledge of the type of user activity. For example, courts have interpreted what constitutes general awareness of infringing activity or "red flag" knowledge to have the same specificity requirements as in notices that identify each allegedly infringing use.

Congress' anticipation that industries would develop standard technical measures has also not come to fruition. The definition of standard technical measures requires that the measures be developed by a broad consensus of online service providers and copyright owners. But there is no incentive for online service providers to work with copyright owners in developing standard technical measures or any filtering technology. Individual industries have developed filtering technology but not with the consensus of online service providers. And online service providers, not wanting to obtain awareness of infringing activity in order to lose their safe harbor, are not incentivized to work with copyright owners in curbing infringing activity.

The requirement that actual knowledge of each infringement be brought to the online service provider's attention has copyright owners complaining that the burden of detecting and monitoring for infringing activity weighs too heavily on the copyright owner and is an unreasonable burden, given the current financial largess of many internet industries. Copyright owners complain that even if compliant takedown notices are sent to online service providers, the same content will be uploaded by another user, requiring a separate notice, an exercise that has been compared to the game of "whack-a-mole." Today, the internet economy looks much different than it did in the 1990s with large companies such as Google, Facebook, eBay, Amazon, and Apple, among others, dominating the landscape. The various chapters in this book demonstrate that there is dissatisfaction both from the online service providers who complain of notice and takedown abuse and from copyright owners who believe that the burden of detecting infringements is disproportionately levied on the copyright owner without enough cooperation from the online service providers to keep infringing content off their sites. In late 2015, the Copyright Office published a notice of inquiry at the request of Congress to study § 512 and held public roundtables.

On May 21, 2020, the Copyright Office published its long awaited 512 (c) report and issued recommendations. The Copyright Office's report looks at Congress' intent in enacting the DMCA, which offered service providers safe harbors to provide incentives for internet platforms and copyright owners to cooperate in order to detect and deal with copyright infringements that take place in the online environment. The report looks at that balance in light of the changes in the internet in the last twenty-plus years and concludes that the current operation of the section 512 safe harbor system is unbalanced, and the burden of deterring piracy has shifted too far to the copyright owner. The Copyright Office makes several recommendations for Congress to consider and highlights areas where current implementation of section 512 does not align with Congress' original intent. The areas that the Copyright Office examines include eligibility qualifications for the service provider safe harbors, repeat infringer policies, knowledge requirement standards, specificity within takedown notices, non-standard notice requirements, subpoenas, and injunctions. The Copyright Office suggests not that Congress make wholesale changes to section 512 but that it revisit language and make modifications. The Copyright Office also suggested practices that have not been used enough and encourages more voluntary cooperation among all stakeholders in order to create standard technical measures to reduce piracy and reliance on notice and take down letters. Finally, the Copyright Office noted that the conclusions on how the current system is working could benefit from further study and verifiable evidence to determine if other changes should be made.

The full report, along with the extensive public comments, empirical studies, and roundtable transcripts, is available on the Copyright Office's website at copyright.gov/policy/section512/.

Sharing Content

The sharing of content between users, and the use of found material online by twenty-first-century creators, whether it is used to create video mashups, music sampling, or collage art is only going to continue. It is not cost-efficient, productive, or tenable for copyright owners to have to police all uses of work, nor is it realistic to expect that creative authorship by individuals who grew up in the internet era will not rely on material found online as a source of inspiration. The sharing generation is accustomed to recording and uploading every moment of their life on Facebook or Instagram, creating Pinterest boards of their interests based on material found online, and sharing playlists with friends. While the music industry has historically had a system of collective licensing for the performance of published music, it may be time to look at similar licensing regimes so that authors, visual artists, and other creators can participate fully in, and financially benefit from, the internet economy. In addition, search engines generate tremendous profits selling advertising space adjacent to content that it is in-line linked to, but not licensed. For the internet to realize the expectations of all artists and maintain the economic incentives promised to authors under the Constitution, Congress may need to develop a real twenty-first-century copyright system and reevaluate the balance between online service providers and copyright owners. This new system would compensate authors to narrow the value gap existing between the money online service providers earn based on the aggregation of copyright owners' works, and the content owners whose content forms the basis of those sites. The US might look to the European Union for guidance based on the recently enacted European Union Copyright Directive as it relates to search engines to see if there are any proposed solutions to this problem that could be adopted by the US.

CASE Act

Several chapters mention recently proposed legislation to create a voluntary, cost-effective, centralized copyright tribunal for copyright claims of lesser value, known as the CASE Act. H.R. 2426, the Copyright Alternative in Small-Claims Enforcement Act of 2019, was introduced in the House in May 2019 alongside a companion bill, S. 1273, in the Senate. Since then, the House bill passed overwhelmingly on October 22, 2019 with a vote of 410–6. While the Senate version of the bill passed the Senate Judiciary Committee, as of this writing, one senator has put a hold on the bill.

The CASE Act would create an affordable, efficient alternative to expensive and drawn-out federal litigation to resolve ordinary copyright disputes. This tribunal would provide creators as well as the companies that are sued for common internet infringements to seek a resolution without expensive legal fees. An important feature of this legislation is that the process would be optional, so if a party does not want to bring or defend a copyright case before the tribunal, it can simply opt out. The streamlined process created by the CASE Act would alleviate the need to hire an attorney and limit statutory damages to $15,000 per claim—one-tenth of the maximum that can be recovered under existing law—as well as limit the total recovery in the case to $30,000.

The CASE Act is a result of a 2013 study Congress asked the Copyright Office to undertake and the bill follows many of the Office's recommendations. The bill would provide the following:

- a copyright small claims board for claims that do not exceed $30,000, with adjudicators with experience in copyright law and alternative dispute resolution;
- a less formal, streamlined process where (1) legal representation is optional, (2) law students can represent parties before the board on a pro bono basis, (3) parties pay their own attorney fees, (4) in-person appearances before the board are not required as proceedings are conducted electronically, and (5) discovery is limited;
- permit the board to award actual damages and statutory damages up to $15,000, but not issue injunctions;
- permit claimants to enforce judgments in a federal court against an uncooperative defendant and mandate that the defendant must pay the claimant's attorneys' fees related to the enforcement action; and
- authorize the Copyright Office to adopt a two-tier system which puts in place even more streamlined rules for claims of $5,000 or less.

Proponents note that the provisions are good for everyone to encourage participation. Specifically, the bill would:

- allow respondents, upon receiving notice, to unconditionally opt out of the small claims process;
- permit respondents to raise all defenses available in federal court, including fair use;
- dramatically limit a respondent's financial exposure—in contrast to federal court litigation— by capping potential damages and insulating them from attorneys' fees awards; and
- discourage bad faith claims, counterclaims, and defenses by (1) imposing attorneys' fees on bad actors, and (2) barring "repeat offenders" from filing claims for a set time period.

Creators support this bill because many are unable to pursue legitimate copyright infringement action in federal court due to the high cost of litigation and the relatively low value of each claim. These infringements come at the expense of licensing revenue for these authors and lead to lack of respect for the copyright system as a whole. While concerns have been raised over the constitutionality of the system and fear of abuse, the bill as proposed seems to address those issues with a voluntary system and provisions to prevent those who would abuse the process. The system may reduce the number of claims that are currently brought in federal court, as copyright owners could bring claims without the need for an attorney. Having a meaningful copyright small claims tribunal may in fact reduce abuse and litigation where settlements have nothing to do with damages, but are the result of the high cost of defense. It may be optimistic, but those accused of infringing may appreciate a system just as much as copyright owners, as the cost of litigation is less, discovery is limited, and the damages, including attorneys' fees, are capped. There would be no need for public appearances, travel costs, or deposition fees, and everything could be handled through papers or teleconferencing. We will see if the one senator who is holding up the bill can be persuaded to bring the bill to the floor either by pressure from other senators or by those interested in the passage of the bill. There is some indication that the senators supporting the bill will be pushing to get the bill to the floor in early summer.

For copyright in the twenty-first century to be effective, a voluntary and streamlined tribunal to enforce copyright infringement of these high-volume, low-value claims generated by the internet is needed. The United Kingdom has had a small claims tribunal for more than ten years and it has reportedly been effective and encourages early settlements of claims.

Termination

The Copyright Act permits authors or their heirs, under certain circumstances, to terminate the exclusive or nonexclusive grant of an author's copyright in a work or of any right under a copyright. The termination right gives authors and/or their heirs a chance to renegotiate terms of their original agreement—or enter into a new agreement—and gives them greater bargaining power. Section 203 of the Copyright Act applies to grants after January 1, 1978 and § 304(c) applies to grants executed before January 1, 1978. Termination is specific to authors and grants by person(s) other than the author cannot be terminated under § 203. Section 203 provides for termination in the thirty-fifth year and § 304(c) offers termination in the fifty-sixth year. The provisions have specific notice requirements and are complex and anyone effectuating termination should carefully read the statute and not rely on the summary notes here. For example, § 304(c) has a termination window calculated within five years beginning fifty-six years from the date the work's copyright was originally secured under the 1909 Copyright Act. For grants under § 203, with no right of publication, the calculation of the termination window is within five years starting thirty-five years from the date of execution of the grant, and for works with a right of publication, the termination is calculated either within five years of either a thirty-five-year or a forty-year period, depending on when publication occurs after the grant. A notice of termination must be served on the termination party (and successors in interest) no less than two years before the selected termination date. To be effective, termination notices must be recorded with the Copyright Office. Terminations will not terminate derivative works that have been started before the termination date but will prevent future terminations. Terminations also do not apply to works created under a work for hire.

As the termination period for grants under the Copyright Act effective in 1978 is just starting to be filed, litigation of issues that could defeat the right to terminate is just beginning. What constitutes a work-for-hire will likely be the biggest area. How this right will help authors negotiate better deals will be seen. Any artist who worked through a loan-out company, a commonplace situation in the entertainment industry, may not be eligible as those are work-for-hire situations. Because of the complexity, it may only apply to authors who have highly valuable properties and can navigate the thicket. A case to watch is a termination notice by the creator of the Philly's much-loved baseball mascot, the Philly Fanatic. It is being contested in part on trademark grounds.

AI and Machine-Assisted Creation

Several chapters looked at the copyrightability of works created with the use of AI and works created with the aid of machines, such as drone photography. They examine the copyright challenges facing works that may not be created by humans, but are based on technology used to develop the machine learning that was created by human authorship. Issues of who is an author and who owns and controls the end product may dominate the conversation in the upcoming years. Issues of who will be responsible if the technology creates infringing works will be another issue. Equally challenging will be the impact on current authors of machine-created works that can compete with their royalty-producing works. While most AI output is used for mundane or repetitive tasks, it is only a matter of time before AI becomes more intuitive and creative.

The Music Modernization Act

The authors and interviewees writing about or discussing music all addressed the tectonic shift when the music industry shifted from physical to digital music and music could be easily downloaded from the internet. With digital technology making perfect copies, music became freely traded on the internet. As downloads increased, musician revenues plummeted. As streaming, and platforms such as Pandora and Spotify, replaced downloads (accounting for almost 75 percent of all music industry revenue), proceeds for musicians declined even more because the statutory rate for streaming is so low ($0.006 to $0.0084 per stream to the owner of the master recording rights, of which some goes to the songwriter, composer, or artist) that only those whose music reaches millions of streams make any money. In response to this reality, and to update current laws to reflect modern consumer preferences and changes in the music marketplace, in 2018, Congress passed the Orrin G. Hatch-Bob Goodlatte Music Modernization Act (MMA), one of the most significant pieces of copyright legislation in decades and the only music bill to pass unanimously in the US history. The full Act comprises actually three laws: the MMA, the Compensating Legacy Artists for their Songs, Service, and Important Contributions to Society Act (CLASSICS) Act, and the Allocation for Music Producers (AMP). The MMA addresses changes in the process for obtaining a compulsory license for digital performance of a work (downloaded or streamed) from a song-by-song basis to a blanket license, thereby better facilitating royalty payments to artist; it creates a process for the use of orphan works and it changes the rate-setting standard used by copyright royalty judges from a policy-oriented to an open-market standard. The CLASSICS Act extends federal copyright protections to pre-February 15, 1972 sound recordings, so legacy artists are paid royalties when their works are played on digital radio; and the AMP codifies the process by which music producers receive royalties via SoundExchange for public performances of per § 114 of the Copyright Act of 1976. This law is so new that its actual impact is still unknown. Not surprisingly, the musicians interviewed in Part V are skeptical about whether it will actually direct more money to them.

Modernization

To have a truly effective twenty-first-century copyright ecosystem, the Copyright Office requires funding and support to best serve the needs of the public in the twenty-first century. The Copyright Office is essential in that it serves the public in the registration and recordation of copyright claims. For the US authors, registration (or a refusal) is a prerequisite for filing a copyright infringement action. Registration serves other benefits as well. A timely registration constitutes prima facie evidence of the validity of the copyright and the facts stated in the certificate of registration. Without a timely registration, copyright owners cannot seek statutory damages or attorney's fees in any litigation. A copyright registration creates a public record regarding authorship and ownership of the work, and a description of the work by title (but no ability to review the deposit). The Copyright Office is also responsible for the recordation of important documents, such as assignments of copyright and security interests that are essential to many transactions involving intellectual property. The Copyright Office has long been underfunded and its technology systems have fallen behind what is needed to serve the public. The Copyright Office published a report on its modernization plan and is making an effort to modernize and improve its recordation functions, in particular to reduce the amount of time it takes to process copyright applications once the deposits are filed with the application. Creators have also complained about the electronic filing system and have been requesting that the Copyright Office allow third parties to create APIs that would integrate copyright registration into an artist's workflow. Photographers would benefit from this ability as they could register images while editing and doing post-production on their digital files. On May 15, 2020, the Copyright Office published a "request for information," seeking information from potential contractors on the capabilities of a new web-based, cloud enterprise copyright system. The description of services requested includes the capacity for external APIs to work with the system.

In addition, the chair of the Senate Judiciary Committee, Senator Thom Tillis, is taking an interest in modernizing the Copyright Office and faults Congress for not supporting the Copyright Office sufficiently in the past. He wants modernization to happen more quickly than projected in the Copyright Office plan and may introduce legislation to provide the Copyright Office with more control over its infrastructure. If the CASE Act is implemented, the Copyright Office will require resources to administer the tribunal.

9.2
WHAT'S NEXT
Predictions from Interviewees and Authors

Joseph T. Baio

What I would like to see happen is the development of stronger and more predictable protections under copyright laws for visual artists, particularly photojournalists.

What is going to happen is the continued erosion of protections—both legal and otherwise—for the same folks, among others.

Daniel J. Brooks

What I would like to see happen to copyright this century is the demise of the transformative use doctrine in fair use.

Dale M. Cendali and Shanti Sadtler Conway

In terms of predications and what we would like to see happen to copyright law in the twenty-first century, we are interested to see if there is more of a focus on strengthening copyright protections based on the rationale that such protection incentivizes creators to innovate and create new works, consistent with the language of article I, section 8, clause 8 of the US Constitution, which provides for authors' rights "[t]o promote the progress of science and useful arts."

Michael Donaldson

The Copyright Act needs to be updated to account for the world we live in now plus all the technological innovations that are coming down the pike. Fair use is the one area that seems to have the flexibility to meet that challenge. Otherwise, there is work to do.

Joseph C. Gratz

We will see a turn toward seeing copyright as an engine of free expression, with an expansive view of fair use and intermediary safe harbors that allows the smallest creators to continue to have access to huge potential audiences.

Brandon J. Huffman

I think we will see more and more litigation over digital creations—specifically digital creations working to create realistic virtual environments or augmenting real environments. As realism improves, so does the temptation to include real-life works. Near the middle of the century, I think we will start to see more debate around the amount of human authorship required for copyright protection as it relates to artificial intelligence-assisted creativity.

Justin Hughes

I predict that in the next ten years, we will see more and more splintering of the old consensus that largely shielded internet service providers (ISP) from liability for online copyright infringement. I see a reassessment of ISP responsibilities for what happens on the internet in the EU's new Directive on Copyright in the Digital Single Market, Chinese law, and a weakening of support for section 230 in the US. I predict more and more automated copyright enforcement, that such automated enforcement will increasingly help small creative professionals, and that all that will happen with minimal negative effects on First Amendment interests.

Terence P. Keegan

In the Future, There Will Be No Looking Back

Judges will begin to enforce the three-year statute of limitations for copyright infringement claims (17 U.S.C. § 507(b)) as strictly and consistently as they do in defamation suits. Instead of simply permitting claims for damages for up to three years before the date a plaintiff has filed suit, courts will begin to bar in their entirety complaints that plaintiffs fail to bring within three years of a defendant's publication. They will still follow the "discovery rule," but judges will begin to require more from plaintiffs who claim to have just found a years-old article featuring their photo.

The shift is already underway—particularly against volume photo plaintiffs, who have been trawling the internet for a decade. In the coming months, courts will begin to charge even first-time litigants with notice of online publications that are only a Google search away.

William T. McGrath

There will be major developments in copyright law with respect to the use of copyright-protected material without permission on social media and in artificial intelligence applications, raising issues of fair use and the scope of the copyright owner's exclusive rights.

Olivera Medenica

Copyright law is a strict liability regime designed in a pre-internet world with the same case law for music being applied to soft sculptures, architecture, photographs, and websites. In the current environment, copyright is a blunt instrument. The Copyright Act's remedies are expensive, time-consuming, and hard to use; its fair use case law is hard to understand and does not fit with the needs of an online world. In the twenty-first century, trolls will proliferate and both creators and users of content will increasingly gain sophistication and seek more friendly alternative licensing regimes like Creative Commons.

Cameron Mizell

As technology makes access to and use of copyrighted material easier for the general public, I would like to see the largest, most influential tech companies lead the way in creating equitable methods of compensating creators and rights holders for use of their work. Ideally legislation would be able to keep up as well, but I have a hard time imagining a world where copyright law can keep up with advancing technology for very long. If the idea of copyright is to encourage innovation, then we will need the most innovative companies to uphold that basic concept through their own technological innovations.

Mickey H. Osterreicher

Like so many things these days, there are two alternate universes for my prediction of what might happen and what I would like to see happen to copyright in the twenty-first century. I would hope that courts return to a more common-sense and protective view of intellectual property rights, especially as it pertains to the work of individual creators. What I fear will happen is that fair use will continue to expand as an exception, until it completely subsumes copyright protection as a rule.

Judith B. Prowda

The elephant in the room in terms of the future of copyright is the problem of orphan works. The historically unprecedented extension of the duration of copyright to life of author plus seventy years, the fact that copyright is automatically awarded to the author upon the creation of a nominated work, and the exponential production of copyrighted material disposed to online distribution, will generate an increasingly unmanageable rights situation where no one will know what they can or cannot use without the risk of draconian penalty. As artistic expression is increasingly created for and consumed exclusively in virtual space, a vast amount of our cultural production will be rendered unusable by the impossibility of resolving licensing issues. In addition, the disappearance of physical media can mark the end of important works' public existence. This is already the case, for example, with major documentary films whose rights have lapsed. The only way the work can be seen is by tracking down an aging VHS tape on eBay. After those inevitably decay, the underlying work may never be legally seen again in our lifetime or even ever again if the master recordings are not painstakingly archived. After we collectively abandon all physical media for future works, even this nostalgic possibility will be no more. The ironic tragedy of a law designed to inspire authors to make sacrifices for the benefit of all.

Mary Rasenberger

Artificial intelligence will bring major challenges to copyright law and to creators in particular in the not-too-distant future. Sophisticated, automated collective licensing solutions will need to be developed for literary, visual, and other works to ensure that copyright owners are paid for the use of their work. Otherwise, it will prove difficult to sustain the meaningful copyright incentives for diverse, middle-class creators in the AI age.

Christopher S. Reed

As for predictions for the future, I am cautiously optimistic that the political climate and evolving business imperatives among key stakeholders will lead to a willingness to explore (or, at least, not immediately dismiss) opportunities for legislative change. As illustrated by the Music Modernization Act, forward-looking legislation is possible when the process is driven by those most affected and presented to Congress as a consensus measure. I remain skeptical that we will ever get there with areas that have traditionally been the source of the most discord— e.g. online enforcement— but at least things appear to be trending in the right direction.

Scott J. Sholder

What I would ideally like to see happen in the twenty-first century is a comprehensive revision to the Copyright Act so the law is in step with rapidly expanding technology and media consumption and creation practices, taking into account phenomena like artificial intelligence, 3D printing, virtual and augmented reality, social media, and "deepfakes." I do not expect this will be likely, absent an unusually productive Congress, so my prediction of what will actually happen is a continued evolution in how courts interpret the existing law in light of rapidly changing technological conditions which may skew more toward favoring content "users" as reflected in recent cases dealing with copyrightable material depicted in video games and the licenses granted by social media terms of use in connection with publicly posted content.

Kenneth N. Swezey and Elizabeth Altman

The coming decades of the twenty-first century will likely be shaped by AI technology—from AI-generated creative content to smart homes to facial recognition software—and, as such, copyright must fill in the gaps where it can, addressing issues such as the authorship of AI creative output as well as other copyright-related concerns, such as the application of the fair use doctrine to the inputting of source material into AI systems and the process by which it learns, adapts, and generates its work.

Francine Ward

A change in who owns a copyright. With artificial intelligence playing a bigger role in our culture, I see humans as the only owners of a copyright being challenged.

Caroline Womack Carroll

The next ten years have the potential to be really big for the entire field of copyright law, especially as we see the expansion of the digital marketplace. My biggest hope is that we begin to develop a more concrete understanding of what the affirmative defense of fair use is and, in turn, how creative works can be used to inspire people while adequately protecting content creators. On a larger scale, I think that we are almost definitely going to have to start taking a hard look at the Digital Millennium Copyright Act (DMCA) as we continue to rely on digital media and the monetization of copyrighted material.

INDEX

social media: cost *vs.* expected damages compensation 107–8; and infringers 104–5; number and identity of infringers 106–7; and number of works misappropriated 105–6; pirating of works on 100–4; post or not to post on 98; pre-posting protection 98; Terms of Service (TOS) 98–100; use it and lose it? 97–108

Solid Oak Sketches v. 2K Games 237; *see also* tattoo cases

Sony 84, 209, 258, 329; *see also* photojournalists, and copyright protection

SoundCloud 172, 173, 174; *see also* music, mashups

Spotify 172, 173, 182, 192, 193, 208, 209, 227, 228, 347; *see also* copyright; internet piracy

Springfield, Rick 172, 183; *see also* remix compulsory licensing for music mashups

Springsteen, Bruce 219, 238; *see also* ownership

Star Athletica, LLC v. Varsity Brands, Inc. 276–77, 284–85; *see also* fashion designs

stature, recognized 130; *see also* Visual Artists Rights Act (VARA)

statutory damages 7, 300–1, 303–5; *see also* damages, copyright infringement

Steeger v. JMS Cleaning Servs. LLC 302; *see also* trolls, copyright

Steinberg v. Columbia Pictures Industries, Inc. 74; *see also* paintings and drawings

Stills, Steven 185; *see also* music

Story, Joseph (Justice) 43; *see also* appropriation art; fair use doctrine

street art: nature of 135–36; and VARA 137–39; *see also* urban murals; Visual Artists Rights Act (VARA)

Strike 3 Holdings LLC v. John Doe subscriber assigned IP address 72.28.136.217 301; *see also* trolls, copyright

"Subconscious Copying: From George Harrison to Sam Smith, a Song Gets in Your Head and Winds up in a New Song" 195–99; *see also* copying, subconscious; Harrison, George

Sullivan, Richard J. (Judge) 298; *see also* copyright; trolls, copyright

Supreme Court: and fair use approach 41–43; and limitation of the Copyright Act 48

takedown notices 289–90; *see also* Digital Millennium Copyright Act (DMCA)

Tanksley v. Daniels, 902 F.3d 165 59; *see also* creative content

Tarzan of the Apes 32; *see also* fictional characters, copyright protection

tattoo cases 237; *see also Solid Oak Sketches v. 2K Games* 237; video games and virtual worlds

termination provision, Copyright Act 341, 344; rights 12–13; Section 203 346; Section 304 346

Terms of Service (TOS): prohibit cashing out 250; prohibit transfers 249–50; social media 98–100; social media companies 99; Twitter 99

Thayer, James Bradley 40–41; *see also* fair use doctrine

Thicke, Robin 230–31; *see also* copying, subconscious

Third Circuit 74, 86, 263–64; *see also* infringement

third-party marketplaces 19–20; accountability of 23–24; regulation of 24–25

Thomson v. Larson 219; *see also* ownership

Tilt Brush 251; *see also* virtual reality

Time magazine 72, 155–56; *see also* fair use doctrine; lawsuits

trademark 245–46; infringement 278; law 5; trade dress 278–79

transformativeness: appropriation art and 147–49; concept of 147; and fair use doctrine 148–49; problems and appropriation art 147–48; *see also* fair use doctrine

trolls, copyright: birth of 299–300; IP address and porn troll case 301–2; representative cases 301–2; setting boundaries 298–99; SDNY cases cracking down on Liebowitz Law Firm 302; sloppy mass-produced litigation 301; statutory damages and too many mouths to feed 300–1; *see also* copyright, trolls

Trump: Donald J. 95, 101, 102, 123; Ivanka 123; *see also* internet piracy

Twitchell, Kent 138; *see also* paintings and drawings; Visual Artists Rights Act (VARA)

2 Live Crew 11, 52–53; *see also* "Oh Hairy Woman"; parody

2 Milly 238; *see also* emote dance cases

UMG Recordings Inc. v. Shelter Capital Partners 23; *see also* online piracy

University of British Columbia's Centre of Gambling Research 258; *see also* loot boxes; video games and virtual worlds

unpublished works, copyright 4, 5, 8, 59, 217; *see also* copyright

Urantia Foundation v. Maaherra 313; *see also* authorship

urban murals: emergence of 139; legitimized in 5Pointz litigation 139–41; *see also* Visual Artists Rights Act

US Copyright Office 6, 8, 11, 12, 13, 25, 34, 59, 60, 91, 123, 168, 179, 211–19, 238, 267–72, 276, 303, 304, 343–48; *see also* copyright

US Patent and Trademark Office (USPTO) 269, 273–74; *see also* US Copyright Office

US Postal Service 106; *see also* infringement, copyright

US Treasury Financial Crimes Enforcement Network (FinCEN) 246–47; *see also* anti-money laundering (AML); money laundering

Van Stry, John 25; *see also* lawsuits; McCrea, Travis

vehicles, challenges in depicting reality *see* video games

Verve Records 189; *see also* Mizell, Cameron